MW00805416

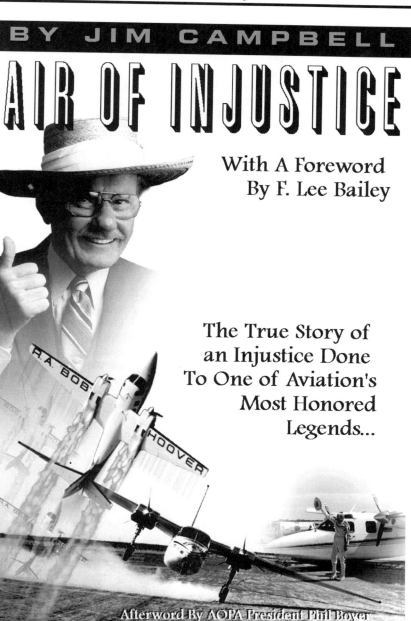

BY JIM CAMPBELL

AIR OF INJUSTICE

With A Foreword
By F. Lee Bailey

The True Story of
an Injustice Done
To One of Aviation's
Most Honored
Legends...

Afterword By AOPA President Phil Boyer

Kindred Spirit Press

P.O. Box 9132 • Winter Haven, FL 33883-9132 • (941) 294-6396 • Fax (941) 294-3678 • Web Address http://www.kindredspirit.com

Some Other Books By Jim Campbell
Flyer's Guide to Ultralights
The Powered Hang-Gliding Manual
The Ultralight Flight Training Handbook
Flyer's Guide to Night Flying
Affordable Flyers: Aircraft YOU Can Afford to Fly!
Kindred Spirit: A Journey Across America
Way Too Far From Home
SportPlane Resource Guide 1st Ed.
SportPlane Resource Guide 2nd Ed.
Air Of Injustice
The Ultralight Resource Guide (late '99)
Bailout! The Emergency Parachute Resource Guide ('00)

Some Other Books By Kindred Spirit Press
SportPlane Resource Guide 1st Ed.
SportPlane Resource Guide 2nd Ed.
Violation: The Aero-Legal Resource Guide
Air Of Injustice
The GPS Resource Guide (late '99)
The Rotax Resource Guide–Two Stroke Edition (late '99)
The Rotax Resource Guide–Four Stroke Edition (late '99)
The Ultralight Resource Guide (late '99)
Bailout! The Emergency Parachute Resource Guide ('00)
Flight Training Resource Guide (Late '00)

Copyright 1999 by Kindred Spirit Press, Inc.

Library of Congress Catalog Card Number 99-63050

ISBN 1-886743-15-0

Printed in the United States of America

10 9 8 7 6 5 4 3 2 1

Graphics by: Elizabeth Tolle
Cover by: Mark Potter, Elizabeth Tolle
Editors: Amy Sumerlin, Jim Campbell, Howard Fried

Published by:
 Kindred Spirit Press, Inc.
P.O. Box 9132
Winter Haven, FL 33883-9132

A Dedication

What does not destroy me, makes me strong.
Freidrich Nietzsche

The aviation world is one of the most lusciously beautiful I've ever known... it is filled with luridly expansive images of cloud and sky and land and sea. It exists in all three dimensions–truly. It can be fast and furious, or slow and peaceful. It can be gloriously colorful or as black and white as an early TV rerun. It can be sleepily peaceful or nerve-tingling, thrilling and even frightening. It's only true constant is change... and that men and women of uncommon character and insight choose to make it a valued part of their lives for precious minutes and hours at a time.

And it is to these men and women that I most particularly dedicate this book... those who conquer fear and uncertainty to take the controls of the world's flying machines and become more than mere mortal human beings. They become aviators.

The best of these; both in his role as a human being as well as a pilot... is the subject of this book, one Robert A. "Bob" Hoover. He is an uncommon gentleman and the best pilot that I have ever seen, personally... and mind you, it is my job, thank the Lord, to work with and know the very, very best.

He has always been a role model (or is that "Roll" Model... grin) and an inspiration; but in the course of the last several years, especially since the beginning of his conflict with the FAA, I have come to find him to be a dear friend, and a phenomenal human being most suitable to pattern one's own life after (especially for those of us who took their time getting their act together). Most important, even when he was accosted for befriending me, he never let it affect our growing friendship. Few men are that genuinely principled... and I look to him as an example of the kind of person I hope to evolve to be. To Bob, personally, I wish to extend my thanks for the way you have allowed me to work with you, for honoring me with your friendship, and the immense privilege of having fought on your behalf. It has been an honor and a privilege beyond measure.

His easy manner, graceful precision and utterly honest personality have endeared him to me and to my fellow flyers by the hundreds of thousands... and I find it fitting and proper to devote such a book to setting his struggle straight in the eyes of the world and letting all know that this is a good and decent man who was treated less than decently by the same government for which he risked his life... time after time after time.

Of all the people who ever seemed good and righteous to me as I made my way through the world, there were only three who always passed the test of time and scrutiny... one a wondrous old Jewish Doctor from Brooklyn who was my much beloved Grandfather; his wisdom and insight into humanity transcended normal capabilities and grew out his wholly empathic soul and endearing desire to leave the world a better place for his having been in it. Another was the patient and surprisingly smart (annoyingly right, more and more as I aged, damn it) fellow who is my Father, a man who set strict standards that seemed impossible, unfair and ridiculous to me as a child--and strangely proper and obligatory as I actually grew up.

The other is Bob Hoover. Outside my own family, I have never met a man I admired more... or was quite so proud to call my friend. My life is so rich to have had these men in my life as either friends or family... or both.

There are others who also deserve to be included among those I have come to admire and learn from, though many of them now fly on far higher plains than you or I. That's the sad part of life; that those we value most are often gone before we get the chance to show them what they mean to us. So... to Tom Jones, Leo Loudenslager, Chuck Cohen, Steve Wittman, Glen Benz, John Denver, Scott Anderson, Randy Gagne, Steve Snyder, and Jim Moser... I hope that heaven is as kind to you as your memories are to me.

Also... I'd be remiss if I did not also dedicate this aero-literary effort to the tens of thousands of men and women of courage and character who came to the defense of Bob, time and time again... especially the extraordinary John Yodice, the incomparable F. Lee Bailey, Norbert Nester (whose picture should adorn the word "courage" in every dictionary), AOPA's *best* President (ever) Phil Boyer, Jimmy Driskell (who truly is Bob's partner and a most amazing man in his own right), the rightfully respected Judge Roger Mullins, the multi-talented and highly-principled Robert Liddell, an uncommonly principaled politician and pilot by the name of Senator James Inhofe, and EAA Founder Paul Poberezny.

One person who truly deserves an amazing amount of credit for this book is Amy Sumerlin, my valued and trusted Editor of many years. Amy is as sweet and dedicated a soul as I know. One of the joys of this business has been my chance to work with her. A true professional, Amy has an abiding love for aviation and the pride she takes in her work has been a credit to us all. Make no mistake about it, Amy is one class act. Kudos also to Howard Fried who, as another victim of the FAA juggernaut, provided excellent editorial advice as this book went to press.

Special thanks must go to my other current and past support staff-members... Mark Potter (who did this book's amazing cover art), Bob Clager, Anya Macias, Francisco Del Toro Rios, Jana Huss, Ed Booth, Dan Moody, Liz Tolle, and Dave Abramawitz. They're a sweet bunch and they've learned to endure my excesses with amazing aplomb.

Additional thanks also go to a few talented photographers and friends who generously shared their work with me, Jim Koepnick of the EAA, Howard Fried, World Airshow News' Dave Weiman, AOPA (especially Drew Steketee!), and Bob Hoover.

Finally; to my family and friends, who have the tough job of knowing and dealing with me. They are a great lot and I love them all dearly... Most especially the lost and confused little girl who used to fly along with me in our biplane and promised to love me forever. As oft happens in life, "Forever" wasn't nearly long enough... but while it did, it was paradise. I miss you...

Blue Skies...

[signature]

James R. Campbell
Winter Haven, FL, Planet Earth
4/1/99

Foreword

What This All Means

Our greatest glory is not in never failing, but in rising up every time we fail.
Ralph Waldo Emerson

One who has lived a full life can always look back on the peaks and valleys of that experience and spot the high points. I have lived - and continue to do so - what many have called a busy and exciting existence. Of the episodes which pop to mind in review, aviation-related occasions stand out, together with events in the world of trials. In one *case* these two worlds came together: *FAA v. Robert A. Hoover.* The trial and conclusion of that case in Oklahoma City in 1994, before a distinguished and able Administrative Law Judge, and against a governmental agency seriously in disarray, comprised a high peak in my personal history that I will long - perhaps ever - remember. This is in part because, although we lawyers almost always like to win, what makes our profession worthwhile is when we win for a highly distinguished and wrongfully accused human being such as Bob Hoover.

As Jim recounts from my speech to the AOPA convention in 1994, although I had been a pilot for 40 years when I had the honor to be the first person, ever, to ride in the copilot's seat during Bob's *Shrike* performance in Hillsboro, Oregon, it was the greatest thrill I had ever encountered in an airplane. Although I was holding on to my seat with an iron grip (we were upside down a lot) I still got a chance to watch the man work his craft, and I do not expect to encounter another pilot like him even though I still fly on a regular basis.

More important, though, is the human being who with very little apparent effort makes airplanes do things that amaze us all. Bob is known as the gentleman of the profession, revered affectionately by all but the lowliest of bureaucrats and their ilk. He is a man of profound courtesy. He has helped more young show pilots than any other performer in history, always advising them as to where the "edge" may be, and how to avoid it even as they astonish the crowds who came to see them.

Jim Campbell has put an enormous amount of work into this book, and it pays off. While offering an in-depth profile of the man that is Bob Hoover, Campbell shows the ugly sequence of events wherein two FAA inspectors decided maliciously, and because they were little men, to bring down that American Icon who was so much bigger than they could ever be. Fortunately, another Inspector who heard them plotting came forward, knowing full well that the Agency would hound him unmercifully for telling the truth. The trial itself offers a rich look at those who dominate the airshow circuit, through the testimony they offered in support of Bob.

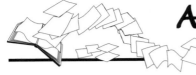

This is a tale which offers much to learn by the community of airmen. Indeed, after winning his trial and then suffering a reversal on appeal, Bob watched with gratitude as aviation people at airshows, with letters and protests, and in every other imaginable way brought home to the grey people of government that what had been done to Bob was unjust, and would not stand. Eventually these folks got the message, and it was a great day in October, 1995, at *another* AOPA convention that Administrator David Hinson (who had no part in the genesis of this debacle) returned Bob's medical certificate to him by satellite broadcast. To fully appreciate the drama of this moment, enjoy this book.

F. Lee Bailey
Manalapan, Florida
June 20, 1999

TABLE OF CONTENTS

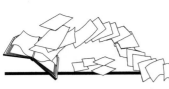

Introduction

Fair Warning: A Few Words from Our Sponsor...

It is not the truth that makes man great, but man who makes the truth great.
Confucius

Greetings, Folks.

The book that you hold in your hand portrays yet another variation of the classic struggle of a single, embattled but ennobled, man *"Fighting City Hall"* ...only in this tale, our erstwhile hero actually wins...

But not without a vicious fight and at great cost.

As the world grows increasingly complex and our governments intrude further and further into our lives, we seem to be losing control over more and more of what we choose to do with them... including the right to set courses for our destiny. Facets of the government not only wind up with increasing responsibility, but seem to be gifted with more authority than we ever intended them to have in setting our lives in directions that may not necessarily be of our choosing... and thus allow them to stand in absolute judgment of whom and what we are.

In the world of aviation, the Federal Aviation Administration (and to a lesser extent, the National Transportation Safety Board) has become the judge, jury and executioner for those who love, live, play and work with the world of aviation. The FAA has an ever-increasing set of ponderous and highly-restrictive rules that govern the conduct and well-being of each pilot who flies through our skies.

Further, it has the absolute power to see those rules through to whatever resolution they deem suitable. When a pilot gets into a row with the FAA, they do not fight them in a normal court like you or I would in a normal legal dispute.

No — they meet the FAA in an "Administrative" court where the FAA has absolute authority over everything. The NTSB has some initial involvement in what happens to a pilot in conflict with the FAA, but every ruling the NTSB may make is subject to immediate reversal by the order of the FAA's omnipresent and omnipotent Administrator.

The FAA wields this power aggressively. Overturning an NTSB decision is *not* an unusual event in the aviation world. In fact, it appears to be the *rule* rather than the exception. Worse, the rights we were all promised as free Americans... i.e., due process, the Bill of Rights, the Constitution, the very Declaration of Independence itself... all those lovely concepts get thrown out the window and scattered to the winds because of the Administrative protocols and privileges the FAA has given itself in order to be officious.

Sound ominous? It is... really. When a pilot is "busted", he or she is not guaranteed counsel... hearsay evidence (he said/she said) is not only admissible but used with abandon; the rules of evidence are a daydream; there are no Miranda warnings; you cannot necessarily plead the "Fifth", and achieving an open hearing to be heard before a jury of your peers is but a pipe-dream. If some guy gets caught selling drugs to school children, he is entitled to far more consideration under the law than *any* pilot who comes afoul of the FAA—no matter how inconsequential the infraction.

That's fact, not hyperbole.

It's also scary... because the power held by this agency over US citizens who happen to be airmen is unparalleled anywhere in North America, and possibly the world.

Consequently, it's a wonder that justice gets done in the world of aviation (and quite often it does not). However, the saving grace in all this is that aviation is still a tight-knit community and most people who work within the FAA are those who love flying and aviation as much or more than the folks they regulate. As such, they tend to offer a degree of fairness and propriety the system does not mandate. That has been the FAA's redeeming quality more often than not. Its people are often far fairer than the system they administrate... and sometimes they are even penalized for acting so.

However, when Feds who are less than fair come into play and decide to act in ways that are counterproductive to the interests of aviation or individual aviators, the system seems to do little or nothing to stop them. In fact, that system allows them to run roughshod over the individual and the collective rights of aviation and aviators. Once a problem started by such errant Feds starts rolling along, there is little to stop it and bureaucratic momentum often keeps it alive a lot longer than common sense would have you think it might.

This is just such a story, where the selfish and errant aims of a few "Bad Feds" and a top-heavy, arrogant bureaucracy unfairly targeted one individual flyer, who might have been grounded in perpetuity, if history was allowed to repeat itself... but it didn't.

Every now and then an unfair system takes on a supremely "fair" man (and one who does not know the meaning of quitting) and his devoted cadre of friends... and that's when all hell breaks loose and even those who make the rules find that they are in for a fight.

Before we dive in to this magnum opus, let me add the following caveat. Because of the intricacies and vagaries of the system, this is a difficult and involved story to tell. When I first tackled this project, I had a feeling it would be an involved process, and it might take a year instead of the two it has consumed, but I had no idea how difficult a task it would eventually turn out to be... involving hundreds of people, over a dozen Federal Agencies or departments, thousands of rules, regs and protocols, and tons of research... just the Freedom of Information Act requests, alone, turned up over 7000 pages of documentation.

So... hold on as I tell the tale, as it may get a bit basic here and there for those of you with prior aviation backgrounds, but since I want every nasty nuance of this story to be understood, I'd rather commit the sin of being too explanatory than being misunderstood. Further, I'm going to throw out all the formality and try to tell this tale as I would if we were sitting at the corner pub, with good friends, discussing a vexing story.

I'm going to be direct, and I'm going to try to make it interesting (which most of it definitely is... though there are minute details that might tend to get a mite laborious

here and there). I'm going to tell you what I learned with as much insight and detail as I can... while also warning you all that I got *very* involved in this story as it unfolded and that I developed some strong personal feelings about how this matter was handled... and the effect it had on aviation and my friend Bob Hoover.

Please note one thing, in particular, as you read this. This is *my* work. If anyone has to take any flak for what appears between these covers, it is I. While I relied on the words, records, and testimony of/from many people; I wish to note that if you have a problem with anything herein, your problem is with me and *not* Bob Hoover, F. Lee Bailey, John Yodice, Norbert Nester or any other of the heroes who made a happy ending possible.

Also be advised that I have played industry pundit for over two decades and my style gets a bit sarcastic now and then. I can be a real wise-ass when a story gets ridiculous and where justice and aviation get treated as a poor stepchild... as it was here... so be forewarned: There is a fairly high disbelief factor at work here but the things herein documented really did happen... and there were far more than what we could cram between a few hundred pages. Sit back and strap in, folks; this story is a heck of a ride.

You see, in 1992, the FAA went after Robert Anderson "Bob" Hoover, a well-known and much-beloved airshow pilot with an amazing history behind him and a cadre of friends and fans that no one else in aviation can claim.

And that's when the FAA finally faced a foe that was bigger and better than they were... America's-pilots and the good old fashioned concept of "justice."

Chapter 1

Oke City '92: Who Knew?

Appreciation is a wonderful thing;
it makes what is excellent in others belong to us as well.
Voltaire

Airshows have become one of the largest outdoor spectator sports in the world, along with major league baseball and auto racing. As a matter of fact, according to the International Council of Airshows, the leading airshow industry association, airshow spectator numbers are second only to auto racing in terms of sheer population... and those numbers continue to grow year to year as the industry matures and learns how to draw more and more people to the excitement and thrills of the greatest shows *over* earth.

As such, this industry has its superstars just like any other. However, few major spectator sports feature superstars whose very lives totally rely on their unerring skills and continual excellence. The tolerance for error in the airshow business is far smaller than any sport I know. An airshow pilot can be killed because of a tenth of a second of error or indecision, from whence the ground then becomes an unyielding, uncompromising taskmaster... often asking for one's life as a consequence.

Men and women who have devoted thousands of hours and hundreds of thousands of dollars honing their skills and developing their aircraft have become the aerial showpersons who have thrilled millions of people a year and are fast becoming some of the most recognized, skillful artisans known to aviation.

Despite much internal political trouble and other problems, one of the premier Airshows in the USA is the annual Aerospace America Airshow held each year in Oklahoma City, OK... which I'm amused to note is also the home of the FAA's National Training Center and a number of other FAA centers ... including the pivotal Civil Aero-Medical Institute (CAMI). Outside Washington, there are few larger concentrations of FAA activity and FAA personnel. It's a *huge* airshow, drawing in tens of thousands of people and the hottest airplanes and performers from all around the world and from both the civilian and the military communities. The 1992 edition was scheduled from Thursday, June 18 to Sunday, June 21. The primary performances were set for Friday, Saturday and Sunday, while Thursday was set aside for press briefings, media rides, practice and getting ready for the big event.

The usual Aerospace America Airshow reads like a "Who's Who" list of airshow stars. While the annual roster does change from year to year, this show can usually count on getting the best and brightest to perform over OKC based on their sheer numbers and the political pull of being in America's heartland as well as the host to some of the FAA's largest nerve centers.

This year was no exception. A truly stellar cast of characters was gathered for what was to be a fine airshow, staffed and managed by some of the cream of the crop of the OKC aviation and political community.

One of the true driving forces behind the 1992 Aerospace America Airshow was a pretty young gal by the name of Kathy Jones. Kathy is a sweetheart... one of those permanently pleasant personalities who is a joy to be around — and one of the few who can maintain such a persona in the midst of a business that not only gets "political" but tends to be a mite cutthroat, to boot. So... well established as the darling of the airshow community both for her expertise and knowledge of the industry as much as her sweet and friendly demeanor, Kathy's job as Show Director was something of a legacy.

Many of her responsibilities were once accomplished by her husband, Tom, a one-time member of the US Aerobatic Team. A burgeoning airshow superstar, "Tommy" tragically died just a few years earlier in the very same show that was now entrusted to her expert care.

Tommy was a truly ebullient personality, known for a quick, if sometimes bizarre, wit and a true gift when it came to aerobatic flight. Tommy was a prankster, a bit of a scamp and an absolute "hoot" to be around. Wherever Tommy was, fun was sure to follow. In 1988, Tommy was a member of the US Aerobatic Team and proud to have helped the team score many a strong showing in that year's World Championships held in Red Deer, Alberta, Canada. It was the first North American World Aerobatic Contest in over a decade and turned into quite an event for the US, which came away with a lot of gold and a US Pilot earning the coveted title of World Champion, Henry Haigh—one of Tommy's heros.

Tommy had come up the aerobatic ladder using a beefy, if somewhat rotund, aerobatic biplane called a Pitts Special. His most recent version at that time, the S2-S, was a nearly 300-hp monster with a rugged steel fuselage, wood wing and fabric covering, known for strength and agility.

He had modified it extensively for airshow and competition work and it had also survived a few near-disasters, once while throwing a propeller at low altitude (leading to a necessarily hasty landing that was mostly a controlled crash) and another while trying to work around weather enroute to an airshow, forcing him to make a landing in a vacant field as the weather went further and further sour.

Although Tommy's bipe had seen him through a series of travails, he grew increasingly aware that the days of the biplane's dominance in world aerobatic competition were nearly over.

At the 1988 World Aerobatic Championship, Tommy became truly enamored with a robust beast of an airplane flown by the Russian Aerobatic Team, the Sukhoi SU-26, a monstrous, radial-engine-powered behemoth known for its rugged strength and lightning-fast maneuverability. It was one tough son-of-a-gun... employing advanced composites and lots of titanium steel to make up one of the toughest airplanes ever built — and a wild one, at heart. It was, literally, a brute.

In little time, Tommy arranged to become one of the first Americans to own this craft, a machine that had powered several Soviet Aerobatic victories for its team and

others in the Communist block.

In 1990, Jones was flying airshows around the country in his "Russian Rage" and despite some teething pains (another failed prop, at one point, as well as the ever-present learning curve intrinsic in learning a complexly-featured airplane), and finally wound up at Oklahoma City for the 1990 rendition of their annual airshow.

Tommy was not only a featured performer, but the "Boss" for many portions of the show *and* the host to a large contingent of Russian performers and pilots who came to show their planes and skills at Oke City.

The combination of an immense workload, as well as playing host to an effervescent group of Russian pilots and his own airshow schedule, proved to be too demanding for the multi-talented but thoroughly exhausted Jones... who made a small error in his aerobatic sequence at the show and was killed as his Sukhoi hit the ground in front of thousands of horrified spectators.

As tragic as this accident was to Kathy, who had lost a husband and a friend, it was a measure of her character that she did not hide away from the world she shared with her husband for several years. Airshows were as much a part of her life as Tommy's... they had even tied the knot in Las Vegas during one of the International Council of Airshows Annual Conventions. So, as she worked though the immense loss of her husband, she remained committed to the world they shared. She took over the reigns of administration for much of the Oklahoma City Airshows... a move that kept her close to a world that was destined to remain a big part of her life.

When Kathy booked an airshow act, they were happy to come and perform, and the 1992 roster was a pretty heavy-duty one... even for OKC.

A show this size requires a super human effort to setup, organize, manage and monitor. The governing organization in OKC had a sizeable staff of volunteers and paid professionals who manage everything from the airshow schedules and crowd control to trash pickup.

One key part of the immense equation is the monitoring conducted by the FAA. Staff members of the FAA check out the performers, the facilities and the airplanes, monitoring the actual show for signs of anything that might be outside safety or regulatory constraints. Most of the time, the people who conduct this activity for the FAA are not remotely qualified to fly airshows themselves (and may not have ever flown a real, live airshow-style aerobatic maneuver *ever*), but are called upon to actually judge and criticize those who do.

Airshow monitoring is generally considered rather cool duty for an FAA Inspector; it is usually somewhat exciting and often brings them into contact with persons of some fame or reputation. Face it — even FAA Inspectors have a number of heros whom they might enjoy meeting. Besides, working an airshow for a few days surely beats flying a desk in some stuffy government office.

This OKC airshow was no exception. The local FSDO (Flight Standards District Office) of the FAA assigned a few Inspectors to the event and many others attended, either by themselves or with family, just for their own enjoyment... but were nonetheless always keeping an eye out for things that might come under their area of responsibility.

Two Inspectors in particular, James Kelln and Clint Boehler, were assigned by the FSDO to monitor the event and participated in many pre-show planning functions with no major complications or concern.

"They really didn't have much to say," says Kathy Jones, "they didn't seem to have any problems with anyone and pretty much kept to themselves."

"So far, so good," she remembered thinking as she made ready to get the 1992 show off to a start. One of the more recent features to be added to the modern airshow is the prevalence of "chalets"... special deluxe areas reserved for corporate sponsors willing to put up some big bucks in return for special consideration and amenities. These corporate chalets have become a boon to cash-strapped airshow organizing committees, who get big money so that some of the more prominent movers and shakers in the local community can treat their employees and clientele to special seats and plush accommodations and play "big-shot" for their friends and business associates. The chalets are usually equipped with a large tent, lots of real, live seats (most airshow spectators have to stand up or pick an inviting bit of the local turf/tarmac from which to observe the goings-on), food, drinks (many offer a full bar, or at least beer), excellent viewing locations and other perks.

These chalets are *the* place to be for an airshow... and usually open their locations to airshow officials, local politicians, the media, and the local FAA (basically anyone with an airshow ID badge).

Many performers also frequent these sites to press the flesh and let these sponsors know that the money and support are appreciated (and let's face it... they are usually the most pleasant spot on the field to wile away the hours before or after a performance). It was there that a number of performers and officials ran into the FAA airshow monitors, often near the food/drink tables and occasionally engaged in conversation or activities that took them out of line of sight with the goings-on of the airshow. Both primary Inspectors, Kelln and Boehler, were seen there a lot and seemed to be having a great time, evincing no great distress with anything they had seen or inspected. They seemed far more interested in chatting with folks than in looking at the show. One other FAA Inspector, Norbert Nester, attending with his son, noted that both of his fellow Inspectors seemed rather wedded to the chalets and once the show was under way, seemed to use this as their base of operations.

There was plenty to see at Oke City... and as usual, there was an incredible collection of acts and features for folks to feast their airshow-hungry eyes and ears upon. Among the superstars to be featured at OKC was none other than Sean Tucker, an effervescent fellow known for one of the rowdiest and fastest-moving biplane aerobatic acts in the world. This guy possesses a strongly positive personality and a love for flying that really shows up when he flies, as he herds a 300+ HP biplane through the skies with incredible abandon—loops, rolls, tumbling, spinning, you name it... the only time his airplane stops gyrating is when they close the hangar doors at the end of the day.

Sean is also a high-powered personality, with an infectious sense of humor. He projects a very optimistic, aggressively friendly persona to all who come into contact with him. A pivotal role model for the airshow community, Sean's operation is a family affair, with his son often employed as an airshow announcer on the ground as his father tumbles through the skies just a few hundred yards away. Sean's also not a bashful guy when it comes to his thoughts and beliefs... regaling those who ask with just what's on his mind with little hesitation or fluff.

FAA Inspector Norbert Nester, who was to play a pivotal role in the Bob Hoover saga, remembers Sean as a unique personality: *"You know Sean is the epitome of a Chris-*

tian family man. He is out there doing a job to the best of his ability and I have never ever seen that man do anything towards the public or another performer or anybody that was anything less than gracious. He is a gentleman, no question about it."

Steve Oliver, a member of Pepsi Skywriters also performed at OKC. Steve and his wife Susan have a unique specialty. In addition to the usual airshow excitement, they boast skills as Skywriters, a talent that seems to have all but disappeared from the planet in the last few years.

Steve has a beautiful old bipe equipped with a smoke system. That system pumps a fair amount of Corvus oil right into the hot exhaust system of the aircraft, enabling it to billow a long trail of thick white smoke. Steve and Susan used that to create a trail that they used carefully and expertly to spell huge letters and words in the sky... and message the crowds over OKC for several hours that weekend. Steve is a quieter sort with a great wit and a calm manner. Married to his airshow partner, Susan (who does most of the sky-writing these days), Steve's life is fully wrapped up in airshows and the classic aircraft that are his particular penchants.

Delmar Benjamin is a pilot who lavishly and expertly built a full-scale replica of one of the most famous and deadly air racers ever designed, the Gee-Bee R-1, which looks something like a barrel strapped to a small set of wings. Benjamin had flummoxed the airshow business with the debut of this airplane only a short time before... as this airplane had a truly deadly history from its 1930 air racing days... putting more than one pilot in peril and in some cases, their very graves.

Benjamin's replica is quite faithful to the original and it was rumored that this pilot-killer would soon do the same to Benjamin, who upon completing the bird went and did what no one expected... thoroughly mastering the Gee-Bee and putting together a thrilling airshow routine that actually made the bulbous, ungainly bird (which appears to all the world like a flying football with a man-sized propeller attached) look good. Since hitting the circuit, the Gee-Bee has become a world-favorite.

Pilots who have seen this act dozens of times still shake their heads in wonder at how this quiet farmer/pilot can master an airplane that even the late great Jimmy Doolittle called a killer. Benjamin, himself, is quite the contrast when compared to the aircraft he flies... being as quiet and unassuming as the Gee-Bee is loud and aggressive. A farmer by trade, he is easily one of the best airshow pilots in the world but speaks his mind with ease and confidence whenever drawn forth and challenged... but only when he feels it appropriate.

Another pivotal act in the 1992 Aerospace America extravaganza was that of the French Connection Airshow team, flown by pilot Daniel Heligoin and Montaine Mallet. This act features a husband and wife of French parentage flying two low-wing wooden French aerobatic trainers in some of the closest formation aerobatics ever done.

One of the more thrilling aspects of their act is lead pilot Daniel Heligoin's opening maneuver... a single violent snap roll (an ultra-fast rolling maneuver that is essentially a horizontal spin) right on take-off and at an altitude that seems destined to grass-stain the wingtips of his CAP-10B aerobatic trainer. Another amazing draw to their act is the mirror image style of formation that they fly... flying a series of maneuvers while one is literally right on top of the other, upside down, so that they are canopy to canopy and eyeball to eyeball. It is a breathtaking routine. Together, they are a formidable couple... Montaine is the business ace of the two while Daniel is definitely the consummate show-

man. Both are very friendly folks and though a bit guarded with strangers, they are warm and endearingly personable folks the minute the ice is broken.

And that was not all... with plenty more pilots, planes, skydivers and other features, it was a jam-packed set of performers as far as the civilian sector was concerned.

In addition to the civilian performers, the military representation was very strong. The US Army Golden Knights parachute team jumped a number of times, displaying freefall and parachute demonstrations that are always a crowd pleaser. The Marine Corp. Harrier AV-8B "Jump-Jet", the only operational V-STOL jet in US military inventories, did a number of demonstrations thrilling attendees with its awesome roar, ability to hover and take-off and land straight up and down just like a helicopter. Russian jets like the MiG 29 showed and carved up the sky with abandon. The Coast Guard demonstrated the CH-47 helicopter. Brutish Army A-10 tank-busters cranked through the skies simulating their lethal ability to take out enemy armor. And a number of historic military aircraft (now owned by well-heeled civilian pilots) flew over OKC and showed off the historic birds that helped us win WWII... all in all, it was a heck of a show!

Still, if there was a top draw it had to be the fellow who climbed into a twin-engine, cabin-class bird each day, throwing his trademark straw hat in the seat beside him as he stepped through the door. An ungainly looking fellow, this tall, quiet guy would start his engines and virtually every pilot (especially), everywhere, would stop whatever it was that they were doing to watch him fly... no matter how many times they had seen him do so.

You see, this fellow was none other than Bob Hoover... one of the most respected pilots in the world and a heck of an airshow pilot... a guy without peer who seem beloved and respected by all... or so we once thought.

Chapter 2

Oke City in Detail: Do We Really Have a Problem Here???

*The secret of life is honesty and fair dealing.
If you can fake that, you've got it made.
Groucho Marx (1890-1977)*

In the midst of all this fun, the stage was soon set for one of aviation's greatest legal travesties.

Robert A. "Bob" Hoover was booked into the Oke City show months before and he was pleased to be attending it, as it was easily one of his favorite affairs... especially in 1992, as it was also a chance for he and his wife of (then) 45 years, Colleen, to spend some time with family and friends.

They made plans for this and invited family and friends to stop by and see Bob perform. Because of this, Bob spent less time socializing at the show than he might normally in order to spend more time with Colleen and his family. Scheduled to fly Friday, Saturday and Sunday, Bob flew in by commercial airliner while his announcer, Jim Driskell, brought the airplane in from the previous airshow location. Jim was nearly always the first person to an airshow site when Bob Hoover was on the schedule, since Jim was the ferry-pilot who brought the plane from show to show.

It was usually Jim's job to get the lay of the land, make sure that all initial paperwork was done, see who was whom, check that the airplane was ready to go and figure out what meetings and inspections might be required so that Bob could deal with the rigors of performing without much of the drudgery and bookkeeping that go hand-and-hand with this involved undertaking. It is a wonderfully symbiotic relationship that has withstood decades of airshow performances and the normal wear and tear that such a high-pressure business brings upon those who take it on.

Jim has been "the Hoov's" sidekick for nearly fifty years and a friend for far longer. Outside of Colleen Hoover (Bob's lovely spouse for over 50 years at this writing), there is probably no one on the face of the earth who knows Bob better or who is in a better position to judge the skills and capabilities of this man.

At the same time, Driskell is no "second-banana"; he is a close friend and assists Bob on a number of levels. Jim is a long-time member of the International Council of Air Shows and served six years as a director for that organization. He has acted as *the* narrator for Bob Hoover at all airshows and air races in which he participates in the United States, Canada and Mexico.

Further, Jim flies Bob's Shrike Commander to and from the various airshow sites and has logged over 7500 hours in that airframe (and nearly three-quarters of a million miles just flying from show to show!).

Jim began his association of 46 years with North American Aviation (which became Rockwell International), in 1940. He held top executive positions in Manufacturing and Personnel. He also taught flying and flew corporate aircraft including turboprops and Sabreliner jets.

"Bob came aboard as an experimental test pilot in 1950. I used to try to get a jump on those things that were coming from engineering to manufacturing... so our paths would cross during that period of time and then he went to customer relations from flight test, eventually becoming head of customer relations. I was Assistant to the Division President until I became Division Director of Personnel Administration and Industrial Security in 1959, where Bob and I both reported to the President of the division. Our offices were side-by-side so we sorta grew up within the company together," Driskell explained.

"In February 1973," he continued, *"Bob's ferry pilot left the company for another job and Bob asked me to fly the Shrike for him down to El Centro... and I did it the next week and the next week... and that was over two decades ago. The second year we were on tour, again in El Centro, and the Navy narrator really did a very poor job. This was embarrassing because Bob had me bring Colleen and some friends down in the Shrike and when Bob came in after the show, Colleen said she didn't think much of the narrator, and while I'm agreeing with her, I said 'that's sure right... hell, if I couldn't do any better than that, I'd quit!'. So he (Bob) says 'Fine... tomorrow you're the narrator' and the next day at Yuma, I was the narrator for both the Shrike and the P-51 and ever since then I've done all the airshows!"*

While Jim oversimplifies his qualifications, I have to tell you that for whatever reason, he has grown into the job well. Narrators have to be a combination of entertainer, technical expert, ad-lib artist and air traffic control operator. It's not an easy job, but it's one that the smooth-talking Driskell does well, despite a somewhat mild voice that one wouldn't normally associate with the job until he steps up to a mike. There, he quickly establishes himself as an expert, a friend, an enthusiast and Bob Hoover's goodwill ambassador to the airshow world.

Airshow performers are quick to admit that their performances are often judged both for the skills inherent in the display as well as those owned by the narrator. Jim's got a knack for giving folksy, dignified and understandable narration that offers a delightful "boost" to an airshow. Since he's a pilot, he has the unerring aptitude to apply *"what's happening up there"* to an audience, no matter whether they are pro pilots, airshow veterans or airshow novices. His peers acknowledge this... and since airshows are subject to the same whims of fate as other endeavors, Jim has been called often by airshow performers who wind up without the services of a narrator to "step in" at a moment's notice and save the show. He does this well. Always.

For Jimmy, Oke City was no different. *"Warm, nice weather, a bit of a wind, nothing really unusual,"* he called it. *"The show went off well... big crowds, decent weather and lots of action."* This filled a jam-packed weekend that left few people feeling bored

with the goings-on.

Jim, of course, was a busy fellow. Not only does he get the bird to the show, but he is the manager for all activities involving the performance so that Bob has little to do but be ready to fly and to do so at the right time. *"I want Bob to be free to relax, fly his best, and not have to think of anything else but that."*

These responsibilities take on some intriguing dimensions. As any large event goes on, things take place to screw up schedules, so one of Jim's primary jobs is to keep up with the changes in the schedule and let Bob know when to fly, who to follow, and what to do as things finally reach a "release time" for the actual performance.

Jim remembers keeping an eye on schedule updates and using the radio to relay data to Bob about when he should start his engines, whom he was to follow each day (which could change at a moment's notice), and whatever other info the "Air Boss" (the person who directs all the airborne activity at an airshow), wanted Bob to have.

He played eyes and ears for Bob so that he concentrate on the task at hand... and Bob is quick to note, *"I listen to Jim... he sees things I don't. He has full access to people I don't and his judgment is impeccable... so I appreciate Jim's inputs."*

Other performers remembered applicable aspects of Aerospace America with great clarity. Sean Tucker's memory of that event is particularly extensive... whether it be about Bob's performance, or the FAA monitors that stood in judgement of all who flew. *"Everything he (Bob) did was as professional as can be. I think Oliver was watching the performance and French Connection, too, because Bob is Bob... we ALL watch him. He is one of the icons that's the greats of aviation and I appreciate every performance he flies.'*

Interestingly, Tucker (as well as other performers), remembered a lot about the FAA Airshow monitor's conduct at Aerospace America... *"I do remember Clint Boehler... most of the time he (was) inside of the performer compound socializing. I can't remember that year if he brought his little girl or not. He has a family. Clint never, ever, at any show I've ever worked at OKC, paid attention to a person's performance. Clint was an amicable sort of fellow who wanted to meet the performers, get their autographs, and hang out with them. So he's in the tent, which when you are in the performer tent, you can't see the show because of the way the compound is set up. It's almost impossible to see, and, because I was watching Bob's performance, I wasn't watching Clint. But, every time I ever saw Boehler, (he) was either at the pilot's briefing or inside the tent having a good time, helping himself to refreshments."*

Sean also remembered that the conditions surrounding the show were tricky but not difficult to deal with *"...Oklahoma City has winds, uh, always. You know you're talking Oklahoma... nothing out of the ordinary that we didn't handle. You know what I'm concerned about mostly is when I'm watching a performer, is make sure they hold to that sacred show line. Don't ever cross that. Mr. Hoover never crossed that. I'm also (as an FAA designated Airshow Competency Evaluator) watching the performance technically (to see) how they perform and whether or not they keep within their margins of safety. Mr. Hoover never exceeded his envelope at all. He was always flying safe, and still entertaining. I can't recall the exact winds, but I know they are normally out of the Southeast, which makes it tough... as the Southeast pushes the wind towards the audience. Bob always corrected accordingly. There was NOT a problem."*

Bob's airplane did have some minor problems during the weekend of the Aerospace America Airshow... which is not all that unexpected, as Hoover's steed was originally designed to be a tough but otherwise sedate twin-engine transport plane... something of a mid-level executive airplane. It was never designed to be an airshow mount, and its use as such came as something of an off-the-cuff suggestion by the original manufacturer, North American Aviation (later known as North American Rockwell), to put together some kind of special demonstration to prop up slow sales. Some 2500 performances later, the Aero-Commander Shrike is literally known as the "airplane that Bob Hoover flies..." as his trademark airshow routine is world famous for its unique nature.

This weekend, the landing gear was giving him some trouble as the rigors of the high G loops and rolls, coupled with warm summer temperatures, caused some minor (but not unusual) problems with the electro-hydraulic landing gear extension/ retraction system. Often associated with excessively hot days, air in the hydraulic system would cause an annoying problem called "cavitation" that often lets the gear hang partially outside the shielded wheel wells of his airplane. This can wreak havoc with the smooth flow of air around the airplane and make subtle changes in the aerodynamic characteristics of the aircraft... not to mention create other problems down the line as the gear is commanded to either retract or extend.

The upshot of this is that as the aircraft is being maneuvered aggressively, some of the responses and stability properties Hoover counts on as he flies this very familiar airplane are changed in response to the new aerodynamics induced by the hanging gear. This is not a big deal, especially when you consider that the fellow flying the airplane was probably more experienced in that airplane than anyone else on the face of the planet.

Hoover had dealt with far worse in less benign airplanes for most of his life... but it can induce some minor, sometimes visible, anomalies in what is usually a very smooth performance on the part of a man who has done this routine thousands of times. It was postulated by Hoover that if there were any visible deviations from the norm of his airshow routine, these could easily be caused by such problems... even though every airshow performer polled and present at the show noted no such difficulties.

Let me repeat that... not a single airshow performer (probably the only real group qualified to judge the man) noted that they saw anything but the "usual Hoover excellence."

Cavitation is not an emergency and it affects the aircraft only minimally. According to Jim Driskell, he had experienced the annoyance of such problems *"just flying along. It's no big deal... on that particular airplane... the hydraulic reservoir is a 'hat-section' and in the protected portion of the hat section there's enough hydraulic fluid in there to give you wing flaps and brakes for a landing. So... you look up there and the hydraulic pressure is way down, its not like the airplane is going to fall out of the sky... or that you can't land or have brakes or anything... but the only time I've known it to happen (consistently) is in extreme heat. And that was an absolutely warm weekend."* Oklahoma in June... oh boy!

Hoover described the problem to the FAA and NTSB as "consistent" (he had it on all three "warm" airshow days). *"The first day, I had it, but... there is a technique to getting it back on line, and sometimes it can be accomplished in 30 seconds and sometimes it can take as long as three or four (minutes).*

The procedure to get the pressure back on line, you see, since it has gone to zero and a gear is hanging down... is cycle the gear and try to get that pump, just like pouring water, priming an oil pump, if you will, an old water pump. You have got to do something to get the pressure back in there, (and) get the oil pouring through.

And you can accomplish that by using your nosewheel steering, which is on the top part of the brakes, and you put your feet on them, and just tap them like this, and keep tapping them until you can see an increase in pressure. It is a mystery to me exactly what uncavitates a pump. But that is how you accomplish it."

Mr. Hoover reported that he stayed in communication with the Air Boss while he was dealing with this minor annoyance and even asked the Air Boss if he had time to redo a maneuver that had been interfered with by the cavitation problem and that the Air Boss had said *"yes."*

So minor was the problem, though, that Bob did not bother to communicate it with Driskell, noting that the two of them had been together so long, that there was no need. Further, Driskell confirmed that had he been so notified by Bob of that fact, that he wouldn't have announced the problem, because it would have been too complicated to hold the average airshow audience's attention.

Regardless, the matter was reportedly never discussed during the show and quickly left everyone's short-term memory as any minor glitch often does. Airshow pilots often have to deal with rough engines, balky electrical systems, argumentative radios and dozens of other annoying but otherwise ridiculously minor glitches that do little but create a need for a few seconds of accommodation as one deals with the problem or changes tactics to eliminate the interference from the problem.

Rough engines may require some leaning or quick maintenance (changing plugs, cleaning out fuel injector nozzles, leaning the mixture, etc). Balky electrical systems may require resetting a circuit breaker, a new battery, a jump-start (and mind you, a number of aerobatic airplanes do not have electrical systems at all in order to keep the flying weight down, lessening potential hindrance with performance from the carriage of unnecessary payload).

Bad radios often necessitate switching over to a back-up/secondary radio, a portable unit or simply "Going NORDO" (no radio) and informing the Air Boss to be ready with a light-gun or other prearranged signal if they need to tell him to terminate or extend an airshow performance. In other words... NO BIG DEAL.

When all was said and done, Bob hopped on a plane to go home with his wife; Jimmy loaded up the Shrike and headed off to the next airshow site; and no one felt anything but a sense of accomplishment over a job well done. There was not an inkling that anything had gone wrong or the hint of any suspicion that such had occurred.

Driskell summed it up best... *"Like always, when you get ready to leave after a show, they gas up your airplane, and give you a pat on the 'to-to', and away you go. No one said anything to me that was bad or wrong. None of the FAA said anything to me. The show officials seemed pleased and I had no idea that anything was wrong... and I didn't see anything that was. When I left, I felt we did a good show... and I still do."*

Chapter 3

The AMAZING Bob Hoover Airshow

Art washes away from the soul the dust of everyday life.
Pablo Picasso

A green and white streak rips across the ground, gaining speed as it leaps off the deck. With both engines roaring at full power, a bit of fear grips the uninitiated as they see the Commander tip to one side... and keep tipping. The Commander starts to roll over and over at an altitude that seems too low to allow for safe completion of the maneuver.

As a matter of fact, one first wonders if he's got enough altitude to allow the wingtips to clear the ground as they reach a point where they are pointed straight at the ground (often called "knife-edge"). But... fear soon gives way to amazement as the Commander appears to do things that no such aircraft should be capable of. Before you know it, the Shrike Commander has rolled all the way around and has righted itself before pointing its nose to the heavens and aiming for the Lord's backyard.

It is poetry; it is art; it is excitement. It is Bob Hoover.

This is Bob Hoover in the amazing Shrike Commander, doing his thing better than any other person in the world — with an act that is truly unique and associated only with the tall fellow sitting in the left seat of the Shrike, whilst an old straw hat sits sedately and unsecured on the right.

There are a few things that initially distinguish Bob Hoover from other performers at the today's airshows. The first is the aircraft that Bob has used primarily over the last few years... the Shrike Commander. The Shrike is a twin-engine, entry-level, executive transport originally designed and manufactured by Bob's former employer, North American Rockwell. The cabin class, piston-engine twin is a comfy, quasi-affordable, mini-airliner designed to be bought and flown by well-healed private pilots and small corporations without the necessary cash for a corporate jet or turbo-prop.

It's a sleek little devil known for crisp handling and good operating economics... but hardly for fire-breathing aerobatic skills. As a matter of fact, the Commander, when first introduced to the flying public, was something of a dud... causing some embarrassment and consternation to the higher-ups at Rockwell (prior to the merger with North American) and abject fear in the marketing department.

As unpurchased aircraft piled up on the ramp at North American, their top test pilot, Bob Hoover, was asked if he could design something of a demonstration show that might spark some interest in the twin-engine Commander series... Well, Bob did have a

routine he wanted to do... and it was strikingly similar to the one he had done with a number of other aircraft such as the P-51 Mustang and the P-38 Lightning, as well as other military fighter aircraft. Despite the less aggressive mission of the Shrike Commander, Bob thought he could adapt this routine to the Commander and set out to do so.

Unveiled at a prominent aviation trade show several decades ago, Bob's show turned sales of the Shrike Commander around immediately and birds literally flew off the ramp at North American Rockwell... and Bob's rep as an amazing pilot and aviation booster grew to even greater prominence. It didn't hurt that he turned the sale of a lackluster product into a near immediate hit with the aviation crowd, by showing them that this aircraft was a very capable one, indeed, in the hands of a good pilot.

The Hoover routine, these days, is a breathtaking event, starting off as previously noted, with a bee-line down the runway and a slow roll on takeoff followed by a turn out and return to the field with his signature touchdown/roll/touchdown, where Bob will seem to land the aircraft briefly, allowing just the *right* landing gear to make contact with Mother Earth before rocketing off the runway again into yet another roll at a dazzlingly low altitude, thence to settle back on the ground momentarily on just the *left* gear before taking off again.

Then he goes out to return and start his first single-engine multiple maneuver. After he shuts down one engine entirely, the crowd can literally see that not only has the propeller come to a complete stop, but the blades have been turned directly into the wind (commonly called the "feathered" position, a low-drag condition that presents the least amount of aerodynamic drag on the aircraft). That done, Bob uses the speed/energy of the aircraft to start a "Barnstormer's Loop", which positions the aircraft with its nose upward and allows it to ascend up and up until it literally flies straight up and over its back to head straight back down where it came from, slowly pulling the nose up again so as to allow for a recovery just above the ground at a speed in the neighborhood of 260 miles per hour.

That ain't all... just as the loop is completed at just above ground level, Bob starts another roll and turns in the direction of the "dead" engine! This roll is much different than the first one we saw on takeoff because Bob pauses for a short time every 45 degrees and flies what is called an "Eight Point Roll."

Now, let me tell you something, folks: A good eight point roll is not the world's easiest maneuver to do. You are fighting a number of forces that are trying to divert you from the planned maneuver, adding insult to injury with short hesitations induced eight times.

Sound hard? It is... especially when you consider the fact that this wonderful twin-engine airplane is not only doing this difficult maneuver in front of God and everybody... but doing it with one engine shut down!

A major difference in Bob's performances is not the fact that Bob flies a twin-engine ship (which is unusual on its face)... but the fact that both engines are rarely operating at the same time throughout the twisting, turning performances that Hoover has been giving for *decades*.

So what, you say? Hmm... Let's think about this for a moment.

OK... according to our notes from "Aerodynamics 101" for those of you who may not understand the rudimentary aspects of multi-engine flight, a twin-engine aircraft with wing-mounted (non-center-line) engines has its share of special requirements. Shutting down one engine not only takes away half of your power, but also increases your

flying problems, as the remaining power is coming from just one side of the aircraft... so the powered side is pushing the nose away from it and toward the side of the dead engine. In other words, the good engine is trying to get the plane to fly "crooked".... and left to its own devices, that's exactly what it will do. This is not a good thing.

This means that if you want to fly straight, you have to use some control to correct the fact that the powered side is trying to pivot the aircraft. So... if you add some rudder (the control surface that turns the nose literally from side to side) to keep the nose straight, you are also adding drag to the mix and further robbing the aircraft of some of the thrust of the engine that is still running.

Every control input causes drag and every attitude change from the most efficient position also causes drag... so instead of losing 50 percent of your power when you lose an engine, you've often lost over 60 percent of the available thrust you might have had by the time you correct for the aerodynamic nastiness this "uneven" or "asymmetric" thrust causes. At this point, flying the airplane becomes a delicate balancing act, because there's rarely enough power left to fly the airplane, normally, much less in abnormal conditions... like upside down or through eight-point hesitation rolls just a few feet off the ground.

To pilots, this maneuver is particularly awesome in that twin-engine aircraft actually require more precision and skill to fly than single-engine aircraft. Many multi-engine pilots take the fact that they have two engines for granted and when one quits, do not exercise proper skill and control, to find themselves in big trouble. With low power, an asymmetric flight/thrust condition, and an aircraft that obviously has other problems, the loss of an engine often makes the accident statistics for multi-engine aircraft worse then their single-engine counterparts.

Think about that... the extra engine often makes such aircraft more dangerous, statistically speaking, than aircraft that rely on just one motor. This happens because it is simply too easy to lose control of a twin with a failed engine if you do not stay ahead of its demands. As a matter of fact, if you do not properly juggle all the requirements of airspeed, energy and attitude properly, you come to a point where you literally lose control of the aircraft and unless critical action is taken, control will remain lost until you hit something. That hurts. Usually, it kills.

Yet another distinction in a Hoover airshow is often lost on the general public but not on people with even a hint of aeronautical knowledge. Bob's performances are known to be some of the smoothest in the business due to the fact that he does not "muscle" his aircraft through dozens of maneuvers using shear horsepower but instead, ekes every bit of energy, inertia and aeronautical advantage out of that aircraft that he can.

The reason that Hoover gets away with so much in this aircraft is because he understands the threats imposed by these conditions intimately. One way to mitigate the loss of an engine is to be in a condition where its loss does not have an immediate and harsh effect on the aircraft.

Therefore, whenever the situation allows, Bob builds up as much speed and altitude as possible and "puts it in the bank" so that when he kills one or both engines, he can "coast" along with the residual kinetic energy stored in that sleek, efficient airframe. Since the airframe is very "clean", aerodynamically speaking, it slows down at a less rapid rate than something a lot more bulbous or obtuse. The combination of the stored speed/

altitude in that multi-thousand pound aircraft can be ridden quite a while before the situation calls for critical measures.

Don't misunderstand me: Such maneuvers must be mentally recalculated hundreds of times per minute and are affected greatly by a number of constantly changing parameters... wind, height above sea level, weather conditions, you name it. It takes an expert to make it all work... an expert who is literally without peer.

So... the artistry and skill of what Hoover does is not lost on many pilots who understand that this kind of mastery is a rare thing indeed.

Yikes! It is easy to get wrapped up in the details of all this... and I guess that's my point. This stuff ain't easy!

But... back to the airshow routine.

As soon as Bob finishes the eight-point hesitation roll, he zooms high up overhead and does two zero-airspeed stalls, reaching such a "slow" attitude that there is not enough air following over and around the wing to support flight... so it falls until it regains the proper airflow and attitude to get back to business. The first of these stalls is done with both engines screaming out as much power as they are able... and it's a cool thing to watch it reach a point where it literally comes to a halt in the sky before the nose pitches down and dives for the earth.

The second of these stalls is done with both engines turned *off... no power*. He builds up a lot of speed prior to shutting the engines down and then zooms skyward again with nothing but the whistle of the wind passing by the aircraft's fuselage and wings to denote that fact that something very cool is about to happen. The air noise is fairly audible at high speed, but as Hoover reaches the zenith of his zoom-style climb toward Valhalla, the noise dissipates to... NOTHING.

Narrator Jim Driskell is a master at dramatizing the keener aspects of this insanity as his voice becomes quieter during the process of the maneuver until he's doing nothing more than a light whisper at the apex of Bob's rocket-like launch, which is now pointing nearly straight up. At the top of this climb, the Shrike slows to a halt, with its pointy proboscis pointed up as if it were the Space Shuttle before it flops down rather speedily and heads *straight* down at the ground, pulling out just above the runway.

The next maneuver is a *sixteen*-point hesitation roll... which means that Bob now has to momentarily hesitate sixteen times — that's every 22.5 degrees — in order for the maneuver to look symmetrical and smooth. But... having done it the eight-point version with one engine shut off, how do you top that? Easy (OK... "easy" only applies if you're Bob Hoover... s'cuse me...), you do the *sixteen*-point hesitation roll with *both* engines shut off! Mind you, I've seen him do this more times than I can count... literally hundreds... but it's still scary as hell to those of us who know what a juggling act this maneuver is from an energy management and aerodynamic control standpoint.

The next series of maneuvers is a real thrill to pilots, especially, who can appreciate what it is that Bob is up to. Hoover's famed "Energy Management Series" involves him powering up both engines again, and climbing up to 2500 feet or so, diving the aircraft toward terra firma — as he shuts off both engines *again*(!)

He then performs another Barnstormer's loop with nearly total silence as he pitches over the top of the big circle in the sky, followed by an eight-point roll, and a 180-degree turn.

After this, he lands (still without power, mind you) and uses the residual energy

of the landing to taxi the bird back to the place that he started... often only requiring a few nudges of the brakes as he comes to stop in front of a predetermined place that he rarely misses (though on truly windy days or on well-sloped/obstructed runways, this has to be one of the hardest maneuvers in his repertoire to accomplish). One of the most memorable aspects of a Hoover/Shrike performance is that silent finish... as Bob comes soaring in with *both* engines out to lunch. The only major sounds you hear are Jim Driskell's low tones trying to describe every bit of action without competing with the whoosh of the unpowered Shrike as it slides on in. As the crowd tensely waits to see if he's going to get to the announcing stand or other pre-planned vantage point, they break into wild applause as he squeaks to a stop that often positions him right in front of the airshow. It's a magical moment.

What most people do not see in all this, though, is the personal maneuvers that come afterward, where he and long-time friend and expert Shrike pilot Jim Driskell grade the entire performance... always striving for excellence, precision, safety and a jolly good show. Jimmy says that Bob *"is his own worst critic... but at least he's qualified to be!"*

Famed lawyer and former Marine Corp. pilot F. Lee Bailey has had an unusual vantage point to all this. He is one of the few people who can lay claim to having flown with Bob Hoover during his trademark routine. He gave a stirring description at the 1994 AOPA Convention in Palm Springs, CA, of Hoover's mastery over gravity and aerodynamics and what it took for him to actually entrust his life to his long-time friend.

"Fifteen years and eight months ago, in Hillsboro, OR, on a rainy evening when the ceiling was on the deck, I sat at dinner across from the legendary airshow pilot and demonstrator for Rockwell Commander's Shrike, Robert A. Hoover, enjoying the exchange of war stories—mostly his, not mine.

And in a moment of magnanimity, Bob, who was not only demonstrating for Rockwell but for Enstrom, then my helicopter company as well, said, "You know, I've never allowed anyone to ride up forward in the co-pilot's seat during the airshow."

'But,' he said, 'I think you could be trusted.'

And I said, 'That's wonderful,' knowing full well that the airshow would not take place. The following day, the occasion being the opening of a new facility at Aero-Air at the Hillsboro Airport, owned by the Ralstons, father and son dealers for both Commander and Enstrom. To my abject horror, the ceiling began to lift. The FAA Inspector came 'round. He said, 'Well, I understand you'll be riding today, if the weather clears, as crew. May I see your license and medical?'

I said 'Guess what? They are back at the hotel some 45 minutes away; there isn't time to go get them. I'll just sit this one out.'

'Ah, come on,' he said, 'everybody knows you have a license, Mr. Bailey. I'll sign you on.'

I called my insurance man (who happened to be my next door neighbor). I have heavy key-man policies, mostly in favor of banks. And I said, 'Gus, my insurance coverage does not allow me to fly in airshows—does it?'

And he said, 'I've got the policy right here, let me look.'

He said, 'Are you being paid?'

I said, 'No.'

He said, 'You're clear, have at it.'

There was no way out.

If you have not had the experience of rolling a Shrike on take-off at 120 kts, you have not lived. Now I had agreed to keep my hands on the seats so they wouldn't get in the way of the controls. Absent that agreement, my hands never would have left the seat: that was the only way to stay in it.

Anybody that tells you that you can put a glass of water on the glare-shield when Bob does his act, is an abject liar. I never once saw the ball in the center of the glass. When we were upside down with one feathered and one wide open, and screaming, nibbling below Vmc, Bob pointed out that absent his long legs we might go into a flat spin. Otherwise it was a delightful ride and, of course, once it was over, I stepped out bursting with triumph, as the first one to have survived that experience. Bob and I have been very close friends ever since, because I always viewed that ride as the time that he saved my life."

As so many will tell you, the full Bob Hoover/Shrike Commander performance is a thing of beauty... more ballet than thrill show, more precision than brute force, more smooth and linear than wild and brash. It is the product of precision and skill and experience... and no so-called cognitive deficit or other medically quantifiable deficiency would ever have allowed this man to keep doing what he's been doing so long and so well without severe consequences. Period.

Chapter 4

Hoover, Huh? So, Just Who IS This Guy? Why All The Fuss?

The art of life is to know how to enjoy a little and to endure much.
William Hazlitt

Who is Bob Hoover? Why is anyone making such a fuss about this guy as to devote a whole book (and not a short one, either) to him? And, mind you, a book that's only about three years of his life (albeit turbulent ones)?

If you've been anywhere near the aviation world for the last fifty years or so, it would be hard not to have heard about Bob Hoover, a man who can easily lay claim to the title "living legend." Hoover is to aviation what John Kennedy was to politics... a beloved symbol of what the best is in an industry where being good is a life or death situation. In the aviation hierarchy, this guy is pretty much at the top of the ladder.

If that's not impressive enough, this is also one of the guys who made our life better by risking his — first in WWII and later as a test pilot who helped advance the aviation art a fair degree by testing the newest, most risky aircraft proposals to ever hit the skies.

As a matter of fact, when Chuck Yeager made that momentous first flight through the Sound Barrier in 1947, it was Bob Hoover who was following him closely and keeping an eye on his welfare... and was very nearly the man who made the flight that made Yeager a household word, had he not been caught buzzing a civilian airfield (fly-boys *will* be fly-boys...) and earned a small slap on the wrist from his superiors.

It is Yeager, himself, who pretty much defines the skill level reached by Hoover. Having occasionally worked with General Yeager for nearly 15 years, I can tell you that this is a man who does not praise others easily. He has a very strong personality, no lack of confidence and ego, and does not suffer fools or amateurs for more than a second (take my word for it).

This is not to unduly criticize the General, because there is no question that it took an extraordinary amount of confidence and skill to strap himself to some very dangerous airplanes and come back, time after time after time... so do understand that when I say "confidence" I do not mistake that for undue arrogance. Regardless, General Yeager tends to praise others sparingly, simply because he has flown with the best and worked with some of the keenest minds in the world, and there are not many people who can measure up to that standard. So when General Yeager called Bob Hoover *"the best pilot I ever saw...,"* understand that there may be no higher praise for a pilot than that.

What has endeared Hoover to the general public, though, whether or not they even remembered his name, are the airshow performances he has given to millions of people — doing things with airplanes that would cause even the best pilots in the world to shake their heads in wonder. And he keeps doing this, year in and year out and is doing so today... even though this legendary airshow pilot, test pilot, fighter pilot and aviation ambassador is now over 77 years old. Wow... 77 years old, huh? That sounds pretty old until you realize that there are a number of older pilots and many older citizens doing critical work who are far older... heck, Dr. Michael DeBakey is still doing critical heart surgery... and he's *OVER* 90 years old.

One story, actually occurring at the same airshow that got him into such hot water to begin with, tells a lot about Hoover and about those who admire him. Further, it involves some pivotal characters in this drama... and may have served as the decision factor for one FAA person to step forward and put his career on the line when it became obvious that Hoover was in trouble.

FAA Inspector Norbert Nester spent one day at the show in the company of his nine-year-old son, Randy. He remembers that *"Bob... was just standing there having a cold drink, when I stepped over to him (without identifying himself as an FAA Inspector) and I asked him if he had just a minute to visit with my son and I. (He was) just as congenial as he could be. I introduced my son... I said, 'Randy, this is Mr. Bob Hoover, and you may not remember it in the future but I would encourage you to remember this day and this time because you are getting to meet one of the all time greats in the aviation industry.*

I didn't expound on all of Bob's records and all that other stuff. I just tried to make an impression on my son that here was a man that really stood well above most everybody else in the industry. He has been recorded in the history books... history is going to be very kind to Mr. Hoover. He was on the forefront and cutting edge of so many aviation events, records and different things he did... so I made it a point for him to realize that he was someone special, that he really should acknowledge this and try to remember.

Bob was a little bit embarrassed by this as he was humble about it all.

He said, 'Well yeah, I've done a few things. It is a pleasure to meet you Randy', and stuck his hand out. I stepped away and I just let them stand there and talk. They visited for oh, I don't know, 5-10 minutes, something like that... and you could see there was some interaction going on between them.

The next thing I know my son comes over and he said, 'Is it okay if I go with Mr. Hoover?' I said, 'Sure, go ahead.' Well, Bob walked him out across the flight line, took him over to his famous Shrike, opened the door, climbed in, and sat down in that airplane with my son for about the next 15 minutes or so. I guess he answered every conceivable question the kid could ever have about flight."

Nester was particularly amused at this event because he specifically remembers Bob asking, *"Have you ever seen a Commander or Shrike?"* Randy looked at him with the straightest face and said *'Nope!'*

"Well, I have to admit being really amused with this, Nester continued, "because Randy had been in a number of Commanders and around those types of planes...

But he looked at Mr. Hoover with the straightest face and got quite the guided tour. You've got to understand my son is pretty sharp, and he knew a golden opportunity when he saw it!

So... Bob Hoover took him over to the Shrike, while I did my best to keep a straight face. Bob told me, 'That kid, he asked about everything in that airplane, no doubt about it'. He spent some time with Randy and made the kid feel really important and special, like a kid should feel when they get a chance to meet somebody like that. When they came back, Bob shook hands with him and he said, 'Randy it is a pleasure to meet you. I was glad we got to visit. Keep up your interest in flying... and off he went, leaving my son feeling like someone special. That's something he'll never forget!"

By the way, Bob did NOT know that this kind was the son of an FAA Inspector at the that time... this is just the way that he is.

That's a great story... and it says a lot about Bob Hoover, the man. The most amazing part of this, though, is the fact that Bob has done this hundreds of times for children all over the world... whether they are the sons of FAA Inspectors or not... each time trying to inspire them to do great things with their lives and to treasure the world of aviation.

So... What Is This Guy's Story?

Bob Hoover was born January 24, 1922, in Nashville, TN. His schooling was uneventful, with grades ranging from C's to B's, though mathematics was occasionally a difficult subject. He started flying at age 16 at Nashville's Berry Field, earning money through odd jobs at a local grocery store.

Enlisting in the Tennessee National Guard after graduation from high school, Bob was selected for Army pilot training, where the loops and rolls he had taught himself during his civilian training were practiced in earnest. Upon graduation, Bob was sent to England. Following the invasion of North Africa by the allies, he was reassigned to Casablanca where he started testing all types of aircraft that had been transported over-seas on ships and then reassembled onsite. This, mind you, at the tender age of 21!

Assigned to the 52nd fighter group, stationed in Sicily, Bob got to fly with one of the only two Spitfire outfits in the Army's Air Force. He flew 58 successful missions, but his luck was not so good on the 59th, getting shot down off the coast of southern France. Hoover spent sixteen months in Stalag Luft 1, in a German prisoner of war camp, where he quickly started planning the first of many escape attempts that quickly earned him the enmity of his captors.

Escaping again shortly before the end of the war, Bob finally made it home by stealing a German fighter plane to help him work his way home. Unfortunately, the air-craft he stole only made it part of the way to safety, because in Bob's rush to escape, he did not have the luxury of stealing an airplane with a full tank of gas...

Following his return to the USA, after the end of the European portion of the war, Bob was soon assigned to the flight test division at Wright field, where he test flew and evaluated many captured Japanese and German airplanes. This experience quickly qualified him for additional testing involving the latest new aircraft being developed by the Air Force. It was during this time that Bob met one of his friends, another highly-regarded test pilot, one Chuck Yeager, who was also starting to make a name for himself.

They worked a number of flight test projects together, including the Bell X-1 supersonic aircraft – the first aircraft designed to break the sound barrier, ultimately succeeding in 1947 with Yeager at the controls, and Bob Hoover flying as the back-up pilot. An interesting footnote about this event, it seems that Bob was originally in line to conduct the supersonic trials of the X-1, but was bounced from the lineup after he had been caught making low passes over a civilian airfield for nonregulation reasons... in other words, he got caught doing a buzz job – one of a pilot's favorite pastimes. Bob was usually a stickler for the rules, but the one time he had some fun, he got caught — and the course of history was changed as a result.

Bob left the Air Force in 1948, accepting a position with General Motors as a test pilot for high-altitude testing of their new line of Allison jet engines, as well as propeller development. Bob spent a year with them, but took a job with North American aviation in 1950 to conduct experimental flight testing for a whole new series of jet airplanes, including the F-86 Sabrejet, the Navy FJ-2 fighter and eventually, the F-100.

These were amazing times for early American Jet aviation, requiring highly-skilled pilots to investigate the performance and control ability of America's first front-line supersonic fighters. It was also dangerous work; during these years Bob had to deal with a number of emergencies and compiled an incredible reputation for being able to bring back airplanes from which other pilots admitted that they would have bailed. He was the first man to fly the XFJ-2 Fury Jet and the Navy's T-28 trainer.

One of Bob's more pleasant duties was to take these fighters to locations all over the world and demonstrate their handling and performance to the fighter pilots who flew them on active duty. Bob developed incredible routines demonstrating the agility, performance, and ultimate capability of these aircraft in ways that impressed virtually everyone who watched him fly. It wasn't long until Bob's name became synonymous with the very top echelon of the pilot community. Beyond the normal call of duty, he also flew combat dive bombing missions with Air Force squadrons in Korea, demonstrating the capabilities of the F-86 over enemy territory.

He has also set a number of world aviation records, including three climb-to-altitude records of a turbo-prop Commander, performed at the Hanover Air Show in West Germany in April 1978. He received the Arthur Godfrey Aviation Award from the Minneapolis Aquatennial for accomplishments in flight testing. In 1981, he received the Flying Tiger Pilot Award for his outstanding contribution to aviation. The Los Angeles Chamber of Commerce awarded him the 1982 Kitty Hawk Award. That same year, he received the Wilkinson Silver Sword for his airshow work.

Another coast-to-coast record was set in a P-51 in five hours and 20 minutes from Los Angeles, CA to Daytona Beach, FL in 1985. Hoover also holds a number of world records in jet aircraft and was awarded the Distinguished Flying Cross, the Soldier's Medal, Air Medal and Purple Heart. He was presented the Aviation Pioneer Award as the world's most notable, decorated and respected living pilot by Parks College in St. Louis.

He received the Lindberg Award at the Smithsonian in May of 1986. In August of 1986, Hoover was honored during Bob Hoover Day at the 34th Annual Oshkosh Celebration by the Experimental Aircraft Association. He is also an Honorary Member of the Fighter Aces Association and the Eagle Squadron Association. In July of 1988, Bob was enshrined in the National Aviation Hall of Fame in Dayton, OH along with other aviation

and space pioneers such as Neil Armstrong, James Doolittle, Barry Goldwater, Charles Lindbergh, Eddie Rickenbacker, The Wright Brothers, Chuck Yeager, Richard Byrd and Howard Hughes.

As Hoover served as the back-up and chase pilot to General Chuck Yeager on the X-1 flights. Yeager participated in the EAA program honoring Hoover along with other leading citizens of the aviation community.

The recipient of countless awards and honors, Hoover is the only man to serve two terms as President of the exclusive Society of Experimental Test Pilots. He was the Captain of the United States Aerobatic Team, which participated in the 1966 International Competition in Moscow.

Hoover has flown over 300 types of aircraft in his career. In 1988, 1989 and 1990, he was selected as the Most Outstanding Airshow Performer of the Year and received the Number One Showmanship Award from the International Council of Air Shows for 1989. He was presented with the annual Cliff Henderson Memorial Award for contributions to aviation for 1989 at the Ohio Hall of Fame.

Bob Hoover, in over fifty years of flying, has performed many thousands of times in more different types of aircraft, in more countries and before many more millions of people than any other pilot in the history of aviation. Hoover is a soft-spoken gentleman, tall, lean and quiet... who never fails to amaze his peers and fans alike for the remarkable skill and enthusiasm he brings to his flying as well as his other business interests.

For the Record – Bob Hoover's Medical History

Bob Hoover is possibly one of the most studied pilots in commercial and general aviation history. This guy has been poked, prodded, x-rayed, inspected, scanned, stitched together, and explored to within an inch of his life. He's a wiry fellow devoid of the tremors and slowness one often associates with a man in their 70s. He does wear hearing aids, which are natural product of decades of military jet flying and the lack of hearing protection afforded jet pilots before the Air Force and the aviation industry became aware of the damage this loud and damaging background noise could do.

He is a fairly energetic person, exercises regularly, enjoys tennis, and jogs occasionally. He is not a smoker and has never dabbled in illicit drug use. Bob wears glasses, though he has done so for quite a long time. His corrected vision is 20/20. He seems to prefer a fairly healthy diet, even experiencing a problem in previous years with low cholesterol rather than high. He leans toward the consumption of fish, chicken, and a pretty fat-free diet, with only sporadic consumption of red meat. He has no allergies to drugs, and eschews medication whenever possible. Bob measures six feet, one inch tall and weighed but 150 pounds at the time he spoke with Dr. Robert Elliott in late '92.

At the time of the first examinations, Bob had been married for 44 years to his wife, Colleen. Their marriage has produced two children, and has turned out to be an extremely stable relationship.

Bob's years as a fighter pilot and test pilot were not exceptionally kind to him physically. During World War II, and while confined as a prisoner of war, Bob suffered a broken jaw. One of his guards had kicked him in the head for attempting to escape. Momentary unconsciousness ensued, but other than the jaw fracture, there were no perma-

nent effects.

In 1954, during flight testing, Bob went down in an aircraft after incurring control difficulties, hitting the ground at approximately 240 knots. He was knocked unconscious for a few seconds, and required hospitalization for the fracture of thoracic vertebra that required Bob be immobilized in a body cast. A traffic accident in 1988 resulted in fractures to his left rib cage with a secondary pneumothorax (punctured lung). Bob was found not to be at fault in this accident.

A shoulder injury during one of his bailouts required repair of the right rotator cuff in 1991. Some two years before the initial series of FAA examinations in late 1992, Bob was subjected to a partial colonectomy, and early in 1992, received a higher than normal PSA count and endured a radical prostatectomy in March. Hoover also underwent laser surgery in 1992 for glaucoma.

Out of all this, Bob suffers a few effects from what was, at times, some difficult medical maladies. About the only lasting effect is some knee pain from hitting the horizontal tail on a bailout when the ejection seat failed.

There is little in Bob's family history that shows any predisposition toward major illness... however, shortly before Bob became firmly embroiled in the FAA debacle, his older brother passed away due to *"bone metastases secondary to prostatic carcinoma."*

The FAA rumor mill has been merciless in discussing Bob Hoover's history with alcohol, as otherwise noted in this book. Much has been made of the fact that in later years Bob developed a pronounced reddening of his nose in combination with an increase in its size and prominence. A few years after this mess hit the fan, a doctor took a look at it, and quickly pronounced it as "rosacea": a fairly advanced form of acne. Antibiotics, taken over a period of time, reduced the inflammation and scarring significantly, and having done that; much of the infamous Hoover nose was reduced in size and coloration.

As to Bob's realistic consumption of alcohol, one must consider that Bob is a product of World War II, a time when fighter pilots and test pilots were a hard-drinking, hard-partying lot who often lived in remote areas or on bases that offered little in the way of entertainment outside of an "O" club, where they could talk, drink, eat, or listen to music. Still, Bob is not known, at least among those who actually know him, as a hard drinker. I have personally attended dozens of social gatherings where there was a lot of serious drinking going on and cannot recall a single time in the last decade that I have seen Hoover drunk. According to those who know him best (as well as my own personal observations), Bob is a gin drinker, good for two or three drinks in an evening. At dinner, he will often drink wine. Bob is quite open about the fact that in his younger days as a fighter pilot and test pilot, he would *"drink it up"* and party with his fellow fliers to relieve the stress of combat and or the risks of flight test. He has no convictions for drunk driving, and his military record reflects no alcohol-related offenses.

Bob Hoover... Personally Speaking

The above data tells you quite a bit about an extraordinary man, but there's another side to this fellow that needs to be explained. I've known Bob Hoover for nearly two decades, becoming particularly close to him over the latter one. I'm very proud to call him a friend. So do many others... and that's the key to this whole thing.

Bob Hoover is possibly the most well-mannered, gentle fellow I have ever encountered. He goes out of his way to keep from being critical; he is uncommonly self-effacing; he has a methodical way about him, he has a great sense of humor; he is loyal to a fault to those he calls his friends. He is also a creature of habit... setting hard and fast rules for his conduct in the air and on the ground and pushing himself to maintain them above all else, but quickly ready to change tactics the minute new information makes it necessary.

At airshows, Bob goes out of his way to make himself accessible to his fans, often staying before or after performances to sign autographs, chat with people, and spend time with them. Bob is particularly well-known for the time he is willing to take with small children, who have little idea of who he truly is but seem instantly enamored of him, regardless.

In fact, among the most famous persons in aviation, we can think of no one who is that accessible to the public as is Bob Hoover. People calling him on the phone just to chat, even though he had never talked to them in their lives, will find on the other end of the phone a man who is giving of his time, respectful of his place in their lives, and very grateful for their support of his career.

To casual acquaintances, it is his gentle manner and friendly demeanor that is most remarkable. They find it hard to believe that such an outstanding pilot could be such a nice guy. A few people have actually asked me if Bob is as nice a guy in private as he has been in public — and are not surprised to find out that indeed, he is.

I've seen Bob in a number of personal and professional roles: I've been a guest in his home, I've worked with him in his office on this book and other projects, and worked with him at dozens of airshows. His gentle mannerisms and peaceful ways never seem to leave him. Even when confronted by brutish or boorish behavior, even when dealing with distasteful tasks, even when pushed to the limit, Bob is slow to anger. Still, he remains polite and professional.

Possibly the most telling story indicative of Bob's overall demeanor occurred in January 1994 as Bob fought for his aeronautical life during the National Transportation Safety Board hearing on his suitability to maintain his flight status. In the midst of this stressful time, one of the FAA attorneys, who had been involved in the attempted destruction of Bob's career and livelihood, walked up to Bob, expressed some admiration for him, and had the gall to ask him for his autograph... whereupon Bob started to comply, hesitated for a second, and politely turned the government attorney down by stating *"I'm sorry, with all that you've tried to do to me, I just can't."*

A lot of people would have blown their stack, using the opportunity to take out their frustrations on this character... but Bob held his ground, politely declined, and remained ever the gentleman.

This is the most remarkable aspect of the Hoover fight: The FAA literally took on one of the nicest guys in the airshow community, as well as one of the most skilled pilots on the face of the planet. In so doing, the FAA alienated the great majority of the general commercial and military aviation community, as well as picking a fight with a man with possibly the most respected man in all of aviation. Nobody thinks the FAA is stupid, but when you look at the face of, their fight with Bob Hoover was possibly the biggest blunder this agency ever took on.

Let me add a few words about Colleen Hoover... I didn't really get to know her until the last few years but I had a feeling that a man with Bob Hoover's accomplishments had to have incredible backing to be able to have persevered and survived one of the riskiest periods in American aviation history. At this point Colleen and Bob have been married over 50 years, and I know why. You only have to see the two of them together to understand it. Both highly intelligent, there is great respect between the two of them and a unique awareness of the pivotal role each plays in the other's life. More than courage, more than skill, more than fast reflexes, I think Bob Hoover has to credit Colleen with his breathtaking rise to the very top rung of the test pilot and airshow pilot community. Watching them together, whether it be out for a nice dinner, or talking over the breakfast table in their home on the hills of Palos Verde Peninsula, one begins to see that there is much love between the two, and despite the familiarity of 50 years, a lot of amusement still takes place. Colleen is a pistol... sometimes a tough cookie, sometimes sweet, and always polite.

But make no mistake about it; her place is alongside Bob... as Bob's place is alongside hers. Colleen has told me stories of how difficult early life was in the 1940s and 1950s, from the time they lived in very primitive housing on remote military bases (that were often little more than desert dust bowls), to Bob's early career as a corporate test pilot. During this time they started to raise a family, struggled with making the transition from military to civilian life, and dealt with a day-to-day terror of Bob's risky job and the ever- present fear that sooner or later one airplane may get the better of him. But they persevered, survived, and thrived.

And Colleen gets to take her fair share of credit for it because this woman, now in her 70s, is an engaging, loyal, smart, dynamic woman... and a perfect partner to one of the best pilots on the face of the good earth.

Chapter 5

FedGate '92: The Conspiracy Begins

If a million people say a foolish thing, it is still a foolish thing.
Anatole France [Jacques Anatole Thibault] (1844-1924)

While no one at Aerospace America seemed to think that anything had gone amiss, there was obviously something wrong in the days and weeks that followed. Over the next few months, Bob flew another 33 airshows without incident or worry until he became aware that someone thought that OKC was something of an aberration. On August 26, the FAA received reports written by two FAA Inspectors who monitored the 1992 Aerospace America Airshow on behalf of the OKC FSDO. Inspectors Clint Boehler and James Kelln seemed to think that something was wrong with Bob's performances as well as with Bob himself. According to a number of sources, Boehler and Kelln, *"closeted themselves in a room in the Oklahoma City FAA Flight Standards District Office and planned a way to have Hoover grounded."*

During their conversation, which was overheard by FAA Inspector, Norbert Nester, Boehler and Kelln conspired to file two separate reports, in which they collaborated and intended to make it appear as if they had not collaborated. These reports alleged that Hoover's flying had deteriorated and that he appeared medically unfit. They further alleged that Hoover was shunned by his colleagues. These statements were filed, and the next day, August 27, 1992, the FAA, acting on the Inspectors' *"strikingly similar and unsubstantiated allegations of substandard performance at an air show more than two months earlier,"* demanded that Hoover undergo psychiatric evaluations by doctors of the FAA's choosing.

Now... these days, it seems that the minute you start alleging any kind of government-involved conspiracy, one either figures that Oliver Stone is in town, or they ignore it as hype and rumor... That's where the story might have stayed had not one FAA Inspector, himself a bit of an upstart, come forward to try to make some sense of the mess that was unfolding. That Inspector was Norbert Nester, a man who remembered Bob Hoover's kindness to his own little boy and could not *"stand there and just let them screw the man."*

Nester recalls the days after the OKE City show pretty well... *"the airshow was uneventful... I watched Hoover's performance. I didn't see anything questionable about it. But... I know there was some discussion about it (afterwards) and one of the statements Boehler made was that the 'old so-and-so got lost and got confused in the middle of the routine and didn't even know what he was doing and wandered around out north of town and finally came back and flew some more. His announcer did not even know what he was up to.' Well, that was the during the time period he had a hydraulic problem and he chose to go out north of town to deal with the hydraulic problem and come back in and continue with his routine. That was one of the comments made by Boehler."*

Another FAA Inspector, by the name of Jay Nelson, came to be mentioned repeatedly as the story unfolded. Nester remembers Nelson as something of an oddity in FAA, though a long-term one. *"Mr. Nelson was well over 60 at the time; he'd had a long tenure with the FAA. I don't know how many years, but a long time, pushing 30. According to stories he told, he had a general aviation background. I guess originally he was probably from Minnesota or Michigan, somewhere up in there.*

He made reference to flying and we are talking way before Part 135 came into existence, back when people chartered airplanes and did a lot of things without any permits or anything special other than hanging out their shingles, for... you know, air taxi type operations. He did that type of thing and flew single engine airplanes going out of Canada. At the time of the airshow, Mr. Nelson was the accident prevention program manager. Later on, that was changed and all of its positions were re-titled. Accident prevention specialists were a term that applied for over a few years. They were the ones that did the public speaking events that promoted aviation and safety. 'Aviation Safety Program Manager' was another term applied to it later on. They were the ones that theoretically worked with the flight schools and talked to them about air space and safe operations and all the things that go into promoting safety. That was really his position.

Part of that position description by virtue of the FAA handbook and manuals... mandate that the individual in that position, number one is an operations Inspector. Number two, they are expected to maintain a medical and maintain proficiency and currency.... Mr. Nelson had not had a medical certificate in many years... twelve, I think." He had not flown an airplane in 12 years!

"Worse.... They have what they call a PACE program, where they go out and do, in essence, complimentary evaluations on pilots. They will have a fly in breakfast or something (where) they will get FAA Inspectors to go out and work with pilots on an 'informal' basis.

This was their (much publicized) 'kinder & gentler' program for enhancing flight safety. They would get the maintenance guys to go out and look at airplanes, where, in theory, they would not write up any violations as a result of what they might find.

Instead, they'd 'enlighten' the owner or operator and say 'hey, look you need to do this or not do that or these are the type of maintenance functions that you can perform as an owner on the airplane and not be a mechanic'.

So... typically an operations person might go out and do a courtesy flight (voluntarily, on the part of the pilot) with them for 10-15 minutes. Maybe, make a takeoff and landing or two or fly an (instrument) approach if the guy was instrument rated and give them a courtesy evaluation and point out not only their weaknesses but point out their strong points, too!"

The idea is to cultivate a good rapport with the public. Jay Nelson could not do that. He did not fly.

Nester continued, explaining that Nelson publicly said *'Oh I do not fly airplanes,*

I have not flown one of those damn things in 12 years and don't ever want to fly another airplane'. He had a heart condition and could not fly. He could not get a medical. Yet the agency kept him in that position for that number of years knowing that every single year that went by he was not performing the job as it was mandated to be done. They kept him!'"

Nester continued with his description of the days that followed the Oke City airshow by saying, *"As far as Jay Nelson goes, he did not even see the performance."*

During the airshow, Nelson was reportedly ensconced inside one of the hangars hosting exhibits. Nester confirmed that... *"Jay Nelson was not even on the flight line. Jay was working from what I referred to as the children's entertainment booth, inside one of the hangars. He did not even watch the airshow... in fact at different times we had talked, and I'd ask him if he saw any of the airshow and he went into his tirade about how many hundreds of kids he'd had come through (his display area) and all that type of thing... and he admitted he had not seen any of the airshow!"*

Nester noted that the first few days after show were quiet ones. *"Initially, there was absolutely nothing said by any FAA (personnel). In fact we did not even know that Boehler had any particular problem with Hoover. Nobody that was working the airshow knew that there was any question about it other than Jim Kelln. I don't even know whether he was even apprized of Boehler seeing or viewing the airshow. Nobody approached Aerospace America and said 'Hey, it appears there that Bob Hoover was having trouble today and think we can visit with him about it or maybe you want to talk him.' Nothing was said. There was never ever a letter of investigation sent to either Mr. Hoover or Aerospace America as a certificate holder, the waiver holder. There were no inquiries, no indication that there was anything wrong anywhere with him. It just didn't exist. In a matter of days after the airshow everything gets back in order, the people go back to their routines and that's when I heard Boehler and Kelln talking about it. In fact, Boehler approached me about Hoover. He said 'did you see how messed up he was?'*

I said, 'Clint I didn't see anything wrong with Hoover's performance'.

He then went into this tyranny of how messed up the guy was and it ended up that there was not too much more said about it. Then I heard him grumbling about it another day or two later. He pointedly made a statement. He said, 'I am going to get that old bastard. He has done so many things and had so many incidents, the fire and other things and never had to pay a price to anything just because of who he is'.

I said, 'Well I don't think that is one I would want to tangle with and I think leave well enough alone. If you did not see anything wrong, you didn't see anything wrong out here this time'. And he kind of grumbled and walked off and that was the end. When you work in a small office like that and by virtue of the design of the office, he had to go up and down the hallways and pass people's offices, and I saw Boehler and Kelln scuttled into Kelln's office and talking at different times. I had reason to go in and talk to Kelln or Boehler about other schools or other issues. I would hear the (other) conversations about Hoover. One particular day as I rounded the corner, I heard Clint Boehler and Jim Kelln talking about writing reports on Hoover. They pointedly made the statement, 'Well we better do them on different machines so that it does not look like it came off the same machine' and Kelln laughed and said 'Yeah, why don't you just write the thing' and he said he would change a few words and sentences so they won't think it is identical. Well even after that you know there was obviously other Inspectors who knew that something was about to be hatched. A considerable amount of discussion along those lines between us privately not in the presence of Kelln or Boehler, either one. And finally Boehler tried to talk this thing out and he goes to the ops unit supervisor with it and it is the subject of discussion in one of our Tuesday morning general meetings, when everyone is there. In fact, the subject was tabled it for the general meeting and when we had our little break out meeting just for the office unit staff, that is when it came up. All the other Inspectors, including myself and every other Inspector other than Kelln, Boehler, and Jay Nelson were opposed to it. We said, 'Look there has been no violation of any of the regulations. There was no infringement or violation of any of the special provisions. Nobody saw anything; leave things alone. You've got no reason to pursue this.'"

Nester seemed to think that the *"problem had gone away... that nothing was to come of what was thought (then) to be something or a minor concern. Believe it or not, collectively, privately, individually, we all talked to the op-unit supervisor and managed to squash it. We got it stopped. There wasn't going to be anything done. Boehler was instructed to forget it, to leave it alone. There is nothing there that justifies any inquiries or any actions. And about that time is when Jay Nelson got involved in it and he and Boehler started talking privately. The next thing you know Jay Nelson is on the telephone calling the Civil Aero-Medical Institute (CAMI). He sings them a tale that would cause anybody's hair to curl on the back of their neck about Hoover's performance. Jay Nelson is the one that did that... even though he never saw Hoover's performance, but he did not tell anybody that. That is where it got out into another realm of the FAA."*

Nester believed that it was Jay Nelson who got Boehler's and Kelln's concerns to be recognized by persons 'over the head' of their direct supervisor. *"I really do not know for certain who he talked to. He (Nelson) had a tendency to go to the top of the pile just because he had been around for a long time. He felt he knew those people well enough that he could get them to pay attention... But he is the culprit that got the story out, that caused the initial problem that caused them to want to re-examine Hoover.*

It was Jay Nelson.... who would come running back in the office and report 'Well, I called CAMI and I talked to them about Hoover and, by God, they are going to take some action on that'. He gloated about what he'd done."

This was not a secret. Norbert believed that *"the office manager, Alan King, and the operations unit supervisor, Frank Allen, knew what (Nelson) was doing, because in later conversation (Nester had with King), Alan acknowledged that he knew Jay was doing it. He said he encouraged Jay to do it. But it was all verbal. There was nothing written. When the story first broke, the very first of it hit, and I am sure you probably know which magazine that came out about Hoover's (being) grounded. US Aviator."*

So... when the story broke that the FAA had some kind of problems with Bob Hoover, the office reaction surprised Nester. Someone had faxed a copy of an early article on Mr. Hoover's dilemma where it was discussed at one of the Tuesday morning general meetings ... *"Alan King stood up and praised Boehler, Kelln and Jay Nelson for their efforts. He said, 'I think that it is absolutely superb that we have people of the character and the diligence to take on an issue of this nature, and by god, if Bob Hoover has messed up, then he needs to be held accountable and I am proud of our people for doing it."*

Nester said that the others in the meeting were a bit surprised at the turnabout and that they *"just sat there... about to gag."*

Chapter 6

Rules & Regs: How Airshows Work– Or Don't

When the old map-makers got to the edge of the world, they used to write,
"Beyond this place, there be dragons."
Barclay Cole (Out of Africa)

The airshow business is not all fun and games... though it sure looks like it from the outside. The thrills, excitement and daredevil stunts would make one think that such a business would be a pretty rowdy pursuit and organized in much the same way. Instead, it is a tightly-controlled, heavily-monitored industry that is both internally and externally regulated. More important, in addition to the regulatory controls placed on this industry, there is an even stronger internal series of controls in place and a strong, voluntary, safety-oriented mandate that may make the airshow industry one of the best managed sporting programs, and potentially the safest, in the world.

Better yet, it is possibly the most self-critical sporting pursuit known... with a huge and highly-motivated hierarchy devoted to safety, evaluation, and research. What this means is this: If something unsafe becomes visible, it is highly likely that members of the industry will take strong steps to eliminate it as potential hazard. Every critical (i.e., life-threatening) aspect of the airshow business has some kind of regulatory oversight... from the pilots, to the aircraft, to the shows themselves. This has made the US airshow industry the world's safest as far as spectators are concerned and definitely kept the airshow industry looking over its shoulder in order to make sure they were on the right path.

By and large, it is *now* a system that works fairly well, despite its imperfections... the most notable of which is the fact that many of those formally in charge of airshow oversight (in the FAA) know very little about the subject that they are regulating. It is entirely possible, for instance, that the very FAA Inspectors who may be called upon to judge an airshow pilot, aircraft or performance may have no practical airshow experi-ence... and may not even have any aerobatic flying skills, or may never have flown an airshow-class aerobatic maneuver in their lives. But then again... these days, the FAA has a lot less to do with the actual regulation and oversight of airshows than the public might think–though they remain the party ultimately responsible for all that happens in the business.

Mind you, there is a very good reason for FAA oversight of airshows and that need is made all too evident by the poorer record of safety among airshows overseas. While airshow flyers certainly are aware of the risks of what they do, the cardinal rule among all performers and those who support them is that no hazard or injury occur to those who watch from the ground.

This grueling facet of the flying business is *tightly* controlled at airshows... to prevent *any* kind of flying that might place an aircraft, damaged or out of control, in any way, close to the spectators. The FAA has worked out a complicated series of guidelines based on aircraft speed and capabilities that determine the directions and speeds certain maneuvers may be flown so as to make sure that anything going wrong happens *away* from a crowd. So... "crowd-lines" and other safety parameters have been established to make sure that if something does go wrong, that it probably does so where there is a minimal chance of spectator involvement.

On August 28, 1988, at Ramstein Air Base, Germany, the worst airshow accident in recent memory took the lives of sixty-seven people and the three Italian pilots that were involved in a mid-air collision, while another 450+ people were heavily injured. A few cardinal rules were broken at this airshow, rules that are in place here in the USA and were not in force overseas. The maneuvers were flown too close to the crowd, and the fatal maneuver involved one jet that, at the point of the collision, was doing a maneuver that aimed his plane at the crowd.

Such maneuvers, in which the flightpath of an aircraft is aimed toward the crowd line at critical portions of the airshow routine, are banned in the USA. A maneuver in which a solo flyer interacted with the formation on a heading that could take it into a crowd if something unforeseen happened arrived at the intersection point off schedule (by a matter of seconds) and appeared to have little room to do much besides strike other members of the team. The airplane plunged, cartwheeling, into the crowd, killing dozens instantly. Any pilot doing anything remotely like it would be busted, big-time, by the FAA or any self-respecting ACE. That part of the system does work... lousy airshow pilots are routinely grounded or "guided" in ways to make sure that they fly safely and competently. And that's the key to what's happening now in the USA... the best of the airshow community judging and regulating the rest.

In the US, we have a good and virtually unblemished record, decades long, that shows we are on the right track. Yes, US airshow pilots do crash and die... but it has been decades since anyone was hurt in a US airshow besides those directly associated with it (i.e., the pilots). On the other hand, the record overseas is not nearly as good. Accidents like the one in Germany, Belgium and other nations have resulted in injuries and deaths to dozens of people as airshow pilots and their aircraft plunged into the innocent crowds who came to be entertained, not threatened.

There is no question that good regulation is needed... and the regulations that are currently in place in the USA are actually pretty good... so long as they are adhered to by persons who are qualified to administer them. So, over the past few years and especially over the past decade, a partnership between the airshow industry and the FAA has created a workable program controlled by the FAA but largely administered by the International Council of Airshows and its "ACE" Program–following the oversight of the FAA and the rules they've established for the airshow community.

The FAA has established a number of regs and documents to guide the airshow industry. They cover a gamut of subjects and leave little to question. Most importantly,

they *are* well written and provide excellent guidance for an involved form of aviation activity.

Advisory Circular (otherwise known as an "AC") 91.45C, "WAIVERS: AVIATION EVENTS" provides prospective aviation event sponsors and other interested parties with information necessary to assist in planning and conducting a safe aviation event. In addition, it provides information on the application process for a Certificate of Waiver or Authorization necessary to host such events.

Advisory Circular 91.48, "ACROBATICS - PRECISION FLYING WITH A PURPOSE" provides information to persons who are interested in acrobatics to improve their piloting skills in recreation, sport, or competitive activity. It also discusses FARs pertaining to aerobatic aircraft airworthiness considerations, acrobatic instruction, operations, and aerobatic flight safety.

Advisory Circular 91.61, "A HAZARD IN AEROBATICS: EFFECTS OF G-FORCES ON PILOTS" provides background information on gravitational forces, their effect on the human body, and their role in safe flying. Suggestions are offered for avoiding problems caused by accelerations encountered in aerobatic maneuvering.

Advisory Circular 105.2C, "SPORT PARACHUTE JUMPING" provides suggestions to improve sport parachuting safety and disseminates information to assist all parties associated with sport parachuting in complying with Federal Aviation Regulations (FAR) Part 105, Parachute Jumping. It also contains a list of aircraft that may be operated with one cabin door removed and includes procedures for obtaining FAA authorization with door removal (kind of important... it's hard to open a door at 100 mph, so leaving them on the ground seems the better part of valor...).

Chapter 31 of FAA Order 8700.1, "ISSUE/RENEW A STATEMENT OF AEROBATIC COMPETENCY" offers guidance to Aviation Safety Inspectors and aerobatic competency evaluators on the issuance or denial of FAA Form 8710-7, the critical Statement of Aerobatic Competency, without which no pilot could perform low-level aerobatics at an airshow.

Chapter 48 of FAA Order 8700.1, "ISSUE A CERTIFICATE OF WAIVER OR AUTHORIZATION FOR AN AEROBATIC PRACTICE AREA OR AN AEROBATIC CONTEST BOX" offers guidance to Aviation Safety Inspectors on the issuance of a Certificate of Waiver or Authorization or the disapproval of an application for a Certificate of Waiver or Authorization for an aerobatic practice area or aerobatic contest box.

Chapter 49 of FAA Order 8700.1, "ISSUE A CERTIFICATE OF WAIVER OR AUTHORIZATION FOR AN AVIATION EVENT" offers guidance to Aviation Safety Inspectors on the issuance of a Certificate of Waiver or Authorization or the disapproval of an application for a Certificate of Waiver or Authorization for an aviation event.

Chapter 50 of FAA Order 8700.1, "SURVEILLANCE OF AN AVIATION EVENT" offers guidance to Aviation Safety Inspectors on how to determine if the holder of a Certificate of Waiver or Authorization is in compliance with the terms set forth in the certificate.

Finally, it all hinges around ***FAA FORM 7711-2, "APPLICATION FOR CERTIFICATE OF WAIVER OR AUTHORIZATION."*** This is the FAA form that must completed and submitted to the local FAA Flight Standards District Office (FSDO) at least 45 days prior to an aviation event. An airshow is not a "legal" event, in that activities that take place during same often constitute a violation of the FARs... so the FAA has to issue a temporary waiver of the rules so that an airshow can happen legally. They explain the public need for same thusly... *"Numerous waivers are issued each year by the Federal*

Aviation Administration (FAA) for the purpose of aviation events or aerial demonstrations."

The FAA defines aviation events to include "airshows, air races, aerobatic contests, parachute demonstration jumps, practice areas designated for aerobatic proficiency or training, and balloon meets and races."

The FAA also defines the aerobatic maneuvers that may be done at these events as "an intentional maneuver in which the aircraft is in sustained inverted flight or is rolled from upright to inverted or from inverted to upright position. All standard aviation event aerobatic maneuvers such as slow rolls, snap rolls, loops, Immelmanns, Cuban eights, spins, hammerhead turns, etc."

As previously noted, these maneuvers are usually not allowed over or near large groups of people... hence the need for the aforementioned waiver. *"Airshow waivers are issued based on the FAA policy that anytime the agency determines a proposed event will be in the public interest in terms of safety and environmental concerns, a waiver will be issued predicated on specific requirements of the event."* In other words... show us a good reason for breaking the rules and we'll let you do so, as long as you follow a new set of rules designed to keep everyone out of harm's way.

The FAA defines a waiver as *"an official document issued by the FAA which authorizes certain operations of aircraft in deviation from a regulation, but under conditions ensuring an equivalent level of safety."* And the FAA has to waiver just about everything... the show site, the airspace, the airplanes... and, of course, the pilots.

Yes... the pilots must also be waivered and are supervised very closely... since if anyone is going to cause a problem, it's likely that an airplane and its pilot will be involved. The waiver situation, pilot-wise, has changed a lot over the last few years as the International Council of Airshows lobbied for more autonomy and self-regulation... and seems to have gotten it... kind of. One of the good parts of this agreement is that highly qualified airshow performers would be used to grade the capabilities of new and upgrading airshow pilots–and each other. In other words, airshow pilots would be judged by those of their peers expert enough to be designated as Aerobatic Competency Evaluators (ACEs).

The ACE program has been critical to airshow safety and as it has matured, has shown that it can (and has) tremendously enhanced the safety of these events.... especially in ways that most FAA Inspectors were simply not qualified to do. Simply put, airshow ACEs have become the judge and jury for airshow pilots in North America (the ACE program is North American in nature... approved and endorsed by the USA's FAA and Transport Canada). Every new or experienced airshow pilot must prove themselves and keep proving themselves... to members of their own peer group. Better, the ACE program is tightly controlled by a series of ethical and professional standards that ARE *strenuously* enforced. ACEs who do something unethical or unwise, quickly find themselves "De-ACE'd." Mind you, this program does have teeth.

I know of one former ACE who was bamboozled by an airshow promoter into designating what was later determined to be an unqualified pilot with errant credentials... and despite the fact that the ACE was lied to (reportedly by a guy with quite a rep as a con-man), he was still held responsible and lost his professional designation as an ACE. ICAS's ACE committee dealt with this (and other situations) forcefully, aggressively and strictly... and proves that these folks are *serious*. The ICAS ACE Manual sets forth its ethical stan-

dards thusly:

A. An ACE must meet the minimum criteria set forth by the ICAS ACE Committee;

B. An ACE shall possess the judgement required to evaluate the aerobatic flying qualities and mental preparation of the applications being evaluated;

C. An ACE shall possess the maturity to properly evaluate the applicant to the proper level of competency and safety as described in the evaluation standards;

D. An ACE shall enjoy the respect of his/her peers and the respect and confidence of the Federal Aviation Administration and/or Transport Canada.

E. An ACE shall abide by the ACE Code of Ethics

    1. Any conflict of interest or the perception of any conflict of interests must be avoided at all times;

    2. All evaluations shall be accomplished in a manner that is fair and equitable to all applicants;

    3. At all times, the ACE shall conduct himself or herself in a manner that reflects on the professionalism of the air show industry and the integrity of the ACE program;

    4. The new performer represents the future of the air show industry. The ACE should guide, encourage and protect the new performer. History has shown the new performer to be at the highest level of personal risk during the first several seasons in the air show environment.

    5. The ACE shall bring any unsafe act or practice to the attention of the individual or individuals involved, the ICAS ACE Committee and/or another appropriate officials.

    6. The ACE is obligated to abide by all terms and conditions of the ACE program.

The cornerstone of the ACE program is the Aerobatic Competency Evaluator... an experienced airshow pilot who often has many years of experience and hundreds of performances under their belt... as well as a good safety record and a reputation for honesty and common sense. ICAS sets forth the minimum requirements for their ACEs as those flyers who:

    1. Have performed not less than 50 performances at waivered/authorized events, provided not less than 25 of these performances were performed at Level One.

    2. Have been an air show pilot performing aerobatic flight at waivered/authorized events for at least eight of last ten years.

    3. Hold an unlimited Level One Aerobatic Competency Card.

    4. Meet a geographic need as determined by the ACE Committee.

Any of the qualifications can be waived by the ACE Committee to meet the demand for a unique type of operation.

Through the ICAS ACE Committee, the FAA allows these senior airshow pilots to issue the certificates once formerly issued by the FAA. The way a person becomes an airshow pilot is a careful and gradual one... requiring one to prove themselves in each aircraft they fly, each maneuver they perform and at an initially "higher" altitude than that allowed for more experienced performers.

For instance; the ACE Manual currently specifies that airshow pilot applicants seeking a "Certificate of Demonstrated Ability" must fulfill the requirements of the ACE Manual's Evaluation Procedures requiring them to:

A. Contact an ACE

The applicant will select a qualified ACE as specified in Section 5, paragraph B of this document and contact him or her to arrange for an evaluation. The applicant can obtain the name, address, and telephone number of the nearest ACE from the list available from ICAS. The applicant may select any qualified ACE he or she wishes in seeking an evaluation.

B. Application

An applicant for a Statement of Aerobatic Competency will receive the evaluation packet from the ICAS office. At the time of the request, the applicant will be asked to identify the evaluating ACE. If the applicant has not selected an ACE, ICAS will provide the applicant with the ICAS list of ACEs. The following materials will be sent to the applicant once the evaluating ACE has been identified:

1. Application for Statement of Aerobatic Competency with ACE name filled out by ICAS

2. Ground Evaluation Standards

3. Air Evaluation Standards

4. Procedures and Pre-evaluation Requirements

C. Preparation

Prior to the ACE evaluation, the applicant should become familiar with the Air and Ground Evaluation Standards used by the ACE in performing an evaluation. By using these standards, the applicant can be sure that he or she is adequately prepared for both the ground (oral) and flight phases of the evaluation.

D. Evaluation Flight Area

Though many ACE's have existing waivered/authorized practice areas as required by the FAA and Transport Canada, and may be very helpful to the applicant, it is not the responsibility of the ACE to provide waivered/authorized airspace for the evaluation. Once the date and location of the evaluation has been confirmed, it is the responsibility of the applicant to ensure the appropriate waivered airspace has been applied for and/or activated. The evaluation airspace must be waivered/authorized to the altitude which the applicant has requested for his or her Aerobatic Competency Card. The ACE may require proof that the waiver is in place. The evaluation site must be accessible to the ACE by surface since the ACE will normally observe the evaluation flight from the ground.

E. Pilot/Aircraft Documents

The applicant must be prepared to provide, if requested, the ACE with appropriate documentation to show that both the pilot and aircraft are authorized by the FAA/Transport Canada for the type of flying contemplated. These documents include, but may not be limited to, the following:

1. Pilot
a. Pilot Certificate with appropriate ratings
b. Current Medical
c. Previous Statement of Aerobatic Competency, if any
d. Current Biannual Flight Review
e. Current Letter of Authorization, if appropriate
f. Applicant's performance sequence (shall include all maneuvers that will be flown at air shows during the next season)

2. Airspace
a. FAA/Transport Canada waiver/authorization covering the time and airspace for the flight evaluation

3. Aircraft
a. Registration
b. Airworthiness Certificate
c. Supplemental Type Certificates and Field Approvals, if appropriate
d. Evidence that the aircraft is structurally capable of performing the contemplated maneuvers safely
e. Current Letter of Authorization, if appropriate.

When an erstwhile airshow pilot is evaluated, the process requires the ACE to not only see them fly in a manner that shows they know what they are doing but tests them on a number of knowledge areas and has established a series of *Evaluation Checklists and Standards* to make sure that these programs are properly conducted:

Ground Evaluation Checklist and Standards **(From the ACE Manual)**
During the Oral Evaluation phase, the ACE must keep in mind that this phase presents an opportunity to review all of the areas of knowledge unique to air show flying. For some pilots, this session may be the only formal review of air show aerodynamics, density altitude effects, physiology, energy, and other specific air show professional knowledge that the pilot may have during the year. For renewal applicants, this will be the only part of the evaluation and renewal process unless the ACE determines a flight evaluation is appropriate or necessary. The ACE must allow sufficient time and attach sufficient importance to this phase so that each applicant will remember the concepts and principles discussed.

A. Air Show Safety Concepts
This first part of the ground checklist concentrates on aerodynamics, density altitude, and physiology. The applicant should have a working knowledge about the relationship of turn and pull out radius to true airspeed and radial "G." The applicant must know the indicated airspeed for his/her aircraft at which the tightest turn and highest pull out can be made. The applicant must understand the constant trading of kinetic energy for potential energy for kinetic energy as used in air show flying. The applicant must know how to determine if a particular maneuver is energy gaining or energy losing under various conditions of density altitude.

The applicant must understand the effect of density altitude upon true airspeed in relation to indicated airspeed, on the performance of aircraft engines, and on the ability to gain and/or maintain energy. The relationship between pull out distances (altitude) and true airspeed should be discussed.

The main point in discussing physiology with each applicant is to impress upon him/her the need to take a good personal physiological inventory before each and every flight. The inclusion of this step in every pre-flight as a conscious effort and the use of this physical state information in planning the flight is critical to safe flying. The ACE should also review the effects of stress, hydration, fatigue, and other human factors.

B. Review of Applicant's Proposed Performance Sequence

The goal in reviewing the entire sequence is to review the design in relationship with the aircraft's capabilities, preservation of energy, adaptability to changes in density altitude and weather, demand on the pilot both physically and mentally, and the flow of the program.

The ACE should proceed through the applicant's written sequence and pause at each maneuver to examine it and discuss it by covering the topics above. The applicant must know the minimum energy state (airspeed and altitude) for various density altitudes which he/she must have as entry parameters for every maneuver in the sequence. This item must be covered for every maneuver in the sequence by the ACE.

The applicant for a Level Three or Level Four waiver will be required to adhere to the maneuver sequence flown during the flight evaluation, as recorded in the information sent to the ICAS office with the completed flight evaluation, in subsequent air show performances. However, variances in the sequence that increase the safety of the performance by compensating for factors such as density altitude, wind and terrain considerations shall be allowed, providing that no new maneuvers that have not been demonstrated are included in such modifications. Maneuvers may be deleted from the sequence.

C. Special Considerations

The ACE should refer to the appropriate checklist item if the applicant is flying a specialty act. A thorough discussion of each item is required. In certain situations, the ACE may have related but not personal experience in a specialty or new act. This is a good chance to ask the applicant to explain the unique facets and safety requirements of his or her specialty or plans for a new air show act. The ACE may also find it helpful to contact another ACE which specializes in a related field such as comedy, transfers or wingwalking. In these situations, the chairman of the ACE Committee will be advised before recommendations are forwarded to the FAA or Transport Canada.

D. Emergency Procedures

An important concept the ACE should bear in mind when reviewing emergencies is the decreasing number of options the pilot has in any given emergency as the total energy level (airspeed and altitude) of the aircraft decreases. Special care should be taken by the ACE to include specialty act circumstances into the discussion of each emergency. Examples include such emergencies as engine failure during a formation maneuver or during a wing walk act. Once again, the concept here is to take the time to think

about these possible emergencies so that the pilot can recall his or her plan when and if the circumstances arise.

When the prospective pilot is evaluated in terms of their actual performance, the checklist maintains its strict adherence to some comprehensive guidelines via the "Air Evaluation Checklist And Standards":

A. Basic Flight Criteria
1. The air evaluation phase is a critical item in the initial certification process. It is also the most subjective. The judgement and experience of the ACE is the primary tool in performing this evaluation. Though the ACE can be helpful in the design of maneuvers, the way in which an aircraft is flown, overall presentation, and other showmanship concepts, the basis for issuing a recommendation is competence and safety.

2. The ACE must be able to make the following statement as honestly as possible in determining whether or not to recommend a certificate. "The performer and his or her routine, as seen during the evaluation flight, do not, in my opinion, present any safety hazards to a potential audience nor to the performer himself or herself." This statement contains the need for preparation, skill, knowledge, and judgement on the part of the applicant.

3. If the ACE cannot make this statement after the evaluation, the evaluation should be graded as unsatisfactory, and the recommendation for a Statement of Aerobatic Competency must be denied.

B. Pre-flight
1. The ACE should use this phase as an evaluation tool. Discussions, while at the aircraft, of the items in the pre-flight checklist can help lead to establishing good pre-flight habits for the performer. The Aerobatic Competency Evaluator checklist items are those unique to air show flying and do not replace, but
rather supplement, the normal pre-flight checklist applicable to the aircraft used.

C. Flight Evaluation
1. The ACE will carefully observe the applicant in flight. The applicant will fly the aircraft in the same configuration that he or she would use in an actual show, including smoke, etc. The ACE should use the application form to make notes for debriefing of the applicant following the flight. When observing the applicant, care should be taken to notice any energy problems with the routine. Indication of pilot disorientation or the need to break the routine to relax and/or recover should be noted. If the applicant is unable to fly the routine as he or she briefed it (including planned breaks), then the applicant could not be expected to successfully execute the routine with the added pressures of a show environment.
2. Unplanned breaks, disorientation, blown maneuvers, loss of total energy, and poor placement of the sequence over the ground are all good indications of lack of planning, training, and skill level, and are unsatisfactory. Never assume that what has been observed will get better or that the pressure of an air show will be less than the evalua-

tion.

3. Should the ACE deny a recommendation, he or she should ensure that the reasons are clearly stated on the application form. The ACE should also recommend a course of action to the applicant which would allow the applicant the opportunity to correct the deficiency.

D. Debriefing

1. The debriefing is the last chance the ACE has to help the applicant be a safe pilot. The ACE should carefully review all notes that he or she made during the evaluation both ground and air phases to gain the maximum benefits of a debriefing. It is also an opportunity to help the applicant with presentation and showmanship concepts. Don't let this valuable opportunity pass without taking full advantage of the time.

That's just a *FRACTION* of what it takes to qualify an airshow pilot... so please don't think that any aspect of the airshow community would tolerate any sub-standard or unsafe actions or pilots. Once a new airshow pilot is given his or her wings, they become a part of a constant evaluation process and are limited as to the maneuvers that they can fly and the altitude at which they can fly them until they earn their way up the skill ladder through the experience of more shows and evaluations. Even the ACE his/herself is restricted from evaluating anyone if there is a hint of potential favoritism or inability to properly execute the evaluation... the ACE Manual stating that:

"A. An ACE designated by the ICAS ACE Committee may recommend the issuance of a Statement of Aerobatic Competency to persons who have met all of the requirements as specified herein and have satisfactory knowledge of the items found in the Air and Ground Evaluation Standards. This includes initial issuance, re-issuance, re-evaluation, and changes in altitude, aircraft and type act.

B. No ACE shall evaluate outside his or her area of competence, experience and background as set forth on the ICAS list that details which type of aircraft and type of act an ACE is qualified to evaluate. ICAS will review each request for evaluation to ensure that the ACE meets this requirement.

C. No ACE shall evaluate team members, family members, employees, aerobatic students* or others who may be financially involved in an ACE's activities for:

1. Initial evaluations

2. Renewals that require a flight evaluation

3. Changes in altitude

4. Changes in Aircraft

* A pilot who receives more than three (3) hours of instruction from an ACE in the preceding 90 days is considered a student of that ACE."

Finally, after educating you about the wonders of the self regulated ACE program, let me add one more reason for filling you in on all this... several of the pilots who flew with Bob Hoover at Aerospace America '92 were ACEs... and not a single one of them found that Bob did anything wrong or remarkable that weekend. In other words, Bob was not only judged by real experts in the field... but by the very best of the real experts in the field... and no one saw a thing that they considered actionable... not a single one.

Chapter 7

33 Shows... Nary A Glitch

No good deed goes unpunished.
Clare Boothe Luce

After Bob's flights at Aerospace America 1992, he went to fly actual airshow performances dozens of times (thirty-three, to be exact) over the next few months (not to mention whatever practice and press shows he did, in addition), somewhat oblivious to what was unfolding back in OKC until the matter reached the bureaucratic equivalent of critical mass. The week after he left OKC, Bob was up in Truckee, CA, for a two-day show followed by two single-day shows, each, thereafter in Harrisburg and Wilkes-Barre, PA, before heading to Oshkosh, WI, for a week-long series of shows that started on July 31 and ended on August 6 (flying five times that week). The author saw each performance and can attest that Bob was flying his standard routines with great precision and care (and I can personally boast to having seen Bob fly several *hundred* times over the years)... and that no discernible problems were evident throughout the week.

Bob's performances at Oshkosh were witnessed by nearly a million people. The annual Oshkosh EAA Fly-In at Oshkosh, WI's Wittman field is the world's largest aviation gathering. It is usually attended by the finest pilots and aviation professionals on the globe. As a matter-of-fact, you can usually count on the FAA Administrator, as well as many senior members of the FAA staff, to be in attendance at this pivotal event. If there were any problems at these shows, there would have been no lack of expert witnesses to them. But... not a word was heard about any of the performances at this high-pressure, high visibility, fast-paced event. As a matter-of-fact, Bob came into contact with a great number of senior FAA and NTSB officials throughout the week as well as his peers in the airshow industry (who tend to watch his performances very carefully... such is the esteem with which he is held, and the awe that many have for what he does).

Even these many years later, we are not aware that anyone took any exception to his actions, his performances, or his competency while Mr. Hoover was maneuvering many thousands of pounds of hurtling metal in close proximity to tens of thousands of people at a time. Throughout the week Bob remained his usual congenial self, greeting friends, talking to fans, signing autographs, and graciously enjoying his reputation as an outstanding pilot and aviation legend. As a matter-of-fact about the only note of discord that can be remotely traced to Hoover during his Oshkosh performances occurred during the playing of the national anthem that preceded one of the Oshkosh daily airshows.

Bob's eyes came upon a few younger fellows who refused to rise (as requested by the airshow announcer), remove their caps, and stand silent as the anthem was played. This is *not* something that Bob Hoover, who lost many friends in combat and military service, tolerated well. So... Bob went up to these young men and politely told them to show some respect for their country, to stand silently, and honor those who sacrificed their lives for them. As always, Bob was courteous, calm and gentle with these kids... but they did as he asked and those who witnessed quietly, smiled in appreciation.

Outside of that kind of thing, Bob flew Oshkosh as he flew all his Oshkosh shows... carefully, expertly, and without incident. When one considers the fact that there were forces within the FAA during this period of time who were pushing to have Hoover grounded, and since the FAA's most cherished mandate is to protect public safety, one would obviously think that such performances would be closely monitored if not disallowed altogether while any question about Mr. Hoover's competency existed.

But no, not a word.

Bob picked up his busy schedule on August 8 with a two-day show in Hutchinson, KS, and headed from there to the Reno National Air Races in Reno, NV. The Reno National Air Races are a world-class air racing event that comes every fall and features a number of classes of unique aircraft that compete against each other around the closed course defined by the immense pylons that constitute the racing area. All kinds of aircraft race here. There are classes for small, 100-horsepower "Formula One" racers, biplanes, a whole class devoted to a world war trainer known alternately as the SNJ or the T-6 (depending upon which branch of service the aircraft first flew for), and occasionally hosts some alternate entertainment, which in the past has included the racing of older classic jets, T-28 trainers, and even helicopters. However, the watershed event of Reno is the annual "Unlimited" Air Races. Pretty much dominated by the fastest former World War II fighters, which are heavily modified and upgraded for the immense speeds and stresses involved in these races, which can reach speeds in the neighborhood of 500 mph), it is here that unlimited air racing fans have come to know and love Bob Hoover.

Bob has been uniquely identified with this event not only because of the shows he performs, but the additional role that he plays as "guardian angel" for the Unlimited Air Racers. Bob not only starts most of the races by leading them to the starting line (usually flying his other trademark aircraft, a yellow P-51 Mustang), but he flies the rest of the race offering "cover" by keeping an eye out for unauthorized air traffic and looking for aviators in trouble. As previously noted, unlimited air racing is the world's fastest sport, populated by a number of modified World War II fighters with pumped up engines and aerodynamic modifications designed to do one thing: make these airplanes as fast as hell. And they do. Four hundred mile-per-hour race speeds are not uncommon and 500 mph is often flirted with... as a matter-of-fact, slower speeds than four hundred are guaranteed losers.

In 1993, Bob flew a grueling sixteen times from September 17-20. It was a tough pace, and we have uncovered no reports indicating that anyone appeared to feel that he was flying below par or in a manner that gave anyone any cause for concern. At Reno '93, he again served his unique role as Safety Pilot for the actual races. Flying his yellow and green North American P-51 Mustang, Bob's job, outside of flying the daily airshow, was to see the races off to a safe start (initiated with his trademark radio call, *"Gentlemen, You Have a Race"* announcement over the race radio frequency) and to oversee their progress

and the individual safety of the racers until they all landed. Bob has been doing this for over 30 years, and has become a virtual institution to this event.

Often, a racer in trouble with engine or other mechanical difficulties would have to be talked through a difficult scenario from a nearby Bob Hoover, who would swoop down from his overhead vantage point to the side of an embattled racer and give them a look-see and as much moral support as he could. From the outside, Bob's expertise could quickly diagnose a situation and tell a pilot, sometimes battling for their very life, what they most needed to know... how to land their stricken bird or when to bail out.

This took an immense amount of skill, because he not only had to diagnose what was going wrong but find ways to tell an embattled pilot how to get down safely all the while flying his own unlimited air racing aircraft in tight formation with the stricken bird and *still* avoid conflicts with all the other racers. This was an amazingly difficult task to accomplish, at times, as most of the in-flight emergencies were engine related, and such engine emergencies usually meant smoke, oil or fire were obscuring the vision of the pilot.

Often times, pilots were talked to the ground without the ability to see where they were going... guided *only* by the cool, calm words of Robert A "Bob" Hoover. To many, it was Bob's help, alone, that kept them alive to race another day. To them, Bob's well-known P-51 Mustang (though he has flown cover in other types of aircraft, including jets, to help with these races) was as beautiful to them as a guardian angel. Bob flew the Mustang for the military, and owned them as a civilian.

The sight of Bob's expertly flown Mustang was a sign to all that one of the most experienced pilots in the world was keeping watch over them. *"When you're in trouble and the whole world has just flat gone to shit... there's no sight more welcome in the whole wide world than Bob Hoover's sliding up alongside your wing to tell you how to save your ass,"* said one of the many outspoken pilots who has raced Unlimited.

Interestingly, another P-51 expert acknowledged by the FAA and the US military as one of the best Mustang pilots in the world calls himself *"a student of Mr. Bob Hoover."* In responding to the FAA's grounding order, this pilot, Lee Lauderback, wrote the FAA in October of 1993 to express his observations of the matter. *"Being the Reno Safety Pilot for 30 years, Mr. Hoover has exemplified himself as an outstanding Aviator, helping to save the life and property of pilots in imminent peril. The Reno Air Races of 1993 were no exception.*

Mr. Hoover's foresight, anticipation, and judgment were instrumental to the safe outcome of over four different emergency situations. Bob Hoover did not write the book on being a Safety Pilot over the years; he is the book.

Bob's ability to convey his knowledge of high-performance aircraft was certainly apparent during the races. He displayed his skill not only in providing a calm atmosphere to a pilot experiencing major difficulties but also in emphasizing the requirement to continue flying the airplane. Having had the opportunity to fly with Mr. Hoover over the past 15 years, and as recently as this year, Bob's insight, intuition, judgment and flying skills are still world class in the aviation community."

By the way, the aforementioned Mr. Lauderback is acknowledged as one of the best pilots in the world... and has served as a corporate pilot for famed golf pro Arnold Palmer, as well as an instructor to new test pilots at the Navy's famed Patuxent River Test Pilots' School. The author has flown with Mr. Lauderback in one of the few authentic TF-

51 (dual cockpit, dual control) Mustangs and can personally attest that this "student of Hoover" seems to have learned his lessons well… he's one hell of a pilot.

So, as we noted, Bob has performed the role of guardian angel dozens of times over the years (in one year alone, he was credited with eight saves!) and more than a few pilots literally owe their lives to him. One of them was William Speer. Even while the Feds were earnestly conspiring to deprive Mr. Hoover of his flying credentials, Mr. Hoover was proving himself to be flying at the top of his form, and for at least three pilots who declared emergencies at Reno 1993, those skills were life savers. Bill Speer tells an extraordinary tale of his rescue, noting that "*I have been a spectator at the Reno Air Races since 1980, and I have witnessed and watched in awe of Mr. Bob Hoover's airshow act as well as his Safety Pilot techniques during the Unlimited Air Races. Not one race at Reno has gone by that I ever saw Mr. Hoover miss a beat. I have witnessed many "Mayday" situations where pilots were in distress and Mr. Hoover was always there to assure the pilot of his options, as well as guide him to a safe runway landing. In many emergency landings the visibility is very poor, due to engine oil and/or coolant on the windshield. It is very comforting to know that Mr. Hoover's there to call out your airspeed and distance to the runway as well as altitude. In most emergency landings you're very busy as well as excited. I've heard many pilots say 'Bob saved my life'.*

This year, Sept. 17th, 1993 was my turn. I'm basically a rookie at Reno. I brought my own airplane (No. 56), a P-51 Mustang for the first time this year to race. On Friday Sept. 17th I won the first Reno heat race, a very exciting, memorable moment; however, when it came time to land the excitement had only just begun. The landing gear would not come down! I announced to the tower that the gear was stuck in the "up" position. I felt very alone and realized that I was in a predicament, to say the least. As soon as my realization of the situation set in, and it was quick, Bob Hoover was there! The depression that was coming up fast never arrived. Mr. Hoover's voice was calm, as well as efficient. He knew that I was low on fuel, having just completed the race (we carry minimum fuel to save weight), so Bob had me bring the power back to below cruise level to conserve fuel and give me time to work on the problem. Mr. Hoover probably knows the P-51 Mustang better than any other pilot today. Bob gave me instructions as well as emergency procedures in order to free the landing gear. Nothing was working, but with his patience and knowledge, we kept trying.

After close to thirty minutes, the gear dropped and locked. At the time I did not believe I would have been hurt, had the gear not come down, but the airplane most certainly would have. And who knows, maybe me too. I owe a lot to Bob, so do many other pilots. His quick thinking is so appreciated and is very hard to come by. You can't buy experience like that. I would like to request a reevaluation and reinstatement of Mr. Hoover's medical certificate to allow him to continue flying. I am sure that other pilots will be grateful in the future."

The Speer incident is but one of dozens of rescues that Bob has accomplished. Many of the rescues that he has been credited with are far more dramatic events than even the tale that Mr. Speer tells. Pilots with failing engines, pilots with airplanes on fire, pilots with landing gear trouble, pilots with all kinds of critical, potentially-fatal failures have come to rely on Bob Hoover for the timely information needed to save their lives or their aircraft. Mind you, he does this while flying his own airplane, as well as inspecting that of a troubled pilot sitting just a few feet away, at hundreds of miles per hour. He takes it all

in and diagnoses the situation in the few seconds that are all that is often available to such stricken aircraft. Such actions require a keen intellect, cool nerves, extraordinary flying skill, and superior cognitive capabilities.

He demonstrated these capabilities in 1993 even while the FAA was getting ready to lower the boom on him. To those who saw him at Reno, the grounding actions of the FAA made no sense at all, when they considered it in retrospect. Experienced Air Racer Delbert D. Williams probably said it best in his October 28, 1993 letter to the FAA. *"In the past three years, Mr. Hoover has talked me down in four Mayday emergency landings in my P-51 Mustang. Being covered up in oil and coolant, his alertness and quick response brought me through every time."*

After Reno, Bob ventured to St. Louis, MO; Kissimmee, FL; and Monterey, Mexico, for a series of two-day shows followed by his final performance back in OKC at Wiley Post Airport on October 17, 1993. Thirty-three amazing shows, with complex aerobatics done as low as a few feet off the ground, without a single mis-hap, and then the FAA lowered the boom... hard.

Chapter 8

Setting the Game into Motion

Life is the art of drawing sufficient conclusions from insufficient premises.
Samuel Butler (1612-1680)

By now the two FAA Inspectors' statements (written by Mr.'s Boehler and Kelln) were making their way through the federal bureaucracy. The statements were short, similar, and brutal. Now they were seeing the light of day, and the extent of the battle that Bob was going to be getting into was starting to reveal itself. Inspector Kelln's statement was filed August 26, 1992, well over two months after the OKC airshow. Typewritten, spanning barely a page, Kelln stated that...

"On June 19 and 21st, 1992, I was assigned to assist in monitoring the Aerospace America 92 airshow in Oklahoma City Will Rogers World Airport.

Mr. R. A. "Bob" Hoover performed at both shows. Mr. Hoover holds commercial pilot certificate No. 448681.

I watched Mr. Hoover performed various airshows over the years, dating back to the middle 1960s and was always impressed with his Aerobatic flying skill and ability. However, at this airshow, beginning with a performance on June 19, 1992, there was a marked difference. Mr. Hoover's performance of his maneuvers at times appeared tentative and imprecise. He repeated several maneuvers after failing to successfully complete them with precision.

On Sunday, June 21st, 1992, I watched his entire performance carefully. The same problems were observed. In addition, I noted that he did not complete his routine within the allotted time. He disappeared from the show area several times and appeared that he was not in communication with his show announcer and that his announcer did not know where Mr. Hoover's aircraft was until it re-entered the airshow area. Mr. Hoover attempted his finale (a both engines stopped, aerobatic sequence and landing with a roll out to his original parking spot) two times and was unsuccessful each time.

Mr. Hoover's behavior on the ground also seemed tentative and he did not appear physically well. It is my opinion that Mr. Hoover's skills and abilities have declined to a degree that affect safety. Mr. Hoover's detailed airman data file shows two violations and five incidents since 1982 (copy attached). This statement is written out of concern for the safety of Mr. Hoover and the public.

It was signed James R. Kelln, aviation safety Inspector, (operations) ASW—FSDO—OKC.

Mr. Boehler, on the other hand, was slightly more verbose. In a page-and-a half typewritten report, Inspector Boehler noted that...

"For the three days of June 19th, 20th, and 21st, 1992, I was assigned as the FAA coordinator for the Aerospace America airshow at Will Rogers World Airport in Oklahoma City Oklahoma.

During this time, I had occasion to observe Mr. Bob Hoover, the well-known Aerobatic pilot, perform his routines for this airshow. It appeared to me that he was not in good form and there were serious discrepancies that gave rise for me to believe he may not be in adequate physical and mental condition commensurate with airshow demands.

My reasons for concluding he was not in command of his activities are as follows:

1. I have known Mr. Hoover for several years and have observed him then and in the present. He now appears somewhat confused when dealing with people, forgets issues, and appears to need the attendance of his staff to keep track of things.

2. When in the air, his timing appears to be off. Maneuvers are not crisp, and no maneuver was performed the same way twice during all shows. At one point, his announcer had no idea where he had flown off to and everyone at show center was looking to see from which direction he would come. We, the FAA, were concerned that he might have been out of the waivered airspace. After a long period of absence, he returned, but his announcer had no idea what maneuver he might perform. This indicated Mr. Hoover was performing freestyle or ad lib. This happened at all performances, the ground announcer calling the planned maneuver, then Mr. Hoover doing some other maneuver. In two of the three performances, Mr. Hoover finalized his act with an engines-out roll out to terminate his departure point, but he failed to reach that point. On one of the attempts, Mr. Hoover was so far away, he restarted his engines and tried again. If he did not do the maneuver just as he thought it should be done, he would leave the plan and try it again, or just do something else.

3. Comments and remarks from other airshow performers indicated a concern for his lack of continuity in performances. Many feel he is not in good physical condition and should not be performing such arduous tasks. Other airshow performers seem to avoid him and he is not included in the group. This is not uncommon when the peers are worried about someone over whom they have no influence.

4. Mr. Hoover appears to be in rather frail physical condition. He had considerable difficulty entering and exiting the aircraft. His range of motion and mobility were weak. His gait seems irregular and he often feels for something before he moves.

5. A review of Mr. Hoover's airman data files indicates a substantial upswing in incidents and violations in the last 10 years. Prior to 1982 Mr. Hoover only had several actions, but since 1982 he is recorded at least five incidents and two violations. It is suspected this may coincide with the decline in awareness, coordination and judgment. There could be a definite relationship between aging and his flight record.

The combination of these factors and having observed Mr. Hoover years prior and now, gives rise to believe his physical condition should be closely examined to determine if he is sufficiently conditioned for the activity in which he is engaged. His performance at the Oklahoma City, Oklahoma, Airshow would cause the reasonable person to question his fitness.

The document was signed by Clint A. Boehler, aviation safety Inspector (opera-

tions) ASW-FSDO-OKC.

This is how the trap was laid. The amazing part of these two documents is that there were a number of holy objectionable statements that, on the face of it, could have quickly been questioned and discounted when the facts attributed could not be verified by outside personnel. For instance, Mr. Boehler's statements referred several times to statements, activities or behaviors observed by Mr. Hoover's fellow airshow pilots. Not a single performer or airshow staff person we have talked to in the six years since that event has ever corroborated a single word of Mr. Boehler's report ... as applied to statements or behaviors directly attributed to them.

Further, Mr. Boehler is not an airshow pilot. Mr. Boehler has never been an airshow pilot. Mr. Boehler does not appear qualified to judge airshow pilots (i.e., not having the skills that a qualified airshow pilot would have) or to consider what is the norm for their behavior—either in terms of their performances or their social interaction. Not a single airshow performer or significant airshow staffer *ever* agreed with the behaviors attributed to them by the ever-so-errant Mr. Boehler.

This is not hyperbole on our part. Numerous statements were filed with the FAA on Bob's behalf, including some telling statements made by the pilots who flew at the very same airshow that Mr. Kelln and Mr. Boehler used as an excuse to prosecute Hoover.

Steven Oliver describes some of his own observations from OKC. *"I was sitting at the runway waiting for take-off to follow Bob as he finished his routine in Oklahoma City (Aerospace America' 92) when I heard him tell Air Boss and his announcer that he didn't have a nosegear light so he would be going around to cycle the gear. Keep in mind that at this time he was on short final with both engines feathered. I can only imagine how busy one must be at this time to get them both running to effect a go-around. It was interesting to have a front row seat and knowing he was going to pull it off but also to actually watch him do it. My point is that there was no question in my mind that Bob had the situation well in control. That's lots of experience and good hands.*

I can certainly appreciate any concern regarding Bob's ability to perform safely giving his age; however, Bob has been doing airshows longer than anyone in the business, he has certainly seen more tragic happenings than most of us, he obviously loves the business as much or more than the rest of us, and I feel that when and if the time comes to retire, Bob will make that decision."

Oliver flew several shows that weekend and told the FAA, *"as an ACE and fellow performer I can honestly say that I have not witnessed a change in Bob or his performance that I feel jeopardizes his safety."*

Steve has flown airshows for twelve years and has known Bob both professionally and personally for even longer. He describes what Hoover does as *"not a gut wrenching 10 G performance, but it's not meant to be. It's a routine that requires a great deal of finesse and years of experience, not jerk-push-pull and being able to stand the pain... I have always been impressed with the level of skill required to get from an airplane what Bob does."*

Writing Dr. Jordan in May, 1993, airshow pilot and ACE Sean Tucker stated that he had seen the FAA monitors' statements regarding Bob's performance at Aerospace America and noted *"I strongly disagree with their observations."*

He described his observations of Mr. Hoover as such. *"I observed Mr. Hoover's performance on all three days of this airshow and did not witness one indication of Mr.*

Hoover compromising his safety or that of the airshow audience. Mr. Hoover did not exceed the structural limits of the aircraft. His technical abilities performing the contemplated maneuvers were executed with the same precision and skill level I have observed on many prior, and more importantly, subsequent occasions (i.e. Reno '92 and Oshkosh '92). The logic of his sequence and energy management were precise and is physiological condition appeared to be normal. In my professional and objective opinion, it was a standard Bob Hoover airshow performance. Unfortunately, sometimes perceptions become reality and this appears to be the case with regards to Mr. Hoover."

Tucker implored the Federal Air Surgeon to look the matter over objectively, with attention to Mr. Hoover's rebuttal arguments to the initial charges presented by Inspectors Kelln and Boehler. He further called attention to the cooperative program built between the International Council of AirShows and the FAA in which the ACE program was founded so that those who were in a better position to judge their peers than the Feds, could do so. *"Dr. Jordan, the FAA implemented the ACE program because they are aware that we are the professionals in the airshow industry. They realize that we can evaluate a performer impartially and provide recommendations for those who have demonstrated a high level of confidence and ethical fitness for the profession. Mr. R. A. "Bob" Hoover definitely remains in that category."*

More Oklahoma City performers join the call for the FAA to reconsider their actions. Another telling letter described Gee-Bee pilot Delmar Benjamin's discussion with Hoover during the airshow over the fence that occurred in his life nearly five decades before. *"I had a long discussion with Mr. Hoover covering his experience with a rocket-powered X-1, and he seemed quite alert and attentive to me."*

Mr. Benjamin has a strikingly different opinion of Mr. Hoover's performance than the FAA Inspectors monitoring the show. *"Concerning his lack of continuity during his act, I have a somewhat different perspective than the Inspector. Mr. Hoover was experiencing cavitation in the hydraulic pump and was dealing with getting the gear down and locked via other means. The fact that the Inspector detected only a lack of continuity in his act is a credit to Mr. Hoover's capability as a pilot. A lesser pilot would have aborted the act and interrupted the show while a professional dealt with a problem and continued the general flow of the show simultaneously. What one Inspector may consider an arduous task is a natural and easy task for one who has spent his entire career in high-performance, complex aircraft. To castigate Mr. Hoover for not terminating his deadstick portion at his departure point is truly absurd, as no other pilot in the world could accomplish the task under perfect conditions. Mr. Hoover is being judged by persons not qualified to the task.*

I, as a performer working with Mr. Hoover at the site, saw no discrepancy in his performance to warrant an investigation. He has passed all tests and met all requirements of the FAA and continued on to perform 25 more shows that season. It is my recommendation that the time has come to abort this investigation due to lack of evidence."

Aviation photographer and airshow vendor "Dixie" Walker knows Hoover awfully well. He wrote Jordan in mid-May of 1993. Walker, who attended Aerospace America 92, is a commercial pilot and has attended a number of performances where Hoover has flown. He found Hoover to be *"in good spirits and good physical condition. Mr. Hoover was talking to people at the airshow crowd line, signing autographs for the people at-*

tending the show, and answering their questions... I observed him talking with many of the performers and airshow officials. I must say he was very sharp and not confused at all. I also know many of the other airshow performers and talked to them at many of the airshows. I have never heard one of them say that they were concerned about Mr. Hoover's performance. Mr. Hoover attends all of the after-show dinners. He is always promoting aviation to its fullest. Many performers seek him out for his advice; they do not avoid him. The FAA also seeks his advice when it comes to show safety. I have never seen Mr. Hoover feeling for something before he moves, nor does he have trouble entering or leaving his plane. I find Mr. Hoover to be very aware and have good judgment. I believe if a man has passed his physical he should be allowed to perform. I would have no problem flying with him, and I am concerned for my safety as well as the public's."*

Further, Hoover announcer Jimmy Driskell weighed in. While noting that Driskell and Hoover have a very close personal friendship, Driskell is a career aviator and knows well the serious implications of any airman flying when he/she is in less than the proper condition. Driskell announced the airshows that were referred to in the statements of Kelln and Boehler.

Jimmy specifically addressed references made in their statements... the first statement he took exception to was *"he was not in communication with his show announcer"*, responding that *"at some airshows, depending on a situation, I have a handheld transceiver monitoring airshow frequencies. But at Aerospace America, I did not, as I was standing shoulder to shoulder with Mr. Tim Daly, the airshow Air Boss. Several times during the weekend I had communication with Mr. Hoover through Tim Daly."*

Driskell further explained to me that this was common knowledge with anyone who was involved in airshow operations, as it was plain to see that the two interface in that fashion. *"If either of them had visited the announcing stand, they could have seen that for themselves. But they never asked me about it and the first I saw of it was contained in those damned reports."*

The next statement he took exception to was the phrase *"performing freestyle or ad lib."* Driskell's report to Jordan stated that, *"the Shrike airshow routine has not changed over the years. The same sequence of maneuvers normally is followed religiously day in and day out. However, there are occasions when it is necessary to change the sequence due to a mechanical problem with the aircraft or due to insufficient speed caused by density altitude. After announcing over 2300 performances by Mr. Hoover, it is quite easy for me to see when he has to make a change to the sequence so I change my description accordingly."*

His next objection occurred where the statement *"after a long period of absence, he returned."* Driskell counters this by saying *"I ascertained through Tim Daly that Mr. Hoover had a mechanical problem of both hydraulic pumps being inoperable due to cavitation. Rather than try to explain this technicality to the audience, I merely stated that Mr. Hoover was making sure that the engine temperatures were "in the green" before returning to the 'show box' knowing that in all likelihood Mr. Hoover would be successful in getting both pumps "back online" – which he did; sometimes it takes longer than others."*

Driskell drove his points home with two final paragraphs... *"over the years, my most important function in our partnership has been to make sure the aircraft is at the next airshow site on time. I can assure you if I thought Mr. Hoover's 'awareness, coordi-*

nation and judgment had declined' or that he was over-stressing the aircraft in any-way, I would be unwilling to ferry the aircraft to the next airshow site. In all the years I have flown with and for Mr. Hoover, I've never known him to fly a sub par performance."

Former World Champion Aerobatic Pilot Leo Loudenslager came forward on May 14, 1993 with a telling letter to Federal Air Surgeon Jon Jordan. Bob Hoover had faxed copies of the FAA's Inspectors reports to him and Loudenslager took great exception. *"It was ridiculous, Jim,"* he told me years later, *"but as hard as we argued for Hoover, we all found ourselves biting our tongues a bit, not wanting to be too confrontational with people with such power."*

Leo and Bob had known each other since 1973... he had watched Hoover fly for nearly a decade previously, and credited Bob with being one of the greatest inspirations in his seeking to become a world-class Aerobatic Pilot. *"I last flew with Mr. Hoover at the Reno Air Races in September of this past year"* he explained to Dr. Jordan, *"Mr. Hoover appeared to be the same pilot that I have known for over 20 years. He was totally professional, focused, and of keen mental capabilities for the four days of the Reno airshow. For example, I was requested to sign autographs with Mr. Hoover for 45 minutes at approximately 1:00 p.m. on Saturday afternoon. A crowd of 300 spectators asking questions, and sometimes being overbearing, can be quite demanding when you're standing in the hot sun with many other duties a performer must accomplish. I remember complimenting Mr. Hoover on his patience and recollection of so many facts and names that were asked of him during this period. I also observed his flight performances on two of the four days of the airshow. Mr. Hoover's flight was flown with his usual trademark precision that I have watched for many years.*

After reading the reports, I find myself confused and disturbed by the apparent difference between the pilot described in June and a pilot that I flew with three months later. I've called performers who observed Mr. Hoover in June. I have found them to be in strong disagreement with the observations. I would be less than candid if I were not to say that many of these performers are afraid over reprisals if they were to be too strong with their differing observations."

Loudenslager's letter should have been a pivotal one. He had enclosed a list of honors at the end of his letter that were but a tiny summary of all that he had accomplished in 20 years of airshow flying. Pivotal in this incredible list of awards and honors and ratings, which he had garnered in an amazing career, were the eighteen metals he had won in world aerobatic competition, half of them gold, as well as the fact that he was a founding committee member and head of the Aerobatic Competency Evaluator task force that literally judged the entire airshow industry at the behest of the FAA, who had come to realize that they did not have the personnel nor the aggregate experience to judge an involved and complex industry. Loudenslager concluded his letter on the somewhat upbeat tone by informing Jordan that *"the combined efforts of the FAA and the industry have led to a greatly improved safety record these past 20 years. Every professional pilot that I know puts safety above all else. I do not know of a more discerning and demanding group in the world. From personal observations, and the observations of the professionals that I have talked to, I find no evidence of the deterioration of Mr. Hoover's flying skills."*

At the Sun 'n Fun airshow in 1996, Loudenslager told me that despite the skills and professional standing of the many pilots who came to Bob's defense years before, there was a fair amount of trepidation on their part... since the FAA holds such power over these pilots, and since many of them made their living in the industry, they were well aware that by contradicting the FAA they put their jobs in danger. Mr. Loudenslager was a Captain for a well-known American air carrier, certified on a number of Boeing and McDonnell Douglas aircraft. Regardless, he and dozens of others came forward fully aware that they could have placed their careers in jeopardy.

Even several years later, as Loudenslager was interviewed for this book, he commented, "*I really have to be careful with what I say about this. Too many Field Inspectors saw this fight over Bob's medical as a threat to their power structure and don't like being reminded of how badly this thing was handled. Too many pilots had to take whatever the FAA dished out to them, and when they took on Hoover, there weren't any of us that weren't willing to stand up and fight for him. They simply picked the wrong guy to attack.*"

Tragically, Leo "The Looper" Loudenslager lost his life when a driver, experiencing a medical problem while behind the wheel of a motor vehicle, collided with his motorcycle head-on. Leo lingered for a month with horrible injuries and finally passed away after a medical error in his care caused his death. So, his comments of the year before can no longer be used against him. One of the last things he told me at the Sun 'n Fun airshow was that "*standing up for Bob was a great privilege and I was proud to have him call me. He is what got me here... and he's still the pilot I measure my flying by.*"

Finally, Bob addressed the Inspector's letters himself in detail. Each of the details has been verified by the comments above and other information that has become well-known since the event. Even years later, I have had no problem getting details of the performances, viewing actual videos, or interviewing dozens of people who, without a single exception, verify all or part of the details that Bob provided.

In his May 12, 1993 letter to Dr. Jordan, Bob detailed the intricacies of hydraulic pump cavitation and its effect on the landing gear. He described the corrective procedure... "*to recover the pressure requires cycling the landing gear lever numerous times, tapping the toe brakes and nosewheel steering, pulling and resetting the circuit breaker. Those procedures create delays on my normal profile time.*"

He testified that "*the control tower and airshow control were advised of my problem and told me not to be concerned about the time extension.*"

He then went on to describe the nature of his performance, "*The routine profile consists of a series of maneuvers with both engines running, which captures a lot of attention because of the size of the airplane. Most pilots declare emergency when an engine is shut down as is the case for my second set of maneuvers, the loop at ground level followed by an eight point hesitation roll into the dead engine. This demonstrates that with proper knowledge of the aircraft and its capabilities and appropriate flying skills, it does not constitute an emergency.*

Many years ago I developed the energy management maneuver which involves climbing the airplane to 3000 feet above the airport at which time both engines are shut off. The airplane is placed into a steep dive, converting altitude into air speed, pulling out at ground level, then completing a loop without power recovering at ground level with enough energy (airspeed) to perform an eight point roll and landing.

Without problems the airplane is to taxi to the parking area. There are factors that occasionally prevent this preciseness. The layout of the airport as regards to the

taxiway turnoff from the landing runway as well as the wind direction and velocity, also of the distance from the runway to the ramp.

The Rockwell Aero Commander is a seven-place business/pleasure aircraft, flown for 25 consecutive years and thousands of exhibitions throughout the United States as well as the major international events. The airplane was not meant to be sold as an Aerobatic plane; however, the manufacturer wanted me to instill confidence in its overall capability by demonstrating that if flown precisely and within the design limits, that it is a very safe plane. It is quite possible that the FAA Inspectors who wrote the letters were not aware of the mechanical difficulties and (it is) unfortunate that they did not have the opportunity to talk with the airshow boss, the control tower, my announcer or the other performers, all of whom were aware of the situation. Throughout the years of testing and demonstration flying, I have always kept safety uppermost in my mind."

There is a lot more detail than what I have listed above. It was easy to uncover; people were quite forthcoming with this information, and as previously noted, there was NO ONE among those we interviewed who agreed with the statements of Inspectors Kelln and Boehler. All of this begs the question: What did these Inspectors REALLY see?

Mind you, we made a number of attempts to contact Mister Boehler and Mr. Kelln over the last few years and our calls were not returned... so your guess is as good as mine.

They allege that other airshow performers were critical of Bob Hoover's performances... yet we can find not a single person who will corroborate the FAA's position, so who the heck were these performers? Did these Inspectors talk to the airboss, the control tower, Jimmy Driskell, Bob Hoover, or any of the actual performers at the show at all? If so, how could they possibly make the statements that they did?

Based on all the evidence I have seen, there is no question in my mind that the statements of Inspectors Kelln and Boehler were flawed, if not outright falsehoods. It would not have taken anyone in authority at FAA looking into their complaints very long to determine that for themselves — and in fact a number of people within the FAA stated that they did so and were promptly ignored by their superiors. So... if this was not the horrible mistake compounded by a series of truly incompetent conclusions and other fact-finding errors, then it sure appears to be a case of outright fraud. Unfortunately, Bob Hoover would suffer the consequences of these *"errors and misconceptions"* for three years before getting his life and livelihood restored to him.

Chapter 9

Political Considerations: The FAA's "Age 60" Rule and Other Bureaucratic Disasters

The truth of the matter is that you always know the right thing to do.
The hard part is doing it.
General H. Norman Schwarzkopf

The FAA has mandated that pilots who reach the Age of 60 years may not have the right to exercise their abilities as they did prior to that time. They say so in FAR 121.383(c)... otherwise known as the "Age 60 Rule."

FAR Sec. 121.383 Airman: Limitations on use of services.
(a) No certificate holder may use any person as an airman nor may any person serve as an airman unless that person—
(1) Holds an appropriate current airman certificate issued by the FAA;
(2) Has any required appropriate current airman and medical certificates in his possession while engaged in operations under this part; and
(3) Is otherwise qualified for the operation for which he is to be used.
(b) Each airman covered by paragraph (a)(2) of this section shall present either or both certificates for inspection upon the request of the Administrator.
(c) No certificate holder may use the services of any person as a pilot on an airplane engaged in operations under this part if that person has reached his 60th birthday. No person may serve as a pilot on an airplane engaged in operations under this part if that person has reached his 60th birthday.
[Doc. No. 6258, 29 FR 19212, Dec. 31, 1964, as amended by Amdt. 121-144, 43 FR 22646, May 25, 1978]

The main thought that crossed the minds of a number of aviators as it became apparent that Hoover was getting a raw deal, was this...

"Why would the FAA perpetrate such a mess??

What can they hope to gain?
What WERE they thinking?"

Certainly, it seemed that the FAA had little to gain from being portrayed as bad guys by virtually every aviation organization and publication in the business. Oh sure, the whole thing started because a few Feds were looking for an easy "trophy bust", but why would this nonsense be perpetrated throughout the most senior levels of FAA management... I mean, what was their motive in this?

There seemed little point in letting this case snowball into the major PR disaster of the year for the FAA and GA community. At a time when the FAA was trying to bridge the gap between aviation users and itself, the Hoover debacle seemed like a world class screw-up. Face it, who needs a fulminating fur-ball of this magnitude when you're trying to show your industry that you're the good guy (this as the then-new FAA Administrator, David Hinson, was trying to portray the FAA as a new "kinder and gentler" agency!).

At the same time, the FAA was under increasing attack by the commercial aviation community for its insistence on the forced retirement of all airline pilots the second they hit Age 60... much to the consternation of the aging airline pilot community who was not necessarily interested in retiring just because the FAA said they had to.

A number of court battles were ongoing (and continue to be fought as we near the end of the millennium) over this matter due to the premise that the FAA was practicing age discrimination and the mitigating fact that *every* airline pilot in the business not only was subject to medical re-examination every six to twelve months but were also in the company of at least one other pilot on their flights... making the potential hazard of a suddenly incapacitated airline pilot to any specific flight a very minor one.

Much salt was added to the FAA's wounds on this matter as a number of prominent aviation emergencies were countered by senior pilots. The day after a critical and tricky take-off accident, one Continental Airlines Pilot was forced to retire because it just happened to be his 60th birthday... and his vast experience — amply demonstrated just hours before — was lost to the aviation industry solely because the FAA thought he was too old. In similarly perplexing accidents, one United Airlines Captain, just weeks after bringing his crippled jumbo jet to a safe landing after part of his fuselage was ripped away, was also forced to retire... at Age 60. And, in one of the most celebrated situations in which the expertise of a pilot was credited with saving *many* lives, United Airlines Captain Al Haynes retired several months after executing one of the most harrowing crash landings in the history of commercial aviation. The experience of Al Haynes... experience that saved dozens of passengers who would most probably have died in the hands of a lesser pilot... was lost to the aviation world because Al had *"simply gotten too old to do the job."*

With these confusing examples staring the aviation world in the face and adding fuel to the Age 60 conflagration, it could not be ignored that a guy like Bob Hoover, pushing his 70s and flying high G acrobatics with as much skill and precision as he demonstrated with each airshow, certainly made the FAA's Age 60 Rule look arbitrary and capricious. Face it, with Hoover out doing airshows, the FAA looked stupid and the "Bob Hoover argument" popped in virtually every fight over the Age 60 rule that came up.

It was impossible to watch Hoover looping and rolling dozens of times per weekend, with precision and alacrity, and believe that the Age 60 rule was anything but arbitrary, discriminatory, unfair and capricious... and the FAA knew it.

Still, the FAA had been pushing the Age 60 doctrine around for nearly thirty years and seemed adamant in defending the indefensible. So... when someone found a way to try to knock Hoover off his pedestal, it seemed like manna from heaven to those in the FAA who were still fighting to maintain the fiction of the Age 60 rule. After all, the FAA had been fighting this battle for decades.

A History Lesson

The history of the Age 60 Rule is a turbulent one... going back to the 1950s and employing entities that one, outwardly, would suspect of alternate loyalties. However, due to the laws of economics and self-interest, the Age 60 Rule map has been cluttered with a number of combatants of conflicting ideologies.

In the early 1950s, several airlines mutually ordained a mandatory pilot retirement age of 60 years. The Airline Pilot's Association initially objected, but comprehensive retirement programs were being discussed and negotiated at that point and other concerns pushed it to the backburner... and pretty much turned ALPA into an "anti-Age 60 Rule" organization.

Starting in 1956, pilots from three different airlines challenged this edict. Mandatory retirement rules at Western, TWA and American airlines were challenged through the use of labor grievance channels. All three challenges were won by the pilots. TWA and American defended themselves using their employee contract as justification while Western relied on "safety" as their sole defense for their reasoning. This was rather decisively rejected by the arbitrator.

About the same time, Air Traffic Controllers were also afforded similar scrutiny. ATC was in a bit of chaos at the time, owing to some catastrophic mid-air collisions, near misses, and other hazards that alarmed the public and their elected reps. Congress then authorized and funded a full review of airman medical certification standards. The Civil Aviation Administration (CAA) contracted with the non-profit Flight Safety Foundation to accomplish this review, while also ordering a separate, expedited examination of the standards applying to air traffic controllers.

Two years later, Congress totally reorganized the CAA, by reassigning economic regulation to the CAB, and creating the Federal Aviation Administration to manage the air traffic systems and overall safety responsibilities. President Eisenhower appointed Gen. Elwood Quesada as the FAA's first Administrator. He had previously served as Chairman of the Airways Modernization Board (created the year before, in 1957, to restructure the air traffic control system) and had been Eisenhower's war-time commander of the European Theater's Tactical Air Forces.

Also in 1958, the two much-anticipated Flight Safety Foundation (medical) reports (the first on air traffic controllers, the second on pilots) were published. The Flight Safety Foundation actually recommended a specific retirement age for air traffic controllers, but specifically recommended no change to pilot medical certification standards.

Additionally, TWA and Western went ahead and acceded to the arbitrations conducted through their labor reps, and reinstated their over Age 60 pilots. American Airlines held firm and adamantly refused to do the same. On December 20, 1958, the pilots at American went out on strike (over both contract renewal and the retirement issues), resulting in the airline having to capitulate to their pilot's demands on Jan. 10, 1959, including acceptance of an arbitrator's ruling on reinstating the over Age 60 pilots.

These were to be some of the last victories for those opposing the Age 60 rule, because at this point things got *political*. In early February of '59, the Chairman of American Airlines, C.R. Smith, who just happened to be a personal friend of Administrator Queseda, wrote a rather intriguing letter to the FAA's Boss. Noting American's loss over the Age 60 issue, Smith sought the FAA's help in putting together a new regulation that would solve his problem.

A month later, the FAA started a thorough revision of Airman Medical Certification Standards, supposedly in response to the Flight Safety Foundation studies. At no time did the FAA give anyone a clue that they were interested in revising pilot aging standards.

As a matter of fact, in April of that year, Administrator Queseda, in a letter written to the President of Notre Dame, the Reverend Theodore Hesburg, stated *"There exists at present no sound scientific evidence that airline piloting, or any other aeronautical activity, becomes critical at any given age."*

However, by June of '59, the FAA started the regulatory process along the lines of the request from American's Smith, ordering a mandatory retirement age of 60 years. The FAA based this action on medical arguments, but ignored the Flight Safety Foundation reports and the ongoing medical standard revision. By the end of 1959, the Age 60 rule was in place.

Of course this was not the last word on the matter. The fight was already being waged as early as January 1960, with an attempt to enjoin the FAA from enforcing the Age 60 Rule plead before a Federal District Court. That attempt went nowhere... and was headlined, bizarrely, with approving comments about General Quesada's war record, as well as the citing of a Washington Post editorial, and quoted an after-dinner speech by Harry F. Guggenheim (where Quesada was in attendance). (*ALPA v Quesada, 182 F. Supp. 595—S.D., N.Y., 1960*). The objectivity of this ruling was, obviously, questionable.

It gets worse. One year later, General Quesada retired... kind of. In January of 1961, General Quesada wound up on the Board of Directors of American Airlines with his buddy C.R. Smith. Imagine that.

With Quesada out of the picture, the FAA initiated the Georgetown Clinical Research Institutes Studies, which was portrayed as a "long-term" (over the course of some 30 years) search for objective criteria with which to replace the arbitrary Age 60 Rule. Mind you, the study protocol appeared to have been patterned on the 1958 Flight Safety Foundation report on air traffic controllers... but not pilots.

The subjects enrolled were primarily air traffic controllers, not pilots. Over the course of nearly five years, nothing much seemed to be happen. In 1965, the FAA killed off the Georgetown study after the initiation of an investigation by the House Government Operations Committee. That Committee found the FAA's study to have collected *no* usable data during its five years of operation, and *no* system or capability to analyze data, if it had any. This little exercise in futility was reported to have cost the taxpayers some $2.5 million dollars... a pretty significant amount of money back in the 60s, mind you.

Congress passed the Age Discrimination in Employment Act (ADEA) in 1968 (in 1979, the ADEA would give way to the Equal Employment Opportunities Commission). Administered by the Secretary of Labor, he declared the Age 60 Rule to be a Bona Fide Occupational Qualification (BFOQ), which allowed the Age 60 Rule to remain in force.

As the decade came to a close, a 1969-70 study of extremely favorable aging data collected from military pilots, flight test pilots, and air carrier pilots was conducted by the Lovelace Foundation in Albuquerque, NM. Studies funded by the National Institutes of Health (NIH) on normal human aging instigated a petition by several pilots for exemptions to the Age 60 Rule.

Two years later, the FAA's considerable docket on the Age 60 Rule appeared to have been "misplaced..." as the legal actions just noted, approached hearing and court actions. Over the next several years, a number of legal skirmishes were fought on this subject, but no acknowledgment of the missing docket was forthcoming.

By 1979, the House Aviation Subcommittee recommended overturning the Age 60 Rule through legislation. This recommendation made it all the way to the floor of the House, but aggressive lobbying by ALPA (with lots of help from organized labor), killed it off to leave it as nothing more than a "study" by the NIH and the National Institute on Aging (NIA).

Two years later, the EEOC rescinded the Department of Labor declaration of the Age 60 Rule as a BFOQ. Further, the NIA/NIH study found no medical basis for the Age 60 Rule. Still, owing something to political expediency, they recommended keeping it in place temporarily, while the FAA agreed to grant waivers to some selected pilots to determine the feasibility of raising or eliminating the Rule.

The FAA responded to the NIH/NIA recommendation, and surprised everyone by proposing inclusion of Flight Engineers under the Age 60 Rule. In a blast from the past, this totally unconnected proposal was initiated at the request of United Airlines, who had just (surprise!!!) lost a court effort to force mandatory retirement of its Flight Engineers at Age 60. If this wasn't a near repeat of the questionable C.R. Smith/American Airlines rule request to Gen. Quesada in 1959, it sure was a *Twilight Zone* like imitation...

The FAA showed their stripes again in 1984. The directors of the NIA and NIH criticized the FAA for refusing to follow the panel's earlier recommendations. As a matter-of-fact, the director of the NIA, after consulting with the NIH, rescinded the panel's earlier recommendations to retain the rule temporarily and thereafter declared (during Congressional testimony) that the agency's policy is that medical science should be able to identify disability, and therefore protect public safety.

During the latter part of 1984, the situation became black and white as Federal Air Surgeon Dr. Frank Austin wrote Dr. Stanley Mohler stating that *"there is no medical basis for the Age 60 rule."* He further expounded that *"I believe this and Admiral Engen, (then the FAA administrator), believes this... it's an economic issue."*

In the meantime, the EEOC started a progressive effort, and a successful one we might add, to convince the non-airline industry to abandon the Age 60 rule. So, in every other facet of aviation (at that time), pilots could fly as long as they liked, even those in far more demanding aviation disciplines... like crop dusting, charter flying, flight instruction, and even... airshow flying.

In 1988, in the case of Aman v. FAA, in the Seven Circuit Court, a pilot's group petition urging further findings on the issue of whether an older pilots greater experience could conceivably overcome any immeasurable the decrement of aging was remanded for future consideration.

Dr. George Kidera, on February 15, 1989, wrote that *"granting qualified pilots over the age of 60 exemptions from the provisions of 14 CFR 121.383 (c), will not com-*

promise safety." Dr. Kidera was one of the original members of the panel that established the Age 60 rule!

In the same year, the General Accounting Office noted that by 1980, 365 airmen had been recertified after bouts with alcoholism but experienced an 18 percent relapse rate. By 1983, there had been 409 re-certifications, with 40 of them issued after one relapse, and three after yet a second relapse.

A number of persons lauded the FAA for allowing these troubled fliers a chance to regain their careers, and in this regard the FAA took a fairly progressive stance ... but why in the case of those who demonstrated the "problem" of alcoholic dependency, and not in the case of older fliers who had not demonstrated any problems at all?

Things started hitting the fan again in 1990. Once again, the Seventh Circuit Court, in Baker v. FAA, found the FAA relying on old statistical studies, in this case one from 1983, to try to deny the inferences of the Aman v. FAA remand. This study compared age, experience, and accidents.

During its presentation to the court, the FAA actually concealed the fact that the author of the study was nothing more than an accountant, **not** a statistician, and the additional fact that the report been severely criticized throughout the scientific community when it was first submitted. As a matter-of-fact, it had been rejected by the FAA's own office of Aviation Safety — who had directed that this study be conducted. This study was never published.

In the same case, ALPA President Henry Duffy said that *"pilots over age 55 comprise only five to six percent of the total membership. The other 95 percent selfishly view the forced retirement of older pilots as their guaranteed path and God given right to their own early promotion!"*

The FAA releases the Hilton study (otherwise known as the CAMI study). "Amazingly," the study finds *"no hint of an increase in accident rates as pilots near Age 60"* and subsequently concluded that the retirement age may safely be raised! The FAA then went through the dog-and-pony show, holding public meetings to gather comments on the Hilton study and the Age 60 rule. Scheduled for only half a day, the meetings went on for days, with nearly 85 percent of speakers showing up to fight the Age 60 rule. Even foreign airlines with waivers to the Age 60 rule wound up attending.

The Professional Pilots Federation, which was formed in 1991, filed an official petition with the FAA to amend and hopefully eliminate the rule. Yet another petition asked for equal status for US pilots as compared to courtesies extended for aircrews flying into the US. In such cases, the FAA allowed one pilot to be over the age of 60, as long as the other was below the age of 60.

Meanwhile, "down under" in Australia, Aussie Chief Justice Wilcox stated *"given the time and effort expended in America examining the Age 60 rule, is remarkable to say so, but it seems to me that none of the cited studies supports any conclusion about the relationship between that rule and aircraft safety."* Believe it or not, the Age 60 rule was killed off in Australia.

By the end of 1995, eying kinks in its own armor, the FAA issues a new order entitled "Commuter Operations and General Certification and Operations requirements." What this little bit of FAA backside camouflage did was impose yet another Age 60 rule for those pilots operating 10- to 30-seat aircraft. These aircraft and the pilots had been previously exempted from Age 60 restrictions. About the same time, the FAA issued a "Dispo-

sition of Comments and Notice of Agency Decisions on the Age 60 Rule" program, but announced no action at that time. All subsequent petitions and individual exemption requests were denied on December 28.

The Professional Pilots Federation filed for review of the FAA's action in the DC Court of Appeals. Less than a month later, the PPF filed an age discrimination case against Federal Express in Memphis, TN, on behalf of pilots who got the boot as soon as they reached Age 60. In the same month, the twelve-nation European Union officially adopted an "Age 65" rule for their airline pilots.

Six months later, the House Appropriations Committee introduced an amendment giving the NTSB the authority to study the Age 60 rule ... but ALPA rallied the troops and the amendment was killed by a vote of 247 to 159. ALPA was not above throwing its weight around, and many thousands of affluent airline pilots represented a very considerable voter block to deal with, and Congress took strong notice of this.

The DC Court of Appeals denied the PPF petition by two to one in July of 1997. Judge Patricia Wald cast the dissenting vote and noted *"more importantly, the Age 60 rule stands as an instance of government-mandated age discrimination for a particular group of employees."*

In the Sixth Circuit, the US Court of Appeals ruled for FedEx, closing formation right behind the DC Court of Appeals. Wasn't that convenient?

In August, the PPF filed for Rehearing with Suggestion for Rehearing En Banc in the DC Court of Appeals. Surprisingly, the court ordered the FAA to respond to the PPF request for rehearing. Their response rehashes old arguments used in the original filing, and a request for a rehearing is eventually denied.

The fight continues... but in the light of the successful and trouble-free flight of Senator John Glenn aboard the Space Shuttle in the Fall of 1998, the whole Age 60 matter is beginning to look pretty silly.... especially while a certain 77-year-old man flies flawless airshows in a twin-engine aircraft that features (among many things) dead-stick, sixteen-point rolls just inches off the ground. Amazing, isn't it?

Chapter 10

Trophy Kills & Fed Wars... How Some Feds Make Sport of Grounding Airmen

Little Things Affect Little Minds.
Benjamin Disraeli

One of the sadder aspects of the immense power wielded by the FAA is the way that it can be abused, and while only a tiny percentage of the FAA Inspector workforce seems to be malevolently inclined, there is no question that the damage they do is extraordinary.

Worse... to a certain small segment of the FAA, abusing their responsibilities and their power seems to be something of a sport. Busting pilots, especially famous or notable ones, has become an underground gag or rite of passage to those Feds who do not understand that the power that they wield is a trust and not a game. Each such bust becomes a notch on their imaginary gun-belt and the growing distrust that has existed for the last decade or so, between the civil pilot population and the FAA, widens ever further.

As a result, it is not unusual to hear that a well-known pilot has had to deal with the Feds over issues, real or imagined, that might have a serious impact on their flying career. Some of the most sought-after targets are airshow pilots, both because of their public visibility and the somewhat naive assumption that guys who fly this wild just can't follow the rules.

Other targets include aviation journalists, famous people from other walks of life (more than one flying celebrity has had to deal with the FAA...), and certainly anyone whom an individual FAA Inspector decides to dislike.

It is a *fact* that a number of the FAA's staff have used their power to "bust" people they don't like, target famous pilots, and throw their weight around for their own personal aggrandizement... and the Hoover matter certainly appears to have started out much in that fashion.

AIR OF INJUSTICE

The Gee-Bee Caper

One of the more recent cases of such abuse surrounded one of the best airshow pilots in the world (surprise!)... and a man who had been active in the defense of Mr. Hoover. Anyone who has seen Delmar Benjamin fly the Gee-Bee R-1 has seen an amazing master at work. There isn't a single pilot who hasn't marveled at the mastery this man has assumed over an aircraft once dubbed far and wide as a "Pilot-Killer" by pilots all over the globe.

As Delmar cranks low-altitude point rolls and breathtakingly low inverted passes in this beast, you know that two things are true: Delmar Benjamin is one hell of a pilot... and that he's got a set of "huevos" that should probably be measured by the metric ton. At the same time, he's a rather convoluted personality; a guy this brassy (in flight) is also a quiet and semi-bashful sort that's really not into trumpeting his achievements or boasting about his abilities. Instead, he's quick to smile, listens as much (or more) than he speaks, and is a genuinely sweet guy... no kidding. Since the Hoover matter came to prominence, Delmar has had a number of run-ins with the FAA.

First, Delmar had to deal with a bizarre Oregon-based problem with a Fed who was not even on the airport at the time an alleged flight took place but nonetheless decided to nail him for a number of items, including flying at an altitude below that which was required (how he could have honestly judged this is not known). They went round and round and after the FAA offered him a three-day suspension, Delmar took it because one should only fight city hall when the stakes demand it... and a three-day suspension wasn't enough for him to destroy his life over.

But later on, Delmar flew the September 1996 Reno Air Races, as he had for five years and pretty much had a ball, as did everyone who got to see this magnificent racer strut its stuff. But... there was to be another problem.

Yet another Fed with an apparent axe to grind (and it was not the first time this particular guy has targeted Benjamin) decided that Delmar was acting in a reckless and dangerous manner... *not* for flying low and upside down. *Not* for the aerobatic routine he's been doing for years and hundreds of performances... No, it was for a simple series of high-speed pylon runs (mind you in an air racing airplane...) that are neither as risky or as radical as the standard high-speed, pulse-pounding unlimited air racing that goes on there *every single year*.

A number of race photographers asked for the pylon runs in order to get realistic race photos of the Gee-Bee doing *what it was designed for* and had signed waivers (we've seen them and signed them for ourselves, in the past) *and* received permission to be in the otherwise off-limits pylon racing areas. Delmar, with the blessing of the airshow staff and at the direct request of the photographers (who were salivating over the photo possibilities...), made a few runs, really strutted his stuff, and then got lambasted by the FAA for it!

A September 20, 1996 investigatory letter authored by Michael Clark of the Reno FSDO stated that *"the aircraft was observed and identified as Gee Bee N2101 flying toward photographers and other personnel at an excessively low altitude and within approximately 100 feet of those persons on three occasions. Operations of this type are contrary to the Federal Aviation Regulations."*

Benjamin and Clark had had discussions about his low-level turns prior to this

event and he was undoubtedly aware of what was transpiring... first because this was a fairly regular request from airshow staff, and further because they had discussed his low-level turns previously and Clark had ordered Delmar to change them to a procedure that Benjamin felt was less safe than what he had been doing previously. According to Delmar, *"Due to the configuration of the aircraft, I avoid pulling towards the ground, which dictates the majority of my turn-arounds be a teardrop (90 - 270) turn back to the airshow center line. This is a non-aerobatic turn designed to conserve energy and get back to show center without delay or loss of speed required for the next maneuver. This method of turn-around is the most energy-efficient maneuver to return to the show environment, which is the runway environment at 99 percent of the airshows I fly."*

Delmar continued... *"This show is flown under a certificate of waiver issued by the FAA encompassing an area of three miles by four miles. Waived in this document are 91.117 (A,B) and 91.119 (B,C). This waives speed and minimum altitude from persons or property for the purpose of conducting the races and airshow demonstrations in a specific designated area. The general public and any other unauthorized persons are strictly prohibited from this area. Any person entering this area must have either race course or press credentials. Reno Air Race personnel shuttle these authorized persons to and from the sterile area by bus. All persons must sign a waiver before being permitted on the bus. Pylon judges and photographers are placed at virtually every pylon in the 3 mile by 4 mile waivered area.*

On September 14, 1996, FAA Inspector Michael Clark gave me the option to modify my turn-around at the west end to avoid pylon eight and its photographers or be grounded. I explained that these persons were placed at that pylon for the purpose of photographing my aircraft under the rules of the waivered airspace. Airshow personnel, on the ground, direct my flight path via a large, highly visible red target for optimal photographic positioning. On this particular occasion the target was placed on the port-a-johns to the north of the pylon... this position falls into the path of every west bound tear drop turn-around performed exactly as in the previous four years. I pointed out that this operation was covered by the waiver and has been safely and legally operating for five years now. The Inspector refused to listen to reason and stated that I avoid turns toward pylon eight or he would shut down the show on Sunday.

Rather than subjecting myself, the air race personnel and Reno's loyal fans to his abusive exercise of power, on Sunday I agreed to modify my west-end turn-around to a left 270, right 90 teardrop turn-around, in accordance with Mr. Clark's direction. This turn-around took place around the Formula One scatter pylon, which is actually behind the extended dead line and results in directing energy during a substantial segment of the turn toward the pit area. Directing this energy away from a three by five mile sterile waivered area and towards a large crowd of racers and airshow fans was absurd and done against my better judgement to appease the Inspector."

Two months later, the FAA sent Benjamin a letter proposing to suspend his ticket for *six* months... which is a lifetime to an airshow pilot, believe you me. Mind you, this is the very same Inspector who threw his weight around a few years earlier, as Delmar tells it. *"This is not the first incident involving Inspector Clark at the Reno Air Races. On September 18, 1993, my logbooks and airworthiness documents were confiscated and removed from the airport premises over night. I received no receipt for them and was left with no documents through the following day. As I was taxiing out to fly my demonstra-*

tion, Inspector Clark pulled in front of my aircraft in a government vehicle, blocking my exit. When I shut down the engine and approached his vehicle he asked to see my aircraft paperwork. I stated that he knew very well that he and his colleagues had the paperwork in their office for inspection. He stated that if I flew without it I would be in violation of the FARs. Due to the time constraints in getting my aircraft in the air on schedule, I ask if he could retrieve my paperwork from his office. He refused even to give me a ride to retrieve them. I ran approximately one half mile to the FAA headquarters and retrieved my logbooks and paperwork from Inspector Morgan, who had examined them and stated they were now in order. Upon returning to the start-up area, Inspector Clark stated that he really didn't want to look at them now. After running a half-mile in extreme heat, I had to commence run-up and cockpit checks while high-speed taxing to the runway. These are very dangerous conditions under which to conduct a low-level acrobatic demonstration in high density air. In spite of the harassment by Inspector Clark and the rigorous work out prior to launch, I flew a safe and flawless demonstration."

Thankfully, this story had a happier ending than most. As the FAA became aware that media was scrutinizing this case (they had received a copy of a **US Aviator** magazine article just prior to going to press), the charges were dropped... But not until after great worry, expense and heartache on the part of Delmar and his family.

"I'm Going to Get Fried"

Another famous aviator really got the screws applied to him... but this time, the flyer was none other than **FLYING** magazine columnist and aviation book author, Howard Fried (widely quoted throughout this book).

Fried, in addition to being a well-known aero-writer, was a designated Pilot examiner for the FAA, a senior flyer who can certify others to fly under the rules established by the Federal Aviation Regulations.

Such positions are only given to highly experienced aviators in order to lessen FAA workloads. Some of the more popular/busy Examiners derive a fairly good income from the checkrides they give to student pilots looking for certification. Howard was one of the busiest such examiners in the country... until the FAA targeted him, too.

Howard recalls the matter vividly. *"In 1992, an Inspector from our local District Office of the FAA (Flight Standards District Office—FSDO), David Sunday, told an operator at the airport where I am based, 'I'm going to get Fried!' (The operator, a freight hauler, has provided me with a notarized affidavit testifying to this statement.) Sunday's opportunity came a few months later when the FAA, in a knee-jerk reaction to an article in the Wall Street Journal criticizing the pilot examiner program, asked each district office to look at the records of their high volume examiners, of which I was one. (I had been conducting over three hundred certification flight tests annually for the past several years.)*

I spent seventeen years as a faithful representative of the Administrator. But, in May of 1992 I was shocked to be informed that my designation as a Pilot Examiner was not to be renewed. It happened like this: Routinely, more than thirty days prior to the annual expiration of my designation, I had always received the paperwork required for renewal. My anniversary date was in May, and the designation must be renewed before

the end of the month. If not, the examiner must start all over again with attendance at the initial course at Oklahoma City (at his own expense). In 1992 I received no such notification or application, so I called and requested it as well as an appointment for meeting and riding with an Inspector for renewal. I was told that the paperwork would be taken care of when I came in, and an appointment was made for me to do so.

Over a period of three weeks I was given three separate appointments, each of which was canceled. The final appointment offered by an Inspector Sunday, who was acting for an Inspector Scarpuzza, the principal Inspector assigned to work with me. It was destined for a day when he knew I could not make it due to a prior commitment. If we didn't get together that day, there was no other time prior to the expiration of my designation in which to do so. I was, however, able to rearrange my schedule to accommodate Sunday's offered time, so I called him back and agreed to come in at that time.

Incidentally, I'm convinced that Inspector Scarpuzza orchestrated an entire attack on me. He merely used Inspector Sunday as a stooge to do his dirty work. The previous year at the time of the renewal of my designation, Scarpuzza had taken away my authority to administer practical tests in three make and model twins and in gliders, claiming that an examiner wasn't needed for these airplanes. However, within six weeks he had conferred that same multi-engine authority on another examiner. Obviously there existed a need for an examiner for those three twins and Scarpuzza had lied when he advised me to the contrary.

The next day Sunday called and canceled that final appointment, saying I'd be getting a letter of explanation, but refusing to tell me what was in the letter. The following day, both by messenger and by registered mail, I received a letter informing me that my designation was not going to be renewed, and advising me that I could come in to the FSDO (with legal counsel if I wished) and appeal this decision.

*This allowed me **one working day** in which to be renewed or I would automatically be disqualified. (In the case of a favored examiner, however, many months **after** his designation had expired, the Detroit FSDO saw fit to "renew" him by retro-dating the paperwork to a date prior to the expiration of his designation thus avoiding the necessity of him having to travel to Oklahoma City and attend the original examiner course)."*

Howard's livelihood was in great danger... *"Immediately after I received the letter denying my renewal, a half-dozen local attorneys offered to accompany me to an appeal meeting at the FSDO the following day (the last working day prior to automatic disqualification). I selected one and we went to the District Office together. The first thing we were told was that I was entitled to due process and specifically 'adequate notice'. I looked across the table to the Office Manager and asked, 'Dave (Hobgood), do you really believe one day is adequate notice?'*

He smiled (smirked), and said, 'Of course it is!'

This set the tone for the balance of the meeting. My attorney suggested that my designation be renewed pending the outcome of an official appeal. This request was denied out of hand, and the appeal process was explained to us. We were also presented with a memo explaining the appeal process, which starts at the District Office, and from which an appeal may be made to the Regional Office (of the FAA). Thereafter, the matter may be appealed to the United States Circuit Court of Appeals. These procedures, too, were disregarded by the agency.

It is my firm belief that had I quietly accepted my fate and not taken an appeal from the decision of the District Office to, in effect, revoke my designation as a pilot examiner (based on three spurious reasons), the matter would have ended right there, and the subsequent vendetta against me would not have been mounted. Of course the fact that I sicced the United States Congress and the Inspector General of the Department of Transportation on them didn't help my cause. It only served to further enrage the Office Manager at the local FSDO. However, I opted to fight by filing an appeal with the Regional Office. For this, to work with my local attorney, I retained the services of the country's most knowledgeable and leading aviation lawyer with respect to regulatory matters, John S. Yodice.

We provided written answers to the three phony charges that the District Office had used as an excuse for taking away my designation, and, under the Freedom of Information Act, we made a demand for my file which is maintained at the District Office. This file, which was fifteen inches thick when I had last seen it a few months earlier, contained hundreds of letters of commendation, many from the FAA itself, as well as both Flight Standards and Air Traffic Control. What we received in response to our demand for the file was only one-half inch thick and contained nothing but a few derogatory entries. (We have copies of over one hundred favorable entries that had been removed from this file.) How convenient...

After a delay of over three months, we received a letter from the Regional Office informing us that they were changing the procedure. In an obvious effort to cover up the mistakes of the District Office by failing to provide me with adequate notice and otherwise failing to follow their own published procedures, the Regional Office stated that we would start all over again by initiating the denial of my designation at the regional level. Then, an appeal may be taken to the National Flight Standards Office in Washington, and thence to the United States Circuit Court of Appeals. This, of course, delayed the entire matter for an additional six months, and it took the bad guys at the District Office out of the picture. This letter dropped two of the charges that the District Office had used as an excuse to revoke my designation, and added two new ones! One of these added charges dealt with a four and one-half year old matter that the District Office Manager way back then had assured me, in his words, 'You may consider the matter closed. You'll hear no more about it.'

It got worse. "We were finally granted a hearing (meeting) before the Regional Flight Standards Manager. This is the same individual who was accused of ordering the destruction of records that might prove embarrassing to the FAA in another matter. John Yodice, Gary Gondek (my local counsel) and I traveled to the regional office to present our case.

Yodice started by asking what happened to all the favorable material that had been in my file, but was no longer there. David Hanley, the Regional Flight Standards Manager, told us that files are regularly culled of stale material. John Yodice then asked, "If that's the case, how is it that five year old derogatory material is still there and three week old stuff is missing?" No attempt was made to answer this question. It was simply ignored. Mind you, Hanley is the same individual accused on the front page of the New York Times of ordering the destruction of files derogatory to the FAA.

The balance of this hearing was taken up with our satisfactorily answering each of the charges that had been used as an excuse to revoke my designation. This included those of the District Office and the new ones added by the Regional Office. At the conclu-

sion of this October meeting at the Regional Office, the Regional Flight Standards Manager, Hanley, said, "I'm tied up the rest of this week and most of next week, but I'll have an answer for you within a week or ten days."

The following month two things happened. First, I and three of the seven pilots who were flying on a contract that I had with a multinational corporation for the delivery of parts for its equipment by air, received Letters of Investigation stating that there was a possible violation of FAR Part 135. Second, Inspector Sunday of my local FSDO told another aviation writer that he ought to try to take over my monthly column in FLYING magazine that deals with flight testing, stating that I was no longer a Pilot Examiner, having been stripped of my designation for violating Part 135! This was before the investigation had even gotten underway!

Sunday further stated to that writer that the editors of FLYING were no doubt unaware of the fact that I was no longer an examiner and the magazine would be embarrassed to have its readers discover this. Evidently since Sunday and his boss, Hobgood, are totally devoid of honor, they believe everyone else is too. When the whole business with my designation first started back in May, I had immediately notified the Editor-in-Chief of FLYING of that fact and his response was, 'I don't care if you're an examiner or a former examiner, just keep writing the column!'

This column has been a sore point with some of the people at the local FSDO since I first started writing it. It is my belief that the reason the investigation of a possible Part 135 violation was started by the FAA, was actually an effort to attack my pilot certificate. Without a pilot certificate, I certainly couldn't be an examiner and thus my appeal of the revocation of my designation would fail. A few weeks after we received the Letters of Investigation, the three pilots who had been flying on the contract received letters stating that at the conclusion of the investigation no violation had been found and the matter was closed. I, however, got a letter stating that the investigation had resulted in a finding that I was guilty of being the operator of an illegal 135 operation and a Civil Penalty of Two Hundred Ninety-One Thousand dollars was being assessed against me!

Please be advised that prior to entering into the contract under which I leased an airplane to the aforementioned multinational corporation for its exclusive use and control, I had described in detail just how I intended to do this to two FAA General Aviation Operations Inspectors, Alfred M. Hunt, and David Sunday himself. Both of them assured me that, as constituted, it did not fall under Part 135. I expected that Hunt would testify truthfully to this fact and that Sunday would, under oath, deny that I ever discussed it with him.

After the lease program had been in operation for a year and one-half, a third Inspector also told me that it was not a 135 operation. At that time, (early fall of 1993), the FAA took the unheard-of step of sending an Airworthiness (maintenance) Inspector (not only) out of his District, but out of his Region(!) with specific instructions to ground the airplane I had leased.

Meanwhile, after waiting for over five months for the answer that had been promised "within a week to ten days", we filed a Mandamus action in the Federal Court system. This action requested that the court order the FAA Regional Manager to do his duty and give us the answer he had promised "within a week to ten days." We immediately received the expected turn-down of our appeal seeking the reinstatement of my designation. This placed us in the position of being able to proceed with an appeal to the National Flight Standards Office in Washington. Even though we were promised the right to present oral argument at that level, we got our turn-down on the written pleadings without benefit of oral argument. This, finally, permitted us to appeal to the Federal Circuit Court of Appeals.

We filed that appeal in the First Circuit (in Washington), and John Yodice argued the matter before the court. The FAA had maintained all along that I was entitled to Due Process, but in their argument to the court the FAA attorney claimed, first, that the court had no jurisdiction to hear the matter, and second, that if the court should take jurisdiction, that I was not entitled to Due Process.

The court did take jurisdiction, but agreed that I was not entitled to Due Process, in essence saying that the United States Constitution doesn't apply to the FAA. This ended my effort to regain my designation, but the matter of the Civil Penalty ($291,000 fine) was left standing. This battle was fought on the local level in the United States District Court for the Southeastern District of Michigan, with Gary Gondek representing me.

For an operation to fall under Part 135 of the regulations, there must be a "holding out", and "operational control." However, I did not hold myself out as available for the transportation of cargo by air, rather the multinational corporation came to me and asked if I could provide them with an airplane. I had NO operational control whatever. I never knew where or when a trip was flown until after the fact, when I was given the data for billing purposes.

In this battle the FAA again demonstrated the same sort of vendetta that has prevailed throughout. In all other cases of which I am aware, an airman against whom a civil penalty is imposed, is permitted to compromise the penalty without an admission of guilt. In my case the FAA told the United States Attorney who was attempting to collect the penalty that she may compromise it out for an inconsequential amount, but only if I was willing to admit that I am guilty of the violation. This I refused to do. The US Attorney filed a motion for summary judgement claiming that there was no issue of material fact on which to base a defense. Had this motion been granted I would have lost and that would have ended it with me owing the United States $291,000. However, the judge denied the motion, which further demonstrated the weakness of the government's case.

After much negotiation with the United States Attorney (who was being guided throughout by an attorney from the regional office of the FAA), the government finally offered to let me settle the matter for $10,000 if I was willing to admit to being guilty of a single count, and $20,000 without the admission of guilt! I countered by saying I would give them the $10,000 but the settlement must include the fact that there was to be no finding of guilt whatever. Otherwise, I was quite willing to take my chances at trial."

They knew they had a shaky case. They accepted the offer and Howard got his life back. Howard spent over $40,000 of his own money (while the FAA was financed by his tax dollars and he lost untold amounts of dollars because of the loss of his designation as a pilot examiner). He also lost the money from the contract with the "multinational corporation", because the FAA advised them to terminate the contract *"because of (Howard's) alleged illegal operation."* Howard had been nearly bankrupted by this matter and simply

had to cut his losses... though one additional matter that horribly compounded the tragedy was the fact that his lovely wife, Myrel, was critically ill and passed away during the course of this debacle.

Michael Taylor

Sometimes the average Joe gets picked for an FAA firing squad... guys like Michael Taylor. In 1997, FAA victim Howard Fried also wrote about the Taylor case and horrified pilots all over the country with what certainly appeared to be yet another FAA miscarriage of Justice.

Herewith, Howard's investigation of the Taylor debacle: ...*Kenneth B., a former naval pilot with over 1065 hours of experience decided to acquire certification as a civilian pilot. He enrolled in a ground school course conducted by Michael J. Taylor, and on completion of this course in 1993 he took and passed the Private Pilot Written Examination with a score of 90%. On January 28, 1995, Mr. B. began to undertake flight instruction from Taylor. Prior to starting this training, Mike Taylor sought the advice and counsel of the local FSDO with respect to just what would be required. He was told that he needed only prep the applicant for the skill requirement (Practical Test) since the experience requirement had already been met.*

Taylor gave Kenney B. 5.8 hours (tach time) dual instruction before permitting him to solo, and Mr. B. had 3.5 tach hours of local solo time before Taylor prepped him for cross-country with 1.5 tach hours of dual instruction.

Please be advised that as a Certificated Flight Instructor I have personally trained and recommended for certification numerous former military pilots, who, having met the experience requirement (regardless of how long in the past), and the knowledge requirement by having passed the appropriate written, required only sufficient training to meet the skill requirement. In some cases this amounted to merely brushing up on the maneuvers.

It should also be noted that between 1969 and 1974 Mr. B., as a naval aviator, flew in excess of 1000 hours in combat aircraft, and executed 185 carrier landings. He was a Landing Safety Officer (LSO) on the USS Forestal. From 1975 through 1981 he was a full performance level FAA center radar controller, and from 1984 through 1995 he was a senior training analyst developing and teaching aviation training programs. He literally "wrote the book" on aerial navigation, and since that time he has been a professional educator.

Mike Taylor is a professional educator and part time flight instructor, formerly with Eastern Airlines. He is the holder of an Airline Transport Pilot Certificate, Certified Flight Instructor Certificate, Flight Engineer Certificate, and Mechanic Certificate. He has sponsored several FAA Safety Programs by arranging for a site for these presentations and otherwise participating, and he has been nominated for Flight Instructor of the Year honors in his local Flight Standards District Office (FSDO).

Are you getting a message here? It seems that the bad guys in the FAA single out for persecution the most prominent of aviators (Bob Hoover, the world's premier aviator; me, the most visible pilot examiner in the world, because of my column in FLYING; and Mike Taylor, one of the more prominent instructors in his district). I suppose these little people in the FAA somehow think that a demonstration of raw power by knocking down a Hoover increases their stature, when what it really does is draw the scorn and contempt of the entire aviation community upon them.

In preparing Ken B. for his Private Pilot practical test, Mike gave Ken training in cross-country operations, although this was not required by the regulations since Ken had already met all the experience requirements for the certificate. (FAR 61.41) A few days after having administered this training, Mike reviewed Ken's planning and dispatched him on a solo cross-country trip, after making the appropriate endorsements and logbook entries. Ken, who owned the airplane, was advised by Mike to top off the fuel tanks at the destination prior to starting the return trip.

However, because of the lateness of the hour, Ken visually checked the remaining fuel and determined that he had enough, including reserve, for the trip home, so he departed without adding fuel. You guessed it. He ran out of fuel some sixteen miles short of his home airport, resulting in an unscheduled, off-airport landing. There was no injury, but the aircraft was severely damaged. This, of course, precipitated an investigation by the Friendly Feds in the form of an Aviation Safety Inspector by the name of George DeMartini, who is alleged to have told Mike Taylor that he was not interested in safety, but rather his job was to find violations, and that's just what he intended to do in this matter!

Actually, the first inkling Mike had that a violation was under consideration was when he received a Letter of Investigation (LOI) from DeMartini stating that a violation may have occurred and Mike may have been involved (the usual boilerplate). The LOI was sent to Mike's correct address by Certified Mail, Return Receipt Requested under date of March 21, 1995. In a spirit of cooperation (I believe this is a mistake. Any effort to cooperate with these evil people is interpreted as a sign of weakness, leading them to push even harder.), Mike Taylor responded to the LOI with an explanation of the training he had given Ken B. He both wrote and telephoned DeMartini in an effort to resolve the matter. However, DeMartini pressed on.

In his investigation, Inspector DeMartini examined Ken B.'s pilot logbook and noted that a few days prior to the cross-country flight in question, Taylor had flown with Ken a total of 1.5 tach hours (the equivalent of 1.8 or more clock hours), and that the training on this flight included cross-country navigation, emergency procedures, and other tasks in the Private Pilot Practical Test Standards. This flight had taken place on February 3, 1995. DeMartini also noted that on the day of the accident flight (February 11, 1995) Taylor had reviewed Mr. B's cross-country planning and preparation prior to signing him off for the trip. Somehow DeMartini seems to hold the impression that there is something wrong with signing a student off for cross-country flight without administering flight instruction on that same day. He makes a big issue of the fact that Batey only got ground instruction on the day of the flight. He also claims that 1.5 tach hours is insufficient time to accomplish all the procedures and maneuvers that both Taylor and Ken B. testified were completed on the day of the flight training. (Taylor claims that even this wasn't really "training" but rather an evaluation of the procedures and maneuvers of an accomplished pilot.)

Taylor says that DeMartini indicated on the telephone that he was not interested in safety, that's the duty of the NTSB. His job, he said, is to find violations and that's just what he is doing. The next Taylor heard of the affair was when he received a

letter by regular mail at his correct home address, and signed by Naomi Tsuda, Associate Regional Counsel for the FAA, stating, "You may not have received the Notice of Proposed Certificate Action allegedly issued by this office on August 2, 1995." This letter was dated November 9, 1995 and was received by Taylor two days later. It should be noted here that this letter proposed to "suspend your Flight Instructor Authorization for a period of ninety (90) days."

The FAA's Regional Counsel's Office claims to have first sent a Notice of Proposed Certificate Action on August 3, 1995 by Registered Mail, Return Receipt Requested. No receipt was returned to the FAA, nor was the letter itself, if indeed such a letter was ever sent. If there was such a letter, it was certainly never received by Taylor. It would have to have been beyond six months of the time of the alleged violation, which occurred on February 3. (The letter, claimed by the FAA to have been written August 2 and mailed August 3 could not possibly have been received by Taylor until August 4th or 5th at the earliest.)

Finally waking up to the fact that DeMartini meant business and that full and complete cooperation was getting him nowhere, Mike Taylor retained the services of an attorney. The next step was an informal conference by telephone, involving Taylor's attorney Garland O. Bell, Inspector DeMartini, and FAA Attorney Tsuda. Bell, also naively (and mistakenly) believing that he was treating with reasonable people attempted to settle the matter informally by explaining just how none of Mike's actions or omissions constituted a violation of any regulations. Mike, not having been informed of its scheduling, did not participate in this telephone conference. The FAA pressed on, and Mike's attorney requested a hearing before an NTSB Administrative Law Judge (ALJ), the next step in the process. It was at this point that the proposed certificate suspension was expanded from his Flight Instructor Certificate only to all of Mike's FAA certificates.

NTSB rule 821.33, the so-called "Stale Complaint Rule" is really a statute of limitations limiting the timeframe within which the FAA may seek sanctions against an airperson to six months from the time a violation is discovered. The rule states that notice of a sanction against an airperson must be received by the airman within six months of the date of the occurrence from which the violation arose. There are two very specific exceptions that allow the FAA to impose sanctions sometime beyond the six month period, neither of which apply in this case. Therefore, based on NTSB Rule 821.33, Mike Taylor's attorney moved for a dismissal of the FAA's complaint against his client. This motion was opposed by the FAA and denied by the ALJ.

Prior to the hearing one of the charges was dropped as being stale, but the other was allowed to stand. At the hearing before the ALJ, Patrick G. Geraghty, both Mike Taylor and Ken B. testified under oath that the training Mr. B. received was adequate. They also both testified that Taylor had instructed Kenny to fill up his fuel tanks prior to starting his return trip. DeMartini testified that the training was inadequate. Taylor's attorney was prevented by the ALJ from cross-examining DeMartini regarding the means by which he had determined the training to be inadequate. Judge Geraghty opted to believe the testimony of DeMartini, who was not present when the training took place, and to disbelieve both Taylor and Ken B. who were there. He therefor ruled in favor of the FAA, but dropped the proposed suspension from ninety to sixty days, but added all of Taylor's FAA certificates as the FAA was now demanding, not merely his Flight Instructor Certificate as was originally proposed.

This decision paved the way for an appeal to the full NTSB, and Taylor appealed. Unless the evidence is overwhelming, the Board is very reluctant to overturn a decision of one of its ALJs, and although in this case the evidence does indeed seem to be overwhelming, the Board opted to uphold Geraghty's decision and it was affirmed by the full Board. The next step is to appeal the Board's decision to the United States Circuit Court of Appeals, and the matter now stands before the Ninth Circuit where a hearing is to be held in the reasonably near future.

The problem now is that the court, of course, won't hear evidence, but may only consider the question of whether or not the Board erred in affirming the decision of the ALJ. In fact the only issue before the court is that of the stale complaint rule. The facts that training was not required, and that even so the training was adequate and complete can't be considered. Here again, the court is very reluctant to overturn the decision of a lower court (in this case the NTSB) without clear and compelling reasons, and there is some law allowing the FAA to circumvent the stale complaint rule where the failure of the Postal Service to deliver the notice was the cause of the delay. We will just have to wait and see what the court does."

Howard concluded his report with the following ominous words and succinctly identified a growing problem facing the world of aviation... *"As a direct result of this activity on the part of the FAA, an adversarial position has arisen between the aviation community and the agency. Because of the high-handed and devious manner in which the agency traps pilots and operators into admitting wrongdoing, we have reached a point at which virtually nobody in the entire aviation community trusts the FAA, and that's too bad because it should be a partnership between the providers and the users."*

There's More...

There are other cases... too many of them to name, and while they admittedly were instigated by the minority of the FAA who constitute the "Bad Fed" element, the damage that these cases have done to the sense of trust and cooperation between the FAA and the pilot community is incredible.

Even I dealt with harassment over the Hoover case... often being subjected to personal attacks over my coverage of the Hoover story, both during and after the matter was finally decided. While this tragedy was at its fever pitch, my personal airplane was "ticketed" with an FAA Condition Notice for having *"decorative N numbers."* The airplane had recently been adorned with a fresh paint job and sported a paint scheme nearly identical to that of a popular series of business jets... and among which there was no record of any similar action. When I called the FAA Inspector (a man with a troubled record with the FAA, no less) in question and identified myself, I was hung up on... and when subsequent contact with his office was made, I was told to *"HOOVER THIS!"* and hung up on again.

The Inspector's Supervisor eventually told me to ignore the notice and the airplane has never drawn such attention again. Such tales are not that common... but unfortunately they are not rare... and that is one of the true shames of this story. If ever two groups needed to cooperate with and respect each other, it's the FAA and the flying population. But... so long as the rules offer such power to wayward Inspectors, further damage to the spirit of cooperation between them will continue.

Chapter 11

Fighting for Reason

All looks yellow to a jaundiced eye.
Alexander Pope

No sooner had Mr. Kelln and Mr. Boehler's statements hit the bureaucratic system, then the wheels started turning. To virtually anyone familiar with the bureaucratic process, there seems to be only two speeds at which things get done... slow and reverse.

In this matter, however, things took on unprecedented speed and urgency... despite the fact that Hoover had flown airshow after airshow after airshow — without any evidence of defect, delay, or inference of a single additional complaint from any of the FAA airshow monitors who were duty bound to report same if they observed such. So, for some reason, once the anticipated statements of the OKC Inspectors were officially filed, it took barely a day for the FAA to spring into action.

These statements were filed on August 26, and the next day, August 27, 1992, the FAA issued a certified letter to Bob Hoover under the authority of Sections 67.31 and 67.25 (c) of the FARs. This letter, issued by Audie W. Davis, a Doctor and Manager of the AeroMedical Certification Division of the Civil AeroMedical Institute (CAMI), said that *"we have recently received information which indicates a reasonable basis to believe that you may not meet the medical standards prescribed in Part 67 of the Federal Aviation regulations (FARs). You may not be called fit to hold any class medical certificate."*

Dr. Davis requested that Bob voluntarily submit to neurological, psychological and psychiatric evaluations in accordance with established specifications outlined by the FAA. They also requested authorizations for the release of required medical information, since the federal government has enacted a privacy act that specifically controls how the FAA and other bureaucratic agencies could utilize, consider, and disclose personal information from any citizen. The letter further noted that *"any expense involved in obtaining such medical information is the responsibility of the airman and not the FAA."*

The letter also ominously intoned that if no reply was received from Mr. Hoover within 30 days of the date of the letter, they would have no alternative but to nullify his medical certificate in accordance with FAR section 67.31. A copy of the letter was sent to Dr. Albert Puskas, Bob's longtime personal physician, and a copy was faxed to him the day the letter was issued, since by then the FAA had disclosed that there could be a problem, according to the information they were using. Enclosed with a report was FAA AC form 8500-11-1, which specified the standards for neurologic evaluation... including all records covering prior hospitalizations and/or other periods of observation or treatment as well as a report by a qualified neurologist. The FAA qualified a neurologist as one who had been certified by the American Board of Psychiatry and Neurology or by the American Board of Neurological Surgery, or an equivalent background for such board certification.

The FAA insisted that a neurologist's report must supply a detailed report of the recent neurological examination, as well as pertinent x-rays, electroencephalograms with activating procedures (procedures used to detect latent abnormalities), or other tests and laboratory procedures as may be indicated. An additional form, FAA form 8500-26, specified the FAA's needs for psychiatric and psychological evaluation. Again, this specification also demanded previous records, specifically psychiatric, of any hospitalization or periods of observation or treatment. It also requested a report by a qualified psychiatrist, defined as one who had been certified by the American Board of Psychiatry and Neurology or an equivalent background for such board certification.

Via a consultation with Federal Air Surgeon Dr. Jordan, the FAA specifically directed Bob to a physician of their choosing. In the interim, Bob consulted with T. Allan McArtor, who not only had been the Administrator of the FAA previously, but had performed as a member of the United States Air Force Thunderbird Aerobatic team. In other words, this was a man with intimate knowledge of both the FAA and the demands of airshow flying. Bob's letter to McArtor was written September 22, and the FAA responded to McArtor's subsequent investigation on October 13, 1992. The letter came from former Air Force General Thomas C. Richards, then the Administrator of the FAA.

Richard stated that the Acting Deputy Federal Air Surgeon, Dr. William Hark, advised him that the request for an evaluation was made after observations of Mr. Hoover's aerial performances, personal appearance, and behavior by two agency Inspectors from the OKC FSDO office. General Richards said that *"these Inspectors expressed concern about Mr. Hoover's mental and physical fitness and for his continued safety. I have read the reports and am satisfied that there was justification for the medical evaluation."*

General Richards never indicated that they had gone to any lengths to investigate the rationale and evidence for the statements provided by the Inspectors, giving those who have read this letter the impression that the statements of Kelln and Boehler went unchallenged and verified. Richards noted that *"Dr. Audie Davis, manager of the AeroMedical certification division, has discussed the case with Mr. Hoover; Dr. Albert Puskas, an aviation medical examiner (AME) familiar with Mr. Hoover; and with Dr. Garrett O'Connor, a Psychiatrist/AME, who evaluated Mr. Hoover on Sept. 28. I understand that Dr. Puskas was supportive of Mr. Hoover but did not consider the evaluation inappropriate."* Mind you, Bob swears, to this day, that he never spoke to or met Dr. Davis.

Refusing to step back from the course that FAA had chartered for Hoover, and ignoring Hoover's continued insistence that the Inspectors who targeted him had never properly investigated the situation before making their accusations, General Richards closed the door on any compromise, saying that *"any further action by the agency will wait (until we have) received an evaluation of Dr. O'Connor's report to Dr. Davis. Dr. Hark assures me that the medical determination will consider flight safety and Mr. Hoover's personal welfare."*

The dye was cast and one of the last remaining opportunities for the FAA to admit that their investigation, and its source, were suspect were swept away by bureaucratic indifference. Bob Hoover, in the interim, had met with Dr. O'Connor. The eight-

page report was submitted to Dr. Davis shortly before Christmas of 1992 and was an illuminating document. The report summed up his examination, the FAA's request for medical information from Hoover, the statements of Kelln and Boehler, another report conducted on October 30th by Dr. Robert Elliott (which included a new testing protocol by the name of "CogScreen", a neurological evaluation done by Dr. Michael Gold on the November 5, 1992), an MRI done the next day, along with the report from November 6, and a SPECT scan from the fourth, as well as an "SMA 24" biochemical profile. Dr. O'Connor also noted discussions with Dr. Puskas (who had been Hoover's Aviation Medical Examiner for two decades) and Jimmy Driskell, Bob's announcer. Additional conversations were had with the FAA's Frank Allen of the OKC FSDO, and Colleen Hoover, Bob's wife of over 44 years. O'Connor saw Hoover for the first time on the 28th of September and did a standard psychiatric interview over the course of two and a half hours.

He stated that *"with the exception of the few relatively minor abnormalities on mental status examination, my valuation of Mr. Hoover was essentially within normal limits from a psychiatric point of view. The abnormalities noted were short term memory deficits, and an impairment of Mr. Hoover's ability to complete backward digit span tests accurately,"* (i.e., counting backwards by a fixed value). Though the abnormalities were termed as "minor" by O'Connor and apparently aware of the scrutiny that his reports were to be given by the FAA, O'Connor referred Hoover to Dr. Robert Elliott for a *"comprehensive psychological evaluation to determine the possible presence of cognitive and/ or neurological abnormalities that might lie outside the range of normal performance in a 70 year old man."*

Originally, before additional information was presented, O'Connor was quoted as stating that Hoover had passed the exam and was "clean." This statement was given to Mr. Hoover and to Dr. Puskas. However, he elicited Hoover's agreement to see Dr. Elliott, by reportedly telling him that he wanted to make sure that he (Hoover) was "squeaky clean." This manner of request differs somewhat from that submitted in December by Dr. O'Connor. O'Connor felt that Elliott's subsequent findings confirmed the deficits noted in the previous evaluation and subsequently referred Hoover yet again to a Dr. Michael Gold for neurological evaluation. O'Connor summarized Gold's findings as revealing *"no abnormalities and Electroencephalographic examination and Magnetic Resonance Imaging (MRI) were within normal limits."*

He did find some abnormalities in a high-tech SPECT brain scan, claiming some abnormalities in the superior parietal areas of the cerebral cortex... later admitting that *"their actual significance is questionable but it is nevertheless interesting."*

Dr. Gold later informed Hoover and Dr. Puskas that there was absolutely nothing wrong with Hoover; he could not find anything suspicious. The report looked into Hoover's background as a pilot and his many achievements, his personal life (including the state of his marriage and personal lives of his children) and some of his previous medical history. The report singled out Bob's use of alcohol in a two-paragraph summary under the heading of *"alcohol history,"* commenting that *"Mr. Hoover has been a drinker all his life, participating as he did in corporate customer relations activities for much of the time. He has been drunk on a number of occasions but denies blackouts and has never been arrested for drunk driving or other conduct associated with alcohol."*

The report also quoted O'Connor's consultation with Mrs. Hoover, who confirmed her husband's statements about his drinking and noted that it had never been a negative factor in their lives, though like other members of his profession that he used to "drink it up" from time to time when he was younger. O'Connor's "Mental Status Examination" made early mention of Bob Hoover's prominent proboscis. For many years, Bob has had a fairly good size nose that is mighty red and noticeable. Some people in the FAA had pointed that as a sign of alcoholism, when in fact the problem is more properly known as acne rosacea, which, as I understand it, is actually a pretty aggressive form of acne, and not an acknowledged indicator of alcoholism.

Rumors of alcoholism had followed Bob, according to various FAA officials... and no one else. Of course, Bob came to prominence in the aviation world through his involvement in the military, often stationed at remote bases and outposts that offered few diversions outside of spending some time with his peers at the officers club. Further, Bob is a product of the World War II generation, a time when the military's pilots were a hard drinking, hard-partying lot who lived extreme lives of aggressive risk, which often gave rise to the need to blow off steam on a regular basis. Surprisingly though, despite after having been at dozens of parties and social events at which alcohol was served and Bob was in attendance, I have personally never seen him drunk, nor has anyone with whom I am associated. So... where the rumors of alcoholism come from, outside of the aforementioned reasons, I have no idea. O'Connor described Hoover as a "tall, stringy, thin individual of 70 years with bright sparkling eyes, a red face and a pronounced purpling rhinofoma." O'Connor also noted that Hoover reported that his father had the same affliction even though he was a tea totaler.

Other details included notes on Hoover's temperament — the absence of depression and a lack of other disorders. Bob was described as entirely compliant with evaluation procedures, and seemed candid and willing to share personal information. It was here that O'Connor noted that Hoover was unable to remember one word out of three after a delay of ten minutes and that he was inconsistent in his ability to perform backward digit span tasks, i.e. counting backwards by a specific amount. Bob was able to achieve the initial three digits correctly in four, five, and six number sequences, but in every case either transposed or mis-identified the remaining digits. This was the finding that O'Connor used to justify his quest for neuropsychological evaluation. Dr. O'Connor reported that Hoover has *"a very positive outlook on life, and regards 'every day as a good day.'"*

A biochemical evaluation showed a few abnormalities outside of the mild anemia and other findings that seemed to be related to his surgery for prostate cancer earlier. The Doctor's synopsis of Elliott's neuropsychological evaluation noted that the tests had taken eight hours (remember that one, folks; we'll get back to it shortly) and there was some verbiage from Elliott claiming that Hoover performed *"within the mildly to moderately impaired range in his attention, working memory, verbal-sequential processing, mental arithmetic, visual spatial orientation and his ability to systematically apply rules to a given problem situation."*

The report also details that Hoover's intellectual functions were intact and overall memory skills were within normal limits when corrected for deviations associated with his age. Hoover apparently scored poorly on something called the Booklet Category Test and the Wisconsin Card Sorting Test, but the greatest concern were shown over an experimental test from the FAA called CogScreen.

O'Connor's summary stated that the CogScreen battery was administered to Hoover at the end of the four hour session at which time Hoover was fatigued and apparently frustrated because he had not anticipated that the overall time for the evaluation would exceed four hours (and in fact, Bob was told the entire testing series would take far less time than that, but as I said, we'll get to that shortly). O'Connor concluded that despite those considerations, he had no doubt that Hoover had performed in a mildly to moderately impaired fashion in a significant number of the test sub-selections.

O'Connor devoted a considerable amount of his report to "Mr. Hoover's Point of View." This part of the report accurately described Hoover's feelings about Kelln and Boehler's report and his explanations for what occurred. It accurately quotes Jimmy Driskell and then detailed his conversation with the FAA's Frank Allen who had observed Mr. Hoover AGAIN at yet another airshow he flew in Oklahoma City in late September.

O'Connor described Allen as a *"qualified pilot observer who had seen Mr. Hoover perform many times over the years."* O'Connor reported that Allen said he could not detect any deficiencies in Mr. Hoover's performance and further noted his conversations with Dr. Albert "Bert" Puskas (and the fact that Puskas had flown with Hoover during an Aerobatic flight a year previously). Dr. Puskas reported an unerring performance by Bob including the astute observation that the aircraft never exceeded 2.2 G's, positive or negative, even in the most complicated centrifugal or centripetal maneuvers. O'Connor concluded this portion of the report noting the fact that Hoover had had a number of incidents with the FAA previously (don't worry, folks, we will get into those, as well). O'Connor described Hoover's past "indiscretions" as having continued a flight following a prop strike at an airshow, unauthorized deadstick landings with passengers on board his aircraft, and of an unauthorized Aerobatic flight with a passenger on board... who just *happened* to be the Administrator of the FAA (and who was not wearing a parachute nor waivered for that performance). Dr. O'Connor's conclusions spanned a little bit over a page. He stated that thorough neuropsychiatric evaluation revealed no psychiatric diagnosis. He stated that comprehensive neuropsychological testing indicated mild to moderate impairment of certain neuropsychological functions which was confirmed on the "Technetium HMPAO (Ceretec) SPECT scan."

O'Connor stated that these so-called abnormalities would not explain the statements made by Kelln and Boehler's reports on his flights at Aerospace America '92, and noted that Bob had flown flawlessly *"on more than 10 occasions"* since that time, one of which was observed by the FAA's Frank Allen, who called the performance *"competent."* Pointing to Dr. Elliott's abnormal findings on neuropsychological testing, O'Connor recalled Elliott's statement that *"these results do not provide specific information about how well a person is likely to perform in different flight situations."* Continuing on the subject, O'Connor concluded that since Hoover has been flying for more than 30 years that we *"required neurological pathways are probably well trained"* and that his judgment appeared to be intact even though some deficit may exist in his ability to process and act upon novel information under certain circumstances.

Referring to the reports that started this matter, O'Connor felt that "something" about Mr. Hoover's behavior in the air and on the ground caught the attention of two *"experienced FAA's Inspectors who acted properly and responsibly by filing detailed reports prefer which reflected their concerns, and which led to this evaluation."*

Dr. O'Connor made no reference to whether or not any of the information that was becoming available at the time — which contradicted the Inspectors' statements — was considered by him. He did note that Hoover had reasonable explanations for most of the observations made by the Inspectors and only one discrepancy about one particular deadstick landing and whether Bob repeated the maneuver (which both Hoover, Driskell and others vehemently deny, and Allen alleges) caught his attention. He further ventured that Hoover's "frail appearance and apparent confusion," which to this date has not been noted by a single other soul attending the event outside of those associated with the FAA (and with which others in the FAA vehemently disagree...), could have been due to fatigue or hot weather. O'Connor discussed the possibility that Hoover, like many individuals advancing in age, maybe in denial of the aging process and would tend to minimize their infirmaries or even misrepresented them because they're unwilling to accept the reality of their declining skills and confidence. Additionally, while he thought that this condition could be present to some degree, he felt Mr. Hoover's previous responses to prior challenges from colon and prostatic cancer indicated that he was capable of dealing with unpleasant medical realities from a mature standpoint and with a minimum of denial.

O'Connor reported that Hoover repeatedly assured him that he would accept the consequences of whatever findings might emerge in the course of this very complete clinical evaluation. O'Connor finished the report by stating *"it is my opinion that Mr. Robert Hoover is currently fit to hold a second-class medical certificate from a neuropsychological and neuropsychiatric point of view and should therefore be permitted to continue his flight activities."*

He also recommended that Hoover's low blood count continue to be monitored by Dr. Puskas and that a repeat SPECT scan be performed in six months to a year to determine if any changes took place. He hypothesized that the most likely explanation for the abnormal findings was some form of nonspecific aging pathology and that *"whether or not this would prove to be progressive and therefore of clinical significance in the future remains to be seen."*

So, O'Connor, while obviously taking much of the FAA's statements at face value, still concluded that Mr. Hoover was qualified to hold a medical certificate — even after a mildly damning examination by Dr. Elliott that included a lengthy, virtually nonstop, eight-plus hour examination, using non-certified, experimental testing (without disclosing same to Mr. Hoover) and leaving him with the impression that he was in for a far shorter ordeal then he was eventually subjected to.

It is the Elliott examination that created a fair amount of controversy later on as the true nature of this procedure was made known, and numerous medical professionals not only thought that the procedure was flawed but aspects of its were highly questionable from a professional and ethical standpoint.

There were some other questionable aspects about all this. Each of the doctors... O'Connor, Elliott, Gold, and Salcedo (who interpreted the SPECT scan results) were selected by the FAA. Hoover had no hand in their appointment. Further, he was the guy who had to foot the bill at an exorbitant cost.

Back to the Elliott examination... Mr. Hoover presented himself to Dr. Bob Elliott on October 30, 1992. Dr. Elliott conducted the psychological evaluation at the behest of Dr. O'Connor, and was a regular consultant to the FAA, deriving a fair portion of his income from FAA referrals. Elliott has been a personal acquaintance of the FAA's chief neuropsychiatric official, Dr. Barton Pakull, for over 16 years. It was later revealed that approximately one-third of Elliott's income is generated by work that he does for the FAA. Elliott also noted at a later date that while testing Hoover, he was attempting to assess

whether there was evidence of neuropathology; never assessed Hoover's ability to perform as a pilot.

Dr. Elliott administered twelve tests. The tests administered included the Wechsler Adult Intelligence Scale - Revised (WAIS-R); the Trail Making Test (Parts A and B); the Booklet Category Test; the Rey Osterrieth Complex Figure Test; the Rey Auditory-Verbal Learning Test; the Wisconsin Card Sorting Test; the Boston Naming Test; the Wechsler Memory Scale - Revised; the Controlled Oral Word Association Test; the Manual Finger Tapping Test; and the FAA Computerized Cognitive Screening Battery (CogScreen).

The use of CogScreen was somewhat problematic. The brainchild of yet another FAA doctor, this un-certified psychological test was seeking industry acceptance and was still judged to be experimental. Dr. Gary Kay, an FAA staff member, was its author and stood to reap significant prestige and possible royalties if the yet-uncertified testing protocol was validated, certified, and used extensively throughout the industry.

Senior members of the FAA medical hierarchy were known to be pushing this protocol as a means by which they could determine and predict the cognitive potential of pilots. According to Elliott's report and the later testimony he provided at an NTSB hearing, Hoover's performance varied. His verbal and perceptual organization skills were intact, but his problems arose in speed, executive functions, using trial and error learning, problem solving and sequencing. Elliott later testified that the results of his standard battery of neuropsychological testing reflected an individual who has difficulty in reasoning processes and thinking through situations, particularly situations that are novel.

But there were some big problems with the tests that he administered. One test, the Wisconsin Card Sorting Test, evaluates a person's ability to use logic and reasoning to figure out how to sort categories. It tests the "executive function" (which is the ability to solve novel problems in an efficient manner). The sixth test Elliott administered to Hoover, Elliott explained that one of the hallmark characteristics of cognitive impairment is the loss of flexibility in the reasoning process; meaning that even though a person is getting feedback that a response is incorrect, they continue to use the same incorrect response continuously.

Elliott was of the opinion that flexibility in terms of reasoning process is probably one of the more critical features in terms of piloting... even though Elliott is not a pilot. Dr. Elliott concluded that Hoover's performance on the Card Sorting Test was "significantly impaired." Elliott testified that figuring out solutions to a novel problem is the piloting skill that correlates to the task of the Wisconsin Card Sorting Test. Elliott also testified that given a novel situation that Hoover has not yet encountered, the impairment would effect his performance. Obviously, Dr. Elliott put a lot of stock in this particular test when he completed his findings on his examination of Mr. Hoover. But there was a big problem here. Elliott administered a non-certified test, and later misled others about its status. He stated several times under later questioning that he did *not* administer a research version of the test, but was using the current "certified" version. When another medical professional researched this fact, it was discovered that this was not true.

This was not the only time that Dr. Elliott misled people. At one point in the examination, Dr. Elliott admitted that he told Bob that nothing that occurred in that testing would be used to determine his fitness to fly, reportedly stating *"...Now, there is nothing that I am going to give you today that is going to have anything to do with your losing your license, so don't worry about that."*

Prior to the test, Elliott stated to Hoover that the examination would probably take about four hours, and thinking this, Bob arrived for the examination with plans for later that day. When it became obvious that the testing would proceed past that point, Bob told Colleen to cancel their appointments. Testing began at 8:00 a.m., and after requesting a break, Hoover received one at mid-day, during which he used the restroom and had a drink of water. Hoover recalled that *"I asked him how much longer (we had to go) and he said, 'We are only halfway through'. So I called my wife to cancel all of our plans, then I went to the bathroom, got a drink of water, and came back... I didn't have another break, I did not have lunch, I didn't have a drink of water or a trip to the bathroom until 5:00."*

What was supposed to be a morning event turned into a day-long marathon, which became fatiguing, frustrating and more than a mite annoying to a man who had been misled by someone who obviously had a considerable portion of his fate in his hands. It certainly did not seem to be an optimal (or fair) testing environment.

Hoover left the examination with some trepidation, knowing he had been misled somewhat but unaware that Dr. Elliott's conduct would later be found to be misleading (repeatedly) to a number of parties, and a potential violation of ethical canons imposed on his profession by his peers. According to famed defense attorney F. Lee Bailey, *"Such unprofessional conduct is a gross violation of the Canons of Ethics which govern the profession of psychology, and actionable under California Law."*

Worse, Elliott later testified that senior persons within the FAA (Dr. Pakull, with the help of a Dr. Richard Gaines), upon hearing his initial report, responded that they might have to get something a little *"tougher"* from him in the future. Whether or not he might have yielded to the temptation is unknown, but the FAA has a network of consultants throughout the country who earn a fair share of their income from FAA referrals. Many of those consultants are selected based on the personal and professional relationships various FAA staffers build up with others in the medical community. Informed sources state that it is a common practice for senior FAA staffers to select friends and even business associates for these financially attractive considerations.

Elliott, as noted, was known to be a friend of Dr. Barton Pakull. As FAA's chief neuropsychiatric official, Pakull was known to be something of a heavyweight and a maverick in the FAA hierarchy, who expected strong cooperation from his consultants. As a rule, consultants who didn't "play ball" with the FAA found themselves losing their "business" in very short order. Dr. Elliott's role in the initial Hoover examination process was not a bright shining moment in the FAA's conduct of this matter.

Still, when all was said and done, Bob did get a clean bill of health. Yes, it was a modestly qualified clean bill of health with what were adjudged to be some minor abnormalities and potential concerns. Regardless, O'Connor's statement of support for Mr. Hoover's being able to resume second-class medical privileges was quite clear–knowing full well that Bob wanted to use those privileges to go out and fly airshows. With that said and done, Hoover justifiably thought the matter was over and for several weeks it certainly appeared to be. However, for some reason or another, the conclusions of the FAA's own doctors, (i.e., those appointed by the FAA), paid for by Hoover, was not enough for senior FAA management.

It seems that they had other plans for Mr. Hoover's future.

...And those plans did not include allowing him to fly again.

Chapter 12

The Noose Tightens

For the truly faithful, no miracle is necessary...
For those who doubt, no miracle is sufficient.
Nancy Gibbs

The year of 1992 went out like a lamb. As reports were filed, discussed, and traded, Robert Anderson Hoover truly thought that the worst of the battle was behind him. After all, even though he had footed the bill, all the doctors he talked to were doctors of the FAA's choosing, and had pretty much cleared him to fly. Everything should have been cool and Bob should have been flying unrestricted in short order... until the FAA's chief psychiatrist, Dr. Barton Pakull, weighed in on the matter.

Pakull, something of an unusual character in the fairly conservative and staid world of the FAA medical bureaucracy, literally overruled his own handpicked experts. As winter turned into spring, the situation reached a point where all parties finally decided they had to talk.

On January 8, 1993, Dr. Richard Gaines, Ph.D., one of FAA's hired guns, reviewed the data on Hoover, including the CogScreen results, in which he stated that the CogScreen protocols were an experimental device and should not be used in making decisions concerning certification issues; he felt, however, that there was clear impairment present.

On March 22, 1993, Pakull reviewed the data that had been provided him and concluded that Hoover had some kind of cognitive deficit partially related to his age.

Come April 14 of 1993, a conference call was arranged between Bob Hoover and his personal aviation medical examiner, Dr. Albert " Bert" Puskas; and a triad from the FAA consisting of Federal Air Surgeon Dr. Jon Jordan, his deputy Dr. William Hark, and the increasingly intransigent Dr. Barton Pakull.

It was not a pleasant call. Pakull reportedly said that he did not believe that Hoover was fit to fly, directly contradicting Dr. O'Connor. Saying that it was he who made decisions in Washington, he dismissed the conclusions of his own experts, calling them simply "tools," and reiterated his stance on Hoover's unsuitability to hold an airman's medical certificate. Thereafter, Pakull pronounced Hoover "grounded."

Hoover was stunned. So was Puskas. Bob couldn't help but think *"these were their own experts... I didn't pick them, they did... how could they possibly ignore their own people's recommendations. I couldn't believe it."*

Hoover was not willing to give up. He argued passionately that he had cooper-

ated in every way possible and had complied with FAA's every request for every test. Further, by this time Bob had performed nearly three dozen times, without incident, and without question. Even one of the Oklahoma City Inspectors who had peripheral involvement in his grounding could not fault one of his latter performances.

With all this thrown in the FAA's face, a compromise was reached. If Hoover would voluntarily surrender his medical certificate and subject himself to further testing (which, of course, he would have to conduct at his own expense, naturally), the FAA would not legally revoke it while the new testing was underway. Mind you, this was a very unusual step for the FAA to take, and Hoover was under no legal compulsion to do so... although it was strongly implied that if he did not, the FAA could then revoke it. Hoover agreed, reluctantly, (knowing full well that this was about as good a deal as he was going to make at this point), and surrendered his certificate to the care of Dr. Puskas.

This was a costly compromise on Hoover's part. Knowing that it'd taken many months to get to this point, and surmising that it would take many months more, Bob was forced to cancel the remainder of his 1993 scheduled airshow appearances, not knowing if or when he would be able to fly and not willing to leave his airshow clients waiting and wondering.

In so doing, Bob gave up the better part of a million dollars in endorsements, sponsorship contracts, and performer fees that he would have earned over the year, for a season that had just barely gotten underway. It was a horrendous financial blow to Hoover's livelihood, and to yearly shows that counted on the additional "gate" that such a famous pilot would draw to their shows because of his attendance.

"It was devastating... not only because my not flying would hurt my finances so much, but for all the people I had to call and disappoint by telling them that I had to cancel my flying for them. I hate to let people down, and I kinda feel like I did," remarked Hoover.

The next stop came nearly two months later, as Hoover was sent to the UCLA Neuropsychiatric Institute. Four doctors consulted on the report submitted to the FAA based on the June 4, 1993 evaluation... Dr. Craig Lyons Uchiyama, Ph.D., was a licensed psychologist and neuropsychology fellow at the UCLA Neuropsychiatric Institute and Hospital, UCLA Center for the Health Sciences; Dr. Paul Satz, Ph.D., was a professor and their chief of neuropsychology. Dr. Rebecca Rausch, Ph.D. was the director for their Neuropsychology Assessment Laboratory. Dr. Gary Tischler was an M.D., and co-director of their Neuropsychology Assessment Laboratory. Their seventeen-page report, surprisingly, supported Hoover's case.

The report trod much familiar ground discussing the reason for the referral, the history of the complaint that had brought him to their offices, and the previous testing conducted by the FAA's experts. This report did note that they examined statements from Leo Loudenslager, Jimmy Driskell, Steve Oliver, Sean Tucker, Delmar Benjamin, and Dixie Walker. They also considered Hoover's own explanation of what occurred in the Aerospace America performances.

A page and a half was devoted to medical and psychosocial histories, including Bob's personal medical history and that of his parents. They reported that Hoover showed up for the tests "immaculately dressed and well groomed" and they noted that Bob remained "cooperative and motivated" throughout the course of testing so that their results would appear to be an adequate reflection of his neuropsychological functioning.

Bob got clobbered with a huge battery of tests, some nineteen in all. And despite what was apparently a more pleasant atmosphere than he endured under Dr. Elliott, Bob reported that it was *"a long process... tiring."*

The UCLA NPI & H report had a problem equating the statements of Kelln and Boehler with all the others that contradicted them and noted *"the question remains as to what the two Inspectors observed that date that made them submit their reports and two, why their reports appear to be in such conflict with other observers of the same situation."*

Still, they did note a series of minor deficits that occurred in a number of tests and examinations but concluded that the deficits currently exhibited by Hoover appeared to be above the threshold required for normal flight and that *"he is able to successfully compensate for such weaknesses."*

The report continued, saying that there appeared to be *"only questionable criterion-based support for questioning Mr. Hoover's flight skills, it is recommended that temporary extension be made on his certification until such time as more clearly documented support of an inability to safely operate an aircraft be demonstrated."*

They summarized that *"Mr. Hoover showed remarkable preservation of many cognitive, social, and judgmental abilities for a man of his station and age. He displayed a consummate knowledge of his profession and managed to address a number of issues relevant to the case as well as to the history of aviation with conversational skill and focus. No tangential thinking or memory lapses were evident. He also impressed these examiners as an individual who pursued his profession with relentless discipline and rigorous attention to health and safety issues. Also, his flight performance since the FAA incident in Oklahoma has apparently been flawless in 27 subsequent shows. This latter issue speaks to the issue of criterion validity, which in behavioral science and medicine, represents a more accepted framework to predict future performance. The reason for this is because it uses test variables more similar to the criterion or outcome variables."*

Adding a bit of counterbalance to the fairly positive tone of the summary, Doctors Uchiyama, Satz, Rausch, and Tischler said that *"in the present case, Mr. Hoover revealed some selected risk signs on neuropsychological performance that could be viewed as signs of accelerated aging or sub clinical (sub threshold) disease. His recent SPECT also revealed some perfusion changes that could be viewed in the same light. Although his other basic cognitive abilities were shown to be well intact, these sub clinical changes should not be ignored nor should they be over-interpreted at this time. Frankly, if they occurred in an individual in another profession, e.g., psychiatry or neuropsychology, they would probably have less significance at this age because of fewer demands on speeded information processing in clinical practice; however, although tasks measuring speed in information-processing declined steadily with age, one might also expect someone of Mr. Hoover's profession to show a slower gradient with age. However, this is not the case.*

On the other hand, one must note that the weight of the evidence favors a criterion validity vs. predictive validity approach. He continues to supply a consummate performance record in his flying. This fact must not be ignored."

The final paragraph seemed to offer a small caveat to the FAA by recommending *"therefore, on this basis, we favor recommendation to reinstate his licensed on the temporary three to six month period, during which his current medical and neuropsycho-*

logical status is closely monitored for potential change. Although such change is un-likely, we are confident that Mr. Hoover would appreciate the importance and signifi-cance of this recommendation for all parties concerned. He is, after all, a remarkable and unique individual who still has so much to give as a human being."

In psychological terms, even after consideration of a number of qualifiers im-plicit in the report, the final report issued by this highly-respected organization was tan-tamount to a rave review. Virtually everyone reading it (outside the FAA) seemed to be-lieve that the previous series of tests conducted by doctors O'Connor, Elliott, Gold, et al, as well as the current report from UCLA's neuropsychology assessment laboratory was pretty much a "slam dunk" for Hoover.

Yup... one would think that, unless one worked for the FAA!

In July and August 1993 the FAA en listed more of their favorite hired guns... Dr. Richard Gaines Ph.D., Dr. Gary Kay Ph.D. (the author of the CogScreen protocol), Dr. Jonathan Pincus M.D., and Dr. John Hastings. Reviewing the UCLA report over the course of two months, these doctors opined that there was demonstrated evidence of brain dysfunction.

Yes, you guessed it... this report wasn't good enough either, and Pakull's consult-ants decided to overrule UCLA. These medical experts were all reportedly "company men," part of the FAA's inner circle of staff and consultants who earned some serious money every time they were tasked with such oversight. Together, they did the unthinkable and blew away the findings of four other doctors, whom their superiors had actually selected! Mind you, these men reviewed the reports on Hoover, without actually examining him themselves. It was at this point that the "odor of Rodentia" made itself, strongly, known to Hoover. *"I expected them to take a hard-line...,"* Hoover says, *"but I didn't expect them to declare war on me."* With a growing sentiment among Hoover's advisers that he was not getting a fair shake, outside experts not selected by the FAA, and found among Hoover's brethren in the aviation community, were brought into the picture.

Even though Bob saw some serious financial reversals because of this, he had riches of another sort to rely on. Bob's reputation as a gentleman and a very friendly personality was known by the thousands of people through the years who had met him. Some of the lucky ones got to call him friend. Those people mobilized themselves and rallied to his side without being asked.

Two of those friends turned out to be pivotal as Bob learned to play the FAA's game. One of them was famed defense lawyer F. Lee Bailey, whose involvement in the infamous Sam Shepard case as well as his defense of Patty Hearst and Ernest Medina earned him a reputation as a shrewd practitioner of the legal part. Beyond that, though, Bailey was an avid aviator, a Marine Corps veteran, and a very dear friend of Bob Hoover. More than that, Bailey was a scrapper... one of those uncommon people who wade into an unfair situation and try to make it right. Having given advice and counsel as Bob's di-lemma with the FAA grew into a full-fledged confrontation, Bailey started to take an active role in helping Bob seek medical certification.

Equally important to the story was another lawyer, one who had not made quite as big splash on the national public radar scope, but nonetheless was one of the most highly-respected aviation litigators in the world. John Yodice, chief counsel to the Air-craft Owners and Pilots Association (AOPA), aviation writer, and pilot, soon waded into the fight by sending out signals to his many contacts that Bob's effort at medical certifica-

tion needed reinforcements... strong reinforcements.

One of the first of Bob's brothers in arms to take a prominent role in the fight with the FAA was Dr. Brent Hisey. A neurosurgeon from Oklahoma City, Dr. Hisey's stepping forward was an uncommonly fortuitous act. Not only was Dr. Hisey a pilot, he was an unlimited air racer, owning and flying a P-51 Mustang. But that's not all — he also served as a Flight Surgeon for the 465th F-16 fighter squadron from Tinker Air Force Base in Oklahoma.

Hisey's life is totally wrapped up in aviation... even to the point of making the incredible investment of purchasing one of the best-known P-51 Mustangs in the world, "Miss America," an aircraft that is literally famous the world over as an air racing icon. *"I grew up watching all the war movies, and seeing the Mustang in action. But when I first saw the Reno Air Races on Wide World of Sports, I realized that these were real Mustangs in real action, and that some of them were still flying."*

He always had the dream to fly, but less-than-perfect eyesight prevented him from joining the Air Force and joining his heroes. Hisey was initially disappointed at the turn-down by the Air Force, and refused any assignment other than flight school. Instead, with his mother's encouragement, the Ardmore, OK, native went to medical school and eventually became a neurosurgeon. After completing the obligatory internship and residency, he looked forward to a successful life as a physician. *"Then one day I watched Top Gun... I was enormously depressed for a week."*

Hisey turned that depression into resolve with his application to the Air National Guard, where he earned a position as a Flight Surgeon, one of the benefits of which was an exciting 100 hours in the supersonic F-16. Earning his private pilots license and later adding an instrument rating, Hisey worked his way up the general aviation ladder, to the point where he had earned sufficient skill and experience to be able to contemplate owning and flying one of the most awesome fighters from World War II... the P-51 Mustang. And he did it, not only purchasing and learning to fly the Mustang, but earning a place among an extremely elite group of aviators — Unlimited Air Racing Pilots. So... Hisey has raced around the pylons at Reno pushing 500 mph, at times just scant feet from the ground: the kind of piloting that requires skill, speed, coordination, and unerring judgment — making Hisey one of the few people in North America who could professionally and medically judge Robert Anderson Hoover.

Hisey met Bob Hoover in September 1993 at the Reno Air Races, an event at which Hoover not only flew but was instrumental in saving the lives of several pilots. After watching him fly several times and upon hearing his explanation of the developing situation, Hisey agreed to review his medical records, which were provided to him by John Yodice.

Hisey understood what should have been FAA's normal concern for aviation safety; however, upon reviewing the records, he felt the data had been misinterpreted. Based upon his observation of Hoover and Hoover's flying performance, he did not understand how Hoover presented a hazard to flight safety. Communicating this to Bob Hoover, he recommended that Bob make himself available for additional series of physical, neurologic and neuropsychological examinations that he and fellow pilot, Dr. David Johnsen (who would evaluate him from a neuropsychological standpoint), would conduct. Johnson and Hisey gave Hoover the works: a complete physical examination, a Neuroopthamologic examination, a neurological examination, a lab work-up and an EKG.

Hisey summarized these examinations and noted the previous brain scans from the previous tests administered by FAA. While FAA's testing indicated some minor causes for concern, Hisey believed that *"these changes were secondary to multiple cerebral vascular accidents or degenerative changes; however, the MRI scan and EEG studies have demonstrated no evidence of either."* In other words, Hisey was not alarmed by the results of the previous SPECT scans, because other testing protocols did not corroborate the conclusions FAA's experts derived from them.

Hisey concluded his report by stating that *"Mr. Hoover has undergone neuropsychiatric retesting in the areas of previously noted deficits. These were retests (done) by Dr. David Johnson, and his testing is within normal ranges for his age group."* Hisey added that Hoover's physical neurological examinations were "normal" and that *"Mr. Hoover is a 71 year old Aviator who on physical, neurologic and laboratory evaluations shows no evidence of the physical or neurologic problem that would interfere with his flying ability or be a threat to flight safety."*

On the last page of Hisey's summary of the situation, he *"found it very unusual that the Inspectors in Oklahoma City did not personally speak with Mr. Hoover or express their concerns to those in charge of the Aerospace America airshow and did not communicate their concerns in writing until August of 1992."*

Another fascinating remark made by Hisey was that *"it appears to me that the physicians who have recommended that Mr. Hoover not be allowed to fly had neither seen nor examined him but have only reviewed the records provided to them. The physicians who have examined him have either deferred to other physicians or have recommended that he'd be allowed to continue flying."*

Looking at the brain scans done by the FAA, Hisey qualified that *"the radiologic studies, specifically the MRI scan, have demonstrated no evidence of structural pathology. The SPECT scans which have to perform have demonstrated only changes and regional blood flow. These studies do not represent cerebral metabolism or cerebral functioning and therefore provide little insight into any pathologic response especially in light of no evidence of vascular changes on either the MRI scan were EEG study."*

Taking aim at the heart of the matter, Dr. Hisey said *"it appears that the major concern for flight safety is whether Mr. Hoover is capable of handling a novel or emergent situation. Unlike most pilots, Mr. Hoover's routine involves the demonstration and safe recovery from emergency procedures such as loss of one or both engines, loss of hydraulic power, unusual flying attitudes, etc... I suppose that there may perhaps be some novel condition and aircraft that he has not experienced and reacted to appropriately; however, after reviewing his flight experience, I am at a loss to think of one. If one is attempting to predict a patient's future response to a situation, the best indicator is how he has performed in past and similar events and in Mr. Hoover's case, this clearly demonstrates that he is capable of handling emerging novel situations in the cockpit.*

The examination of Mr. Hoover by myself and Dr. David Johnson showed no evidence of significant physical, neurologic or cognitive dysfunction that would impair his ability to operate an aircraft in any situation."

Hisey and Johnsen formalized their opinion conclusively with one final line: *"Mr. Hoover is fit to hold his Class Two medical certificate and continue his flying career."*

Once again, Hoover got a clean bill of health, and frankly, one of the most posi-

tive and least evasive reports on the matter thus far. Remember that Hisey was not one of FAA's paid stooges... and while he obviously had a great deal of admiration and respect for the man, numerous written communications prior to and during this examination process showed Hisey's willingness to act against Hoover if he found reason to do so. Hisey is one of the few men in the country who could "walk the walk" with Hoover and had even flown some of the same airplanes that established Hoover as one of the greatest aviators in the world. Of all the aviation/medical experts who could have evaluated Hoover, it is hard to think of someone more qualified this Doctor/Air-Racer/Military Flight Surgeon/ Neurosurgeon/honest man.

At this point, Hoover had been endorsed and encouraged to continue his flight status by no less than three groups of medical and/or aviation experts. Remember this. Three times, three positive results, nearly a dozen doctors. One would naturally conclude that Hoover's problems were over, and while I am sure that you, the reader, must feel like I'm beating a dead horse with this issue through the overt repetition of the situation, not a soul on the outside of the situation — even those with a rapid distrust and/or dislike for the FAA — really felt that the FAA had any choice but to return this aviation icon to flight status and the airshow world that was anxious to have him back in the air.

But... it all went to hell. Hoover and his advisers took this evidence, all these positive reports, and demanded return of his medical certificate, which he had given up voluntarily to the care of Dr. Puskas, who accepted it on behalf of the FAA. Pakull wouldn't have it.

On December 14, 1993, the FAA responded to Hoover's demands with an Emergency Order of Revocation, alleging that Bob did not meet the medical standards in the Federal Aviation Regulations... and set the stage for one of the most derisive battles in general aviation's history.

Chapter 12

Medical Mumbo-Jumbo #1...The "System"

The meaning of things lies not in the things themselves, but in our attitude towards them.
Antoine de Saint Exupery

Every pilot has to qualify for the "privilege" of flight in a number of ways. It is not enough to simply learn to fly and take a test to prove that you can safely act as a pilot. No... the FAA has decided that every pilot must maintain specific medical qualifications... and keep doing so at regular intervals throughout the years that they fly.

The FAA likes to compare the need for a medical certificate with an aircraft's need for an annual or other scheduled/periodic inspections. For all but the most critical flying applications, the need for such inspections appears to be somewhat superfluous. The actual incidents of aircraft accidents or hazards caused by pilot incapacitation are statistically insignificant. And, as a matter of fact, if one looks at other transportation industries, one notes that the drivers and or pilots of other motorized vehicles operate in even tighter parameters than pilots, and they are not required to have any kind of medical certification.

One of my favorite examples of this was given to me by EAA Founder and former President, Paul Poberezny (who is also, incidentally, an accomplished pilot flying well into his 70s). He notes that drivers of school buses, who often face each other from opposite sides of the highway at closure rates exceeding 100 to 130 mph. and are responsible for dozens of lives at a time, require no medical certification or other physical inspection and may pass each other with bare inches between them (depending on what passes for a median/barrier at the time). However, aviation seems to have a reputation for intricacy, and so it seems perfectly reasonable to bureaucrats that even recreational pilots and pilots involved in noncritical commercial applications be scrutinized in this fashion.

The System

Of course, since the FAA has decreed that pilots must be medically qualified to exercise the privileges of their certificates, a whole new level of bureaucracy is required to

set those standards and enforce them. In 1926, the Air Commerce Act mandated all pilots be medically qualified to fly. The qualifying conditions for any class of medical certificate were specified as *"disease and conditions that could cause sudden incapacitation or death, or could otherwise compromise aviation safety."* The standards not only apply to pilots, but air traffic controllers and other aviation professionals.

The focal point for all this activity is the FAA's Office of Aviation Medicine. The "OAM" oversees applicable aspects of Accident Investigation, AeroMedical Certification, AeroMedical Education, Aviation Industry Substance Abuse Prevention Programs, the Aviation Medical Examiner Program, Air Traffic Controller health, Employee Substance Abuse, Occupational Health, and Research. Under the control of the FAA is "CAMI," the FAA's Civil AeroMedical Institute, which serves primarily in a research capacity.

CAMI

The Federal Air Surgeon, Jon L. Jordan, describes the Civil AeroMedical Institute as *"A National Resource. Better known as CAMI, (it) was created 35 years ago in response to a recognized need in the aviation industry for scientific research related to aviation safety factors. From this initial singular thrust, the Institute evolved to include its present structure comprising four major programs: airman medical certification, AeroMedical education, research, and occupational health. Like virtually all of the Federal Aviation Administration's functions, the work accomplished at the Institute addresses the safety concerns of the general public and of the aviation industry."*

CAMI's major aviation safety functions include Airman Medical Certification... and *"protects the public safety by helping to ensure that pilots are medically fit to fly. The Civil AeroMedical Institute administers the national program for the medical certification of airmen who are required to meet medical standards. To keep aviation safe, medical standards are determined and maintained for the nation's pilots. No other governmental entity assures there are ongoing minimum health standards of the nation's 650,000 civil airmen, including 68,000 airline pilots. Without this critical safety function, pilots with significant undetected medical problems could operate civil aircraft, thereby placing themselves, their passengers, and others at risk."*

CAMI also oversees AeroMedical Education, contributing directly to aviation safety through a program that trains all 6265 (worldwide) FAA-designated AMEs. CAMI insures that AMEs maintain detailed knowledge and understanding of the FAA medical certification standards, regulations, policies, and procedures. This includes the necessity of maintaining *"quality standards for AME selection, training, and performance to ensure that only the best AMEs are retained in the program."* CAMI also provides safety training relating to the physiology of flight, global survival, high altitude indoctrination, and cabin safety for pilots, flight attendants, and others, as well as developing/distributing safety information to the civil aviation community.

CAMI has a strong research component that does work that relates to passenger safety and the safe performance of airmen, including general aviation pilots, airline pilots, air traffic controllers, and other aviation safety-related workers. Such research includes efforts in "Human Factors" ...including human performance under various conditions of impairment, human error analysis and remediation, training analysis, impact of

advanced automation systems on operator requirements and performance, the effects of workload, stress, and fatigue of air traffic controllers, the relationships of various indices of airman performance to age, and the development of selection and training methods.

CAMI's AeroMedical Research programs investigate the biomedical, bioengineering, chemical, and clinical aspects of civil aviation safety. Three main areas of research relate to toxicology and accident investigation, aviation physiology, and protection and survival. CAMI is equipped with an amazing array of specialized facilities including a hypobaric test chamber, protective breathing equipment and water survival test laboratories, a dynamic impact test facility, an aircraft evacuation simulator, a spatial disorientation lab, a reconfigurable general aviation simple/complex aircraft flight simulator, double-wall sound booths for auditory/communications research, and computerized radar simulation equipment for assessing air traffic control procedures.

AME's

The amended Federal Aviation Act of 1958 gave the FAA's administrator the power to delegate medical exam authority to qualified private physicians. These private physicians, after conducting a medical examination according to FAA criteria, were empowered to issue medical certificates to qualified applicants. AME's, by and large, are medical doctors and osteopaths in private practice who must hold a current valid medical license issued by the state licensing authority in the location where they intend to perform their examinations.

There are approximately 5400 civilian AME's located in nine US regions, and another 350 international AME's located in 81 countries. There are also 500 Federal AME's acting on behalf of the military, Coast Guard, NASA, and other federal agencies. AME's perform nearly a half a million medical examinations every year for over 17,000 air traffic controllers and nearly 650,000 pilots in the US and overseas. By and large, AME physicians are engaged in family practice (some 56 percent), with 19 percent specializing in internal medicine, seven percent in general surgery, four percent in aviation medicine, three percent in ophthalmology, one percent in psychiatry, and ten percent scattered among other medical disciplines and specialties.

Applicants become AME's by providing references from three local physicians or an official statement from their respective state licensing authority regarding their professional standing in the medical community. The applicants must be engaged in the practice of clinical medicine at an established office address that is readily available to the general public. Applicants must also have a properly equipped office (for which a required equipment list is determined by the regional Flight Surgeon) in which to conduct their examinations. The FAA gives special consideration to applicants who have been Military Flight Surgeons or have specific training and expertise in aviation medicine. When they become AME's for the first time, they are restricted to the issuance of Class Two and Class Three physicals only until they have performed as an AME for a period of at least three years.

The FAA has a specific training program for every AME, covered in FAA Order 8520.2D. The erstwhile AME applicant must first complete a five-day basic AME seminar and a medical certification standards and procedures workshop, and a staff member from his or her office must also complete a one-day medical certification standards and procedures workshop. The basic AME seminars (with the attendant workshop) are conducted four times a year at the FAA's Civil AeroMedical Institute in Oklahoma City, OK.

The initial training program is designed to help the applicant:

1. Recognize the importance of the AME's role in the overall goal of achieving aviation safety,

2. Develop a clear understanding and recognize the importance of the medical certification process in the AME's responsibilities in the process,

3. Learn the airmen medical certification standards and FAA policies and regulations,

4. Review the latest medical and technical information and clinical examination techniques in every medical specialty field that an AME will need to use to ensure that airmen meet the medical certification standards for the class of airmen medical certificate applied for,

5. Recognize the basis for disqualification of the airmen with a medical problem and conditions necessitating deferral or denial as outlined in the Federal Aviation Regulations, and

6. Understand, and be able to explain to airmen, the denial process to include steps necessary for certification appeal rights.

7. The AeroMedical Education Division of CAMI has designated the basic AME seminar as a continuing medical education activity that is valid for 38.75 credit hours in Category One of the physicians recognition award of the American Medical Association.

The FAA charges no fees for the seminars and workshops; however, all applicants and/or staff must pay all the personal expenses associated with their training. Once an AME is designated, they are required to maintain their designation by attending a two-and-a half-day regular AME seminar every three years. Further, one of the AME's staff members must also attend a one-day medical certification standards and procedures workshop every three years. Additionally, regular AME seminars are conducted throughout the country, designed to maintain AME's currency on examination procedures, the AeroMedical Certification process, the latest medical technical information and clinical examination techniques applicable to airmen medical certification... as well as the arduous task of keeping the FAA's paperwork straight (particularly the Application for Airmen Medical Certificate, FAA Form 8500-8).

Once again, participation in these regular AME seminars allow physicians to earn additional educational credits (26 credit hours in Category One of the physicians recognition award of the AMA) associated with the practice of general medicine. Other, non-mandatory seminars are held throughout the year in locations around the country. The three-and-one-half-day seminars are held in conjunction with the Aerospace Medical Association (Asthma), and may be devoted to subjects such as Cardiology, Neurology, Neuropsychology, Psychiatry, Aviation Physiology, Human Factors, Ophthalmology, Otolaryngology, Endocrinology, and other topics.

For services, an AME may charge whatever the traffic will bear for a medical certificate. There isn't really much cost differentiation for an examination among the three classes of medical certificates, unless additional tests or protocols (such as the EKG required of commercial pilots after age 35) are required. The FAA's only mandate on AME medical examination fees is that they be *"commensurate with fees charged for similar services in the locality of practice."*

Since AME's are not federal employees, they're not entitled to protection under the Federal Tort Claims Act... but an AME can call upon the FAA for legal advice and counsel if the need arises. Regional Flight Surgeons for each of the nine regions of the US are available to assist AME's regarding legal questions, as are the Regional FAA attorneys. However, if an AME does get dragged into court, they're responsible for their own defense and legal fees.

Not all AME's simply give Class One, Class Two or Class Three physicals... many AME's are called upon by the FAA to aid regional or national headquarters in determining problems for which they are specially qualified, or in giving lectures to other medical professionals, as well as speaking to the aviation public on medical matters... especially during FAA aviation safety seminars conducted for pilots throughout the country. AME's are often called upon to assist in accident investigations if it is believed that medical concerns played a part in the cause or aftermath of such an incident. Still other AME's are utilized to determine the efficacy of transporting acutely ill/incapacitated patients by air.

Finally, there is a fairly erudite group of AME's who serve as consultants to the FAA. Most of these are among the medical specialists and will be consulted according to their medical specialty to help the FAA determine the fate of pilots who may be seeking certification after having been turned down. The busier consultants for the FAA tend to be a rather exclusive clique... chosen not only for their expertise, but (according to many within the FAA's hallowed halls), for connections and relationships to those in power within the FAA.

Class Struggle

So... most pilots (with the exception of balloon, ultralight, and some glider operations) are required to hold one of three classes of Medical Certificate. These certificates are designed to make sure that flyers are medically qualified to operate their aircraft and should not have to deal with medical complications that might make them unsafe as pilots. The basic physical is a simple one... eyesight, hearing, reflexes, urine test, basic physical and a specific questionnaire that pilots are required to complete or update, in total, each time they ask for medical certification. A pilot (or would-be pilot) simply contacts the physician's office for an appointment and upon arrival completes an application form before undertaking the physical examination. Once the applicant meets the medical exam standards, the AME issues a medical certificate.

If there are problems with the exam, the AME may refuse to issue such a certificate. At that point, the applicant is forced to deal with the FAR Part 67 mandated appeal process. In most cases this is a very simple process. And to be fair, the FAA ultimately refuses few medical applications. If the AME refuses to issue the certificate, the paperwork is forwarded to the FAA, where it is processed (with the exception of "special issuance" cases) within 15 working days of receipt of all necessary medical information.

The first appeal actually goes to the Federal Air Surgeon (via the Oklahoma City office) to request an authorization for the "special issuance" of a medical certificate. This might result in a medical certificate that might contain restrictions or limits. Some of these limits may be contingent upon the successful completion of additional medical testing, restricted to a specific (shorter) time-period, or otherwise restricted. The FAA has issued medical certificates under its "special issuance" criteria for a number of pilots with

other conditions. Pilots missing limbs or appendages, pilots with hearing deficiencies, pilots with color blindness, and pilots with a number of maladies have been given medical certificates to fly airplanes, sometimes with little or no restriction, so long as they demonstrate their ability to function in the flying environment. Such pilots are issued a "Certificate of Demonstrated Ability."

The restrictions do make a lot of sense in most cases. For instance, a pilot with a hearing deficiency may be allowed to pilot an aircraft... but only in uncontrolled airspace where his/her need to contact a control tower or other or radio controlled authority is moot. Pilots with color blindness may not be allowed to fly in instrument conditions or exercise other privileges that require their ability to differentiate some colors.

Some restrictions are simple. Pilots with less than 20/20 vision may be required to wear glasses. Pilots with partial hearing loss may be required to wear a hearing aid. And pilots with some handicaps may be required to use external resources to help them fly in airplane. I have been privileged to work with a number of pilots who have suffered the loss of arms or legs and have subsequently been certified to fly airplanes with the use of mechanical accouterments or special controls.

Thus, in most cases, the FAA is not only reasonable in working with people who want to fly, but will often go to extraordinary measures to help people earn their wings. The fly in the ointment occurs, however, when the process becomes "political."

For those poor souls who are not given a special issuance certificate following a refusal of medical privileges, an appeal to the National Transportation Safety Board must be made. If a pilot is denied, outright, a medical certificate by an AME, the pilot may (within 30 days after the date of the denial), apply in writing to the FAA's Federal Air Surgeon for reconsideration of that denial. If the denial is upheld by the FAA, then one resorts to the NTSB for its consideration of any appeal. This process is expensive, time-consuming, and frankly, rigged in favor of the FAA. No matter what the NTSB may say on appeal, the FAA has the final say in every decision. In other words, the FAA Administrator has the right to overrule any decision made against it by the NTSB. However, if the NTSB concurs with the FAA's denial action, an applicant's only recourse is to request a hearing in Federal District Court, and failing that, the Supreme Court. Unfortunately, things happen during the course of one's life and should a pilot's medical condition change, he/she is expected to report that immediately to the FAA.

Private (not-flying-for-hire) pilots and persons flying in a non-commercial application may hold a Class Three, which is the most lenient of the classes and poses the least restrictive and invasive series of exams. The Class Three certificate is good for up to three years for applicants under age 40 and two years for those 40 and over, and can also serve as a Student Pilot certificate for new flyers (one version of the certificate has room for the required Instructor Endorsements for solo and cross-country privileges).

To obtain this combination certificate, the applicant must not only meet the medical standards but also must be at least 16 years old and be able to read, speak, and understand the English language. If these requirements are met, the AME will issue the combined certificate... though the combined medical/student pilot certificate will not be good for flight duties until properly endorsed by the student's instructor.

A Second Class Certificate is the minimum necessary for Commercial privileges. It is good for one year but may be useful for up to two more years as it becomes a Class Three after the first year passes. The test does involve more scrutiny during the physical

examination but not tremendously so. This grade of certificate is (at least) required of crop dusters, charter pilots, corporate pilots, and anyone else who flies commercially.

The First Class is the most restrictive and closely monitored certificate available. Few commercial operations require First Class privileges unless one is in command of aircraft operating under FAR (Federal Aviation Regulation) Part 121 (airline). It is good for up to six months and like the rest, devolves to a Class Two or Three as it matures past the original six to twelve month shelf-life.

The "Boss"

The FAA's current Federal Air Surgeon (the most senior executive rank in the Office of Aviation Medicine) is an affable and rather accomplished man. Dr. Jon L. Jordan was selected as the FAA's Federal Air Surgeon in September 1991.

According to the official FAA bio, Jordan hails from West Virginia and received his early education in the Michigan and West Virginia school systems. He earned a Bachelor of Arts degree from West Virginia University in Morgantown, WV in 1958 and an MD degree in 1963 from the Medical College of Virginia, Richmond, VA. After serving a general rotating internship at Petersburg General Hospital, Petersburg, Virginia, he attended the University of Virginia School of Law and graduated from that institution with an LLB degree in 1967 (later converted to a JD degree).

During semester breaks and after graduating from law school, he practiced medicine in Williamson, KY. He joined the US Army Medical Corps in 1967 and following receipt of training at Fort Rucker, AL, served as a flight surgeon at Fort Lewis, WA and Chief of Aviation Medicine at Madigan General Hospital, Tacoma, WA. He left the Army with the rank of Major in 1969 to head the Projects Development Branch of the FAA's Office of Aviation Medicine in Washington, DC. Dr. Jordan was subsequently promoted to Chief, Medical Standards Division in 1976 and to Deputy Federal Air Surgeon in November 1979.

Long recognized as a leader in Government and Civil Aviation Medicine, Dr. Jordan received the FAA Superior Achievement Award in 1985 and the Presidential Rank Meritorious Executive Award in 1992. In addition, he received the John A. Tamisiea Award from the Civil Aviation Medical Association in 1988 for his outstanding contributions to the science and art of Aviation Medicine and the Airlines Medical Directors Association Award in 1995 for his outstanding contributions and eminent leadership in aviation medicine. Dr. Jordan is licensed to practice medicine in both West Virginia and Virginia and is a member of the bar in Virginia and the District of Columbia. He is a Fellow of the Aerospace Medical Association and a member of the International Academy of Aviation and Space Medicine.

Both from my own experiences as well as those of the insiders that have worked with him, Jordan is a rather nice guy who adheres to the rules with strict accuracy. Something of a career bureaucrat, Jordan definitely knows for whom he works, but has been known to buck the system here and there... but rarely when a serious controversy is involved (which he may have his reasons for... there are rumors that a previous FAS was booted for just that reason).

AIR OF INJUSTICE

Chapter 14

MORE Medical Mumbo-Jumbo... Tests, Protocols, Consultants, and "F.M."

He who knows others is wise; He who knows himself is enlightened.
Tao Te Ching

One of the most difficult tasks that I faced when I decided to write this book was wading through all the medical mumbo jumbo that the FAA threw at this case as it proceeded. The world of medicine has come up with a language all of its own. The world of aviation has its own language as well. It's a toss-up as to which is the most confusing to the other... and to those uninitiated into either jargon-dominated discipline. Coupled, the two of them not only have two separate languages fighting it out for dominance, but the resulting confusion is immense.

Well, the combination of two highly technical disciplines made the technical discovery in this case extraordinary—and the ability of the public to *really* understand what was happening was significantly undermined. And of course, when the whole process got mired in the court system, one also had to translate yet another jargon concentrated discipline... the law. It's amazing that anyone knew what anybody was talking about.

Unfortunately, the situation is even more difficult to understand because on the medical side of this particular case much of the data is neurological or psychological in nature... which basically means that the "jargon" quotient is particularly arcane. I'll do my best to walk you through most of the major testing protocols and medical testimony that came out of this case. But... because of the immense amount of paperwork involved and all the medical jargon that got thrown into this mess, I'm going to try to boil it down to the brass tacks. That's not going to be easy. It becomes even more difficult when you consider that even medicine is not a precise science... so much of it is subject to interpretation and question.

In any neurological or psychological examination, medicine has derived a series of basic tests and criteria that are used as "first base" before proceeding on and fine-tuning the examination process. Bob Hoover was subjected to a battery of them. Not just once, but many times. And... it was up to the FAA and a battery of hand-picked consultants to justify their objectives.

Who "Owns" The Consultants?

Several of these tests prompted many to ask a few questions as to their selection and relevance (especially in light of the fact that no one could quite show where Mr. Hoover was actually exhibiting any *real* problems in his flying performances… annoying, that). Even more asked questions about who ordered and evaluated these tests… especially those not directly working for the FAA.

The FAA uses an eclectic network of consultants who reportedly offer exceptional expertise in desired medical specialties. The need for consultants and experts is unquestioned. Much of the very senior AeroMedical staff in FAA are qualified physicians, but are not involved in actual practice, instead pursuing a bureaucratic side of their medical disciplines. Even those assigned to a particular specialty—cardiology, neuropsychiatry—etc. have to spend much of their work dealing with the legalities and bureaucracy they administer, rather than practicing actual medicine.

Indeed, Federal Air Surgeon Jon Jordan is not only a medical doctor, but has earned a law degree, which probably serves him exceptionally well in his current responsibilities. So… it is up to a number of qualified experts to help the FAA make the right decisions. Let's face it, if a senior FAA cardiology expert, who spends most of his days dealing with paperwork, is questioned on the minutiae and specifics of new and arcane medical technologies, he is probably not qualified to discuss them articulately. Mind you, this is not a criticism… these subjects are formidably complex under the most basic circumstances, and no one person, even within a particular specialty, can be counted upon to know it all. This is where FAA needs help, and quite a lot of it. Thus, the FAA's need for, and reliance upon, consultants.

There is not a lot of official rhyme or reason behind the FAA's selection of outside experts. One of the things that we have noticed is that the FAA appears to be very impressed with published works, degrees and titles. They do not seem to be nearly as impressed with those who spend more time in actual medical practice than in getting their name published or publicized. The FAA was loath to talk to us about this matter, especially when they understood it was in connection with this book, but outside the FAA there are few people who are as intimately familiar with the FAA AeroMedical establishment as the AOPA's Gary Crump. AOPA, the world's largest pilot's organization, has an office specifically dedicated to helping its individual membership with questions or problems of an AeroMedical nature. Every month, over 1000 pilots and airmen call AOPA for advice, information, and intervention in seeing that their medical problems are dealt with fairly and competently. Gary Crump manages this office, and has personally overseen the medical concerns of tens of thousands of pilots. (As an aside, I must note that of the hundreds of AOPA members I have talked to, the great majority of them who have had to ask AOPA for some kind of assistance, have noted that it is *this* office that they call. This is unfortunate, but with the FAA's recent backlog of pending medical applications having reached the astonishing number of nearly 50,000; the need for AOPA's expertise and clout becomes readily apparent).

Gary notes that the FAA's current consultancy system has been *"used for some time."* Crump was not aware of any specific set of standards in regards to the FAA selection of consultants, outside of the fact that they *"be appropriately qualified, and be available to the FAA as necessary."* When questioned about the neuropsychiatric aspects of the

AA AeroMedical establishment, Crump said that *"all that derives from Pakull.... He's the onsummate bureaucrat, and applies a strict bureaucratic mindset to everything he does. As conservative as he has become, he naturally selects consultants that are as conservative as he."*

The FAA AeroMedical consultancy selection process seems ripe for abuse. Senior AA officials are free to select friends and associates, or others, who may tend to agree with whatever their sponsor requires. Further, the FAA is obviously looking for information that will sustain or enhance their decisions and processes. Consultants who go against the grain or repetitively disagree with the FAA are likely *not* to be selected to consult in the future. This is not necessarily a unique fault with the FAA, but human nature, and unless some kind of check and balance is in place, one can't help but think that consultants have a vested interest in agreeing with the FAA.

Quite a few medical professionals derive large amounts of their income from onsultancy fees with the FAA. Others also receive additional compensation in the form of research grants and special projects that can often be fairly lucrative. While the great many of these medical professionals are unlikely to render untrue or false results in order to please the FAA, it is hard to conceive that their reliance upon the government for such incomes would not color their judgment process. This is a human process, after all, but the astonishing thing here is that there does not appear to be any outside check and balance or external oversight apparatus to make sure that the FAA's consultants are rendering objective and proper judgments that are fair and impartial. The potential for conflict is ponderous.

In questioning conducted by Hoover counsel F. Lee Bailey, one FAA consultant admitted to being asked to change an evaluation by a Senior FAA staffer, and that change appears to have come about... leaving many of us to wonder how prevalent a practice this is and how many pilots are unfairly denied their rights and/or livelihood, as a result.

Sometimes, though, it seems that even Senior levels of the FAA, itself, act in ways that appear to be ripe for claims of conflict of interest.

CogScreen

One of the most pivotal tests in this case turned out to be the product of a high-level FAA Doctor (neuropsychologist) closely associated with the headquarters staff in Washington DC, by the name of Gary Kay. Dr. Kay researched and designed a series of tests to evaluate cognitive function that he nicknamed "CogScreen." Even though the test was experimental at the time that Mr. Hoover was subjected to it, there seemed to be a great deal of persistence on the part of the FAA to see this test used and positively portrayed.

While there are many questions about the efficacy and accuracy of CogScreen, one of the most intriguing questions that came up throughout the entire process was the fact that CogScreen as presented in the Bob Hoover case wasn't a certified test (then). Further, one must note that FAA Senior Doctor Gary Kay had a lot to gain through its validation and adoption by the FAA and other agencies. In other words, if the test became successful and popular, he stood to make a lot of money. Can you say "conflict of interest" (again), anybody? So... the more the FAA insisted on its use, the more it mentioned it, the

more times its use was noted in official circles, the more that one of the FAA's own people stood to gain. Just as important, remember that the FAA was constantly taking heat over their stance on aging pilots and the "Age 60" rule... so it was a godsend that one of their own developed a tool that might potentially be used to validate their position... a conveniently symbiotic relationship, no?

Dr. Kay's "CogScreen-AeroMedical Edition" (CogScreen-AE) was reportedly developed to detect subtle changes in cognitive functioning in pilots and was the product of an eight-year international research effort. The company marketing this test series advertises it as *"an economical and well validated approach for testing the neuro-psychological functioning of current aviators and pilots seeking medical recertification, as well as for establishing a baseline level of cognitive functioning for trainees or recently hired pilots."* It is a computer-based test. Administered on-screen, the test scores itself automatically and contains a series of *"self-contained cognitive tasks to assess deficits or changes in attention, immediate and short-term memory, visual-perceptual functions, sequencing functions, logical problem solving, calculation skills, reaction time, simultaneous information processing abilities, and executive functions."*

The results are interpreted from any one of seven different report formats. These include a summary report of raw test scores; graphs and tables showing percentile and 'T' scores relative to a specified pilot normative sample; a data export file; or a detailed data output report listing test items, responses, and response times. The test currently reportedly takes about 45-60 minutes to complete and is "suitable for *"Aviators 25-73 with 12 years or more of education."*

Three guesses where they got the test data for the 73-year-old pilot?

The FAA loves CogScreen... and has referred to its use repetitively in a number of studies and projects. Many in the flying community, however, grew immediately suspicious of the "Big Brother" onus of a test that supposedly evaluated whether someone was thinking right, especially after one rumor was circulated in which a number of Doctors apparently took the test to sample its capabilities... and wound up scoring poorly (this report is true).

Even the catalog entry published by Psychological Assessment Resources Inc (apparently acquired by them in 1995) boasts some far-reaching capabilities of concern to many, stating that the CogScreen is "Useful for establishing a baseline level of cognitive functioning for trainees or recently hired pilots." 1984, anyone?

The $870 test kit claims that *"the original US aviator normative sample included data from 584 airline pilots. Supplemental data are provided for three additional normative samples: major airline pilots from a large US carrier, major airline pilots from smaller US carriers, and pilots from a regional commuter carrier. Age-corrected and non-age-corrected normative profiles can be generated based on these four pilot groups. Profiles can also be generated to compare an individual's current CS-AE scores with previous testing sessions. More than 900 commercial aviators participated in CogScreen studies. Validity studies demonstrated expected relationships between CogScreen-AE and analogous, non-computerized neuropsychological tests. Contrasted-group validity studies demonstrated differential performance related to different neurobehavioral syndromes. Criterion-related studies demonstrated high levels of sensitivity and specificity in comparison to conventional tests. Performance on CogScreen has been validated as a predictor of actual flight performance."*

Those are pretty lofty claims... and the FAA has apparently embraced this testing protocol aggressively... which, of course, certainly does Dr. Kay's bankbook no harm at all. The FAA has practically endorsed CogScreen, publishing studies in which it was used extensively and thereby signaling the AeroMedical community that this is a test that they approve of and use. The FAA's use appears to be far-reaching. CogScreen was utilized extensively in a report published by CAMI, "Age 60 Rule Research, Part IV: Experimental Evaluation of Pilot Performance," a report coauthored by Dr. Kay. The report stated that *"The purpose of this study was to examine the feasibility of developing an individually based pilot performance assessment, as well as design an experimental methodology to empirically examine the relationship between pilot aging and performance. Pilot performance was measured with both domain dependent, as well as domain-independent assessments to test a decrement with compensation model of expertise and aging."*

Another CAMI report utilized CogScreen to determine *alcohol* related effects on aviators. Entitled "Some Performance Effects of Age and Low Blood Alcohol Levels on a Computerized Neuropsychological Test," the study *"explored a multifaceted application of the sensitivity of the battery to potential differences in performance capabilities, current civil aviation interest in the performance effects of low levels of blood alcohol, and the potential significance of age on cognitive performance."*

Even DOT jumped on the bandwagon... in "Improving Transportation for a Maturing Society," published by the US Department of Transportation Office of the Assistant Secretary for Transportation Policy, the DOT report discussed aging factors for operators in the transportation industry and how those factors might adequately be evaluated. Concerns about the capabilities of aging transportation operators were heavily investigated in the 21,000 word report and a number of DOT research programs and tools explained. The report specified that *"...the FAA has one such tool under development, CogScreen-AE. It is a computer-administered test for use in the medical recertification evaluation of pilots with known or suspected neurological and/or psychiatric conditions. It measures the underlying perceptual, cognitive and information processing abilities associated with flying. This tool has potential for use in testing the mental capacities of all operators of all ages but can be used to identify mental changes more common to older pilots. If this tool is successful it may be adaptable for other modal applications."*

The DOT also proclaimed that *"CogScreen is now used as a supplemental test option by neuropsychologists doing evaluations of airman on behalf of the FAA; other applications include both military and civilian entities that use CogScreen as a baseline documentation of cognitive performance on entry into an aviation job."*

So... FAA had lined up behind CogScreen, DOT jumped on, too... and aviators worldwide were now potentially subject to being tested on their cognitive capabilities, based on a test whose most famous/infamous use occurred during the Hoover controversy. The Hoover case must have seemed like a golden opportunity for CogScreen's proponents... a wonderful way to validate and draw attention to a test that could solve a number of their problems and was the personal brainchild of one of their own.

"Legal" Tests?

One other concern that was repeatedly raised throughout this matter must be mentioned, albeit briefly, as it is discussed extensively during the court battles. But... much psych testing is awfully subjective. Not all tests work for all people and a number of

varying conditions do affect their outcome from day to day. More important, who has established the validity of these tests and how well did they do so? In the case of the efforts of Dr. Elliott, that job appears to have been botched.

One major embarrassment that occurred in the Hoover matter was the revelation that Dr. Elliott used a research version of the Wisconsin Card Sort test–though he first denied that any such thing occurred. It was only after Dr. Antoinette Appel called the company that published the test, that Dr. Elliott was convinced that the test he used was a research version. In other words... it was a non-certified test that other medical professionals insist should never have been used until it had been accepted for professional use.

Appel stated that the computer version of the Wisconsin Card Sort test used by Elliott had been released only as a research version, and went on to say that this version is worthless for diagnostic purposes. She reported that it even took *her* 10 times longer to complete the test. Mind you, this was the test series in which Hoover had been promised that nothing he was asked or tested on would be utilized or have any bearing on his ability to fly, and was conducted during an appointment that was far longer than he had been led to expect. Appel testified that a number of studies demonstrate a marked drop-off in testing performance after 90 minutes — referring to Elliott's lengthy testing environment. She said this drop-off also occurs if the patient does not eat (Hoover did not) or if there is tension between examiner and patient (Hoover *knew* his neck on was on the block and admitted, later, that he did not feel he could trust Elliott). Appel also felt that practice effect did not account for Hoover's improvement in subsequent testings.

Finally.... as to the actual relevance of this testing: Appel mentioned reading an article by none other than Dr. Kay, which essentially said that there had been no studies regarding the relationship between testing performance and actual aviator performance. Mind you, this article was written in 1990 and Kay had since written other articles that seemed to contradict his earlier writings...

So which was it? Good test? Bad test? Relevant test? Irrelevant test? One thing's for sure... there seemed to be plenty of room for doubt throughout the whole scenario, and this so-called "exact" science sure seemed to be open to a lot of interpretation. Additionally, research version or not, much of Elliott's results certainly must be called into question... and all the data gathered therein considered suspect.

One final note: Dr. Appel, who is certainly as learned and respected as any of the FAA's consultants, stated that "...*the best test for determining cognitive function is performance.*" The FAA *hated* that concept and fought it throughout the three-year ordeal.

Bob Hoover repeatedly stated that the tests he performed for them seemed to be "weird" and bore little relation to the skills he used while flying... and that if they really wanted to see if he was impaired in any way, all that they had to do was "*saddle up,*" fly along with him (ostensibly in a simulator) and let them see him *in action*.

Bob admitted to frustration with the testing process and wondered whether "*any of it really amounted to anything... Jim, they can throw whatever they want at me (in terms of emergency or unusual conditions) ...but for God's sake, test my flying... not my drawing, or whether I can remember silly numbers, or how I do on some computer. Just watch me fly!*"

Chapter 15

The Boom Lowers... Grounded?

People only see what they are prepared to see.
Ralph Waldo Emerson

And so... the FAA prevailed in what seemed to be a longshot, due to the wealth of positive information on Bob's behalf. All that work, all that positive support, all the experts so supportive and speaking so clearly... It was all flushed away. What the German's best fighter pilots and prison camps in World War II could not do, what decades of flight tests could not do, what countless dangerous airplanes and the whims of gravity could not do, the almighty FAA had done. Bob Hoover was grounded. Bob was told he could no longer fly... by the same government he had risked his life for hundreds of times.

The grounding set into force a rather well-regimented set of bureaucratic procedures, the first of which was a certified letter to Bob from the FAA's Assistant Chief Counsel, Susan Caron. Since Bob had voluntarily surrendered his medical certificate to the FAA through Dr. Puskas, he was entitled to have it back and, in fact, the FAA would have been forced to give it to him if they had not taken other actions. The FAA's fastest, most concrete, way of dealing with a matter was to revoke Hoover's medical certificate through a series of powers that allowed them to circumvent normal American jurisprudence. By asserting that their actions were of an emergency nature, i.e., of urgent importance to aviation safety, the FAA could jerk his ticket without having to give him any kind of legal opportunity to be tested before the revocation. That is exactly what they did.

Dated December 14, 1993, Ms. Caron's letter formerly set the "**Emergency Order of Revocation**" in motion as part of FAA Docket No. 94AGC10007. The three-page letter formally reiterated the FAA's case as follows...

The Administrator of the Federal Aviation Administration (FAA) has determined that:

1. On February 12, 1992, you applied for a second-class airman medical certificate and were examined by A. Puskas, M.D., an FAA designated Aviation Medical Examiner, who withheld issuance of the certificate pending further evaluation.

2. On March 2, 1992, Audie W. Davis, M.D., Manager, of the FAA Aeromedical Certification Division, issued you a second-class airman medical certificate.

3. You have a cognitive deficit as demonstrated on neuropsychological testing.

4. The Federal Air Surgeon finds that you are unable to safely perform the duties or exercise the privileges of your airman certificate; or that you may reasonably be expected to be unable to do so within two years because you have:

a. A neurologic condition (cognitive deficit); and

b. An organic, functional, or structural disease, defect, or limitation (cognitive deficit).

5. Based on the foregoing, you do not meet the medical standards of paragraphs (d)(2)(ii) and (f)(2) of sections 67.15 and 67.17 of the Federal Aviation Regulations, 14 C.F.R. 67.15 and 67.17(d)(2)(ii) and (f)(2).

The Administrator has determined that, by reason of the foregoing circumstances, safety in air commerce or air transportation and the public interest require the revocation of all airman medical certificates held by you. Further, the Administrator finds that an emergency exists and that safety in air commerce or air transportation and the public interest require the immediate effectiveness of this order.

NOW, THEREFORE, IT IS ORDERED, pursuant to the authority vested in the Administrator by sections 609 and 1005(a) of the Federal Aviation Act, as amended, that:

1. Effective immediately, all airman medical certificates held by you, including the medical certificate issued to you on or about March 2, 1992, are hereby revoked on an emergency basis;

2. All airman medical certificates held by you shall be surrendered immediately by mail or delivery to:

Assistant Chief Counsel, Attn: Susan S. Caron, AGC-310
Enforcement Division, Federal Aviation Administration
800 Independence Avenue, S.W., Washington, D.C. 20591

Hays V. Hettinger, Assistant Chief Counsel
Enforcement Division, Office of the Chief Counsel

As required, the letter also outlined the Appeals process that pilots may use when such an order is forced upon them. It listed that process as follows:

You may appeal from this order within 10 days from the date it is served by filing a notice of appeal with the Office of the Administrative Law Judges, National Transportation Safety Board, Room 5531, 490 L'Enfant Plaza East, S.W., Washington, D.C. 20594. The Federal Aviation Act of 1958, as amended, provides that the date of mailing should be considered as the time when service is made. 49 U.S.C. App. 5 1485(c). Due to the fact that your certificate has been revoked on an emergency basis, the Emergency

Order of Revocation will remain in effect during the pendency of any proceedings before the National Transportation Safety Board (NTSB). Part 821 of the Board's Rules of Practice in Air Safety Proceedings applies to such an appeal. An original and three (3) copies of your appeal must be filed with the NTSB. In the event you appeal, a copy of your Notice of Appeal must be furnished to the Office of the Chief Counsel at the address noted in the Emergency Order.

Whether or not you choose to appeal from this Emergency Order, you must surrender your certificates to:

> *Assistant Chief Counsel, Attn: Susan S. Caron, AGC-310*
> *Enforcement Division, Federal Aviation Administration*
> *800 Independence Avenue, S.W., Washington, D.C. 20591*

In the event of an appeal to the NTSB, a copy of this order will be filed with the NTSB and will serve as the Administrator's complaint.

Bob, of course, knew that this was coming, and long before the certified letter was dropped on his doorstep, a faxed copy was in his hands and the hands of friends F. Lee Bailey and John Yodice. Bailey and Yodice started formulating a plan of attack for the defense of Bob's flying rights.

The one positive caveat in this situation is that when the FAA invokes its otherwise unconstitutional emergency powers to deprive any airman of their rights and privileges, a "fast-track" process ensues to allow an airman to get their day in court in a fairly speedy fashion. Under 49 U.S.C. Section 1133, the NTSB's Administrative Law Judges hear, consider and issue initial decisions on all appeals from FAA certificate and civil penalty actions involving pilots, engineers, mechanics and repairman also covered under this appeal process are petitions for Certification that are denied by the FAA.

The process is, admittedly, quite orderly. Once an appeal or petition is filed by an airman to the Office of Judges, the appeal/petition is assigned a Docket Number and acknowledged by the case manager for the Administrative Law Judges. The FAA has to file a copy of the order issued to the airman and designates the order as an FAA complaint. The airman has to file answers to the FAA's charges in order to either admit or deny their assertions/charges.

At this point, request for discovery of information can be filed by both the FAA and the airman. Within 60 days, a hearing is set by the judge assigned to the case at a place convenient to both the FAA and to the airman, though the timeframe may be expanded if the airman requires so. That done, a hearing is held, a decision is issued, and the judge either affirms, modifies or reverses the FAA's order.

If either party is not happy with those results, a second appeal, this time to the Full Board, may be made. The second appeal must be filed with the NTSB's Docket section and sent to the NTSB's general counsel. An appeal brief must be filed by the appealing party and a reply brief will be filed by those in opposition. Thereafter, the Board may issue an order affirming, modifying or reversing the Judge's decision or the case may be remanded back to the judge for further proceedings.

This allows for the losing party to petition once again for reconsideration, if

necessary; whereby a reply to that petition by the opposing party will usually take place. The board will then roll on the petition for reconsideration... although a request for a stay of the Board's order will occur if a losing party notifies them of their intention to proceed with a third appeal – this time to the US Court of Appeals.

The third appeal process is serious hardball, legally speaking. The aggrieved party files a petition in the US Court of Appeals, forcing the NTSB to forward a certificate of record to the Court of Appeals, along with the full Docket, if requested. Briefs are then filed before the court by both parties, followed by an oral argument in the Court of Appeals. The US Court of Appeals will thereafter issue a decision on petition either affirming, modifying, or reversing the board's decision, or amending the case back to the Board. After that, the only authority beyond this is a direct appeal to the US Supreme Court — though there is no guarantee that the court will even hear the party's petition, and of course any actions before the Supreme Court of the United States are about as serious and complex a legal proceeding as one can engage in.

Everyone associated with this matter told this writer that no one expected this situation to get this combative, and with each succeeding battle, each felt that sooner or later a combination of reason and/or bad PR for the FAA and the NTSB would force them to rethink their positions and allow Hoover to get back to flying status... but upon the official revocation of Bob's medical, there was only one thing to do – fight.

No time was wasted in seeking a resolution to this matter. By 6:15 PM of the very date that Bob's certificate was revoked, Bailey and Yodice were not only on the case but had tele-faxed an appeal of the Emergency Order to the NTSB stating, as part of NTSB Docket # SE-13417, reading as follows:

"Robert Anderson Hoover, respondent, by his undersigned counsel, pursuant to Section 21.55 of the Board's Rules of Practice, hereby appeals the Administrator's EMERGENCY ORDER OF REVOCATION dated December 14, 1993, revoking respondent's Second Class Medical Certificate. Respondent denies the allegations of the Administrator's EMERGENCY ORDER and prays that it be reversed."

It was signed by both Yodice and Bailey, who took up position on either side of Bob, just like his wingmen had in WWII... though none of them believed that the battle that they were now waging was about to turn into a full-scale war.

So... yet another battle was set, but Bob had fought wars before and always lived to fly again... but he was *"damned if I could have believed I'd be fighting my own countrymen."*

Chapter 16

Ready, Set...

*"The man who never makes a mistake always takes orders from one who does.
No man or woman who tries to pursue an ideal
in his or her own way, is without enemies."*
Daisy Bates

Preparations for Bob's day in court were in process before the ink dried on the appeal to the FAA's grounding order, with famed Aviation Attorney John Yodice really burning the midnight oil with requests for discovery, depositions and responding to the same from the FAA. It was a detailed and arduous process, requiring a lot of faxing, mailing and phone calls to coordinate all the details in just the short time available before they would appear before the NTSB.

The process seemed to be quite contentious. Examination of the paperwork that went back and forth between Yodice/Bailey and the FAA shows Yodice working quickly and expediently to file the necessary subpoenas, interrogatories, and discovery requests that needed to be presented in the few short days before the Oklahoma City festivities. On the other hand, the FAA seemed to resent Yodice's requests and complained steadily throughout, complaining that they had insufficient time to deal with them, though they knew full well that they were dealing with an Emergency Hearing and the attendant "short fuse" that is part and parcel of such procedures.

So contentious were the intervening paperwork wars that both sides wound up filing various "Motions To Compel" in order to gain access to what they requested. What was particularly uncalled for was the number of instances in which the FAA used regular mail instead of express mail services or fax transmission as circumstances would seem to have dictated. On January 7, 1994, NTSB Administrative Law Judge William R. Mullins saw fit to sustain an order compelling the Administrator of the FAA to respond to Yodice/Bailey's requests for a second set of interrogatories and production of documents. A few days later (January 10), the FAA responded with a Motion for Protective Order seeking to stall the scheduled depositions of Ray Hughes (though we must note with amusement that the FAA's motion refers to Ray Hughes alternately as Mr. Hughes and Dr. Hughes, when in fact the gentleman they're talking about is the fellow who flew with Bob Hoover on a T-28 practice flight and was a certificated Airframe and Powerplant technician) and Dr. Simon.

On the same day, the FAA renewed its Motion to Compel Discovery and seemed

to insist on being treated expeditiously, though in fact they did not seem to be treating their adversaries with the same urgency.

Bob's primary defense team, as expected, consisted of two of the most expert litigators in the world, who also possessed unusually expert knowledge of aviation and the FAA/NTSB administrative/legal process. Particularly adept in this arena was John Yodice. The chief counsel for the powerful Aircraft Owners and Pilots Association, the largest pilots organization in the world, Yodice conducted most of the preparation for the NTSB hearing and put together an extraordinary argument for the world-renowned F. Lee Bailey to argue before the NTSB.

Before Yodice got heavily involved in the Hoover case, he notified AOPA president Phil Boyer that this defense was likely to take a great deal of his time and keep him away from a lot of the important and pressing business he conducted for AOPA. Boyer gave his blessings to Yodice, noting that *"a case like this was sure to have a great effect on aviation... and while it was obviously in Bob's best interest to have an expert like John Yodice in his camp, we also felt it was in the best interests of our hundreds of thousands of members to have a man of his expertise arguing such a pivotal case."*

In addition to running Yodice Associates, a world-class aviation law firm, and serving as chief counsel for AOPA, Yodice is an avid aviator. A 5000-hour pilot, Yodice has a commercial pilot's license, an instrument rating, and is a fixed-wing flight instructor (CFI-A) and holds additional ratings as a seaplane pilot and helicopter pilot. His flying career started in 1960, and he currently operates a Cessna Turbo 310 based at Washington National Airport that is used to travel for his practice of law. For pure fun, Yodice also owns a simple 65-horsepower Piper J-3 Cub. Yodice is also a featured magazine columnist in AOPA's *Pilot* magazine, where his "Pilot Counsel" column has, for years, given aero-legal advice to aviators in need of the best expertise available.

One well-known aviation personality who knows him best calls him a "superb litigator." Howard J Fried was a columnist for *FLYING* magazine for many years and the author of numerous books and magazine articles. He has a law degree and was a Designated Pilot Examiner for the FAA for many years. Running afoul of the FAA himself, Fried called his friend John Yodice to assist in his defense and though it was a losing case from the get-go (not on the merits but because of the fact that the Feds had stacked the deck against Fried in a way that made it financially unfeasible to even think of fighting the case to a proper conclusion), Yodice fought valiantly and aggressively. *"He does his homework, is very well-prepared and when he goes into action, he has the ability to carefully pick the time and place to play hardball and when he does, he does it well. Still, he also knows when to be conciliatory... he did a superb job for me in a losing cause and I really can't say much more than that... he is a nice guy, is awfully good at his job and he knows it—as he should. He's very, very thorough in his preparation and that's his greatest strength... when he represented me, he was far better prepared than the FAA's counsel. He works well with Judges but is hard as a rock with opposing attorneys as the situation requires... he's quite a guy."*

Hoover's legal team caught a major break right from the start. The Hoover case was to be heard (by virtue of where the matter was based—OKC) by NTSB Law Judge William Roger Mullins. Mullins had something of a rep as a maverick... being a person who was not only a pilot, but appeared to be willing to swim upstream against the oncoming tide of pressure often felt in cases in which the FAA felt it had a stake. Mullins is

rumored to be the record-holder in terms of the times he has found against the FAA... but is reportedly also the record holder in terms of how many times that FAA has had him reversed on appeal.

Most important, though, Mullins has a rep for fairness and a willingness to listen to arduous, detailed testimony with great patience to capture all the intricacies of what were often highly-complex issues. If there were a better Judge to hear this case than Mullins, we are not aware of whom he or she might be.

Judge William "Roger" Mullins is a graduate of Panhandle State University, Goodwell, OK, (BA, 1963) and the University of Colorado School of Law (JD, 1969). He was admitted to the practice of law in Oklahoma and Colorado in 1970, and he was admitted to practice before the US Supreme Court in 1975.

Judge Mullins was appointed as an Administrative Law Judge of the NTSB in January 1989. Before his appointment to the NTSB, he was an Administrative Law Judge of the Occupational Safety and Health Review Commission.

For 15 years before his appointment as a Federal Administrative Law Judge, Judge Mullins was an Associate District Judge, 8th Judicial District, State of Oklahoma. He was engaged in the private practice of law from 1969 to 1971, and was employed as a public school teacher in Oklahoma and Colorado from 1965 to 1967. Judge Mullins served on active military duty in the United States Army from 1963 to 1965 as a Lieutenant assigned to the 4th Infantry Division, Fort Lewis, WA. In March 1994, he retired from the US Army Reserve as a full Colonel. His last five years of reserve military service were as a military judge. Judge Mullins is also a general aviation pilot and holds a commercial pilot certificate. His affection for aviation is strong and he tries to fly regularly both for pure enjoyment as well as to maintain competency.

Mullins travels the country within a specific geographic area hearing cases for the NTSB and spends many weeks out of the year on the road. Since many of the cases that he hears are scheduled with little time to prepare, he is supported by a regional office staff that tries to keep up with the demands of his very mobile occupation. Howard Fried also has high praise for Mullins... *"a fairer Judge does not exist in the NTSB Administrative legal system... Roger is a class act and an uncommonly fair man."*

The Hoover case had another serious "Ace" up its sleeve. Like Yodice, Hoover friend F. Lee Bailey had provided much counsel and guidance to Bob throughout the months that led up to the actual hearing. Renowned for his courtroom expertise, F. Lee Bailey was not only the litigator's litigator, but as a former Marine Corps aviator, and avid aviation enthusiast, Bailey brought both his usual passion for the law as well as his passion for aviation to this case.

F. Lee Bailey is a partner in the law firms of Bailey, Fishman & Leonard in Boston, MA, and Bailey, Fishman, Freeman & Ferrin in West Palm Beach, FL. Bailey is a member of the bars of Massachusetts, Florida, the United States Supreme Court, and all 12 United States Courts of Appeals. A participant in many notable defense cases, Mr. Bailey was designated Counselor to the Chief Judge, United States Court of Military Appeals in 1992, selected by then Defense Secretary Dick Chaney to sit on the Code Committee in 1992, and appointed to the Advisory Board of the Alfred A. Cunninghan Aviation Museum in 1990. Mr. Bailey is a well-published author of a number of esoteric legal tomes such as the *Complete Manual of Criminal Forms 3d, Criminal Trial Techniques, Handling Misdemeanor Cases 2d, Handling Narcotic & Drug Cases, Crimes of Violence-Homicide &*

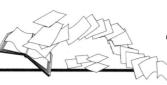

Assault, Crimes of Violence-Rape & Other Sex Crimes, and *Defending Business & White Collar Crimes 2d*.

He is also the author of a number of popular books covering his experience as a lawyer and as a pilot, such as *The Defense Never Rests, Cleared for the Approach: F. Lee Bailey in Defense of Flying, For the Defense, To Be a Trial Lawyer, Secrets*, and others.

Bailey has oft been associated with some of the most celebrated (or infamous) cases in legal history. He achieved great fame for his successful defense in the retrial of Dr. Samuel Sheppard (often referred to as the inspiration for *The Fugitive*), the trial of the "Boston Strangler", SLA kidnaping victim Patty Hearst, Captain Ernest Medina (in his court-martial for his involvement in the incident at My Lai), and, of course, O.J. Simpson.

Not just slightly controversial, Bailey is a vocal and intimidating presence in a courtroom, in front of a camera or in any venue in which he chooses... but little known is his willingness to put his money where his mouth is, doing some rarely recognized pro-bono work in a number of cases where he felt his services might be properly utilized.

One of the many cat-fights that occurred between Hoover's legal team and the FAA was fought over the deposition given by Gen. Thomas Stafford... an extremely accomplished military aviator and the commander of many space missions, including the Apollo 10 flight to and around the moon, and the Apollo-Soyuz international space flight. General Stafford was getting ready to head overseas and had but a few days in the states before disappearing for the better part of a month. As such, his availability for deposition was extremely limited, and upon learning this, Hoover's legal team set an immediate deposition of the General.

A few of the General's statements in the deposition were quite intriguing. Hoover's legal representative for the deposition, an attorney by the name of Raymond E. Tompkins (of the OKC firm of Daugherty, Bradford, Haught, and Tompkins), established that General Stafford was leaving the United States the next day for an extensive trip overseas to New Zealand, Australia, Singapore and Thailand. He was not expected back in the United States until January 20, nearly a week after the start of the hearing. While the onus of this deposition was on General Stafford's direct observations of Bob Hoover at the 1992 Aerospace America airshow, which he not only attended but in which he held a leadership role, there were some fascinating discussions about General Stafford's personal history and some of his many accomplishments.

During the course of the deposition General Stafford indicated that he had a pivotal role in the development of the B-2 bomber, *"...In early '79, in a hotel room in Chicago, on a piece of stationery, I wrote down the specifications, range, radar cross-section, payload, and gross takeoff weight, and started the B-2 bomber program."*

How many of you knew that?

Stafford also detailed the fact that he, himself, had several dozen hours flight time in the Shrike Commander and direct personal knowledge of the systems and engineering of the aircraft because of a position he had held with Gulfstream, who had purchased the Commander line. Stafford had met Hoover in the Fall of 1958, while he was a student at the Test Pilot's school at Edwards Air Force Base, during which he was a part of a number of meetings with defense contractors throughout the Los Angeles area. At this time, Hoover was chief test pilot for North American, which later merged with Rockwell to become North American Rockwell. During questioning, General Stafford indicated

that he had flown with Hoover in both the Shrike Commander and the Sabreliner.

Tompkins then got down the business... *"When you were with him and could observe his flying ability, how would you describe it?"*

Stafford responded: *"Absolutely superb."*

Tompkins: *"Would you describe him as a precise pilot?"*

Stafford: *"Very much so. I was an instructor in the test pilot school, and I taught people how to fly with the proper airspeed indicator to 1/8 of a knot, and an altitude within ten feet. So I think I'm pretty critical on people who fly airplanes, and he's the tops."*

Tompkins: *"Could you describe him as a disciplined flyer?"*

Stafford: *"Yes."*

Tompkins: *"A superior pilot?"*

Stafford: *"Absolutely."*

As the honorary chairman of Aerospace America, Stafford was in attendance at the 1992 Aerospace America airshow on Saturday and Sunday. Stafford described Bob's performance as *"normal for Bob Hoover."* Under extended questioning, Stafford noted that Hoover appeared to be acting normally and that he observed no evidence of impairment or anything otherwise different in his longtime colleague. Stafford continued... *"When I observed him there, which is the last time I saw Mr. Hoover, there at the airshow, his ability was the same as I have always seen. He was superb in the way he made the airplane perform."*

Tompkins questioned further: *"Was there any difference at all, insofar as you are aware, here under oath today, in the manner in which Mr. Hoover has performed in any other airshow that you have observed him in and the airshow which occurred in Oklahoma City in June of 1992?"*

Stafford: *"No, no."*

Tompkins: *"You found nothing in his performance as a pilot or in his ability as a pilot that would give you pause as to his continued abilities to be a superb pilot?"*

Stafford: *"I have seen nothing of any abnormality there."*

Tompkins: *"Was there anything in Mr. Hoover's flight performance in Oklahoma City or in his post-flight performance, after he landed, which would cause you to believe that he had compromised in any way his own physical safety?"*

Stafford: *"His own safety?"*

Tompkins: *"Yes, sir."*

Stafford: *"No way."*

Tompkins: *"Anything that would indicate that he might have—he might by reason of his demeanor his actions or his flight performance have compromised the safety of anybody at the air show that was in the crowd?"*

Stafford: *"No. Bob is a strict professional. If he had any he would be the first to say, 'I don't feel like flying.'"*

Tompkins: *"Based on your understanding of the Shrike aircraft and its capabilities, did Mr. Hoover in any way exceed the structural limits on the aircraft during the course of his maneuvers?"*

Stafford: *"I don't see how he could have. It was standard maneuvers that he did all the way through, and I can't see any difference what he did in '92 and the previous years when I have seen him there."*

Tompkins: *"Was there anything... that you noted that would give you any reason to believe there has been any changes in Mr. Hoover's personality or demeanor, from your past knowledge of him?"*

Tompkins: *"Gen. Stafford, would you allow your family to fly with Bob Hoover?"*

Stafford: *"Absolutely."*

Tompkins: *"And let me ask you this: Would you fly as a crew member with Bob Hoover during one of these air shows and one of those performances, if you were asked or allowed to do so?"*

Stafford: *"Certainly."*

Tompkins: *You have no doubt in your mind as to his ability and his acumen or skill as a pilot?*

Stafford: *"None whatsoever."*

Not everyone involved in the upcoming NTSB hearing had even the minimally allotted few weeks prepare for it. FAA Inspector Norbert Nester, subpoenaed by Bailey, barely found out about it all in time to attend... and noted some interesting details about how he came to testify.

"Believe it, or not, I was attending a class at the Aeronautical Center the week that Hoover was being represented by Bailey and Yodice at the initial NTSB hearings in front of Judge Mullins. I was not even working in the FSDO office. I was going to school that week."

Being in school, Nester was not privy to much of the political preparation the FAA was making as the NTSB hearing came about. Nester later discovered, *"Interesting(ly) enough, the FAA actually issued a memorandum... it was not a local memorandum out of the FSDO office, and it was not out of the Aeronautical Center. I think it originated at the regional level. It specifically said all FAA Inspectors are prohibited from the observing, viewing or attending the proceedings regarding Bob Hoover this week here in Oklahoma City."*

Nester's first word about his upcoming appearance at the NTSB hearing came as a surprise. Norbert left his classes Friday afternoon and shortly after supper time (and well beyond the end of the standard business day), Nester received a telephone call from Frank Allen.

"He says 'Hi guy, how are you doing?', then he says 'I've got a little job for you tomorrow.'"

Nester said, *"What do you mean you have a little job for me tomorrow? Tomorrow is Saturday; I'm off. I don't anything scheduled for tomorrow, I've been in school all week, don't even know what is going on in my office."*

Allen then informed him that, *"Well, you're going to have to go do this one"*, and Nester said, *"Well, what is it?"*

It is then that Allen informed him that *"Well, I have a subpoena for you."*

Norbert replied *"A subpoena, what the hell are you talking about?"*

Allen: *"You have been subpoenaed to provide testimony down there at Bob Hoover's hearing."*

Nester: *"Okay, so where did this all come from?"*

Allen: *"Well, it was served on me during the office, and I accepted it on your behalf earlier this afternoon."*

Nester was pretty chagrined... unaware of why he was subpoenaed and despite the fact that he held some strong opinions about the justification for the FAA's case about Hoover, he was unaware that anyone might be aware that he held any opinions. *"I never did really know why it was that I was subpoenaed... I (was) under the impression in talking to my supervisor that the government had subpoenaed me to go testify. Really... this was my impression. It never occurred to me that Hoover or Bailey or anybody would be the ones that did it."*

Nester, working under the impression that the government wanted him to testify on their behalf questioned Allen... *"Okay, what is the deal?"* he asked. Allen told him, *"you need to talk to a woman named Susan Caron... She is with the government and she wants to talk with you before you get in there."*

Nester continued to believe that he was now going to be under FAA orders for this testimony, *"You have to understand the way he is doing that, he is just furthering my belief that I am being called by the government. I was supposed to call and talk to a government attorney before I went. Well, if you were going to bring somebody in wouldn't you talk to them and give them some idea what testimony you were going to try to cover and that type of stuff?"*

Allen gave him her number at a local hotel and a conversation ensued... *"So I* called this Susan gal." Nester recounted, "I get her on the phone. She identified herself as being attorney that was, I don't think she used the term prosecuting, but defending the government's position against Hoover in this particular proceeding. I said what is he going to talk about? She said 'Well, if you are put on the stand tomorrow what do you know about Hoover and what do you know about the case and what do you know about this?'"

Nester said "Lady, I don't anything about the case. I worked the airshow; I didn't see anything wrong with what happened. I don't understand why Hoover is being pursued. I have been at school for the past week, I have not watched the news; I have no clue to where this thing stands at the moment."

According to Nester, "Caron said 'Well, if you were put on the stand and were pointedly asked 'Did you observe anything wrong with Hoover,' what would you reply? 'I told her no, absolutely not. She said 'well, how about the airshow?' No, there was nothing wrong with it. How about the complaints against Hoover?"

This is where Nester opened up to his feelings on the Hoover matter, telling Caron that "Well, you probably are not going to like it... but I think it is a crock of crap. I think it is the biggest bunch of bogus nonsense that could have ever been. I think that the people that are perpetuating it ought to be hung."

Caron wasn't thrilled.

"...Needless to say I went through a bit of litany there for about 20 minutes with her and she asked me a series of questions and things. Finally, she just kept probing and probing and asking questions and I said 'wait a minute, I said who actually subpoenaed me here?'"

Things got very interesting at that point, as Caron reportedly revealed that "Oh, well, Mr. Bailey did."

Nester replied, "then what in the hell am I talking to you for? And she said 'Well you are a government employee, I have the right to talk to you.'"

Nester was somewhat annoyed at this point, telling Caron "Okay, so you are telling me after we are into 30 minutes worth of conversation and you have questioned me about everything that you ever wanted to know, that you are not the one who is calling me to testify tomorrow, that I am being subpoenaed by the opposition so to speak, by Mr. Bailey."

Nester said that Caron confirmed that and that he ended the conversation on the following note... "Okay Susan, now I have told you how I feel; I told you what I think about the government; I told you what I think about Mr. Hoover and the performance and everything about it. Now I know a real catch 22. I am damned if I do and damned if I don't. If I walk in there tomorrow and they ask me the same kind of questions that you just asked me, what kind of answer do I give them?"

(She said) "Well, what do you mean?" I said, "Let's face it, I am a government employee. I am being called to testify in a very controversial proceeding that is obviously getting international attention. Now if I say anything derogatory towards the government or about the government or the government employees that their practices or anything else, I am going to get crucified. The government is going to be on me like the duck on a June bug. The other side of it is if I don't tell what I know Mr. Bailey is going be all over me like ugly on an ape. So what do I do? Do I slit my throat and go tell the truth or do I conveniently not remember anything in hopes I can skate by?"

According to Norbert, Caron counseled him that, *"...as an attorney I have to tell you, that you have no choice, you have to go tell the truth."*

Nester then said, *"this is one hell of a position to be put into."*

That's how the conversation ended, with Nester confounded at the situation he suddenly found himself in at 10:30 the night before the hearing...

"I have recounted this to more than one individual, and it really is a predicament when you are in that position. The thing that astounded me was the fact that they were so god awful devious and would not say who actually called me. They questioned me, and they took the tape." Nester was due to be at the hearing the next morning at 8 a.m.

Nester had little time to consider what was coming... *"My tit was in the ringer. No question about it... I was smart enough to know that I did not need any more trouble with the FAA, and that I needed someone to look after me because the Feds were not going to look after me. They were looking to crucify me for what I was about to say... So I contacted a private attorney who had done some work for me at different times and I said, 'Look, I am desperate. This is what the situation is, I have been called to testify, I have been called by Bailey, not by the government. I have already been told by Susan (Caron) that she is going to take great objections as to what I am going to say. This is really a bad situation. I need a personal attorney to go with me that will walk in and somehow on another set the stage and let it be known that I am not real pleased about being here but I am doing what I have to do by the law. I don't want any repercussions after the fact.'*

In essence that is what exactly happened. I took the gentlemen with me. I met Bailey downstairs when he and Hoover came in and things. I explained to him, I said, 'Look, obviously you have called me, I understand.'

He said "yes, that is right, I am the one who issued the subpoena for you." I said "Can you give me some time frame as to when you think they are going to want me on the stand?' He said "Yeah, I've got Dr. Hisey... on this morning and it is probably going to be afternoon (before Nester would be needed)."

I said, 'well, if you do not mind I really need to go, you know be close to home and things. My wife is expecting a child just any day and she has no way of getting a hold of me right here but let me go take care of a couple of things I need to do and if you will give me time I will be back'. He said 'fine, go ahead, be back up here at noon'. It was during that time period that I managed to get an attorney and so he went back with me that afternoon.

But the evening before, after I had talked to Susan Caron, before I thought about the attorney, I thought about Walt Hammell. Walt is a very outspoken intelligent individual and he has an engineering degree and a lot of other things and he has an interest in Hoover and what was going on. I said 'Walt, I have a personal favor to ask.' And he said, 'what is that?' I said, 'I have been called to testify and be at these proceedings tomorrow. If you know there is a memorandum out that says everybody is prohibited from going. And he said "yeah, but they can kiss my butt what I do on my day off is my business and if I want to go down there on Saturday is my business. If I want to go down there on Saturday and watch it, I am going to watch it."

I said 'Well, Walt I know I am going to have trouble out of this. Will you please come down there so if at a later date if I have to I can call upon you and you can say I was

present, I heard the testimony.

He said, 'sure I will do that'. Well, sure enough, Walt met me down there the next day. I left and I came back with my attorney.

It ended up that I went back, we sat in a little tavern next door, deli or whatever the hell you want to call it. I watched the famous Mr. Bailey scarf down a couple of hot dogs and as he was talking to me and asking me specific questions. Surprisingly, Lee did not ask me but about three or four questions when we were sitting there and he was eating lunch. Hoover was not even at the table. We sat down, just the attorney that went with me, Bailey and myself. He asked me three or four questions and told me what he would say about this, this and this and that was it and he said okay, we are going back in, we are going to reconvene at 1:00.

We went next door, went upstairs in that building and immediately news cameras and all that shit (were present) because I was walking in there with them. I walked past the news people to go back into the holding room where they have potential witnesses. I'll tell you how distracted I was, I didn't realize that when I walked in there, (that) I knew the people that were sitting there but I couldn't have told you who they were to save my life. I really couldn't.

Two of them were (airshow pilots) Sean Tucker and Steve Oliver. We sat back in the back and visited and the next thing I know, in the courtroom I go. I provide the testimony and that is all history for you. From that point on I was dismissed, I left, went home for the remainder of the weekend and wondered what was going on..."

Chapter 17

A Trial by Fire... The T-28 "Test"

As I grow older, I pay less attention to what men say. I just watch what they do.
Andrew Carnegie (1835-1919)

With the growing hoopla developing over Bob's abilities, it was a combination of bad luck, deteriorating metallurgy, and Hoover's own innate skills that should have been more than adequate proof of his own airworthiness.

Hoover had not actively flown in some ten months prior to his first big show-down with the FAA and NTSB in Oklahoma City. There, he hoped to prove his skills under the watchful eyes of an NTSB Administrative Law Judge, the FAA's own representatives and a very supportive number of his peers. Former World Aerobatic Champion (1980), Leo Loudenslager, was to serve as his safety pilot throughout the test performance and provide data on his capabilities, skill, reaction times, and judgment.

About ten days before the initial OKC NTSB Hearing, Bob elected to get some practice in, under the watchful eye of his friend Ray Hughes, and to videotape his airshow routine from the back cockpit. Ray worked for Great American Aircraft's Bob Grant, who did most of the maintenance on Bob's aircraft and kept them in shape for airshows. An airframe and power plant mechanic as well as a licensed pilot, Ray was thrilled to be asked to go along on the flight, realizing that *"you just don't get that many chances to fly with a guy like Hoover... and I was excited to get the chance-again."*

Bob remembers that, *"I had a call from my friend Lee Bailey, who suggested that if I had an opportunity, I should try to get a flight in a T-28 and have somebody photograph from the back seat my going through one of my aerobatic routines so that I could show the court that I had not lost any of my touch as the FAA has alleged."*

Bob's T-28 was grounded for the time-being, since it was out of license (such aircraft are required to undergo an extensive inspection, yearly, in order to be flown) and since Hoover had no other reason to go to that expense, he elected to borrow another ship, though that flight had to be done by Wednesday since the insurance was scheduled to expire after that date. He set out to shake out *"the dust,"* noting that he had not flown since October of 1992.

This particular Navy T-28B is a typical example of a rather unglamourous old military trainer that seats two, in tandem, and is powered by a huge radial engine swinging an even larger propeller that easily stands taller than the average person. The massive prop, alone, weighs a few hundred pounds. It's a rugged, sturdy aircraft designed to take the abuse of student fighter pilots and the rigors of aerobatic training... not to mention Navy landings.

While the average Navy fighter jock may choose to deny it, Navy pilots are taught to land airplanes in terms that emphasize positioning, timing and attention to airspeed and descent parameters... critical concerns when it comes to placing an aircraft doing well over 100 mph (in landing mode) on the deck of a pitching aircraft carrier that is being affected by waves, weather and the fact that the whole thing is about as small as a fixed wing aircraft could possibly hope to hit— and "hit" is often the operative word to describe such landings.

Aircraft carrier landing areas are so small, in fact, that fixed wing aircraft using them are equipped with huge tail hooks used to grab arresting cables strung across the deck (necessary to slow it down before it pitches over the end of the deck and into the ocean). Such landings are tough on these airplanes, since Navy pilots are looking to "plant" the aircraft at the proper place (within inches of a targeted spot) without necessarily being dainty about it. So... all Navy aircraft, especially the trainers (which often have to put up with the inglorious machinations of a student pilot who is often the least dainty of all) are built to take abuse... an amazing amount of it... and to damage such structures takes an amazing amount of force. Remember that point for a few minutes, folks. And, mind you, the T-28 series is possibly one of the "beefiest" piston powered military trainers ever produced.

Hoover is well acquainted with the bird and is undoubtedly one of the world's experts on this aircraft... having actually helped write the Navy operations manual (NATOPS) for the T-28, and used the same aircraft, off and on, for an arduous low-level aerobatic act for many years. It's not a strange aircraft... it's an old friend, and Hoover is as familiar with the old bird as any person living.

Come Wednesday, January 5, 1993, Bob arranged to fly ex-navy T-28B Trainer NX171BA out of Torrance, CA, with fellow pilot Ray Hughes sitting in the back. Hughes was an experienced T-28 mechanic and pilot, who would be serving as the "legal" Pilot in Command for the flight, he having the legal wherewithal and license necessary to fly such older warbirds, and still holding both a valid pilot's license and medical certificate... though Bob was destined to do all the flying.

Hoover and Hughes looked the dark blue trainer over, carefully, prior to flight, started it without difficulty, and got taxi clearance from the Torrance airport before the flight out over the Pacific ocean to an aerobatic practice area about halfway between the California coast and Catalina Island.

Since Torrance has highly restrictive noise abatement rules in order to appease surrounding homeowners, Bob conducted a high-rate climb over the airport (a normal procedure for noisy aircraft like the T-28) to get high and minimize the chance of setting off noise alarms at the airport (difficult not to do, as the North American T-28 was never designed with thoughts of quieting it down... only in making sure it could train pilots for the arduous task of navy piloting duties, and that meant *lots* of noisy horsepower).

According to Hoover's official report, *"Prior to take off the engine was warmed up until the oil temperature and pressure were in the green. The engine run-up and magneto check were normal without a drop in RPM. After take-off clearance was received, the power application was smooth with a normal take off and climb over the top of the Torrance airport at 2500 feet."*

Bob and Ray continued climbing and pointed the bird out over the 60-degree waters of the Pacific. In unrestricted airspace over the ocean, Bob started with a four-point roll to the right, an eight-point to the left and a sixteen-point roll at 7000 feet, nearly a mile and a half above the ocean and over 10 miles southwest of Torrance.

Hughes started the videotape as the routine started and kept filming as Bob worked through his entire repertoire. As Bob was getting ready to finish off a 4G Cuban 8 maneuver, a red warning "chip light" illuminated in the first half off the maneuver. Bob immediately pulled the nose of the aircraft up to slow it (and keep engine RPM down since he expected the engine propeller governor to fail in short order... which might send the prop revving into a very dangerous "overspeed" condition that could rip the front end of the airplane apart), retain as much altitude as possible, and turned back to Torrance. Bob expected immediate trouble and set into action to counter each of his perceived threats...

Hughes told me that, *"Bob asked me to check my gauges in the back cockpit to see if they were telling me the same things that his were telling him, although while trying to keep the engine running in a way that would keep it from tearing itself to bits. A little while after the chip light came on, I could see that the engine oil temperature was rapidly rising and the oil pressure was falling... not a good sign. Soon the engine temperature was pegged out and the engine started back firing and coughing and running rough. Bob kept trying to pretty much nurse it along and turned back toward the airport. At this point I think we were about seven miles from the coast."*

A chip light is a great little gadget to have in any cockpit... although they seem to be rarer and rarer these days among fixed-wing, piston-powered airplanes. The military, in their wisdom, installed such in the massive T-28... just so that pilots could be warned of impending havoc. The chip detector is a small magnetic probe that senses and warns the pilot of extraneous metallic particles in the engine... or "making metal" as many pilots term the failure. Metal chips and particles are the result of a number of failure modes and of course having that kind of trash ripping through the inside a 1425-hp engine was cause for serious concern... the internal wear and erosion caused by such particles can turn an engine into an expensive and potentially explosive slag heap in just seconds. This concern was Bob's second priority... the first was keeping the airplane in the air until he could find a safe place to land.

"The engine was just eating itself apart, oil pressure drop(ped), engine temperature went above the red line, I had cowl flaps wide open (to cool the engine), and when it started back firing, it would cut out... I started manipulating the mixture control and the primer. Obviously the propeller control had no effect even though I had it full aft (to keep the engine rpm down since the prop governor had failed... an engine "overspeed" is also highly destructive)... I told Ray to declare a May-Day and notify the tower that we were going to attempt to make a straight-in approach from my present location... they said they'd be watching for us."

Hoover was able to climb a few thousand feet by babying the engine and eking whatever thrust he could get out of it since his position would not normally have left enough glide room to get back to the runway... he needed all the altitude he could get... which he would trade for additional room to stretch the glide back to the runway. At some point in this scenario, the Trojan caught fire and Bob eventually wound up shutting the engine down fully, though the prop continued to rotate due to the airflow of their descent (the T-28's prop is also massive and the air blowing past it, kept it turning... much like

what one happens when air is blown through a pinwheel).

Unfortunately, this continued rotation created a tremendous non-aerodynamic "drag" effect and caused the airplane to descend much faster and slow down at a higher rate than would be present with a stopped prop. The aerodynamic effects required a real balancing act on the part of a pilot — who was not only trying to find a place to land, maintain control of the airplane and look for signs of other hazards (like fire...), but to make the second-to-second calculations and trade-offs necessary to accomplish the mission (namely, staying alive, *and* without hurting anyone).

Another complication in this story is the nature of the airplane itself. The Trojan is a flying tank... a big, bulbous airplane with lots of power, lots of weight (nearly five tons), minimal streamlining... and it's a *lousy* glider. It looks as if someone took a huge barrel, stretched it some and stuffed some wings and prop on it. Dainty, it ain't. This airplane was designed for lots of power and, frankly, it needs it.

Bob remembers another judgment he was called upon to render... whether to ditch it in the ocean or try to make the airport. The area around Torrance is heavily, even densely, populated and any attempt to land on anything in the immediate vicinity of the airport was likely to result in severe injuries (at least) to the pilots and possibly to others on the ground. The beach area is not very hospitable to landing and what areas there are often inhabited by folks enjoying the charms of the shoreline... even in January (remember this was *Southern* California). Therefore, as Bob approached the shoreline at speeds nearing 150 mph (just minutes after the onset of the failure), he had to look ahead and judge whether he could make the airport or take the chance of ditching a nearly 10,000-pound airplane in the 60-degree waters of the Pacific... where if he didn't get picked up right away, survival was fairly problematic. Though 60 degrees may sound warm, it isn't... especially when one just can't get out when one chooses.

The reason that I bring up all these factors is simple... Bob was called upon to make hundreds of judgments and decisions in the two to three minutes from the first sight of that alarming chip light to the crossing of the coast line and an imminent landing... or crash. Reaction timing was important (and apparently not a factor here, as Bob apparently hesitated not at all, doing what he had to do and delegating a few other chores to Hughes—showing that he knew enough not to bite off any more than he had to). This mind you, was happening to the same guy that Inspectors Boehler, Kelln, a number of non-flying government-paid Doctors and the all-powerful FAA was trying to tell the entire world was too old to fly... and that he was slowing down in his "old age."

So... how did he make out? Beautifully.

"One of the better landings that I can recall," said Hoover and not a single witness who saw this incident disagrees with that assessment.

Bob elected to keep the landing gear retracted until the last minute to allow the aircraft to fly as efficiently as possible during the critical glide back to the airport. Too soon deployed, the extra drag of the wide and gangly landing gear would have resulted in a forced impact short of the landing area and high probability of injury or death. Too late and the aircraft would belly onto the runway, with the ever-present possibility of significant airframe damage and even a fire (remember now, he had a damaged engine that had reduced itself to slag... and had even been on fire... the resultant belly landing and scraping down a hard runway at over 100 mph was not about to do anyone any good at all).

But Bob made it... he lowered the gear right before crossing the threshold of the

runway, and greased that behemoth to the runway like it was on rails... no kidding... and none too soon. As he crossed the edge of the runway, with the gear just poised to touch down, the engine (with the prop still "wind-milling" reluctantly along) gave up the ghost, and seized *violently*.

That huge three-bladed prop came to a total stop as the internal workings of the engine became so "slagged" and choked with disintegrating metal that no further rotation was possible... and the force of that prop coming to a sudden stop resulted in such incredible physical forces on the aircraft that the entire front of the aircraft-grade, Mil/Spec steel and aluminum airframe was physically *twisted*, wing mounting bolts (the monstrously thick bolts that hold the wings on the airplane!) were compromised, the prop shaft (made of an extraordinary aviation grade of steel that is really tough stuff) physically twisted and almost snapped in two as the aircraft lurched laterally in sympathy with the immense forces involved. Because Bob had sufficient speed to not only land the airplane under full control, but to offer sufficient roll control to counter that momentous lurch, he was able to keep the aircraft level as it settled to the runway. Bob summarized the whole event simply... *"When the engine seized, it was about as violent a reaction as you could get in an airplane... the whole airplane just lurched... and then I kissed it on the wheels... I had plenty of speed so there wasn't any problem with lateral control as a result of the seizure."*

Several years later, with the full import of the danger that they had collectively faced now fading from memory, Hughes called the flight, *"A fascinating, amazing experience... terrifying at the time, (but) looking back on it now I really think it was an invaluable... flying opportunity that gave me the opportunity to see the true importance of experience and skill and staying calm in an emergency... and how that can all benefit you. It was very fortunate of me to have such a very competent pilot and I fear had he not been there that things could have turned out quite different and I really have to credit him with being cool and collected enough to handle things so well and in probably saving my life."*

Hughes laments that his only regret is that, *"as soon as the overspeed started, I shut the camera off, and gave my full attention to the airplane and helping Bob... it's a shame that I didn't think to keep a record of everything that occurred because people would have been amazed at just how smoothly Bob took it all in and dealt with it. Also, the noises and the stuff that was happening with the engine was really dramatic... with every backfire it would blow off great amounts of smoke through the exhaust stacks and would also blow out the carburetor inlet which is right on the top of the cowling where it would cover the cockpit in this dense cloud of smoke and oil and junk flying everywhere. It was quite a ride.*

We literally made the airport by only a few feet... by not putting the landing gear out until he had to and I don't think he even did that until we crossed the edge of the airport boundary, about six feet off the ground... and about two seconds after they came down, the wheels touched the ground. If we'd had another hundred yards to go, I think we wouldn't have made the runway. It was actually an ideal learning situation... because I feel that in the future I can draw from that and maybe Bob's lesson will get to save me again."

It's an amazing story, and it took but a few minutes for the whole drama to transpire. But... the facts of the matter are a mite more complex than the short period

might suggest. Bob wrestled a big, heavy, damaged, and not-too-aerodynamically-gifted airplane back to earth with sound judgment, excellent reactions and consummate skill. Hughes' videotape, though turned off during the worst part of the emergency, was turned on again shortly after the aircraft came to rest, where onlookers were incredulous of the damage done to that monstrous military bird. Gravity, physics, aerodynamics, and metallurgy all conspired to turn that bird into a flaming piece of junk... but Bob Hoover saved it... along with his and Ray's life. The only true tragedy that occurred that day was that there was no one from the FAA there to see it!

Bob wryly notes that he'd *"have given anything if those two guys from Oklahoma City had been there to see it..."*

Countless pilots, including some prominent industry luminaries, who know of this accident shake their heads and more than a few openly wondered whether they might have survived if they had been put in command of such an emergency... but none states that he could have done a better job than Robert Anderson Hoover... the man that Chuck Yeager called *"the best pilot I ever saw."*

Chapter 18

Back to OKC:
The NTSB Hearing–Day One

"A court is a place where what was confused before
becomes more unsettled than ever."
Henry Waldorf Francis

The process of dealing with the FAA when there is a conflict over what they mandate can be a complicated one... especially when it comes time to draw in the National Transportation Safety Board, who serves as the adjudicating agency in disputes with the FAA. As previously noted, when a pilot comes afoul of the FAA, normal jurisprudence goes out the window and a strict and an outwardly unconstitutional set of rules comes into play because all such actions are deemed "Administrative" even though the results that arise often deprive persons/pilots of their rights to life, liberty and the pursuit of happiness.

In an Administrative action before the NTSB, the concept of "Due Process" often seems to be a stranger therein...

Nonetheless, Bob Hoover was finally going to get something of a "day in court" even if it seemed like it might turn out to be of the Kangaroo variety. On December 15, 1993, Bob was granted an emergency hearing. It was to be held before an NTSB Law Judge in OKC on January 13, 1994, barely a month after the final boom was lowered by the FAA on December 14. The hearing was held in Room 1020 of the US Tax Court (such hearings are often held in available Federal and State court buildings) on 420 W. Main St, in Oklahoma City.

The hearing's preliminaries began with the lawyers for the respective sides introducing themselves. Susan Caron, Greg Winton, and Bob Vente were representing the FAA, and John Yodice and F. Lee Bailey were representing Mr. Hoover. NTSB Law Judge William Roger Mullins, a man with an uncommon reputation for fairness, and no particular love for FAA's occasionally excessive machinations, presided over the matter.

As the case got underway, Judge Mullins took charge right from the beginning and laid down the ground rules.

Judge Mullins*: "Let me—before we start, let me go over just a couple of little ground rules that I wish we could—that you would observe.*

First of all, because of the number of attorneys that are in the courtroom, I

don't want to have to be dealing with each of you as you might have urge to jump up and say something. I would like for one designee for each side to sort of do the objecting or responding to objections, and just one of you taking care of examining and/or cross-examining witnesses, unless there is some particular reason that you would let us know in advance. That way the court reporter won't get too confused about who is doing what, and I won't be confused about who I am supposed to be addressing any responses that I might have to.

Second, I would like for you to observe the standard courtroom procedure of each of you will have two shots at a witness, examination, redirect, cross examination, cross-examination.

If there is an objection, the opposing side will have an opportunity to respond. The other side will have an opportunity. The person making the motion will have an opportunity to rebut that response. But I don't want to go on ad infinitum with the objections and the arguments and/or examination of witnesses. And if we could sort of follow those generally and accepted rules of procedure, I would appreciate it."

At this point, Gregory Winton spoke up and indicated that he would be handling objections for the FAA... and was soon to be kept busy doing so.

Some additional paperwork matters were cleared as Judge Mullins cautioned both sides as to their handling of paperwork and evidence, making sure that they note (to Mullins) what they were referring to so the Judge was kept abreast of the data before final arguments.

The FAA also indicated that they would be calling no "fact" witnesses (those who were to testify about specific events and circumstances) but would have a number of expert witnesses who would call upon their expertise to support FAA legal arguments.

At this point, Bailey indicated they he would prefer that the expert witnesses not be privy to the testimony of others (so as not to potentially contaminate their own remarks and findings) and asked that they be separated from the courtroom during such testimony. Mullins consented, though one neurological expert/consultant was allowed to remain in the room to aid the Attorneys as they conducted their case.

Before the reshuffling, the FAA introduced neuropsychologist Dr. Gary Kay, neurologist Dr. John Hastings, and neuropsychologist Dr. Robert Elliott to Judge Mullins. Bailey then introduced neuropsychologist Dr. Antoinette Appel and named her as the Defense consultant who would remain in the courtroom.

Judge Mullins then directed the witnesses, *"Gentlemen, the rule has been requested which requires that you remain outside of the hearing room until such time as you are called to testify. You are admonished that you may not discuss this case with each other or any other person until the hearing is concluded. You are further admonished that on recess, you may discuss it with the attorneys, but you may not discuss it with the attorneys in the presence of the other witnesses,"* whereupon they left the room.

At this point, Bailey brought up one more piece of initial important business that was to have a significant impact on the case and give the FAA's Attorneys a fair amount of heartburn over the next few days.

Bailey: *"We filed a motion asking that Mr. Hoover be permitted to demonstrate now, a year and a half after it was thought that he might be deteriorating, his continued ability*

to function at a very high level. The motion was not responded to, and when we got a ruling from Your Honor, I believe I learned through Mr. Yodice that it was treated as moot, because of no objection.

We went to the expense of bringing the plane down from Peoria, of bringing an instructor up, an American Airlines captain who was an aerobatic specialist, recognized by the FAA, named Leo Loudenslager, and another one from St. Louis to instruct him, and going through all of the routines in order to make Mr. Hoover current, because he has not been allowed to fly since he gave his medical certificate temporarily to Dr. Puskas at the request of Federal Air Surgeon Jon Jordan.

Belatedly, the FAA now comes in says, 'Well, not only would it not be relevant, but we are going to prevent you from doing that by refusing to give you the kind of waiver we have always given Mr. Hoover in the past.'

Winton said this was because of safety considerations — even though one of the finest aerobatic pilots ever to have lived, Leo Loudenslager, would be on board as safety pilot, the FAA, he said, thought it just too risky for Hoover to be the sole manipulator of an aircraft that would be lower than 1500' and going at speeds in excess of 150 mph. He also reiterated that the flight would be irrelevant — the case, he said, was about Hoover's medical qualifications."

Judge Mullins: *"Let me ask you a question. Does the FAA, when it issues a waiver for aerobatic show(s) ever question that individual whether or not he is going to be physically controlling the airplane? And do they ever limit the number of people on board to just one?"*

Winton: *"As far as I know, personal information regarding this issue, we have not issued a waiver for aerobatic flight below 1500' with a passenger on board. Most waivers issued at an airshow type surrounding—"*

Mullins: *"Not a passenger. What about another pilot?"*

Winton: *"Another pilot, not that I am aware of. However, I cannot tell you dispositively (as read from the transcript... we assume he meant "this positively") whether or not that has been issued."*

Bailey: *"You certainly cannot, because I am that pilot. I was the first person ever to fly in the right seat with Mr. Hoover in his airshow. The only other person to have done it was T. Alan McArtor, except for the instructors employed for the case. And I got the waiver from the FAA without even producing a medical, because I had forgotten to bring it to the show."*

Mullins said he did not have the authority to direct the FAA to issue a waiver. He said if it were necessary, Hoover could do the show at 1500', his attorney could videotape it using a zoom lens, and show in Court.

Winton: *"We never received a formal written request for the waiver, just for the record. And secondly, your mention of having a qualified pilot on board, if Mr. Hoover is on board an aircraft, he is considered a passenger, whether he operates the controls of that*

aircraft or otherwise, because he is not qualified to act as pilot in command."

Mullins: *"Is that not in contradiction to some cases that I hear routinely where nonmedically qualified instructor pilots are on board airplanes, giving instruction?"*

Winton: *"They can give instruction. However, they cannot log that time or act as pilot in command during that time. The individual —"*

Mullins: *"Well, I don't think Mr. Hoover is going to log this time or act as pilot in command, if I understand the argument."*

He restated that he didn't have the authority to order to the FAA to give a waiver, and after some discussion about the trial, mostly housekeeping matters, such as how long this trial should take (three days), when they would recess for lunch, etc., went on. "First Blood" was accorded the Administrator's representative, Ms. Caron.

Opening Statement on Behalf of The FAA Administrator

Caron: *"Your Honor, it is not often that we come to an enforcement proceeding where we start off on our opening remarks by praising the Respondent, but in this case, I think everybody in this courtroom probably has been dazzled by Mr. Hoover's performances, and it wasn't easily that we came to these circumstances, and we have taken all that into consideration."*

However, Caron went on to say, none of that was at issue... only his medical qualifications. *"The Administrator is prepared to show with a preponderance of the evidence,"* she continued, *"that Mr. Hoover no longer has those qualifications. We will do that by showing that through the testimony of three competent neuropsychologists, one of them who examined Mr. Hoover and all of whom have vast experience in examining pilots for neuropsychological and cognitive functioning, that his performance on three different sets of neuropsychological functioning is substandard and is contrary to the safe operation of an aircraft during the duration of the certificate."*

She also said that the FAA would present the testimony of two nuclear medicine experts and two neurologists.

Caron: *"We anticipate that much will be done at this hearing to try to distract all of us from the issue that is at hand, and I think that is why it is important that we all stay focused, that the issue here is medical qualification, and that is the only issue."*

Opening Statement on Behalf of the Respondent (Bailey)

Bailey: *While it is seemly that the Administrator has commenced how opening commending the Respondent for perhaps the first time in such proceedings, it is unfortunate that we cannot reciprocate, because, Your Honor, as the evidence will show by an over-*

whelming margin, this case has ugly roots and an ugly track. And at the end of the day, the evidence will show that this is simply an all-out effort to get Mr. Hoover grounded one way or the other for reasons I hope become clear as we litigate.

By way of background, Mr. Hoover has a very extensive background as a test pilot for North American, Rockwell, a demonstration pilot for other manufacturers, and in connection with those duties, developed some 25 years ago a show with a twin-engine plane known as the Aero Commander, later purchased by Rockwell and called the Rockwell Commander, Model 500, designation S. which means Shrike, the last one produced before production was discontinued in the '70s.

This was the first business airplane ever flown by a President of the United States and got considerable publicity when one propeller was removed in Oklahoma City and it was flown to Washington on the other propeller.

Mr. Hoover developed an act at the request of his bosses, to show that while this was a business transportation machine and nothing more, it was one with extremely safe margins between what it was licensed to do in the ordinary operation and what it could do in extraordinary circumstances.

And toward that end, he devised an acrobatic act which involves basically opening the throttles wide at take-off and welding them in the open position, never to be touched again; doing a slow roll on take-off; performing various acrobatic maneuvers, alternately feathering one engine or both; and in a grand finale, coming down at a very high rate of speed, leveling out right over the runway—I shall never forget it—pulling up into a loop; then doing an 8- or 16-point roll; and coming around and landing and stopping in front of the crowd where the airport configuration permitted that, all with the engines feathered for the last part of the act that I have described.

In order to accomplish this, only two modifications were made to the airplane apart from standard issue. Normally if a Rockwell Commander has an engine feathered, the only way to unfeather it is to start the engine with the starter, let the oil pressure build up, and get out in the dome and bring the blades back in a normal operating position.

Because Mr. Hoover had no engines and thus no hydraulic pumps in part of his act, unfeathering accumulators were installed so that by moving a control, he could unfeather the props, and they would start the engines by themselves.

The second modification was a blow-down air bottle. The Aero Commander comes equipped with a back-up landing gear system in case of the hydraulic system such as loss of all the fluid, whereby the landing gear can be lowered and locked in a position with a blast from an air bottle that is kept at a certain pressure in the left engine cell of most of these aircraft.

Mr. Hoover had a modification made so that he had additional blow-down power, because he had to lower his landing gear in the final phase of his act without the engines running. Other than that, it was a standard airplane.

It has become the hallmark of airshows all over the United States. It could be categorized, if tried by an amateur, as a very dangerous piece of flying, not because the maneuvers themselves are so extraordinary, although they are close to the edge without question, but because it is conducted close to the ground. Mr. Hoover, of course, has conducted shows for years and years and years with nary a mishap. That does not mean, however, that there are not malfunctions in the airplane from time to time.

AIR OF INJUSTICE

One of the worst problems since the airplane was not intended to operate inverted or doing rolls is that air may get in the hydraulic system, causing the pumps to cavitate, which in turn will permit the landing gear to leak out of their wells while doing slow rolls. This is a somewhat calamitous event in terms of the air flow over the surfaces, and when that happens, as it did during the relevant air shows, we will show beyond the pale, Mr. Hoover has to interrupt what he is doing and try and get the pumps working again, so that the plane will function normally, and that happened here.

On June 19, 20 and 21, an airshow was conducted in Oklahoma City where many performers were present, and one way or another Your Honor will hear from virtually all of them.

Mr. Hoover did have, as the air boss and his ground handler, Mr. Jim Driskell, who will be a witness in this case, will tell you, problems with the cavitation of the pump, and on one occasion a nose gear light failed to come on, which caused him to abort a landing and go around until he could get a safe indication.

Other than that, the flying that was done, which is recorded, thank goodness, on videotape by a local TV station, which will be available for Your Honor to view, is as good as Mr. Hoover has ever done in the opinions of those who know his flying standards well.

After this series of three days of performances was concluded, Mr. Hoover went on to perform some 33 other airshows before he was ever directed to stop. Now, the most serious part of this case is what will amount one way or the other to gross misconduct, either a violation of Title 18, Section 1001, or negligence in the performance of the duty exposing the public to severe risk.

On August 26, more than two months after these airshows took place, two FAA Inspectors on the same day, apparently with the same typewriter or word processor, and in the same format, sent letters describing Mr. Hoover's performance as erratic, his condition as frail, his personality as sour, and suggesting that he was deteriorating mentally. This is the first record we have ever seen of these complaints. Meanwhile, of course, Mr. Hoover, unaware of all this, continues to fly his airshows.

As a result of these descriptions, which we will show, number one, were at least uninformed since the Inspectors never bothered to question anyone who would have known if there was any reason for a difference in this performance or these performances and the other performances they had seen in years past, including the air boss who knew, other performers on the special frequency who were operating in the waivered zone those days who knew, Mr. Driskell who knew, and the tower, if they had bothered to want to know, or if they had seen anything wrong.

We will show, by the way, the tower has no recollection of anything memorable about the entire event.

Because of these reports allegedly, Mr. Hoover was asked to submit to certain tests which he did in the latter part of 1992. One of the tests was administered by Dr. Robert Elliott who was sitting here when we opened this morning and is now sequestered with the other witnesses.

He found Mr. Hoover's performance in a couple of the tests that will be described to you, I am afraid, in excoriating and excruciating detail to be substandard, and made a comment in his report that a neurological exam would be appropriate to rule out any cognitive defects.

The evidence will show that Dr. Elliott did two things. First of all, he improperly administered one of the tests, using a version which was plainly marked on its face, *Experimental Only*, and declining to use the accepted version.

Number two, Mr. Hoover, who had made plans for the day and had no forewarning of what this was going to entail, was suddenly told that he would be there all day; that he would have to go out and cancel his plans; and the atmosphere for conducting this kind of test was far less than ideal.

Nonetheless, Dr. Elliott merely suggested that a neurologist, not a psychologist like himself, but that a neurologist make appropriate studies to rule out any degeneration that might impair his ability to fly his airplane.

A neurological examination was made by Dr. Michael Gold, all of this under the supervision of Dr. Garrett O'Connor, a psychiatrist, all of these people chosen by the FAA. The Respondent had nothing to do with their selection, nor did they purport to be neutrals.

A Dr. Salcedo ran what is called a SPECT scan. This is an imaging of the brain which in his case is performed by using Ceretec, a nuclear fluid, injecting it into the system and watching it appear in the brain and filming it, much as you may have seen in CAT scans and MRIs and other forms of imaging diagnostic technology.

And he found very minor deviations, and reported them to Dr. Gold. They were not viewed as significant. Dr. O'Connor in viewing the psychological report of Dr. Elliott; the SPECT scan as interpreted by Dr. Gold, the neurologist, issued his opinion: Give the man or let him keep his medical certificate. Mr. Hoover thought that he had survived the ordeal.

On April 14, 1993, when all of this was concluded, Mr. Hoover, Dr. Puskas, a Dr. Hack, I believe; Barton Pakull, who is now the FAA's point man and whose name will swerve around almost every development in this case from this day forward, and the Air Surgeon, Dr. Jordan, got on the telephone. And they said, we are going to deny your medical certificate.

And Mr. Hoover said, 'Well, wait a minute; these people said in their opinion, I am clean.'

Dr. Pakull said, 'These people are only tools; I make the decisions here, and I am saying you can't fly.'

Mr. Hoover said, 'Look, I have done a lot for the FAA over the years; you owe me at least another examination; I am willing to submit to any examination.' The FAA acquiesced, and Mr. Hoover agreed to stop flying during the period of time that it took to conduct this examination and tendered his medical certificate to his air surgeon, Dr. Puskas, who had been examining him for years, and will assure the Court that in his view, Mr. Hoover is perfectly fit to fly. A second battery was arranged. This time Dr. Paul Satz of the University of California in Los Angeles, a, I believe, psychiatrist and neurologist, was given the overall assignment.

A Dr. Mena who does radiology was given the assignment of repeating the SPECT scan, and this time he used two different media. The first was xenon, a gas which is inhaled, and the second was the same Ceretec that was used in the first exam by Dr. Salcedo.

The up — oh, an extensive battery of tests was run by another psychologist, again selected by the FAA, Dr. Uchiyama, I believe his name is.

Once again, Hoover was cleared. Dr. Pakull then went to neuropsychologists

and a neurologist who have extensive ties with the FAA and have had, and enlisted their opinions, which said that Mr. Hoover is impaired, based on the psychological tests that he took.

One of the tests — and I don't know how this is going to wash out, because the position of the FAA has changed considerably from time to time. One of the tests administered originally by Dr. Elliott is called a CogScreen test. Dr. Kay who is sitting over here is a consultant, has considerable knowledge of that, although he himself wrote earlier this year, it is not ready for use.

It is primarily a test of airline pilot-ability being developed. I think it has been sold to a private company recently, and I understand the FAA would like to use it. Whether or not there is any reliance on that, I can't really predict, because we have been told both ways.

To rule out any question about the SPECT scans, we, through Dr. Toni Appel, a psychologist, neuropsychologist from Fort Lauderdale, contacted Dr. Theodore Simon in Dallas, believed by Dr. Appel at least and apparently many others to be a leading authority on SPECT scan interpretation — he is associated with the Cooper Clinic, the nuclear medicine and aerobic institute, as I believe it is called, at 12200 Preston Road in North Dallas.

We asked Mr. Hoover to go out and sign authorizations so that he could get either the originals or prints of — and a negative yields a colored print here, where you see sections as the camera keeps rotating, various directions, and they will be described by Dr. Simon in his deposition.

These finally arrived at his office in two different segments, one set, then the other, late last week. I learned on Friday that he was able to reach a conclusion as a result of that, and arranged to notify the FAA. Yesterday we took his deposition. I have videotaped it, so that Your Honor can view the witness in attempting to determine his credibility. The FAA participated by telephone, and they are clearly heard on the videotape.

The deposition itself, with attendant exhibits, will arrive sometime today, and you will learn that Dr. Simon has ruled out any significance of the neurological examination as it is described in the SPECT scan, except for that which apparently the others failed to consider, even though it is plainly in their report: old trauma.

Mr. Hoover was a prisoner of war for a long period of time, having been shot down over Europe, was in Stalag 1 where he was mistreated physically. He has been in some serious accidents, one in 1947 in an airplane that comes to mind and one much more recently in an automobile.

And although he is not impaired in any way, the evidence of this trauma shows up in the SPECT scan. And Dr. Simon has said it has no bearing upon his ability to function, as the issues in this case are concerned. That testimony will be presented to you.

In addition, one of the FAA's experts from Georgetown, which you will see has sort of taken over this case in a way — oh, one thing ~ want to bring to Your Honor's attention. Up until we engaged a radiologist to read these centigrams as they are sometimes called, the FAA never even bothered to look at them.

They received them yesterday morning by Fed Ex, notified us that two witnesses, one a psychologist and one a neurologist, would be looking at them and might be their witnesses and apparently magically now are coming forward with something help-ful to the FAA. I simply want the Court to understand they showed no interest in these SPECTograms as indicative of anything until we made it plain we were going to bring it to Your Honor's attention in a way that would favor Mr. Hoover.

One of the experts, a Dr. Pincus, expressed the opinion that the neurological exams done by the FAA's own selected neurologists were deficient in several important particulars. No request was made by the FAA for a supplemental neurological exam to address those specific tests, which in Dr. Pincus' view, would relate to cognitive ability and activity in the frontal part of the brain which is essential to Mr. Hoover's function.

Mr. Hoover flew in the Reno Air Races with another at the controls as safety pilot for the racers, as he has often done in the past. The evidence will show that his vast experience with trouble — and bear in mind, his whole act is one emergency after an-other—that is what he is there to demonstrate.

But experience has shown that his whole history with solving problems in the air has been invaluable from time to time when these racers, running around at power settings that are punishing their engines and sometimes cause them to blow up and all other malfunctions, can be extremely helpful in talking them down to the ground in the best possible condition. And that is what he was doing out there.

There he met for the first time Dr. Brent Hisey, a neurologist from Oklahoma City, who is Air Surgeon to an Air National Guard unit here that flies F-16s, and a pilot himself. And he learned of Mr. Hoover's difficulties and the fact that doctors were clear-ing him and the FAA was running out and getting people to contradict them.

And he said, 'Look, I don't work for the FAA; I don't have any ties to them. If you shouldn't be flying, you shouldn't be flying; I will be the first to tell you so. But I will give you an exhaustive and complete neurological examination, and I will arrange for a col-league, Dr. David Johnsen, to give you the battery of psychological tests which could be helpful to the diagnosis.'

And this fall those tests were performed, including every single one of the items listed by Dr. Pincus as deficient in the first battery of tests.

Drs. Hisey and Johnsen will testify, as will Dr. Appel, that there is nothing wrong with Mr. Hoover; that there is no evidence upon which one could conclude that he is impaired in any way, and that to disregard the continuing high level of performance of his motor skills and completely subjugate them to theories of psychological testing which have never been visited on any airman, are not used to screen out candidates for flying jobs, are not used on airline pilots, and have given rise to a tremendous amount of specu-lation in this case — and I am not sure this is shown, all by the party with the burden of proof.

The testimony will be very solid that there is nothing wrong with this man, and he is more than fit to fly. Now, he has been, after signing contracts in reliance on the fact that he passed all their tests and thought he was in good shape until he learned that Dr. Pakull viewed these people as only tools and in no way binding on him, signed a bunch of contracts this summer for air show performances, and had to cancel them all because the FAA continues to hold his certificate.

We tried to resolve it in an amicable way, with constant visits with the FAA, negotiations and talks, and when that failed, we demanded the certificate back. They revoked it the next day, and that gave rise to the complaint that is now before you, Your

Honor.

But I will say that at the end of the day— and reports have continued to be generated by all of the experts who have never seen Mr. Hoover, but who are supportive of Dr. Pakull's determination to keep him on the ground, now suggesting without any precedent whatsoever that even though he is normal for a man of 71, he should be judged as a 40-year-old, or at least that should be given some thought. That will come before you as a proposition of law somewhere in the case.

I would suggest to you, Your Honor, that at the conclusion of the case, you will have the gravest of doubts as to the credibility of the claims made by the original Inspectors on August 26, 1992, of aberrational conduct, and the gravest of doubts as to the effort that has gone into the single-minded purpose of keeping Mr. Hoover on the ground, no matter what the medical evidence keeps coming up with. Thank you."

Chapter 19

The FAA Goes On the Attack With Dr. Elliott

If the first button of one's coat is wrongly buttoned, all the rest will be crooked.
Giordano Bruno

Dr. Robert Elliott Testifies

Elliott was called as an expert witness for the complainant, the FAA. Elliott, whose curriculum vitae is seemingly a mile long, took the stand on the first day of the NTSB hearing - January 13, 1994.

Elliott received his BS in Psychology from California State University at Pepperdine and his doctorate in counseling psychology from the University of South Carolina. He boasted that he was a fellow in the National Academy of Neuropsychology and a Diplomat in the American Board of Neuropsychology ... one of only 14 people in the US to hold diplomat status in both boards. But all of his credentials and awards and lines on his resume never prepared him for Bob Hoover, F. Lee Bailey... or the truth.

The FAA wanted to make it clear at the top that Elliott was no stranger to aviation. In addition to being a consultant for the FAA, the good doctor had served as a consultant for various airlines since 1976, evaluating pilots for fitness for duty. As a matter of fact, Elliott testified that he spent 50% of his time examining airmen.

According to Elliott, his tie-in with Hoover came at the request of Dr. Garrett O'Connor, a psychiatrist/FAA consultant in Los Angeles. Elliott said O'Connor examined Hoover and subsequently expressed concerns about some clinical matters and therefore felt further evaluation was necessary.

Elliott explained on the stand that O'Connor indicated to him there had been an allegation that Hoover had had some difficulty in a *"particular airshow"* and that two FAA observers had noted *"some maneuver & other difficulties"* and that those were *"justifiable enough that he needed to be evaluated..."*

Shortly thereafter, apparently, Elliott and Hoover spoke on the phone and arranged a time to meet. The meeting took place at Elliott's office. After three hours of talking about various subjects (from incidents with the FAA to his career to his medical and family history and more), Elliott said, they finally commenced neuropsychological testing.

After an attempt to enter a seemingly endless array of exhibits (to which Judge Mullins said that, in essence, he didn't have time to read a million pages), the prosecution finally attempted to tender the document "Comprehensive Norms for an Expanded Halstead-Reitan Battery", published by Psychological Assessment Resources, authored by Robert Heaton, Igor Grant, and Charles Matthews — a document to which he would refer for the remainder of his testimony.

Again, Bailey objected... *"I think this is an imposition. Just to load up the record; no quality, just quantity."* Judge Mullins agreed. The prosecution was told to direct Elliott to specific pages, introducing only those. After all this was agreed upon, Elliott explained Heaton's norms — which, he said, were *"an attempt to establish levels of proficiency for individuals ... in certain ages with specified amount of education."* ...Although Elliott quickly admitted that the task of a pilot is not addressed anywhere in the Heaton norms.

The Reitan norms, evidently, are more stringent than the Heaton norms, with a single point cut-off: either you're brain damaged or you're not, according to Reitan — no matter what your age or level of education. Elliott said for Hoover, in order to assess neuropathology, he used both sets of norms.

Elliott was then questioned about all neuropsychological tests given to Hoover. **Weschler Adult Intelligence Scale, Revised** — measures overall level of functioning, as well providing information on verbal and motor performance skills specifically. Hoover, Elliott said, performed at an average or — when working with his hands and more visual kinds of processes, his performance was above-average (when compared to others his age, Elliott testified).

Trailmaking Test - assesses a person's ability to sequence/sequencing skills. Requires motor skills and adequate attention span. Interestingly, the judge noted that the evidence described the results of this test as "nonsignificant" and subsequently asked, *"Why are we talking about it, if it is nonsignificant?"*

Elliott attempted to explain this away by saying that compared to others the same age and with the same education as Hoover (how his score was looked at for the Weschler test — with Heaton norms), Hoover scored in the nonsignificant range... but when compared to pilots and the general population, Hoover was impaired — severely impaired, he went on to say.

Booklet Category Test - assesses a person's ability to think through a problem and use feedback to change a mode or response style to solve a problem. For example, on the easiest task, you have a series of Roman numerals, and you have to match the correct number with the correct Roman numeral. There are seven subtests within this test, and within each subtest the task remains the same, but the stimuli progressively changes a little. You need to keep up with the reasoning process to solve the problem. Additionally, memory is tested at the end, asking you to remember the processes employed earlier on.

When looking at the results, the prosecution said that the copy of the protocol - Hoover's performance on this test — looked *"like mumbo-jumbo..."*

"We accept that definition," Bailey said.

Elliott then went on to explain the protocol, per the prosecution's request — testifying that his performance in this test was *"very impaired"* and slow... going on to say that his performance was *"as bad as I have seen in terms of performance in a pilot in my 20-some years in evaluating pilots."*

Ray Osterrieth Complex Figure Test - assesses person's ability to look at a design, repli-

cate the design, and then, unannounced, replicate the design after 30 minutes. Hoover's performance was satisfactory.

Rey Auditory-Verbal Learning Test – assesses short-term, immediate, and long-term memory. Also looks at person's ability to learn over time — the learning curve. Person is orally given a list of 15 words and then asked to repeat them back, in no particular order. Hoover remembered two and also gave two that weren't on the list. Elliott stressed that this was particularly important — but what wasn't discussed and what I wondered about was this: were the *"intrusions"* (Note: the words not on the list) variations of words that were on the list? Or did they rhyme?

He did, however, try this test five times, and remembered seven words in that trial. Although Elliott stressed that Hoover's performance was poor and that it showed a poor learning curve, he admitted that, according to Heaton norms, his performance was *"nonsignificant."*

Wisconsin Card Sorting Test –computer test. The person is given a series of four designs at the top of the computer screen and a series of "essentially the same cards" below that. By use of the computer keys, you move the card off the bottom of the screen below one of the four cards at the top, which remain the same throughout the whole test. They are matched in terms of color or form or number and you have to figure that out. After every response, the computer tells you whether it was a correct or incorrect response through a beep or a buzz. Elliott was stopped here — before he discussed Hoover's performance on this test — by Bailey with a request for a voir dire, as he felt this test was inadmissible.

"It (the test) has been computerized by the owner of the test and described as a research edition and still is. Isn't that correct?" asked Bailey.

"The current edition of the test is designated as a computer version, not a research edition," responded Elliott. Shortly thereafter, Bailey said, *"I am going to suggest to you, Doctor, that this program has never been shipped as a non-research version according to the company that owns it, and ask you whether or not you can demonstrate to the contrary. I am holding a manual that was just sent to us, and it says, Research Edition."*

Even after this statement, Elliott was quite firm in his opinion that this was not the case. The doctor then explained that this test assesses a person's ability to use logic and reasoning to figure out how to sort categories. Hoover's score, according to Elliott, was *"significantly impaired."*

After this, the prosecution finally turned over the raw data on this test, and Bailey asked for another voir dire. Bailey began telling the doctor and the court what to look at. *"...The page I am trying to get you to look at, Doctor, says Wisconsin Card-Sorting Test, Computer Version 2, Research Edition."*

Elliott: *" That is correct."*

Bailey: *"Why does the test itself say that that is what it is? The computer printed that out, didn't it?"*

Elliott: *"That is correct. The -"*

Bailey: *"Are you saying the computer lied?"*

Elliott tried to explain this by saying that after Hoover took the test, he inputted the responses into the computer and the information/report generated by this – which gave him information on age-and-education-corrected scores – is what said *"research edition"* (later saying that this information wasn't available at the time he administered the test).

Bailey: *"Why did you include this in your report? You have just told us a little earlier, whether you realize it or not, that you did not use a research edition in testing Mr. Hoover."*

After direct examination resumed, and Elliott explained how impaired Hoover's performance was in this test, Bailey again interrupted. *"Excuse me. Your Honor, may I interrupt? We have just spoken with the manufacturer, and they are willing to send a letter that they have never shipped anything but a research version."*

Even after this, the prosecution insisted upon discussing Hoover's results in this test before going on to the next test.

Boston Naming Test – measures verbal fluency. Hoover did "fine."

Weschler Memory Scale, Revised Version – Memory test. Elliott described Hoover's performance as "variable."

Controlled Oral Word Association Test – *"generate as many words as you can that start with the letter F,"* for example. Hoover did *"very well."*

Finger-Tapping Test –assesses fine motor coordination and response speed. This is a little counter with a finger-tapping lever - person has to tap as rapidly as possible. Elliott said Hoover's performance suggested significant impairment.

The prosecution then stated that they had just covered ten different neuropsychological tests and only "three-and-a-half" showed significant impairment...

"How can you make a neurological assessment when only three out of ten appear to reflect significant results using the Heaton norms?" Bailey asked.

Elliott explained that response time, clinical observations, and the peaks and valleys in his performance were all taken into account.

But the prosecution wasn't done yet. They began to ask Elliott to describe another neuropsychological test battery he had administered, the CogScreen... but Bailey quickly jumped in, objecting to any evidence whatsoever relating to the CogScreen.

Bailey explained that it is an experimental test, and they had been told it would not be used in the case. *"...Mr. Hoover took it because this witness told him it was experimental, and he was trying to sell it to the FAA... It was unfair to tell Mr. Hoover that it was experimental and then to use it against him."*

The objection was sustained.

Judge Mullins: *"...It is experimental. He has read from a treatise here that it doesn't have any validity, at least established validity in the medical field. It is experimental only. I don't want to hear anything about it... I have ruled, Counsel. Let's move on."*

The Prosecution then asked Elliott to reflect on all of the results from all of the tests — except the CogScreen, of course — and what they said about Hoover. Elliott said that the tests showed he was an individual *"who has difficulty in reasoning process and thinking through situations, particularly in situations that are novel, that if you start changing the parameters of the problem that he is exposed to, he has increased difficul-*

ties as the complexity increases." He also said Hoover was slow and had trouble *"following what the continuity of the problem is."*

Interestingly, prosecution then asked if Elliott was making a recommendation to an airline based on similar scores (as Hoover's), *"what recommendation would you make to an airline regarding fitness for duty?"*

Elliott: *"I would say based on this information that I have that this is a person who is showing evidence of cognitive deficits and not suitable for flight fitness."*

Again, Bailey objected. *"Excuse me, Your Honor. On reflection, I move to strike that. We are not dealing with an airline here, and that is not what he told Garrett O'Connor. He never suggested he wasn't fit to fly, and what he would tell an airline is irrelevant. This is not an airline pilot."*

Judge Mullins concurred: *"I think the objection is well-founded. This is not a commercial airline test that we are going through today. It is whether or not he is qualified to hold any medical certificate issued by the FAA, and that is not the questions that counsel asked."*

Prosecution then changed the question around, and Elliott testified that Hoover was not medically certifiable. The recommendations to Garrett O'Connor, however, were only that he should be referred to a neurologist to identify or screen out neuropathology or any sort of degenerative disease process — not if he should lose his medical.

Next, Elliott was asked to testify about testing done on Hoover by another physician, Dr. Craig Uchiyama at UCLA. Uchiyama administered a series of personality and neuropsychological tests, including the Mini-Mental Status Exam, the WAIS-R, the CALCP Computerized Reaction Time Test, Trailmaking test, Wisconsin Card Sorting Test, Boston Naming Test, Verbal Fluency Test, Ray Osterrieth Complex Figure, Hooper Visual Organization, Weschler Memory Scale, the Rey Auditory-Verbal Learning Test, Finger Oscillation Test (finger tapping test, same as Elliott's), the Dynameter Test, and the Minnesota Multiphasic Personality Inventory, the sentence completion test, draw-a-person test, Thematic Apperception Test, and Bender-Gestalt. (Some of these tests were new; others were the same ones given by Elliott.)

Hoover showed improvement on the tests that Elliott had previously given him (the Wisconsin Card Sorting Test, for example), showed *"significant improvement,"* but Elliott said this was due to *"practice effect,"* which means a person should improve on subsequent testings. He also said the tests done at UCLA continued to show evidence of cognitive dysfunction.

Dr. Uchiyama said Hoover's results provided some risk signs and some impairment. He recommended the reinstatement of Hoover's license for a temporary time while Hoover continued current medical and neuropsychological status monitoring. Elliott was then asked about the testing done by Dr. David Johnsen - and the prosecution made a big point (they had had Elliott look over Johnsen's vitae) that Johnsen was a clinical psychologist, not a neuropsychologist.

Hoover had taken some tests with Johnsen that he had taken with Elliott and Uchiyama - the Category Test, the Trailmaking Test, and the Wisconsin Card-Sorting Test. Johnsen also administered the California Verbal Learning Test, a test Hoover had never taken before.

Elliott testified that this was not adequate testing and that any improvement on

the ones he had previously taken would be due to "practice effect" (i.e., the more you do something, "by practicing", the better you get at it). Also in Johnsen's report was some criticism of Elliott's test methods - aspects of testing that he felt could compromise the validity of the performance. Hoover had told Johnsen that he was upset because the testing took much longer than expected (which necessitated a change in previously-made plans) and Hoover said he was not given any breaks. Elliott said he did not agree with these criticisms –that Hoover was given breaks and the opportunity to discontinue testing and come back later to finish.

Johnsen also asserted, in his report, that Hoover may have felt anxiety about these tests – and that his performance on them could determine his ability to fly – and that could have affected the results. Elliott, of course, then asserted that Hoover had not exhibited any signs of anxiety. Dr. Johnsen's conclusion was that Hoover was not suffering from any significant cognitive dysfunction — with which, of course, Elliott disagreed. Then the prosecution raised an interesting question. *"Much has been made so far... about Mr. Hoover's ability to perform on subsequent flights after a certain point. Do you have any explanation how someone with this type of impairment could still function at a certain task level?"*

Elliott: *"Yes. Mr. Hoover is obviously a gifted aviator that has been doing the routines that he has been involved in (at) airshows for a period of 30 years plus. We know in psychology and neuropsychology that somebody who has practiced, even sometimes a complex skill, over a long period of time is likely to maintain that skill, sometimes even with cognitive impairment apparent."*

However, Elliott then went on to say that he *"would project that given a novel situation that he has not yet encountered, that there is a high likelihood that we would see the impairment having an effect on his performance."* Elliott finished his testimony by repeating his beliefs that Hoover had a neurological condition and that this condition makes him unable to safely perform his duties/exercise his privileges of his airmen's certificate and that he believed this condition would still be present two years from now - and that his opinion was based on Hoover's case history and *"appropriate medical judgment relating to his neuropsychological condition."*

The Cross-Examination of Dr. Elliott

Bailey, upon cross-examination of Elliott, quickly went for the jugular vein.

Bailey: *"I take it that your Marine aviation position had very little to do with the operation of airplanes."*

To this, Elliott explained he was a mechanic so the position had a lot to do with the operation of airplanes. Next, Bailey said: *"Do you fly an airplane?"*

"Yes, I do."
"How long have you had a license?"
"I have a student pilot's license."
"A student pilot's license."
"Yes."

(The above exchange simply set the stage for Bailey to take away from Elliott's

credibility to judge a pilot's ability to safely fly an airplane.) Bailey then asked how many pilots Elliott had examined had been trained as test pilots and for whom Elliott had tested them, to which Elliott replied a couple dozen, for some aircraft manufacturers, Boeing, McDonnell Douglas, Lockheed, and some military test pilots. Elliott said these pilots had been assessed for the Age 60 Rule, and Hoover commented that the Age 60 Rule has application to and only to commercial airline pilots.

"How many of these pilots were denied a medical based on your recommendation for impairments such as the kind you claim here?" asked Bailey.

Elliott: *"None."*

Bailey: *"Not a single one. Mr. Hoover is the first of his class, isn't he?"*

Elliott: *"What do you mean by class?"*

Bailey: *"The first test pilot for whom you have ever recommended today, not in your original report, of course, but today that he not be allowed to fly. He is the first one, isn't he?"*

Elliott: *"Other pilots that I have assessed in the past have been test pilots at points in their career."*

Bailey: *"And how many of those — I asked you before, and you said none — did you recommend be grounded, to put it in simple terms?"*

Elliott: *"None."*

Bailey: *"Now let's go to aerobatic pilots. How many of those do you know?"*

Elliott: *"I don't think I specifically when I have evaluated pilots asked them whether they were aerobatic qualified."*

Bailey: *"How many pilots who are aerobatic specialists have you tested to your knowledge? I suggest the answer is none."*

Elliott: *"Are you asking me?"*

Bailey: *"Yes."*

Elliott: *"The answer is I don't know."*

Bailey: *"You mean, they may have slipped by without you realizing they were aerobatic specialists?"*

Elliott: *"Pilots that I have assessed may have been aerobatic pilots, but the question wasn't asked."*

Bailey: *"Ah, so obviously then you have never concentrated on this specialty in flying in your testing procedures, prior to Mr. Hoover, have you?"*

Of course, Elliott had no choice but to agree with Bailey – was there any other choice? Next, Bailey asked Elliott if he ever had any personal familiarity with manipulating aircraft controls, other than as a student pilot – to which he answered he had had a few hours in simulators — and if he had ever studied the requirements of an aerobatic pilot – to which Elliott responded (no surprise) that he had made no personal studies.

Bailey then tackled another interesting angle, asking Elliott what discipline he believed instructors are supposed to inculcate in private pilots. Elliott didn't understand the question, so Bailey said, *"Is your instructor trying to teach you to follow the rules? (by "rules", Bailey meant the handbook, the FAR's, and the limitations of the aircraft.)*

Elliott said, *"Of course."*

Bailey followed this by asking for agreement that the same held true for commercial pilots – i.e. that they had to be taught to follow the rules - whatever all the rules might be.

Bailey: *" Would you agree that commercial pilots are trained rigorously and religiously, but also trained in simulators only to be prepared to confront an emergency and to deal with it?"*

Elliott: *"They are trained to handle situations that have been — that they have been prepared for. There may be situations that they may encounter that are not — they have not been trained for."*

Bailey: *"But is it not the daily regimen of the airline captain, based on your long experience that you claim with these people, to fly the routine and avoid the emergency?"*

Elliott: *"That is their goal. That is correct."*

Just where was Bailey going with this line of questioning? Read on. You'll see.

Bailey: *" No, would you take a look, please, at the history of test pilots. Do you know what they do?"*

Elliott responded that he did, *"generally speaking,"* and that he had known probably dozen or two test pilots.

Bailey: *"And have you discussed with them at some length the things that they do as opposed to commercial airline pilots who follow schedules and routines whenever they can?"*

Elliott said he had talked to some about that.

Bailey: *"Who writes the books that require other pilots to follow the limitations? Do you know?"*

Elliott: *"The FAA."*

Bailey: *"Is that what you think?"*

Elliott: *"That the FAA writes the books that set up the rules and regulations, yes."*

Bailey: *"For each aircraft. Who writes the handbook for —"*

Elliott: *"Oh, the manufacturer."*

Bailey: *"The manufacturer, for FAA approval hopefully down the line. Where does the data come from that describes the parameters that find their way into these books?"*

Elliott: *"It comes from pilots that have tested the equipment."*
     This, of course, is exactly what Bailey wanted Elliott to say –that it was test pilots like Hoover who made up the rules! Satisfied that he made his point, Bailey changed his line of questioning, next asking if there were cases during Elliott's testing of Hoover where Hoover was slow but accurate. Elliott said yes.

Bailey: *"Do you understand that a test pilot does not have a handbook to guide him?"*
     Elliott said no, he didn't understand that, so Bailey explained:

Bailey: *"Well, if nobody has written a handbook on a brand new airplane, it is very diffi-cult to read it and understand where the limits are, isn't it? Do you understand that question?"*
     After Elliott agreed that he understood this, Bailey continued, *"Do you under-stand that this a far different regimen than the bus driver who is driving a commercial airline?"*

Elliott: *"There are aspects of the job that are similar, and there are aspects that are different."*

Bailey: *"All right. Tell me about the similarities, and then we will get to the differences. What is similar between a test pilot, flight testing a new prototype to deliver data to the manufacturer, and a fellow who is flying American Airlines from Dallas to LA every day?..."*

Elliott: *"The major similarity would be they are both operating similar kind of system; they are flying the same – generally speaking, flying the same air space. They are flying under some of the same regulations."*
     When asked the differences, Elliott said that test pilots are pushing the aircraft to its limits. Bailey then pushed things a little farther. *"Now tell me about the articles that have been published on the subject of test pilots who have taken batteries of tests similar to the ones you have given."*
     Elliott couldn't.

Bailey: *"Well, certainly in preparation for this case, knowing the issues to be decided and the nature of the Respondent, you looked for them didn't you?"*

Elliott: *"My primary focus was on establishing whether there was cognitive deficits in an*

individual that had been referred to me, not to establish his flight performance."

Bailey: *"Is it your position that no matter how well Mr. Hoover flies for the next ten years, even if it is flawless, that we should yield to your paper and pencil tests and determine him to be unfit today?"*

Elliott: *"I think medical fitness is the issue that I should stand on, regardless of his flight proficiency."*

Next, Bailey asked how many airmen had ever been grounded from aerobatics for turning out results similar to the tests given by Elliott to Hoover.

Elliott: *"I can't cite that."*

Bailey, of course, wasn't ready to let up. *"And you have no explanation for the fact, I take it, that over the last year and a half, when he is supposed to have been deteriorating, his flying skills have remained at peak performance, should that be evidence."*

Elliott: *"I think that it is very apparent again that we have a very over-practiced skill that Mr. Hoover is very good at, and I think that certainly speaks to that issue."*

Bailey: *"...your view is that if he should be surprised in the air by something he hadn't experienced and hadn't expected, that he might not be able to think fast enough and clearly enough to deal with the situation effectively. Is that what you meant to say?"*

Elliott agreed that was an accurate statement.

Bailey: *"Thank you. Now, where were you last Wednesday night, Doctor?"*

Elliott: *"I was in Redondo Beach."*

Bailey: *"Do you know where Mr. Hoover was?"*

Of course, Elliott did not know... so Bailey told him... boy, did he tell him.
Where was he?
Ten miles out over the Pacific, practicing for the trial, when the engine malfunctioned and an emergency descended upon himself and the pilot in command. With consummate skill, Bailey said he brought the aircraft back to Torrance Airport and set it *"on the numbers,"* whereupon the aircraft *"destroyed itself on the spot."*

Bailey: *"Well, now, that wouldn't really square, assuming all of this is proven up to the satisfaction of the Court, with the speculation on your part that this fellow is not good at handling the unexpected, would it?"*

Elliott was firm, however –refusing to give in.

Bailey: *"If he goes out and solves new and bizarre emergencies every day of the week for the next ten years, you are not going to change, are you, Doctor?"*

Elliott: *"The information I have is what I rely upon at this time."*

It took a couple of tries, but Bailey finally got an answer to his next question:

"...you can't cite a single example where you can trace these alleged defects to failure to perform any aerobatics or testing, can you?"

The answer, as you may imagine, was that he couldn't think of such a case.

Next, Bailey questioned Elliott about the telephone conversation he had with Hoover prior to their scheduled meeting. *"Isn't it true that you told Mr. Hoover that he could expect to spend about four hours testing?"*

Elliott: *"No."*

Bailey: *"Can you think of any other reason he would have arranged with his wife to leave at noon to go to Palm Springs where he has a home?"*

Basically, Elliott wouldn't comment on this, but, seemingly satisfied he had made his point, Bailey went on... not in any specific direction, mind you — rather, in several... obviously opening doors for later points.

The subjects of these questions included everything from in what esteem the FAA held him to how he became acquainted with Bart Pakull of the FAA to how he dictated his reports to his role in the Age 60 (for airline pilots) rule to how Elliott had received the history of the alleged aberrational flying by Mr. Hoover to who had recommended Elliott to examine Hoover — Garrett O'Connor or Bart Pakull. And then he went back to the reports of Hoover's "history" — including the report from O'Connor and the FAA Inspectors who reported about Hoover's flying at the airshow in question.

Bailey: *"Do you remember anything about them (the reports), something that struck you?"*

Elliott: *"No."*

Bailey also asked if Elliott had known, prior to being assigned the case, what type of flying Hoover did at airshows. Elliott testified that he knew he was an aerobatic pilot who had done some *"very unique stunts and was well known for those..."*

Back to the reports. *"Now, when you read these reports by these two Inspectors, to what extent did you accept their observations as germane to the studies you intended to do?"*

Elliott said they were *"just another piece of information that I considered."*

Bailey: *"Did you know whether or not these were experienced observers of airshows of this type?"*

Elliott: *"No, I did not."*

Bailey: *"Did you notice that they alleged personality changes, that he was not getting along with people, relying on staff to answer questions, and things of that sort, that would be of interest to you?"*

Elliott: *"I made–I remember there were some comments about more psychological aspects. Correct."*

Bailey: *"Do you remember thinking, 'If all these things are true, this fellow could be dangerous if he continues to do airshows'?"*

Elliott: *"My mind didn't think in that way, no"*

Bailey: *"Didn't think in that way, and you probably didn't take note of the fact that these minions of the FAA took two months and three days to notify anybody about this very difficult situation. You didn't know that."*

Elliott: *"No, I didn't."*

Bailey: *"Well, sir, if you read the report, I suggest you did know it, because it was dated August 26 in both cases; both were typed in the same typewriter. They mirrored each other, and they described incidents on June 19, 20, and 21. Did you note that?"*

Elliott: *"It wasn't relevant to the issue why I was seeing Mr. Hoover."*

Bailey: *"Didn't you think it somewhat alarming that this fellow, who apparently had been detected in a rapidly degenerating condition, was still out there flying? Or did you know?"*

Elliott: *"Well, at the time he made the appointment, I didn't know."*
Bailey then commented that Elliott did, however, know, *"the minute you started talking with him;"* Elliott agreed with this statement.

Bailey: *"He told you, first of all, that he had an explanation for problems he had had with his airplane when they were making the observations. He told you that. Right?"*
Elliott agreed.

Bailey: *"You got no corroboration from anywhere other than the two Inspectors that what Mr. Hoover said was anything less than the gospel truth, did you?"*
Again, he agreed.

Bailey: *"My next question is: when he gave you a rational explanation for aberrational flying, if we call it that, did you accept it or reject it?"*

Elliott: *"I noted it."*

Bailey: *"Did it make any difference to you whether he was telling the truth or whether the Inspectors were telling the truth, since obviously they couldn't both have been telling the truth?"*
Elliott said it was not his responsibility to judge the legitimacy of the truthfulness of either party. Next, Bailey asked Elliott if he had felt his responsibility to re-evaluate Hoover was very serious, both to the FAA and the public; Elliott said he did.

Bailey: *"Is it your position today that when you concluded your examination, you were*

satisfied that this person who was in the business of performing highly delicate aerobatic maneuvers was impaired to do so?"

Elliott asked him to repeat the question.

Bailey: *"You have testified here today he is not fit to hold a second class medical certificate, have you not?"*

Elliott: *"That is correct."*

Bailey: *"All right. Was that your position on October 30, 1992, when you reported to Dr. O'Connor your findings and said only, 'We should rule out neurological damage'?"*

Elliott: *"That was not my recommendation at the — I mean, that was — my statement at the time was that we should be referring him for a neurological evaluation."*

Bailey continued by quoting verbatim from Elliott's own report, which noted the original Inspectors' reports and that *"Mr. Hoover has reasonable explanations for each of these allegations."* Elliott's report also noted that Hoover had indicated to him that he had flown successfully in several airshows after the one in question.

Bailey: *"So you must have appreciated the fact that from June 19, 20, and 21, 1992, until the day you saw him, he was out flying airshows. Correct?"*

Elliott agreed.

Bailey: *"Was it your understanding that these airshows were flown in such a way that the public might be in jeopardy from (his) cashing it in halfway through a loop?"*

Elliott: *"I didn't know the nature of the airshows."*

Bailey: *"Weren't you concerned?"*

Elliott: *"At the particular point, I can't say that — that was not on my mind."*

Bailey appeared amazed — the public could be at risk, but it *wasn't* on Elliott's mind... obviously making a point here.

Bailey: *"With all your experience in aviation, are you telling us you didn't appreciate the fact that they (the FAA) were asking you whether he was fit to fly in your opinion?"*

Elliott: *"That was not what I was asked."*

Bailey continued quoting from Elliott's report, which then said that Hoover's tests indicated that he was performing in the *"mild to moderately impaired range."*

Bailey: *"Now, have you ever related any of these mild to moderately impaired functions to the business of flying a twin engine airplane through aerobatics?"*

Elliott said that those skills were standard and contained in literature that talks about tasks involved in flying. Bailey then asked if someone in the cockpit with Hoover would have noticed *"something going on"*, to which Elliott replied, *"Not necessarily."*

Bailey: *"So even though you can see it, the rest of the world cannot, because his flying continues to be flawless. Is that your position?"*

Elliott testified that because flying was a well-practiced skill to Hoover, problems in his cognitive functioning would not necessarily have been noticed by anyone else.

Bailey wasn't through yet. *"Then you pass the football in essence, don't you? You say in your recommendation 'I can't make a determination as to whether or not there is neuropathology or degenerative disease present. He should be referred to a neurologist who can rule it out.' Right?"*

Elliott agreed.

Bailey: *"I don't see anywhere in here where you warn the FAA that this man in your opinion was so impaired that he wasn't fit to fly. Do you see it?"*

Elliott: *"I was not contacted by the FAA at this point. I was responding to Dr. Garrett O'Connor."*

To this, Bailey reminded him — by citing two specific places — that Elliott's own report mentioned the FAA: *"You knew he was there for an FAA evaluation,"* he said.

Bailey: *"Did you on October 30, Dr. Elliott, have an impression that this man was a danger to himself or the public if he continued to perform aerobatics?"*

Elliott: *"I had not fully formed my opinion at that time."*

Hmmm... Interesting. Bailey then asked him if he had seen Hoover since that time, or if he had given him any further tests — and he had done neither. He then asked him if he had spoken to any of the other physicians who had examined Hoover. Elliott had spoken to three: O'Connor and Dr. Bert Puskas, who was then identified as the flight surgeon who had given Hoover his second class medical and who had never requested that it be withdrawn.

The third was Dr. Mike Gold, who was the neurologist who, as Bailey put it, *"is the guy who did what you recommended: rule out degenerative process, isn't he?"*

Bailey: *"Now, have you filed a subsequent report saying what I forgot to say or wasn't asked to say or for some reason didn't say was this guy should be grounded? Have you filed such a report?"*

Elliott had not.

Bailey: *"When did somebody come to you and say, 'We need something a little tougher in your opinion, Doctor, than what you wrote?' Was that recent?"*

Elliott did not know an exact date, but Bailey requested that he look through his notes to provide this when he took the witness stand the next day. Elliott said he would "attempt to."

The hearing was then recessed to allow for a flight exhibition by Hoover — accompanied by Leo Loudenslager — as one way to show his fitness for flight. The flight was witnessed by, among others, the lawyers on behalf of complainant and respondent and Judge Mullins. The hearing reconvened the next morning... and the fight started anew...

Chapter 20

The Morning After...

Few things are harder to put up with than the annoyance of a good example.
Mark Twain (Samuel Clemens)

Hoover's flight demonstration went well. Flawlessly, in fact. With World Aerobatic Champ Leo Loudenslager flying as safety pilot, Hoover put on the same routine that he had for years, and with precious little practice beforehand, making him about as "rusty" as he had ever been in his life – not the best circumstances for a critical demonstration. Still, it went well and it was a quiet group of Feds who filed back into court the next day, not thrilled with the fact that Hoover's excellence in the air would obviously impact their case. As soon as the proceedings were back on the record, Mr. Winton had an objection.

Winton: *"Your Honor, the Administrator objects to your consideration of any of the flight performance demonstration that was conducted yesterday."*

Winton's reasons for this were that the flight demonstration was not relevant to the issue of Hoover's medical qualifications. Additionally, he said that the probative value was outweighed by the unstructured viewing, the lack of rules and regs with regard to the viewing, and — this is a biggie — *"the fact that the listed witnesses which were supposed to be or will be testifying here today were present yesterday, discussing their testimony with Your Honor without the presence of the Administrator's counsel, without the full and adequate opportunity for cross-examination at any time."* It was obvious that Mullins didn't like the accusation. *"Mr. Winton, who are you suggesting discussed their testimony with me yesterday outside of the presence of the Administrator?"*

Winton: *"Your Honor, Mr. Jim Driskell for — specifically."*

After some thought to whom Driskell even was, Mullins remembered. *"There was a — I know who you are talking about. Mr. Driskell was there yesterday. He described to me each of the maneuvers that was done during the airshow as he would do them, I assume, at an airshow. He didn't talk about his testimony. All he talked about to me was what was going on with the airplane."*

Winton continued to object, saying that that would be part of Driskell's testimony.

Mullins: *"Well, he needn't testify about what when on yesterday, because I saw what went on yesterday."* But Mullins wasn't done yet... by any means.

"I am offended that the Administrator suggests that I was hearing evidence outside of the presence of the Administrator. I went out there for a few... There was a gentleman who came up and was introduced to me as someone who would tell me what was going on with the maneuvers, and that is exactly what happened. I am also — I don't understand why the Administrator thinks that cognition is not an element. The Administrator is the one that says that the Respondent has a cognitive deficit. I saw a demonstration of cognition out there yesterday, and I can't help but think that that has some relevance to these proceedings. Your objection is overruled."

And despite their objection being overruled, the complainant wasn't done yet, either. They then offered a tape of a news show from the previous day — which showed the flight demonstration — as evidence. Winton said it showed Driskell explaining *"to the Judge part of his testimony which will be heard."*

Bailey got involved at this point. *"The offensive conduct continues. For the record, we waited while the FAA belatedly made an appearance, almost forcing us into sunset which would have made the demonstration illegal, and we waited at the suggestion of the Court."* He further explained that Driskell had been introduced as a person with the only two-way radio on the field (and therefore the only person who could communicate with the aircraft), and who would *"explain what maneuver would be expected so that the Court would have some idea of what it was seeing, and hopefully evaluating."*

"Furthermore," Bailey continued, *"not only did the Administrator bring his witness out, who is now on the stand, to observe the proceedings, about which there may be some discussion, but observed that Mr. Driskell was with the Court and at no time objected or came over to participate in the conversation. Let the record further show that when Mr. Driskell was talking to the Court, no member of the defense team was present, listening in."* Mullins again took over, after thanking Bailey for his comments. He reiterated that when Driskell was explaining the maneuvers, two of the Administrator's representatives were "within 30'" of Driskell and himself, stating that if there were a legitimate objection, they should have walked over and voiced it right then. He did say, however, that the Complainant could enter the tape. ...But Bailey had suspicions.

"This specious conduct, Your Honor, should not go unanswered. Is the tape being offered to impeach the Court or in any way try to disqualify him?" — continuing that the Complainant's behavior was not seasonable or professional.

Judge Mullins: *"Is it the Administrator's position that you want me to recuse myself because of this?"*

Winton: *"We would request that, Your Honor."*

Judge Mullins: *"All right. The request is overruled."*
... And the hearing was finally able to proceed.

The Return of Dr. Elliott

Dr. Robert Elliott once again took the stand... and Bailey gave the Administrator a taste of his own medicine.

Bailey: *"Dr. Elliott, with whom have you discussed this case since we adjourned at 3:00 o'clock yesterday?"*

Elliott testified that he had "briefly" discussed the case with the attorneys, regarding Hoover's flight performance — and nothing else.

Bailey: *"Well, you seemed to be rather busily engaged in conversation with them while we were at the airport waiting. Do you recall that?"*

Elliott once again said that only brief comments were made.

Bailey: *"Did counsel bring to your attention that it was improper for you to have any discussion with them until cross-examination was concluded?"*

Elliott: *"Yes."*

Bailey then began questioning Elliott again about his reports.

Bailey: *"Did you read this report before you signed it?"*

Elliott: *"Yes."*

Bailey: *"Do you have any familiarity with the United States airplane manufacturers, types, et cetera?"*

Elliott: *"Basic."*

Bailey: *"Do you have any familiarity with the airplane you saw yesterday?"*

Elliott: *"No."*

Bailey: *"Would you tell me why your report describes an airplane that has never been manufactured in this country?"*

When Elliott said that he didn't understand the question, Bailey explained that the report referred to an "Arrow Commander" when it is actually an "Aero Commander."

Bailey: *"Doesn't that suggest a lack of familiarity with US aircraft and aviation to you?"*

Bailey wanted to again discuss the fact that Elliott's opinion of Hoover's fitness seemed to have changed between Hoover's testing and Elliott's current testimony.

Bailey: *"Did you deliberately withhold from the report an opinion that he (Hoover) was unfit to hold a second class medical?"*

Elliott: *"I didn't have an opinion at that time. The issue I was dealing with was cognitive deficits."*

Bailey: *"You didn't have an opinion at that time. You have since acquired an opinion. Correct?"*

Elliott: *"I have since been asked for an opinion."*

Bailey: *"...Well, is it just a coincidence that the testimony that you might have given a year ago which was not favorable to the FAA's position has become favorable somewhere in the interim? Is that a coincidence?"*

Everyone in that court room got Bailey's drift, so he then changed directions.

Bailey: *"Now, Doctor, yesterday I challenged your right to use the Wisconsin Card-Sorting Test on the grounds that you had avoided the recognized manual test and had gone for (the) experimental or research version, and you asserted unequivocally that that wasn't true, didn't you?"*

Elliott said Bailey's statement was correct — later agreeing that he did not know it was a research version until, after Bailey's inquiry the day before, he contacted technical services at PAR. Bailey then read the following statement, asking for Elliott's opinion of it.

"There have been no studies of the relationship between normal cognitive functioning as measured by standardized neurological measures or PABs and actual aviator performance."

Elliott disagreed.

Bailey continued. .. *"The authors reported, however, that there were no studies in which test batteries had been validated against actual flight performance of experienced pilots. Further, they concluded that it was likely that the skills required to train successfully as a pilot were different from those skills used by experienced pilots when actually flying."*

Bailey attributed these statements to the article "Measuring Performance Decrements in Aviation Personnel Infected with the Human Immunodeficiency Virus" written in February 1993 by a team of four physicians, including Dr. Gary Kay. Elliott contended that further research had been done since the time that article had been written. *"...Kay has done research with Russian pilots and looked at the relationship between cognitive functioning and actual performance off the black box,"* he said.

Bailey: *"These are, of course, aerobatic pilots you are talking about, the Russians."*

Elliott, as you may have imagined, didn't know if they were aerobatic pilots, airshow pilots or test pilots. Bailey asked Elliott specific questions about the testing given Hoover, such as "what color is the circle?" (in a specific item number) or "What objects are in the third box?" or "how many are there?" Elliott couldn't recall the answers to most of the questions.

Bailey: *"Now, do you realize that your memory has just enabled you to flunk the Wisconsin Card-Sorting Test?"*

Bailey continued, wanting to know the correlation between performing well or poorly on this test and being able to fly aerobatically.

Elliott: *"I can't cite any."*

Bailey then went on to the category test — where, as Elliott explained, the person taking the test had to be able to match on *"some sort of criteria, much like the*

Wisconsin Card-Sorting Test."

Bailey: *"...what is it that a pilot does that would draw on the skills necessary to figure out what the author of the test had in mind when he conceived these answers?"*

Elliott: *"To figure out solutions to a novel problem situation."*

Bailey: *"Did you know Mr. Hoover had a novel problem yesterday flying the airplane?"*

Elliott: *"No."*

    After establishing that Elliott did not know what a cowl flap was, Bailey continued. *"...did you notice that one of Mr. Hoover's maneuvers required that he shut down the engines and then perform a series of aerobatics and wind right back where he started with no power at all?..."*

Elliott: *"I noticed he did that."*

Bailey: *"Did you notice or did you learn that his cowl flap jammed open, creating drag that the program was not intended to deal with? Did you know that?"*

Elliott: *"No."*

Bailey: *"Did you observe that Mr. Hoover successfully completed the maneuver he began?... Now tell me about the deficiency that made him unable to deal with an unexpected circumstance and how it relates to the category test, if you can."*

    How did Elliott respond? I bet you can guess. *"Well, I can't comment on that."*

    Next subject. Bailey began talking about some of Elliott's earlier testimony, when he had told the Court that Dr. Dave Johnsen, the Oklahoma City psychologist, had used the computerized version of the Wisconsin Card-sorting Test. Bailey contended that what Elliott had said was false and that he had known it to be false when he said it. Elliott responded by saying, *"Well, I can't recall if my testimony was on scoring or on administration."* Again, feeling assured that he had made his point, Bailey went on to the next subject still pertaining to the Wisconsin Card-Sorting test.

Bailey: *"Would it surprise you to learn that a trained neurologist, the most senior in the United States, takes six times as long to do it on the computer, Doctor, who knows the test backwards and forwards?"*

Elliott: *"I would be very surprised."*

    Again, Bailey changed the subject. He expressed amazement that Elliott never mentioned Hoover's medical unfitness in his report. To this, Elliott explained that he was only asked to express an opinion regarding cognitive deficits.

Bailey: *"And you didn't think that for the protection of the public, you owed it to anyone to say, 'By the way, my expertise tells me that this guy is a walking accident'; didn't think you had any duty. Is that right?"*

Elliott: *"I did not have a duty. That is correct."*

Bailey: *"You, I take it then, approved of the conduct of the FAA Inspectors who observed this possible accident about to happen and didn't tell anyone for two months. That is kind of in the same vein, is it?"*

Elliott said he didn't know what the action of the FAA was. Bailey next asked Elliott if Pakull from the FAA had kept him informed about the status of Hoover's file after his testing of him Hoover, namely, that Dr. O'Connor had tested Hoover and recommended that he get his ticket back but Pakull overruled him and said not to give it to him. Elliott testified that he did not know that, and did not know that Hoover had protested Pakull's conduct and had requested a second battery of tests nor, he said, did he know that Hoover had complained about the way he had treated him and administered the testing.

Bailey: *"Did you know that he said he was there from 8:00 to 5:00 without anything to eat and only one break, long enough to go to the bathroom?"*

Elliott: *"I am not sure what he said, but he wasn't there from 8:00 to 5:00."*

Bailey: *"Oh? You have, of course, your bill this morning, which will tell us what you charged for that day."*

Elliott: *"That is correct."*

Bailey: *"Yes. And what did you charge?"* Elliott said $1700.

Bailey: *"$1700. How many hours was that? When did you log in and out?"*
Elliott testified that testing was from 8:00 to 3:30.

Bailey: *"By the way, during that day, did you assure him that nothing that was going on that day was going to impinge on his right to fly?"*

Elliott: *"Yes, I did."*

Bailey: *"Doesn't turn out to be true, does it? You are here supporting the notion that he can't fly, aren't you?"*
Bailey also said that if he was telling the truth right now, he was indeed lying to Hoover on the day of testing. Elliott merely repeated the same old line that he was only asked to evaluate his cognitive deficits.

Bailey: *"And you felt that it was proper, even though you felt he was medically unfit, you felt it proper for you to say to him, 'Nothing that is going on here today will jeopardize your medical certificate.' Is that right?"*
I bet you can guess the response: The same old line about merely looking for cognitive deficits. But then Bailey wanted to know something about those cognitive deficits, especially seeing that Hoover had successfully flown a plane the day before (even

aking care of a problem situation) — namely, when were the cognitive deficits that Hoover was supposed to have supposed to begin interfering with his flying ability.

Elliott: *"I can't predict that."*

Bailey: *"You cannot deny the fact that Mr. Hoover may well be safe to do what he did yesterday afternoon for more than two years hence, can you?"*

Again, he couldn't predict that.

Bailey: *"You also cannot tell this Court that he has not been flying with the exact same condition for the past 20 years, because you don't have a baseline, do you, Doctor?"*

Elliott: *"That is correct."* (But wait, dear readers, it gets better!)

Bailey: *"Oh, now, I want you to assume, Doctor, that if I was subjected to a battery like you administered to Mr. Hoover by an unethical, unscrupulous neuropsychologist and scores (sic) badly, would you agree, number one, that by displaying a hostile attitude and otherwise vexing the subject, you could affect the scores of these performance tests?"*

Elliott: *"I would say there are many conditions that could affect the scores."*

Bailey: *"Okay. Assume that because the doctor unwittingly uses a research version or for other reasons the subject is unfairly given a low score. As I understand it, he can never escape that condemnation, because any improvement will be attributed by doctors like you to practice effect. Is that the situation?"*

Elliott: *"I can't speak for other doctors."*

Bailey: *"Well, if Mr. Hoover has twice performed within normal range on the Wisconsin Card-Sorting test and once performed poorly when you elected, unwittingly, you say, to administer it through a computer, a research version, is it the fact that all of the improvement can only be attributed to practice effect, or is it possible that the earlier test was defective because of the person who administered it? Is it possible?"*

Elliott said his tests showed a valid administration of neuropsychological tools.

Bailey: *"So whatever defect prevented him from doing better on Wisconsin that day, he somehow practiced his way out of before Dr. Uchiyama tested him seven months later. Is that your position?"*

Elliott responded that his level of functioning on those tests were still in the impaired range.

Bailey: *"Well, that is according to whose standards. It wasn't the Heaton standard, was it?"*

Elliott said that was correct.

Bailey: *"By the way, you several times referred the Court to a pilot standard. Where did*

you get your pilot standard from the literature?"

Elliott said he got the information from case studies by Dr. Gary Kay as well as his own experience with pilots.

Bailey: *"Do you understand that we are here, trying to find out if what you learned in your testing, even if it was done correctly, has any relevance whatsoever to this man's ability to fly an airplane?"*

Elliott: *"My understanding is that we are dealing with a medical fitness issue."*

Bailey countered with a statement that quoted one of the Government's experts as saying that there is no data to show a correlation between the cognitive functions measured by Elliott's tests and aviation skills.

Elliott: *"I disagree that there is no information available to take a look at successful flying and cognitive functions."*

Bailey later questioned Elliott's tele-conversation with Dr. Barton Pakull in July. *"I am asking you why you would call him in July to make further corrections to your report."*

Elliott: *"Well, the call in July would have been to discuss the case, or he must have contacted me."*

Bailey feigned amazement that it appeared that Elliott really couldn't remember who called whom. *"You now remember that,"* he said. *"A moment ago, you couldn't remember."*

Bailey: *"Do you have any memory impairment that you know of?"*

Elliott: *"No."*

Bailey left that line of questions and asked Elliott if Pakull had told him during this conversation that he had commissioned another battery of tests to be given to Hoover and that the experts once again told him Hoover was fit to fly, but once again he rejected them all. Elliott said they had not discussed that and that he was unaware of it.

Bailey: *"Did you know he was out looking for supportive opinions at that time, people who would agree with him?"*

When Elliott responded *"No"*, Bailey asked, *"Well, then, what were you two folks talking about, Doctor?"*

Elliott: *"My recollection of the conversation had to do with his level of performance."*

After a few general questions, Bailey asked a biggie: *"Isn't it the truth, Doctor, what you were asked to do was change your opinion to suit Dr. Pakull?"*

Elliott did not agree with that, of course. A few minutes later, Bailey returned to the conversation with Pakull and who called whom.

Bailey: *"And the next day you talked to Bart Pakull"*

Elliott: *"That is correct."*

Bailey: *"For how long?"*

Elliott: *"I don't know."*

Bailey: *"Did you call him?"*

Elliott: *"I don't know."* (Hmmm)

Bailey: *"You would have a phone bill, I take it, if you did."*

Elliott: *"If it was on my phone bill, then I would have called him. My suspicion is he probably did. I don't know."*

Bailey: *"Okay. You don't remember now."*

Elliott: *"I don't recall."*

Bailey: *"A few moments ago, you did recall he called you. Do you know that?"*

Even a neuropsychologist can have a bad memory, I guess… Bailey then began asking Elliott about a conference call between Elliott, Gaines, Pakull, and Jordan.

Bailey: *"Did you learn during the conference that Dr. Gaines was one of the people that Dr. Pakull had solicited to support his position on the issue?"*

Elliott: *"I don't know. I couldn't characterize their conversation. I don't know what he was asking of Dr. Gaines."*

Elliott further explained that he simply knew that Gaines had reviewed some of Hoover's medical records.

Elliott: *"Dr. Pakull had requested a copy of the original SPECT scans from Dr. Michael Gold, and that is the only notes I have on the content of the conversation."*

Not surprisingly, given his earlier display of a faulty memory (grin), Elliott couldn't seem to remember anything else about that conference call, including if he was asked to participate in the case as a witness. Bailey was ready to discuss the last subject, which was why Elliott had not cooperated with Dr. Appell when she had requested data from him. Elliott tried to explain it away with the reasoning that he did not realize that this was a fast-track proceeding, therefore requiring expediency. He also said he left the day after the request was made and didn't have access to a fax machine (via which Hoover would have sent him to release the information as necessary).

Bailey: *"Did you ask to have Mr. Hoover meet you at the office and sign it, so you could get the data and ship it to her?"*

Elliott: *"No."*

Bailey's last comment, which was struck after FAA counsel objected, was this: *"Wouldn't you say, sir, that you were more of a team player than a witness in this case?"* And now FAA counsel needed to re-direct.

Re-Direct Examination of Dr. Elliott

Caron first asked Elliott if neuropsychological testing should be interpreted differently if the person being tested was a test pilot, to which Elliott said no, all people holding the same class medical certificate should be held to the same standards, regardless of the skills that they are required to utilize in flight. Caron then asked if Hoover' flight the day before changed his opinion of Hoover's neuropsychological status. Elliott said no, because it was a very practiced skill and he alleged that Hoover has simply learned to compensate for his cognitive deficits. The only other things that were touched on in the re-direct was that no one, according to Elliott, is able to predict when those cognitive deficits could cause a problem. Elliott also testified that he had given a similar battery of tests about 800 times. Elliott was then excused from the stand, and a recess was taken. When they were back on the record, Bailey began a description of the latest offensive action of the opposing side. He said that he had just been informed that the FAA intended to call a psychologist from Texas to say that Hoover had Alzheimer's disease.

Bailey: *"Quite apart from the fact that that is patently offensive, since he was examined very thoroughly several times and the issue has never been raised until now, we are totally unprepared to go forward and litigate that. There are many ways to detect Alzheimer's disease. The FAA comes too late. It is not part of their charges, and we think that the evidence ought to be excluded."*

He went on to describe canons of ethics in neuropsychology that prohibit expressing opinions on someone's impairment when the neuropsychologist who would be expressing these opinions have not examined the subject (and, he added, had been given that opportunity and declined it).

Bailey: *"Mr. Hoover has never been asked to be examined by Dr. Gaines or Dr. Pincus or Dr. Kay. Now, to permit them to come into this Court and flout their own canons of ethics in order to deprive this person of the right to fly seems to me grossly unjust."*

FAA Counsel countered by saying *"...we are not using any of our neuropsychologists who have not examined Mr. Hoover to specifically say that they, based on the examinations, find that he is inadequate to hold the second class medical certificate..."*

Bailey then expressed confusion — what were they going to testify to, then? The Judge, however, said he would not disallow their testimony based upon this... although he said he felt it important that each of the witnesses be asked about the *"ethical functions"* when they were on the stand... but he also said: *"...Now, please respond if you would, Mr. Winton, to the Alzheimer thing."* Winton tried to explain that the Alzheimer thing was not new and that the doctor was not going to testify that Hoover actually had Alzheimers but that the SPECT scans indicated an Alzheimer's-type of degenerative cognitive impairment. Thereafter, the Judge said he wanted to take everything under consideration for a while.

Chapter 21

The Attack Continues...
Gaines & Pincus

*It is hard to believe that a man is telling the truth
when you know that you would lie if you were in his place.*
H. L. Mencken

Again, the FAA had chosen a medical witness whose curriculum vitae was a mile long. Dr. Richard Gaines has a bachelor's and masters from the University of Southern Cal and a Ph.D. in psychology from the University of New Mexico. He is board-certified in neuropsychology; and, like Elliott, is also a diplomate in neuropsychology. They also pointed out that a good deal of his active duty military service was primarily aviation-related—doing research in psychology and aviation — and, lucky for the FAA, he was able to testify that he had worked with test pilots at the Navy Test Pilot School.

According to Gaines, he had examined between 1100 and 1200 pilots over the previous 20 years. He is also a pilot with about 3000 hours.

Caron: *"Do you believe it is important for someone who is administering neuropsychological testing to have received training on administering that testing?"*

Gaines: *"Oh, yes... If we don't know how to administer the tests, they are not administered in the standardized fashion, then the results — you wouldn't have any idea what the results meant."*

(That little exchange was meant to bolster the previous testimony from Dr. Elliott, whom Gaines then said had received the proper training required.)

Caron: *"Dr. Gaines, are there identifiable functions, cognitive functions that a pilot must have in order to safely operate in the cockpit?"*

Gaines agreed, and said that the previously-mentioned Banich article, "A Neuropsychological Screening of Aviators, A Review," are representative of these functions. *"There have been other task analyses, and they produce pretty much the same kind of results,"* Gaines explained.

The Banich article, according to Gaines, lists six major functions: perceptual motor abilities, spatial abilities, working memory, attention, processing flexibility, and planning sequences.

Caron: *"In evaluating those functions if you have a set of test scores, how do you determine whether someone has performed sufficiently on the neuropsychological testing in comparison to those tasks that a pilot must perform? What do you compare them to?"*

Gaines: *"Norms."*

Gaines then explained that this normative data "paints a picture" of the overall abilities in the particular cognitive areas. *"There are different sets of norms: general population norms, age norms, and norms for specific — relatively specific groups. And we try to pick the norms which seem most relevant,"* Gaines said.

Next, FAA Counsel began questioning Gaines about an article he had written in the Bulletin of the Nat'l Academy of Neuropsychology; it was a primarily a case study called "Inefficiency of Cockpit Simulators for Identifying Cognitive Deficits."

The article dealt with a Boeing 767 Captain who was referred for evaluation after having made a *"fairly innocuous mistake"* in a simulator. Evaluation discovered that the aviator had Alzheimer's.

Gaines: *"... And the point of the article was that the simulator itself was not a very good screen of performance, cognitive performance. He had been flying as a Captain up until a week or so before when I saw him, and also the other concern in this article was that using age-corrected norms would have made this man look a lot better than he really was... if we age-corrected the norms, he would probably look like he was in the normative group, but he still had Alzheimer's disease."*

FAA Counsel then began to ask Gaines questions about his opinions of Hoover's test results. He stated that he was concerned about some of the results that seemed to exclude Hoover from the necessary criteria to hold a second class medical. When they began to discuss the Wisconsin Card-Sorting Test, Bailey jumped in.

Bailey reiterated his point that any discussion of the Wisconsin Card-Sorting results should not be allowed, because Elliott had *"unwittingly"* given Hoover a research version of the test. He reminded the Court in a voir dire with Gaines that even Dr. Appell, the most senior neuropsychologist in the nation, took six times longer to complete the computerized (research) version as compared to the manual version.

During this voir dire, it became apparent that Gaines held the same misconception as Elliott regarding the test and therefore had not understood that Hoover was given a research version. Bailey also reminded Gaines at this point, with the Judge's permission, about the neuropsychological canons of ethics and what it said about offering an opinion of someone's neuropsychological health without the benefit of an examination.

FAA Counsel said they only wanted to ask Gaines one question about the Wisconsin Card-Sorting Test *"for continuity"* and then would move on. The one question asked Gaines to look at a screen from this test and tell the Court whether it said *"research version"* ...of course it didn't... but that didn't change the fact that the company that produces this test, as uncovered in the cross-examination of Elliott, had verified that they had never shipped anything but a research version of the computerized test.

Nonetheless, Judge Mullins looked at the situation a little differently: *"But apparently that is the basis for the Administrator's — it is the basis for what we are here for almost, it seems, and I am going to overrule your objection. I think it is not a matter of admissibility as much as it is a matter of weight."*

And so the door was re-opened to discuss this battery of tests. And again, practice effect was brought up as seemingly the only reason (according to the FAA) that Hoover could have improved on subsequent tests.

Gaines also gave an opinion — despite the ethical canons — that Hoover "fell into the impaired range on several critical areas of cognitive skills." He stated that he felt that Hoover did not meet the criteria to be recertified — and that he believed (although he had never examined him) that Hoover had some organic condition that had caused a decrease in cognitive function and that represented an increased risk of unsafe flying.

He also agreed with Elliott that Hoover would still be impaired in two years and the fact that he flew successfully the previous day did not change his opinion because of the potential of a problem with a novel situation: *"There is always the eventuality that some new and novel circumstance will occur that will not be resolved because of some inability to shift set, to demonstrate cognitive flexibility that is required to handle some unforeseen circumstance."*

FAA Counsel then tried to begin questioning Gaines about a case with which he had been involved, regarding an airline pilot with Alzheimer's.

Bailey: *"Your Honor, I don't know how this commercial airline pilot's Alzheimer's disease relates to Mr. Hoover in any way. I object to the line of questioning."*

The objection was sustained, and Caron then passed the witness.

Bailey: *"On that point, Your Honor, since tomorrow is our last day, I am beginning to get a drift, before I begin cross, that the Government may not call the Inspectors who triggered this whole event. If that is so, I would like to be told now, so I can subpoena them. If I don't learn it until tomorrow, we won't get them."*

The Judge told Bailey that the FAA had already indicated that they did not intend to call those two — surprise, surprise — and Bailey apologized for not catching that, and said he would therefore ask for subpoenas.

Gaines Cross-Examination

Bailey: *"Your concern is that although he routinely performs with a high degree of skill in an act which is unique in aviation, flying business planes or aerobatics, that he may encounter some unforeseen situation and because of his performance on the Wisconsin Card-Sorting Test, may not be able to deal with it?"*

Gaines: *"Not just with the Wisconsin Card-Sorting test, but yes."*

Bailey asked Gaines if an emergency was created to surprise Hoover and he handled it with aplomb, leaving no room for error, would that change his mind. Gaines said it would not, if it were a routine emergency that all pilots practice. Upon further questioning, Gaines said even the successful handling of a novel emergency would not change his opinion.

Bailey then brought up a fairly recent (at the time of the trial) emergency that Hoover had handled well– when a chip light came on in a T-28 Hoover was piloting (with Mr. Hughes, in the back seat) ten miles out over the Pacific.

Bailey: *"What would you expect an unimpaired pilot to do in the circumstances?"*

Gaines: *"I am not offering myself as an expert pilot."*

Bailey: *"No. You are an expert testifying about what pilots do when they are impaired and unimpaired, as I understand your testimony."*
Gaines disagreed.

Bailey: *"Isn't it fair to say that none of the tests that you have described have ever been shown to have predictive value as to whether or not a pilot can handle an emergency properly?"*

Gaines: *"There is no research to that effect."*

Bailey: *"...In other words, once you have an opinion, no set of facts is going to contravene it."*
Again, Gaines disagreed, saying that the tests only represent an increased probability of a circumstance where an error will be made.

Bailey: *"Increased over what? What is the probability in the average pilot and from what study do you know that?"*

Gaines: *"I don't know."*
Bailey then asked what studies showed whether an average pilot would behave appropriately when confronted with an emergency; Gaines had no knowledge of one.
Bailey (after confirming that Gaines had seen Hoover perform): *"Wouldn't you say that on an absolute scale, he (Hoover) is more likely to successfully handle an emergency than the average pilot?"*
Gaines said yes, provided Hoover *"is flying in the same airplane, doing the same things."*
...But Gaines still said his opinion would not change, repeating that the tests only represented an increased risk.

Bailey: *"All right. If Mr. Hoover ordinarily would solve 999 emergencies correctly, more than the average pilot, and now he can solve only 998, that is an increased risk, isn't it?"*

Gaines: *"I guess so. Yes."*
Gaines remained firm that his opinion would not change no matter how many emergencies were solved correctly by Hoover, so Bailey changed his questioning a bit.

Bailey: *"How do you know that he didn't have about the same condition when he was 50 that he has now? Have you got any data on that, Doctor?"*
Gaines eventually said he didn't know such a thing, although *"I don't know anybody who hasn't changed between 50 and 70."*
Gaines still remained adamant that his opinion would not change.

Bailey: *"Do you give any credence at all to the testimony of expert pilots who have watched him fly over that period of time and see no change?"*

Gaines: *"No."*

Bailey: *"You mean, they are all liars?"*
Gaines said no.

Bailey: *"Give me instances where neuropsychologists have predicted accidents that didn't occur..."*
He didn't know.

Bailey: *"So we really don't have any way of knowing that your opinion has a value in this case beyond mere speculation. Isn't that a fair statement?"*
Of course, Gaines did not agree. Bailey then asked Gaines' opinion of an article by Dr. Kay, which was identified for the record during cross-examination of Elliott (and which FAA Counsel did not seem to remember... more poor memories... better have their cognitive functioning tested...), and which stated that standard test batteries did not enable one to predict conduct in skilled airmen. Gaines asserted Kay's statements were no longer accurate.

Bailey: *"Oh, was it accurate in February of '93 when it was published?"*

Gaines: *"Probably not then."*
Gaines, of course, could not tell the Court when it ceased being accurate... and so Bailey moved on.

Bailey: *"Now, how long have you known Dr. Barton Pakull?"*
Gaines said he had known him about 15 years and had been a consultant for the FAA for ten or twelve years, reviewing records for them. Bailey asked how many times he had testified for airmen against the Administrator.

Gaines: *"Well, having, a contract, that would represent a fairly significant conflict of interest."*
Bailey subsequently asked what Gaines' rate of pay was, and Gaines said $260/day (remember, Elliott was paid $1700), but also said his contract had lapsed before he looked at the Hoover case and therefore had not been paid for any of his time on this case. Bailey then asked Gaines when Pakull had contacted about the case. He only remembered that it was sometime after he received Dr. Elliott's work-up.

Bailey: *"Did he mention the name?"*

Gaines: *"I don't even recall that. He may have."*

Bailey: *"Well, now, earlier, Doctor, you had to look at a piece of paper to find out when you were certified. Do you have any memory problems?"*

Gaines: *"Well, probably not more than one would expect for my age."*

Bailey: *"Okay. Are you telling us that the head psychiatrist of the FAA called you abou the most famous pilot in America and you forgot his name?"*

Gaines: *"No. I didn't say I forgot his name. I don't recall if he told me the name or not. Tsk, tsk... maybe bad memories are contagious..."*

Bailey: *"Did he tell you that he was dissatisfied with the opinion of Dr. O'Connor and the others who participated in the evaluation, the results of which was a recommendation that Mr. Hoover continue to fly?"*

Gaines said no, but he did say he had heard there were questions about *"some performance."* Bailey asked him if that report would be material to his opinions of this case — particularly if the whole story had been made up.

Gaines: *"It doesn't change the data."*

Bailey asked Gaines if he had ever requested an examination of Hoover and he said no, he had not – he had only looked at the data and commented that it looked as i impairment was represented. He also said he did not know that Pakull was looking for support of his opinion in this case. Bailey then began questioning Gaines about that July conference call that included, among others, Gaines, Pakull, and Elliott. At first, it ap peared Gaines remembered very little of the conversation.

Bailey explained his interest in the conversation: *"I think the relevance is this Your Honor. I think that at the time these doctors well knew there wasn't sufficien scientific basis, and that is why no action was taken... And I am anxious to know whether or not that is this doctor's view."*

Gaines: *"...Quite the contrary. The discussions were that the scientific evidence was very negative, and the conversations that were had were representing reluctance on the part of the air surgeon and/or the people in the air surgeon's office, just because of the stature of the case."*

Bailey then reiterated his position that if someone – namely, Elliott – had felt Hoover was impaired enough such that his medical certificate should be rescinded, his opinion should have been stated right away rather than allowing to fly longer... reluc tance or no reluctance.

Gaines: Re-Direct Examination

Caron asked Gaines if a pilot needs perceptual motor abilities, spatial abilities, working memory, attentional performance, processing flexibility, and planning or sequenc ing abilities — in normal and emergency flight.

It doesn't take a brain surgeon (literally...) to see that Caron was leading Gaines to say yes. When that was established, Gaines testified that he believed all of those task were effectively tested in Hoover.

Gaines then said he was most concerned with Hoover's results with processing flexibility, working memory, and some attentional measures. Again, he was seemingly le

to say that those abilities were necessary for a pilot to have to effectively handle an emergency.

Finally, Gaines testified that although he doesn't know when the cognitive impairment began in Hoover that didn't lessen his opinion that the current presence of the impairment and that said impairment should be a factor in his loss of flight privileges.

Gaines: Re-Cross Examination

Bailey: *"If you had these tests dated 1973 and the same results in 1993, with a 20-year span of flawless flying, would that change your view as to the value of this data in predicting the likelihood for failure by an airman?"*

When Bailey said the numbers would be comparable adjusted for age and education, Gaines admitted that it might change his opinion.

Examination: Jonathan Pincus

Pincus is yet another neurologist called by the FAA with another cookie-cutter curriculum vitae: long and distinguished... even some Yale education and a book authorship thrown in. He, too (of course), is board certified in neurology.

It quickly became obvious that Pincus' testimony would rely heavily on SPECT scan evidence, which he explained *"measured cerebral blood flow."*

"Cerebral blood flow is very much influenced by brain activity, so that in parts of the brain that are working hard, there will be more flow, and certain parts of the brain that are not working will have less flow," he explained. Pincus was asked what he had learned from Hoover's history.

Pincus: *"The — his career, as best I could tell from the records I had, has been an extremely distinguished one. However, in the last few years, there was a report by one of the Federal observers who said that he had been cited for several violations in the past ten years...*

It said that he had been involved in five incidents and two violation since 1982, and the... Inspector who wrote this, indicated that there had been – that this represented an increasing pace of such incidents, violations."

He then said that this might indicate a pattern of decreased capacity, function. When asked what other information he learned from Hoover's history, Pincus launched into a dissertation of the Inspectors' report of the airshow in question and Dr. O'Connor's report – and the abnormalities he believed to be shown in that report –particularly regarding memory issues.

Pincus also brought up a subject undiscussed up to this point: drinking. He testified that there was inconsistency in what Hoover had told O'Connor and Elliott about hangovers. Additionally, according to Pincus, O'Connor noted that Hoover had rhinophyma... here described as a large, red, discolored nose... which, he continued to say, was often seen in people who engage in excessive drinking. It was obvious what he was trying to say about Hoover.

Pincus then said that Dr. O'Connor was *"very much disturbed"* by the testing,

and therefore felt he needed additional testing.

Pincus also testified that O'Connor had ordered a number of tests, including blood tests, and these tests did not have normal results. "There was a mild anemia. His hematocrit was low; his hemoglobin was low. His red blood cell count was slightly low and his mean corpuscular volume was elevated," he explained.

Again Pincus brought up drinking, stating that that seemed to be the cause of Hoover's anemia: *"That is the usual cause of a macrocytic anemia, and that is seen frequently in people who drink, because people who drink don't take in enough vitamins and sometimes don't absorb what they take in from their gastrointestinal track."*

Pincus then discussed Dr. Gold's examination of Hoover, which wasn't as complete as he would have liked (*"He didn't concentrate on many of the cortical signs that I believe would have been indicated..."*). However, Gold did order a SPECT scan and Pincus felt that was important, because, he said, its results were abnormal. Gold also ordered an MRI scan, which, Pincus said, showed sulcal widening — a sign of brain atrophy.

He said all of the testing, to include Elliott's, showed *"neurological, cortical brain impairment."* Additional testing, including a second SPECT scan, showed more definite abnormalities, and another neurologist who examined Hoover said ankle reflexes were absent, having been lost sometime between Nov. 1992 and Oct. 1993. This, Pincus testified, meant peripheral nerves were not working properly. Again, he seemingly attempted to blame this lack of a reflex on drinking: *"...And it is something that is seen in people who have been — who are vitamin deficient and who have been drinking."*

He even attempted to correlate his weight and drinking. He said that Hoover was 6'1" or 6'2" and weighed 150 to 160 lbs. This meant he consumed about 1800 calories/day and if he drank two alcoholic drinks per day (about 500 to 600 calories), he was not obtaining adequate amounts of protein, vitamins, etc.

He concluded by stating that he was "convinced" there is neurologic dysfunction: *"The cause of that dysfunction, I am not sure... I think alcohol is the most important factor in this."*

Pincus: *"The chances of having an accident are increased because of his brain impairment, the same as a person who has been drinking, and an experienced drinker and an experienced driver has an increased chance of having an accident, even though he is able to carry out his driving most of the time."*

He continued, when asked for an interpretation of the tests: *"...I think that it was — he was — it was unsafe to have him being a pilot of a plane at that time, and I think it is unsafe now."*

Pincus: Cross-Examination

Bailey began by asking Pincus how long he had known Pakull, to which Pincus answered only about a month. He also testified that he had no affiliation with the FAA... except that the University of Georgetown School of Medicine, where Pincus is Professor and Chairman of the Dept. of Neurology, does receive grants from the FAA.

Bailey: *"Which department?"*

Pincus: *"Neurology."*

Want to see a great example of Bailey's talent? Read what happened next... When asked what these grants were for, Pincus said for the development of the CogScreen test, for which Dr. Kay is in charge. Pincus testified that he knew Kay very well.

Bailey: *"Do you agree with this statement? 'There have been no studies of the relationship between normal cognitive function as measured by standardized neuropsychological measures or PABs and actual aviator performance.'"*

FAA Counsel Winton objected to any questioning about CogScreen as it was not mentioned during the witness' testimony.

Bailey: *"The question has nothing to do with CogScreen. I have read it now for the third time, and every time you have interrupted before the witness can be required to answer."*

Winton then said that the article dealt with Gary Kay's studies with the CogScreen.

Bailey: *"The article has to do with people with AIDS flying airplanes, Mr. Winton..."*

The Judge then overruled the objection, but Pincus needed the question repeated... more bad memories...

Bailey: *"You don't remember a question I asked you one minute ago?"*

Pincus said he did not agree. Bailey then began questioning Pincus about his familiarity with aviation, about which he said he knew "virtually nothing."

Bailey: *"How great a reaction time is necessary to avoid an accident when flying an airplane?"*

Pincus: *"I don't know."*

Bailey then asked if the reaction time needed would be greater than driving an automobile.

Pincus: *"I think you have to have a better reaction time than an automobile."*

Bailey: *"Based on what?... You are speculating, aren't you?"*

Pincus agreed.

Bailey: *"Assume that Mr. Hoover, whom you have delineated as keeping his driver's license, thank you, is driving down a road at 60 miles per hour, the legal limit, and another person driving down the road at the same legal limit veers over to his side of the road. What kind of reaction time is necessary to save himself, if you know, assuming the vehicles are 100 feet apart?"*

Pincus: *"That would require a little mathematical calculation that I am not going to make right now."*

Bailey: *"You can't figure out how long it takes to go 100 feet at 120 miles per hour, Doctor?"*

Pincus still maintained that he did not want to figure it out.

Bailey: *"You haven't the slightest idea whether or not one who is able to drive an automobile might also be able to fly an airplane, do you?"*
    Pincus said that, based upon his looking inside a cockpit and seeing *"lots of switches, many switches, and little lights that go on and off,"* he believes it is more complicated to fly an airplane than to drive a car. Next, Bailey made it clear that Pincus had not been thoroughly briefed on Hoover's history, as he had not mentioned a *"calamitous air crash"* in an F-100, the results of which included a concussion and a broken back.
    Then Bailey began asking Pincus about a baseline for Hoover — i.e., that he had no way of knowing that Hoover would have performed differently on any of the tests when he was 50.

Pincus: *"I think that we do."*

Bailey: *"Was he given some tests that you know about when he was 50?"*

Pincus: *"No. But he was not cited for violations."*

Bailey: *"Ah. Now let's talk about the violations. I suggest to you, Doctor, that you are not terribly careful about your homework. Is that a fair statement?"*
    Pincus said no.

Bailey: *"Well, you didn't know about the crash. Do you know about the '87 crash, Doctor?"*

Pincus: *"The '87 crash?"*
    Bailey said it sounded as if he had never heard of it, and Pincus said he was right.

Bailey: *"Was there a crash in '87?"*

Pincus: *"The automobile crash, you mean?"*

Bailey: *"Yes."*
    Pincus remembered now; Bailey asked if he knew how severe it was.

Pincus: *"It was in Florida."*

Bailey: *"I asked you how severe it was; you said it was in Florida."*
    Pincus then said he didn't have those records and Bailey said that was some of the homework he didn't do.

Pincus: *"They weren't made available to the lawyers for the FAA."*

Bailey: *"They what? The FAA couldn't get records of an automobile crash investigated by the police. Is that what you are telling us?"*

Eventually, Pincus said he never saw a police report and didn't even seem to know whether police had investigated. Bailey asked him how bad the crash was.

Pincus: *"It caused a collapsed lung and a fair amount of pain after the recovery. I have no data on the crash, but he, when he was in California, sought medical attention because of the pain in his chest."*

Bailey finally brought the subject of violations back up.

Pincus: *"He was cited by the FAA for violations, five separate incidents, five incidents and two violations, since 1982, and since he was cited by – these were mentioned by a Federal Aviation Administration official, I assume that they had to do with flying."*

Bailey: *"Oh, well, did you know in one of those cases a lawyer for the FAA said, 'I am going to prosecute you because I want to get a promotion out of it and you are famous.' Did you know that?"*

Pincus did not know that.

Bailey: *"Okay. Which of the violations involved deficiencies in flying?"* He wanted to know about each one, one by one, from the homework Pincus had done.

Pincus: *"I don't have the details. All I have is the statement by the Federal Aviation Agency official that there were such, and that there had been an increasing pace of these things since 1982."*

Bailey: *"Does it make any difference whether these violations showed deteriorating motor skills in some fashion, or whether they were the product of carrying too many people in the airplane?"*

Pincus said it made no difference; what was important was the increasing pace of the violations.

Bailey: *"I see. Then I take it that one who speeds has created a neurologically significant piece of history."*

Pincus: *"I am glad you mentioned that, because that is very true."*

Bailey: *"That is very true. People who speed."*

Pincus: *"People who have repeated violations for speeding do. Yes."*

Bailey: *"It is not that they just want to go faster."*

Pincus: *"Why do they want to go faster, Mr. Bailey?"*

Bailey closed the door on that little tangent, and asked him if he had asked for any of the violation records in order to determine their nature. Pincus said he had not and agreed that he felt that not doing that bit of homework made no difference.

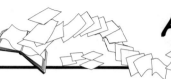

Bailey: *"Okay. Now, is it true that you really feel Mr. Hoover should be grounded simply because he is 71?"*

Pincus said that was not true.

Bailey: *"I see. All right. When you read the original records, July 27, 1993, did Mr. Pakull tell you that he had twice overruled groups of Doctors hired by the FAA to evaluate Mr. Hoover who had recommended that he keep his medical certificate?"*

Pincus said no.

Bailey: *"Didn't tell you that. Groups of doctors, yes. You didn't realize that Dr. Pakull was trying to shore up his opinion that Hoover shouldn't fly in the face of his own selected experts' contrary opinion, did you? Didn't know that."*

Pincus: *"I still don't."*

Bailey: *"Can you think of any reason he might not have informed you of the number of people who said that Mr. Hoover should be allowed to fly?"*

Pincus said that he was perplexed by this line of questioning. Bailey, after stating for the record that every time a question was asked, Pincus looked at the FAA Counsel, asked him about Dr. Gold's examination. *"You have told us today that it was superficial."*

Pincus corrected him, saying it was, instead, *"perfunctory."*

Bailey: *"Not quite as offensive as superficial. Right?"*

Pincus agreed.

Bailey: *"Did you call Dr. Gold, by the way, and tell him of his deficiencies?"*

Pincus had not; he did, however, put those deficiencies in writing for Pakull.

Bailey: *"All right. You said that, 'All of these tests reveal deficits in functions that are mediated through the frontal lobes. For this reason it would be important in performing a neurologic examination to concentrate on those parts of the neurologic examination that reflect frontal lobe dysfunction.*

For instance, eye tracking, number one; limitation of upward gaze, number two...;'" and Bailey continued listing six more items, *"but none of these were performed by Dr. Gold. True?"*

Pincus: *"True."*

Bailey: *"So you had no way of knowing how Mr. Hoover would have fared if the doctor had chosen to perform those tests."*

Pincus said that was fair. Bailey then commented that the solution would have been to perform those missing tests, and he asked Pincus if he had ever asked to see Hoover in an effort to be fair to him.

Pincus had not, nor had he asked that another competent neurologist (other than Dr. Gold) perform those tests.

Bailey: *"Do you know whether the FAA ever attempted to follow up your suggestion that its neurologist had been deficient and peremptory in his tests because he left out all these important things?"*

Pincus didn't know. Bailey then pointed out a typo in Pincus' reports –*"aerobiotic pilot"* and asked if that was *"another one of (his) little slips."* Bailey said he would go over the others eventually.

Bailey: *"And to your knowledge had anyone at FAA sent for the SPECT scans prior to the time you were asked to do your report?"*

Pincus said he had seen the scans.

Bailey: *"When? When?"*

Pincus said it was sometime between his first and second reports.

Bailey: *"You are kidding. Did you know that the FAA was demanding that we produce them, because they didn't have them? Where did you get them?"*

Pincus said he believed Pakull gave them to him, but he didn't recall when.

Bailey: *"Can you think of any reason that the FAA would be asking the Judge to issue subpoenas to the fellow who did them on the eve of trial if Dr. Pakull had them?"*

Pincus said there were two SPECT scans and he had seen only one of them.

Bailey: *"Wouldn't it be very important to look at both of them?"*

Pincus said it was not, because he didn't interpret SPECT scans; he left that for others to do. He did say when prompted, however, that he could have performed the tests that Dr. Gold had omitted. Bailey then asked Pincus if he had known at any point that the FAA had not intended to call anyone to testify about the SPECT scans. Pincus said he had thought they did have an expert to testify about that.

Bailey: *"It appears that they didn't bother to get one until we took the deposition of such a person. I am wondering if you knew that they intended to eliminate that part of the scientific evidence in that case, because you seem to have relied on somebody's interpretation of the SPECT scans to a degree."*

Pincus said yes. Bailey then asked Pincus if he knew that the FAA had never asked Hoover to submit to the omitted tests; Pincus said no. He then asked Pincus if he knew that Hoover had voluntarily submitted to those tests with Dr. Brent Hisey. Pincus did know this and he also testified that he knew Hoover had performed satisfactorily.

Bailey: *"Now, one of the reasons that I asked you whether or not you were involved as an advocate, advising the FAA lawyers on the presentation of their case and the arguments that they might make is because you filed a report on December 22 of last year, did you not?"*

Pincus said he did.

Bailey: *"With Dr. Pakull, and you were then confronted with the fact that your wishes had been carried out but only in the enemy camp, weren't you?"*

Pincus at first did not respond, but then said yes. He did also say, however, that the use of the term "enemy camp" was unfair. He continued by saying that the findings of Hisey's tests weren't what he expected and he wondered if they were done properly. Bailey then states that these tests – the ones Pincus said should be done – were done (albeit by a doctor friendly to Hoover) and though these tests showed satisfactory results, Pincus would not change his opinion because of who gave the tests. Next, Bailey brings up one of Pincus' statements – that in order to fly an airplane, a 70-year-old should be held to the standards of a 40-year-old.

Bailey: *"Do you know any basis upon which pilots are required to perform at levels, age levels lower that their chronological age in order to meet standards?"*

Pincus replied that it should depend on the purpose of the test, and continued that *"very few pilots are 70 years of age and older..."* Bailey asked Pincus how many 70 year-olds are flying. Pincus didn't know. *"I have never, ever seen a commercial pilot who was – who looked as if he was 70 years of age."*

After explaining the Age-60 Rule to him, Bailey again asked Pincus how many 70 year-olds were flying.

Pincus: *"I don't know."*

Bailey: *"More homework undone, Doctor?"*

Bailey then commented about Pincus' opinion in his report that there should be questions about Dr. Hisey's report, as the two (Hoover and Hisey) had met through a social contact and because they had something in common — they were both pilots.

Bailey: *"Now, I want you to assume that Dr. Hisey said to Mr. Hoover, after learning of the ongoing controversy, 'I will be glad as a physician actively working with the Air Force to give you a very stringent exam with the clear understanding that if I have any suspicion that you shouldn't be flying, I will put it in writing'."*

Pincus asked if that were a hypothetical question, and Bailey told him no, that was really how it happened — he (Pincus) just hadn't bothered to learn about it. Pincus eventually said that there would be nothing wrong with that approach... but maintained that there could still be questions about objectivity.

Pincus: *"In addition, there is a problem of experience in carrying out the tests."* ...and then explained that the problem was that Dr. Hisey was a neurosurgeon, and neurosurgeons don't usually involve themselves in the diagnostic process... and therefore Pincus was not sure Hisey had carried them out properly.

Bailey disagreed: *"...A neurosurgeon working with the Air Force is likely to be there to give the benefit of his expertise from a neurological standpoint and not a surgical standpoint. Would you agree?"*

Pincus: *"No."*
Bailey: *"No. You think he is there to operate on pilots."*

Pincus was steadfast – their training is for surgery, he said.

Bailey: *"Do you know anything about Dr. Hisey's background or experience?"*
Pincus had seen his curriculum vitae, but nothing beyond that.

Bailey: *"Do you have one scintilla of evidence that his testing procedures was defective in any particular?"*
Pincus didn't even have a description of Hisey's testing procedure.

Bailey: *"Did you ever ask for one?"*

Pincus: *"No. I didn't think that would be proper."*
Pincus, who had several times used the excuse *"I am a doctor, not a lawyer,"* continued by saying that had he contacted Hisey to ask for this, that would have been *"interfering in the judicial process."* Bailey commented that he was beginning to sound *"more like a lawyer every minute..."* and then reminded him that the FAA lawyers could have requested the information on Hisey's tests in a proper fashion.

Bailey: *"The fact is, Doctor, this is simply another occasion where you didn't bother to do your homework. Isn't that so?"*
Pincus, of course, said no. Referring again to the Wisconsin Card-Sort, Category test, and Trails Test, Bailey asked *"what studies have looked at where this sort of data has been used to successfully predict deficient flying abilities in a pilot?"* Pincus said he believed Dr. Kay had information on that.

Bailey: *"...have you ever predicted dysfunction on a pilot and failure to fly properly based on this kind of evidence?"*
Pincus had not. Nor, he said, had he ever seen a case like this before... *"I have never even heard of another 70 year-old show pilot,"* he said. Bailey, after pointing out another typo in the Pincus report, quoted Pincus *"'...Would a 40 year-old pilot who tested normally for a 70 year-old but abnormally for a 40 year-old be considered safe? If not, why not? The question answers itself.' Is that your argument, that Mr. Hoover should be treated as a 40 year-old?"*

Pincus: *"If a 40 year-old were to test normally for a 70 year-old, he would be several standard deviations beyond that of a 40 year-old, and he would be considered abnormal and impaired."*

Bailey: *"How is that relevant to the fact that Mr. Hoover, according to some doctors, tests normal for a 70-year-old?"*
Pincus said that as people get older, their capacities, intellectual capacities and physical capacities, deteriorate... adding that *"(this is not true of everyone, but that is true statistically)."*

Bailey: *"You mean, my cross-examination is slipping?"*
Pincus said he didn't know what it used to be like... and then said *"It doesn't matter what the age is. If a person is 70 and is able to be unimpaired and to be completely effective, I have no problem with that... It is the impairment that bothers me."*

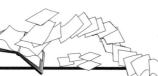

Bailey: *"Do you know that the impairment did not show up in the 33 airshows in 1992 following the complaint by the Inspectors?"*

He did know that... and he also knew that it (the impairment) hadn't shown up in the flight the day before or in Reno the previous September... and that Hoover had a sudden, unanticipated emergency descend upon him a week earlier when he was 10 miles out over the Pacific. But he said the fact that Hoover had handled this emergency flawlessly wasn't really relevant, because he was talking about likelihoods and probability. After an exchange where Pincus asserted that the same "things" (i.e., exhaustive testing) would be done to a doctor who is believed to be impaired (by his colleagues), Pincus said that, on the basis of his experience, he believed that Hoover is not going to be able to fly properly in the next two years.

Bailey: *"What should we look for in his motor functions to see whether or not there is any impairment resulting from these tests which has any bearing at all on flying? What should we look for?"*

Pincus: *"I think you could do a lot worse than use a CogScreen, but I am not allowed to say that."*

Bailey repeated his question –what should one look for in his flying? *"What should the check pilot look for in Bob Hoover's handling of the controls which would show that he has some dysfunction as a pilot? Do you have an answer?"*

Pincus: *"I really don't have an answer to that. That is beyond my area of expertise."*

That was all of the questions Bailey had for this witness, but the Judge had a couple. His first was a request for a lay definition of cognitive deficit. Pincus explained it as a disturbance of the brain that interferes with thinking.

Judge Mullins: *"Does it not deal with performance in addition to thinking? Or when you say thinking, are you talking about a whole sphere of human activity?"*

Pincus explained that there were different kinds of cognitive dysfunction a person could have. When asked by the Judge how all this differs from Alzheimer's, Pincus replied that in Alzheimer's, memory is more impaired. He continued by saying that Hoover's problems could be Alzheimer's – he only knew that Hoover was impaired but did not know the cause of the impairment. However, he said, Alzheimer's typically showed a steady deterioration that did not seem to be present in Hoover's case.

This witness was then excused, and a recess was taken. When they came back on the record, the Judge explained that Bailey's earlier objection about the Administrator bringing in a doctor to discuss the possibility of Hoover having Alzheimer's, after consideration, was sustained. If the witness was indeed to testify about this subject, then he should not be brought forth, because the possibility of the presence of this disease had never before been discussed in this case.

The Judge brought up an interesting issue: *"...I assume if Alzheimer's is an issue, then there wouldn't be an issue of practice effect, because you wouldn't remember that you practiced it, I assume. I don't know that."*

Judge Mullins: *"...and my ruling goes to the issue of Alzheimer, not Dr. DeVous. I just*

on't want to open that up."

At that time, Winton of the FAA explained that they did have one other doctor *ho was en route – but not yet there – whom they may wish to call and wanted to reserve *hat right should they feel it necessary in rebuttal. Otherwise, they wished to rest their *ase.

It was now 4:00, and the Court had use of the courtroom until 7:00. All involved *ad hoped to be done with the case that day, but it was painfully obvious it was to go on... *erhaps even into the following week. To break the tension (or so it seemed), the Judge *hen said: *"Well, that lady back there in the back said if we quit early, she was going to *uy my dinner, so, you know – for the record, I guess I should identify her as my wife."*

Knowing that he would keep the Court busy until the last possible minute, Bailey *aid, *"They say the steak is real good here after 7:00."*

Chapter 22

Bob Hoover Speaks...

Behold the turtle. He only makes progress when he sticks his neck out.
James Bryant Conant

The testimony of the most important witness, you see, would keep the Court listening... it was time for Robert A. "Bob" Hoover to come to the stand.

Yes, it was now time for Hoover to impress the Court and all who were there with his "curriculum vitae," as it were... which was just as long and impressive as Elliott's and Pincus' and all the others. Hoover had learned to fly at 16, and joined the Tennessee Air National Guard when he was 18. His unit, he said, was the first to go active before WWII. He then received normal flight training to become a fighter pilot, going overseas earlier than most units. He ended up flying British Spitfires *"because there weren't enough of our airplanes for us to fly."* He flight-tested airplanes that were shipped over in crates and then assembled and he finally went into combat.

He was shot down in his 59th mission, and spent the rest of the war in a prison camp — Stalag I. *"I was a maverick,"* he said. *"I wanted out, and I spent every waking hour plotting and planning on how to escape. And I was often mistreated, because the escape attempts would fail... and I was frequently kicked and beaten from time to time."* (He said he had been kicked in the face and the jaw.) Hoover went on to relate that he was in the camp for 15 months, getting out within the last two weeks of the war by diversion tactics.

Bailey then left the war stories momentarily to ask Hoover about the nose. He asked him what sort of nose his father had. *"It looked exactly like mine,"* Hoover said, and when asked if his father had drank, he explained that he had been a teetotaler. Bailey then asked if Hoover had had any medical problems relating to his nose.

Hoover: *"...I have had two skin cancers removed on my nose and skin grafts on the tip of my nose, as you can see."*

Back to the war stories. Bailey asked Hoover what he did after prison camp, and Hoover said that he went to Wright Field and completed Air Force test pilot school.

Bailey: *"Now, how does one get into Air Force test pilot school? Is there any competition for that job, or is it the luck of the draw, or what?"*

Hoover told the Court that there is competition, and certain requirements —

including the equivalent of two years of college to get into it — which Hoover did not have.

Bailey: *"You think they perhaps looked the other way a little bit on that requirement?"*

Hoover: *"I don't know. They perhaps did. I can tell you for sure the Navy did when I went through the Navy test pilot school."*

Bailey then asked how Hoover had done in mathematics in high school (to which he replied *"very poorly"*) and if he had ever been a *"book-learning sort of person"* (*"not really"*). He then asked Hoover to tell the Court about his days at Wright Field.

His first assignment there was dive testing on the P-47, which including designing a system of recovery where the pilot could manually create some flaps on the stabilizer — which allowed the plane to effect a recovery out of compressibility — i.e., make it controllable when it might not otherwise be so. Two pilots had been killed on this project before Hoover took over and completed it. Next, he was one of the early people to fly the Bell P-59 jet, the first jet in the US, and some testing on the P-80, the next operational jet. He did ram jet testing, where there were jet engines on the wingtips as well as on the main engine — he was the first pilot to test a P-51 that was designed that way.

Hoover: *"I flew all kinds of planes. I was the Air Force pilot on the P-82, which was a twin Mustang. We had a little bit of everything there that was left over from — airplanes that never went into production."* Additionally, Hoover had done the military flight testing for the military equivalent of certification for many airplanes that did go into production. *"I was on practically every airplane that North American built back in those years,"* he explained.

When Hoover left the Air Force, he became a test pilot for General Motors, testing jet engines at altitude and experimental airplanes (such as the F-9F, which he told the Court had an Allison engine in it... good memory, eh?). He joined North American in 1950.

Bailey: *"You mentioned Naval flight testing school. What kind of training did you receive from the Navy?"*

Hoover: *"Well, the Navy requested me. North American was going to start a Navy factory in Columbus, OH, and they said they wanted someone that they — they wanted to choose the test pilot that would be representing North American Aviation for the Navy, and they wanted me trained and they wanted me to go aboard a ship. And I took all of the training that they had, and again I went through their test pilot school which I must tell you was very difficult. Academic-wise, it was much, much more severe than the courses I had at the Air Force test pilot school."*

Hoover told the Court that he hadn't been there a week when he went to the commandant and told him he couldn't handle calculus. North American and the Navy wanted him so badly because of his flight skills that the instructors coached and tutored him, often *"burning the midnight oil"* to pass. Once through the school, Hoover entered the F-86 program, doing much of the spin testing, dive testing, and high mach number flying. *"I went through every facet of that airplane's development,"* he said.

Barnstorming

By J.R. "Zoom" Campbell

In Defense of Bob

FLYING GROUNDED!

The inside story of how the FAA got Bob Hoover.

BY F. LEE BAILEY

World's Most Widely Read Aviation

THE WALL STREET JOURNAL.

1994 Dow Jones & Company, Inc. All

HOMEBUILDERS' CORNER

NEVER A DULL MOMENT

For every problem that is solved, or good thing that happens, something else comes along that slows progress. Most of the time it's so unnecessary. It makes me wonder why we can't all move in the same direction, promoting aviation. Here's a look at just some of the issues.

The most asked...
the past few...
much...

BOB HOO...

$2 Per Copy · First August Issue 1994 · 46th Year, No. 16

General Aviation News & Flyer

The Nation's Aviation Newspaper — Since 1949
76 Pages

Bailey: Case against Hoover was 'cooked up'

By JAMES...

demonstrably and righteously than Robert A. "Bob" Hoover... one of the finest pilots in the world and a

TOM POBEREZNY
President, EAA

Hoover. Over... people "not... 's appeal to... of Appeals...

ontravention...

As a matter of fa... that this current problem... the result of a criminal conspiracy... rt of people within the FAA to "hit"... up... the Feds, in their infinite igno-... e somehow had the brass cojones... to ground Bob Hoover.

Their evidence??? When you examine the

The Bob Hoover story woke the aviation media up... if only for a little while. Rumors started almost as soon as Boehler and Kelln filed their paperwork and started making serious news as soon as the NTSB hearing was set. With the favorable decision in Oklahoma City overruled by the FAA, even though the most lackadaisical aviation writer could see that something was seriously amiss.

In very little time, articles started showing up in the Aviation Media bringing forth details of the travesty that was in the making. Articles appearing in AOPA Pilot Magazine, FLYING magazine, Atlantic Flyer, Sport Aviation, Pacific Flyer, General Aviation News & Flyer, World Airshow News, US Aviator (published by the author), and many others got the ball rolling and started letting the aviation public know that the FAA had run amok. Many articles used the Hoover fight as the justification for demanding Pilot's Rights reforms and regulatory relief from an often heavy handed FAA.

FAA Administrator Dave Hinson inherited the Bob Hoover scandal from his predecessor, General Thomas Richards.

The hue and cry over the Hoover Affair was awesome... at aviation gatherings, T-Shirts, signs, bumper stickers, pins and buttons proclaimed loudly that the great majority of the aviation public was quite sure that Bob Hoover should be flying and NOT grounded.

During the Hoover fight, Steve Oliver, F. Lee Bailey, Bob Hoover, Sean Tucker, Leo Loudenslager, and aviation writer/publisher Dave Weiman give the camera man a thumbs-up in hopes for a victory in the Hoover fight.

A major distinction in Bob's performances is not just the fact that Bob flies a twin-engine ship... but the fact that both engines are rarely operating at the same time throughout the twisting, turning performances that Hoover has been giving for decades.

The original Commander, when first introduced to the flying public, was something of a dud... causing some embarrassment and consternation to the higher-ups at Rockwell (prior to the merger with North American) and abject fear in the marketing department. Hoover's airshow demonstration turned it into a hit.

It is Jim Driskell's job to get the lay of the land, make sure that all initial paperwork is done, see who's whom, check that the airplane is ready to go and figure out what meetings and inspections might be required so that Bob could deal with the rigors of performing without much of the drudgery and bookkeeping that go hand-and-hand with this involved undertaking. It is a wonderfully symbiotic relationship that has withstood decades of airshow performances.

The Hoover routine is breathtaking. It starts off with a bee-line down the runway and a slow roll on takeoff followed by a turn-out and return to the field with his signature touchdown/roll/touchdown. Bob then lands the aircraft briefly, allowing just the right landing gear to make contact with Mother Earth before rocketing off the runway again into yet another roll at a dazzlingly low altitude, thence to settle back on the ground momentarily on just the left gear before taking off again.

While there is obviously no disliking Roger Mullins for his courageous ruling against the FAA and on behalf of Hoover, it is worth noting that, win or lose, aviation attorneys from all around the country have commented most favorably on his fairness and common-sense. One of the few breaks that Hoover received was being heard by this uncommonly fair man.

Bob's performances are known to be some of the smoothest in the business due to the fact that he does not "muscle" his aircraft through maneuvers using shear horsepower, but instead, ekes every bit of energy, inertia and aeronautical advantage out of that aircraft that he can.

Australia's Dr. Robert Liddell was one of the early Doubting Thomases as regards the FAA's case and went ahead with Hoover's Australian certification despite immense pressure from his superiors and the FAA!

Dr. Jon Jordan (left) FAA's top medical professional... is both a medical doctor as well as a lawyer. To the far right, is FAA Associate Administrator Tony Broderick, a man who did not appear to distinguish himself favorably during the Hoover fight.

Aero-writer Howard Fried (l) has also felt the enmity of the FAA. He battled them in court with the expert help of AOPA Chief Counsel John Yodice (r), considered by many to be the most expert aviation attorney in America.

Dr. Robert Poole is one of Jon Jordan's more senior deputies... and was the man who wound up delivering long sought welcome news to Mr. Hoover at the end of a tiresome three year legal battle.

Aviation Attorney and Writer Glenn McGovern wrote extensively on the Hoover matter and oft questioned FAA's motives and legality in the Hoover matter... much to their chagrin. Glenn is the author of US Aviator magazine's "Pilot's Bill of Rights" petition.

Supporting players for one of the FAA's "Meet the Boss" sessions. Administrator Hinson rarely dealt with the public in the forums without a number of his deputies in attendance... who often were the ones who got to answer questions put to Hinson.

Bob has a very loyal cadre of fans and friends... just a few of the thousands of them are shown here in a group photo at the 1996 Arlington Airshow during a cookout/party.

One of the most memorable aspects of a Hoover/Shrike performance is that silent finish... As the crowd waits to see if he's going to get to the announcing stand or other pre-planned vantage point; they break into wild applause as he squeaks to a stop that often positions him right in front of the announcer. It's a magical moment.

After he comes to a stop, Bob repositions his trademark straw hat and prepares to receive the applause of the crowd.

As so many will tell you, the full Bob Hoover/Shrike Commander performance is a thing of beauty... more ballet than thrill show, more precision than brute force, more smooth and linear than wild and brash. It is the product of precision, skill and experience...

Leo Loudenslager was the World Aerobatic Champion in 1980 and flew along with Hoover for the infamous 1993 Oklahoma City demo for NTSB Law Judge Mullins. Leo was a tireless Hoover advocate. Sadly, he lost his life a few years later in a motorcycle accident.

Tommy Jones was the life and breath of Aerospace America, until he lost his life in a horrific airshow accident apparently caused by his fatigue in both managing AND flying in the show. He was an amazing person.

The effervescent Sean Tucker is always in motion.... An ACE and one of the best airshow performers in the world, Tucker worked aggressively on Bob's behalf. This guy possesses a love for flying that really shows when he flies, as he herds a 300+ HP biplane through the skies with incredible abandon—loops, rolls, tumbling, spinning, you name it... the only time his airplane stops gyrating is when they close the hangar doors at the end of the day.

Bob remembers that, "I had a call from my friend Lee Bailey, who suggested that if I had an opportunity, I should try to get a flight in a T-28 and have somebody photograph from the back seat my going through one of my aerobatic routines so that I could show the court that I had not lost any of my touch as the FAA had alleged."

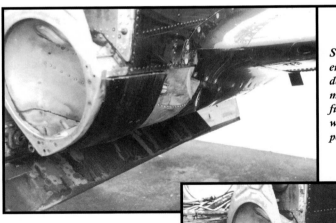

So catastrophic was the engine failure that the sudden stoppage of that immense propeller twisted the fuselage just forward of the wing... and the wing attach points were also damaged.

Bob summarized the whole event simply... "When the engine seized, it was about as violent a reaction as you could get in an airplane... the whole airplane just lurched..."

Bob Hoover is a very busy man... but no matter how crazy his schedule seems, he always makes time for the children... who somehow seem to know that they are in the presence of someone pretty great.

EAA President Tom Poberezny was a vocal Hoover advocate and one of the organizers of the "Friends of Bob" attempt to help raise money to counter Bob's immense legal expenses.

AOPA's indefatigable President Phil Boyer travels the country regularly hosting dozens of annual Town Meetings. "I never gave a speech, never had any kind of gathering or get-together in which if I didn't mention it as part of the formal presentation, the very first or second question from the audience would be about Bob Hoover and our involvement in what was going on."

Under the best of circumstances, this is what the prop shaft SHOULD look like. Compare this picture of a healthy engine/shaft with the two below. That huge prop came to a total stop as the internal workings of the engine became so "slagged" with disintegrating metal that no further rotation was possible. The force of the prop coming to a sudden stop twisted the entire front of the aircraft!

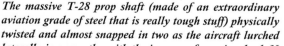

The massive T-28 prop shaft (made of an extraordinary aviation grade of steel that is really tough stuff) physically twisted and almost snapped in two as the aircraft lurched laterally in sympathy with the immense forces involved. Note the twists in the grooved portion of the prop shaft... and imagine what kind of energy it took to twist something that strong that far! Bob remembered that, "When the engine seized, it was about as violent a reaction as you could get in an airplane... the whole airplane just lurched... and then I kissed it on the wheels... I had plenty of speed so there wasn't any problem with lateral control as a result of the seizure."

What endears Bob Hoover to the general public, whether or not they even remember his name, are the airshow performances he has given for millions—doing things with airplanes that would cause even the best pilots in the world to shake their heads in wonder.

One of the most prized opportunities for any airman is to get their picture taken with Bob Hoover... as this picture from Australia (and the smiles on everyone) shows. The lovely woman in the center of the photo is none other than Colleen Hoover.

Bob is most at home at airshows... where he is free to talk flying with pilots from all over the world, like this Russian flyer he met at a Florida Fly-In in 1996. No matter their background or experience level, Bob treats them all with respect and courtesy... and is nearly as well known for his good graces as he is for his flying.

You Can't Tie An Eagle Down
A Song by Barb MacLeod

There comes a time when injustice draws a line in the sand,
When the laws that protect us deal a dark upper hand;
We can close ranks together at the line, or we can fall,
For the hand dealt an ace may be awaiting us all.

There's a twin Shrike Commander doing loops in the blue,
Floating on feathered engines, diving low, pulling through;
The man at her throttles is a prince among his peers,
Has the heart of an eagle and the grace born of years.

Oh, you just can't (oh no, you can't)
Tie an eagle down (tie an eagle down),
Clip his graceful wings (take away his wings),
Keep his spirit bound (stake him to the ground);
We are one voice (we are one voice)
All the nation 'round (all the nation 'round);
We stand and say to the FAA,
You let him fly, or you tell us why;
Though you may try, you just can't tie an eagle down!

He's been an ace of the airshows two decades and more,
And a champion flier for a long time before;
Bob Hoover's in Oklahoma, got the feds on his tail;
They say he's losing his touch, getting old, looking frail.

An endless chain of opinions, rulings and appeals;
A good man is grounded in the turning of the wheels;
In other lands he is legal, but at home he cannot fly;
They've tied down the eagle, and his home is the sky.

Oh, you just can't (oh no, you can't)
Tie an eagle down (tie an eagle down),
Clip his graceful wings (take away his wings),
Keep his spirit bound (stake him to the ground);
We are one voice (we are one voice)
All the nation 'round (all the nation 'round);
We stand and say to the FAA,
You let him fly, or you tell us why;

Though you may try, you just can't tie an eagle down!

But they gave him his freedom in the hour of the game
When they held all the cards, bent the rules to their aim;
The Washington Shuffle's just a play for saving face,
And the stand that we made changed the terms of disgrace.

There comes a time when injustice draws a line in the sand,
When the laws that protect us deal a dark upper hand;
We can close ranks together at the line or we can fall,
For the hand dealt an ace may be awaiting us all.

Oh, you just can't (oh, no you can't)
Keep a good man down (keep a good man down),
Take his golden years (take his silver wings),
Take away his crown (tie an eagle down);
We are one voice (we are one voice)
All the nation 'round (all the world around),
He got away from the FAA;
They won't say why, but they let him fly;
Though they were sly, they couldn't tie Bob Hoover down!

There's a twin Shrike Commander climbing high in the blue,
Looping down to the numbers as no twin ought to do;
The man at her throttles is a prince among his peers,
Has the heart of an eagle and the grace born of years.

Oh, you just can't
Tie an eagle down,
Clip his graceful wings,
Keep his spirit bound;
We are one voice
All the nation 'round;
We stand and say to the FAA,
You let him fly, or you tell us why;
Though you may try, you just can't tie an eagle down!
Though you may try, you just can't tie an eagle down!

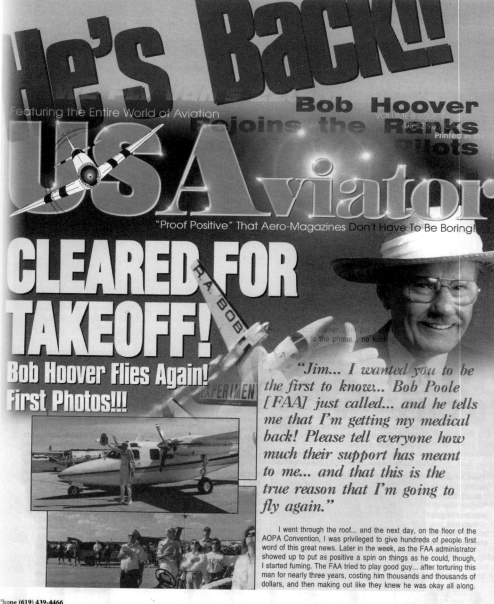

He's BACK!!

Bob Hoover Rejoins the Ranks of Pilots

Featuring the Entire World of Aviation

USAviator

"Proof Positive" That Aero-Magazines Don't Have To Be Boring!

CLEARED FOR TAKEOFF!

Bob Hoover Flies Again!
First Photos!!!

"Jim... I wanted you to be the first to know... Bob Poole [FAA] just called... and he tells me that I'm getting my medical back! Please tell everyone how much their support has meant to me... and that this is the true reason that I'm going to fly again."

I went through the roof... and the next day, on the floor of the AOPA Convention, I was privileged to give hundreds of people first word of this great news. Later in the week, as the FAA administrator showed up to put as positive a spin on things as he could, though, I started fuming. The FAA tried to play good guy... after torturing this man for nearly three years, costing him thousands and thousands of dollars, and then making out like they knew he was okay all along.

Phone (619) 439-4466   Pacific Flyer November 1995 - Page A3

Hoover Vindicated!

After Another Battery Of Tests, Hoover Gets His 2nd Class Medical — With Restrictions

Not all "Man Fights City hall" stories have a happy ending. After three years, the FAA finally changed its mind. The pressure mounted, as the evidence was getting too ponderous to refute, and a new round of tests basically gave the FAA a reasonable basis/excuse to admit that Hoover could fly. All of a sudden, despite the stresses and upsets of a punishing three-year battle against seemingly impossible odds, Bob's condition had "improved" and the FAA decided to issue Bob a conditional medical certificate under its "Special Issuance" guidelines.

Additionally, he made the first flight on the T-28 and tested some bombers, and he tested the heaviest airplane ever put on a carrier, the AJ-1... all for the Navy. He also tested the OV-10 Bronco turbo-prop insurgency counter, which was used in Vietnam. One of the biggest projects in his flight testing career came after that.

Hoover: *"... the F-100 was a very important segment of my flight test career, because this was our first supersonic airplane in level flight... But, remember, I had been on the X-1 rocket research program with Chuck Yeager before I left the Air Force. And now we were able to do it with a jet airplane instead of a rocket-powered airplane and able to go faster than sound on level flight. It was a very big accomplishment back then at very high risk. We lost quite a number of pilots in that program."*

Bailey: *"...I take it that in the course of all your test pilot work, you received extensive training in handling unforeseen emergencies."*

Hoover: *"Oh, it was a daily routine."*

Bailey: *"Do you feel any diminution in your ability to handle emergencies today as against 1955 when you packed in the F-100?"*

Hoover: *"None whatsoever. If anything, I have accumulated knowledge in the memory bank that I can draw upon. At the Reno Races each year, I sit there and assist — this year I think there were eight pilots that I helped save.*

What that means is that these people are running engines at real high power, way above and beyond what they were designed for, and you can anticipate that we are going to have an emergency every time we fly, and I have been the safety pilot there for 30 years. And even without my license, I was flying a P-51 with a qualified pilot in the back seat or the front seat, and this year I helped eight airplanes get down, and I have letters from some of them. I have had letters from people saying that I have saved their life. And I have talked them down when they were on fire and absolutely no visibility forward at all, every little detail until I got them on the ground."

Hoover then told the Court about an emergency he had once had in the F-100, in 1955. He was flying a brand new engine design, and there was a terrible explosion at 41,000'. The fire was so enormous it came out the nose of the airplane, enveloped it, and bounced his feet right off the rudder pedals.

The people with whom he was in touch said that they didn't believe he could survive a landing without an engine. He told them he was not going to bail out — he was going to try to save that airplane, and, at the same time, millions of dollars. The gear collapsed and it was a near-fatal landing — Hoover lost consciousness at one point and when he came to he knew he had broken his back. He was out of commission for six weeks after the accident, but later went back to the F-100 program. He was proud that the availability of the wreckage allowed the designers to re-configure the hydraulic pump capacity, which they determined was the problem. After the F-100 program, Hoover was promoted to management — but on the basis that he could stay in the cockpit as well.

Hoover: *"I was director of customer relations. I was in marketing, public relations, ad-*

vertising, but always in the cockpit, and I became the demonstration pilot for the corporation... I performed just about any place you can imagine, demonstrating the capabilities of our airplanes, all different types, everything we built."

Hoover also said he flew at the Paris Air Show, and other airshows all over the world. Bailey asked him when he started doing aerobatic flying. Hoover said it was when he was at North American, taking the airplanes out of their design limits and then writing the handbooks for other pilots who would then fly the airplane... basically, a certification process. Rockwell Standard Co. bought out North American in 1968, and they asked Hoover to *"see what he could do"* with the Aero Commander (later called the Rockwell Commander) — an aircraft on which they had been losing $13 million/year. Hoover explained that he revived an aerobatic demonstration he had utilized in the P-38's in WWII for the Commander — it was the same demonstration the Court had seen the day before.

Hoover: *"Once I demonstrated (that routine) before the public, the airplane started selling like hotcakes..."*

After establishing that Hoover had also done routines in other airplanes, such as the Sabre Liner, and that he had performed aerobatically so many times — all over the world — that it would be practically impossible to say how many times he had done it, Bailey returned to the subject of a potential problem in handling an emergency.

Bailey: *"Now, is the act which you do in any way dependent upon what I will call the cleanliness of the airplane, the aerodynamic cleanliness; that is, your ability without power to execute certain maneuvers and wind up back where you started."*

Hoover said it is.

Bailey: *"Did something happen yesterday that was unusual that could have affected the flight?"*

Hoover said that one of the cowl flaps on the aircraft, which are located atop the engine cells (there for cooling the engine cells), failed and went wide open. This created an enormous amount of drag. *"I had to draw upon some skills that you wouldn't normally use."* He also testified that he had never had a cowl problem like that before... although he had had to deal with unusual occurrences and/or in-flight emergencies many times throughout his career.

Hoover asked Bailey if the airplane had any special features in the demonstration airplane, and he said it did have a couple of STCs, to include: a blow-down bottle for additional brake pressure for use when the engines are off, and accumulators, to feather and unfeather the engines. Next, Bailey asked Hoover to tell the Court about in-flight procedures during his performance. First, he said the throttles are left wide open and rarely touched after that. The propeller controls, however, get exercised considerably — every time he shuts an engine down, he pulls back on the lever to feather the propeller.

Bailey asked which of the maneuvers took the aircraft closest to its design limits. Hoover explained that it would be the energy management maneuver, where he climbs to between 3000' and 3500', rolls the airplane, and then begins downhill — and then shuts down the engines. He does a loop, a roll, a 180-degree turn, and then comes back in and lands... with no instruments. *"It is all judgment, all in the eyeballs and the seat of your pants,"* he said, adding that every flight is different... and that everything he does must be

right. Bailey asked Hoover if he had ever had problems with the hydraulic system before, and he said he had many times. When this pressure drops, the gear hangs down — which in turn causes drag, and it's difficult for him to get any speed.

Bailey: *"Now, from time to time, Mr. Hoover, are you dissatisfied with maneuvers that you perform in an airshow? Do you sometimes feel you didn't do them the way you intended to do them, or to the level of skill?"*

Hoover: *"Well, yes. You are correct. The next weekend after having been here in Oklahoma City, I performed in Truckee, CA. The wind was gusting to 50 knots, and that is up in the mountains... I could not do the maneuver you saw me do yesterday, which has been my trade for all these many years, because the air was so rough and the wind was so strong, that I didn't feel it was a safe maneuver to perform."*

Hoover continued, now talking about the June 1992 airshow in question. *"...This was the second day of flying, and everything was just perfect. And I set up my pattern and put the gear handle down. The main gear came down, and I had a red light on the nose gear, and I called and said, 'I am taking it around'.*

And I got one engine going, I got the other one going, and I took it out, and I took it out, and I was circling around to make a normal landing. I now had the gear down, and I asked the air boss, 'Do I have adequate time to repeat the maneuver, or do you wish me to land now?' And — that was one of the allegations against me, that I took extra time. I was given extra time, and I repeated the maneuver. I did not remember it, and I can equate that to someone who has been on stage. Can you remember when somebody coughed and you have done thousands of performances?"

After a discourse that disclosed that these performances had been taped by a local TV station and that Hoover had it in his possession (Bailey mentioned that they weren't planning to show it but left it as an option depending upon cross-examination), Bailey asked Hoover if he had been ill at any time during that airshow.

Hoover: *"Oh, absolutely not."*

Bailey: *"Do you recall any time when you were unfriendly to any of your colleagues in the business during that show?"*

Hoover: *"Oh, absolutely not."*

Bailey: *"Do you have to rely on staff members to help you remember things during that show?"*

Hoover: *"I do not, and I can tell you for a fact that what happens — I am a — I try to be a very friendly person, and if we are standing in a group of people and all their questions are addressed at me... I will turn around to one of the people who are working for me, Jim Driskell or Kelly Pettit... or Tim Bonnell and say, 'Why don't you tell that?' I want them in the conversation... I want to be friendly and get everybody in. That is my nature."*

Bailey then asked Hoover if he knew the two FAA Inspectors who had turned in the report. Hoover said he may have met them somewhere along the way, but he didn't

recall them. Bailey also asked him if anyone from the FAA questioned him at all during that airshow. He testified that no one had. Next, Bailey inquired as to who was in charge of the box of air space used by the performers at an airshow, and who operated the box by radio. Hoover explained that the FAA Inspectors are in charge of the box, and an air boss — someone hired by the promoters of the airshow —handled the communications. When asked, Hoover continued that if a pilot must leave the box, he must answer to the control tower. Bailey then asked Hoover what role Jim Driskell played in a Bob Hoover airshow.

Hoover: *"He has been my narrator for a great many years, and he also ferried my airplane. Up until the last — until '92, I was operating as many as three airplanes, and I would fly one of them to the show site. I would fly the Sabre Liner, and Jim would fly the Aero Commander."* He was the announcer for the airshow in question.

Bailey: *"Okay. When you had problems during this show, did it occur just one time or more than one time, the cavitation?"*

Hoover: *"My problem was consistent (later saying he had it on all three days). The first day, I had it, but… there is a technique to getting it back on line, and sometimes it can be accomplished in 30 seconds and sometimes it can take as long as three or four minutes. And the procedure to get the pressure back on line, you see, it has gone to zero and a gear is hanging down, so now what you have got to do is cycle the gear and try and get that pump, just like pouring water, priming an oil pump, if you will, an old water pump. You have got to do something to get the pressure back in there, get the oil pouring through.*

And you can accomplish that by using your nosewheel steering, which is on the top part of the brakes, and you put your feet, and you just tap them like this, and you keep tapping them. And you do it, whatever you can do, and it is a mystery to me exactly what uncavitates a pump. But that is how you accomplish it."

When asked, Hoover explained that he had been in communication with the air boss when he was having these problems; Hoover reiterated that he had asked the air boss if he had time to redo the maneuver and that the air boss had said yes. Bailey then asked if he had discussed the problems with Driskell, and Hoover said no; the two had been together so long, there was no need. Driskell wouldn't announce the problem, because it would have been too complicated to hold their attention, he said.

Bailey: *"Was there any time during those three days where Mr. Driskell didn't know where you were?"*

Hoover: *"I would question that that would ever be the case, because he has been watching me. He has seen this thing thousands of times."* He also said that Driskell always has the power to communicate with him if he would have a question. Bailey then said he wanted to discuss the prior Wednesday's flight, when Hoover was flying a T-28 Navy Trainer *"—the type I made the first flight on many years ago,"* Hoover explained. He also said he hadn't flown that type of plane in three years. Ray Hughes, a pilot and A & P, was with him.

Bailey: *"What was your purpose in flying on that day?"*

Hoover: *"Well, I wanted to get some videotape... two things really. I wanted to get more comfortable. Remember, I haven't been flying a lot. I hadn't flown since September at Reno, and I just wanted to feel more comfortable about everything, knowing that all these things were going to happen real soon.*

I had planned on flying the P-51 the next day. It is a dual control P-51, and I intended to have Lockheed test pilot Skip Holm fly with me, because since I have had this medical certificate withdrawn, each time I fly, I have to have a qualified person with me. And in the case of the T-28, I had Ray Hughes..."

Hoover also said that when he got into the sanctioned box, he practiced point rolls while Hughes videotaped him to see how precise he could be. He did four-, eight-, and sixteen-point rolls. He also did a loop; but when he started to do his cuban-eight, a chip warning light (which detects foreign metal in the oil system) came on. This meant an engine failure was imminent.

When this happened, Hoover said, he headed back to Torrance. He continued, *"and I said, 'We have a prop overspeed,' and it went over 1000 RPM above where it is supposed to go. You know the engine is going to tear itself apart catastrophically within seconds or maybe minutes if you are lucky, and in this case I was lucky.*

I got the governor under control. Apparently some metal had gotten into the governor itself, let it go and then spit it out, and I was able to control the prop. But the damage was already done to the engine. It backfired; it started smoking. And it started stopping, and then I would get it going again, and I was working everything to keep that engine running, all the time heading toward Torrance..."

Hoover continued his tale, saying that he got everything under control at about seven miles off the coast. *"...it was the smoothest landing I ever made in my life,"* he said... but that wasn't the end of the trouble. *"I kissed it off, and right at that time, with the nose still in the air, the engine seized. The prop stopped, and I taxied off the runway on a high-speed taxiway... The severity of this emergency was that the airplane is in bad shape..."*

Hoover then described some of the damage, which included sheared wing bolts, destroyed engine mounts, a broken cowling, and a buckled fuselage. Bailey then offered photos of this aircraft as evidence and the proceedings recessed for the day shortly after that.

The next day, the Judge began with a statement that reiterated his point about Driskell narrating Hoover's earlier flight (i.e., that the FAA had wanted him to recuse himself because he had talked to a witness) and firmly said that their objection was over-ruled — again saying that the videotape showed two FAA lawyers standing very close when Driskell was explaining Hoover's maneuvers to Judge Mullins. After that, the FAA's Mr. Winton threw out yet another objection, saying that they had become aware that Bailey intended to call the two FAA Inspectors who wrote the original reports, as well as a third Inspector who would then be called to discredit the first two. Winton, of course, felt this would only waste the Court's time, stating that their story was no longer even relevant because the FAA had offered a sufficient (in his opinion, mind you) amount of medical testimony to "prove" that Hoover should be medically disqualified from holding a pilot's medical certificate. Bailey, of course, begged to differ.

Bailey: *"... But what he (the third Inspector) will testify is that the FAA Inspectors com-*

plained that Bob Hoover was too important and too old and should be grounded in their judgment and they sat down deliberately to concoct a story to try to get him grounded and he heard them say: 'We can't let anyone know that we put this together as a couple.' That is evidence, and if that is not relevant in this case: fraud, collusion, a violation of the federal statute against false statements to a Federal officer, I can't think of anything more relevant.

A more important question is when did the FAA learn this and who in the FAA knew about it. Perhaps the FSDO officer can tell us that. I think this evidence is critical, particularly since you heard Dr. Pincus say part of the history on which he based his opinion was the bad flying in 1992 which turns out to be, as we had suspected all along — and I told you in opening without even knowing that this witness existed — a fraud."

Again, Winton stated that none of the three expert medical witnesses relied on the statements of the Inspectors. The Judge had an interesting way to look at it.

Judge Mullins: *"The Administrator has alleged cognitive deficit which by Webster's Dictionary means an inability to perform. Now the Administrator wants to continue this trial without any reference to any objective deficit of Mr. Hoover... That concerns me...*

...His ability to perform relates to cognition. Any statements about his ability to perform, I believe — and as witnessed by my looking at the airshow tape I think are relevant. I just don't know whether — how that balances with the medical testimony. All the medical testimony so far says he has a deficit but no one has ever seen the deficit, apparently, unless we are talking about these statements from these Inspectors..."

And he then overruled the objection. Bailey then said in the interest of time he was going to release Driskell, Hoover's announcer, as a fact witness but still wanted him to testify regarding the innocence of the conversation he had with the Judge during Hoover's flight demonstration. Winton objected, and the Judge agreed, saying it wasn't necessary: *"I don't want to waste my time because I am satisfied I spoke the truth,"* he said.

Bailey: *"In addition to that, we subpoenaed one of the complaining Inspectors and tried to serve the other who has been fired, I am told, but is in any event, no longer employed by the FAA; we haven't found him. I am releasing those witnesses because I believe they should come in with counsel. I believe they are guilty of a federal offense and I intend to pursue it when this matter is over."*

With that, Hoover then returned to the stand to continue his testimony. They began by stating that they had a videotape of Hoover's flight in the T-28 described earlier, when he had an emergency mid-flight and that they wanted to show this tape. As you may have guessed, Winton quickly objected, saying that the tape's authenticity was *"questionable"* and that *"If we are going to go on viewing tapes of Mr. Hoover with apparent emergencies every time he gets in an aircraft, again, we will be here all day long,"* Winton said.

Bailey: *"May that remark be stricken: Emergencies every time he gets in an aircraft. What are you talking about?"*

After he found out that the tape was only five minutes long, the Judge overruled the objection, and the Court began to watch the tape. The tape showed Hoover doing

point rolls, a loop, and half a Cuban-eight before the emergency occurred and then the tape showed the damaged aircraft after the landing (subsequent to the engine seizing).

Next, Hoover's testimony resumed, with Bailey asking Hoover about other accidents he had been in — such as the accident in the F-100 (in 1955) they had discussed earlier, and an accident that had banged him up and caused dental damage when an engine caught fire in an F-84 in 1947. It was necessary for him to eject during this emergency, but the ejection seat didn't work.

Hoover: *"I ended up with the airplane completely out of control going straight down and I had to climb out and go over the side. I should say I was sucked out as soon as I opened things up and I went right into the tail with both legs, broke both legs right at the knees, and busted up my face, and then I was free-falling and pulled the ripcord and landed on two broken legs, and I was out in the desert for maybe four hours before a farmer happened to find me."*

Bailey then asked Hoover about a 1987 automobile accident.

Hoover: *"I was hit broadside. I was driving an automobile and at an intersection and a car was coming through fast and hit me and broke all the ribs on this side and my lung was punctured."*

Bailey then shifted gears, and again asked Hoover about the 1992 airshow, asking if anyone had ever questioned him about his performance after that show; no one had.

Bailey: *"You are now aware that two Inspectors signed similar letters claiming that you were deficient, frail, unfriendly, etc. When did you first get notice that you had been complained of?"* Hoover said he had received a form letter from FAA Doctor Audie Davis stating this.

Hoover: *"...and I immediately went to my American medical doctor who had been a flight surgeon for many years and I said, 'Gee whiz, I didn't do anything wrong or anything different than any other performance', but I didn't know about the letters. And so finally Dr. Davis sent the letters out to Dr. Puskas."*

After this, Hoover said, he went to see Dr. O'Connor. As a side subject here, Bailey asked Hoover if he selected Doctors O'Connor, Gold, Salcedo, or Elliott. Hoover had not — but did have to pay them to examine him. He then testified that after the routine of psychiatric tests, O'Connor called Hoover's wife and told her that Hoover *"had passed his exam and was clean."* Hoover said O'Connor also said the same thing to Jim Driskell.

Hoover: *"And then he called me up, he said, 'I would like to see you and Dr. Puskas together,' so I visited with him. And he said, 'I want to make this squeaky clean; I can't find anything wrong,' but he said, 'I would like to have you go and take these other tests so that nowhere downstream in your career will you ever be involved with anybody questioning your ability'. And he said, 'Would you be willing to do that?' And I said, 'Well, I don't really want to, but if you think that is the right thing to do, I will do it.' And so I hesitantly went to Dr. Elliott."*

Hoover testified that he spoke to Elliott the day prior to testing, and Dr. Elliott told him it would be no longer than four hours. He also said it was a stressful experience

for him because it was a test he had never taken and he didn't know anything about it. Continuing, Hoover said he was not given one break that day.

Hoover: *"So at that point in time — it is now 12:00 — I have not had a drink of water or a trip to the bathroom, so I said, 'Dr. Elliott, I would like to make a trip to the bathroom and use the telephone.' I asked him how much longer, and he said, 'We are only halfway through.' So I advised my wife to cancel all of our plans and I went to the bathroom, got a drink of water, came back, and I didn't get out of that office, I didn't have another break, I did not have lunch, I didn't have a drink of water or a trip to the bathroom until 5:00. He said 3:30; that is not right. My wife could tell you that is not true."* Hoover also testified that Elliott said nothing he was doing would impinge on his right to fly.

Hoover: *"... and he said, Now, there is nothing I am going to give you today that is going to have anything to do with your losing your license, so don't worry about that."* Hoover also said that Elliott never told him he was unfit to fly.

Bailey: *"Did Dr. Elliott explain to you what the tests were about or how they should be handled?"*

Hoover: *"He did not."*

Bailey: *"Once the tests began, did his demeanor change in any way from the admiration he expressed (Elliott had told Hoover his career was quite impressive) earlier in the day?"*

Hoover: *"Well, I didn't think he was very friendly right from the very beginning."*

Bailey: *"When you were having trouble answering the questions on the tests, did he give you an explanation or encouragement or tell you what you were doing wrong?"*

Hoover said he did not. Bailey then asked Hoover who his lawyer had been at the time. Hoover said it was Vern Lawyer (his real name, he also pointed out), a gentleman Hoover had met through Bailey, and whom he (Hoover) had assisted with an accident case. After that, the two, Hoover and Lawyer, had become friendly. On April 14, 1993, Hoover testified, he was with Dr. Puskas when Pakull and Puskas spoke on a speaker phone. It was then that Hoover found out that, despite O'Connor's recommendation, the FAA was going to attempt to deny his certificate. At the same time, Puskas spoke to Dr. Gold and Gold stated unequivocally that there was absolutely nothing wrong; he couldn't find anything that was the least bit suspicious. Then, Hoover continued, the call came in, and Pakull told him he was not medically fit to fly. Hoover told him he had been cleared by Dr. Davis and had flown 33 times since the airshow in question. Although Davis had told him to go ahead and book '93, none of this changed Pakull's mind.

Bailey: *"Had you, in fact, booked contracts to perform in '93?"*

Hoover: *"Yes, sir, and it cost me an enormous amount of money because I had to cancel every airshow in '93. I have had zero income since this came up."*

Bailey then asked Hoover to continue testifying about the conversation with

Puskas and Jordan. Hoover said Pakull told him to turn his certificate over to Puskas, and he (Hoover) asked him to give him an opportunity: *"Send me to any experts you wish,"* he said, *"and I will go to them, take any tests you wish."* He also told Pakull that he had already passed the tests and he didn't understand why he couldn't accept them.

Hoover: *"He said, 'Those doctors are all tools,' and he said, 'I make the decisions here in Washington...' and those were his exact words. From that point on I started pleading with Dr. Jordan. I said, 'Dr. Jordan, do you realize how much time and effort and money it has cost me to be supportive of FAA?' I said, 'I have given hundreds of safety lectures all over this country, I have put on flight demonstrations at facility dedications for FAA. I think you owe me a favor. Give me an opportunity to go to some other doctors of your choosing.' And so he chose Dr. Satz at UCLA. And I told him, I said, 'Dr. Jordan, I really appreciate this, I will go take those tests, I will get the appointment as quickly as I can,' which I did. And when I talked with Dr. Satz, he was a very friendly person and he told me he couldn't find anything wrong with me."*

Hoover also submitted to tests from Dr. Uchiyama and additional SPECT scans that were administered by Dr. Mena, and Hoover testified that they also gave him a *"clean bill of health."*

Bailey: *"Now, did you know when you asked Dr. Jordan to be examined again that no matter how well you performed, Dr. Pakull intended to deny your certificate period?"*

Hoover said he had that suspicion all along and that is indeed what happened. Bailey then began asking Hoover about his flight at Reno.

Bailey: *"At any time when you were flying the P-51 did the pilot who was with you — whoever that was — suggest any abnormality in your flying?"*

Hoover: *"No, sir."*

Bailey then asked Hoover for how long and in what capacity he had known Leo Loudenslager, the pilot who had flown with him during the flight demonstration for the Court. Hoover explained that Loudenslager was a world champion (who represented the US in Europe and beat the Russians) in a little aerobatic airplane of his own design, structure, and construction. It was also mentioned that he is a Captain for a major airline. Hoover recounted an earlier conversation with Loudenslager.

"He said, 'We will do your airshow circuit and I will be your safety pilot'. He said, 'This is the worst thing I have ever heard of.' And he put into motion through a Mr. Tony Broderick, for permission to fly with me, and I think Mr. Broderick okayed it verbally but as it went downstream within FAA, they stopped it."

Bailey then said he wanted to stop for a minute and ask about his experience within the community of aviators who travel from show to show.

Bailey: *"First of all, do you get to know these people personally?"*

Hoover said indeed so, and that the community was *"not too large."*

Bailey: *"Do you become familiar with the ordinary standards of performance from one star to another, so to speak?"*

Hoover: *"We police each other, and being the senior citizen on the block, I have been responsible, I believe, for saving a lot of lives. When I see someone doing something the least bit hazardous for their health, flying too low or snapping too quick, I caution them about it: I want you to be as old as I am, put a little air underneath that airplane, give yourself a little cushion, a little room to breathe. In case you have a problem or you make a mistake or rough air or you have got high density altitude where the airplane doesn't perform correctly, give yourself some breathing room."*

Next, Bailey asked Hoover if he was familiar with an accident in an F-86 that had happened at El Toro a year or so before the case, and if it had caused increased policing within their own ranks. Hoover said it had, so Bailey asked what the procedure was if a deficiency was detected.

Hoover: *"We go talk to him and we can ground him, we have that authority to do so"* — explaining that an ACE (aerobatics competency evaluator) could do this.

Bailey: *"Now, Mr. Hoover, there has been some testimony suggesting that you are impaired in some fashion. Have you ever felt impaired in flying an airplane other than mechanical accidents that you have described — I mean physically or mentally impaired to the point where your performance could not be brought to standard?"*

Hoover: *"Never."*

Bailey: *"If you ever sense that you are impaired, Mr. Hoover, what do you intend to do?"*

Hoover: *"I will quit."*

Bailey and Hoover then clarified that Bailey took Hoover's case, with the help of Yodice, when his original attorney, Mr. Lawyer, had a heart attack.

Bailey: *"Do you recall, whether in agreeing to take your case and protect your license, I imposed a condition? That is to say if I thought there was something wrong, what I would do."*

Hoover: *"You stated that if you didn't think that I was safe you were going to tell me, and I said I will accept that."*

Bailey then switched gears again, and asked Hoover if he had become aware of a doctor named Hisey at the Reno air races; Hoover said he had.

Hoover: *"Mr. Bill Rhinchild, he and his wife each race up there in P-51s. It is the first and only time that a husband and wife have been competitive in a high speed race, over 400 miles an hour in that course."*

Bill Rhinchild, Hoover continued, introduced Dr. Hisey to him.

Hoover: *"Dr. Hisey said, 'I am not associated with the FAA and I can — just watching you and observing you, I don't think there is anything in the world wrong with you'. He said, 'I would like you to come to Oklahoma City and let me and my doctors examine you and you will get the most thorough examination you have ever had in your life and I will*

stand up and be counted.'"

Like Bailey, Hisey also told Hoover that if he found a deficiency, he would tell him and make every effort to get him grounded. Hisey subsequently introduced Hoover to Dr. Johnson, who imposed the same condition if he found a deficiency. Hoover went to Oklahoma City for this testing. Hoover also testified that he had, subsequent to that period of time, become acquainted with Dr. Appel, and they had discussed Hoover's history and situation. Next, Hoover testified that he had asked some of the people who had been at Reno that year to submit written evaluations regarding their view of the consistency of his performance. The following people signed those documents:

Lee Lauderback: Owner of a dual-control P-51, jet-qualified, a Navy instructor pilot. Flew with Hoover at Reno. The airplane they were flying had a problem and they weren't able to fly it after the second or third day, so another man offered them the use of his plane (also a dual-control P-51). This man, Robert Patterson, was Hoover's mechanic when Patterson was 16 years old and is now an instructor pilot.

William Speer: *"Bill had an emergency and I was on him real quick and we saved the airplane,"* Hoover said.

The last to sign the document was **Delbert Williams:** *"I have talked him down a dozen times in the last 30 years. They are running those engines wide open and they are not designed to go at the kind of power that they are pulling out of them and they frequently destruct themselves,"* Hoover explained.

Bob Hoover's Cross-Examination

One might guess they didn't have any better points to bring out, so the FAA first brought up the subject of Hoover's demonstration flight and the question of "where was" the Judge?

Hoover: *"I do not recall the Judge being there after I got out of the airplane when I was discussing my flap problem with the other people."*

Winton questioned Hoover about the skin cancer he had on his nose: *"Did you ever mention this cancerous condition to any of the doctors that testified here today?"*

Bailey: *"Excuse me. Do we know what doctors have testified here today. I haven't seen any."*

Winton: *"I am sorry. The doctors that have testified over the last couple of days, specifically Dr. Elliott."*

Hoover: *"Well, they are not medical doctors, but for your information, any medical doctor could look at my nose and see where I have had skin grafts if they know their business at all."*

Winton then asked about the accidents Hoover had had in 1947 and 1955, and whether he had lost consciousness either time. Hoover said he did not remember doing so in 1947—reiterating, however, that it was quite a serious blow — but that he had in

1955. Therefore, Winton asked if he had indicated that each time he filled out an application for medical certification for the FAA. Hoover said that his doctor was aware of the accidents but that he could not recall if he had noted the accidents on each application. Winton then pointed out that Hoover did not check the box noting that he had ever been unconscious on the 1991 application. Winton then switched the subject to alcohol. *"Did you admit to (to Dr. Elliott), I think, having two drinks a day?"*

Hoover: *"I may have stated that."*
Winton then asked about hangovers.

Hoover: *"Well, I am sure when I was young and first started to drink that yes, I did have hangovers, but you are talking about ancient history."* Hoover continued, saying that he hadn't had a hangover in 25 years — and that he hadn't had that much to drink.

Winton: *"You also mentioned on direct examination that you were — I believe you had a problem with mathematics, that maybe you were a little slow in that area."*
Hoover agreed.

Winton: *"But you were able to overcome that, weren't you?"*

Hoover: *"Well, I managed to come out almost number one in the class at the test pilot school and I was the only person there that didn't have a master's degree in my class."*

Winton: *"So you consider your performance might be superior then. Right?"*

Hoover: *"Absolutely."*

Winton: *"Both academic and flying abilities?"*

Hoover: *"Absolutely."*
Winton then said he wanted to concentrate on Hoover's flight experience, and began to ask him about the T-28 and how many hours he had in the aircraft. Hoover said, *"In my days of flight testing we didn't have the sophisticated instrumentation and the flights were maybe 10 or 15 minutes, just take it up and find out whether it is going to hold together and bring it back."*
Winton asked if he dealt with any other emergencies in the T-28.

Hoover: *"Well, I had the butterfly valve get swallowed in the carburetor and made a dead-stick landing with it. Another time I had a governor fail and it ate the engine up and it was similar to last Wednesday's flight."*
Hoover testified, after being asked, that he had had three dead-stick landings in the T-28. Winton then said he wanted to ask him about his experiences at the Reno AirRaces, where Hoover had been safety pilot for 30 years.

Winton: *"And people push their aircraft pretty hard at those races, don't they, sir?"*
Hoover said they do indeed.

Winton: *"So it is almost expected that somebody would have an emergency. Isn't that right?"*

Winton asked what types of airplanes are flown at Reno; Hoover said always a P-51 or a T-33.

Winton: *"Lee Lauderback, what aircraft did he have an emergency in?"*

Hoover: *"Lee Lauderback did not have an emergency; he was my safety pilot and I did the flying and he rode with me."* He said the same was also true with Robert Patterson.

Winton: *"And William Speer?"*

Hoover: *"He was flying a P-51 and had the emergency which is listed there. That describes his emergency and how I saved the day for him."*

Hoover said, when Winton asked, that Delbert Williams was a race pilot, who has flown P-51s and other airplanes, and who has had a number of emergencies during which Hoover helped him.

Winton: *"So is it fair to say that the purpose of your being there, one of the primary purposes, is to help pilots deal with emergencies?"*

Hoover said that was correct.

Winton: *"And they rely on your experience as a test pilot and as an aerobatics pilot to help these people with that. Is that right?"*

Hoover: *"That is true."*

Winton asked how much time Hoover had in a P-51.

Hoover: *"I have no idea but I would venture to say that I have more time than any living person."*

Winton then asked if he had experienced many emergencies in a P-51, and Hoover said he certainly had.

Winton: *"So would it be fair to say that an emergency in a P-51 would be something common to you?"*

Hoover: *"An emergency is never common to anybody. My adrenaline flows just like everybody else; I have just been able to deal with it perhaps a little more quickly and swiftly than others who aren't with us today."*

Winton then asked Hoover how many years he had flown the Aero Commander; Hoover said he had flown that type of airplane for 25 years — later guessing that he had flown the routine he had shown the Court earlier at least 2000 times. He had made modifications over the years and he also stated that the weather conditions change his routine from show to show.

They then discussed the emergency that had occurred during the routine for the Court, and Hoover made it clear that he didn't really consider it an emergency; it was just

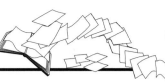

something with which to deal. And although any other pilot probably would have, he at no time felt in danger (or he would have landed the plane), and he was P.I.C. at all times during the flight. The only things Leo Loudenslager did during the flight was handle the mike and start the engines. During the emergency in the T-28, with Ray Hughes, Hoover testified that he was at the controls from the time he started the engine to the time he landed. Winton then brought up the previously-discussed cavitation problem and asked how many times it happened; Hoover estimated two or three times a year. When Winton asked how long it took him to correct the problem, Hoover said anywhere from 30 seconds to four minutes. He also testified, however, that no one would notice the difference.

When the subject of Dr. Elliott's testing had to come up again, Hoover testified that he tested from 8:00 a.m. until noon, when he (Hoover) asked for a break. Again he said he was not offered a break for a trip to the restroom or coffee or lunch. Winton then brought up Dr. Appel, and asked him if he had met her in her office; Hoover said he had not. He also said, after he was asked, that she did not perform any tests that were similar to the tests that Doctors Elliott, Johnsen, and the UCLA doctors had performed.

Winton's Last Question: *"Mr. Hoover, let me ask you this, with all due respect — you have many hours of experience flying many different aircraft — do you feel, in your opinion, that you have experienced every possible emergency that one could be confronted with in aviation?"*

Hoover: *"I do not."*

Winton: *"Thank you. No further questions."*

Judge Mullins: *"Mr. Hoover, how many total hours of flying time do you have?"*

Hoover: *"Sir, I would guess at maybe 20,000 hours, again, because of the short flights when I was active in testing every day."*

After a short recess, Bailey addressed the Judge and told him that he unwittingly omitted a matter on direct that he felt should be addressed — the five incidents and two violation previously mentioned by one of the FAA's expert witnesses, Dr. Pincus.

Bailey's Re-Direct of Hoover

Hoover took the stand again, and was asked about these violations and incidents.

Bailey: *"Do you know anything about any five incidents, as we sit here?"*

Hoover: *"I can recall three."*

Bailey then asked Hoover to tell the Court about those three. The first occurred, he said in Erie, PA, about 1986. *"My practice for a great many years,"* he said, *"was to give demonstration flights to the members of the press. Now, I would accept five passengers and fly as many as maybe ten flights prior to the airshow start time and give members of the press an opportunity to get footage for TV or have them along to write stories or what-have-you. The demonstration consisted of showing them single-engine operation*

of the airplane, showing them how docile it was in low-speed flight, and then show them what it was like to land without engines, so I would shut off both engines — absolutely no aerobatics — and set up a pattern and land the airplane, and then after the airplane was on the ground on its wheels, I would crank the engine up and taxi in."

Hoover continued his testimony, saying that the airshow in Erie was no different except that the airshow sponsor told him that the FAA Inspector had asked who the headliner was — Hoover, of course.

Hoover: "He (the FAA Inspector) said, 'Well, I am going to knock him — and I won't use his profanity — I am going to knock him right off his pedestal because nobody, no one deserves to be treated like that, and I am going to be the one to knock the royalty out of him and I will get him grounded.' This man had the audacity to ask me for my autograph and have his picture taken with me, and then he violated me."

Bailey asked if the violation was for "dead-sticking" with passengers, but Hoover said the Inspector claimed he was doing aerobatics with the passengers. Hoover said that he was on the board of directors for Evergreen Int'l Airlines at the time, and so was defended by their counsel. All of the passengers who had been aboard were contacted, and as everyone for Hoover's defense would have had to go to Pittsburgh between Christmas and New Year's, he decided not to fight it any further. He did, however, go to the Administrator at that time, Allen McArtor, and tell him the situation.

Hoover: "And he (McArtor) said, 'Since it didn't happen on my watch (the incident had occurred before he became Administrator), I can't erase the situation but,' he said, 'would you accept being grounded.' But a very important thing to that, Mr. Bailey, is that the man who wrote me up was fired by FAA because of mental instability."

In the end, Hoover accepted a sanction of being grounded for 30 days. This sanction, however, also covered the second violation. Hoover explained that he was performing at Oshkosh and someone from the FAA said he flew over the terminal building.

Hoover: "I couldn't have flown over the terminal building because my crowd line — Your Honor, there are 500' lines for certain speeds of airplanes. At 156 knots and below, you have to be 500' separated from the crowd line; your faster airplanes up to 250 knots go out to 1000'; and then the jet airplanes go out to 1500'. And I couldn't have been over the terminal building and be on my crowd line which was 1000' because the terminal building was over here."

Bailey: "What happened to that alleged violation?"

Hoover: "Well, that was sandwiched in with the other one and I accepted the 30-day grounding, and he let me choose the time. The Administrator said, 'When is convenient for you to accept this just to get it out of your hair?' I said, 'How about right now?' It was December 1."

Bailey commented that it was off-season, and then asked about the third violation. Hoover testified that it occurred at Deer Valley Airport near Phoenix, close to the end of a show. He said he still had two maneuvers to perform, a touchdown/roll and a touchdown on the other wheel. Right then, he said, a lightplane flew illegally through the

airshow box. The tower told Hoover to pull up, and he climbed to 2000'. When they told him it was clear, he turned around to come back in and he did so, he testified, a little fast.

Hoover: *"The flaps on a P-51 are such that they will not deploy themselves, they will only come down as the speed is decreased, so you can therefore use them as speed breaks. And so I put the flap handle down to slow up because my next maneuver was a touchdown-roll-touchdown, and I pressed for the runway. I was out of sequence, and being out of sequence means normally you put the gear handle down and then the flaps.*

And so I pressed for the runway and I was waiting for that left wheel to touch and all of a sudden I got a (makes noise). I ticked all four blades of that prop. Now, normally when you have a prop strike the blades are curled back and it will shake, it will shake real bad. In this case there was absolutely no shake. The buzz saw got each one of them exactly the same amount about like that, and it was no change in performance, so I just pulled up, dropped the landing gear, did the routine that I had planned to do, and took off and then did my last maneuver, which was a roll."

Long story short, the FAA Inspector who was on the scene filed a report that he flew the airplane in a condition other than how it left the factory, but Hoover contended that it hadn't hurt anything. Hoover went to L. A. and when he was told he would be grounded for six months, asked what his rights were. He also had the option of simply paying a fine or fighting the charge all the way up to the NTSB. As it was during airshow season, Hoover believed it was simpler to just pay the fine. Bailey then asked him if he had ever had a violation where lack of skilled performance was at issue, and Hoover said *"Never."*

The FAA "Re-Cross" Examination of Hoover

Winton: *"I just want to clarify something. The P-51 incident that you just mentioned, you were setting up to do a touchdown-roll-touchdown, is that what you described?"*
Hoover agreed.

Winton: *"And for whatever reason you were out of sequence being you pulled the flaps down before the gear."*
Hoover said yes.

Winton: *"So you are descending to the runway to do the first touchdown and you realize at the time because the prop had hit the runway that the gear wasn't down."*

Hoover: *"That is correct."*

Winton: *"How many other times have you forgotten or didn't put the gear down before landing?"*

Hoover: *"You know, as well as I, there are those who have and those who will."*
Hoover went on to explain that he had gone out of sequence before, because as a test pilot, things are happening all the time. Winton then asked Hoover if he thought his cavitation problem was an emergency, and Hoover said no.

Chapter 23

The "Friends of Bob" Weigh In

Few things are harder to put up with than the annoyance of a good example.
Mark Twain (Samuel Clemens)

World Aerobatic Champion
Leo Loudenslager Testifies

Leo Loudenslager was then called to the stand, after Bailey told the Court that he put several tapes of airshow performances, a tape of the flight demonstration, and the deposition of Dr. Ted Simon (on which Winton's voice is heard conducting the examination and on which it was apparent, Bailey asserted, that the SPECT scans came to him during the deposition), were being admitted. When Loudenslager finally made it to the stand, he testified that he had been a pilot for 28 years and that he was a Captain for American Airlines.

Loudenslager: *"I started in the Lockheed Electra, the L-188, the BAC-111, the 727 B –"*

Winton: *"Your Honor, I will object to any testimony by Mr. Loudenslager as it has no relevance to the issue of medical certification of Mr. Hoover."*

Judge Mullins: *"Why don't we do this, why don't we I just give you a continuing objection? The Administrator obviously has taken the position that this determination can be made strictly and only through medical examination when I have a — I disagree because I look up Webster's where it says cognition and it talks about performance and I think testimony about performance, whether it be through medical tests or through actual performance, is relevant, and I have said that over and over 'til I am tired of it. I will give you a continuing objection to that ruling and let's just move on."*

Winton: *"I just wanted to note my objection for the record. I know you know that."*

Judge Mullins: *"Well, it is on the record, please. Let's go on."*

Loudenslager: *"A 707, DC-10, MD-80 aircraft."*

Bailey: *"In your occupation as an airline pilot how is the ability to perform safely moni-*
tored among your colleagues and yourself?"

Loudenslager: *"Well, there are primarily two systems: the checks and balances between*
the multiple members on the crew station, and of course, the annual checks that we have
through simulator tests at our Dallas/Ft. Worth facility."

Bailey: *"As an airline pilot can you ever remember being given a Wisconsin Card-Sorting*
test?"

Loudenslager: *"No, sir."*

Bailey: *"A trail-making test?"*

Loudenslager: *"No, sir."*

Bailey: *"A categories test?"*

Loudenslager: *"No, sir."*

Bailey: *"Do you have any other occupation?"*
Loudenslager explained that he also flew airshows, and that he was the seven-
time national and 1980 World Absolute Aerobatic Champion and that he built the airplane he flies.
He said he first observed Hoover at the 1964 Reno Air Races, when Loudenslager
was a 19-year-old Air Force mechanic and a private pilot. He said he had known him for
more than as an observer for probably 20 years, and that he had observed Hoover's performances countless times.
Bailey then asked what an ACE (aerobatic competency evaluator) was and what
the origin of that position was. Loudenslager explained that Bernie Geier of the FAA and
Charlie Hillard initiated the program based on the premise that those most qualified to
judge an aerobatic competitions were those who performed aerobatics daily. Loudenslager
was one of the founding members of this FAA-sanctioned program. Bailey then asked
Loudenslager about a 1993 F-86 accident.

Loudenslager: *"The cause of the accident was the failure really of the program to prop-*
erly monitor this program. We went back and we found that there was falsification of
records, that the pilot did not have the level of experience that he had stated, and there
were several people who were concerned there on-site with the performance, several
ACEs or aerobatic competency evaluators were concerned, as were others, that the flying
they were seeing was perhaps subject to an accident."
The specific cause, he said, was that the pilot did not gain enough altitude at the
top of a loop and the speed control over the loop, not leaving enough room for pull-out at
the bottom for safety. Since this accident, changes in the ACE program were made so that
if anyone saw anything unsafe, they are to go to an ACE and the ACEs will convene.

Loudenslager: *"the one they feel best represents them, to take appropriate action. That may be go to the FAA, that may be go to the show monitor, they may be going to the pilot themselves, or all these things."*

Loudenslager then testified that he had seen no change in Hoover's performance over the span of years that he had known him and that he had done none of the flying during the flight demonstration earlier that week.

Bailey: *"Did you observe his manipulation of the controls, his timing, his coordination, etcetera?"*

Loudenslager: *"Yes, sir."*

Bailey: *"Did you see any deficit whatsoever in Mr. Hoover's ability to perform his act?"*

Loudenslager: *"None."*

Bailey then asked if Loudenslager was aware of a cowl flap malfunction during the flight demonstration, and Loudenslager said he was. Bailey asked what effect that problem had on the airframe as far as aerobatics were concerned.

Loudenslager: *"Well, it compounds the problem. Drag — it is not a safety issue, it is a drag issue. The cowl flaps can be open from all speed ranges but what it does require the pilot do is it requires the pilot to add to the basic numbers, the basic parameters that you have to allow yourself to do the maneuvers required."*

Loudenslager testified that he observed Hoover making those adjustments, with no difficulty.

Bailey: "Mr. Loudenslager, as an ACE, if the day comes around when the ravages of age to get to Mr. Hoover, would you have the slightest hesitation to try to cause him to be grounded?"

Loudenslager: *"No, sir. May I elaborate on that?"*

Bailey said he could.

Loudenslager: *"My personal thing is my soul comes before anything, any friendship, but I would go back and when I went into this business and I think the professionals in this business, the one thing that I told myself as an aerobatic pilot personally, if my peer group — and by that I mean the people that I really respect in the business — were to ever approach me and tell me that I was doing something that concerned them, I would take that advice and basically modify whatever it was to meet their objections.*

I had that happen two times in my career. One of them was Bob Hoover — and I can't remember the year but I do remember the location, it was El Paso, TX — and he said, 'Leo just wasn't there on that.' I felt fine about it personally but because it was Bob Hoover that was concerned, I changed it the next day. The other one was Bob Herendeen. It was a competition in a four-minute routine and he said, 'You concern me'. So I changed the format of the four-minute routine. It is a standard that I hold myself to and I would hold the same standard with another aviator."

Loudenslager also said that no other ACE would hesitate to make efforts to ground Hoover if they felt that was necessary.

Loudenslager's Cross-Examination

Winton: *"Thank you, Mr. Loudenslager. You are an airline captain and an aerobatic pilot?"*

Loudenslager said that was correct.

Winton: *"You don't have a degree in clinical psychology, do you?"*

Loudenslager said no.

Winton: *"You are not a neuropsychologist?"*

Loudenslager: *"No, sir."*

Winton: *"Not a neurologist?"*

Loudenslager: *"No, sir."*

Winton: *"Neurosurgeon, maybe?"*

Loudenslager: *"No, sir."*

Winton: *"And you have not reached a clinical diagnosis based on a battery of neuropsychological tests performed on Mr. Hoover."* (Author: Can we spell smart ass, kids?)

Bailey objected to this ridiculous line of questioning. The Judge, for whatever reason, overruled this objection — but did comment that if Loudenslager didn't have any of those degrees it is assumed he hasn't administered any of the tests that those degrees would be required to give. But, of course, Winton still wouldn't give up. He then asked, *"So you don't have an opinion based on a reasonable degree of medical certainty as to his cognitive ability to perform the functions required of a second class airman medical certificate, do you, sir?"*

Bailey again objected, saying you can't ask a lay person a question to a degree o[f] medical certainty. This objection was sustained. He still didn't give up, though — Winto[n] asked Loudenslager if he had any opinions of the neurological tests that had been given t[o] Hoover. Loudenslager said he did not have an opinion — had never even seen the reports[.]

Testimony of David Johnsen

Unlike much of the previous testimony, which was prefaced by lengthy discus[-] sion of the witnesses' curriculum vitaes, Bailey pointed out where in the exhibits Johnsen['s] C.V. could be found and said he would keep this line of questioning brief.

Johnsen testified that he had been a clinical psychologist (which, he explained, i[s] a psychologist who works primarily with the assessment and treatment of mental disorders) since 1987, when he received his doctorate in the field. He had received his Bachelors in psychology in 1976 and his Masters in 1978. Johnsen also said that his specialty within clinical psychology is neurological assessment, and that he is licensed by the State of Oklahoma to perform neuropsychological assessments.

Vente, another FAA lawyer who would be handling this portion of the trial, felt this discussion of Johnsen's background was too brief and requested a voir dire. (A Voir Dire being something of a verbal recitation of one's expertise and its relevance to the matters at hand, this was an appropriate if somewhat overdramatized request).

Johnson's Voir Dire

Vente asked Johnsen what his medical license was for, and Johnsen again said clinical psychology.

Vente: *"It is not in neuropsychology. Is that correct?"*

Johnsen: *"No. In —"*

Vente rudely cut Johnsen off, and began to ask another question. Bailey objected, and the Judge sustained the objection... but Vente was persistent, and began to ask the next question. The Judge interrupted, and told Vente to allow Johnsen to finish his first answer.

Johnsen: *"In the licensing process in Oklahoma I am licensed as a clinical psychologist. What you have to do is if you are going to perform certain types of assessment or treatments, you have to demonstrate proficiency in those, so in the licensing process you state that you do neuropsychological assessments or whatever and then have to undergo examination in that area, and then it is listed on — with the state board of examiners for psychologists."*

Vente then resumed his attack, asking Johnsen if he were a member of the National Academy of Neuropsychology or International Neuropsychology Society. Johnsen was not. Next, Vente asked him what the requirements for board certification in neuropsychology were, and Johnsen testified that he was not sure. Vente asked him if he were board certified in neuropsychology or psychology and *"Are you board certified in anything then?"*

When Johnsen said no, Vente objected to his testimony, stating that there is some question as to his expertise in this area.

Judge Mullins: *"Why? Because he is not board certified?"*

Vente: *"Just for the record, Your Honor."*

Judge Mullins overruled the objection.

Johnsen's Direct Examination (Resumed)

Bailey asked how Johnsen came to meet Hoover. Johnsen said Dr. Brent Hisey contacted him, explained the loss of Hoover's medical certificate, and asked him if he would be willing to look over Hoover's records and see if *"it made sense"* to him.

Johnsen said he reviewed the reports by Dr. Elliott and a report by Dr. Satz (which included the testing by Dr. Uchiyama) from UCLA.

Johnsen also gave Hoover some testing on his own. He re-administered the category test, the Halstead-Reitan Neuropsychological battery, the trail-making test, trails A and B- of the Halstead-Reitan Neuropsychological battery, and the Wisconsin card-sorting test.

Bailey: *"Which one?"*

Johnsen: *"The card version; the computerized version is a research edition only."*

Bailey: *"Is it ethical to you as a research edition of a testing program to perform actual tests on a patient for a legal issue?"*

Johnsen said he felt it would not be unethical to administer the tests, but *"to make statement as to their clinical utility or to make statements as far as someone's ability to function based on a research test without proper norms and data, no that is not."*

Bailey asked about Hoover's performance. Johnsen said he also administered the California Verbal Learning Test and that he performed at an average level compared to people of his own age. That was true, in fact, on all of the tests.

Johnsen: *"The category test — now, what I administered was the actual category test from the Halstead-Reitan battery. There is a booklet category test, which is produced by Psychological Assessment Resources. There is some question as to the similarity between the two. I know a great many individuals use booklet categories. Ralph Reitan of the Halstead Reitan Group says that he questions the use of the norms with booklet categories versus the actual category test."*

Bailey: *"The author of the test then suggests the one that you administered."*

Johnsen said yes.

Bailey said that others had given opinions that, based largely upon the same tests that Johnsen described and administered, Hoover has a cognitive defect or impairment that will influence his flying skills... and then asked Johnsen had found anything to suggest the same opinion.

Johnsen said no.

Bailey asked Johnsen if he had cautioned Hoover prior to testing that regardless of the results, he would call *"it as he saw it."*

Johnsen: *"I made it very clear to Dr. Hisey when he first approached me about considering doing this test and then I reiterated this to Mr. Hoover that, as I do in any case involving this kind of litigation, it doesn't matter whose side is on who, that what data I get is the data that they will receive and I made it very clear that if I did not feel he was safe to fly, I would make that very clear for his protection and mine."*

Johnsen continued, saying that if he had not been truthful about the tests, in Hoover's favor, it could cost Hoover his life and it would come back on him. Johnsen testified, then that *"I feel very strongly he is qualified to hold a second class certificate"* and that he will remain qualified for the next two years).

Johnsen's Cross Examination

Vente first brought up Johnsen's comments about the category tests, as far as the booklet and computer versions.

Johnsen: *"Well, it is — I say computer version. It is not a computer version, it is more of a slide projector system where the same images are put on a category test screen. It is like a slide projector versus looking at them in a book. And there have been questions raised about the compatibility of the norms. My personal feeling is that they probably are very compatible."*

Vente then asked if he saw pilots frequently in his practice. Johnsen said not frequently.

Vente: *"So I imagine you don't consult for the airlines or anything like that?"*

Johnsen: *"Oh, no."*

Johnsen explained, saying that if he saw a pilot it *"was certainly not because he has gone crossways with the FAA."* It is probably, he said, because he was a pilot who had some other kind of problem that brought him into Johnsen's office.

Vente then began referring to Johnsen's report to Dr. Hisey.

Johnsen testified that Hisey asked him to look over the tests and asked what tests could be considered to retest Hoover, if any.

Johnsen: *"... and I felt like there are so many factors that can go into a poor performance on certain tests that it would not make sense to do an entire battery again, so I re-administered those test that he had done poorly on. The purpose was to try to understand why he had, according to Dr. Elliott's report, done poorly."*

Vente asked Johnsen how many tests were administered during the UCLA study. After looking at the report, Johnsen testified that there had been 17 actual tests, not including the Fulstein, a mini mental status test (not a formal test).

Vente: *"Thank you. And Dr. Johnsen, how many did you give to Mr. Hoover?"*

Johnsen said he had given him four.

Vente: *"Four tests. Would you say that your evaluation was somewhat less comprehensive than Dr. Elliott's or Dr. Uchiyama's?"*

Johnsen: *"Less comprehensive, less repetitious. There is really no sense to re-administer tests that he had shown good performance on time and time again."*

Vente: *"So you only gave him tests that he had shown poor performance on that report."*

Johnsen: *"Correct, the four that he had apparently done poorly on, and as I stated before, it was a question of what are the factors that contributed to poor performance. Were they neuropsychological deficits or were they other things, emotional."*

Vente asked what new tests Johnsen gave Hoover. Johnsen said it was the California Verbal Learning Test, which, he said, is similar to the Rey Auditory-Verbal Learning Test (Hoover had taken the Rey test).

Then the familiar tune of *"practice effect"* was once again brought up.

Vente: *"Given what we know about practice effect and what the Judge knows about practice effect, did you really expect to more accurately determine Mr. Hoover's cognitive abilities by giving him tests that he had already received at least once, if not twice, in the previous year?"*

Johnsen: *"Well, I felt that what practice effect might be there would certainly be minimal, particularly on the category test since there was a one-year lapse between when he had been given the test and took it again. With the trail-making test, my experience has been that there isn't that significant of a practice effect when you are talking about neuro-cognitive deficit simply because if the brain cannot perform a certain activity continuing presenting it to the individual to try to get them to do it, if the brain is not capable of performing it, it is not going to do it."*

Vente then asked, talking about the Trails B test: *"So you are telling me that someone who hasn't seen it twice before wouldn't get any benefit from that?"*

Johnsen testified that there might be less anxiety associated with the tests, which could cause a slight improvement — but it would not be significant. He also testified that although the California Auditory and Rey Auditory tests are similar, there would be no practice effect.

The last points Vente made included how Hoover did on Johnsen's testing of the California Auditory (he remembered two of sixteen words immediately after being given them), which is how he had done in Uchiyama's tests. He also asked Johnsen what Uchiyama had determined from his testing of Hoover. Johnsen said that Uchiyama evaluated selected risk signs and recommended reinstating him with a three to six month medical certificate, with close monitoring for potential change. When Vente finished his cross examination, the Judge said he had a question.

Judge Mullins: *"Doctor, there has been testimony here that during Dr. Elliott's tests there were some — Mr. Hoover was unaware of the time requirements, that there wasn't a lunch break, that he was there for seven to nine hours. What impact, in your opinion, would that have on the scores that he gave to Dr. Elliott?"*

Johnsen: *"I think it would have a significant impact and one of the reasons why I re-administered those tests was because emotional factors can have a significant effect with effective cognition. So if it is a question that his brain is not able to perform certain activities, we would need to know that, but then if there were a question of emotional duress interfering with that, you would expect that time when he was not under similar duress that he would give better performance."*

udge Mullins: *"One other question. All of the other doctors that I have heard testify ave discounted any demonstration or performance factors, objective observation, of Mr. ʻoover, and yet your report seemed to say that that is a factor. Would you explain your ʻatement where you say: 'In Mr. Hoover's case the need to predict his performance is reatly reduced by the fact that he subsequently demonstrated excellent performance n 25 separate occasions?'"*

Johnsen said that if what caused his poor performance during the alleged inci- ent were an organic problem or a problem with his brain, you would not expect those roblems to disappear on subsequent airshows — once the brain is damaged, he said, it is oing to stay damaged.

ohnsen: *"...So for him to go out and perform in 25 subsequent airshows and not have ny problem, no problem such as what was alleged had happened during the first air- how, you would think well, something other than his brain being damaged or being ʻmehow dysfunctional had to have caused that."*

Continuing, Johnsen testified that the best predictor of behavior is past behav- ʻr, barring that something somehow changes. *"For us to give tests and then say based on ʻese tests this individual cannot perform these activities and yet he went out and per- ʻrmed those activities, not just once or twice but 25 subsequent times, to me reduces the ʻsumptions and the generalizations that we can make based on these test data because ʻe have got the actual occurrence going on."*

Johnsen's Re-Direct Examination

ailey: *"Have you ever subjected a person to nine hours of straight testing with one reak for water and urination?"*

Johnsen said no.

ailey: *"Have you ever heard of it being done?"*

Johnsen said only from Hoover.

Bailey asked if he would place any confidence in a battery obtained in such a way.

ohnsen: *"I would place greatly reduced confidence, certainly from the tests that were btained later on. Maybe the tests that were given initially would have greater validity, ut those that occurred later on, I would have questions as to what kind of emotional nterference and stress were playing a part in deficit performance."*

Bailey then asked, because one of the witnesses seemed to be critical of Hoover ʻr wanting to perform airshows in his 70s, if Johnsen knew of any active pilots older than ʻoover. Johnsen said he knew of a CFII who is 90 years old. He also said he had recently ʻone to an airshow where they gave an award to the oldest pilot who had flown there. This ʻllow was 84 and had flown there in a T-28, *"which is certainly a more demanding plane ʻhan what I fly."*

ailey: *"Is there any technology that says that somewhere in your 70s you lose your ʻbility to fly an airplane that you once had?"*

Johnsen said there was not. One other pilot, Steve Wittman, was also mentioned.

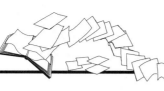

AIR OF INJUSTICE

Wittman is the pilot for whom Wittman Field at Oshkosh is named. Johnsen was not sur
of his exact age, but knew that he was at least 90 — and still an active pilot.

Johnsen's Re-Cross Examination

Vente: *"Have you administered a battery of psychological tests to Mr. Wittman?"*
Johnsen said he had not.

Vente: *"Let me see if you agree with me on this. If someone is impaired by alcohol, ca*
someone operate a car without incident?"
Johnsen said they may, but the risks were much greater. Johnsen was then ex
cused as a witness and Dr. Brent Hisey was called to the stand.

Dr. Brent Hisey's Direct Examination

Again, Bailey said he did not intend to completely go through Hisey's C.V. Hise
testified that he is a neurosurgeon and had been so since 1989. He is also a flight surgeor
(and chief medical officer) with the 464th Tactical Fighter Squadron at Tinker AFB for th
Air Force Reserve. He is board certified by the American Board of Neurologic Surger
(hopefully that made Vente happy!).

Hisey is also a pilot, with a variety of experience — including aerobatics (Pitt
Special), warbird time, and over 100 hours in an F-16. Additionally, he testified that on
routine basis he sees approximately 20 pilots a month since 1989, when he began hi
career as a flight surgeon with the Air Force Reserve. When asked if he was able to issu
medical certificates, Hisey said he was able to certify pilots for the F-16 Falcon. Whe
asked how he met Hoover, Hisey said through mutual acquaintances at the Reno Ai
Races that year — but had seen him perform in the 60's at Tinker AFB and on numerou
occasions at Aerospace America in Oklahoma. He testified that he never saw Hoover per
form in a non-standard manner.

Bailey asked how it was that he came to examine Hoover. Hisey said that Hoove
explained his situation to him and asked if he would review the case and offer his opinion

Hisey: *"I told Mr. Hoover that I would review his case and offer a judgment based on two*
premises: One, that I was provided complete access to his medical records and what had
taken place with this incident; and number two, that he submit to a thorough examina
tion by myself and Dr. David Johnsen. And then based on our findings we would issue ar
opinion, either for Mr. Hoover or against Mr. Hoover, whether we felt he was safe to fly.

Bailey asked if he would have been a party to permitting a renowned pilot to fly
out of sympathy or for any reason if he thought he (Hoover) was impaired. Johnsen said
he would not — and that, had he done such a thing, he would have been subject to a
court martial and would probably lose his credentials and license.

Bailey asked if Hisey reviewed a letter within Hoover's records from Dr. Pincus
which suggested that Dr. Gold's examination was significantly superficial because it lacked
at least 12 different tests. Hisey said he had, and that he felt those missing tests would
have been relevant because there had been question about the function of Hoover's fron

l lobes. After reviewing the records, Hisey and Johnsen arranged for Hoover to come to klahoma City for testing.

ailey: *"Do you believe that it is possible to pick up deficiencies that occur because of age ˟ disease or any other cause based on actual performance by the pilot?"*

Hisey said yes.

ailey: *"If there is an impediment that arises from any source whatsoever that is not ɪrable, can the performance be restored once it is impaired?"*

isey: *"If it was due to an incurable pathologic process, probably not."*

When asked to detail his examination, Hisey said he did a physical examination, ɪneurologic examination, and a laboratory examination. The laboratory examination con- sted of a complete blood count, blood chemistries, a urinalysis, a prostate-specific anti- ɘn, and his EKG.

The neurologic examination evaluated the brain and spinal cord functions, spe- fically looking at Hoover's frontal lobes. This was done by looking at certain reflexes in ɪe brain, where the frontal lobes are responsible for inhibiting primitive reflexes to allow ɔnduction of higher intellectual processes.

ailey: *"Yesterday Dr. Pincus suggested that because you were a neurosurgeon and not a ɘurologist that you might not perform them (the tests) correctly. Do you know in your ˟ofession whether there is any basis for such an assertion?"*

isey: *"There is no basis whatsoever."*

ailey: *"Did you perform each of the tests... that were in the Pincus report as having been ɪissing from Dr. Gold?"*

Hisey said he had, and that the results were all within normal limits. The only ɔnormality in his tests was an increased cholesterol level on his blood studies. Hisey ɪen testified that he examined Hoover again, just the day before. Vente objected, because ɘ didn't know anything about this examination, but the objection was overruled. Hisey ɪid he could do this same examination — which looked at Hoover's reflexes — in the ɔurtroom if the Court so wished. Bailey then said he wanted to do this right then, be- ɪuse Pincus had testified that Hisey had not correctly performed these reflex tests be- ɪuse he was a neurosurgeon, not a neurologist. Vente said he needed his neurologist — Dr. Hastings — to be present, and Bailey did not object to this.

The Judge broke in at this point, and said he had no objection to this testing, but ɪked that they limit it to just two tests in the interest of time. As it was time for lunch, ɪisey would conduct these after the lunch break. When they returned from lunch, how- ɪer, Bailey had a special request. The wife of his next witness — FAA Inspector Norbert ɘster – was due to go into labor imminently and asked that he interrupt Hisey's testi- ɪony and call Nester so that he could quickly leave to be with his wife.

udge Mullins: *"Certainly."*

Norbert Nester's Direct Examination

FAA Inspector Nester was accompanied by David Batton, his own counsel, wh
stated that Nester was here pursuant to a subpoena and that Nester feared for his job if h
told the truth. *"I believe whatever they are going to put on for impeachment purpose
puts his job in severe jeopardy,"* Batton said. Caron, one of the FAA's attorneys, said tha
she was uncomfortable with Nester testifying: *"... because I don't want to jeopardize M.
Nester's rights. I want Mr. Nester to tell the truth."* She admitted that she really didn
know how to handle this situation.

Nester was still called, after Batton reminded the Court that Nester was not ther
of his own free will and Bailey said that he was sure the FAA knew that any retributio
against the witness would be a violation of the Obstruction of Justice statute. Nester too
the stand, and testified that he was an FAA Safety Inspector for the Oklahoma FSDO. H
is an ATP-multi-engine, rated in a DC-9, with commercial single-engine privileges. H
has logged approximately 6500 hours.

Bailey asked if Nester was present at the airshow in question. Nester said he wa:
as one of the airshow monitors for the FSDO. He saw Hoover perform that weekend, an
had even introduced himself and his son to Hoover in the performers' tent. Nester sai
Hoover was very amiable and very cordial. In fact, Hoover took more than a passing inte
est in Nester's son, and spoke to him for 10 or 15 minutes — and even showed his son th
Shrike and explained some things to him. Nester said it made his son feel very specia
Nester testified that he saw nothing unusual about Hoover's flying. Bailey then asked
Nester knew Clint Boehler. Nester said Boehler had been an Inspector for the Oklahom
City FSDO until about October of '93. He testified that he also knew James Kelln, a
Inspector in the operations unit of that same office. Bailey asked what Boehler looke
like, and Nester said he was short in stature, early 50s, balding, and a bit on the heavyse
side. Bailey asked if he had ever made a comment about tall, thin people.

Nester: *"One morning when I walked in and spoke to him, he said, 'I hate people lik
you.' And I was somewhat taken aback and said, 'Why?' And he said, 'Because you ar
built like what everybody expects a pilot to be: tall and skinny.' And I said, 'I am sorry fo
the build, but you know, that is just the way it turned out.' And he said, 'Well, I don't lik
being short and paunchy and middle-aged and balding.' And that is kind of where t
stopped."*

Bailey asked if Boehler had said anything to Nester after the airshow in questior

Nester: *"He initially asked me if I had observed anything unusual about Hoover's perfor
mance, and I said no. I likened him to a figure skater or something else, I didn't see an;
glaring errors. You know, I am not a qualified judge but I didn't see anything that jumpe
out at me, it all appeared to be smooth and rhythmical and continuous."*

Nester testified that Boehler (who, to the best of Nester's knowledge, is not a
aerobatic pilot), however, said he had noticed some thing he considered substandard, o
not expected of Hoover.

Bailey asked if Boehler had said anything else to Nester.

Nester: *"He indicated that Mr. Hoover had had a number of incidents or violations of th
FAR, specifically in-flight fires and he had run out of gas on various occasions, and
don't know how he came to that conclusion, but that is what he said, and he said, 'He ha*

ever had to stand accountable for anything.'"

Nester also testified that Boehler said, *"Well, it is about time for him to have to e accountable."*

Nester: *"I said, 'Well, I guess if there is something there you see that you can pursue, go head. I don't believe I want the dubious distinction of being the man that was noted for rying to stop Bob Hoover.'"*

Bailey: *"And his response was?"*

Nester: *"A bit of a strange chuckle and glint in his eye and he said, 'Well, we will see.'"*

A few days later, Nester testified, he went by James Kelln's office, and Boehler was n there. Nester said that they were discussing their perceptions of the deficiencies of Hoover's performance at the airshow in question. They were discussing writing reports bout this.

Nester: *"He (Kelln) said in a joking kind of way and offhanded fashion, I think to inject ome levity, but it was to the effect of the words were: 'We had better write them and take look at them so nobody can compare them and make them think that we sat and did hem together, so it would look like they were done side by side.'"*

Nester said he did not tell anyone of this incident, nor had he seen the reports.

Bailey: *"Was there an offer to read them to you recently?"*

Nester said yes. *"Yesterday evening — I assume this is Susan that is sitting in ront of me, FAA's representative, called and spoke to me at my home,"* he said. Nester aid that Caron had been very open about everything and she was the one who told Nester hat Bailey was subpoenaing him.

Bailey: *"Did she tell you there was a rule in this case that lawyers were not supposed to ell one witness what another witness had testified to until after they were excused?"*

Nester: *"She did not cover that specific area."*

Nester said that Caron had filled him in on the medical reports. *"She said that ll of the reports came to the same conclusion, that there was a deficiency with Mr. Hoover,"* he explained.

Bailey: *"Did she tell you that there were reports that were exactly the opposite of that?"*

Nester: *"No, sir."*

Bailey: *"Mr. Nester, are you concerned there may be some form of retaliation for your ppearance and giving of your testimony today?"*

Nester: *"Very much so."*

Bailey then began to ask Nester about a complaint currently open against Nester. Nester said there had been allegations that he had acted in a manner that could be per-

ceived as accepting favors or putting himself in a bad position with the public. Nester sai
he was suspended for five days without pay, but that his attorney was appealing the matte
for him through the grievance process.

Nester's Cross Examination

Caron asked Nester what they had discussed the night before on the telephone
Nester said that she had been very open and honest with him and that she had told him t
be very empathetic and to only testify to that which he had seen or heard — no hearsay

Caron: *"And did I tell you to be completely honest and forthright?"*

Nester: *"Yes, ma'am, you did."*

Caron: *"The information that you are presenting to the Court right now, how come yo*
never gave me that information before?"

Nester: *"I did not know you or know that you were the one that was working on the case*
for one. The primary reason is because of the political nature of our office and the pres
sures that are put upon people and the fact that it would have been discounted ver
quickly due to my junior position, you might say. I may be a GS-13 just like Mr. Boehle
was, and Mr. Kelln was a GS-14, but due to their years of service, I am sure that it woul
have been swept away very quietly. You know, you have no position in this, we wi
handle it."

It was for those reasons, he said, he never went to anyone within the FAA wit
the information.

Caron: *"In connection with your litigation, did you ever reveal that to your attorney so*
could be conveyed to the FAA?"

Nester said no.

Caron: *"Why not?"*

Nester: *"For fear of the reprisals that would come out of my office for overstepping m*
bounds and circumventing the normal chain of command, as they perceive it."

At this time, Nester was excused and Dr. Hisey returned to the stand.

Hisey's Direct Examination (Resumed)

Bailey: *"Dr. Hisey, we are going to bypass any demonstration of neurology, becaus*
despite the speculation of Dr. Pincus, no one has given any evidence that any of you
tests were incorrect. As a result of your total examination, were you able to form a
impression of Mr. Hoover as a 70-year-old man?"

Hisey said he had. *"My opinion of Mr. Hoover, based on his physical, neurologic*
and laboratory examination, was that he was of average physical stature and had a

average neurologic examination for a 71-year-old male."

He continued, saying that he felt *"Mr. Hoover was qualified and fit to hold a second class medical certificate and to continue his flying career."*

Hisey also stated that he was aware that a second class medical was good for one year and becomes a third class for the second year.

Hisey: *"Mr. Hoover is completely competent and fit to hold a second class medical certificate and he should hold such."*

Bailey: *"If he were a military pilot, would you hesitate to certify him for duty?"*

Hisey: *"None whatsoever."*

Hisey's Cross-Examination

Apparently, Vente wanted to hammer the complaints Pincus had voiced about Hisey not being qualified to do neurological testing because he was "only" a neurosurgeon.

Vente: *"...Dr. Hisey, you are not a neurologist, are you?"*

Hisey: *"No, sir."*

After he was asked, Hisey explained that neurosurgery is a field that deals with the surgical treatment of diseases that involve the brain, spinal cord, peripheral nerves, and their coverings. Vente then asked about his choice of Johnsen to do the neuropsychological testing. He asked if Johnsen was a neuropsychologist; Hisey said no.

Vente: *"Do you recognize the difference between the two disciplines?"*

Hisey: *"There is a difference in their certification. Is there a difference in the way they administer tests? No, sir."*

Vente then asked about his physical examination of Hoover. He asked if Hoover had told him about head trauma from the 1947 and 1954 accidents. Hisey said Hoover had told him about it but that he had said it was not significant injury.

Vente: *"Doctor, isn't it true that normal EEGs and MRIs do not necessarily exclude the possibility of neurologic disease?"*

Hisey said that was true. Vente then asked if he had reviewed the SPEC scans, and if he had noticed that one of them showed profusion on both parietal regions. Hisey had seen it.

Vente: *"Isn't it true that this type of showing profusion over both parietal regions can be consistent with degenerative brain disease?"*

Hisey: *"It can be consistent with it."*

Changing subjects, Vente again wanted to make a point about how few tests

Johnsen administered to Hoover (four) and so had Hisey physically count the number of tests given by the UCLA crew from their report —19.

Vente then began to play *"let's find it in the report"* and kept asking Hisey what the other doctors' findings were... the point being that O'Connor and Uchiyama had recommended a return of the medical certificate — but not for two years and contingent upon close monitoring of his medical status and spec scans — which, of course, is not consistent with an unrestricted medical certificate. Vente then asked about a statement Hisey had made in his report, where he said he was *"at a loss to think of a novel condition or emergency that Mr. Hoover had not yet experienced."*

Hisey: *"Well, if we look at what possible conditions Mr. Hoover could experience in the air, that a pilot would experience that would cause a failure of his ability to control the aircraft. Could he have a catastrophic failure of the wings and the wings come off? Yes, that would be some condition that is out of his control. What is within his control that he has not experienced? He experiences engine shutdowns, which is probably the worst thing that could happen to a pilot, he experiences that with regularity. He flies with the aircraft in unusual attitudes, close to the ground. He has suffered numerous mechanical failures in his aircraft throughout his career that he has successfully managed. So I suppose there could be something that I have overlooked, however, I was at a loss to think of one."*

Hisey's Re-Direct Examination

Bailey asked Hisey if the follow-up SPECT scans that O'Connor had recommended had happened, and Hisey said they had. He also, after he was asked, said that the close monitoring that Dr. Uchiyama had suggested had taken place. As far as Hisey knew, all suggestions offered by the physicians who had examined Hoover prior to Hisey had taken place. Bailey again asked if there was any reason to restrict Hoover's medical certificate.

Hisey: *"There is absolutely no evidence that would document any reason to restrict Mr. Hoover's medical certificate."*

Hisey was then excused and Sean Tucker called to the stand.

Sean Tucker Direct Examination

Sean Tucker testified that his occupation was that of an airshow pilot, and he had began in 1976 for three years and then began again in 1988 — and that was his full-time occupation.

Tucker testified that he flies a highly-modified Pitts S2S, and that he had flown probably well over 300 performances in his career. In 1988 he won the National Advanced Championship; in 1992 he was awarded the Bill Barber award for showmanship and the Art Scholl award, also for showmanship, and was voted favorite male performer by *General Aviation News & Flyer*. He was the first aerobatic pilot to receive both the Barber and Scholl award in the same year.

Tucker testified that he had watched Hoover fly ever since he was a child. He

ad known a professional level since the mid-80's, and since 1990, as a friend.

ucker: *"At every airshow I pay attention to other aerobatic performances. It is my ob, I am an airshow performer. You can, number one, learn from them. Also paying ttention to safety details."* Tucker has also, he said, observed Hoover's performances. *I can honestly say that at every show that I have performed at with Mr. Hoover I have atched Mr. Hoover fly."*

Tucker said that he has not seen any deterioration in Mr. Hoover's performance ince the time he resumed his airshow career in 1988.

ailey: *"Do you have an opportunity to observe his demeanor, his mental attitude, his hysical state?"*

Tucker said yes, and that they were fine — alert and in good health. ailey then brought up the airshow in question and Tucker said he flew with Hoover in hat airshow. He observed his performances and interacted with him personally that reekend.

ucker: *"Professionally, Mr. Hoover performed and interacted no differently than the revious shows that I have flown with Mr. Hoover or the subsequent shows that I have own with Mr. Hoover."*

He reiterated that he did not see anything unusual about his performance or is personal interactions. Bailey then asked if Tucker knew Boehler. Tucker said he did, ecause of Boehler's position as a monitor at the Aerospace America airshow. He never net Kelln. Tucker testified that he had seen their reports. Yodice read some of it aloud, nd Tucker said he did not agree with the statements — that said Hoover was not in ood form, among other things — contained therein. The report said that his timing ras off, and Tucker didn't agree with that, either.

ailey: *"What was your observation regarding the crispness of the maneuvers that Mr. Ioover performed?"*

ucker: *"Airshow flying is probably the toughest flying that there is in aviation, airshow 'ying — you need to be very disciplined to be an airshow pilot. If Mr. Hoover at any time ver, ever made a mistake, all of us pilots — because we look up to him so high, he is held n such high regard, I might have missed it but another certainly wouldn't have missed . We are talking about one maneuver. I think Mr. Hoover is not allowed ever, in terms, f how high a regard we hold him, to make those kind of — to be sloppy, to just go hrough the motions because of who he is as an aviator.*

And at Oklahoma City he flew no differently than I have ever flown with Mr. Ioover before from 1988 on up to after Oklahoma City. I flew with him at Oshkosh onvention in that year in 1992 and I flew with Mr. Hoover at the Reno air races and his naneuvers were precise, they were crisp, there was continuity, there was harmony, the olls were coordinated, he wasn't off heading in pulling up on his maneuvers and his ooping portions; there was complete harmony in his routine. And if there would have een one bobble, we would have noticed it because he is Bob Hoover."

Bailey said that the reports said other airshow performers indicated concern for

his lack of continuity and performance. Tucker testified that that was not the case, as he mingled with the other performers throughout the weekend and would have heard such comments.

Bailey asked if Tucker was an ACE, and he said yes, that he had been so since 1990 — since the inception of the program. As such, Tucker would have followed procedures outlined by that program if he had seen anything unusual in Hoover's performance. Bailey asked if he had ever had to do such a thing as an ACE, and Tucker testified that he had. He went to the FAA about a Canadian gentleman with whom he had flown at a Florida airshow when Tucker felt his flying was marginal — and he then described a couple of other such times. He described ACEs as the "Airshow police," and said it was not an easy job.

After he was asked, Tucker explained that he had heard about Hoover's difficulty with the FAA from Hoover himself. Once he heard about it, he conferred with two other ACE designees, Leo Loudenslager and Steve Oliver.

Tucker: *"...we wanted to make sure we didn't miss anything, that is why we talked... I the FAA said something, I wanted to make sure I was — my head wasn't in the sand, and we definitely talked about it."*

Bailey: *"As a result of the discussion, what did you conclude?"*

Tucker: *"Well, my personal opinion is I don't know why these Inspectors wrote these letters the way they did but they are completely — from what I and how I evaluated Mr. Hoover, during that show, it was completely different from the letters they wrote."*
Tucker discussed a time when Hoover told him he was concerned about him.

Tucker: *"...in 1991 I flew an airshow with Bob and he had to come up to me and he told me that I am out of line on my flying and he was concerned about — what he calls it, he said he was concerned about me busting my buttons. I was diving for a ribbon, doing an inverted ribbon cut at 200 miles an hour and Bob dropped everything and just came running up to me and really chewed me out because, number one, he cares about airshow safety, and number two, he cares about Sean Tucker. This whole thing is peer review, this whole thing is how are we going to keep this business going is the professionals are going to pay attention to the other professionals to make sure we do it correctly."*

Tucker's Cross-Examination

Winton: *"Good afternoon, Mr. Tucker."* (saccharin sweet, I think) *"It is a pleasure meeting you. Thank you for coming. Sir, do you have a degree in physiology, by chance?"*
Tucker said no.

Winton: *"We all appreciate your concern with the ACE program and the input they have had, and my question to you is you indicated that the FAA helped design the program. Is that what you said?"*
Tucker said the FAA came to the professionals at the International Council of Airshows and the two organizations worked together to develop the program.

Winton: *"And usually you determine airshow safety by observing your peers throughout their performance. Am I correct?"*

Tucker agreed.

Winton: *"So it is more of an observation of the proficiency of the airmen and the aviator skills."*

Tucker: *"The skill level, yes, sir."*

Winton decided to use another approach, and asked if the FAA had given ACEs the burden of determining the medical qualifications of their peers.
Tucker said that you can tell if a pilot is physically down from the way he flies — by looking at what kind of G's he's pulling or what kind of corners he's doing. Winton then asked if Tucker knew of any heart ailments Hoover may have. Tucker did not know of any.

Winton: *"And what if I told you that he had a heart ailment that you couldn't see, you couldn't detect, but it could at any time bring an onset of a heart attack, would you as an ACE program manager ... would you consider him safe to fly knowing that at any moment he could have a problem?"* Tucker testified that he would go up to Hoover and address that problem.

Winton then began to discuss — at length – *"bad flying days"* ...what causes them (fatigue, for instance) and if all pilots had them. Tucker contended they weren't a problem in the airshow industry, saying it was a very disciplined profession.

Winton: *"So let me ask you this: Have you ever, due to a medical reason, whether fatigue or head cold or otherwise, decide that you weren't going to fly your routine?"*

Tucker, much to Winton's seeming surprise, said he had, due to fatigue. He continued, saying that his reaction time may have been off — and said that all airshow pilots have to evaluate themselves before an airshow or even before practicing for an airshow.

Yodice apologetically objected here, saying that he knew Winton should have wide latitude in a cross-examination, but he stated that it was difficult to see a connection between these questions and the direct examination or even an impeachment of the witness — and he also stated the time factor and *"this seems to be going on and on."*

The Judge sustained the objection, told Winton to bring out the connection to aerobatic flying.

Winton reminded Tucker of his last statement and then said, "So reaction time, you feel, is important for flying in an airshow. Am I right?"

Tucker agreed.

Winton asked if Tucker, as an ACE, would be concerned if he knew another pilot's reaction time was off. Tucker responded that he would be.

Next, Winton asked how many performances Tucker had flown with Hoover. Tucker estimated the number to be between 50 and 75, and his position in the airshow lineup (i.e., before or after Hoover) varied from show to show. Winton asked if Tucker watched all of the other acts during airshows, and he said he makes every attempt to — but admitted that interruptions sometimes prevent this – *"but I try to pay attention during every show with the majority of the performers or just about all of the performers,"* he explained. Winton latched onto this, and asked if he remembered watching every

one of Hoover's performances — from takeoff to touchdown — at Oshkosh in 1992. Tucker said he probably did not. Winton then asked about Tucker's letter regarding Hoover's performance at the airshow in question, quoting: *"The logic of his sequence and energy management were precise, and his physiological condition appeared to be normal."*

Tucker: *"And I indicated that I don't think you could be unhealthy and fly an airshow sequence. I just don't think it is possible.*

And when I am speaking of logic, it — everything tied in well, and it flowed, there was harmony. Energy management is what airshow flying is all about. And there is — if there is plenty of energy to go to the next maneuver, then you can complete that maneuver and come back around and complete the next maneuver."

After that, Winton kept trying to ask Tucker questions applicable to a pilot's medical status — and Bailey's attorneys kept reminding them that Tucker was not a medical witness. Winton seemed to be satisfied when Tucker did say, after he was asked, that yes he would be concerned if a doctor told him that Hoover's reaction time was impaired. However, Tucker did qualify his answer, saying he would want to understand the parameters of the doctor's definition of impaired.

Tucker's Re-Direct Examination

Yodice: *"Mr. Tucker, you were asked a lot of questions ... that were in a hypothetical vein... And now I would like to bring your testimony down to the issues in the case. Now, FAA is seeking to revoke — or has revoked and is seeking to sustain Mr. Hoover's revocation on the basis that he is not thinking well enough to fly safely.*

Now, in your opinion, in connection with the times that you have observed his performances, the times that you have interacted with him personally, over the periods of years to which you have testified, do you have any doubt of whether he thinks well enough to fly safely?"

Tucker: *"I have no doubt of that; I firmly believe that Mr. Hoover can fly safely and he will not jeopardize his safety or the safety of the airshow audience."*

Tucker's Re-Cross-Examination

Evidently Winton still hadn't figured out that Tucker wasn't a medical witness. Since Tucker had said that he would be concerned if a physician told him Hoover's reaction time was impaired, Winton dug up Dr. Uchiyama's report, which stated... guess what... and quoted it to him. When he still didn't get the answer he wanted (Tucker said that he would want to know about the tests to which Uchiyama was referring), Winton rephrased the question.

Winton: *"If a physician told you this, would you be concerned about Mr. Hoover's safety as an airshow performer and the safety of others, as a member of the ACE program?"*
Tucker said yes, and Winton had no further questions. Steve Oliver was the next witness called.

Steve Oliver's Direct Examination

Oliver had just begun to testify, stating that he was a professional airshow pilot when Winton voiced an objection — stating that there were many airshow pilots who could testify about his past performances.

In the end, in the interest of time, it was decided that Oliver would only testify to new things — but Yodice did say that he wanted sufficient corroboration from Oliver about the Inspectors' statements — and *"the fact that they are incorrect."*

When Oliver's testimony continued, he stated that he had been an airshow pilot for 30 years. He said he had known Hoover personally since the mid-80's and *"of him, for a long, long time."* He said he had personally interacted with Hoover over the course of the relationship.

Yodice then asked him if he had seen any degradation in Hoover's performances, and Oliver said he had not. Yodice asked Oliver how Hoover's performances were in terms of quality.

Oliver: *"Pretty awesome. I don't know of anybody that can watch Mr. Hoover fly without awe; an unbelievably smooth performance and eliciting from airplanes performances that are way, way beyond what I could ever hope to do."*

Yodice asked Oliver what he thought the general status of Hoover mental and physical health was.

Oliver: *"Well, I think he is very active. I see no problems of any kind. We interact in the daytime during the airshow and at evening time at functions that are meant for airshow performers to go into the course of their duties, and I see him in both places, and Mr. Hoover is Mr. Hoover."*

Oliver also said that he had not seen any degradation in these characteristics. When asked about the FAA proceedings, Oliver said, *"I have never observed anything that would give me any cause for alarm or to think that there was a problem area of any kind."*

Yodice asked him about the airshow in question, and Oliver testified that he flew in that show, had observed two of Hoover's performances — and had interacted with him. He had no recollection of anything being unusual with Hoover and he said that if anything had been wrong, it would have stood out. Additionally, Oliver testified that he too was an ACE, and that he had seen Hoover fly since the airshow in question and had also interacted with him since then.

Oliver: *"Without trying to be redundant, sir, it is: Mr. Hoover was Mr. Hoover. I have never seen anything that stands out that says, you know, that there is any problem or anything like that. He is like any other performer or any other person that I know that I interact with: you would remember something that wasn't right; you don't spend time thinking about things that are right."*

Oliver also testified to hearing the conversation between Hoover and the tower about when he didn't have a green nosegear light and told them he was going around. He remembered thinking that he would like to have seen Hoover taking care of these problems — you would have had to have been moving fast... and *"there was no doubt he was*

going to do it (take care of the problem) but I had a ring-side seat to watch this thing happen."

Yodice asked Oliver if he had seen the Inspectors' reports about Hoover's performances that weekend, and he had. Yodice read him some of the statements from those reports, and Oliver consistently said he did not agree.

Oliver: *"...what I am trying to say is I have never seen Mr. Hoover have anything that, even for a second, would concern me about his flying capabilities."*

He also said that he never heard a word of concern from any of the other performers (or ACE designees) who worked that weekend.

Oliver's Cross-Examination

Winton first asked Oliver what aircraft he flew and what kind of routine he did. Oliver testified that he flew a highly-modified Dehaviland Chipmunk. His routine consisted of 10 to 20 minutes of loops, rolls, vertical rolls, ups, snap rolls, and more. He later said, after he was asked, that the only maneuvers he repeats in a routine are turn-arounds and hammerheads. As he had asked Tucker, Winton asked Oliver if he had had times over his 36 years of flying when he hadn't felt at his best — due to fatigue or a bad lunch or whatever and if it would affect his performance.

Oliver: *"It would only affect my performance in that would still fall within the parameters that I set for safety. I would cancel and have canceled an airshow because I got the flu the night before."*

Winton then asked him what skills he felt were necessary for him to adequately perform his maneuvers.

Oliver: *"Experience first; a realization, thorough understanding of your own; weather conditions."*

Winton asked if the ability to divide your attention would be necessary to perform in an airshow.

Oliver: *"Yes, but I would stipulate I don't know what you — your idea of dividing attention, how far that goes."*

Winton continued on this for a while, making the point that an airshow pilot is concentrating on staying in the box, and maintaining the correct airspeed and all the correct settings all at the same time.

Winton: *"Okay. I am just trying to get that: that you are dividing your attention between every — all these things at once. Is that a fair statement?"*

Oliver said that was fair, so Winton began asking about reaction time, asking if it were critical to flying in an airshow. Oliver said of course it was. Winton then asked Oliver about the ACE program, and what Oliver's responsibilities were within that program.

Oliver: *"In a nutshell: protecting the public, protecting ourselves, protecting the industry."*

Winton then began asking about Oliver's earlier statements that Hoover appeared healthy at the airshow in question — if Hoover hadn't, Oliver said, that is what would have stuck out in his mind.

Winton: *"... So if there were something wrong with me, let's say, that could affect my performance in an aircraft in an airshow situation, that would affect the safety of the public and me, as a pilot, and the industry, that you couldn't see, how would you make that determination?"*

Oliver: *"Mr. Winton, in your case, I couldn't; I don't know you. I don't know anything about you. I have never been around you. I can assure you that if we run around together or if I have had the opportunity to spend lots and lots of time with you so that I know how you normally are, at that point, if you were different, I would be aware of it, I assume."*

So Winton tried a different approach. He asked Oliver if there were something *"on the inside of Mr. Hoover"* — that he didn't know about — was affecting him and his airshow, would he be concerned with his safety and the safety of others (how could he be concerned if he didn't know about it?).

Oliver: *"I am — that was so long, I am not sure."*

Yodice objected at this point, and Winton withdrew the question... but brought up the ol' hypothetical heart problem again. Of course Oliver would be concerned. He said he would also be concerned, when Winton simply changed the same question around and asked if he would be concerned if he developed some medical condition after he had received a medical certificate but before it expired. Of course he would be concerned. When Oliver said yes, Winton again asked the same question, this time making the condition something that would affect his ability to divide his attention.

Oliver: *"Well, we are getting into kind of an area that — your questions are getting harder and harder to answer because I may not be sure exactly what you are saying and you may not hear exactly what I am saying. I think the bottom line is this: If there is a safety issue of any kind that I perceive, as an ACE and as a fellow performer and as a friend, be it medical or the fact that you just had a fight with your wife, that is a moot point. If I myself saw anything that concerned me, I would address with that person, no matter who they were, that issue."*

Winton still wasn't satisfied, and so he asked the same type of question in a different way — would Oliver be concerned if a doctor told him there was a problem — but one that he couldn't see — with one of his fellow pilots that could affect that pilot's ability to divide his attention? Oliver said he would be, but that doctor would have to be someone he trusted in order for him to lend credence to a diagnosis such as that. Evidently that still wasn't the right answer, because Winton still pushed it... until Yodice finally objected, asking how many times Winton could ask the same question. The objection had no sooner been sustained when, guess what? He asked it again. And another objection.

And he slid in one more time, with just a couple of different words. Again, Oliver repeated that yes, he would be *"based upon the degree of legitimacy of that particular*

doctor's report..."

At this time, Oliver was excused and a little bit of administrative business was taken care of. They admitted the deposition of Dr. Simon, witness for the Defendant. Because they admitted this, however, the FAA was allowed to bring forth Dr. Ziessmann for a rebuttal — out of turn.

Bailey also offered the deposition of General Tom Stafford, and the FAA objected — but this objection was overruled. The Administrator offered reports on Hoover's history with the FAA (i.e., problems, such as nose-gear failure, only going back ten years). Bailey had one final deposition to offer, that of Ray Hughes — the gentleman who was with Hoover when he had the T-28 emergency. However, Bailey said there had been no evidence presented to contradict Hoover's story of that night, and when the Judge agreed with that statement, Bailey withdrew the offer of the deposition.

At this point, the Administrator called Dr. Ziessman to the stand.

Chapter 24

The Experts Start Finishing Up...

"Control your emotion or it will control you."
Samurai maxim

Dr. Ziessman's Direct Examination

Instead of going through Ziessman's entire 25-page curriculum vitae, the FAA did the most sensible thing they had done in months – they asked Ziessman for just a brief overview of his work. Ziessman explained that he was a nuclear medicine physician and the Director of Nuclear Medicine and a professor of radiology at Georgetown University. Of course, he is board certified by the American Board of Nuclear Medicine.

When asked, Ziessman explained that radiology is an imaging specialty of which nuclear medicine is one sub-specialty. Within this specialty, Ziessman said that he was quite familiar with SPECT scans, having worked with them for eleven years.

Ziessman testified that these scans are used to study more than brains; the scans are a process by which cross-sectional images are acquired and processed. Brain SPECTs capture multiple images of the brain after a radioactive drug is administered. These images show the distribution of blood flow in the brain. The blood flow, Ziessman said, represents normal or abnormal brain activity.

Winton then began to show Ziessman SPECT scan reports on Hoover performed by Dr. Mena and Dr. Salcedo. What he wasn't going to discuss, however, was Mena's revised report – revised in favor of Hoover. Bailey objected. Winton said it was not an intentional omission, and said Ziessman would see it.

When he finally began looking at the scans, Ziessman said that the report showed overall global regional cerebral blood flow within normal limits, but right-frontal bilateral temporal and left-parietal hypoprofusion (lack of blood flow).

Ziessman testified that Dr. Mena's original conclusion was that these results were consistent with multiple strokes or degenerative changes in those areas. His revised report said *"Normal Variance?,"* meaning, Ziessman said, that he didn't know if the results were normal or abnormal.

Ziessman then testified that Dr. Salcedo's report said that it was a *"border-line examination suggesting the possibility"* of bi-parietal areas of hypoprofusion, and that the findings should be correlated with neuro-anatomical findings. And with the patient's condition, if clinical conditions persist, *"one may wish to consider a six-month follow-up*

exam."

Ziessman was then asked if Salcedo's report mentioned trauma, and Ziessman said it did not. Continuing his recital of Salcedo's findings, Ziessman said Hoover's superior parietal area demonstrated a mild deficiency in a symmetrical fashion, but that the remainder of the cortex appeared normal. There was symmetry and normal uptake in the basal ganglia and cerebellar hemisphere (say all of that three times fast!)

Ziessman was then asked if he had been present at the time of Dr. Simon's deposition and he had, via phone. He had also reviewed the transcripts of that deposition. He also testified that he had consulted with Dr. Michael DeVous about Hoover's SPECT scans. DeVous, he said, is an internationally-renowned expert in brain imaging. Winton began asking if DeVous' opinions of Hoover's SPECT scans mirrored his own, but, after an objection, the Judge reminded the Court that we hadn't even heard Ziessman's own findings.

Ziessman: "*My findings were, first of all, that this is an abnormal study,*" he began. He then said that these abnormalities were hyprofusion of both parietal lobes, both temporal lobes. He explained that the lack of blood flow in these areas suggests decreased metabolism — decreased function — in that part of the brain. He said there was also decreased profusion in the temporal lobes, too.

Ziessman said that he agreed with Salcedo's findings, and that the findings weren't consistent with what one would expect from trauma… he considered a degenerative disease of the brain more likely.

DeVous, Ziessman said, shared his findings… as did Dr. Simon, although he said Simon's scans produced different color patterns and qualities. Dr. Mena's test, Ziessman said, only showed abnormalities in one parietal lobe, but Ziessman said he saw them in both lobes. Nonetheless, he said, they still showed similar results… although they were done six or seven months apart.

Ziessman's Cross-Examination

Bailey: "*Dr. Ziessman, as a scientist, are you often suspicious of unusual coincidences?*"
Ziessman said that certainly happens.

Bailey asked if there had been any unusual coincidences that resulted in his appearance in court, and Ziessman said that Bailey would have to point them out to him. Bailey asked if he knew Dr. Pincus, and Ziessman said yes. When asked what he did, Ziessman said Pincus was the Chief of Neurology at Georgetown University. Bailey said that as such, he should be able to read SPECT scans competently, to which Ziessman said that Pincus doesn't routinely read SPECT scans, and that he has had Ziessman and his group interpret SPECT scans. Bailey asked when he had first seen the SPECT scans in this case, and Ziessman said it had been the day of Dr. Simon's deposition.

Bailey: "*Yes. So Dr. Pincus apparently, although he had them in his possession in July, never consulted you. Is that right?*"
Ziessman agreed, and then Bailey asked if Pincus had recommended him (Ziessman) to the FAA as an expert. Ziessman said he didn't know. Bailey asked how they did select him, then. Ziessman had talked to an associate of Pincus… so, he said, it was possible that he had been selected via Pincus' recommendations. (*Author's Note: Big reach*

here, eh?)

Bailey: *"Yes. This is the same Georgetown that has the FAA grant, if I am not mistaken. Is that right?"*
Ziessman said he didn't know anything about a grant (of course).

Bailey: *"...Now, then, did you know that the FAA did not think enough of the SPECT scan evidence to use it in its case in chief in this prosecution? Did you know that?"*

Ziessman: *"I don't understand the question, but I don't think I know the answer to it, either."*

Bailey: *"All right. It is obvious to you, is it not, that the SPECT scans have been in the FAA's custody, through its experts, since October of '92 and again in May of '93. Is that apparent?"*
Zeissman had no idea, so Bailey said to assume that the FAA ordered the studies that included the SPECT scans, and asked Zeissman if that helped. Zeissman didn't respond.

Bailey: *"That is overwhelming evidence in this case. Okay? Now you were never consulted until the FAA was ordered to attend the deposition, if they chose —"*
Winton objected, saying the question had already been asked and answered, but Judge Mullins told him to let Bailey finish the question. Zeissman agreed that he had never been consulted prior to the Simon deposition.

Bailey: *"What I am trying to develop is that Dr. Pincus never asked him to read the SPECT scans, even though he had them in his possession, as he testified."*
Bailey then asked Zeissman if he knew who Simon was. Zeissman testified that Simon is the Head of Nuclear Medicine at Humana Hospital in Houston. He knew who he was, but didn't know him personally. Zeissman said Simon was respected in his field... but Zeissman also said that he thought Simon's opinions were *"in error."*
Bailey then ran down the list, asking Zeissman what he thought of the various opinions. Salcedo, he said, was correct, but didn't go far enough. Of Gold, who said that Hoover should be allowed to fly, Zeissman said he didn't know of his opinions. Dr. Mena's testing led him to believe that Hoover should be allowed to fly. Of Mena, Zeissman said, *"I am a specialist in nuclear medicine and interpreting images; I am not a neurologist."*

Bailey: *"I understand that. But we are going to talk in a minute about coincidence. All right? Now, do you understand that when the FAA was suddenly confronted with the fact that Mr. Hoover was going to produce Dr. Simon in this case, even though they didn't intend to go into SPECT scans with an expert, you were selected to be their consultant? Do you understand that?"*

Zeissman: *"I think so,"* he said, saying that he understood that the FAA chose their consultants, which also included DeVous.

Bailey: *"Right. And unlike the selection of most experts, they had to give your names before you had seen the materials. Did you know that?"*

Zeissman said he did not, and Bailey then asked him how many times he had been called as an expert before he had formed an opinion. Zeissman said it was unusual for him to be called as an expert at all.

Bailey: *"... but due to the constraints of time, you understand they had no choice but to give us your name before you saw anything. Right?"*

Zeissman said he would take Bailey's word for it.

Bailey: *"Now, Dr. Zeissman, I just want to know: Is it pure coincidence that two blind selections turned out to be helpful to the FAA?"*

Winton objected to the use of the term *"blind selection,"* so Bailey simply asked if he had agreed to give an opinion favorable to the FAA before he had seen the opinions. Zeissman said he had not.

Bailey: *"Did you know that if you gave an opinion unfavorable, they wouldn't hire you any more in this case?*

Winton, as you may imagine, objected to this, and it was sustained. Zeissman did agree, however, that he probably would not have been brought out to give an opinion favorable to Hoover... but he also said that *"it wasn't my choice to come to this trial."*

Bailey: *"I understand. But 'lo and behold, having selected two experts without knowing what they would say when they were qualified to have an opinion, the FAA got two good opinions. Does that strike you as a coincidence?"*

Zeissman: *"It must strike you as a coincidence."*

Bailey: *"Well, it strikes me as an extraordinarily lucky maneuver. Wouldn't you think?"*

Zeissman didn't respond. Bailey then asked him what Hoover's brain looked like 10 years ago. Zeissman did not know. Bailey asked if he knew about the crashes and trauma he had been through, and Zeissman said he had heard that Hoover had had trauma.

Bailey: *"The Germans beat him up in a prison camp: you knew that?"*

Zeissman: *"I had heard that."*

Bailey: *"He bailed out of an airplane at a very high rate of speed and cracked his head when the tail of the airplane broke his legs: you know that?"*

Zeissman, after a short intermission resulting from Winton objecting to this line of questions, said, *"I don't know the details of his injuries."*

Bailey: *"So you would say there is possibility that in the history of this subject, there has been trauma, would you not?"*

Zeissman said that there was no question that he had had trauma, but *"the question is whether it caused these abnormalities of the profusions."*

Bailey: *"Do you understand that Dr. Simon has said that it certainly could have?"*
Zeissman said yes, that is what Simon said.

Bailey: *"And you are attempting to rule it out only on the basis of symmetry. Isn't that true?"*

Zeissman: *"I am not ruling it out. I am saying that the most likely diagnosis here of these particular findings is a degenerative disease of the brain. These are characteristic findings of that, and not characteristic of trauma."*
Bailey asked at what age a brain begins to degenerate.

Zeissman: *"Well, the brain is dying off at—starting to lose cells at a, you know, fairly early age. And that is continuous. However, I am not talking about normal aging processes, and a normal elderly patient would not have a brain scan like this."*
Bailey asked if he were calling Hoover elderly, and then asked how old he was. The doctor said he was 49.

Bailey: *"Did you ever see this 71-year-old man fly an airplane?"*
After Winton objected because Zeissman was "here to testify about SPECT scans" (which was overruled), the doctor testified that he had not... and that was the end of the cross examination – but Judge Mullins had a few questions of his own, concerning Dr. Salcedo's report.
The Judge said that the report said *"if clinical symptoms persist, one may wish to consider a six-month follow-up examination."* Judge Mullins wanted to know what he meant by *"clinical symptoms."*

Zeissman: *"I think what he means is that images aren't ever interpreted by a clinician by themselves, or rarely, at least; they are usually interpreted in correlation with a patient's history and physical findings and other tests."*

Judge Mullins: *"Okay. The evidence seems to be in this case that there is just no history of any cognitive deficit, at least from an objective standpoint; it has all been determined from these neuro-psychological tests that have been administered. Just – there haven't been — is he referring to symptoms that are — that one might observe objectively? The other subsequent tests that people keep talking about... they are not valid because of a, quote, 'practice effect'?"*
Zeissman said he wasn't positive about what Salcedo meant, but that he did know that a follow-up scan might show further progression, which would confirm a degenerative problem with Hoover, and he thought that is what Salcedo meant. After that, Zeissman was excused and free to go, and Bailey called his next witness, Dr. Appel.

Antoinette Appel's Testimony

When she came to the stand, Appel testified that she was a neuropsychologist, and had been so since 1972. She said that as far as the American Psychological Association is able to ascertain, she holds the first degree in neuropsychology awarded in the US.

When asked what kind of practice she had, Appel testified that she evaluated an treated people who are thought to have something wrong with their brains, a large por tion of which have been involved in traumatic incidents. Additionally, she is the founde of the Distressed Professionals Program, evaluating professionals whose licenses migh be in jeopardy. Bailey asked Appel the question the Judge had asked Zeissman abou Salcedo's comment.

Appel: *"…What Dr. Salcedo was suggesting was that a correlation be established betwee the patient's clinical complaints and findings and the radiological or nuclear medicin evidence and that that occur on more than one occasion; that the past history and pas complaints be considered with reference to the first set of imaging and that if a follow u of imaging were to occur, that the patient's complaints and findings be related to that…"*

Bailey asked her if she used SPECT scans in his practice, and Appel said yes – an had done so for about four or five years. Bailey then asked if she had done any studies tha would address Salcedo's suggestion.

Appel: *"Obviously, yes. If — as people read Dr. Ted Simon's deposition, they will discove that I am the person who recommended Dr. Simon. Subsequent to that and subsequen to the completion of the review of these and after his deposition, I agreed to participat with him in a formal study in which I will do the neuropsychological evaluation on th patients for whom he has already collected SPECT scan data, some of whom are bon fide normals and some of whom are trauma. And it will be done blind; I will have no ide which is which."*

The purpose of such a study, Appel said, is because at this time there is no answer to the question of the correlation of neuropsychological test data and SPECT scan data. Bailey said that Ziessman had testified that trauma was an unlikely cause of what the scans showed because of symmetry, and asked if Appel agreed with that. Appel said she did not, because her experience with over 12,000 people who had head injuries had shown that symmetrical injuries were frequently found. After this, Bailey ques- tioned Appel about when he first engaged Appel as a consultant. Appel said it was the week before Christmas 1993, and that Bailey provided Appel with the records of the other doctors' examinations of Hoover— which she had reviewed.

Bailey: *"And now, has there ever been, to your knowledge, a version on computer of th Wisconsin Test which was intended for anything but research use?"*

Appel said there had not been.

Bailey: *"When you heard Dr. Elliott testify the other day that he had such a version, di you at my request call the people who own the program?"*

Appel said she did; she called Psychological Assessment Resources, the only com pany that has ever owned, made, and/or distributed that computer program. At her be quest, Appel testified, PAR sent a letter verifying that that the computer program was for research use only. Bailey offered this as evidence, Winton objected, and the Judge over ruled.

Additionally, Appel testified that she got received a copy of this research versior to see if it was the same as the non-computerized version, both in administration and performance. Appel said she has given the regular version of this test more than 5000 times, but only gave the computerized version to herself. Appel further testified that when she gives the manual version to herself, she is able to complete it in five minutes with no errors. On the computerized version, it took her a little over 40 minutes. When asked what she attributed the difference in time to, Appel responded:

Appel: *"The task is different. Okay? And the way that they have got it set up – that PAR has it set up, with a key input as opposed to a light pen input, which would have its own problems, given their light pen, it is just an unusual way of doing it. It is not putting it under the key card in question; it is using F, G, H, and J, I think four keys in a row, and having that represent. There are tiny, tiny little codes that can be placed on key caps. The light pen does not work so well, because it is, contrary to everyone else's light-pen, not on contact, but on release."*

When asked what the test was worth, Appel bluntly said nothing. Bailey then asked Appel about Elliott's testing methods, where he tested from 8 to 5 with only one break for a drink of water and to go to the bathroom. He asked if those were proper methods, and what degenerative effects could result from such methods.

Appel: *"There are any number of studies of performance that have been run by psychologists that demonstrate a marked drop-off in performance after 90 minutes. And that is why, if you look at university schedules, for example, courses break at 90 minutes. If they don't break sooner than that, performance simply breaks off.*

And most neuropsychologists I know schedule breaks and insist that patients get up, walk around, go to the bathroom, have a cup of coffee, do whatever. But we fill the breaks in. We also definitely break for lunch because people – your blood sugar varies. And we are not trying to measure blood sugar; we are trying to measure brain function."

She added that performance goes down hill if you don't eat and Apell also mentioned that any kind of tension between the tester and examinee can also have a deleterious effect on test results. When Bailey asked Appel what the ethical propriety was of telling an examinee that the test would have no effect whatsoever on the retention of the job, when knowing that it indeed would.

Appel: *"As the author of planks that are incorporated in the APA Ethical Principles and Code of Conduct, so as someone who has – is well familiar with that code, I need to tell you that I believe my colleagues will find that to be unethical behavior and actionable against the licensee."*

Bailey then asked Appel about what she thought about the other tests given by Elliott and Dr. Johnson, and what she thought about practice effect.

Appel: *"Okay. First of all, the category test was given a year apart. And so if we were to give a category test every couple of weeks, yes, there would be practice effect. But most neuropsychologists, beginning with Morazzo (phonetic) would agree that a year is appropriate."*

Appel went on to say that if in fact Hoover did have a degenerative disease, *"all the practice effect in the world"* wouldn't matter because his brain would be getting worse. Additionally, Appel said she did not agree with Elliott's assessment of his own records,

citing a possible scoring error, particularly a reverse-digit span that had been discussed in the courtroom. Elliott said Hoover's span was three, when, according to Elliott's records, it was four – which was within normal limits.

Bailey stopped here, and asked the doctor if she knew Elliott before the trial. Appel said she had spoken to him on the phone sometime around 1989 for American Board of Professional Neuropsychology business. She again called him in regards to this matter, with a request for his raw data so that she could examine it.

Appel: *"He told me that he was not in the office, that he would not accept the release that I had from Mr. Hoover and was willing to fax to him, that he would insist on an original copy and that he was not going to go to his office and get the data Xeroxed and he was leaving for Hawaii and I would have to wait until after he came back. And when he did come back, I still didn't get it."*

Bailey then asked about predicting behaviors based on the results of these kinds of tests. Appel quoted from a February 1993 article from *Aviation, Space, and Environmental Medicine magazine,* which said, *"There have been no studies of the relationship between normal cognitive function as measured by standardized neuropsychological measures,"* and also said that, *"there were no studies in which test batteries had been validated against actual flight performance of experienced pilots."*

She also quoted from a study done by Dr. Kay. *"Out of a group of 10,000 examinees, 500 would be expected to truly have a cognitive impairment. The tests would correctly identify 450 of those impaired examinees and would fail to identify 50 examinees with cognitive impairment. Of the 9500 non-impaired examinees, 950 would be identified incorrectly as having cognitive impairment. According to the formula, the probability of the presence of disease, given a positive test result under these conditions, is 32.1%."*

Additionally, Appel quoted another study that said all but one of the pilots had been misclassified were in the third (51 to 60 years) and fourth (over 61 years) age group. Bailey asked if she felt there was any need to be concerned about Hoover's cognitive function.

Appel: *"I don't believe so. And I tested that by taking the test scores acquired after Dr. Elliott's exam and plotting them as an interesting function, using the PAR normative data program for the Halstead-Reitan. I assumed that they – the very same numbers: that Bob Hoover on that data was 46 – or 42, 46, 50, 52, 54, 58, 62, 64, 66, 68, 70, and 71 years old. And based on those assumptions, Mr. Hoover's category test results, as done by Dr. Johnson, were as well as a neurologically normal – that is, unimpaired – 65-year-old. Or he has a six-year advantage."*

Appel continued, saying that her other tests showed similar results – trails A as a 55 year old, trails B — as a 63 year old, and his dominant hand peg board, as a normal, neurologically unimpaired 44 year old. She also testified that she told Bailey right up front that if she had tested Hoover and looked over the data and had come to the conclusion that Hoover should not fly, she would tell Bailey, Hoover, and the Court, if necessary, just that.

Appel said she had also tested Hoover in another way – she had been Hoover's constant shadow for the last 72 hours – during the trial, which Appel said had to be *"horrendous conditions of pressure because in fact, Mr. Hoover has sat here while we*

have talked about him… and in addition to his being normal on the two mental status examinations that I administered, I failed to see a single piece of aberrant behavior in those 72 hours. And in point of fact, the laboratory of observation is the best laboratory."

Bailey asked if Appel had the experience and expertise to make such judgments and to recognize if Hisey did the test correctly and/or were the results as Hisey had testified. Appel said he had completed a fellowship at Mount Sinai, served as Dr. Bender's last fellow, and then served as the primary consultant to the dept. of neurosurgery. He has also taught neuro-ophthalmology and neurology.

After that preface, she said she felt Hisey did the test correctly and she agreed with Hisey's conclusions. Bailey then asked Appel to comment on the importance of assessing sudden change versus slow aging on reaction time.

Appel: *"Much has been made about reaction time. But the human condition is such that we accommodate to slow change. And as we get older, our tissues use intersticial fluid, and the initiation of movement takes longer. But we learn that, and we have to learn that or we would stub our toe… So as we get older, we begin to initiate movements slightly earlier so that the gradual onset in all of us – and if I take a 35-year-old and compare him to a 25-year-old, on reaction time, the 35-year-old is going to be slower… We are just not as fast, but we adapt to that. And we don't go around killing ourselves. I don't know how else to answer that."*

Bailey asked Appel about Pincus' statement that he would license Hoover to drive a car but not a school bus. Appel saw fallacy in that, saying that if Pincus were correct, the school buses should stay off the streets because Hoover could put his car into a school bus.

Bailey asked Hoover if a pilot doing an established aerobatic routine would need to react any faster than someone driving a car. Appel said no. She also reiterated that no study has been able to show an association between success on the types of tests that Hoover had taken and prediction of the behavior of experienced pilots.

Bailey: *"Now, Doctor, the last question. Three witnesses testifying for the FAA said they had reached their conclusions and they would not change them, no matter what the facts showed, as to his actual performance, no matter over what period of time. My question to you: Is that a professional attitude for these people to take?"*

Appel: *"No, Mr. Bailey. And I told you when Dr. Hisey did his neurological exam last night – and I have been sitting next to you throughout these proceedings. If it had been abnormal, either you would have been foolish to call me or I would have been telling the Court that it was abnormal."*

Appel also stated firmly that she does take his ability to operate an aircraft into account because *"the behavior is much more important than the tests because I can't establish that these tests do what we claim we would like them to do."*

Bailey then asked Appel if she had any hesitation in recommending to Judge Mullins that Hoover be allowed to fly; Appel said she had no hesitation whatsoever, and that she saw nothing in his examination that would suggest that he was at any increased

risk over the next two years.

Appel's Cross-Examination

Winton asked Appel how often she testified in court. Appel answered that as a neuropsychologist, a substantial portion of her patients have sustained injuries and there fore end up in the litigation process.

Winton: *"So you indicated that most of your experience was with traumatic injuries, criminal justice, and determination for agencies for qualification of personnel?"*

Appel: *"No, I didn't say that. I said that I do cases that happen to appear before those kinds of agencies. I see a whole host of neurological problems because I see people that someone thinks has a problem with the brain or central nervous system. I told you I had approximately 12,000 cases in my personal history of closed-head injury types of things. But I have over 20,000 cases in the warehouse. I hope I look younger than I really am."*

Winton asked Appel how long she had been there preparing for the trial, and Appel said it was approximately 72 hours, not including sleep time. About half the time she had put into the case total had taken place since he arrived, much of which was spent following Hoover around. What it finally became evident that Winton was getting at, once he had asked how many depositions and trials Appel attended and if she prepared that way for all her cases (to which Appel said it wasn't always necessary because she often takes copious notes during an exam), was this: *"And Doctor, because you spend all this time preparing records, reading reports, writing reports, preparing for deposition, traveling, preparing for litigation, do you have much time to read new articles, let's say, in the field of neuropsychology?"*

Appel said she probably reads ten journals per month. Winton asked how many journals there were, and Appel said hundreds... Winton was trying to make that ten sound pitiful.

Appel: *"Except I subscribe to **The Neuropsychology Psych Abstracts**, and so I get a review of the entire field every three months in terms of the abstracts. And I have a service running where, on a monthly basis, someone goes down and keys in certain key terms on the Silver Platter, which is a computer-retrieval service, and pumps it onto my computer, prints it out, and I have the abstracts. And that way, at least I – if there is another article, I go read it."*

Winton continued to press, saying that she must have spent so much time preparing for litigation that she must not have read a follow-up article to an article by Dr. Kay that Appel had referred to in her earlier testimony, when she had said that there was no correlation neuropsychological testing and the ability to fly.

Winton: *"And did you do any research to follow up on what studies have been performed after that article came out, Doctor?"*

Appel: *"If you are telling me there is another article, I might remind you, because I am the initiator of the request for production, that we requested all articles offered by Dr.*

Gary Kay on the subject."

Although Appel remained firm and stated that she had not received any other articles, Winton continued with the same line, saying that she spent too much time preparing for litigation and not enough time reading.

Winton: *"…Knowing that it was possible that the data was based on 1990 studies, you made no effort to plug in key words into your computer system that you just mentioned to find out if any other data had come up since then?"*

Appel said Winton was wrong – she had done one better. She had called Dr. Kay. *"I called Dr. Gary Kay. And I asked him for any new data, and he told me you guys owned it, that the FAA owned it, and that he couldn't release it to me."*

Appel: *"… and then we submitted a request for production for discovery, and I still didn't get it. So I am sitting here with the articles that were made available."*

Bailey therefore objected to this line of questioning, but Winton continued.

Winton: *"So you are not surprised that that article was based on 1990 studies. Am I correct?"*

Appel said that would not surprise her.

Winton: *"And you wouldn't have a problem accepting that there may be additional studies that came in after that. Am I right?"*

Appel: *"I have no basis for assuming that there are additional studies. And, in fact, I requested any data that might exist. And I will repeat again –"*

Bailey: *"I am going to move the Court to direct Counsel for the FAA to state whether or not there are additional articles by Gary Kay that have not been turned over."*

The Judge stated that if the questioning continued, Winton would have to reveal the document, and he also said that if the documents come up and they have been asked for and they weren't provided, then the Administrator is going to have "some problems." Winton said he understood that, and he wouldn't have asked the question otherwise.

Winton: *"Doctor, you are not questioning the validity of your field, that neuropsychological testing does not relate to everyday functioning, are you?"*

Appel said that there is truly little data that relates this type of testing to everyday functioning. She also said there was a recent article listing these studies in **The Neuropsychology Handbook** by Shalume and Merrill. She also said that the single most predictive measure of everyday functioning is IQ, and she quoted from the above-mentioned article: *"And the overwhelming majority of these studies rely on IQ, and not on neuropsychological assessment in terms of the Halstead-Reitan or the Luria-Nebraska to assess everyday functioning."*

Then, Winton began asking about the never-before-seen article again… not only, it seemed, had it not been produced, but it seemed to be about the CogScreen, which had already been declared off-limits. Of course, Bailey objected, and Mullins sustained the objection and told him to move on — with no more reference to that article. It looked as if Winton was going to begin questioning Appel about an article by Banich entitled "Testing the Tests", when Judge Mullins called a recess until the next morning, saying that he had reached a mental saturation point.

When the Court reconvened the next morning, Bailey said that he withdrew the taped deposition of Dr. Ted Simon because it was an hour long. The video of Hoover's performance the previous week had not been withdrawn.

Next, Caron stated that she wanted to make an objection for the record. Her objection was that Appel made references to certain articles that related directly to the development of CogScreen... which the FAA had been prevented from using in rebuttal evidence. Mullins overruled the objection, but said he did want to stay away from CogScreen.

After this, the cross-examination of Dr. Appel continued. When it did, Winton withdrew his last question, stating they referred to Caron's recent arguments. Bailey said he wanted to know what the question was and why he wanted it noted on the record – stating he didn't want to see this one on appeal. Mullins also wanted to know what the question was.

Winton: *"It was the last question regarding an article published, I believe, in '93 based on 1990 studies, and my question was if she was aware of any studies since then regarding the testing of pilots and the correlation between neuropsychological testing and the ability to perform."*

Bailey: *"Aha. Counsel now refers to an article which apparently the FAA withheld despite an order to deliver it to the Respondent."*

Bailey also demanded that all of Dr. Kay's information on this subject, including unpublished information on his computer, be turned over to the Respondent.

Judge Mullins: *"This whole issue revolves around the fact that other than just a listing on a CV, the Respondent has asked for anything Dr. Kay has published since that time or has written, and apparently that was not responded to in the discovery requests."*

Winton: *"Your Honor, anything that was published by Dr. Kay regarding CogScreen which was asked for was submitted to the respondent. Apparently this article — it is not an article. It was a presentation at an aeromedical seminar in Miami, and there was no article published or accepted. Therefore, we cannot present it, Your Honor."*

Bailey: *"If it please the Court, let the record not be warped. Dr. Appel called Dr. Kay and was told there was such an article, but he said, 'I can't give it to you; I don't have the right to do that.' And so we filed a very specific demand in discovery for the article, and the government failed to deliver it."*

After this, Mullins said to move on.

Winton: *"Doctor, would you agree with this statement, that the comatose individual has little to no cognitive functioning?"*

Appel explained that the answer to that question is not known, because there really is no way to measure a comatose person's cognition. When asked, she did say she

would probably agree with the statement that a comatose person without any signs of voluntary functioning would have little to no cognitive functioning.

Winton then asked if she agreed that cognitive functioning is required to perform a task on command, and Appel said no, referring to the fact that it is possible to train humans and animals to make voluntary responses – conditioned responses – on demand, with the presentation of some stimulus.

To get more specific (and smart-alecky), Winton asked if cognitive functioning was required to tie a shoe, drive a car, or fly a plane. Appel said it was. Winton then asked if Appel were a pilot. Appel said no.

Winton: *"You have never flown aerobatics."*

Appel: *"I haven't flown aerobatics, but if you read my CV, you are well aware of the fact that I am a graduate of the National Aeronautics and Space Administration's biospace technology training program."*

Winton: *"But you have never personally flown aerobatics."*
Appel said that was correct.

Winton: *"...and in between all the time that you spend rendering your services as an expert witness, do you have any time left to study aerobatic pilots for cognitive or neuropsychological testing in your office?"*

Appel : *"I don't know whether I have seen aerobatic pilots. I know just off the top of my head, I can think of two folks in the last year or so that I knew were pilots. I can assure you that there are more pilots in my patient database, but I really don't –*
You need to understand something. When I am evaluating someone's neuropsychological status, it doesn't matter to me whether they are a pilot, a doctor, a lawyer, or the person who cleans up my office. They get basically the same evaluation, because I am interested in answering certain kinds of questions. So it doesn't matter whether it is a pilot."

Winton continued the same question, asking how many pilots she had studied. When Appel said she didn't know, Winton asked her if she had ever tested Sean Tucker or Steve Oliver or Leo Loudenslager. Appel had not.

Winton: *"...do you recall Sean Tucker, the world renowned aerobatic expert and member of the ACE program, testify to what he feels are the necessary abilities required to safely perform in an airshow?"*

Appel said to correct her if she were wrong, but she believed Tucker didn't understood what the technical terms meant. Winton then went on, asking if she remembered Steve Oliver's testimony, which Appel did.

Winton: *"Do you recall him testifying that while he is concerned with staying within that airshow box, he is also concerned with maintaining certain altitudes? Do you recall that, Doctor?"*

Appel said he probably did say that, but she didn't remember his exact words.

Winton asked if Oliver had said he had to pay attention to staying within the airshow box, and maintaining his airspeed in addition to the altitude. Appel said yes.

Winton: *"Doctor, does that require the divided attention for the safe performance of an airshow?"*

Appel: *"I don't know what you mean by divided attention. If you mean simultaneously monitoring various instruments, the answer to that appears to be no. If you mean taking the input from all of that information and somehow synthesizing it, the answer appears to be yes."*

Winton: *"Thank you, Doctor. Did I mention anything about instruments in any of my questions?"*

Appel: *"I have –"*
Apparently quite loudly, Winton then said, *"Did I?."*

Bailey: *"All right. May counsel be instructed to behave like a gentleman."*

Judge Mullins: *"Mr. Winton –"*

Winton: *"I will."*

Judge Mullins: *" – you needn't scream. I think – I am certainly hearing you just fine. I think the witness can hear you."*
Winton said he was sorry… he was just getting excited because Appel wasn't answering his questions. Mullins said that was no reason to get excited, and he should move on. After continuing to grapple with the question for a few minutes because Appel said *"divided attention"* was not a psychological term, Winton repeated the question and Appel said paying attention to those three items did not necessarily require the ability to divide attention.
Winton then said that the *"not necessarily"* answer apparently disagreed with Oliver's testimony – and reiterated that Oliver is an expert aerobatic pilot and Appel was not even a pilot. Bailey objected, stating *"testimony by counsel"* and that Winton's statements were argumentative.

Judge Mullins: *"Well, this lady is not an aerobatic pilot. Mr. Oliver is not a neuropsychologist. And you are trying to compare the two of them, and we will be here all day if you continue to do that. So in that sense it is argumentative. The objection is sustained."*

Winton: *"Do you recall Mr. Steven Oliver indicate that he feels reaction time is crucial in the safety of his performance during an airshow?"*
Appel said yes.

Winton: *"And do you recall Mr. Hoover testifying that during his airshow, he deals with many, many changing conditions?"*

Appel said yes.

Winton: *"And even though he has been performing this same aerobatic routine for at least the last 25 years with the exception of taking out the spin that he felt was unsafe, that he has to deal with changing air density, changing wind conditions, and sometimes unexpected emergencies. Do you recall him testifying about that?"*

Appel said yes again.

Winton: *"Let me ask you this, Doctor. Would that be considered – Mr. Hoover's airshow performance, considering all those factors at once, would that be considered a conceptually demanding job in a neuropsychological sense?"*

Appel: *"For the – the literature suggests that initially for novice aviator, it is much more difficult than for an experienced aviator. The literature demonstrates a progression –"*

Winton: *"Judge, I don't think I am getting an answer."*

Judge Mullins: *"Well, why don't you let the witness… I mean, you are asking some difficult questions, and you are obviously not getting the answer you want. This is an answer."*

Winton said fine, and Appel continued.

Appel: *"There is a progression in the degree of difficulty and demand on the performer that varies with experience. And I don't know what scale we would measure that on, but I have no reason to disbelieve my colleagues who have measured it. The scales appear to be reasonable and rational."*

Winton: *"Okay. If Mr. Hoover experienced an emergency in the performance of his airshow that he has never experienced in his life and he deals with it in the proper manner, while he is still considering the changes in the wind conditions and the air density, would that be considered a conceptually demanding job in the field of neuropsychology?"*

Bailey objected, stating that Appel was not a pilot witness and the question was therefore silly and unfair. However, Judge Mullins overruled.

Appel: *"Insofar as I can answer it, obviously the simultaneous consideration of various inputs is more difficult than the consideration of a single input."*

Winton wasn't satisfied. *"Doctor, yes or no? Is that considered a conceptually demanding job in the field of neuropsychology?"*

Bailey: *"I am sorry, Your Honor. I object to the form. Is that – I don't know what 'that' is, and I don't think the witness does."*

Mullins sustained the objection, so Winton repeated the question.

Winton: *"During Mr. Hoover's performance which he has performed over the last 25 years which is his routine performance, taking into consideration all of the weather conditions – do you understand weather conditions?"*

Appel said yes.

Winton: *"Taking into consideration all of the weather conditions affecting his performance and dealing with a simultaneous emergency which he has never before experienced in his life, dealing with that safely and adequately, would that be considered a conceptually demanding job in the field of neuropsychology? Yes or no, please, if you could."*

Appel: *"There is no measure for conceptually demanding. Would it conceptually be more difficult than considering a single thing? Yes. But I don't know how to answer your question, because –"*

Winton cut her off, saying that was *"fine."*

Bailey: *"I am going to ask that this counsel stop thanking witnesses and saying 'let me ask you this' and get back to what should be a cross-examination."*

The Judge said to move on, please, and Winton thanked him, too.

Bailey: *"May I know what the purpose of thanking the Court is?"*

Winton simply continued, asking if Appel knew Dr. Robert Heaton, Ph.D.

Appel said she did know him, and he was generally respected within the neuropsychological community. Winton then asked if Appel was familiar with the book, **The Comprehensive Norms for Expanded Halstead-Reitan Battery**.

Appel said absolutely, and Winton asked her to look at the trails B portion of this battery, and tell the Court what the purpose of that test is. Appel said it is a combination of speed and keeping two sequences in mind at the same time by alternation between number and letter. She also testified, when asked, that this test is generally recognized in the field of neuropsychology.

Winton: *"Okay. So if I am correct, I would have to divide my attention between the number sequences and the letter sequences simultaneously in order to accomplish what I have to do on this test. Is that right?"*

Appel: *"You would have to keep the sequences in mind simultaneously. I am not sure that that requires dividing attention."*

Winton then asked if the test was a timed one, and when Appel said yes, Winton asked why. Appel said that was the dependent variable, the measure.

Winton: *"The measure. So you are measuring, let's say, my time to react while I am dividing attention between numbers and letters in a sequence."*

Appel: *"It is not a reaction time. It is a motor speed. It is not a reaction time."*

Winton continued with his questioning for a bit, and Appel was firm with her explanation that motor speed was not reaction time. Next, Winton announced he had a new exhibit, which was the cover page from Heaton, Grant, and Matthew's tables of comprehensive norms. Appel, after Winton asked, said that these norms were accepted within the neuropsychological community – by some people, including herself.

Bailey interjected, saying that the version he had had been marked up, but Winton simply continued. He wanted to talk about the Trails B battery again. He asked Appel if it

ever changed – were the numbers ever in different places, for example. Appel testified that other than there being versions – one for right-handed people and one for left-handed people – they remain the same.

Winton: *"And would you indicate whether or not there would be any practice effect between taking this once, seeing the test another time, and seeing the test a third time, all within six-month intervals?"*

Appel said there is mixed literature on that subject, but the general reading and her opinion was that practice effect on the Trails B was minimal. Winton began to continue his questioning, and Bailey interjected.

Bailey: *"If it please the Court, I have a motion to make. Yesterday I very unwisely acquiesced in the accommodation of a prosecution witness who said that he had to go home, so we took him out of turn. I should not have made that mistake, because Dr. Appel's father who is 85 is being honored tonight, and the time was changed to accommodate her so that she could make an airplane and get back.*

Due to the ineptitude of counsel, wasting the Court's time with what is under the guise of cross-examination and is not, she had to stay over. There are limits, and if she misses that appearance because of this conduct, it will be a shame. I ask that you give him some limits as to when he may terminate this charade."

The Judge told Winton to move on, and said if need be, they would continue the trial to allow Appel to make her father's event and come back. Continuing, Winton asked Appel if she agreed with Heaton's statement that *"Especially at extreme age and education levels, T-scores are not good reflections of the adequacy of a test performance in absolute terms."* Appel said she did not agree. Winton continued to quote Heaton, stating that a raw test score of 80 errors is about average for a 75-year-old high school graduate, but, paraphrased, that still showed *"relatively weak"* conceptual skills – and that the average 75-year-old high school graduate *"is not likely to perform well in a conceptually demanding job."*

Appel explained that although she recognized Heaton as knowledgeable in the field of neuropsychology, she reserved the right to disagree with him and did so with regard to this statement. He then began to question her about Hoover's scores on this battery. Appel testified that Hoover's performance was about 5th or 6th percentile – a scaled score of 5. Winton asked if that meant that out of 100 people taking the test, Hoover would be number six. When Appel concurred, Winton asked if that were substandard.

Appel: *"Well, if it had been administered correctly, I don't know what the results –"*

Winton: *"I am sorry, Doctor –"*

Appel: *" – would have been. But for that, yes."*

Winton asked if substandard meant impaired, and Appel said under some circumstances. Winton asked Appel what Hoover's percentile was on Dr. Uchiyama's Trails B battery, and Appel testified that it also fell into about the 6th percentile. Not satisfied, Winton then asked Appel what percentile Hoover's performance on Dr. Johnsen's test fell into. Appel testified his score was in the 19th percentile.

Winton: *"Okay. Is that the type of performance that you would expect from a top aviator, naval graduate, and test pilot? Yes or no, Doctor? Is that you would expect from a performer of that magnitude?"*

Appel: *"I think that your question is misleading, because these are population norms. These are not age-specific norms, and these are not even group-specific norms."*

After that, Appel explained that the normal range is from the 16th percentile on up, so Hoover's performance could be perfectly acceptable. Still not satisfied, Winton said he wanted to ask about one more test, the Category test. When asked, Appel testified that Hoover erred 112 times, which put his scores in the 1st percentile.

Winton: *"First percentile. Does that mean, Doctor, out of 100 people who would take the test, Mr. Hoover would be at the absolute bottom? Is that a correct statement?"*

Appel had to agree that that is what the 1st percentile meant, so Winton charged on, asking about Dr. Johnsen's category test. Appel testified that Hoover's scores were in the 6th percentile. Again, Winton asked if those were scores you would expect from a top aviator. Appel answered that there is no demonstrated relationship between these scores and being an aviator.

Winton whined that the doctor wasn't answering his questions, so the Judge said, to simplify things and speed things up, Appel should only answer yes, no, or *"I can't answer that."*

Well, Winton continued to ask the same question – are those the kinds of scores that she would expect to see from a superior performer such as she considered Hoover. Guess what? Things being as they were, Dr. Appel couldn't answer that. Winton whined some more, but the Judge said the question had been asked and answered. Seemingly defeated, Winton said he had no further questions for Dr. Appel, nor did Bailey. She was excused.

At this time, both the Administrator and the Respondent rested their cases and began their closing arguments. Winton admitted two previously discussed pieces of evidence (standard business)… but then something interesting happened.

Bailey: *"May the record reflect that on the close of evidence, Mr. Winton approached the Respondent for his autograph."*

(Author Note: This REALLY Happened! Mighty strange, if you ask me!)

Chapter 25

The Beginning of the End... Closing Arguments

"It is error alone which needs the support of government.
Truth can stand by itself."
Thomas Jefferson

Caron did the FAA's closing arguments, and she began by describing Part 67 of the FARs, which discusses performance (in the air, as a special medical flight test) being used to show that an airman can safely utilize his certificate. Caron argued that because Part 67 does not provide for consideration of performance outside of Section 6719, this case, which did not involve a special issuance, must not (her words, of course) be based on a consideration of performance. Therefore, she said, medical evidence must be used to establish the condition... despite what she called *"the impressive show"* that Hoover's supporters had put on as a tribute to his career. Even ACEs, she said, know nothing of medical qualifications.

She then contended that Hoover seemed to want special consideration because of his stature, and there was simply no room within the regulations for that, especially considering what she called the *"overwhelming"* medical evidence. She argued that Dr. Elliott's testing showed mild to moderate impairment and that what was said about the use of the research version of the Category Test being unethical could also be said about the Respondent's witness, Dr. Johnsen.

After that, she said that even Sean Tucker and Leo Loudenslager had agreed that it was necessary to divide attention when piloting, insinuating that Hoover would not be able to do that. She then merely reiterated the results of the FAA's medical witnesses, all which seemingly showed Hoover to be cognitively impaired *"to the extent that; he should no longer be flying."* She added that Dr. Appel *"even conceded that Mr. Hoover is impaired on the tests that Dr. Uchiyama administered, as well as the tests that Dr. Johnsen administered."* (Funny, we don't remember her testifying to that!)

Bailey Closes

Bailey's closing was pretty confrontational... and it was obvious that this immensely professional man was also fighting a battle that he believed in personally.

Bailey closed by saying:

"Your Honor may recall that on the morning of Thursday, the 13th day of January, 1994, a day which will live in infamy in the aviation history of the United States — I told you that this was an ugly case and had a foul odor about it.

It was not until yesterday that the odor was able to be defined.

But it will ever be known as a great tragedy that one of the finest contributors to American aviation was the victim of a series of moral and ethical pygmies. How Mr. Hoover could have had such bad luck is almost unfathomable.

But first in the notable absence of these witnesses who did not have the courage to come to this Court and face cross-examination should be the subject of the most devastating inferences a judge can draw. The little fat man, Clint Boehler, who set this whole conspiracy in motion, has not been with us during this trial, but his deeds are uncontradicted. And it is very sad and a stroke of good luck that Mr. Norbert Nester, who one way or another will probably pay for his virtue in this agency riddled as is a rabbit warren with retribution and small people, nonetheless because of the kindness visited upon his son two years ago was willing — he didn't come forward to us, but he was willing once subpoenaed to tell the truth.

Let's take this fellow down. Why is it that the bureaucrats of this world always think since they can't be a celebrity that the next best thing is to assassinate one? Clearly that has recurred in Mr. Hoover's history, and he is the victim of his own personality. He is just too nice a guy to have acted when he should.

Mr. Boehler told Mr. Nester, 'He has got to be accountable like everybody else, and I am going to do something about it'. The next thing we know, he and Mr. Kelln, another of easy virtue, are conspiring to send in separate reports and make them look like they were independently generated. That is a quote from an Inspector of the Federal Aviation Administration which the Administrator is unable to contradict. And so two months and three days after what, if the reports had been genuine, would have been a period of inordinate risk to the public in general, because of a degenerating airman who could no longer fly properly but somehow was doing so, a completely fabricated report was sent to the medical department.

Having no jurisdiction to pass upon the capability of Mr. Hoover to perform as an aerobat, that having been delivered over to responsible citizens like Mr. Loudenslager and Mr. Oliver and Mr. Tucker, these corrupt Inspectors, committing the felony of violating Title 18, United States Code Section 1001, carrying five years and $10,000 fine, just a little more serious than perjury before this Court, filed a report which was false and known to be false.

They recited facts which have been overwhelmingly contradicted by the evidence, and the Administrator knew that these reports were false. Why do I say the Administrator knew? Because if you will look at Barton Pakull's report, he said, 'We are not going to consider whether or not the original complaint was valid: we are only going to look at Dr. Elliott's tests'. And so, belatedly, Mr. Hoover is asked to submit, and being a nice guy, he walks in blind to the physicians selected by the Administrator through Dr. Jordan and Dr. Pakull. And Dr. O'Connor is a decent man, and he examines him and ultimately says he can fly, but he selects Dr. Elliott. And here was the second misfortune which Mr. Hoover could never have anticipated and was not equipped to deal with.

Dr. Elliott, as you have been told, not only lied to this Court about the fact that he used a research version of a test upon which he put great emphasis; he changed his report at the behest of Barton Pakull, who has not appeared before you, who has not the courage to answer questions put by the Respondent, but who has orchestrated this entire fraud from the safety of his seat in the pit of the bureaucracy.

And Dr. Elliott, for nine straight hours, sat on this fellow with his tests and violated the fundamental code of ethics, and incidentally the tortious laws of malpractice of the State of California. The informed consent which was his right to administer these tests is vitiated by his admission that he lied to Mr. Hoover by saying, This will having nothing to do with your ability to pursue your vocation.

Indeed, if you strike Dr. Elliott's tests — and they deserve to be stricken, as you have been told by two ethical and responsible psychologists — this leaves nothing except the parroting effect of Dr. Gaines, a contract hired gun for the FAA, who dependably comes forward with whatever Dr. Pakull seems to be seeking, and Dr. Pincus, who doesn't bother to do his homework but speculates that Dr. Hisey performed inadequately as a neurologist.

And the third and final misfortune is that Mr. Hoover never knew, as he in good faith went through the first battery of tests and was cleared, and then having been told by Dr. Pakull who does not come and appear before Your Honor, 'These are tools; I am the Fuhrer in this regime, and I overrule them all, and I take your certificate'.

Mr. Hoover says, 'The FAA owes me a few; how about another battery of tests'. And they give it to him without telling him it won't make any difference. 'If they clear you, we will overrule them in the same way', because there is no intellectual honesty at this level of medicine in the FAA.

And then we come to court, and we ask ourselves, 'How could the FAA possibly not have looked behind the scurrilous statements by Kelln and Boehler'. They are so suspicious on their face, they fairly demand to be investigated.

Who were the people at the air show that they were quoting when they said Mr. Hoover was frail and unfriendly and so forth? Obviously not Mr. Nester. Obviously not Mr. Oliver or Mr. Loudenslager. No. The statements could have been demonstrated to be false by any honest lawyer or Inspector who was interested in the truth, and we have not had the good fortune of finding such people on the other side of this case.

What was the purpose, Your Honor, once Mr. Nester came forward, shaken as he was, in trying to persuade Mr. Nester, number one, that he was hitching his wagon to a falling star, by telling him fraudulently and falsely, 'All the doctors agree Mr. Hoover is impaired', when, Your Honor, all the lawyers in this case have known since before the trial that the doctors don't agree at all on that subject?

Why is a lay witness being told this by a lawyer who obviously is going to be destroyed or at least her case destroyed if he testifies, a question I haven't heard answered, and if you don't hear it answered in the rebuttal to this argument, you will know that the answer is too unpleasant to articulate.

Now, down to the bottom line. Despite the gross misconduct of the principal players here, we have a greater concern, and that is: Is Mr. Hoover safe to fly? He is a member of a small community, and you have had a good look at the cream of their crop. Who was it that decided the FAA didn't have the competence to pick out the losers in this dangerous game of aerobatics, dangerous because, according to the Johnny Ringo syndrome. Trying to get in with the celebrities by taking inordinate chances has ever been the risk and the disease of this profession. It was the Leo Loudenslagers, the Steve Olivers and the Sean Tuckers of this world, and the Bob Hoovers.

Who was it that continually went to performers and said, 'Look, you are crowding the edge; I know where it is, you need learn where it is; and you are getting too close?' That was Bob Hoover.

We rely in most of the professions in the United States on the self-policing effect of the top professionals who are concerned about their integrity, the integrity of the industry which they serve, and their fellows. We like to be a clean bunch. We don't always succeed, but we like to be.

What is the protection against the day that Mr. Hoover or the 90-year-old CFI-II in Oklahoma City is no longer able to hack it? The protection is not a pencil-pushing doctor with argyle socks who doesn't seem to know that lying to patients is improper and hammers people with tests long beyond the human endurance. That is of no value, and none has been demonstrated.

Indeed, the Government did not seek to call the statement: "These tests cannot be shown to predict aviation skills." And I assume that is because he is hobbled with a tendency toward candor. But in any event, the statements stands unrebutted before the Court. There is no meaningful correlation between performance on these tests and the ability to fly an airplane.

The honest experts told you that the best evidence of capability is past performance, and until there is reason to believe there has been a change, it will ever be.

Because the FAA sat on its back side, first in filing the complaint through the two dishonest Inspectors, and then in acting on the complaint at the highest levels of aviation medicine, Mr. Hoover was able to pack in not 25 but as he testified 33 different performances between the day when he was fraudulently described as having been improperly flying his airplane — and Your Honor viewed Exhibit 6 this morning which I hope persuaded you that his precision on June 20, 19 or 21, 1992, was very comparable to what you saw in the afternoon of January 13.

Those of us who care about Bob Hoover, who is a mark in history — because Chuck Yeager was right. He is not only the greatest pilot that Chuck Yeager has ever known. He is the greatest pilot that any of us have ever known. His skills may go on for years and years. We don't know.

But the one thing that this Court can depend upon, the law can depend upon, and the FAA can depend upon, even though it is beyond the realm of its meager expertise in the area, is that if Bob Hoover ever begins to fall, as he was told repeatedly by his lawyers and his doctors, we will be the first to take action.

I think that Your Honor should be persuaded of several things. First, unlike the rather nasty and unfriendly people that come in to try to destroy this man, the aviation community, at least those who survive long enough to fly for 10, 20, 30 years and appear before you, are nice people.

Watching them put up with the kind of cross examination to which they were subjected, trying their best to be polite and answer questions candidly, is a good index of the fact that these are healthy personalities, responsible human beings, who care about each other and about the industry in which they star.

On the other hand, those who would rip down Mr. Hoover either haven't seen the inside of a cockpit, or having seen it are persuaded that there are too many dials and

buttons to be easily comprehended, if I may quote one of the witnesses from the Georgetown team that seems to be married to the FAA through one or another grant—

'Every time the FAA needs a witness, it simply marches into Georgetown, and with everlasting good fortune, plucks one out who happens to agree with whatever point is needed in the litigation.'

All that aside, every person who is credible, Your Honor — and I suggest to you that Dr. Johnsen and Dr. Hisey, the only people who had no links to the Administrator, tested Mr. Hoover, as I have defended Mr. Hoover. If we find that you ought to be on the ground, it is time to retire, and we will take steps to see that that happens.

On the other hand, if we find that this is nonsense — and we now know that it had a fraudulent beginning and a very unethically managed middle and end.

If we find it to be nonsense, we will stand up for you. Here is a man who can fly an F-16, who has cleared pilot after pilot after pilot to do that, and I didn't hear any evidence that any of the people that he cleared had packed it in because they turned out to be flawed neurologically, and here is a very responsible clinical psychologist who ran the tests and told Your Honor,   There is no problem here.

Dr. Appel, I think, established one thing: that although we would love to have a magic button, just as we would love to have a situation in that witness box where when a witness spoke, a red light would come on if the witness were lying and a green light if the witness were telling the truth; that would make Your Honor's job ever so much easier.

If there were a battery of tests which had any established value in predicting the likelihood of failure of cognitive ability while at the controls of an airplane, particularly while demonstrating emergencies in that airplane, hopefully we will all run to meet it. And people apparently are working hard to do that.

Indeed, I think Dr. Appel said that the work of Dr. Kay, whom the FAA couldn't afford to call as a witness, is responsible and to be commended, but we are not there yet.

In deciding whether or not people like Bob Hoover and his ilk should be continued to allow to perform, to teach, and to serve aviation in the United States, this man for whom speculation was offered to this Court by the most irresponsible of witnesses that he might not be able to handle an emergency, even though he has just done so and is trusted more than any other human being, even after the FAA denominated him as problem ridden, to stay in the air in one of the most dangerous and demanding air shows of the United States, the Reno Air Races, to pull from his memory bank instant(ly) the aid that pilots in distress need to try to save themselves and in some cases their airplanes, should be the overwhelming evidence that shows this Court that the aviation community is not much concerned about the malfunctions or the malfeasance of the Federal Aviation Administration which every pilot of great years has come to know and suspect, but they depend upon themselves.

And despite the fact that Barton Pakull manipulated his way into grounding Mr. Hoover, it was in September 1993 that the aviation community selected this great icon of American aviation and acrobatic performance to be its safety valve and its policy of insurance, to salvage whatever could be salvaged of each emergency that arose. And they arise every single year, as I am sure Your Honor knows, in these races where everything, including the engines, the airplanes and every system within them and the pilots themselves, are pushed to the limits and sometimes beyond.

No greater testimonial, no greater evidentiary, no greater probative value could

ever be offered to a Court than having been alerted, put on notice that there was a claim of disability, at the Reno Air Races the pilot community decided not to change horses, but to stay with what it relied upon.

It is perfectly clear that no one in good conscience can assert to this Court or should be allowed to be believed in asserting to this Court that Robert Anderson Hoover cannot now fly his airplane or is unlikely to be able to do so within two years because of any cognitive defect that has anything at all to do with aviation.

I think that the overwhelming evidence in this case, Your Honor, is that he has been unjustifiably and fraudulently assaulted by two dishonest aviation Inspectors, a sloppy psychologist without whom we wouldn't be here, and a thoroughly dishonest, in my view, chief psychiatrist of the FAA who arrogates to himself an expertise he does not possess.

Whatever people he appoints to examine Mr. Hoover, he dependably overrules and posits himself as some kind of super authority because having decided to ground Mr. Hoover, he will not be deterred from that course by any facts or truths that arise as obstacles.

I must say that this case, an attack upon one of the greatest contributors to America, can only be compared to the assault visited upon figure skater (Nancy Kerrigan) with a crowbar to the kneecap for what it has done to Mr. Hoover or tried to do — hopefully Your Honor will correct it now, although the damage has been extensive.

I suggest that when a lawyer for the FAA rises to respond to my remarks, that he or she do so having in mind that they bear the mantle of shame, shame, shame.

Thank you."

Judge Mullins Rules

After all of that, the court recessed. When it reconvened, the Judge gave his oral initial decision and order. After the requisite description of the trial (who was present, etc) and description of the events that led up to it, Judge Mullins gave his opinions. Mullins discussed Elliott's testing, including the lack of notice given of the importance of the tests (being told that it would in no way impact his medical certificate), the use of the research Version of the Category Test, and the fact that the testing lasted nine hours with no breaks.

He merely commented that the rest of the FAA's doctors agreed with Elliott's findings.

When he discussed the viewing of Hoover's airshow routine, he said "it occurred to me that my flying skills compared to his are about like my golf skills compared to Jack Nicklaus; there is just no comparison."

Mullins commented that no matter what his decision was, he believed the hearing would also be presented to the Full Board, simply because of the notoriety a case like this has. Mullins also thought that Hoover's testimony that the doctor who had been Hoover's AME for 20 or 25 years, had told Hoover to fight the charges because they weren't true. Mullins commented that yes that was hearsay, but the Administrator had done nothing to prove that it wasn't true. He also thought it was important that Loudenslager, Tucker, and Oliver had seen many of Hoover's 33 performances following the Oklahoma airshow, but, according to their testimony, had never seen any degradation in his ability to fly.

Mullins then mentioned the three doctors that Bailey had called as witnesses, and that they felt there was no reason that he could not hold a medical certificate. He felt it was important to note that Appel testified that it took her ten times longer to complete the Research Version of the Category test. Then, he announced that he was going to rule in Hoover's favor, and he would tell the Court why.

He discussed Dr. O'Connor, Dr. Uchiyama, Dr. Davis, Dr. Satz, and Dr. Hisey's opinions – all of which recommended that Hoover continue to fly. He noted that Dr. O'Connor recommended a SPECT scan and a blood count to show any change. When these tests were done six months later, no changes were shown. Mullins then said that these doctors said that it was also important to consider Hoover's ability, training, and skills. He then said that all three of the Administrator's key witnesses refuted this belief, saying that his ability had nothing to do with Hoover's cognitive function. *"And I cannot agree with that,"* Judge Mullins said, *"and I think that taking that position in and of itself almost is discrediting to those doctors."*

He also brought up that Dr. Elliott and Dr. Gaines depend on the Administrator for their livelihood, and that Dr. Pincus worked for Georgetown, which received a grant from the FAA. He also thought it was interesting that Dr. Pincus testified that *"the most important thing in his sort of medical diagnosis was the history. And yet he refused to consider the history that Mr. Hoover has not a single episode of any demonstrated cognitive deficit in any of his day-to-day airshow activities."*

Finally, he reiterated that Dr. Elliott's findings were discredited and...

"For all of these reasons, it will be my order that the Administrator's emergency order of revocation will be overruled."

Bob won, Bailey won, Yodice won... We all won... until the FAA stepped in, and fired the parting shot. And then, ***nobody*** won.

Chapter 26

Who Needs the NTSB?
The FAA Has the Last Word

Speak when you're angry, and you'll make the best speech you'll ever regret.
Lawrence J. Peter

Just twelve short days after Judge Mullins ruled that the FAA had not proven that Hoover had a cognitive deficit that would inhibit his ability to fly safely, thereby overturning its emergency revocation, the FAA filed its rather argumentative appeal brief.

The beginning of the appeal was merely a statement of their side of this saga — beginning with his examination by Dr. A. Puskas in February 1992, who withheld Hoover's certificate *"pending further investigation"*, continuing with the statement that *"You have cognitive deficit as demonstrated on neuropsychological testing"* and that the Federal Air Surgeon therefore finds that *"you are unable to safely perform the duties or exercise the privileges of your airman certificate; or that you may be reasonably be expected to be unable to do so within two years"* because of said condition.

It went on to recap the process — that Hoover filed an appeal and a hearing on the matter was held January 13 through 16, 1994... wherein Mullins, much to their chagrin, reversed the Administrator's emergency order of revocation. These, of course, were "facts" we'd all heard before; kind of a mashed-up, Swiss cheese version of the actual events.

In the attached Statement of the Case, the FAA began its tale by stating that Hoover had flown in the Aerospace America airshow in June 1992. His performance was seen, the appeal said, by Aviation Safety Inspectors James Kelln and Clint Boehler who waited two months, even this appeal was forced to admit, *before* submitting statements that questioned Hoover's performance and physical and mental condition.

In August 1992, Dr. Audie Davis, Manager, AeroMedical Certification Division, requested that Hoover submit results of current neurological, psychological, and psychiatric evaluations. Davis, the appeal said, indicated a reasonable basis to question whether Hoover met FAA medical standards.

Subsequently, Hoover went to Dr. Garrett O'Connor, a psychiatrist. Again, the FAA was forced to admit that Hoover's psychiatric examination was within normal limits — except, the appeal eagerly noted, for Hoover's short term memory deficits and *"inability to accurately complete backward digit span tasks."*

Dr. Elliott

On the basis of these shortcomings, Hoover was then referred to the infamous Dr. Robert Elliott — who was to become the FAA's leading witness. Elliott was to determine the presence of any cognitive or neuropsychological abnormalities. Elliott was just the kind of witness the FAA loved: His curriculum vitae was longer than Route 66, and according to this appeal, he was *"frequently asked by airlines to evaluate personnel, primarily pilots, for neuropsychological or neurological fitness for duty."*

In order to make Elliott sound objective, the appeal noted that he had never before testified on behalf of the FAA — but had testified against the FAA during formal hearings on the "Age 60" rule. Contradicting Hoover's testimony during the hearing, the appeal said that Elliott had advised Hoover of the length of his examination prior to Hoover's visit and that he had offered Hoover numerous breaks... and, Elliott said, had offered to continue the testing on another day if Hoover so wished.

The FAA appeal admitted that Elliott had told Hoover that this testing would not affect his medical certificate. But, it continued, this statement was true at the time – because *"he had not been asked for an opinion regarding Respondent's qualification for a second-class medical certificate."* The appeal went on and on about Elliott, basically giving a *Reader's Digest* version of the entire testimony... with a few well-chosen tidbits tossed in for good measure.

"Elliott testified that there has been much research in relating tasks that implicate a pilot's cognitive function to standard neuropsychological tests." Elliott had identified an article by John Flanagan that this article served as a *"take off platform"* for other researchers who have studied the link between aviation psychology and piloting skills. A footnote within the appeal almost snidely noted that Mullins did not note this article — "or other relevant documents"— as evidence. *"Apparently,"* the FAA appeal said, *"the ALJ accepted Respondent's counsel's warning that articles relevant to the issue at hand would simply clutter the record."*

The dissertation about Elliott continued, again explaining the norms he used to categorize Hoover, as well as the tests that he had used... but the appeal did not even mention the fact that Elliott had forced a Research Version of the Category test (on computer) upon Hoover. Instead, the appeal only mentioned that Hoover scored in the *"significantly impaired range"* on this test, with *"slow and laborious"* performance. In fact, another footnote said that *"Elliott believes that the computer version is a more accurate measure of performance because it provides more precise information and allows less interference from the examiner."*

The appeal continued, with a description of how Hoover performed on each of the tests Elliott gave to him... never again mentioning Hoover's testimony that the testing went on twice as long as he was led to believe it would take... with but just one bathroom break and no time for lunch. What Elliott appeared to be testing, some might believe, was Hoover's blood sugar levels... and not his cognitive abilities. But, of course, this was the Swiss cheese version of the Hoover tale to this point.

No need for details such as this.

Yeah, right...

Another snide footnote mentioned that Elliott also administered the CogScreen test, a battery of neuropsychological tests specifically designed to measure a pilot

cognitive functioning. It again noted that Mullins did not allow this evidence of a test *owned* by one of the FAA's own senior people (who were obviously anxious to see this test gain validity and acceptance... and what better way than a *very* high profile case such as this?). In summation, the appeal said that Hoover's performance was *"strongly suggestive of cognitive deficits"* (still strongly contradicting the FAA's own early reports), and Elliott therefore recommended that Respondent consult a neurologist to rule out neuropathy or a degenerative disease. Following Dr. Elliott's recommendation, the appeal reiterated, Dr. Michael Gold examined Hoover. It was now November 1992, and his neurological examination, EEG, and MRI studies, all showed normal results (much, we are sure, to the FAA's chagrin). Dr. Alberto Salcedo took over at this point, and conducted brain SPECT scans, which were *"borderline suggestive of biparietal areas of hypoperfusion/ hypometabolism."*

At this point, Dr. Garrett O'Connor came back into the picture and, on the basis of the above test results, *recommended* that Hoover be given his second-class medical. O'Connor, did, however, also recommend that Hoover repeat the SPECT scans in six months to a year to see if any changes had taken place. According to the appeal, Dr. Elliott felt that this type of recommendation was not consistent with an unrestricted medical certificate.

On April 14, 1993, a conference telephone call was held between Dr. Jon Jordan, the Federal Air Surgeon; Dr. William Hark, Deputy Federal Air Surgeon; Dr. Barton Pakull, FAA Chief Psychiatrist; Hoover; and Dr. Albert Puskas, Hoover's original Aviation Medical Examiner. During this conversation, the appeal said, Jordan advised Hoover that on the basis of psychometric testing, he was not qualified to hold any medical certificate. Hoover disagreed, and Jordan said he would allow the submission of additional information. Subsequently, Dr. Craig Uchiyama, of the UCLA Neuropsychiatric Institute and Hospital for neuropsychological assessment, examined Hoover. Even before this, Hoover had undergone another SPECT brain scan, which, the FAA contended, revealed multiple strokes or degenerative changes in those areas.

During the hearing, the appeal said, Dr. Elliott discussed Dr. Uchiyama's testing of Hoover. Any improvement shown in these tests — and the Wisconsin Card Sort Test, for example, showed significant improvement — was simply dismissed by Hoover as *"practice effect."*

Dr. Uchiyama did question Hoover's ability to deal with emergency situations, but nevertheless recommended a three-to six-month temporary extension of his medical certificate, while Hoover's current medical and neuropsychological status remained closely monitored. After Uchiyama, Hoover went to Dr. David Johnsen. Elliott quickly dismissed any opinions given by Johnsen, saying that Johnsen was not affiliated with any neuropsychological associations, and he only administered four tests — three of which Hoover had already taken — so any improvement, he contended, would only be due to practice effect. Elliott compared Hoover's performance to a table prepared by Dr. Gary Kay, and he said that this comparison was evidence that Hoover was significantly impaired... and therefore should not hold a second-class medical.

Dr. Richard Gaines

Counsel for the FAA *loved* Dr. Gaines. Gaines seemed so impressive that one

imagines that they would have let him date their daughter... He was sufficiently board certified, had done aviation and psychology-related research, and he held a pilot certificate with glider and instrument ratings. Additionally, he had evaluated between 11,000 and 12,000 pilots over 20 years, and conducted neuropsychological testing on pilots for many airlines. More importantly, he had been a consultant to the FAA for 10 to 12 years... i.e., he was on "the team"... you know what I mean? (Of course, the FAA appeal didn't put it quite that way...)

Gaines testified that there are several published task analyses of piloting skills, and these functions, which included perceptual motor abilities, attention, processing flexibility, and several others. These functions, Gaines said, were tested in Hoover through his neuropsychological evaluations. He also agreed that any improvement in subsequent testing would only be due to practice effect. Basically, it seemed that he said whatever the FAA wanted him to say.... which included saying that Hoover was not medically qualified for a medical certificate. Big surprise, that.

Dr. Pincus

Dr. Pincus, a professor and Chairman of the Department of Neurology at Georgetown University, also testified for the FAA. But guess what! He's on the team, too... Georgetown, even the appeal had to admit, has a grant from the FAA for the development of the CogScreen testing program (under Dr. Gary Kay). Remember that line about not biting the hand that feeds you?

His curriculum vitae, detailed as the others were in the appeal, was equally impressive. Dr. Pincus took Dr. Elliott's and Dr. O'Connor's neurological examinations, in conjunction with Hoover's MRI and brain SPECT scans, into account when he concurred that *"He was convinced of the presence of cognitive dysfunction,"* and that Hoover was unable to safely pilot an aircraft.

The FAA's Version of Hoover's Case

The FAA appeal said that Hoover testified in detail about his early background in aviation, as well as his days as a military and civilian test pilot. Hoover testified that he did not believe his piloting skills had diminished, and that he had even helped save eight pilots during the 1993 Reno Air Races (*after* the so-called "bad" performance at Aerospace America... remarkable "recovery", that).

The FAA appeal discussed Hoover's testimony about his accidents that had occurred in his career and how he had lost consciousness on some occasions. Hoover, the appeal said, also testified that he had performed his airshow maneuvers thousands of times and had encountered and handled in-flight emergencies and problems on many occasions. He also explained that he frequently had problems with his aircraft's hydraulic system.

On the second day of the airshow in question, this hydraulic pump cavitation problem surfaced (as it had done before), and he took extra time to complete his maneuvers because of it. Hoover *"denied the FAA Inspectors' allegations, adding that at no time did anyone with the FAA approach him to discuss any problems."*

When confronted about his ability to handle an emergency, Hoover testified regarding an emergency he had encountered just one week before this hearing when flying

n a T-28 with Ray Hughes. During flight, a chip warning light came on, indicating imminent engine failure. Hoover successfully landed the aircraft, which suffered a catastrophic engine seizure on roll out, resulting in devastating damage.

Another snide footnote admitted that Ray Hughes' testimony (which was taken by way of a deposition in California) generally corroborated Hoover's story about the incident, but the Administrator was not given adequate notice of the deposition. Ultimately, the deposition was not offered.

When discussing his neurological examinations, Hoover testified that he had nothing to do with the selection of Drs. O'Connor, Gold, Salcedo, or Elliott. He testified that O'Connor told him he was "clean" and only recommended further testing so that no one would ever question his ability. Elliott, Hoover testified, told him that his testing would take no more than four hours, and that it would not affect his medical certificate. The testing lasted all day, Hoover said, and he was not able to get a drink or go to the bathroom until 5:00 p.m., when the testing finally ended.

During the hearing, Hoover recounted the conference call between himself, Dr. Puskas, Dr. Jordan, Dr. Hark, and Dr. Pakull. According to the appeal, Pakull told him he was not fit to fly, whereas Dr. Davis had given him a clean bill of health, and advised him to accept contracts for the 1993 season.

Hoover also testified that Dr. Pakull said the other doctors were just his "tools" — at which point Hoover asked to see other doctors. Jordan agreed, and Hoover consulted Dr. Satz, who also gave Hoover a clean bill of health. The appeal continued with their version of Hoover's testimony, discussing Hoover's explanation of the ACE program. Basically, he explained that the airshow performers generally police themselves, and an ACE has the ability to ground a pilot. He also affirmed that if he ever felt his piloting skills had become impaired, he would stop flying.

Hoover met Dr. Hisey at the 1993 Reno Air Races, and Hisey agreed to examine Hoover. He subsequently referred Hoover to Dr. Johnsen, who did additional neuropsychological tests. Hoover also testified that his airshow performance does not change unless conditions dictate, and that he feels more comfortable in his Shrike than he does in some automobiles. During the airshow for the hearing, Leo Loudenslager, a world famous airshow and champion aerobatic pilot, operated the radios and he operated the controls. He agreed that quick reaction time can be critical to properly handle an emergency. Finally, the appeal said, Hoover explained his FAA write-ups, and asserted that one of the incidents was motivated by FAA counsel's desire to prosecute a celebrity.

The appeal then set to discredit Dr. Johnsen — first by saying that he is not a neuropsychologist, not board certified, and not a member of any neuropsychological associations. The FAA also did not like Johnsen's opinion that the best predictor of behavior was past behavior.

After this, it was time to discredit Dr. Hisey, who had interpreted Hoover's physical and neurological testing as normal. In particular, they did not like Hisey's testimony that he relied on Johnsen's neuropsychological evaluation (earlier discredited, of course) when he came to his conclusions.

It was then time to bring up the touchy subject of Norbert Nester, the FAA Aviation Safety Inspector who was subpoenaed to testify on behalf of Hoover. First, Nester testified that he was on duty during the airshow in question, and never saw anything unusual about Hoover's performances.

On the other hand, Boehler, another Inspector, had claimed Hoover' performance was substandard and it was time *"he stand accountable like everyone else.* A few days later, Nester testified, he heard Boehler and Kelln, yet another Inspector talking about writing reports on Hoover... and they were to make sure that they looke different so it would seem as if they had been written independently. The appeal mentione that Nester testified that he expected retaliation for his testimony, and that his life wa already becoming difficult there. The FAA had recently, in an unrelated manner suspended him for five days for *"accepting favors."* He also testified that he had no contacted anyone within the FAA regarding his allegations against Boehler and Kelln.

World Aerobatic Champion Leo Loudenslager was the next subject within th appeal. It mentioned, in a very direct manner, that Loudenslager had never undergon neuropsychological testing. It also said that he had known Hoover for 20 years and ha watched his performance at the airshow in question.

Loudenslager also testified that an ACE is the most qualified to judge an airsho performance, and, as an ACE, had never seen a deficit in Hoover's flying — includin, during the performance flown for Judge Mullins (where Hoover easily dealt with a *unexpected* cowl flap problem). Loudenslager also testified that he would not hesitate t ground Hoover if he felt his age was affecting his performance. Here, the FAA was quick t note that Loudenslager had no medical training and therefore could not offer an opinio as to Hoover's neurological testing.

Sean Tucker, also a top airshow performer and an ACE, testified for Hoover a well. He testified that he had known Hoover personally for over a decade, and had neve noticed any deterioration in his flying. He did not agree with the FAA Inspectors statements concerning Hoover's performance at the airshow in question. He too testifie that he would not hesitate to ground Hoover if he felt he was unfit to fly.

To knock his testimony, the FAA appeal noted that Tucker did not have a degre in physiology and that he had agreed that timing, effective decision-making, and an ability to divide attention are critical to an airshow performer. The appeal also said that Tucker *"when shown Dr. Uchiyama's conclusion that Respondent was impaired in divide attention and tasks that require speeded information delivery, expressed concern for th safety..."* (Funny, I don't remember Tucker's testimony quite that way...)

Yet another top airshow performer and ACE, Steven Oliver, was next. He had als known Hoover since the mid-1980's, and had observed him many times. He had never see any sort of deterioration, and he hadn't noticed anything out of the ordinary with regard to Hoover at the airshow in question. He too would approach Hoover if he were concerne about his safety.

Dr. Simon, whose testimony was offered by way of videotaped deposition, is specialist in nuclear medicine who reviewed, in addition to other documents, the SPEC scans and reports generated by Dr. Salcedo and Dr. Mena (he, however, never examine Hoover). He testified that many processes, such as strokes, can be visualized through thes scans. He also testified that Hoover's scans did not show areas of decreased activity tha would suggest degeneration, stroke, or dementia; rather, he said, any abnormalities see were consistent with trauma. Simon's testimony never was placed into evidence, primaril because the FAA allegedly received late notice of the deposition. The FAA also alleged tha Simon used several exhibits that had not been provided to them.

Dr. Antoinette Appel, a neuropsychologist, testified on behalf of Hoover. Sh

asserted that there was no correlation between neuropsychological test data and SPECT scan data. She also testified that the computer version of the Wisconsin Card Sort test had been released only as a research version, and went on to say (much to the FAA's disapproval, I am sure) that said version is worthless for diagnostic purposes and that it even took her 10 times longer to complete the test.

She further testified that a number of studies demonstrate a marked drop-off in testing performance after 90 minutes — referencing Elliott's testing environment. She said this drop-off also occurs if the patient does not eat or if there is tension between examiner and patient. She also felt that practice effect did not account for Hoover's improvement in subsequent testings.

When asked about the predictive value of neuropsychological testing, Appel quoted an article by Dr. Kay, which said, in essence, that there had been no studies regarding the relationship between testing performance and actual aviator performance. Here, the appeal noted that Appel was unaware that this article was written in 1990 (and that additional research had been done. In the hearing, if you recall, it came out that Kay had written subsequent research that perhaps did not agree with the above statement. Appel, on behalf of Hoover, had requested all research done on the subject, but she had been told that none was available to her... it was all in the FAA's possession. The appeal, as you may guess, did not mention *any* of this.).

Appel further testified that the best test for determining cognitive function is performance, and she explained that she had not left Hoover's side during the previous 72 hours, and had not seen a single piece of aberrant behavior (the appeal did not finish her quote, which went on to explain how stressful and trying those 72 hours must have been). Appel was firm in her belief that Hoover was medically qualified to fly and would be so for the next two years.

Dr. Harvey Zeissman testified in rebuttal on behalf of the FAA. Dr. Ziessman has a curriculum vitae that the FAA loved for their physicians: He was the Director of Nuclear Medicine and professor of radiology at Georgetown University (the FAA does love Georgetown)... and, thank heavens, he was board certified.

He routinely interprets SPECT scans, and was authoring a book on brain perfusion imaging. After finally cutting to the chase, Ziessman testified that he believed (and had contacted Dr. DeVous and was in agreement with him) that Hoover's scans (done by Dr. Mena) showed abnormalities of hyperfusion – reduced blood flow – of both parietal and temporal lobes and that they therefore did not reflect a normal aging process.

The appeal then summarized Judge Mullins' decision to return Hoover to flying status. The appeal said that his decision *"seemed to rest primarily on his belief that Respondent's continued ability to not only operate an aircraft but to operate an aircraft in realms that even the best pilots couldn't do."*

The appeal then listed its issues as the following (for your reading pleasure, these were translated into English from the Legalese utilized in the appeal):

1. They believed that the preponderance of the evidence supported the FAA position.
2. They believed Judge Mullins erred in making credibility decisions regarding the expert witness testimony.
3. They believed that Judge Mullins erred in excluding relevant evidence.
4. They believed that Judge Mullins erred in giving weights to videotapes of previous flight

demonstrations.

The appeal also asserted that *"the only real question for debate should have been limited to whether the documented cognitive impairment is inconsistent with the medical qualifications necessary to hold an unrestricted second-class medical certificate."*

Again, the appeal noted the supposed poor performance by Hoover on the various neuropsychological tests and said that *"it is even more disturbing when it is evaluated using normative data that is appropriately used to evaluate the complex tasks associated with operating an aircraft."*... and, again, went on to explain the norms used to evaluate Hoover — you know, good ol' Heaton and Halstead-Reitan. After discussing this, the appeal asserted that Judge Mullins relied on Dr. O'Connor's report, and that he read the report *"far too broadly"* and that he *"obviously misinterpreted"* Dr. O'Connor's report (well, you know, I guess you just can't do anything well without those all-important board certifications...). The appeal again reiterated the FAA's belief that Hoover's improvement when tested by Dr. Uchiyama, was solely attributable to practice effect... and that Hoover still didn't do too well on those tests. The appeal also noted that *"at best, Dr. Uchiyama's report might be construed as a recommendation for a restricted medical certificate."*

Again it was time to knock Dr. Johnsen and his lack of board certification, again note that Hoover performed badly... and again to note that Hoover's substantial improvement on the Wisconsin Card Sort Test was only attributable to practice effect.

It was then time to bring up Hoover's SPECT scans — again. The FAA was firm in their assertion that his SPECT scans showed bilateral temporal hypoperfusion, right dorsofrontal hypoperfusion, and left dorsoparietal hypoperfusion... which was consistent, they said, with his MRI (which supposedly showed *"atrophy to brain"*) and that was not consistent with normal aging and *"highly predictive of Alzheimer's Disease."*

FAA's Dr. Pincus said that these findings, on the other hand, were not consistent with the traumas – including at least one incident where he lost consciousness – that Hoover had described. All of the FAA medical witnesses agreed – of course – that his various tests showed evidence of a cognitive deficit.

On the contrary, the appeal asserted, the evidence presented by Hoover's legal team to rebut this case was *"scant and focuses primarily on evidence documenting Respondent's career and contributions to aviation,"* continuing that Hoover's medical evidence was in no way conclusive. The appeal even went so far as to say that Dr. Appel merely *"manipulated"* research for her purposes.

The appeal noted that Judge Mullins *"implies that Dr. Elliott's, Dr. Gaines,' and Dr. Pincus' testimony was not credible because the doctors had financial interests with the FAA"* (Gosh, I wonder why he would have thought that...). The appeal quickly continued that *"not only did the ALJ grossly misinterpret the record regarding the Administrator's expert witnesses' testimony, but he misapplied Board precedent regarding expert witness testimony"*–also saying that Mullins did not give any fair consideration to those witnesses' testimony based on *"the logic, depth, and persuasiveness of their testimony"* because of their dependence on the FAA for their livelihood.

(Gosh, I feel as "silly" as Mullins... I just can't imagine how depending on an entity for one's livelihood, to a strong extent, could not slant one's opinions toward that entity! I thought impartiality was important!)

Regardless, the appeal was adamant that Mullins was mistaken in his judgment

the credibility of these witnesses. Next, the appeal set about to defend Dr. Elliott, who ad, at least in my opinion, been badly battered in the hearing, most notably because he tilized a research version of the Wisconsin Card Sort Test and he kept Hoover in testing nger than he said he would — and without reasonable breaks, no less. The appeal argued 1at the Wisconsin Card Sort test — even as a research version — remains a valid measure f the use of logic and reasoning and other cognitive functions. In regards to the length of sting and resultant stress for Hoover (which, it had been argued, would negatively affect st results), the appeal asserted that Hoover was *"quite relaxed"* and had been told how ng testing would take. He also said that he did offer Hoover breaks. Moreover, the appeal aid, Hoover did poorly on both the tests administered at the beginning as those dministered in the end of testing.

As far as Hoover's testimony that Elliott had told him that his tests would not fect his medical certificate, the appeal only said that Elliott was only testing him to test r cognitive impairment — not his fitness as a pilot because he had not been asked for ach an opinion. It also said that Hoover *"was well aware that Dr. Elliott could discuss the esults of his test with the FAA."*

Regarding Mullins' obvious incredulousness during the hearing that the FAA octors seemingly refused to accept Hoover's exemplary airshow performances — even uring the hearing — was representative of his cognitive functioning. The appeal, owever, said that these witnesses *"did not testify that piloting performance should be xcluded as a factor in evaluating Respondent's neuropsychological condition"* (again, 1at's not how I remember it!). The appeal's argument was that Hoover's cognitive npairment merely had not yet been manifested in his flying performance because *omebody who has practiced a complex skill over a long period of time is likely to aintain that skill, sometimes even with cognitive impairments becoming evident"* (quote from Elliott). The appeal summed up by simply saying that Mullins erred in his adgment of the credibility the FAA medical witnesses, and then it was time to jump on Iullins for excluding what they considered (of course) relevant evidence.

The CogScreen test, which Hoover's counsel had objected to at the hearing ecause it was an experimental test — and Mullins had sustained, was discussed first. The ppeal argued that Mullins should have permitted the FAA's expert witnesses to establish 1e validity and relevancy of the test. This test was important to their case because Hoover erformed poorly on it and this performance was consistent with his other europsychological test results.

The appeal said that Mullins also erred in his exclusion of other technical ocuments on which the FAA medical witnesses relied upon for their opinions. And of ourse, those weren't his only errors, according to the FAA. They said — in the interest of airness — that he erred in excluding rebuttal testimony to Hoover's deposition of Dr. imon. This would have included testimony by Dr. DeVous, who was prepared to testify 1at Hoover's SPECT scans were indicative of Alzheimer's. (If you recall, Bailey had bjected to any such testimony because of shortness of notice, and Mullins had sustained.)

Of course, the appeal had to complain about Hoover's flight demonstration as art of the proceedings, saying that Part 67 of the FAR's does not provide for an evaluation f piloting skills to determine medical qualification except at the discretion of the Federal ir Surgeon (you know, the guy who wouldn't have done any such thing to help Hoover)… nd it said that this flight performance had *"no probative value to resolution of the issue*

of Respondent's qualification for an unrestricted medical certificate."

Mullins, it said, took a great risk contrary to the interests of aviation safety I letting Hoover fly.

Oh please...

The appeal also brought up the FAA Counsel's assertion that Mullin observations at the flight demonstration were *"highly prejudicial,"* (If you recall, Jimm Driskell explained Hoover's maneuvers to Mullins as they were being performed. Mullir was firm during the hearing and said that nothing underhanded had occurred — and th only conversation was Driskell explaining to him what Hoover was doing. Nothing more The appeal said FAA counsel was *"not privy to many of the communications,"* althoug Mullins said during the hearing that they certainly could have listened to Driskell explanations, but had not approached them.

Additionally, the appeal alleged that by allowing the demonstration to be filme by the local media, the demonstration took on a circus-like atmosphere. Basically, th appeal made it clear that the FAA did not like this flight demonstration — or th admittance of videotapes of Hoover's prior performances and performances at the airsho in question (saying those were not authenticated and had *"no probative value"* either). only because seeing them made it obvious that Hoover had no cognitive problems.

In the appeal's conclusion, it said that Mullins committed errors in restrictir the FAA's usable evidence and that he *"failed to fully consider the overwhelming weigh of the evidence that was before him"* — and made *"inappropriate credibilir determinations..."* which basically portrayed Mullins as an unwise, possibly errant judici figure... rather than what he truly is: Perhaps the best Administrative Law Judge ever t work the Circuit (according to many of those who practice before him... win or lose).

Chapter 27

Australia Beckons... Renewal and Validation Down Under

Obstacles don't have to stop you. If you run into a wall, don't turn around and give up. Figure out how to climb it, go through it, or work around it.
Michael Jordan

While a number of people are said to have come up with the idea, it appears that FAA Inspector Norbert Nester was the first to suggest that if Bob couldn't fly airshows in the United States of America, his home, then maybe he should consider flying airshows in some other country, if allowed. As the true import of the medical fight wore on, Bob's desire to fly increased dramatically. However, through the good graces of some uncommonly open-minded bureaucrats in Australia, as well as some budding airshow organizers with a good idea, Bob got to resume his career (though on a somewhat subdued scale) in, of all places, Valleyfield, Tasmania!

The organizers of Australia's SkyRace '94 had contacted Hoover some time before his medical fight hit the fan. As the combination airshow/air race grew closer, the desire to have Hoover fly the show and participate in the race (like he did at Reno Air Races), grew ever greater. So great, in fact, that they set about to see if the rules might not be "bent" a bit to get Hoover back in the air. Notified that Bob's medical certificate was very much in contention, the race organizers contacted their Director of Aviation Medicine and set in force a chain of events that restored Bob to flight status... even though it was on the wrong side of the globe from his own corner of the world.

Under normal circumstances, the fact that Bob's medical certificate was in dispute back here in the States would mean that most other nations would probably have never given Bob the chance to fly. But the (then) head of Australian aviation medicine (and a highly accomplished airline transport rated pilot/medical doctor) by the name of Dr. Robert Liddell had other ideas. It was his contention that if Bob could pass Australian aviation medical standards, earn an Australian pilots license, and demonstrate Aerobatic competency according to the same standards every Australian airshow pilot flies by, then there was no reason that Hoover would not be allowed to display his skills *"down under."*

Therefore, Dr. Liddell started a series of events that was certain to cause him no end of consternation. Liddell is an amazing character all to himself. A graduate of the University of Western Australia from Perth, Liddell studied medicine there. Thereafter, he

worked with the Royal Flying Doctor Service in Western Australia and also earned a commercial pilot's license during that time. He went on to become the Medical Director bu left to pursue an alternate career as a pilot as well as a physician. Taking a job with Dan Air, an airline in the United Kingdom, he not only served as their Medical Director bu flew 727's for them for a little over six years! Liddell seemed to have a good time of it. *"Oh yeah, it was a good job because I would fly two to three days a week and do medicin two to three days a week. Probably the best job I ever had."*

Liddell left Dan-Air at the end of 1988 and took a job as the equivalent of the US Federal Air Surgeon in Australia (called Director of Aviation Medicine). He held that po sition until he resigned in November of 1996 due to his concerns about his superior' (Leroy Keith) priorities for aviation safety. Liddell remembers that the airshow organiz ers for the 1994 Country Club Casino SkyRace-Tasmania event *"rang me in my office an said 'we are putting this air race together; however, we've got a bit of a problem. We'v advertised where this ace aerobatic pilot is coming out as an attraction for the air rac but he has lost his FAA medical certification. If he hasn't got a medical certificate, h can't fly. Is there anything we can do about it?'"*

Liddell was intrigued... *"So I spoke a little more about the problem. The story was getting was there were a great number of people who felt there was no reason wh Bob shouldn't be flying, and the medical certification thing was possibly a personalit clash between people in the FAA and himself. So I asked him to jump through (some hoops to prove he was capable of flying (but not the extra tests the FAA requested, lik psychometric testing, as there was no scientific validation as to how to interpret th results in a pilot). So I contacted Larry Marinelli, who is an examiner for the Australia Civil Aviation Authority in Los Angeles. I said, 'Would you be prepared to do an examina tion for us on Bob Hoover to see if he makes out.'*

We certainly were not going to ask him to do psychological testing because w did not ask anyone else to do it. It would be discriminating to suddenly pick on on person out of the blue. Especially when there were no apparent, demonstrable, defects i his flying. And what we would attempt to do in Australia is that if we had concerns abou a person's cognitive function, we would give him a flying test because that is what the are being asked to do. I then rang Bob (whom) I had never met or spoken to previousl and I didn't really know much about him really. I introduced myself and I said we hav a medical examiner in L.A., Dr. Marinelli, and he said, 'I know him, I will go there.'

I said, 'Would you like to give him a ring and go have a medical and see if yo measure up to our standards?' So he did, and he did measure up, and Larry Marinell advised me of that. And so he said, 'Okay, on the strength of that we will give you th medical certificate but it will be an Australian medical certificate so it can only validate an Australian license.' He then realized he would have to get an Australian commercia license to do the display. Knowing that would be the case, I felt any concerns which existed about his competence and ability would be covered by the fact that he woul have to fly and pass a flight test with an examiner. Being in a strange country with slightly different air rules, if he could demonstrate he could pass a commercial license test, learn the rules, pass the test, and then pass the flight test, I wasn't likely to be having too many concerns about his cognitive function. Larry had indicated that his physical condition was okay.

So basically he was certified. He came out, did the tests and passed. I was aware

the FAA had some information which Bob had copies of, some of it possibly; however, not all of it. But he had copies. I would suspect the great majority of his reports were not very complimentary. There were some areas I suppose that were at the most concern to the FAA — were a SPECT scan, which showed the significant serial atrophy. However, I spoke to a neurosurgeon colleague of mine, who is an AeroMedical specialist in the United Kingdom, about this and he felt the test was not definitive in any way and did not relate to a person's performance. He felt performance was the final evidence, as I did, of someone's abilities. The other thing was the quality of that investigation (the FAA's) turned out to be so poor, and that some distance down the track another radiologist looked at it and said he was embarrassed to think anybody ever bothered to report on it."

Hoover remarked that Liddell had been very *"very thorough"* in their initial consultations, but Liddell remained very open, affable and never appeared evasive. Hoover said that *"after that first conversation, I began to feel very good about him... he seemed like he was very honest... and as an experienced pilot, he was a man I could relate to."*

Dr. Larry Marinelli was the Southern California based Aviation Medical Examiner who also had authorization to conduct medical examinations on behalf of the nation of Australia. He became an indispensable party in the effort to get Hoover back to flying. Marinelli was pretty positive about the effort he undertook, and so was another AME who was qualified to work with the Australian Medical requirements, Dr. Gary Ferris... *"It didn't take long to see that this was a man in command of his faculties... and that if this pilot had any serious problems, I simply wasn't aware of it. I just never saw any real evidence to suggest what all the fuss was about. It seemed that he'd gotten a bad break and once I determined that, it was a pleasure to even the score in his favor."*

Hoover had a medical certificate in Australia, but now he had to get an Australian Pilot's license and qualify to fly shows under their rules. Still, Hoover was pumped up and looking forward to getting back in the saddle and was to be accompanied by his wife, Colleen, on this excursion down under. The process of re-certifying Bob Hoover, Australian-Style, went well. In a follow-up report to US Federal Air Surgeon Jon Jordan, Dr. Liddell reported that, *"On arrival in Australia, Mr. Hoover passed the Australian Air Law examination for a commercial license; he then undertook the flight test with a flying operations Inspector which he passed at the commercial pilot license level. As result of these procedures Mr. Hoover was granted Australian Commercial Pilot's License."*

The Australian operations Inspector who oversaw Hoover through the flying tests and the airshow examination was a very well-known and highly-experienced pilot by the name of Barry J. Diamond. Diamond held both Australian and US Airline Transport Pilot licenses and also held Australian certification for agricultural work, low-level Aerobatics, a commercial helicopter pilots license, and type ratings in the Cessna Citation business jet and other turbine aircraft. Prior to joining the Australian Civil Aviation Authority, Mr. Diamond had done some 20 years as a Naval Aviator in the Royal Australian Navy and logged over 500 carrier landings on HMAS Melbourne in a McDonnell Douglas A-4 SkyHawk. Diamond's experience included quite a bit of experience as an airshow pilot flying the A-4 (an aircraft that the US Navy Blue Angels used for many years, with good effect). Diamond also served as a flight instructor in an exchange program with the Royal Australian Air Force and was a team member in a low-level military aerobatic formation flying act using the Macchi jet trainer.

Hoover arrived in Australia and tackled the licensing requirements head-on. Aus-

tralian aviation writer and historian Terry Gwynn-Jones got the opportunity to sit in on Hoover's pre-test briefing for his commercial pilot's license... a test for which he had only two days to study. Gwynn-Jones wrote a thoroughly enjoyable summary of the preparation and noted that Hoover had said *"I have a conference table covered with books and a great bunch of young pilots from the Tasmania Aero Club who helped me... and taught me how to cross reference."* Hoover passed the Commercial Pilot's License law exam written test with a grade of 84 percent.

One had to feel a bit of sympathy and amusement with Mr. Diamond's predicament... that he was put in the position to evaluate a man with 52 years of aviation experience and 32,000 hours of flight time – although the very first evaluation had nothing to do with his immense skills and aerobatic excellence. This test would concentrate on the kind of basic airmanship every brand-new commercial pilot had to demonstrate as they started their flying careers. But Barry Diamond did it with good humor, asking him questions about heading control, basic airmanship, and the kinds of things that a 150-hour pilot would often struggle to answer... though noting at one point to Mr. Hoover, *"Heck, I feel embarrassed having to say this to you."*

Eventually a flight test was conducted after a very thorough pre-flight and Barry Diamond's reports on Hoover's competency were very positive. More important, after that point Hoover became Australia's newest commercial pilot. Hoover seemed quite satisfied with his accomplishments, and with the way that he was treated. *"It went just fine... Barry's a real professional and was probably a little more stricter than they are back home, which I think was very appropriate."*

Barry was equally complementary, according to the Gwynn-Jones report... *"Bob made the test easy for me by the professional manner in which he approached the whole thing. We covered every item and on the visual nav... with no aids... he just picked up the map and was identifying points in the country he has never seen before."*

Then, the fun started. Mr. Diamond found himself in the unique position of then having to judge Hoover's aerobatic competency in an aerobatic routine that no one else in the world, Mr. Diamond included, was remotely capable of matching. When Gwynn-Jones asked Diamond what it was like to be upside-down at 150 feet in a light twin, with no engines operating and someone else at the controls, he replied, *"Honestly, at no stage did I feel uncomfortable. I watched him fly to the lowest limits (altitude) of his performance. There was no fumbling or faltering although I must admit that after the deadstick eight-point roll on the downwind leg I was a bit concerned that we might not make it back to the field... I should have known better... we crossed the fence at Ag-plane height and he said to me 'I want to finish up by the big Marquee'. And that's right where we stopped... We set our own standards here (Australia). They are equal to any in the world. Bob Hoover easily exceeded those standards. It was a privilege to see him in action."*

Mr. Diamond's official report noted that he conducted the flight tests on March 3-4, 1994. These flight checks, conducted in VH-UJM, an Aero Commander Shrike AC500S aircraft, started with an initial check flown to a minimum display altitude 1500 feet AGL, while the second day included aerobatic maneuvers down to "ground level". In addition to the commercial maneuvers necessary for his license, Hoover showed Diamond an aileron roll after take-off, a single engine loop and eight-point hesitation roll into the dead engine, the zero airspeed stall with both propellers feathered, another zero airspeed stall at full power, a no-engine sixteen point hesitation roll, and deadstick loops, eight-point

esitation roles and his trademark deadstick landing.

Diamond noted that *"all maneuvers were flown smoothly and accurately and well within the aircraft's maximum normal acceleration limits. Mr. Hoover was at all times oriented with a display axis and never faltered in aircraft or engine handling. Mr. Hoover showed no visible indications of stress throughout the flight checks..."*

Diamond summarized Hoover's subsequent airshow performances briefly. *"I observed Mr. Hoover's displays in the AC500S on the Fifth and Sixth of March 1994. Both displays appeared faultless from the ground and following the "Dead Stick" Landing, Mr. Hoover stopped the aircraft at the nominated point on each location."*

Newly minted as an Australian commercial pilot and fully evaluated as an airshow pilot once again, Hoover looked forward to SkyRace '94 with great anticipation. In addition to a number of racing classes and a strong airshow roster, the highlight of the race was to be a $50,000 unlimited class air race. The racing action was sure to be fast and furious, and SkyRace officials made great and consistent use of Hoover's unparalleled experience as a guiding force in the Reno Air Races to help the Australian version conduct itself with safety and excitement. A number of pilots sought him out for advice and were rewarded with extensive discussions about air race technique, safety criteria, emergency procedures, and some of the many many things he had seen in his career. The Gwynn-Jones report on SkyRace quotes Hoover in saying *"you gotta listen to what I say about safety. We are going to make this whole thing squeaky clean. No hitches. Every pilot must be sure that they know where every other pilot is throughout the race."*

Pilots, of widely varying backgrounds and experience levels, were glued to his every word... both to the excellent technical advice that he imparted, with little urging, as well as his good humor and stories of his many experiences as a test pilot and Reno race legend. But one of his most quoted lines from throughout the event was the advice he gave to one and all with a twinkle in his eye... ***"Turn Left... and Go like Hell!"***

Hoover was insistent about preserving a very high level of safety throughout this event... Gwynn-Jones noted that when several pilots seemed confused about making safe over-taking passes Hoover responded with a clear but common-sense answer... *"you don't pass unless there is enough room to drive a Boeing 747 between (you and) the aircraft ahead. And remember (that) you've got radios. Use them to talk to each other if need be."*

For his own part, Hoover's performances went flawlessly and the narrative of those performances is filled with superlatives... also noting that where Barry Diamond and his fellow check pilots were applauding Hoover's skill, one flyer, a fellow by the name of John Lindsay, was heard to remark that *"flyers like that are made in heaven."*

Hoover played pace pilot, just like he did at Reno... even to the point of starting each heat with his customary race command *"Gentlemen, You Have a Race."* From there, Bob would pitch up, climb a little ways above it all and watch the race from overhead, playing guardian angel in case any of the pilots might have a problem and have need of his services to get to the ground safely. Bob flew race patrol in the T-28, the same type of aircraft in which he had demonstrated his skills a few days before the Oklahoma City Nearing some months before. All in all, everyone associated with the event agreed that Hoover's attendance and participation not only made the event a great success but his own performances and activities showed that this master of the sky had lost none of his touch." Hoover, of course, was elated. *"I had a ball... and I couldn't have asked for a nicer group of people or a more professional group of pilots... it was a great way to get*

back to business!"

Thereafter, Bob flew a fair number of shows in Australia... all without incident but not without some rumor and controversy. Dr. Liddell kept the FAA's Federal Air Surgeon Dr. Jordan well-informed throughout the period and filed regular updates with the USA... often chiding them politely for continuing their grounding of Mr. Hoover. In April of 1995, Liddell updated Jordan thusly... *"As you may well require ongoing assessment regarding Mr. Bob Hoover should he again apply for an FAA licence I thought that I should appraise you of his activities in Australia over the last few months.*

As I think you're aware, Bob Hoover has an Australian Commercial and Private Pilot's licence and has flown in air displays in Australia in the last two years. This year he has traveled to Australia twice and flown in two separate major aviating events in the country. The first was the air races in Tasmania which ran from the 16-19 February 1995. At this event Bob Hoover flew his Aero Commander display every day and also displayed various other Second World War high performance aircraft all of which he flew in an exemplary fashion with a very high quality and polished performance. He returned to Australia in March to perform at the Air Shows Down Under aviation event which ran from the 21-26 March at Avalon in Victoria. This event is run once every three years and is the major aviating event in the southern hemisphere. Once again Bob Hoover flew his Aero Commander display each day of the air pageant as well as flying a wide variety of other aircraft on each day. Again his displays were conducted to a very high level of precision and expertise.

I am aware that one of the concerns that existed in your office regarding Mr Hoover's certification related to his ability to react in a timely fashion to an emergency. In light of this I felt that I should place on record a minor incident that occurred during one of his displays at Avalon. Mr Hoover was in the middle of one of his display routines and was at the time in the Aero Commander inverted over the main runway with both engines fully feathered when air traffic control cleared a Tornado jet fighter to line up for take off on the active runway. Mr Hoover, despite the fact that he was in an unusual attitude conducting a precision manoeuver, came up on the radio immediately and advised the tower to keep the runway clear as he was about to perform a dead stick landing on that runway.

This incident I believe indicates that Bob Hoover is capable of a high level of concentration and presence of mind whilst flying a difficult acrobatic routine. I think that you should be aware of the incident for any future deliberations."

On the 10th of October of 1995, Liddell wrote Jon Jordan again... *"To keep you informed of the situation regarding Bob Hoover and his Australian Certification I am writing regarding an aerial display which Bob Hoover performed in Brisbane on the 1st 2nd and 3rd of September (1995) this year.*

Mr Hoover performed his usual routine in the Aero Commander and also flew an acrobatic routine in the T-28. Apart from his initial low level acrobatic check flight conducted with a CASA Flying Operations Inspector on the Friday before the air display Mr Hoover flew all the sequences during the air display solo.

His performances were flown to a high degree of precision and accuracy despite a requirement by the local Flying Operations Inspector that an area of housing close to the display flight line be avoided during the display sequence. This requirement made the display line slightly unusual, however Mr Hoover handled the requirement and his

offset display without any difficulty. In relation to Mr Hoover's supposed cognitive deficit I would like to recount to you a comment made to me by Mr Hoover following his display performance on the Saturday.

'Mr. Hoover approached me after completing his display in the Aero Commander and confided that his workload was considerably higher whilst using aircraft which were not his normal display aircraft that he has utilized in the United States. He commented that in his own aircraft, after completion of the eight point hesitation roll performed with both engines fully feathered, to restart the engines he had to move the propeller levers to the full fine position which activated micro-switches that automatically oper-ated the unfeathering pumps allowing the propellers to turn and the engines to restart.

This modification with the unfeathering pumps allowed him to concentrate on positioning the aircraft so that a dead stick landing could be affected should the engines fail to start. It also allowed him a free right hand to operate the landing gear lever should a dead stick landing appear necessary. The aircraft that Mr Hoover was using in Austra-lia had a manually operated unfeathering pump so that after placing the propeller levers in the full feathered position it was necessary to hold the unfeathering pump button with the right hand and at the same time observe the engines for a restart. Whilst performing this task he was also required to monitor the airspeed and position the aircraft through a 180 degree turn back to the airfield should a dead stick landing become necessary.

The dilemma he found himself in with this arrangement was the decision as to when to abandon the attempts at a restart and to remove his right hand from the unfeathering pump to activate the undercarriage in time for the undercarriage to cycle and achieve a safe dead stick landing. These considerations were especially relevant to him on the day of our discussion due to the aircraft's engines being a little slower in starting than one would normally anticipate. I bring these comments to your attention as a fellow Specialist in Aviation Medicine to enable you to have more insight into the thought processes required with the type of display that Mr Hoover is conducting and as evidence of his demonstrated cognitive abilities in this area."

This did not endear Liddell to the FAA... and pressure was exerted on Liddell to change his tune. *"I actually received a certain amount of pressure from the FAA through our system about what were we doing certifying Hoover when they won't and, in fact, the boss of the Civil Aviation Safety Authority, the new authority that was formed, (the whole of Civil Aviation Authority was split up into various Air Services, where you've got the Air Traffic Control separate from CASA or Civil Aviation Safety Authority). The new boss (of CASA) was a guy called Leroy Keith who was from the USA. He was Ex-FAA, ex-Douglas Aircraft and he had a relationship with (FAA Administrator) Hinson and (Tony) Broderick (a Senior FAA official who resigned shortly after the ValuJet controversy broke)."*

And so he went off and he came back and said 'Leroy didn't really mean that, he meant maybe you should consider it' and I said 'well it's been considered.' I believe at a later stage Hinson actually came out to Australia and I think there was some query about it... and he said 'you guys are not making it easy for us in the FAA by certifying Hoover. It's creating all sorts of hassles for us.' That wasn't my consideration. I mean, I didn't exist to make life easy for the FAA. I mean, my reason for existing was to make sure that pilots received medical certification fairly... there were some comments by the FAA that we didn't have access to all the medical information, and that may have been true, but I had access to enough information to make me realize that there was enough

dichotomy of opinion that it didn't matter what else they had (because) it wasn't going to throw the lever severely one way or the other. Also, I knew of what appeared to be some sort of a plot or personality difference with people in the FAA who just didn't want to have Bob Hoover flying and had made comments to that extent in public... uh, some of them (were) in the medical profession and some of them weren't. I think that from my point of view, the evidence was in the flying performances and in meeting Bob Hoover... and realizing that the guy was very much switched on and was a truly professional pilot.

I did have some concerns about the whole thing, of course... but Bob's flying was too great to ignore. Since Bob Hoover's been flying within Australia, probably 15 young aerobatic pilots have been killed in airshows (as of 1997). No one would say a word (about those), but of course if Bob had an accident flying this critical sort of aviation, all those other people would have stood up and said 'I told you so', which is nonsense because accidents do occur (albeit rarely) at airshows. Then... I saw him fly. In retrospect, I realized that I had seen a video of him pouring a drink (while) doing his barrel roll... and I was quite impressed... I was quite anxious to see some of the things he was doing, you gotta have a good chance here of having a crack up doing this. (It) doesn't matter what your medical status is... if he had an accident doing something which I would consider very extremely critical flying, no matter whoever was doing it and most people can't. That's the bottom line. There were comments made on some of his testing like 'Well, he might be all right, but we don't know if he's got the intellectual ability to handle an emergency.' But, I was thinking what greater emergency in aviation can there be than going inverted in a six-seat twin engine aircraft with both engines not spinning... so I can't really go from there to a 'better' emergency!"

The Anaheim Meeting

Liddell recalled meeting Jordan at a conference in Anaheim, California in 1995, and taking the initiative of bringing up the Hoover matter directly. This action should have signaled the beginning of a significant turn-around in the FAA's recalcitrant opposition to reinstating Hoover.

"I personally met Jon Jordan and said, 'Can't we get the lawyers out of this and just have a meeting with Bob?'" He'd never met Bob and he actually went out on a limb doing that because there is an amount of hot water that floats around the FAA..."

So they met. *"...the meeting was very amicable and Jon said, 'Yeah, we'll look at it again.' He said he wasn't making any promises in terms of certification but they would look at it again. What we were trying to do, was trying to get him treated like any other pilot rather than this special case stuff. And I don't believe that Jon had come to that meeting with any foregoing conclusions or anything and I think he was quite genuine when he said he would look at it again. Now, Bob Hoover doesn't think what I think, I think Bob thinks Jon Jordan didn't play the game... as fairly as he might have, but what we're not privy to, of course, is the impressions that he got from the other side and, uh, I think Jon Jordan's got legal training* (Editor's Note: Jordan is also a lawyer) *and I think that means that he's probably more reluctant than a lot of us to put his neck in the noose. For instance... I've heard that Pakull said that Hoover would never fly again... I don't know what he's (Pakull) still doing working for the FAA...*

Bob and I weren't privy to what stuff Jon had. I suppose Jon was seeing it as 'if I certify the guy. He goes out and crashes on his first thing, I'm finished'. No doubt in the world, especially if he goes into a crowd... and (various people), of course, would be dancing on Jordan's grave. So Jordan's decision is going to be colored by all this sort of stuff and I, for one, would realize that this couldn't be an easy deal.

I'm a different personality from Jon. I say, well, we're gonna do it because A + A = 2A... that sort of thing. But that doesn't detract from the fact that other people have different ways of handling their careers and that's their business. I would only say that it's unfortunate that some people might have to suffer because of the fact that the top man perhaps wasn't prepared to go out on a limb. But, I say that in full cognizance of the fact that he had pressures that I'm surely not aware of.... but I just don't see Jon Jordan as the total villain here."

Hoover seems a mite more negative about the event. "I'd been through a whole series of expensive tests and asked him (Jordan) straight out... 'What's the most important test I can take to prove to you that I'm OK?' I wanted to accomplish one thing at a time and have a promise from Jordan that if I passed, that I could fly. Once I had that, I started spending money getting my plane ready for Oshkosh, believing he'd keep his word and that I would pass all his tests."

Jordan reportedly told him that the Brain Scan was the most important thing he wanted to see from Hoover, with psych testing to follow if he passed. Hoover communicated with Dr. Gary Ferris, who had been instrumental in dealing with some of the Australian matters (and is a highly qualified Aerospace Medicine Specialist with additional credentials in Radiology — including Interventional Radiology — basically revolving around vascular studies, nuclear medicine and trauma). Ferris spent many, many hours working on the Hoover matter with a near-heroic effort. "I never worked so hard on a case in all my life... not just the medical stuff, but I knew all the players on both sides and played 'point man' ...making sure that papers weren't lost, the right forms were submitted... you name it. It took hundreds of hours... it was terribly involved," he remembered.

Ferris enlisted the expertise of Dr. Darwood B. Hance right away to conduct the additional brain scan... and Hoover went through that with flying colors. Ferris gets quite concerned though, when he is reminded that Hoover's initial brain scan looked so suspect and was repeatedly used by the FAA to "prove" Hoover's inability to hold a medical certificate... "They let him sleep through the procedure and on top of it, he wasn't counseled properly on the procedure and winds up drinking caffeine (coffee) before the test... and they are worried that the first brain scan showed diminished perfusion in some areas? Those are absolute no-nos. That's nuts... those two factors alone will totally defeat the whole point of the brain scan. That means the test was totally invalid. I don't think that it was malicious or anything but the technical service doesn't get paid if the test isn't done right. No one probably wanted to say anything because they'd have to do it over...

Still, the FACT he did so well on the second is more than sufficient indication that they were dealing with flawed data... Jim, the brain scan we did on Bob is the best example of a brain scan in his (Hance) teaching files on a 73 year old man! Bob not only came through very well... They use it now as a teaching file at the University of California! Totally normal. I mean... what did they want from this man that he hadn't already proven again and again?"

As far as Hoover is concerned, though, there was a major breach of faith that occurred between he and Jordan when he went through the additional brain scan and Jordan still wouldn't relent... *"I was trying to be very clear, very polite with him, but I didn't want to take a whole bunch of expensive tests if failing one would stop everything... so I deliberately asked which one was the 'make or break' and I truly remember him saying it was the brain scan... and when I passed it, I was to be allowed to take the next one. He didn't follow through. I felt very let-down..."*

Hoover said that he'd been promised that he could do all the new testing on the West Coast, even though Jordan originally wanted him to go back to the East Coast and see some others of his choosing (in other words, FAA chosen consultants). They compromised when Bob said that he would go to people that Jordan selected... but closer to home, to keep the travel and expenses down (please note that by this time, Bob's losses and expenses numbered in the many thousands of dollars and he simply had to cut his losses as much as possible). But one thing appeared clear (according to Hoover and others with him)... if Bob passed the tests, then he could fly at Oshkosh.

The deal was a rocky one and the so-called rules seemed to keep changing. After passing the Brain Scan, Bob was told to go to San Diego to undergo psych testing from Dr. Heaton, instead of in LA (which we hear has its share of world class psych experts). This presented a number of difficulties since Heaton was preparing to leave town for a trip to Australia and originally indicated that he wasn't available... until the FAA convinced him otherwise (and yes, Bob paid for Heaton, too). Finally, Hoover took the tests (including CogScreen) and passed them... again. Mind you, Hoover objected to the CogScreen test as well, but the FAA was adamant in seeing Bob take it. It took two days, but Heaton reported to Hoover that he was getting *"a clean bill of health."*

Hoover asked Heaton to call Jordan right away and report that... after which Bob called the Federal Air Surgeon and requested his medical back so that he could be on his way to Oshkosh (which was coming up quick... and for which he'd just spent serious bucks in getting this previously dormant plane ready to fly airshows again). Jordan refused... reportedly saying that he *"had to see it in writing,"* while Hoover grew ever more frustrated... knowing that Heaton was leaving for Australia right away and feeling that he was being put off. Jordan promised to *"have someone call him (Heaton)"* but the much-hoped-for breakthrough never came off. Bob's disappointment grew even more profound later on... *"Jordan has since denied that this agreement even took place... we had an agreement and he broke it."* Please note that other medical professionals associated with this series of affairs do support Hoover's recollection.

Liddell summed up some of his feelings on the matter by saying that *"You know, I think there are many people that have suffered transgressions at the hands of regulators whether it be the medical department or the operations area and many of those people have just had to give up their career and be frustrated and feel badly done by. You know, my concern is maybe hopefully we can save the odd one by just being fair. We don't want people to be flying who are dangerous and most people don't want to fly if they are dangerous, but when they have some bureaucrat telling them that they can't fly when everything else is telling them they can — sometimes the bureaucrat will be right, but sometimes that individual will be right and they are the ones that we've gotta try and be fair to."*

Chapter 28

FOB... The Friends of Bob

"If it can't be expressed in figures, it is not science; it is opinion."
Robert Heinlein in *"Time Enough for Love"*

I really don't think the FAA had any idea of the sh*t-storm they were generating in their actions against Hoover. Aviation and aviators are some of the most disorganized and complacent folks on the planet... hard to motivate and even harder to gather together for any reason... until it gets *really* serious. Apparently, the aviation community thought this matter was serious. Never in general aviation history did the world of aviation appear so single-minded and united over one problem.

A series of news items and magazine articles alerted the flying world to the dilemma facing him, the (then) fledgling Internet became a breeding ground for basic information (and much disinformation...) and at airshows and Fly-Ins all over the world, the word of Bob Hoover's predicament grew... and grew.

The worlds of Sport and General Aviation are pretty much overseen by two primary pilots' organizations — the politically active Aircraft Owners and Pilots Association (AOPA—currently the largest aviation organization in the world) and the Experimental Aircraft Association (EAA). As the Bob Hoover debacle became a predominantly public event, both organizations started hearing from their membership more and more, asking them what they were going to do about the problem. In both cases these organizations stepped up to the plate. Other aviation organizations covering the commercial and professional areas and aviation also got involved at various times in this matter because of Hoover's popularity with their membership and the obvious fact that such a great pilot deserved their support.

EAA's value came not so much from what they did or not say or do on Hoover's behalf, but for the stage they provided several times a year via the huge international Fly-In in Oshkosh, WI, or the other regional Fly-Ins that occurred throughout the year. These Fly-ins served as gathering and rallying points for aviators and focal points for certain events that were to prove pivotal to the public visibility of Bob's plight.

Over 45 years old, the EAA got its start in early 1953 under the guidance of current Chairman of the Board, Paul H. Poberezny. It grew from an initial meeting of 36 flyers to a 170,000-member international organization covering much of the world of recreational aviation. Its headquarters and EAA Air Adventure Museum now occupy a 150,000 square foot, multimillion dollar facility on the south side of Oshkosh, Wisconsin.

The association's first newsletter, called the Experimenter, has grown into five complete publications covering everything from ultralights to warbirds and a number of special divisions of EAA have been established to aid devotees of classic aircraft, ultralights, aerobatics, warbirds and SportPlane builders.

The first EAA Fly-In was held in September of 1953, in conjunction with the Milwaukee Air Pageant, which Paul Poberezny had helped organize in 1950. Fewer than 50 airplanes were registered at the inaugural event, but today over 12,000 airplanes flock to the week-long Fly-In hosted each year at Wittman Regional Airport in Oshkosh. The Convention outgrew Milwaukee and moved to Rockford Municipal Airport in Illinois in 1960. Continued growth prompted EAA to move to its current location in 1970. Now known as EAA AirVenture Oshkosh, one of the world's largest aviation events, the week-long Fly-In is attended by over 800,000 people.

EAA Headquarters has also evolved greatly through the years. For the first 11 years, EAA's home office was located in Paul Poberezny's basement. In 1964, EAA's offices moved into a new building in nearby Franklin, another Milwaukee suburb. By the late 1970's, however, space was at a premium at the Franklin site. After studying several sites and receiving invitations from many cities throughout the nation, the EAA Board of Directors decided to keep the Convention in Oshkosh and build a new headquarters there. Groundbreaking for the new EAA Aviation Center took place during the 1982 Fly-In Convention. The museum portion of the Aviation Center opened in January 1983, while the headquarters became operational in January 1984. In July 1989, the EAA Air Adventure Museum officially opened the "Eagle Hangar" a 44,000 square foot addition that houses the EAA Aviation Foundation's collection of World War II-era aircraft and memorabilia. Founded and administered for many years by Paul Poberezny, the association is now run by his son, Tom.

The history of AOPA is even more illustrious. This 360,000-member association also grew from humble roots and has become the preeminent aviation organization in the world... and the most politically active one, to boot. The Aircraft Owners and Pilots Association, a not-for-profit organization dedicated to general aviation, was incorporated on May 15, 1939. Right from the beginning, AOPA fought to keep general aviation fun, safe and affordable, but had to deal with slow growth during its early years, though it now counts as members well over half of the entire current pilot population in the USA.

AOPA got its start with a deal struck with Ziff-Davis Publishing Company even before its incorporation. AOPA had a special section in each issue of POPULAR AVIATION, the predecessor of FLYING Magazine, to communicate with its membership. It was a risky deal, though, since Ziff-Davis had a clause that threatened cancellation of the deal if AOPA membership didn't reach 2500 in the first year. Its five founding fathers met in April, 1939, to work out the details, and spent hours trying to decide a name for the organization. Founder P.T. Sharples favored "Pilots, Incorporated" to give the group a *"serious tone."* The debate raged on well into the night. Finally, founder C. Townsend Ludington yawned - by this time it was about 2:30 in the morning - and announced, "Gentlemen, I am tired, so I'm going to bed. I propose we name it just what it is - the Aircraft Owners and Pilots Association." There was unanimous approval—and everyone went to bed.

J.B. "Doc" Hartranft was AOPA's first employee, taking the title executive director and moving the offices from Philadelphia to Chicago, right next to the Ziff-Davis publishing house. From there, Hartranft got busy with the details of building the associa-

tion. AOPA's first political activity was to urge passage of a Senate bill that would establish the Civilian Pilot Training Program. This piece of legislation allowed thousands of people to earn their pilot certificates under a government subsidy and stimulated general aviation activity and aircraft sales. It also provided a solid aviation education for those who would later serve in the air forces of World War II.

AOPA also secured a reduction in the cost of the medical examination fee (from $10 to $6), urged the Civil Aeronautics Authority (CAA) to construct more airports to handle the increased flying activity, and conducted the first study of the various state aviation fuel tax policies. Discussions with the National Advisory Council for Aeronautics (NACA - the predecessor of NASA) centered on design parameters for an easily affordable single-engine airplane. A drive was also started to recognize general aviation's improving safety record, to help reduce insurance rates. AOPA's first year ended with a membership of 2000. Just three months later, that figure had doubled, and local pilot groups called "AOPA Units" were formed around the country. War was obviously on the way, so in 1940 AOPA formed the "AOPA Air Guard" to introduce civilian pilots to military rules and procedures, and form a manpower base from which the air forces could draw more pilots.

Some 5000 pilots participated. On December 7, 1941, America's entry into World War II brought a drastic change in civil flying. The government sought to ban *all* civilian flying, but AOPA helped in establishing an identification program that persuaded the CAA and the military to allow properly registered pilots to fly in all airspace, except border areas now called Air Defense Identification Zones. AOPA offices moved from New York to the Washington, DC area in 1942. When the war ended, membership again started, with about 20,000 active AOPA members by the end of 1946. The years following World War II were years of explosive growth in aviation, and AOPA staff members worked long hours to help bureaucrats and lawmakers understand the special needs of general aviation pilots.

The issue of required equipment surfaced early, when the CAA proposed shortly after the war that communications equipment be required for everyone. AOPA initially opposed this requirement, in part because the tube-laden radios of the day were very heavy and compromised a light airplane's useful load. Ultimately, a compromise required communication radios only in the busiest airspace. By late 1948, AOPA was helping educate pilots about the new-fangled VHF navigation tool called "VOR", and published manuals on the subject. The association also helped in test programs for VOR and ILS equipment.

The late 1940's were also when AOPA assumed a major role in legislative lobbying. To help members of Congress understand general aviation, Hantranft pushed for formation of the Congressional Flying Club, which still exists. He persuaded manufacturers to donate aircraft, and volunteers to teach both ground school and flight. In 1948, Hartranft hired the legendary Max Karant, formerly managing editor of FLYING Magazine, to serve as assistant general manager of AOPA and editorial director for AOPA PILOT magazine. During the next three decades, the team of Hantranft and Karant helped to quadruple AOPA membership from 50,000 to more than 200,000 by the mid 1970's.

As the 1950's rolled around, AOPA found itself in a leadership role whenever general aviation was threatened. Several midair collisions between airliners and general aviation aircraft led to a vigorous debate over a proposal by the Air Line Pilots Association (ALPA) to ban general aviation from any airport used by air carriers. Partly because of this battle, the "party-line" UNICOM - a term invented by Hartranft and Karant - was brought into being to help pilots know of each other's presence.

AOPA created the AOPA Air Safety Foundation in 1950, and within 10 years there would be thousands of pilots who took advantage of the "180-degree" rating that provided basic instrument instruction for non-instrument rated pilots. The AOPA Air Safety Foundation has gone on to become the world's largest and most effective nonprofit organization devoted solely to general aviation safety. Offices moved several times in the 1950's, the first move from downtown Washington, DC to suburban Bethesda, MD.

Major battles fought on behalf of general aviation pilots in the 50's included reductions in life insurance rates, charting of VOR stations and retaining highways on sectional aeronautical charts. A military plan to scrap the evolving VOR-DME system in favor of TACAN only led to a pitched battle that resulted in a compromise still in use today. An "experimental" type of airspace that was the forerunner of today's Class B airspace was proposed in the mid-1950's for Washington National Airport. It would have extended 15 nautical miles from the airport in all directions and up to 3000 feet AGL. A full mile of visibility would have been required for VFR operations, as well as a speed limit of 180 miles per hour. AOPA successfully fought to keep Washington National Airport open to general aviation, and it was many years before Terminal Control Areas (also forerunners of Class B airspace) were instituted. In 1958, AOPA PILOT magazine made its debut as a stand-alone magazine. Boom times came to general aviation in the 1960's, with aircraft manufacturers introducing new models left and right and producing an average of 9000 airplanes a year. With the increased flying activity, communications became more important. AOPA pushed for additional radio frequencies for aviation. A plan to close many Flight Service Stations was muted, and the first AOPA Airports USA airport directory was issued. The International Council of Aircraft Owners and Pilots Association was created in 1962, with the first members including Canada, Australia and the Union of South Africa.

Various battles were fought over air traffic control, including proposals for mandatory transponders and new types of controlled airspace called "Terminal Area Radar Service." By 1964, the Atlanta airport was offering these services and the program would soon be expanded nationwide. Two midair collisions in 1967 and another in 1969 (near Indianapolis between an Allegheny Airlines DC-9 and a Piper Cherokee) led to urgent calls for creation of the now famous (or infamous) Terminal Control Areas around busy airports. AOPA worked in each case to maintain access for general aviation pilots, and spent much of the 1970's trying to keep aviation safe without grounding many GA pilots.

By the end of the 1960's, AOPA membership had climbed to 141,000. The years of the 1970's would include some of the most important political battles AOPA had ever fought, including those over TCAs, the Airport and Airways Development Act, fuel crisis fallout and ever-tightening Federal regulations. Proposals to squeeze more taxes and fees from "fat cat" general aviation pilots were fought back many times during the 70's. A Nixon proposal to "raid" the aviation trust fund was also stopped. The 1973 oil embargo took all of AOPA's persuasive power to prevent catastrophic cuts in general aviation activity, because as Hartranft pointed out, "while general aviation has 98% of all aircraft, it uses only 8.6% of civil aviation fuels (while) 91.4% is used by the airlines."

In May, 1977, former FAA Assistant Administrator John L. Baker took over reins of the association. Just two years later, at the end of the decade, more than 245,000 pilots were members of AOPA, and general aviation was a raging bull in the marketplace. More than 18,000 airplanes would be delivered in 1979. The AOPA Political Action Committee

was formed in 1980 for more lobbying effectiveness. It would be needed, as an increasing number of politicians involved themselves in aviation technical matters in the name of aviation safety. Air traffic controllers went on strike on August 3, 1981, and ATC underwent the most massive changes seen to date. General aviation was singled out for virtual elimination from the ATC system until AOPA helped work out a flow-control method that allowed IFR flights.

In May, 1983, AOPA made its last move, from the Bethesda, MD, offices to new offices on the Frederick, MD, municipal airport. It symbolized the growth of the association, which now had 265,000 members and was recognized as one of the most effective voices for any group in Washington.

Additional airspace restrictions – including ARSAs – were proposed, and AOPA fought to keep regulation to the minimum necessary for safety. AOPA urged that the FAA establish an office to monitor traffic in terminal areas, install more ILS, provide more airport improvement program funds to outlying reliever and potential reliever airports, build more runways at existing airports, and designate more military airports as joint-use facilities.

By 1989, AOPA membership was close to the 300,000 mark and as the 1990's opened, the fight for general aviation airports accelerated. Closings and restrictions threatened many airports around the country, with development pressures and noise complaints heaping work on AOPA's plate.

Long-term battles – some still undecided – have raged since 1990 at many popular airports. As losses of public-use airports continued at the rate of about one per week, AOPA launched a major program to educate pilots about potential dangers to their local airports. A new "Airport Community Relations" book and a "Flying Friendly" video produced in 1995 helped pilots win support at their home fields.

AOPA staffers fought hundreds of battles for pilots in the first half of the 1990's, including funding for DUATS and effective opposition for both a "shoot-em-down" proposal from US Customs and a suggestion for costly renewals of pilot certificates.

The biggest "win" for all of general aviation, however, was the 1994 passage of product liability reform legislation, which led directly to an announcement from Cessna that production would resume. In 1991, another milestone in AOPA history occurred when Phil Boyer, former Senior Vice President with ABC Television, assumed the reins of the association from John Baker. Under his leadership, membership has grown to its current total of about 360,000 and AOPA influence has expanded proportionately.

AOPA was particularly active right from the get-go in the Hoover affair, since their chief counsel, John Yodice, became part of Hoover's defense team. John asked AOPA's permission early on to become strongly involved in the matter but knew that it would take time and attention away from his duties for AOPA. AOPA President Phil Boyer, the most politically active president that this organization had ever seen, gave him the go-ahead right away. *"I saw this as an issue that our membership was going to be very concerned about and even more so for a long time. We were getting phone calls about this practically from day one, from pilots who have two major concerns... the first was that Hoover was a truly beloved character and had endeared himself to aviators all over the world producing some very strong feelings, and the other was the fact that if the FAA could ground Bob Hoover for reasons that didn't seem to be all that apparent to the general public, then many feared that they would have had no protection from an FAA*

that might target them next."

Hoover's legal fight was sure to be a costly one, and some more senior members of the aviation community immediately put together a "Friends of Bob" organization to raise funds to help Bob mount a legal defense, and to help him politically as circumstances arose. Many thousands of dollars came into the account, and though it came nowhere near to paying the full extent of the financial damage that Bob suffered over the course of the three-year battle, it certainly helped keep his legal team funded. The "Friends of Bob Hoover" fund was administered by the Wayne Smith Co., from a Washington, DC business address and dispersed funds for Bob's legal bills.

One other interesting aspect of this is that Bob's primary legal team actually received a fraction of what they might normally receive for such a defense... both were good friends of Bob Hoover, and were well aware that this defense was not just important to Bob Hoover, but would probably greatly affect the rest of aviation.

All over aviation, pilots rallied to Hoover's defense. Letters poured in to political officials, FAA managers and offices, media persons, and aviation associations. In no time at all, aviators made it very clear to the *"powers that be"* that they supported Hoover strongly and that they were getting *"pretty pissed"* at what they thought to be an arbitrary and unfounded grounding of an American hero. Such efforts manifested themselves in many ways... often with individual FAA offices and Inspectors soon receiving scorn and ridicule from the pilot community for the actions taken against Hoover in Oklahoma City. FAA public events, meetings, and speeches were often peppered with questions and statements about the Hoover matter and the strong feelings that the aviation community was trying to portray on behalf of Hoover's defense.

Let me make something clear here... the aviation community is not very well organized. It has come up against many problems over the years, and only been able to mount light to moderate political pressure in its own defense. It is fairly fragmented, not all that well-organized (though that situation is changing, mostly under the guidance of AOPA), and frankly does not do a very good job of defending its interests. Three of the biggest threats to aviation in recent memory — airspace access limitations, user fees, and product liability problems (the costs of which were making aviation prohibitively expensive) — provoked what can honestly only be called lukewarm responses from a disaffected community that had pretty much given up on its ability to affect any great changes on their behalf.

All that changed with the FAA's grounding of Bob Hoover. As the Bob Hoover controversy became front-page news for the aviation community, the FAA was hit with a virtual storm of bad feelings, revulsion, political activism, and the most intense criticism it had seen in many years. Outside the growing clamor created by many articles from the aviation press, one turning point often noted by many in the public perception of this case was F. Lee Bailey's speech to the 1994 AOPA Expo in Palm Springs, CA. While thoroughly enmeshed in the bizarre circus of the O.J. Simpson legal defense at the time, Bailey arrived at the Expo to perform duty as the Opening Day Keynote Speaker. His outspoken, highly confrontational speech truly energized those few aviators who, at that point, still had not understood the importance of the Hoover matter. It is doubtful that anyone leaving that speech was willing to take the Hoover case lightly thereafter and if the FAA had any doubts about what kind of fight of they were in previously, there could be few remaining.

Working without notes, Bailey's command of the English language and his memory for detail were coupled with a speaking style that can only be summarized as dynamic." Bailey opened his speech with the amusing anecdote of his flight in the cockpit of the Shrike commander as Bob Hoover flew a performance and quickly launched into a summary of the case and how he got involved in it. *"I was therefore somewhat horrified to learn, about a year-and-a-half ago, shortly after the demise of a great pilot, great trial lawyer and mutual friend, Verne Lawyer, that Bob had been troubled by the FAA. And I began to look into the case and the more I looked, the more angry I got. To encapsulate the background of this case, it appears, from the uncontradicted evidence, since the FAA hid its witnesses to the event, if they were witnesses, from the trial judge who heard the case last January, that on June 19, 1992 at Oklahoma City, Bob performed three days in a row. All of those who could be found to testify, and those who were qualified to comment—the other airshow pilots—said it was vintage Hoover, which means flawless."*

A stirring narrative followed... in which Bailey relived the details of the Oklahoma City performances, the NTSB hearing, and the legalities that followed. The speech was merciless, and at least one FAA employee in attendance was seen scowling as point after point was recounted by Bailey. Despite the strong personality inherent in Mr. Bailey, he was generous in his praise of his co-counsel. *"I immediately got John Yodice on our team. He is, in my view, the most expert lawyer in these matters. I handle some enforcement actions, but try a whole range of cases and don't know both the players and the rules like the back of my hand as John does."*

Bailey seemed incredulous of how the FAA built its case and the foundation upon which it rested. *"...the FAA had staked out a position and this is the nub of the controversy and something that I hope will strike terror into the hearts of everyone here who's got a medical in his or her pocket and wants to keep it: the neuro-psychological profession, which is the one involved here. One neuro-psychologist has given opinion on the witness stand that Bob was impaired. Although at the time he examined him, he was part of a group that recommended giving the license back. And not until many months later, at the request of the FAA, did he change his opinion. And to this day, the whole case rests on his shoulders.*

That profession, like most others, has a bible and it's called the DSM-4, republished as recently as last July. Many things in that bible are of no interest to you, but when it comes to the question of impairment, under the Federal Air Regulations and your right to have a medical certificate, one element is critical. The FAA has decided to rewrite the bible by eliminating one of its most important precepts, and that is that no matter what results may be obtained in any kind of paper and pencil or oral testing, if there is no conduct to show up an impairment then, there is no diagnosable impairment. That is to say, unless you, in some way, exhibit extraordinary, or strange or bizarre, or limited conduct, you cannot be diagnosed as impaired under their rules.

[The] FAA said, 'we disagree with that, we make our own rules.' And it turns out they have for much too long. The people in the FAA that had to do with this case are so completely undisciplined as to shock a rather liberal lawyer. They said we are going to do without the impairment and urged upon one of the finest trial judges I have seen in this country, a man with 15-years' experience on the State of Oklahoma and then Federal benches, that regardless of the ability of the subject to perform flawlessly, they could

rule him out as impaired on paper tests, which were improperly administered as a resu[t] of false statements made to Bob to induce him to take the test, i.e. these tests canno[t] cannot influence your right to fly. The man who made that statement turned out to b[e] the only witness against him who had examined him."

Bailey also brought out one of the more ridiculous incidents to occur during th[e] Oklahoma City NTSB hearing... *"We started the trial by having Bob do his airshow befor[e] Judge Mullins, who himself is a Baron pilot. And it was, with Leo Loudenslager in th[e] right seat as safety pilot, flawless, once again. The prosecution sat around clapping ironically, and after trying to take his ticket, asked for his autograph. (This is a strang[e] bunch of birds out there wearing the FAA license.)"*

The testimony of Norbert Nester was singled out. *"There came to our attentio[n] a courageous man and I and many in my profession are just waiting, just waiting for th[e] FAA to try to take one bite out of his backside that they yearn to do. He came forward an[d] he said, 'I may lose my job for this, but,' he said, 'I can't forget that on June 20, 1992 [at] Oklahoma City, I was one of the Inspectors assigned to the case. I went out with my so[n] and had a chance to introduce him to the great Bob Hoover. And Bob took him to th[e] airplane and explained all the controls and instruments and made him the happies[t] child in the state.'"*

He said, *'In view of that, I have to put my neck on the line. The two Inspector[s] who wrote that complaint tried to get me to join them even though I told them in m[y] view his flying was as perfect as always. And one of them said, 'You know, guys like you...* (Norbert Nester like Bob Hoover is a tall, handsome ectomorph) *'... and Hoover reall[y] piss me off.'*

He said, *'I don't like being short, fat, and bald and you guys look like pilots an[d] everybody admires you. He's been around long enough; someone's got to take him down. I would have given my good right arm (having in mind that I am left-handed) for th[e] chance to cross-examine this morally-destitute Inspector but he was not produced, no[r] was his co-conspirator. No action, of course, has been taken against these people, despit[e] the violation of numerous Federal statutes by placing in the United States' mail false an[d] fraudulent reports which were intended to, and did, mislead the regulators in their inves[-] tigation."*

Bailey held the audience spellbound, but summarized the matter dramatically urging his listeners to take all so very seriously, *"I hope that you will be alert to every ste[p] of the proceedings. We have printed enough copies of this brief and will print more [if] necessary so that everyone that would like to take the time to get really down to the nu[t] of what the evidence was, what law was applied and what should have happened in thi[s] case, that is the brief to the Federal court, we'll make it available to anyone on request Just send those requests through AOPA and they'll be answered.*

I can only sum up the Hoover case in its present status as I did to Judge Mullin[s] in Oklahoma City late in January in 1994. I said then and I tell you: This case has rubbe[d] luster from American aviation and is in its most literal and reverent sense, a God-damne[d] shame. Thank you very much."

Bailey received thunderous applause, and if the "Let Bob Fly" movement wasn'[t] in full swing by then, it surely was by the time Bailey left the podium. There is little doub[t] in anyone's mind, that this was one of the pivotal moments in the way the aviation publi[c] started to wake up and take notice of what was occurring to Robert Hoover.

Chapter 29

Let Bob Fly! The Aviation Media Wakes Up—Kinda...

*It is dangerous to be right in matters on
which the established authorities are wrong.*
Voltaire

The world of aviation has long been plagued by the fact that the media that covers it has not distinguished itself in terms of its objective editorial standards. Most of the aviation magazines are dedicated to glowing prose about this product, or that person, or such and such a company... just so long as they are a potential advertiser. While major threats and hard news stories are not totally ignored by the aviation press at large, it has often taken a pretty strong set of circumstances to wake them up from their marketing oriented slumber and get them to do some real journalism for a change. Mind you, there are a number of very good aviation journalists and editors out there, but the true fact of the matter is that those who speak their mind and try to act as activists for a stronger and safer aviation world are a small minority of the whole.

Surprisingly, though, the Bob Hoover story woke them all up... if only for a little while. Rumors started almost as soon as Boehler and Kelln filed their paperwork and started making serious news as soon when the NTSB hearing was set. With the favorable decision in Oklahoma City overruled by the FAA, even the most detached and lackadaisical aviation writer could see that something was seriously amiss. In very little time, articles started showing up in the aviation media bringing forth details of the travesty that was in the making. Articles appearing in *AOPA Pilot Magazine, FLYING magazine, Atlantic Flyer, Sport Aviation magazine, Pacific Flyer, General Aviation News & Flyer, World Airshow News,* **US Aviator** (published by the author), and many others got the ball rolling and started letting the aviation public know that the FAA had run amok.

As publisher of **US Aviator**, I arrived at the conclusion early on that this was going to be a huge story... and had the potential to affect virtually every airman in the country. This feeling was reinforced as I inspected quite a bit of the paperwork that was available at the time, in addtion to my many consultations with Mr. Hoover, and a great number of conversations with people who had been at Oklahoma City's Aerospace America Airshow in 1992. I also talked with some FAA officials who were willing to speak to me anonymously.

With no real evidence (at that point, or since) of a significant impairment on the part of Bob Hoover, it was obvious that this was going to be a major Pilot's Rights issue. For far too long, the FAA's bureaucratic/administrative legal system had unfairly targeted pilots who were either innocent of charges, or guilty of minor or inconsequential infractions, and run rough-shod over by the FAA's "kangaroo court" legal system.

In the past, such actions were largely un- or under-challenged... simply because in such legal matters the FAA/NTSB is literally judge, jury, and the eventual executioner. With the FAA's targeting of Bob Hoover, the system itself went on trial. For an aviator of such a high caliber and impeccable character to be questioned by people who were not remotely qualified to judge him, and to produce no compelling evidence of an honest-to-goodness impairment, looked to us at **US Aviator** as one of the FAA's biggest legal and public relations mistakes of all-time.

I have to admit to you right here and now that **US Aviator** magazine has long been an advocate for significant changes in the way the FAA penalizes pilots who run afoul of the Federal Aviation Regulations. While Bob Hoover —the person— was a dear friend and an unquestioned hero to me and my staff, it was obvious that this battle could and would be pivotal in terms of how the FAA was able to administer its rules over the aviation population for the foreseeable future.

We jumped on the story... with both feet. Luckily, we weren't the only ones who saw that this was more than the story of a favored and even beloved figure being unfairly targeted by a seemingly faceless bureaucracy, but a chance for an entire population to stand up and say "enough"!

So... before the first onslaught of stories started appearing among the aviation press, we went to work. For the better part of three years, it was a rare issue of **US Aviator** that didn't feature a letter, a story, or some other remark about the progress and conduct of this case. In short, we didn't let this story go until it had a positive resolution, and thereafter, we've used (and used...) this story as an example of the many problems aviation faces in dealing with the bureaucracy with too much of the wrong kind of power over it.

Don't mistake me; we were far from the only ones to feature this story prominently and often. *World Airshow News* publisher David Weiman, a prominent aviation writer (who specializes in airshow reporting), owned a publication that covered the airshow industry. He was a strong and vigorous advocate for Hoover's reinstatement, and took a hard look into what the FAA was doing to him.

Via his column in *Atlantic Flyer*, expert pilot and aviation columnist Robert Cadwalader wrote numerous insightful articles about every facet of this case and its repercussions. Indeed, he was the first to note the plight of FAA Inspector Norbert Nester as the FAA's displeasure at his positive testimony in support of Mr. Hoover turned out to have very negative connotations for Nester's career. Cadwalader's efforts were easily some of the most expert and passionate to be written about this affair.

The official AOPA magazine, *AOPA Pilot*, distinguished itself with some excellent writing. Often authored by Hoover counsel and legal Top-Gun John Yodice, he not only presented the affair in excruciating detail, but brought home the immense importance of this case to individual airman all across the country via a publication that is probably the largest industry periodical in existence.

The Experimental Aviation Association's *Sport Aviation* magazine carried regular updates about the matter and EAA President Tom Poberezny used his editorial pulpit,

often, to decry what was occurring to Hoover, and the aviation industry at large.

But... *easily* one of the most compelling articles written was also authored by a lawyer who represented Mr. Hoover: F. Lee Bailey wrote a strong indictment of the FAA's actions in FLYING magazine.

Much as I hate to admit it (as the Owner of a competitive publication), the May 1994 F. Lee Bailey article in FLYING magazine was yet another pivotal event in the public awakening of the General Aviation population—and possibly the most important magazine article written throughout the entire fight. Entitled "Grounded! The Inside Story of How the FAA Got Bob Hoover," Bailey's article mercilessly detailed the case from its beginnings in June 1992 to where it stood at that time. In fact, Bailey's cool recitation of the facts soon yielded what appeared to be a very angry lawyer upset at a grave injustice.

At the time this had been written, Bailey's brilliant and successful defense of Hoover had just been overturned by the NTSB, a matter which in fact, surprised him. Indeed, Bailey appeared to admit that much of what the FAA did surprised him both in terms of the dishonesty he felt he witnessed as well has its innate unfairness.

The article was a great read... especially with his descriptions of some of the more intricate machinations that surrounded the Oklahoma City hearing. Bailey discussed Bob Hoover's flight performance in front of Judge Mullins and wrote that "*as everyone expected, Hoover's performance was satin-smooth, though none of us on the ground realized that Bob was fighting an extraordinary yaw problem as he flew his maneuvers. The cowl flaps — which protrude sharply into the slipstream from the upper surface of the engine nacelles–produce drag at higher airspeeds. The flaps on the left nacelle had stuck in the open position, requiring constant rudder pressure to counter the drag. The FAA's claim that Bob's "impairment" prevented him from dealing with unexpected flight situations took another hit in the solar plexus. The judge watched carefully but said little. As a Baron pilot and veteran airshow spectator, he had watched Hoover before. I thought he was favorably impressed.*"

Bailey often takes some delight in ridiculing his adversaries when they screw up... and this article contained more than a few examples of this propensity. Skewering one of the FAA's doctors who had faulted Bob for some alleged short-term memory loss Bailey noted that he was "*totally unable to explain why he had directed that I repeat the question I had asked him only 60 seconds earlier, which some might define as the same affliction.*"

Bailey concluded that "*the FAA's lawyers had run out of gas and rested their case without calling the other doctors who supported their case nor the FAA Inspectors who made the original complaint. In other circumstances I would have moved for a ruling that their evidence was woefully short of proving Hoover's disability by 'A Preponderance of the Evidence.' But this trial was no ordinary case. The King was on trial, and to a lesser degree, age itself was on trial. Victory could not be claimed upon legal niceties. We had not come to court to beat the FAA on these issues, but to bury it.*

The FAA's witnesses had not come across as 'nice' people. To counter their offering, we called three of the most pleasant personalities America has ever produced: Leo Loudenslager, Sean Tucker and Steve Oliver. Each is an airshow pilot of consummate skill, and yet each is the kind of person you would like to invite to your own home, and often. It soon became apparent that the real protection of our airshow performers is not FAA Inspectors, but the 'ACE' people."

Bailey said that *"the balance of the trial was — in my own biased judgment — no less than a slaughter."*

Bailey recounted his use of the testimony of Norbert Nester, the FAA Inspector who had witnessed much of the behind-the-scenes goings-on at the OKC FSDO. *"With no contact or conversation, we served a subpoena upon FAA Inspector Norbert Nester. We expected that if he were courageous enough to tell the truth under oath, he could blow a large hole in the very roots of the case. When she learned of his identity, FAA lead counsel Susan Caron spent more than an hour on the phone with him before we ever saw or heard him. She told him — according to his sworn and uncontradicted testimony — that all the doctors had found Hoover unfit to fly. Twice she approached the trial judge to warn that if Nester took the stand, it would be her unpleasant duty to cause him some possible difficulty. Her concerns turned out to be a bluff."*

Of course, Nester's testimony was a bombshell, but Bailey described the indignant passion he brought to his closing arguments. *"I blistered, with every color of rhetoric I could muster, the fraudulent, contrived and manipulated case with every accountable villain hiding from the witness stand; a disgraceful insult to one of America's great aviation resources, and a shame to the Federal Aviation Administration. The FAA had a right to respond to this indictment. It refused to do so."*

Bailey described his lack of surprise when Judge Mullins ordered Bob back to flight status and aptly called Mullins *"one of the most able judges I have seen in 40 years of trials."*

Thinking the record was *"bulletproof"*, Bailey indicated that he was not worried when the FAA appealed to NTSB. As he expected, *"I lost no sleep over what I thought was a perfunctory proceeding. Pointing out that no appellate court could dismantle judicial findings so solidly wired to the evidence, I expected Bob to have his medical certificate returned to him on February 18, the date upon which the Board was required to decide the case. John Yodice was a little less sanguine about the slam-dunk win I thought we had. Yodice has been watching the Board operate for many years. I should have listened."*

Bailey closed his seven-page article with the bad news.

"At 6:10 p.m. on the fateful Friday, Yodice called my office. 'The news is not good,' he said, his voice filled with anger. 'They have reversed.' I was stunned!

In one of the most difficult phone calls I have ever placed, I called Bob. He was crushed, as he had every right to be. His hard-won prize had been snatched away.

When I got to read the Board's opinion, I could hardly hold the pages in front of me. Every rule of judicial review was trashed. Judge Mullins was repeatedly excoriated for things that never happened. To properly dissect this outrageous opinion and order would far exceed the limitations of this article, but the Hoover case is far from over.

More important than the rights of any single pilot is the machinery protecting those rights. I have been uneasy for years because I have repeatedly been told the FAA wins 90 percent of its cases before the Board. It is now clear why. Both the composition of the Board and the power it has grabbed for itself over the years need strong Congressional scrutiny, and some redesign. This is no place to be if due process of law is viewed as a check and control, for due process did not find its way into this appeal. In my opinion, what the Board did to Robert A. Hoover has rubbed luster from the word 'justice', and is, in its most literal sense, a rotten shame."

Bailey's article became a cornerstone of aviation conversations all over the country, and indeed, the world. As the Spring of 1994 proceeded, the appearance of the Bailey/ FLYING magazine article was possibly the most damaging early shot fired in the direction of the FAA's 800 Independence Avenue, Washington DC headquarters. It was certainly not the last, but it has to be one of the biggest "hits" the FAA has taken in recent memory, and certainly the largest in association with a general aviation issue. In so doing, Bailey played Paul Revere, not only riding to Hoover's rescue, but letting pilots worldwide know that "The Feds Were Coming, The Feds Were Coming."

It didn't take long for the aviation media to sense the justifiable paranoia of pilots who saw the FAA targeting Hoover, and were wondering if they were next. It was AOPA Senior Vice President Drew Steketee who may have summed up the growing concern most succinctly in a January 1997 letter to the author. *"This battle was fought not only for Bob Hoover, but for the principal involved. And since Bob is 'the pilots' pilot,' if it can happen to Bob Hoover, it can happen to anyone."*

Some of the more outspoken industry pundits saw the dangers inherent in the Hoover case early on, especially to those aviators who were facing their more mature years. Shortly after the FAA's reversal of the originally favorable NTSB ruling, AOPA Pilot Magazine Editor Mark R. Twombly opined that *"Bob Hoover was forced down by a daunting series of psychological tests designed to measure his cognitive ability. Using a lot of serious scientific terminology to make their case, the government's expert medical witnesses successfully argued that Hoover no longer is mentally up to the task of flying low-level airshow routines. It's not that he can't perform the maneuvers — he put on a demonstration for an NTSB judge. It's that, according to the experts who administered and interpreted the tests for the government, Hoover may not be able to cope with a serious emergency in the midst of his routine.*

Regardless of how one feels about the treatment Hoover received at the hands of the FAA and NTSB, his case could have far-reaching repercussions. For example, one of the FAA's defenses against relaxing its rule requiring airline pilots retire upon reaching Age 60 is that there is no way to accurately determine if a pilot is or is not able to continue to perform in the left seat. Yet, that is exactly how they got Hoover. Will there now be a call for the FAA to institutionalize cognitive ability tests as a possible avenue to doing away with the Age 60 rule?

If that were to happen, it might not be so good for all other pilots. It's not hard to imagine a scenario in which political pressure forces the FAA to require such tests for all pilots reaching a certain age. That would be traumatic, very expensive (Who do you suppose would be billed for such tests?), and undoubtedly would lead to big reductions in the pilot population. All of this is speculation and what-ifs, but thinking about what did happen to Hoover and could happen to each of us has to make you shudder."

Just days after the 1994 Oshkosh EAA Fly-In came to a close, one of the most publicly visible articles to appear about the Hoover controversy was published in a non-aviation media outlet... none other than the *Wall Street Journal*. Appropriately titled *"The Case of The Ace on Ice: Fliers Protest Veteran's Grounding,"* the article was subtitled *"Air-Show Star Bob Hoover, 72, Is Unfit to Fly, FAA Says; Fans Say He Was Framed."*

Daniel Pearl, a WSJ Staff Reporter ventured to Oshkosh and got an ear and eyeful of the controversy that was, by then, in full swing over the Hoover grounding. Pearl recounted some of Bob's war history and his contributions to the world of aviation before

regaling his readers with an outsider's view of the FAA v. Hoover fight.

Pearl wrote that Hoover, then 72, was *"aching to perform"* at the EAA convention in front of their annual gathering of (then) 800,000 people. Explaining that every pilot needs a medical certificate to fly solo and that the FAA had revoked Hoover's after ordering tests on him previously, Pearl indicated that the NTSB had upheld FAA's decision to ground him, saying the aging airmen had a "cognitive deficit" and shouldn't be performing airshows. Pearl succinctly quoted the reaction from the majority of Hoovers fans – *"phooey,"* they said.

Mr. Pearl documented the reaction of Oshkosh pilots, *"Pilots have peppered government officials with protest letters and telephone calls. At Oshkosh, many fans wore buttons reading 'Of Course I Support Bob Hoover, Don't You?' and some charged, red faced, into the Safety Board's tent to say, 'you ought to be ashamed of yourselves.'"*

Quoting the ever-quotable F. Lee Bailey, Pearl said that Bailey was prepared to leave the O.J. Simpson case for a few days to take Hoover's case to the US Court of Appeals, but had yet to send Hoover a bill. *"One of the finest contributors to American aviation was the victim of a series of moral and ethical pig needs,"* said Bailey.

Oshkosh 1994 was the scene of an endearing tribute to Hoover. *The Wall Street Journal* article noted the repeated standing ovations Hoover received and the fact that Air Force Chief of Staff Merrill McPeak had bumped into Hoover behind the amphitheater and offered to give him the Air Force's fitness test in order to support his cause.

Pearl explained that Hoover had earned $500,000 a year as a stunt pilot and was upset to be parked on the ground with 8000 other planes surrounding him, and no opportunity to fly. Additional details about the Oklahoma City airshow, the FAA Inspectors who started the problem and Norbert Nester's testimony filled in some background while describing the "mind games" Hoover was forced to endure while undergoing psychological and physiological testing. Unfortunately, the old saw about Bob's nose was also brought up. The story explained that an FAA neurologist suggested that irregularities in Hoover's brain scan may have been caused by years of drinking, but the WSJ story did explain that Bob got his nose genetically and not alcoholically. This well-balanced story included a quote from James Harris, who ran an association of flight surgeons who disputed the pro-Hoover sentiment by stating that pilots with Mr. Hoovers experience can fly *"by rote,"* until something goes wrong. *"If he crashes into a crowd, killing a lot of people you know who's going to get to the blame,"* continued Harris.

Pearl countered with the possibility that Hoover was a victim of a larger FAA crackdown on older pilots. *"If they catch the biggest fish in the pond, the little fishies will be really impressed,"* said Charles Webber, a Southern California aviation writer who had been involved with numerous skirmishes with the FAA over matters of pilots rights. Another telling quote came from Duane Cole, then 80 years old, a well-known aerobatic pilot who had been grounded after heart surgery. Duane said that *"pilots don't have the same rights as criminals... if you can drive a car why do you need a medical to fly a little airplane from town to town?"*

Pearl closed his article with the notation that more than 99 percent of recreational pilots get their medical certificate renewed and that several active pilots were approaching the age of 100 years. He reported that Mr. Hoover was unsure that he would be interested in *"looping and rolling that long,"* but that he would retire if he ever had a string of poor shows and couldn't regain his form.

Due to the immense numbers of people, many of whom of course were not fliers, who read the Wall Street Journal, this article had a strong impact and brought the Hoover case to the attention of the national media and to many politicians who had heretofore ignored it or not heard of it. Most important, it put the FAA even more visibly on the chopping block, to either defend their actions or reconsider them.

As the pressure built, there was no doubt that many in the FAA were beginning to think that a change was in order.

Many articles used the Hoover fight as the justification for demanding Pilot's Rights reforms and regulatory relief from an often heavy handed FAA. Writing in his "Pilot Law" column for the *California Pilot* newsletter, attorney Jay White expounded that *"When the FAA unilaterally labeled Hoover's situation as a medical problem rather than a pilot proficiency problem, the cards were stacked against him. That is because of the way the system works.*

Here is how the system works against a pilot caught in the FAA's net:

First, in a medical certificate revocation case in which FAA claims that a pilot is not medically qualified, the pilot has the burden of prevailing by a 'preponderance of the evidence' that he/she is qualified to hold a medical certificate. This differs from FAR enforcement procedures in which the FAA has the burden of proving a pilot has committed a violation. Rarely is a pilot able to present sufficient medical evidence to overcome this procedural burden. Hoover, however, was able to present sufficient medical evidence to persuade the law judge that the FAA's medical evaluation was wrong. The judge ordered the FAA to reinstate Hoover's certificate.

FAA was not pleased with this decision and took the next step, an appeal to the full five-member National Transportation Safety Board. This Board has investigative and appeal jurisdiction over a wide range of transportation facilities including railroads, the US Coast Guard, aviation and pipelines. Rarely do members have any substantial aviation experience. The Board has in effect abdicated its duty to review, reverse or modify FAA orders. Sadly, rather than conduct an objective review, the Board usually rubber stamps FAA's orders. That is apparently what happened in Bob Hoover's case.

Hoover has taken the next step of exercising his right to appeal the Board's decision to the courts. His battle is still very much uphill. According to court rules the Court will uphold the Board's decision if it is supported by "substantial evidence in the record." This standard rarely favors a pilot. The court will review the record of the proceedings mainly for errors of law rather than the merits of the case.

What can other pilots do to avoid troubles similar to Bob Hoover's? Before attempting to answer that question, we must identify the problem. The main problem is that Congress gave FAA too much discretionary authority to make and enforce its own regulations and procedures. There is no effective review or appeal procedure which assures that a pilot or other certificate holder will receive a fair hearing.

The solution lies in further action by Congress to curtail FAA's power. Congress can require that FAA's regulations and procedures be fair and reasonable, and that there be an effective appeal procedure This change can be effected IF PILOTS THROUGHOUT THE NATION WILL RISE UP IN CONCERT AND TELL THEIR SENATORS AND CONGRESSIONAL REPRESENTATIVES THAT THE LAW MUST BE CHANGED. The big question then becomes: Are we concerned enough to force Congress to do that?"

EAA's Tom Poberezny, often known for treading the middle of the road and not wanting to upset the apple cart, was aggressive. *"On October 31 (1994) Bob's case was heard before the Appellate Court. People who attended told me his defense was well presented and felt there were reasons for optimism... though knowledgeable legal experts felt his chances of winning were limited. Normally, a decision from the Court minimally takes 45 to 60 days. Everyone was shocked when a decision, against Bob, was handed down in 3 days! It makes you wonder how much of the decision was already made before the hearing. ...If FAA thinks the Bob Hoover case will go away, they are in for a rude awakening. Whether they like it or not, FAA more than ever is looked upon as an organization that is going in the opposite direction from the "kinder and gentler FAA" that has been promoted over the past couple of years. Pilots are concerned. This issue, combined with new medical standards and ATC Corporation proposals, has everyone frustrated."*

Lest I leave the impression that all the aviation media lined up behind Hoover, let me offer you what appeared to the one major exception to the rule... an exception the FAA quoted repeatedly.

Private Pilot magazine Editor, J. Patrick O'Leary, penned a piece on the situation, entitled *"Forget Bob Hoover Already,"* in which he expressed annoyance with the *"public relations machine"* that supported Hoover. Blaming a lazy press for not doing their homework and the fact that Hoover's lawyers were exceptionally vocal, he seemed to be saying that the FAA knew what it was doing and that we (the aero-public) were being duped by slick PR. O'Leary claimed that *"there is nothing in the public record to indicate that the FAA or the Federal courts were out of line."* He also opined, *"That we who claim to be aviation journalists were either too lazy or too biased to walk down to the federal building and make copies of these documents and review them to balance our coverage of events says a lot about the disservice we've done to general aviation."*

He based this lack of balance on the fact that he had read *"Computer transcripts of the decisions of both the initial hearing and the appeal were available through AvSig on CompuServe."* He did not indicate that he had read the full transcript of the original NTSB Hearing and all the evidence of the FAA's false statements, uncertified tests, errors in fact, or the simple fact that all the early medical decisions reached by FAA designated Doctors seemed to favor Hoover's reinstatement. Personally; I think that if he did, he might have reached a different conclusion (something he seemed to verify when I met him several years later). Further; "balance" is a nebulous concept when the facts just don't support an alternative argument. O'Leary is a very pleasant and personable man, so the article seemed somewhat out of character and confrontational, in a way that did not please a lot of the aviation public. He got quite the shock when the mail poured in after that editorial... as quite a number of his readers expressed severe displeasure over it and argumentative statements like *"Am I the only one who's tired of this?,"* and *"It is highly unlikely that you or I will be singled out by overzealous FAA inspectors."*

Personally; while the facts, public record (the FULL record) and other evidence did not support O'Leary's contention that the FAA had acted properly, I was glad to see alternate viewpoints expressed, disagreeable though they might be. But; saddest aspect of this article was not that someone expressed an unpopular viewpoint, but that the FAA exploited it repeatedly as evidence that they had acted properly and correctly.

In other words... the rest of the aviation media/public: journalists, pilots, aviation professionals, aviation associations, lawyers and aviation experts were all wrong... but O'Leary was right... because he supported the FAA's position. Yeah, right... ***Not!***

Chapter 30

RIP: The Court of Appeals and Other Exercises in Futility

*It is only with the heart that one can see rightly,
what is essential is invisible to the eye.*
Antoine de Saint-Exupery

Since the FAA was successful in getting the original NTSB ruling overturned, all eyes were turned to the US Court of Appeals. Lee Bailey addressed this situation eloquently (but then again, when hasn't Bailey been eloquent? Bailey wields the English language as Picasso wielded a brush...) at the 1994 AOPA Expo... *"Now, we are in the United States Court of Appeals for the District of Columbia, and on Monday the 31st of October, we will be the fourth of four cases which that Court will devote 15 minutes per side of oral argument, in a rather narrow window. What we must show at this level, although we never got a chance to be heard except through written briefs before the NTSB, [is] what I thought was the most bullet-proof judicial opinion coming out of a trial court, finding the bad guys to be liars and all the facts in our favor were simply trashed by five political appointees with no judicial experience and obviously little appreciation for the realities of aviation.*

Their opinion was written by a former FAA lawyer named Vivian Weisner and smacks of a brief far more than any judicial writing. But much of the review is closed off at that point. One who would challenge a ruling of the NTSB, or a comparable administrative board, must show a federal constitutional violation and we believe we have a mixture of two. There has never been a case decided anywhere on cognitive impairment of an airman, without the necessary fourth element and that is some conduct which does not meet the norm. This is the first. A trial balloon carved out to nail one person and, therefore, we say it is not only a denial of due process of law, which is one prong of the constitutional rights that all of you, at least assumptively possess, but also the equal protection of the laws.

One of the great principals that we are taught right off the bat in law school is that justice is an elusive concept and somewhat personal: what's just to you might not be just to her. Justice is always to be pursued and admired, but it is not the God of the Common Law. The God of the Common Law is consistency and all that means is that if we shaft you, we will shaft your neighbor that same way. But it is a rule, and it has been broken in this case.

Whether or not three Federal judges, one of whom was once a candidate for the United States Supreme Court, Judge Ginsberg (not the female judge who is up there but one who was considered sometime before she became a candidate), is on the panel along with two other distinguished judges. And what we are going to have to try to show them is that regardless of one's age, for which there is no law outside the airline profession... I believe Steve Wittman has a low-level waiver at the age of 90, I know while we were on trial a person who was about that age was getting his CFII certificate renewed by the FAA.

When the Inspector indicated that his motive at least included a reference to 'that old bastard who got all the credit' and he apparently had gone through his life with none and his resentment of that fact, it became very obvious that age discrimination had wormed its way into the controversy. Coupling that to a special rule to be applied against a special target is supposed to be what America is exactly against and its legal profession is supposed to protect. And that hasn't happened in this case.

Now on a more global basis, we will take the Hoover case wherever we can and that certainly includes, if necessary, the United States Supreme Court. Someone, at some point, is going to have to put a stop to this outrage. By all accounts the Dean of Airshow Pilots in the history of the United States, an icon in aviation who has probably inspired more skilled pilots to be nice people as well as skilled pilots than anyone ever, and a jewel in the crown of what we call American aviation, has been wrongfully and unfairly sullied and somewhere it must be set right. But equally important, as Bob will tell you, this fight is important because a runaway agency of bureaucrats who do not care apparently for the rules, or even in some cases human decency, must be arrested and hopefully rearranged so that these kind of tactics are not visited on anyone less able to fight than a Bob Hoover in the future."

So... how did they do with the US Court of Appeals?

The short answer: After Hoover won the hearing before Mullins, the FAA appealed, and the NTSB set aside the ALJ's decision, siding with the FAA's edict that Hoover was not fit to fly. This meant, of course, it was again Hoover's turn to appeal.

...Which also meant, of course, that it was again time for the FAA to argue its position anew in a brief (and oral argument, of course) issued to the US Court of Appeals.

The legalese written here was nothing new. It began with a discussion of the Federal Aviation Regulations concerning pilot medical certification and the neurological requirements for an unrestricted second-class medical certificate. It also reiterated the authority of the FAA to revoke a pilot's certifications in an emergency situation.

When it got around to actually talking about Hoover, the brief began by stating what a wonderful pilot Hoover was, even acknowledging him as the "Dean" of airshow pilots. When the airshow in question came up, the subject of his performance was positively skipped over, saying only that two Inspectors submitted reports about him, which in turn caused the FAA to ask Hoover to submit to a neurological examination.

From here, the FAA repeated its stories and support for their physicians, just like a school child who has repeated a poem so many times he can say it from memory: Elliott is wonderful. Hoover did badly on Elliott's tests (no mention, of course, of his allegedly poor testing environment). Hoover's SPECT scans indicated hypoperfusion (no mention, of course that this hypoperfusion could have been caused by trauma many years ago – and

he'd been flying just fine since then, thank you very much). Testing, the FAA doctors said, indicated cognitive impairment. Then it was time to discuss the hearing before Judge Mullins, where the appeal again said that Hoover had a cognitive impairment. The brief summarized Hoover's arguments as follows: He did not perform badly at the airshow in question, and *"he argued that the two FAA Inspectors 'conspired' to get him, and that one of them 'hates' tall, skinny men."* (Makes him sound rather paranoid, doesn't it?)

As for Dr. Elliott's testing, it only said that Hoover *"claimed"* he didn't know the testing would take all day, he was under a lot of stress, and Dr. Elliott didn't offer him enough breaks (that all sounds rather chocolate coated, doesn't it?). Additionally, it said *"several airshow performers"* (not "top" airshow performers, or ACE airshow performers, or even *"venerable"* airshow performers... just *"several."* It could have been some no-name wing-walker from Hoboken) testified that they saw nothing wrong with Hoover's performance.

As expected, it skimmed over Hoover's physicians' testimony, saying only that they testified that Hoover was average for his age and/or that his scans did not raise cause for concern. It then discussed Mullins' decision, saying he noted Hoover's flying demonstration and the testimony of other pilots. It also mentioned Mullins' credibility findings about the FAA doctors who had monetary interests with them.

It then discussed the NTSB's reversal of that decision because the Board *"found the FAA had presented 'overwhelming evidence of a cognitive deficit that makes [Hoover] unqualified to hold an unrestricted airman medical certificate'"*... and the Board held that Hoover never rebutted this evidence.

The Board, the brief said, held that Mullins erred by accepting *"Hoover's overly broad and unsubstantiated suggestions as to the veracity of the expert opinions offered"* by the FAA and that he (Mullins) did not review the medical records carefully enough, which again, they asserted proved that Hoover had a cognitive deficit that left him unfit to hold an unrestricted second class medical certificate. It was then time within the brief to list a summary of the FAA's argument — basically beating a dead horse for legal purposes — about Hoover's medical impairments and the credibility of their doctors.

When it came time to address Hoover's actual flight performances, the brief said the *"NTSB correctly recognized that whether Hoover is a skilled pilot or can perform well in a demonstration is not the issue here"*... saying that the FAA must deny a certificate if the applicant has a condition that could be expected to create an *"unacceptable risk."*

It inferred that Mullins ruled for Hoover because he was *"star-struck"*—*"the ALJ ruled for Hoover in large part because he was impressed by Hoover's skills and experience"*, again saying that he didn't take the risk factor from a cognitive impairment into account. Hoover's flying abilities, it said, were *"over-learned skills"* that Hoover may be able to compensate for in *"the short term..."*

Then the appeal began to discuss Hoover's neuropsychological testing again and how even the experimental tests that Bailey had objected to were useful to determine Hoover's cognitive skills (or rather, as the FAA would have it, cognitive impairment). The discussion of the tests and the doctors' testimony continued, page after page of the same things we'd heard in the testimony and read in the earlier appeal... all of which was summarized by the FAA's statement that the *"Board properly rejected the ALJ's unfounded rejection of the FAA's expert witnesses."*

In the end, the brief said that *"at bottom, Hoover cannot escape the record and the objective medical evidence in this case"*, concluding that the Board's ruling is plainly supported by *"substantial evidence"* and *"should be affirmed."* So... the decision by the Appellate court on November 3 denied Bob Hoover's appeal (oral arguments were presented on October 31, 1994). Bob Hoover had 90 days to file petition for certiorari review with the US Supreme court. This petition was filed on February 1, 1995. The FAA and the NTSB were allowed to reply to the petition but they did not. The Supreme Court then was to decide on whether to review it or not. In early April, the Supreme Court decided *not* to review it. (It was not entirely unexpected that the Supreme Court would not review this type of case). Hoover's legal possibilities were at an end... and if Bob was going to get to fly again, another route to restoring his privileges was going to have to be taken.

US Aviator magazine aviation writer and attorney Glenn McGovern penned the opinion piece on the matter after the Court of Appeals bailed out on Bob. Glenn is a trial attorney, pilot, aircraft owner and AOPA Panel Member who often represents pilots in FAA Enforcement Proceedings. Living with his wife Elizabeth, and three little co-pilots, in New Orleans, LA, Glenn flies a Cessna 206 and recently completed a major expedition to Alaska in the bird, before losing it in a 1998 flood that destroyed the aircraft.

Herewith Glenn's summation of the matter:

An Aviation Attorney's Perspective
Administrator Versus Hoover: Why We All Lost...

Bob Hoover was recognized as one of the top airshow pilots in the world. He was represented by two of the most respected attorneys in the world, John S. Yodice and F. Lee Bailey. Legal support in the form of amicus curiae (friend of the court) briefs were filed by the top aviation organizations in the US, including AOPA, EAA, Lawyers Pilots Bar Association, and the National Transportation Safety Board Bar Association in a noble effort to protect other pilots' medical certificates.

Medical experts testified on behalf of Mr. Hoover, even going so far as to criticize the questionable tactics and ethics of the opposing FAA-hired medical consultants. An experienced, respected Administrative Law Judge (ALJ), Judge Mullins, maintained the FAA medical witnesses' testimony lacked credibility by having monetary interests with the FAA and because they refused to rely on Hoover's demonstrated flying skills. The Administrative Law Judge believed Hoover's doctors to be more credible and interpreted their testimony that Hoover should have an unrestricted medical.

The NTSB disagreed and found that some of Hoover's doctors did not find that Hoover should have an unrestricted medical certificate since some discussed in depositions and medical reports having Hoover possibly re-tested in six months or a period less than two years. Hoover's MRI and EEG were clean. There was conflicting medical testimony as to his SPECT scans (which measure blood flow to parts of the brain). Therefore, the NTSB found Hoover did not successfully rebut the FAA doctor's testimony that Hoover may be unfit to fly within two years' time period.

The original investigation of Hoover's medical incompetence was called into question by two FAA Inspectors, namely Clint Boehler and James Kelln, who allegedly conspired to have Hoover grounded and then covered up their collaboration. Their re-

ports alleged Hoover's flying had deteriorated at an airshow in June 19-21, 1992, at the Air and Space Show in Oklahoma City, Oklahoma. Boehler and Kelln never testified at the administrative hearing. Norbert Nester, a fellow FSDO Inspector, testified at the hearing as to the other Inspectors' actions, verifying their conspiracy to issue separate independent reports of Hoover's alleged incompetency at the airshow.

Expert airshow pilots testified that on the dates in question, Hoover's airshow act in Oklahoma was flawless, as usual. The Administrative Law Judge allowed an actual performance of Hoover as part of the hearing, with Hoover flying with a qualified airshow pilot on board. The NTSB sharply criticized the ALJ for allowing this demonstration since Hoover's medical was revoked, even though an extremely competent pilot-in-command was on board the aircraft. Again, Hoover's performance was flawless. Even the counsel for the FAA lauded the performance and asked for Hoover's autograph at the end of the demonstration, despite the fact that the FAA counsel had previously tried to block the performance. (The demonstration was held at the only airport where FAA approval was not required to do low-level aerobatics.)

The NTSB reversed the ALJ's decision, ruling against Hoover and upholding the revocation of Hoover's medical certificate. The NTSB reversed the ALJ, stating that Hoover's demonstrated ability was irrelevant and the ALJ did not allow in and properly evaluate medical testimony proffered in the record.

The US Court of Appeals for the District of Columbia denied a petition for review of the NTSB decision of February 18, 1994, and its appeal judgment filed on Nov 3, 1994, held: "petitioner's license was properly revoked..."

Not just Bob Hoover, acknowledged by both sides in the legal appeals as "Dean of Airshow Pilots", lost in this case. We all did and are just as vulnerable as Hoover.

Cause For Concern

A complete analysis of the case here is beyond the scope and breadth of this article. The purpose of this article is to highlight a few points that concern myself as a pilot and as an attorney who represents pilots. They are a few new "rules" that arise from the Hoover decision that concern me — and should concern you.

Rule #1: Medical experts for the FAA are allowed to deviate from accepted medical, ethical, and state law standards yet remain credible.

On page A400 of the ALJ trial transcript, Dr. Elliott, an FAA-hired consultant, allegedly told Hoover the neuropsychological tests would take four hours, and that: "... nothing I'm going to give you today that is going to have anything to do with your losing your license, so don't worry about that." (Transcript A402)

Dr. Elliott admitted misrepresenting to Hoover about the impact of the tests on his medical. (Transcript A180)

In fact, Hoover testified the testing took place beginning at 8:00 am and continued until 5:00 pm with only a break for a drink of water and a restroom stop at mid-day. (Transcript A400)

It was argued by Hoover's attorneys that California law provides obtaining a consent to examine by the use of false pretenses vitiates the patient's consent. (Hoover

Brief, Court of Appeals p 23). Such actions were also alleged violations of the APA Ethical Code. (Transcript A571)

The testing of Hoover in a continuous manner, without food and only brief breaks at noon and not again until 5:00 pm can have a deleterious effect on test results, and cause a marked deterioration in performance on the tests, according to Dr. Appel. (Transcript A569-570)

Dr. Elliott also refused to provide test data to Dr. Appel despite the fact that Hoover signed a consent for medical information to be given to Dr. Elliott by Dr. Appel. (Transcript A573-575, Dr. Elliott A198)

Dr. Elliott also testified he had given Hoover a computer version of the Wisconsin Card Sorting Test, but it was not a research version. Dr. Appel contacted the manufacturer and learned that only research versions had been shipped by the manufacturer. Dr. Elliott then admitted on the second day of trial that he administered a research version. (Transcript A54,57,156) Dr. Appel also testified that Dr. Elliott had not computed Hoover's scores properly and therefore he did not fail 8 out of the battery of 11 neuropsychological tests as Dr. Elliott testified. Yet the NTSB Board reversed the ALJ's finding regarding Dr. Elliott's lack of credibility.

Rule #2: There are no rules of evidence in NTSB administrative proceedings so all evidence can be admitted against the pilot.

The ALJ rejected the CogScreen (Computerized Cognitive Screening Battery, an FAA-funded test) experimental cognitive testing methods used by Dr. Elliott, as inadmissible due to the test's experimental nature. The NTSB reversed the ALJ and found that the Federal Rules of Evidence do not apply and any relevant evidence should be admitted. (JA 982-983) Since Hoover was found by Dr. Elliott to have a weak performance on at least eight of the CogScreen tests, this was offered and accepted by the NTSB as ample evidence of his impairment. (JA 710)

It should be of concern to all pilots that the Federal Rules of Evidence do not apply to NTSB decisions. FAA Counsel argued that the test would be allowed into evidence under the Federal Rules, but the Federal Rules don't apply anyhow, thus requiring the admission of this experimental test into evidence. (JA 983)

Rule #3: Any appeal from an NTSB decision is extremely limited.

A pilot is entitled to a hearing before an ALJ. He can then appeal to the NTSB. He can then appeal to the US Courts of Appeals — such as Hoover did. But this type of appeal is extremely limited. The test is whether the NTSB could have fairly and reasonably found the facts as it did. Robinson v. NTSB, 28 F 3d 210 (DC Cir 1994). Again, such an appeal is extremely limited and provides limited judicial review — limited protection for the pilot appealing a NTSB decision.

Rule #4: The NTSB accepts all FAA Medical witnesses as credible automatically provided they are qualified as experts.

The NTSB now automatically accepts the testimony of any medical expert as truthful after the expertise of a witness is established. Qualifying someone as an expert is usually relatively easy upon showing the expert will aid the trier of fact. The Board can only then evaluate the expert testimony on the basis of logic, depth, and persuasiveness.

Petition of Doe, 4 NTSB 84, 90 (1983), aff'd, 732 F 2d 163 (9th Cir 1984).

In other words, once an expert is qualified, the Board cannot find he or she is lying or is biased due to monetary contractual considerations, as a matter of law, under this line of cases. This view is somewhat unique to NTSB proceedings and ignores what occurs in the real world. (Real trial lawyers don't fight with guns, they fight in court with hired experts.) It also greatly limits the trier of fact, the ALJ, as to what he can rule — thus forcing the ALJ to accept questionable (perhaps extremely highly-overpaid), expert testimony. The ALJ's main job, the judging of credibility of the witnesses, is severely destroyed under Doe and its prodigy. A pilot now appears to have little protection from "pseudo" testing methods that have limited acceptability.

Rule #5: The system of pilot medical review needs revision.

The whole process of pilot certification and appeals needs serious review. Misconduct by FAA Inspectors was overlooked as being irrelevant. (FAA Appeal Brief, p 34). Questionable testing procedures were used under improper circumstances, but were totally overlooked, despite possible violations of ethical standards that could have affected the results of the tests. The review powers of the ALJ's are unreasonably curtailed due to NTSB decisions.

Additionally, the whole process is too expensive in that it requires an individual pilot to exceed the medical expert resources of the FAA — and then probably still lose. The proposed changes to the medical rules will greatly broaden the FAA's discretion to revoke a medical certificate on psychological grounds. The controversial CogScreen test was developed by the FAA (who funded the Georgetown University research that developed the test). We all may face CogScreen after the Hoover case.

Conclusion: We All Lost

Was safety enhanced? Why did the Civil Aviation Authority in Australia grant Hoover a commercial medical after examination when it knew the FAA denied him a medical certificate? What of the impropriety of the FAA Inspectors who triggered this case? More questions are raised than are answered by the Hoover matter. Why did Hoover's AME, a highly-respected doctor who cleared Hoover to fly, tell Hoover to fight the revocation of his medical in a telephone conference call if there was no medical impropriety? Is CogScreen to be used in all commercial pilots future medical examinations? Is lack of functional impairment and a pilot's ability totally irrelevant? Are different medical standards to be applied to all commercial pilots depending upon the perceived risks of the pilots' primary type of flying? Will all cropduster pilots, helicopter instrument pilots, Learjet pilots, (and perhaps ALJ's who rule against the FAA), be routinely CogScreened?

One thing is certain. Pilots' trust in the FAA and NTSB has been lost. New rules have been created, for better or worse.

Chapter 31

Payback: The FAA Learns Some Hard and Embarrassing Lessons...

"Injustice anywhere is a threat to justice everywhere."
Martin Luther King, Jr.

Amazing things happened as the Hoover case went more and more public... Pilots and other aviation professionals, who (until this matter became truly public) tended to be a fairly silent lot, even when their most sacred of oxen were being gored, all of a sudden seemed to come to something of a group understanding... they'd had enough!

No place was this more evident than at the "Meet The Boss" conferences that occurred at the two major EAA Fly-ins each year. At the Sun 'n Fun fly-in each spring, and at the much larger Oshkosh EAA fly-in each summer, it had become customary for the FAA Administrator or a person with significant authority from the FAA to give a speech, answer questions, and deal directly with their constituency.

The format has been somewhat formulaic. The current FAA Administrator gets to speak to the audience from behind the lectern, as his or her image is projected in a larger-than-life fashion on a huge video screen to the rear of the auditorium. This room is often filled with pilots, aircraft owners, aviation journalists, EAA members, various VIPs from the FAA, NTSB, and various aviation associations, as well as a number of people who simply have an interest in aviation. These conferences are often packed to the gills, and tend to become a wonderful place for anyone with a grievance or a "hard" question to try to get a serious answer from the "Boss." But to keep in mind that "try" is the operative word here...

While retired Gen. Thomas C. Richards initially ruled the FAA when the Hoover matter was instigated, his term was a short one (and ended with the departure of the outgoing Bush administration), and it fell upon the shoulders of new FAA Administrator David Hinson to deal with the aftermath of the Hoover decision. Hinson made a habit of being accompanied by at least half a dozen associate administrators or other senior FAA officials, to whom he often diverted questions according to the expertise espoused by each. If a person had a question about air traffic control matters, Hinson would rarely answer such a question directly but referred to the Associate Administrator who handled air traffic responsibilities... and so on for medical questions, legal questions, airport questions, etc.

The FAA presence is always professional, somewhat uniform (even to the point of wearing similar golf shirts and slacks), and is usually preceded by an introduction by either the EAA president (these days, Tom Poberezny), or the fly-in director. Depending on the severity of the matters at hand, the FAA Administrator usually launches into a speech of varying length, describing current events, recent initiatives, and whatever they feel they need to get off their chests right away.

We must note that the Administrator's speech length seems to be closely associated with the anticipated controversy ahead. In other words, if the Administrator expects many questions, the speech gets longer, and the time available for questioning is appropriately shorter. Nobody said the Feds were dummies.

The proceedings are closely controlled. Once the FAA Administrator opens the meeting to questions, only those who have caught the attention of one or two FAA personnel with mobile microphones are allowed to address the Administrator, and the selection process seems a bit less than arbitrary. Often-times, questioners with reputations for tough questions are shut out, or forced to endure long waits before they get answers to their questions. However, once one gets the chance to ask a question, anything goes... and while the Administrator can often give a "political" answer (in other words, an answer that has little to do with the target of the question), or pass the question off to an underling, Hinson (in particular) often met such questions head-on and attempted to answer them in the first year of the Hoover controversy – but became increasingly less specific as the controversy wore on. One other customary feature of these events was the fact that as the questioning proceeded, the questions often got more and more difficult.

Meet The Boss—1994

Heading into Oshkosh 1994, the FAA could not have been feeling comfortable with having to face the public. In the case of the 1993 "Meet the Boss" forum could more likely have been entitled "Beat the Boss" as a number of pilots, fed up with FAA double-talk and a lack of fair play, took on Acting FAA Administrator Joseph Del Balzo and gave him a serious tongue-lashing... a political anathema, for sure.

By the Summer of 1994, questions were being asked quite publicly about the Hoover matter. At Oshkosh 1994, Hinson answered the easy questions, referred the hard ones to his deputy assistants, and answered the unpleasant, emotional ones with what was to become his usual *"Please send me a letter or give Tony (Broderick) your name and address and I will get back to you."* Hinson rarely seemed to honor that commitment, although no one really knows whether that occurred through carelessness or the fact that these tasks were usually detailed to an underling, who might promptly forget all about it. Aviation Lawyer/writer Glenn McGovern noted that such statements always seemed like a "nice touch."

McGovern also noted that Oshkosh 1994 was where Hinson perfected his soon-to-be common technique of answering Hoover questions with "I can't talk about that now for legal reasons." He only used it once in 1993 when he was asked about the Bob Hoover case (and shortly before he was officially confirmed as FAA Administrator). Hinson's comment then was he could not talk about the matter since it was in litigation. He got plenty of boos for that one and the dissatisfaction of the pilot community over getting put

off began to grow.

These meetings became intriguing ways to judge the climate of the pilot community. As the Hoover fight wore on, pilots started showing up with buttons and t-shirts proclaiming such sentiments as "Let Bob Fly" and other protestations. Speakers became more evasive as the questions got more pointed... and the "Meet the Boss" meetings became battle grounds for all that was wrong with aviation.

Meet The Boss—Spring '95

Aero-Writer McGovern wrote about the 1995 Sun 'n Fun Fly-In for **US Aviator** and started his coverage off with the admonition... *"There were no... bright spots at the Sun 'n Fun FAA forum this year. In fact, the Administrator and his staff were extremely low-keyed; Hinson looked fatigued. It was almost depressing."*

McGovern noted our concern about the plight of FAA Inspector Norbert Nester, who was already in very hot water with the FAA for coming to Hoover's defense and writing the Administrator about his misgivings and intimate observations of the Hoover fiasco. *"Questions came first from* **US Aviator**'s *own editor, Jim Campbell. Campbell asked about the Norbert Nester letter, wherein Nester, an FAA employee/Inspector and witness for Bob Hoover, accused the FAA of certain falsifications regarding the Bob Hoover medical/legal fiasco in a published letter to Hinson. Campbell pointed out that Bob Hoover is flying airshows outside the country with top airshow pilots, who are of the opinion that Hoover is flying at peak performance. Campbell asked why, taking that into consideration, the FAA still does not allow Hoover to fly. In response, Hinson said that the FAA is engaged in conversations with Mr. Hoover and that they have "proposals" and are working with him. The audience was silent and unresponsive."*

Not content to see the FAA dust off the public this way, McGovern decided to air some of the FAA's own dirty laundry and expose what appeared to be a double standard. Glenn launched into questions about an embarrassing incident in which Hinson was personally involved, regarding an aircraft incident...

"I tactfully asked about a 'hypothetical FAA Administrator' (i.e., Hinson), who went into Illiama, AK, in an FAA King Air; this aircraft was allegedly damaged while taxiing in loose gravel with Hinson riding in the left seat of said King Air, accompanied by an Anchorage FAA Office pilot in the right seat. Hinson was asked, after going through the resulting FAA investigation and experience, whether his views on FAA pilot enforcement had changed, and whether he had filed a NASA 277 Form. Hinson responded jokingly that he would give a "hypothetical answer." A roar of laughter ensued in the auditorium. An offer to represent him pro bono if the FAA came after him was made, to which Hinson responded in a good-natured manner, 'Of course, of course.'

Hinson stated that he was not pilot in command; therefore, he did not file a NASA Form, which gives a pilot or crew member immunity from FAA enforcement proceedings. Hinson then commented seriously, 'Of course, it changes your views, after you go through such an experience and investigation', referring to the investigation conducted by officials of the FAA after the incident occurred. The investigation concluded that although Hinson was in the left seat of the King Air, was qualified in the aircraft, and was operating the throttles while taxing, he was not pilot in command in the air-

craft.

(Clintonese logic at its best?)

The poor pilot in command in the right seat, an FAA employee who works for the Anchorage Office, and an unpaid Good Samaritan mechanic who improperly attempted repairs to the turboprop's damaged propeller, were not suspended nor fined, but *'counseled.'* Hinson stated that he has *'been flying since 1954, and like every other pilot that's flown, made mistakes, and have done things that I would not do again'."*

Glenn included some comments about our questions of one major FAA cooperative initiative that started well and then went nowhere..." *Jim Campbell of* **US Aviator** *then reminded Hinson of the large user group meeting in Kansas City some time ago. The FAA met with various members of a multitude of user groups who came to Kansas City at their own expense. Campbell said that there were very progressive proposals made and promises were made by FAA personnel to implement those changes. Campbell commented that 'nothing came out of it'. He questioned why the FAA held such a golden opportunity to institute revisions and nothing happened; in effect, Campbell said, the FAA 'blew it'."*

McGovern noted that David Hinson sighed and *again* turned to Tony Broderick. Broderick replied that it was a good experience for the FAA to have received that information from users, and that the FAA staff was working on revisions.

McGovern continued:

"Hinson stated, 'the FAA does need to do more'. He urged aviators 'not to be discouraged because they have participated making their opinions known to the FAA and nothing appeared to come out of it'. (Perhaps the FAA should consult Dr. May, cult consultant, on whether we pilots should be upset.) Hinson stated that 'the solution is more dialogue, not less' and aviators need to 'talk to us.'

At the end of the forum, my daughter Celeste asked me, 'How many of these FAA 'Meet the Boss' forums have you attended?' I told her I had attended a number of them over the past eight years at both Oshkosh and Sun 'n Fun. She looked puzzled and said; 'I don't know why you go to these every year. Nobody from the FAA wants to do what the pilots say, and all the pilots do is complain. The airshows are more fun.'"

Meet the Boss—Summer '95

The "Meet The Boss" confab at Oshkosh was expected to be a bit of an FAA bloodletting, as recent events had come together in embarrassing ways for the Feds, and they were none-too-pleased to have to deal with them.

US Aviator's coverage noted that *"Almost everyone agrees there should be changes in the FAA.... Pilots complain of heavy-handed FAA enforcement and a lack of basic pilots' rights. Even Congress wants to make changes in the FAA due to its plethora of problems: the Bob Hoover fiasco, ATC radar/communication vacuum tube equipment failures, Dr. May and his "FAA executive cult," the sexual harassment suits that followed, the Broderick bogus parts publicity, and "Primetime" and "Dateline" investigations of the FAA's practices, to name a few. But David Hinson and his bureaucratic entourage resisted the inevitable changes that are coming to the agency. It was no surprise, then, that the public relations tactics used by the FAA at the "Meet the Boss" forum at 1995's EAA convention* *vere different. A public relations offensive was launched at Oshkosh. On July 31, 1995, David Hinson first held a press conference announcing changes for the self-certification of Recreational Pilots, then he met the public at the Meet the Boss forum."*

Once again, Glenn McGovern penned the political coverage for **US Aviator**, noting that *"This year, Hinson further refined his public relations technique by adding some new tactics. Of course, he still employed his 'I can't talk about that for legal reasons' when asked about the proposed changes in Part 67 medical standards. But he displayed a new technique of sarcastic comeback when dealing with a question from US Aviator's Jim Campbell, reminding Campbell that not everyone agreed with him! Hinson also brought along Democratic Congressman Oberstar to give a supportive speech that in effect said, 'Sure the FAA's got problems but give 'em more money. I trust David Hinson. The agency will work them out.'*

Hinson went even further, giving out awards to new aircraft manufacturer Chris Heintz of Zenair for their certification of the CH 2000 airplane, and to EAAers who helped make a new Advisory Circular and video for homebuilders about test-flying experimentals. This made him look like a nice guy and afforded less time for hard questions."

Pilots were disappointed with Hinson's presentation and tactics. An FAA Inspector summed it up best afterward: *"Hinson had some good, positive announcements, but they somehow got lost in Hinson and Dr. Jordan's poor handling of the Part 67 medical revisions and the Hoover mess. Hinson is getting bad advice and is totally insulated from the pilots' feelings."*

Glenn reported that *"Hinson opened the floor for questions, wiped away perspiration, and took a slug of water, expecting the worst—and it came. The first question was asked: 'Would [you] bottom line it and state when [you] are going to reinstate Bob Hoover?' Hinson looked down at the lectern, frowned, then smiled with teeth clenched as applause erupted for over 40 seconds. The Administrator then said in conjunction with Mr. Hoover's working directly with the FAA, that he directed the flight surgeon to engage in a third alternate set of medical advice from very experienced and reputable physicians who have not been involved in this, so that they may offer an independent, unemotional opinion. He asserted that we would have that opinion from a completely good, different set of medical references within eight weeks. If Mr. Hoover was deemed okay, he could fly. Applause erupted again. Hinson recognized that 'Bob is here and [he] has known him for a long time.' Hinson stated the man is about his issues, his business; and if anyone wanted to talk to him, please do so, because Hinson wouldn't speculate about his condition."*

Next Hinson stated, 'Let's call on this next gentleman because he has been very patient,' pointing to Jim Campbell, publisher/editor-in-chief of **US Aviator**. *Campbell asked, 'In light of several problems with the FAA in the past, of the 'gang that can't shoot straight' [i.e. the FAA], including the Dr. May 'cult,' incidents involving the San Antonio FSDO, prosecution of A&P students, reports of FAA Inspectors exceeding their authority by breaking into airplanes, such as Mr. Peshak, and the Bob Hoover case... it seems that these are incidents where the FAA breaks faith with general aviation. It used to be that general aviation pilots had breakfast on Sundays with FAA personnel at fly-ins.*

Now, the trust is broken.'

Campbell continued, saying that 'hearsay evidence is used against pilots in enforcement proceedings, pilots do not have a right to counsel and are denied other basic constitutional rights, and there is no trust that will ever occur until this is changed. There is a Pilot's Bill of Rights, which was given to you. Is there some way that we could get together with you on this and work together?' Long, loud applause and hoots emanated from the crowd. Campbell further questioned Hinson as the applause subsided. *'Is the FAA ready for a new NPRM for the Pilot's Bill of Rights?'* Hinson lost his patience and snapped, *'Jim, you have a viewpoint but it is not shared by everybody.'*

A loud round of boos immediately ensued with people chanting, 'Yes, it is' (indeed, Hinson was forced to step back from the podium for a few moments as the yelling, catcalls and chanting demonstrated that he had made an error going on the attack against such comments).

The Administrator was taken slightly aback: 'We have to operate in a regulatory law environment. You make it too simple. It would take more than a simple NPRM to do this.' Hinson agreed that he shared the concern about mutual trust, but that *'It is not as easy to implement as he [Campbell] stated.'* Then, as Hinson has done before, he suggested that Campbell write to him to explain his position further, as he is not an attorney. A brief round of applause broke out again when Hinson promised to meet with Campbell concerning the Pilot's Bill of Rights. Hinson broke this promise last year."

He broke it again in 1996... and 1997.

General Aviation News & Flyer columnist, Darryl Phillips (one of the more outspoken industry pundits we've run across with exceptional expertise in avionics matters) opined *"Anyway, Mr. Hinson eventually got to the questions. It was much the same as last year. The first question was about Bob Hoover. As you've no doubt read elsewhere, a third panel of doctors will issue a recommendation as to his fitness to fly.*

There had been a rumor circulating at Oshkosh that FAA would return Mr. Hoover's certificate in a flightline ceremony and Bob would lead off the airshow, but like so many other rumors it proved to be untrue. My guess is, if the medical certificate is returned at all, it will be at the AOPA convention this fall in Atlantic City. But FAA will never have a more positive PR opportunity than Oshkosh 95. **They blew it.**

Last year the matter of the Pilot's Bill of Rights was raised. It came up again this time, and again Hinson said he would be happy to discuss it privately. Not much progress on that score."

The ever-insightful McGovern targeted some of the reasons for Hinson's seeming aloofness from the general aviation community and the reason he seemed reluctant to deal with certain issues head-on. *"To compound the problem, Hinson seems to have surrounded himself by Assistant Administrators who attempt to insulate and protect him from any controversy. Apparently, they do this to keep him away from issues that may cause him political problems. Hinson's administration is like the proverbial ostrich protecting itself by sticking its head in the sand. Ostriches can't fly; Hinson's policies will not help general aviation pilots fly either."*

After the forum, Glenn noted that a pilot complaining about Hinson's performance asked me, *'Should I write FAA Administrator Hinson a letter?'*

'Nope,' I said.

'Why not?' he persisted. I replied, *"Tony Broderick gets in there before anybody, so [Hinson] will probably never see the letter."*

My own coverage was fairly brief but related some of the political machination that led up to the 1995 Oshkosh convention... Entitled "What About Bob", I noted that

Bob had gotten screwed out of a medical certificate again, "...*and in an infuriating man-ner. Bob spent thousands of dollars on new tests with doctors the FAA selected, with the reported assurance by air surgeon Jon Jordan that if there was no deterioration from previous testing, Bob would get his medical reinstated. Bob made the mistake of believing him. Bob hustled like mad to make Oshkosh, even spending more thousands (of dollars) getting his airplane ready for a possible airshow appearance. But after reportedly scoring well on these arduous tests, Jordan copped out and turned him down... kinda.*

According to Bob, he was turned down just prior to Oshkosh... which I immediately posted to the Internet, America Online, CompuServe, and then broadcast far and wide, even appearing on a national radio talk show for a solid hour pleading Bob's case. Jordan reportedly called Bob back after hearing of my efforts, expressing anger that Bob had talked to me 'and broken faith' with him. Then Jordan tried to tell Bob he had not been turned down after all, but that his case would be referred to an independent review board outside the FAA... which, of course, would still be chosen by the FAA and be all too aware that the FAA has turned him down repeatedly in the past. Sounds real objective, doesn't it?

So... there is a tiny ray of hope in that Administrator Hinson has indeed promised to designate an outside panel to review Bob's grounding and report their findings to Hinson. Yes, this panel will be appointed by the FAA and we real people will have no say in the matter... nor does Bob, for that matter. Frankly, all this really seems to be is yet another delaying tactic designed to see if the public will lose interest in this case. I don't expect we will, but the FAA will find that out shortly. Worse, though, is this: Bob has now missed Oshkosh and will assuredly miss the Reno Air Races... two of his favorite venues, and a real blow to his airshow business cash flow. I don't know how many hundreds of thousands of dollars Bob has been deprived of by now, but I assure you the amount has to be considerable. In the meantime, Bob is still flying shows in Australia and Mexico... and rumor has it that shows in Japan are pending."

It wasn't the FAA's best moment... but the stage appeared to be set for the FAA to do *something*... and it already appeared virtually certain that they would have to relent or provide incontrovertible evidence to keep him grounded. The public pressure was peaking, pilots and aviation fans were writing their political reps in record numbers and the fight was even getting air time on television and radio, making the FAA's anti-Hoover stand a public embarrassment to a Clinton Administration that really hated such things – no matter how small the conflagration seemed to be. Something appeared to be ready to break... and knowing the FAA's interest in trying to minimize the damage, it appeared that if they weren't going to get Bob flying for Oshkosh, then the next big PR opportunity would be the upcoming Fall AOPA Expo in Atlantic City, NJ.

Chapter 32

Exercises in "Posterior" Camouflage (F.A.A.=C.Y.A.)

The trouble with being in the rat race is that even if you win, you're still a rat.
Lily Tomlin

There is no question that the FAA was feeling the heat created by the Hoover grounding. It is also no secret that many FAA employees distanced themselves from the decisions of their superiors as much as possible and informal surveys indicated that such Feds were in the majority. All over the country, Feds who were questioned about the Hoover case voiced the party line publicly but privately voiced great doubt about the credibility of their employer's case. Out of forty-seven FAA employees surveyed, informally, between 1994 and 1996, all but eight of those questioned seemed to have problems with the Hoover case... fully. Thirty-six simply said that Hoover should have gotten a chance to fly again. On July 12th '95, as pressure mounted to reinstate Hoover, the FAA decided that it was time to try to repair its somewhat tarnished image. Unfortunately, their biggest effort at that time seemed quite one-sided and a bit creative (or maybe "selective" is a better word) in its retelling of the facts of the matter. Worse, the FAA decided that the press they had gotten from the media had been inaccurate and unfair (though to this day, no member of the press we know has ever been given any specific facts to dispute), and sought to re-write the previously documented history of the case.

The FAA statement was simply entitled "***Robert A. (Bob) Hoover***":

On March 31, 1995, the Supreme Court of the United States declined to review the airman medical certification case of Mr. Robert A. (Bob) Hoover. This exhausted the famous aviator's administrative and legal options for contesting the Federal Aviation Administration's (FAA) revocation of his airman medical certificate. The furor created by the agency's action has been most unfortunate, particularly because much of it has been based on misunderstanding created largely by articles written in the aviation press by persons who remain very loyal and partisan to Mr. Hoover or, when legal remedies failed, who apparently sought to obtain reversal through public outcry.

As a regulatory agency, the FAA must meet its responsibilities for public safety even when unpopular, but it is limited in its ability to explain and defend its decisions in the face of determined attack and distortion of its actions and motives. This paper represents an effort, within the bounds of Mr. Hoover's privacy as delineated by public disclo-

sures in his legal briefs and hearing before the National Transportation Safety Board (NTSB), to provide the interested public with the FAA perspective. It is not intended to open debate of the agency's legislative mandate to issue airman certificates "...when the Administrator finds, after investigation, that the individual is qualified for, and physically able to perform the duties related to, the position to be authorized by the certificate."

The Aerospace America Air Show in Oklahoma City during the weekend of June 19 through 21, 1992, was, as usual, attended by Federal Aviation Administration (FAA) officials. Two veteran Aviation Safety Inspectors, individuals with many years of service to the agency, viewed the aerial performances from separate vantage points. After Mr. Hoover's first routine, each independently concluded that something appeared wrong. They later wrote that Hoover was "not in good form," "there were serious discrepancies," 'his timing appears to be off," "maneuvers are not crisp," "his maneuvers at times appeared tentative and imprecise." Each of the Inspectors viewed additional performances and observed Mr. Hoover's personal appearance and activities, finally suggesting that he appeared frail with an unsure gait and unwell physically; possibly inadequate for the demands of his air show performances. The question of a decline in his awareness, coordination, and judgment was raised.

Because of their concern for the safety of Mr. Hoover and of the public, the Inspectors discussed their observations with their supervisor and with a fellow FAA employee, an accident prevention specialist. There was agreement that the Inspectors' concerns and observations should be brought to the attention of FAA medical officials. At no time was enforcement action initiated or even contemplated regarding Mr. Hoover's flying activities. The only issues were his health and fitness.

About 2 days after the air show, the accident prevention specialist visited the FAA AeroMedical Certification Division (AMCD) in Oklahoma City and discussed with a staff physician the concerns about Mr. Hoover. A medical evaluation was suggested by the specialist, and the physician asked that a written report of the observations made by the safety Inspectors be submitted. Two months later, on August 26, the Inspectors provided formal statements to the AMCD describing Mr. Hoover's performances and appearance. While this delay was unfortunate, it was a result of the press of other business combined with a natural reluctance to begin an investigation which ultimately might identify an adverse health condition that could end the career of a world-famous, much admired aviator.

There was, of course, appropriate dialogue between the safety Inspectors and exchanges with the accident prevention specialist and their supervisor throughout their consideration of the air show observations. The Inspectors, following proper procedures, however, composed their personal reports separately to ensure objectivity. At Mr. Hoover's hearing before an administrative law judge (ALJ) of the NTSB and in a later magazine article, Mr. Hoover's well-known counsel, Mr. F. Lee Bailey, introduced dubious testimony by another employee who, at the hearing, for the first time implied a plot by the Inspectors to "get" Hoover, supposedly because the Inspectors disliked tall, thin men. The FAA has absolutely no basis to believe that the two Inspectors, long-time government employees, acted maliciously, and this absurd charge properly was ignored by the NTSB.

A letter written later and made public by Mr. Bailey's witness demonstrates his

onfusion regarding the agency's concerns for Mr. Hoover. Since the Oklahoma City air how, these concerns have been about medical fitness; not about improper flying proce-dures. The witness' innuendo that the Inspectors' reports of their observations at the air how were not credible, is belied by Mr. Hoover's own testimony at the hearing. The vitness stated that there was nothing unusual about the performance while Mr. Hoover icknowledged that there were discrepancies but that they were due to a cavitation prob-em with his aircraft. The hearing transcript includes material further suggesting that his witness' testimony was not reliable.

On receipt of the Inspectors' reports, the AMCD immediately wrote to Mr. Hoover equesting that he undergo neurological, psychological, and psychiatric evaluations ac-ording to standard protocols used by the FAA for many years. Mr. Hoover agreed to indergo such testing, and, in coordination with his long-time, personal aviation medical xaminer (AME), it was arranged for a respected psychiatrist, well-known to the agency nd to the medical community, to conduct and coordinate the evaluations. In the re-ponse to a letter about the case from a former administrator of the FAA to the then urrent administrator, it was agreed that any final action on the case would come only ifter review of the complete file by officials in Washington.

Mr. Hoover first visited the psychiatrist for evaluation on September 28, 1992, nd relatively minor abnormalities were found on the mental status examination. Based n these findings, Mr. Hoover was referred by the psychiatrist to an experienced and vell-qualified neuropsychologist for a more comprehensive evaluation. In addition to an Q test, nine standard neuropsychological tests were performed, four of which demon-trated abnormal findings. A developmental version of "CogScreen," a new tool for the valuation of mental function also was administered with consistent findings. The neu-opsychologist concluded that the results were strongly suggestive of cognitive deficits nd that Mr. Hoover was performing in the mild to moderately impaired range in critical reas of cognitive function even though his overall intellectual capabilities were intact. Ie recommended consultation with a neurologist to look for a medical cause for these mpairments. Both the psychiatrist and the neuropsychologist have together and indi-idually examined a great many commercial pilots and are recognized as very well quali-ied in their fields. Neither are consultants to the FAA nor do they have financial or other onflicting arrangements with the agency. (Author's Note: Elliott is reported to have arned as much as $50K a year for his FAA Consults...).

In November 1992, Mr. Hoover was referred by the psychiatrist to a neurologist vho found no abnormalities on gross, clinical neurological examination; on lectroencephalography (EEG); or on magnetic resonance imaging (MRI). Technetium SPECT brain scanning, however, a refined imaging technique, was borderline suggestive f biparietal areas of hypoperfusion/hypometabolism of the cerebral cortex.

After review of the consultants' reports and completion of his rather extensive nterviews, the psychiatrist reported to the FAA on December 21, 1992, that his findings n clinical examination and the results of the comprehensive neuropsychological test-ng, as well as the SPECT scans, "all came up with identical findings of mild neuropsy-hological deficits." Nevertheless, his opinion was that Mr. Hoover was currently fit to old a second-class airman medical certificate but with the recommendation that new SPECT scans be performed in 6 months to a year because he (the psychiatrist) was con-erned that the abnormal findings were some form of "non specific aging pathology," *which might be progressive.*

The medical file with all reports and recommendations was forwarded to the Federal Air Surgeon for review and a determination of eligibility for medical certification. Despite the recommendation received, abnormal findings on neurological testing usually preclude medical certification of pilots. Further, Mr. Hoover customarily performed his flight demonstrations in proximity to thousands of members of the public. Accordingly, additional opinions were sought from the Federal Air Surgeon's staff, outside consultants, and appropriate other experts in pertinent medical fields. The intense discussions included the participation of the neuropsychologist who administered the original test batteries to Mr. Hoover.

One of the most experienced neuropsychologists in aviation, a consultant to the FAA who has examined well over a thousand pilots in his own practice and is a pilot himself, reviewed the raw data and the evaluation reports. His report, dated January 8, 1993, concluded that, based on the very complete neuropsychological evaluation and the data provided, Mr. Hoover clearly had a mild to moderate impairment of cognitive skills, including those of problem solving, mental flexibility, and the ability to modify responses based on feedback. In this consultant's opinion, the level of impairment was incompatible with the cognitive performance expected of a pilot.

Noting the consensus of staff and outside specialists that Mr. Hoover's test results reflected significant pathology, the Federal Air Surgeon concluded that this represented a risk to aviation safety and advised Mr. Hoover and his personal AME by telephone that medical certification could not be continued. In response to Mr. Hoover's personal request, however, the Federal Air Surgeon agreed to hold any formal certificate action in abeyance while Mr. Hoover sought additional medical opinions. Mr. Hoover voluntarily handed over the medical certificate to the temporary custody of his personal AME to ensure safety.

Consulting with a neuropsychologist of his own selection at a major university, Mr. Hoover then underwent new neuropsychological and intelligence testing. Five of 13 tests were repeats of those previously administered by the original neuropsychologist. In his report dated June 4, 1993, the consultant indicated that Mr. Hoover was "showing deficits in several discrete neuropsychological domains." He was "functioning in the impaired range in the areas of reaction time to sequential stimuli, language discrimination reaction time, response reversal-word reaction time, formed discrimination reaction time, divided attention, verbal impaired associated learning, and bilateral grip strength." This psychologist also noted "specific deficits on other tasks that required speeded information processing and cognitive flexibility when faced with competing information." He noted that because of these deficits and because performance was likely to deteriorate with age, "the possibility of long term continued flight appears unlikely." He also noted that a repeat SPECT scan report from June 1, 1993, indicated "focal hypoperfusion," and that the results were consistent with the neuropsychological test results. Mr. Hoover's consultant recommended that Mr. Hoover's "license" be reinstated "on a temporary 3-6 month period during which his current medical and neuropsychological status is closely monitored for potential change."

The FAA's neuropsychological consultant reviewed the results of the new tests in July 1993. He confirmed that the scores did, indeed, reflect impairment and was of the opinion that this was inconsistent with aviation safety. The FAA consultant disagreed

ith the recommendations of Mr. Hoover's neuropsychologist and pointed out that the reas of impairment involved functions critical to the type of flying Mr. Hoover engages . The FAA consultant further observed that the independent psychological test evaluaons as well as the SPECT scans were all consistent in their findings. An FAA consultnt in neurology then reviewed the medical findings. In a report dated August 4, 1993, e neurologist concluded that "there is sufficient evidence of impairment in Mr. Hoover's europsychological performance that he represents an unacceptable risk to aviation fety." Another university-based and prominent neuropsychologist, one of the developrs of CogScreen, reviewed the available information and, on August 24, concluded that edical certification would place Mr. Hoover and others at risk.

Mr. Hoover provided still another evaluation in October 1993, this time from a eurosurgeon and a psychologist with whom he consulted. The psychologist's concluion, despite some abnormal findings, was that Mr. Hoover was not suffering significant ognitive dysfunction. The psychologist did note that on one test Mr. Hoover's score ould be considered "mildly impaired" when compared with people his own age and ignificantly if compared to 40 year old males. The agency's consultant neuropsycholost, however, reviewed the new report and pointed out in December 1993 that this psyhologist had repeated some earlier tests and that the very modest improvement in the cores that the psychologist suggested was likely due to practice effect. This is a phenomnon where test scores improve simply because the individual has taken the same test epeatedly.

Other neuropsychologists and neurologists were consulted, both formally and formally. On the basis of their observations and recommendations, the Federal Air urgeon could only conclude that Mr. Hoover's continued airman medical certification as not appropriate. Of prime importance in the decision was the evidence of impairent on neuropsychological testing, abnormal findings on the SPECT scan consistent ith the neuropsychological test results, and concern for the presence of a significant nderlying neurological disorder, the progression of which well might not be detected efore a critical failure in Mr. Hoover's performance. The observations of the Aviation afety Inspectors, while important in respect to the initiation of the investigation of Mr. oover's medical qualifications, did not play a major role in the Federal Air Surgeon's ecision. At a meeting on December 13, 1993, however, the Federal Air Surgeon's posion was discussed with an attorney representing Mr. Hoover, and he was offered yet nother opportunity to obtain additional medical evaluations. The FAA was prepared to uggest new tests, not previously administered to Mr. Hoover, that might reduce practice ffect and identify any changes in his condition that may have occurred over the past ear. The attorney, however, questioned the utility and expense of additional testing and uggested that litigation now probably was necessary.

Within 24 hours, through his attorney, Mr. Hoover asked for return of his medial certificate. The FAA then issued an Order of Revocation of the certificate based on his edical condition.

Mr. Hoover's attorney quickly filed with the NTSB a notice of appeal from the AA's order. A hearing on the matter was held before an ALJ in Oklahoma City, comencing on January 16, 1994.

From letters and comments in the media, it is evident that the administrative rocess for appeals from enforcement decisions of the FAA is poorly understood. The

NTSB, having review authority over those decisions, uses an ALJ system. These ALJ's ar
employees of the NTSB and operate in accordance with rules promulgated by the NTSI
The ALJ's hold formal hearings at which they receive evidence from both sides of th
issue, review the evidence, and make an initial decision. Either side may appeal the ALJ
decision to the full NTSB for a **final determination in** the administrative process, an
the FAA normally will do so in the case of an adverse decision in a medical certificatio
case. The full NTSB bases its determination on the record compiled by the ALJ and o
appeal briefs filed by the opposing sides.

The NTSB rules, as with any court, are designed to ensure fairness in admissio
and consideration of the evidence and to protect the rights of the individual as well as th
safety of the public as represented by the FAA. The ALJ is bound to remain within th
limits of the NTSB rules in the discharge of his or her responsibilities.

Mr. Hoover's hearing was held in Oklahoma City, Oklahoma. During the 4 day
of hearings, the FAA presented the testimony of the chairman of a university departmer
of neurology, the neuropsychologist who had conducted the original neuropsycholog
cal tests and reviewed the results of the various other test batteries administered to M
Hoover, another neuropsychologist familiar with those test results, and an expert i
nuclear medicine. For Mr. Hoover, a neuropsychologist, a clinical psychologist, and
neurosurgeon testified. Other witnesses described Mr. Hoover's well-known and non di
puted pilot skills, and Mr. Hoover provided his own description of the airshow of June 1.
21, 1992, which was in issue only in that it set in motion an evaluation of Mr. Hoover
medical qualifications. One witness, an FAA employee, implied that there was a plot b
other agency Inspectors to "get" Mr. Hoover because he was tall and thin. The hearin
was marked by a flight demonstration by Mr. Hoover.

The ALJ ruled in Mr. Hoover's favor. The decision was based on the ALJ's inter
pretation of recommendations made by the examining physicians and neuropsychologist
what he perceived as the FAA witnesses' refusal to recognize the relevance to cognitiv
function of Mr. Hoover's performance in piloting airplanes; and the lack of credibility
the FAA witnesses, largely because of what he saw as a monetary relationship with th
FAA. During the course of the hearing, the ALJ made evidentiary rulings that exclude
evidence submitted by the FAA in support of the validity of CogScreen and the CogScree
test results. In addition, the ALJ refused to put into evidence the actual scientific article
that had been misquoted by one of Mr. Hoover's witnesses.

The FAA filed a Notice of Appeal to the full NTSB from the ALJ's decision, an
both parties filed briefs with the NTSB setting out their arguments. On February 1i
1994, in a unanimous decision, the NTSB reversed the decision of the ALJ, upholding th
revocation order of the FAA. The Board concluded that the ALJ's findings were belied b
the evidence and that his analysis of the case was clearly deficient. The Board found tho
many of the ALJ's evidentiary rulings were legally deficient, and, were it not for the fac
that the Board was convinced that the evidence demanded affirmation of the revocatio
order, the Board would be inclined to remand the case for a new hearing before a differ
ent ALJ.

Specifically, the Board found that the ALJ erred in excluding scientific article
offered by the FAA in response to the testimony of Mr. Hoover's psychologist and i
excluding the CogScreen evidence. The Board indicated it was perplexed by the ALJ
apparent belief that the Board didn't want him to review all the medical evidence full

before rendering a decision. The Board also expressed "grave doubts" concerning the ALJ's decision to let Mr. Hoover fly after the FAA's Order of Revocation based on the Federal Air Surgeon having found him not medically qualified. It was critical of the ALJ for ex parte communications with Mr. Hoover's witnesses during the flight. In summary, the Board found that the testimony of the FAA expert witnesses was far more persuasive than the testimony of Mr. Hoover's witnesses and concluded that the FAA had proved by a preponderance of the evidence that Mr. Hoover had a cognitive deficit which makes him unqualified to hold an unrestricted second-class airman medical certificate.

Mr. Hoover petitioned on April 15, 1994, for a review by the United States Court of Appeals for the District of Columbia. This review includes scrutiny of the actions of the NTSB in the case as well as those of the FAA. During this interval, there were many articles in the aviation media about the case, most based on interviews with Mr. Hoover or his supporters and attorneys. Some castigated the NTSB; others complained of some imagined collusion between that body and the FAA. Many charged that Mr. Hoover's rights somehow were violated. Letters of complaint were written to Members of Congress, usually accompanied by clippings of published articles as "proof" of their charges. Even Mr. Hoover's attorney wrote letters to many elected representatives while preparing his case for presentation to the Court of Appeals.

Briefs were filed by both sides, and oral arguments were heard by the Court on October 31, 1994. Only 72 hours later, on November 3, the Court of Appeals denied Mr. Hoover's petition for review, supporting the Board's reversal of the ALJ. The Court stated, "There is substantial evidence in the administrative record to support the National Transportation Safety Board's conclusion that the Administrator proved by a preponderance of the evidence that [Mr. Hoover's] license was properly revoked..."

Despite the clarity of the message sent by the Court of Appeals, Mr. Hoover asked for review by the United States Supreme Court. The Court denied certiorari (declined to hear the case) on March 30, 1995. The FAA regrets the unfortunate reaction of many of the public to this very visible medical certification case and, more importantly, is very concerned about the apparent willingness of this public to accept and believe unsubstantiated charges of invidious behavior by the agency. Editor J. Patrick O'Leary of Private Pilot, however, recently suggested in his column that the public's perception of unfairness in this case reflected its reading of what the aviation press printed, and the aviation press was largely getting its information from Mr. Hoover and his supporters. Mr. O'Leary noted that the FAA presented its story in open court without a public relations campaign and that the hearing transcripts indicated the system had not "gone bad." The FAA will always pursue its necessary enforcement responsibilities thoroughly, fairly, to the best of its abilities, and with consideration for individual privacy.

Within the requirements of safety, an admittedly subjective concept, the FAA strives to facilitate individual participation in flight, whether as an airline or other commercial pilot, general aviation private pilot, or stellar performer such as Bob Hoover. Only occasionally is it necessary to restrict or prohibit pilot privileges, and the FAA does so only after careful consideration of the facts and circumstances and with great reluctance. So it was with Mr. Robert A. (Bob) Hoover.

The summary pretty much fell on deaf ears. All throughout the industry, formerly stalwart defenders of the FAA began to openly question its decisions in the Hoover matter and the FAA started talking, in earnest, to the Hoover camp to find a way to put this public relations disaster behind them. Yes... the facade was crumbling... *FAST.*

Chapter 33

More Chinks in the Armor...
The Facade Cracks Wide Open

*We must use time creatively,
and forever realize that the time is always ripe to do right.*
Nelson Mandela

The FAA's increasing defensiveness took some serious blows as 1994 came to an end and 1995 came in like a lion. To many, it appeared that the FAA case was getting weaker and weaker (amply demonstrated with each airshow Bob flew, flawlessly, down under) but some of the most damaging chinks in their armor came courtesy of their own minions.

Notes On A Review Of The Hoover Papers...

In September of 1994, an extremely well-known British neurosurgeon, a Mr. J.L. Firth (Brit physicians who also earn the title of Professor do not commonly use the appellation of "Doctor", but use "Mister" instead), was invited by Australia's Dr. Robert Liddell to go over the medical file on Bob and render his expert judgement. In addition to his medical expertise, it should be noted that Mr. Firth is also a competition aerobatic pilot and is better qualified than most to be able to render a judgment both on Mr. Hoover's health as well as the potential effects of this airshow routine on his physiology.

Mr. Firth's report looked at various assertions made in the FAA case and commented on them individually. The report consisted of:

1. Delay in filing the reports of Mr. Hoover's alleged inability.
The FAA/NTSB seems to have failed in their responsibility of care both to Mr. Hoover and the American public in that they did not apprehend Mr. Hoover immediately after the Oklahoma Show. If the agents on the spot had any doubt as to his competence he should have been grounded immediately, on the spot, when expert witnesses were on hand. This was essential, if only to cover the FAA's position. To allow him to fly 33 further shows when the FAA's opinion was that he was dangerous brings the whole system of safety surveillance into disrepute. The FAA needs first to address this anomaly and the

dangerous acts that, by implication, at this time are going unreported. Failure in their primary duty of care both to individual and to the public is implicit in their case. Either way, whether Mr. Hoover was at risk or not, they admit that they were negligent both of his and the public's safety and interest. All the more so if, as they allege, Mr. Hoover IS a menace. Sadly, as an admirer of the FAA, they have placed themselves in a "heads they (the FAA) lose, tails he (Mr. Hoover) he wins" situation.

2. What do the observers at the subsequent shows indicate?

At worst Mr. Hoover may have been "off form" at Oklahoma. If so he needed immediate advice to this effect (which at the very least would have demonstrated the FAA as an efficient, caring organization). In the event they have allowed him to confirm his competence in the subsequent series of Airshows before the most expert, critical and outspoken audience and jury in the world—the American Aerobatic and Airshow Circuit (as is remembered only too well). This constituency has effectively advised the Good and Great in the past when it was time for them to bow out.

3. Detailed clinical history and neurological examination by clinically experienced, practiced aviation neurologists have found Mr. Hoover fit to fly.

4. Neuropsychological review is at best unreliable as a test.

A useful tool in the right context, it is less than useless as a test of pilot competence (to our universal disappointment), and in practice may actually be misleading. Its specificity and sensitivity are such that it is inappropriate to use or represent such an assessment as a test. Sadly the FAA has sought to do just that.

5. Neuro-imaging is designed to be coordinated with, and is dependent for its interpretation on, clinical assessment.

6. There are no normals. If one is human one is abnormal to a greater or lesser degree.

7. There are also no absolutes.

Aviation, like life itself, is a risky business. If absolutes are required, no one should fly. It is always easier to say "no." The business of aviation neurology in this context is to accept that an individual can fail at any time (like any other component of the aviation system), but rather than stop all aviation, to logically establish the risk status of each component, here Mr. Hoover. No one has a crystal ball. Our responsibility is to provide reasoned opinion, not summary proscription.

8. If a pilot of demonstrated ability such as Mr. Hoover is to be grounded then by analogy no pilot over 45 years of age should be allowed to fly.

9. The problem is firstly to establish pilot competence (which the FAA accepted in allowing him to fly after Oklahoma and confirmed by their observation of his competence at the 33 subsequent Airshows) and then to relate the individual to some arbitrary level of acceptable future risk, attempting to establish whether the individual satisfies that requirement or not.

10. The minimum requirement for commercial, fee-paying scheduled passenger operation is a risk of not more than $1:10^{-7}$ hours. Mr. Hoover is not seeking such a license.

11. The risk target in military and non-scheduled commercial operations is $1:10^{-6}$ hours. This is the area of his interest, though the $1:10^{-5}$ hours General Aviation safety level is more appropriate to his present activities (for which a Commercial License is required).

12. It is understood that Mr. Hoover is neurologically asymptomatic.

13. Neurologically he has lost his ankle reflexes, in common with most of the adult human population afflicted with the near universal spondylosis which reflects the human condition. There is no suggestion of a systemic peripheral neuropathy. If he had a cortical, intracranial lesion/s as suggested by the FAA's testimony he would have enhanced leg and peripheral upper limb reflexes, which their evidence shows he does not.

14. The Neuro-imaging evoked as evidence of his incompetence is of such poor discrimination, as well as of such low specificity and sensitivity, that it cannot and should not be interpreted in isolation. Indeed their very interpretation depends on the clinical circumstances.

14.1. Mr. Hoover's SPECT appearances are those of a worried individual denied the ability to exercise his legs and buttocks. Had he done so he would have engaged the wrath of the technician conducting the scan for degrading a resting scan. But at the same time had he done so he would have produced related activity in the high parietal and parasagittal areas, the absence of which in his resting scan is considered abnormal (and no one would have noticed).

14.2. The MR appearances reported are within the range of the "normal", accepting that with improving neuro-imaging "abnormalities" can be found in all scans. The key to MR interpretation is the clinical circumstance. "Abnormal" scans are seen in volunteers of indubitable normality. The cortical "atrophy" and punctate high signal (vascular) lesions reported are commonplace in the human middle-aged adult air pilot population.

15. That his parietal cortical function is normal was manifest today when on a social occasion he unwittingly and spontaneously demonstrated locomotor, cerebellar, and association tract skills using the areas in question which would have been a credit to an athlete half his age.

16. There is no doubt as to his static neurological competence.

17. What of his "cognitive" abilities? An opportunity to review him clinically would be welcome. Today however, under observation, he displayed none of the hallmarks of the age or neuro-degenerative dementias or focal deficits so familiar to the neuro-clinician and which are more reliable diagnostically than the whole gamut of neuropsychometry.

18. When in his familiar and practiced element, the air and current air operations, he

could be expected to perform even better. This explains the dichotomy between the aviation and clinical evidence on the one hand, and opinions of those who have not examined him and who have attempted to use neuro-psychometrics as tests rather than tools, or even worse merely re-evaluated the opinions of others rather than going back to the patient—the cardinal rule of the neuro-sciences.

19. RWL's (Liddell) strict attention to his responsibility for maintaining safety in Australian Airspace is commended.

By establishing Mr. Hoover's actual competence and risk, excluding emotion, CAAA has taken the responsible as well as the reasonable option in Australia's interest and in the light of the legislative requirements, however difficult a position this may have placed relationships between the CAAA and FAA.

20. His neurological review, the FAA's lack of adverse comment on the long series of subsequent shows and RWL's observation at Launceston establish his static competence. What of his risk of future acute incapacitation?

The risk factors are:

20.1. Age: *This has several constituents*

20.1.1. *An individual neuro-aging factor, in that all dement with age. Unfortunately for regulating authorities as well as neuroclinicians, there is no constant relationship between age, dementia and a particular individual. Mr. Hoover's performance in heavy/ fast/multi-threat and conflicting LA road traffic under conditions of multiple distraction was impressive today.*

20.1.2. Stroke Risk.

The overall age-related risk reaches the $1:10^{-6}$ hour level in his cohort. However he is fit, lean, does not smoke, is not hypertensive and has no stigmats of hyper-cholesterolaemia. His clinical stroke risk status is that of one <65 years of age.

20.1.3. Increased seizure risk with age.

The low risk in the 20-65 year age group is replaced by an increasing incidence >65 which reflects the increase in cerebral pathology with age. Mr. Hoover is therefore at risk on two scores:

a. Stroke-related seizure. He is at a lower-than-cohort risk for this as a consequence of 20.1.2., above.

b. Cerebral neoplasms.

There is no clinical suggestion of this. He has the superficial hallmarks of one who has spent much time in the sun, but a relationship between solar-related skin reaction malignancy and cerebral or systemic neoplasia has not been established.

20.2. Past History:

20.2.1. Head injury.

It is understood that he had a significant head injury in 1944. No seizure risk factors are reported. Even if they had been present the passage of >18 years indicates that he is likely to be at no greater risk than his peers.

An alternative concern is whether he might still display post-traumatic frontal disturbance. His empathy, continence and legendary courtesy, confirmed today, indicates that this is not a factor.

20.2.2. The suggested alcoholism inferred from a degree of MR demonstrated cortical atrophy.

One would not expect Mr. Hoover to have imbibed any less than his fellow Americans. The fact is that a degree of such atrophy is commonplace in CT and MR-imaging of aircrew. The mechanism has yet to be determined. What is certain is that it is no indicator of aviation competence or the lack thereof. One would wish to view the images, but the statements made suggest a common MR finding which in isolation has no clinical or prognostic value.

21. CLINICAL IMPRESSION

21.1. One cannot express a legally-useful opinion (which holds for many interested parties in this case) without reviewing him both formally and clinically.

21.2. Several general points can be made.

21.3. A non-clinical test of prognostic and "stand-alone" statistical or individual validity in this situation does not exist. If it did, aviation neurologists and other neuro-persons would be superfluous.

21.4. Mr. Hoover appears to represent a risk between the 10^{-6} and 10^{-7} hours levels. This is less than the ALTP requirement but compatible with a CPL and the status of thousands of CPL-holders worldwide.

21.5. In his very demanding field appropriate caution by the Authority is reasonable. This would be best exercised by 6/12 neurological history and review coupled with the degree of ground surveillance of in flight performance maintained in and by the unlimited aerobatic community.

Old pilots of current aerobatic world-championship winning ability and performance, older indeed than Mr. Hoover, are an established feature of the American aviation scene. The members of this community are practiced in their observation, criticism, advice and restriction, when, where and as appropriate.

21.6. A time will come when Mr. Hoover will discontinue his present aviation regime. This would be best determined by personal preference, expectant aviation neurological assessment and expert peer review.

21.7. CAAA's present adherence to the regulations is reasonable.

21.8. The FAA are in a difficult position.

21.8.1. Here an interest has to be declared. For the last 20 years we have been striving to put the neurological dimensions of aircrew licensing on a logical basis. The FAA has

been outstanding in its support of this programme. The present case is completely out of character and out of keeping with their fair, constructive and workmanlike approach, to date.

21.8.2. There is a problem in assessing the effects of age. Age is, above all others, the condition in which one has to "treat the man not the scan." This basic principle and sound practice has been ignored in this case. It has to be said by the same token that many pilots, many years younger than Mr. Hoover, quietly give up their pilot status before reaching 65 of age, realizing that the years have caught up with them. It is an area where pilot status and ability, not the calendar, is the key.

21.8.3. Distressingly, the FAA appears to have failed in its duty of care, both to Mr. Hoover and to the American public, by delaying action on what they now suggest is a serious matter whilst allowing another 33 airshows to proceed without alerting Mr. Hoover, the local organizing authorities or even their own Inspectors at those airshows which followed. The latter seem to have been left in ignorance that there was an area of concern, one to which they should pay particular attention and one on which they should report back to the FAA. This was essential to protect the FAA's interest should there have been an incident at one of those shows. With Mr. Hoover continuing to fly it was mandatory that the FAA observers be able to give contemporary witness as to the continuing quality and safety of Mr. Hoover's flying and general conduct and to demonstrate the FAA's care, operational competence and control over the situation whilst the matter was under review. In the event Mr. Hoover's performance at the subsequent airshows, de facto, established beyond doubt his continuing competence as concern was not reported by the FAA agents present at and reviewing those later events.

21.8.4. Inexplicably the FAA have abandoned their established, reasoned and successful practice of assessing individual aircrew in objective, clinical and engineering terms as components of the overall Aviation System.

21.8.5.1. The detailed clinical and operational assessments available on which to establish both Mr. Hoover's present competence and future risk appear to have been rejected.

21.8.5.2. In contrast clinical tools of doubtful and debatable validity in the particular situation under review have been introduced, interpreted in isolation and represented as infallible tests. Fallible and subjective assessments have been substituted for long-established, well-tried, generally-accepted and hithertofore successful practical methods.

21.8.5. There are several options by which the matter could and still can be resolved fairly and to the FAA's credit.

21.8.5.1. These would be best discussed informally over the telephone.

21.8.5.2. Meanwhile the case has been allowed to degenerate into the ultimate "one for experience" and not only the case celebre par excellence.

21.8.5.3. However if it forces us all to a realistic re-appraisal of Age as a risk factor then something constructive can yet come from this sorry affair and the case could prove a valuable milestone in the development of fair and appropriate means of assessment in the older pilot cohorts.
Signed: **John Firth, Consultant Neurosurgeon**

Because of the foreign origin of this report, it got little play until it was published in **US Aviator** magazine and/or the rest of the aviation media got a hold of it, published it, and commented on it. But... as time wore on and other data was added to the mix, the FAA's case continued to be whittled down in terms of credibility. Still, it was a lot easier for the FAA to discount a foreign Doctor who could not easily rise to his own defense (and, in fact, some clumsy attempts were made to diminish the impact of the report), than if they had to refute someone a bit more local.

Then... one of the FAA's own broke ranks.

The Smoking Gun?

As Hoover's Australian performances caused greater and greater consternation, OKC FAA Inspector Norbert Nester really deflated the FAA bureaucracy with a shot across the bow via a letter to the FAA Administrator, David Hinson.

Fed up with the way the FAA had handled the matter, Nester made a decision that would ultimately impact him strongly. Nester is one brave and forthright guy, but he concluded that "right is right," and put his experiences into writing and sent copies of the letter to members of the media, to boot.

Dated November 27, 1994, Nester's letter stated.

"Dear Mr. Hinson, It is only after two years of remaining relatively quiet regarding the malfeasance that was directed at R.A. "Bob" Hoover that I finally write to you. As the Aviation Safety Inspector employed by the Flight Standards District office in Oklahoma City, OK. who was subpoenaed by F. Lee Bailey to appear at the initial NTSB Administrative Hearings with the Honorable Judge Mullins presiding I am profoundly disturbed at the complete breakdown in our American System of Aviation Regulation.

I have written a number of enforcement investigative reports that have been submitted to the southwest region legal counsel for action all of which had a sound foundation for pursuit by the agency as mandated by FAA Orders. Some of these reports involved the use of alcohol by pilots which ended in serious accidents with substantial injury to the pilot and passengers; others involved documented violations of the Federal Aviation Regulations that called for revocation of the Airman Certificate and each of these EIR's was settled with a lesser penalty that would not be supported by FAA Order 2150.3. Some of these reports are as much as three years old and have not yet been adjudicated to date. One report that comes to mind involved the night drops of sport parachute jumpers in an area that lies between the primary arrival and departure routes to the Will Rogers World Airport. The surveillance that led to this report was generated after years of complaint by local citizens, Airline Pilots and Local FAR 141 Schools in the area. In this particular case our Legal Department chose not to pursue the case when the alleged violators Attorney claimed it was a personal vendetta by myself as the Inspector.

All of the above and many more cases that can very easily be verified by Inspectors in my office are what brings me to write to you. At no time did the Agency bring forward a witness that refuted my testimony or could offer any FAA order or Regulation that would support the Action being taken against Bob Hoover. As an Aviation Safety Inspector I believe that I am bound to adhere to established guidance and not go on a crusade solely for my personal gratification at the expense of the public. To do so would be considered a malfeasance and would subject me to the established disciplinary actions of this agency. To date that has not occurred to the three Inspectors involved in this matter. Clint Boehler, the Inspector who concocted and perpetrated this whole affair, has resigned from the FAA because of his self professed inability to work with this agency and then he was given a Pilot Examiner Designation when he failed to meet the Criteria as set forth in the then current FAA Order 8710.3A. All of this was done by our Office Manager and Operations Unit supervisor against the overwhelming and vehement objections of numerous Inspectors. To make matters worse, the qualification for the designation was done with Agency funds after Mr. Boehler had announced his intended departure from the agency. Thus we have misappropriation of US Government Funds and this has been condoned by all levels of FAA Management because this has been brought to their attention and no action has been taken to correct this matter.

Mr. James Kelln is a GS-14 Inspector who has continued to work in the office and been granted virtually anything he has asked for. Mr. Kelln is the Inspector who corroborated Mr. Boehlers' story and stated that they should be careful so that it would not appear that they had conspired against Bob Hoover. This was only one of the times that I observed the previously named Inspectors double up on an individual airman or operator or even a co-worker solely for the pleasure of creating havoc in the office or for someone.

The real culprit is Mr. Glen Jay Nelson, the Accident Prevention Program Manager in the OKC FSDO as he did not even observe Bob Hoovers' performance because he was inside a hangar during the Airshow involved with a non-FAA-related children's entertainment booth. For your enlightenment when the OKC FSDO management had all but decided there was no technical merit or foundation to the claims made by the first two Inspectors and had decided not to pursue any action regarding Bob Hoover; Glenn Jay Nelson chose to take the only action that would almost guarantee Bob Hoovers' grounding and that was to contact the Airman Medical Branch, and deliver a story that would be sure to cause doubt in the mind of anyone regarding an airman's abilities.

Ironically, Mr. Nelson, as the Accident Prevention Program Manager is compelled by FAA SW Order 3710 to maintain technical proficiency within his specialty. This includes participating in the flight program as an air crew member and meet the medical and flight currency requirements as set forth in agency orders governing the operation of FAA and/or rental aircraft. Mr. Glenn Jay Nelson has not met these requirements for the last thirteen years. As recently as two weeks before the Reno, Nevada Air Races this year, Mr. Nelson was on the telephone conspiring with Dick Angelo, his counterpart in Reno, to cause Bob Hoover more grief and public humiliation. I fail to see where his actions promote aviation safety or could possibly be in the public interest.

From a technical point of view, Bob Hoover did nothing at the Aerospace America Airshow to initiate this type of wrath. He was never sent a letter of investigation regarding an alleged violation on his part, the Aerospace America Management was never con-

tacted regarding his performance either during or after the Airshow and he was never questioned during the event about his alleged questionable performance. I do not believe this is in accordance with any handbook, policy, order or regulation that I have ever viewed or been made aware of since becoming an Aviation Safety Inspector.

Furthermore, Ms. Susan Caron's statements in the NTSB Hearing regarding my impending testimony were uncalled-for, unprofessional, without ethics, and I am appalled that anyone who demonstrated this behavior would be allowed to continue to represent this agency at the national level or remain a member of the bar association.

As a government employee I have been deluged with Mission Statements, Policy Statements, and Memorandum, from Vice President Gore, Secretary Pena, Yourself, the Southwest Region Director, The Director of Flight Standards in the Southwest Region, and local office Managers regarding subjects ranging from reinventing government to sexual harassment and cultural diversity in the work place, demanding that I as a government employee adhere to policy. I have yet to see the FAA adhere to established policy when it was convenient or less troublesome for them to do otherwise, generally to the detriment of employees or the public.

I have received innumerable telephone calls regarding the Bob Hoover Case and am asked almost daily about it and have heard comments from all levels in the aviation community. I can tell you without reservation the mishandling by the FAA of Bob Hoover has been divisive to the aviation world; both between agency employees themselves and the entire aviation world as the American Civil War was to this country, and will probably take as many years to heal.

It was said in one of the many proceedings that Bob Hoovers' hours and years of experience mean nothing with regard to his ability to handle an emergency. If that is true then there is no need for any pilot to adhere to FAR Parts 61, 121, 135, 141 regarding recency of experience, training, and testing, as experience means nothing as it relates to a pilot's ability to handle potential emergencies. I personally am not ready to discount the belief that experience is required to attain certain levels of proficiency. I further do not believe Mr. Hoover has ever failed to demonstrate his ability or proficiency when requested to do so, here in Oklahoma after a year of not being able to practice.

I have been told by many it took a lot of guts to testify as I did; however, I don't think so. I did it because in the words of Wilford Brimley the Actor/Spokesman for Quaker Oats "Cause It's The Right Thing To Do." I'm sure that offered the opportunity to continue to fly and perform Bob Hoover has the common sense, mental capacity, and years of experience to know when to retire gracefully from public performance. I further believe he would willingly accept closer medical scrutiny during his advancing years and this agency could benefit immensely from his knowledge and cooperation.

If for no other reason than to demonstrate to thousands of pilots world wide that the FAA is not purely bureaucratic and that we are truly here to foster and promote safety and not merely to fester and provoke the public, I challenge you as a government employee and public servant to exercise the authority of your position as administrator to settle this matter in a dignified manner with Bob Hoover as he is a "National Treasure." Just because it's the right thing to do!

Sincerely, Norbert J. Nester, Aviation Safety Inspector (Operations), Oklahoma City Flight Standards District Office

The letter hit the aviation world like a rifle shot and the universal reaction only confirmed what the evidence had suggested all along: Bob had been set up. The reaction was one of anger, incredulity, and a growing sense of unrest in the aviation community. Many realized that Hoover was getting less than proper treatment and the aviation community started getting very loud in their disapproval of the matter.

"God" Speaks

The FAA's vendetta against Bob Hoover took some even stranger turns—and targets—shortly thereafter. We received both written and verbal reports that Hoover Attorney F. Lee Bailey was threatened by a senior member of the FAA AeroMedical staff.

We learned that in early December 1994, the FAA's somewhat flamboyant Neuropsychiatric expert, Dr. Barton Pakull, attended an aviation-related meeting. Following the meeting, during a conversation, Dr. Pakull indicated that the Hoover case was causing him some difficulty and that he was not pleased with that. He also mentioned that he had lawyers to protect him from Hoover's lawyer. When F. Lee Bailey, the well-known attorney who had represented Hoover was discussed specifically, it was casually mentioned that they believed that he had once had a problem with alcohol, whereupon (according to one of the witnesses), Dr. Pakull responded with a *"Great deal of emotion... stated that he had heard the same thing, and that he 'want(s) to get that son of a bitch.'"*

I called Dr. Pakull in early February '95 at his office at the FAA's headquarters in Washington DC; Pakull admitted that he had attended the meeting in question and gotten together with some people thereafter, but refused to confirm or deny that he had made the above-mentioned statement about Mr. Bailey and that he would not comment on it further.

Obviously, this statement made it appear that there was some obvious bias at work in the FAA. Further, it cast a negative light on the FAA's protestations that the Hoover case was a legitimate action pursued in order to guarantee public safety. Additionally, any public official who would make such a statement has to be taken with a grain of salt... And since Pakull's decision was so pivotal in the original grounding order, the whole case was immediately suspect... again.

Upon confirming this incident with two witnesses, **US Aviator** magazine called upon the FAA to investigate the matter and determine what occurred. We demanded that if the comment was found to be true and there was apparent bias on the part of Dr. Pakull, we suggested that the powers-that-be set aside the Hoover verdict immediately. We also suggested that Pakull be reassigned to other duties or dismissed from FAA service. The FAA failed to respond to our request for an investigation, and nothing was heard for several months thereafter...

At the 1995 Sun 'n Fun Fly-In, I put the FAA's Jon Jordan on the hot seat and specifically questioned him about the Pakull matter. Jordan defended his staffer valiantly (as one would expect him to do) and reported that Pakull had denied to him what he refused to deny to us... and that's when things took a very interesting turn. One of the witnesses stood up and verified the report in front of the entire assembly! Initially, we had not used the names of those reporting to us, at their request, since they feared repercussions from the FAA. However, another person summoned up a fair amount of courage in the face of these denials and sought to set the matter straight. Frank Goeddeke, a flight

instructor and aviation professional, stood up and told Jordan face-to-face that Pakull *had* threatened Bailey... he had been there and he heard it.

Goeddeke later borrowed a page from the Norbert Nester play-book and also wrote FAA Administrator David Hinson a rather damning letter...

"Dear Mr. Hinson: Thank you for speaking at my graduation ceremony last November. Your speech about how integrity is our greatest asset in our aviation careers was well taken. I was glad, too, when I later discovered the words 'Professional Integrity' written on the side of my class ring. Years from now, even after the words are worn off, I will remember what it used to say, as well as your speech. I will also remember one of your employees, Dr. Barton Pakull, as an example of a person without integrity.

I was never very fond of the FAA's policy toward recovering alcoholics in general aviation. I have always thought a shorter abstention period than the current two years would be sufficient. One time, after the famed airline crew drinking and flying event, I called the FAA's 800 safety number to report what I thought was a safety hazard: The FAA treats drunk pilots better than they treat admitted, recovered alcoholics. I was patched through several people and finally spoke with Dr. Pakull. I have a few friends who are recovered alcoholic airline pilots, who speak highly of him. During our telephone conversation, Dr. Pakull identified himself to me as "God", stating that he "know[s] everything." To me, that explained why the FAA was treating drunks better than admitted, recovered alcoholics.

In December 1994 I attended the annual Pearl Harbor Pilots Association meeting and found myself sitting next to Dr. Pakull at a restaurant table with several others. This was the first time I had met Dr. Pakull face to face. He asked me if I was the one who made a name badge for Dr. Jordan, which reads, "Jon Jordan, M.D., Honorary Member, Dr. Pakull Fan Club" (I am told that Dr. Jordan has worn this badge at work). I confirmed that I was, and further, that I thought Bob Hoover had one too.

The conversation then turned to Mr. Hoover and finally to Mr. Hoover's lawyer, F. Lee Bailey. One gentleman remarked that he had heard Mr. Bailey was drinking too much, to which Dr. Pakull replied, with great emotion: "I know, and I want to get that son of a bitch" or "I know, and I'm going to get that son of a bitch." Dr. Pakull made it clear through the tone of his voice that he meant to take away Mr. Bailey's FAA medical certificate, apparently because of excessive drinking.

Later Dr. Pakull stated that I reminded him of some aviation writer who once wrote a poison pen letter. He joked about how he grounded this writer, who had to write about gliders for a while because he didn't have a medical certificate to fly powered aircraft. Although he could not immediately remember the name of the individual, after I suggested the name, Dr. Pakull confirmed it.

When I returned home I wrote a letter to Mr. Bailey warning him of Dr. Pakull's intentions. I did not hear anything back until I met Mr. "Zoom" Campbell at the FAA public hearings in Orlando in January. Zoom stated he was initiating an investigation.

At the April Sun 'n Fun I found out that Dr. Jordan had investigated by asking Dr. Pakull if he made the remarks. Dr. Pakull denied it. Dr. Jordan also stated that Dr. Pakull was "above reproach," so I wonder just how objective of an investigation it was.

I also found out from "Zoom" Campbell that one other person who was at the Washington event confirmed Dr. Pakull had made the remarks, but Zoom refuses to tell me who this person is.

[Author's Note: I have promised the other verifying person that I would protect his identity in order to protect him from repercussions.]

It is bad enough that Dr. Pakull thinks of himself as "God." But when he threatens to use his official powers to ground the attorney defending a client from him, it is not only unprofessional and unethical, it is also, I suspect, illegal. This goes above the Bob Hoover case to become a crime against the American people and the US system of justice. Further, to openly discuss the medical case of another airman, the aviation writer, is equally wrong.

It is unfortunate the American public is stuck with a public servant like Dr. Pakull. His policies have no rational basis and he openly abuses his power. Thank you for your valuable time in listening to my complaint. If I can answer any questions or provide more information, please ask.

Sincerely, Frank Goeddeke, Jr.

Goeddeke's letter also shocked the public and hundreds of letters flooded into **US Aviator** after we published details of this story from people absolutely incensed that a man like this was allowed to pass judgment on others. One of the more interesting aspects of the letter were Goeddeke's comments about his having grounded an aviation writer some time ago... and that detail personally bothered me to no end... as I WAS THAT WRITER... and had to suffer at the hands of this bureaucracy for quite a while until the situation was finally remedied.

This was one of the reasons that I became so passionately involved with the Hoover case... because I not only worried that others might be treated as unfairly as Bob had been... I *had* actually been one of those so unfairly treated and had an inkling of what Bob was fighting. What goes around comes around... and often does so many times.

More important, the facade created by the FAA's constant and consistent denials of anything but professional interests in this case began to crumble at an ever increasing rate. Rumors spread, stories started and slowly but surely, facts were unearthed and widely communicated that showed, somewhat conclusively, that something was rotten at 800 Independence Avenue (FAA Headquarters).

Chapter 34

The Light at the End of the Tunnel: It All Starts Sinking In...

"The best way to escape from a problem is to solve it."
Alan Saporta

No kidding, the pressure really was reaching a fever pitch. Something had to give—or so everyone thought... and had thought, again and again, only to be disappointed as the Summer 1995 came and went, and the fall proceeded apace.

In addition to all the press, airshow, aero-organization and other pressures exerted on Bob's behalf, one of the more pivotal aspects of the case revolved around the thousands of people who sat down and wrote letters... lots of letters... to the FAA, to their elected officials, to the media, to the President, to the aviation associations and the aviation press... and to anyone whom the writer thought might be able to help them right a horrible wrong. Over the course of the Hoover scandal, the urgency and indignance expressed aggressively by tens of thousands of letters and phone calls grew and grew, and the FAA knew that there was a serious undercurrent of strong dissatisfaction with them that was reaching dangerous levels for those who wished to continue in government service.

More important, the public dissatisfaction with the Hoover affair was pealing through the layers of insulation that separated various levels of FAA bureaucracy from each other. It was strongly rumored that even FAA Administrator David Hinson was not all that up to speed on the Hoover matter, trusting his deputies to do their jobs without questioning the hows and whys of the matter.

However, as the pressure mounted, Hinson was quoted as asking a number of people throughout aviation, including Association Presidents Phil Boyer, Tom Poberezny and others about their feelings and insight into the situation. They told him, in no uncertain terms... but no one seemed to feel that Hinson was fully in the loop about the matter... and it was yet one more letter that ultimately may have brought him fully into the matter in a way that eventually determined its resolution.

AOPA President Phil Boyer travels the country regularly hosting dozens of annual "Town Meetings" for pilots all over the USA. About a week out of every month is spent doing so. He remembers the Hoover matter being a major source of discussion. *"I*

never gave a speech, never had any kind of gathering or get-together in which if I didn't mention it as part of the formal presentation, the very first or second question from the audience would be about Bob Hoover and our involvement in what was going on." In the fall of 1995, his on-going conversations with David Hinson took on a frank and "extremely candid" tone... a tone that grew to become "extremely sympathetic." As it became increasingly obvious that something positive was in the making, Boyer sensed that Hinson was seeking more information from outside the FAA. *"...He was an Administrator that had a hell of a lot on his plate... including a relationship with the Secretary of Transportation that wasn't the best in the world... so I wasn't surprised if he wasn't fully informed."*

Boyer also recalls, *"I remember that he asked... 'What can I do to show your membership that I really care about general aviation?' I told him that there was one easy way to do that... Give Hoover his license back."*

The Letters... A Sampling

10/15/93

Dear Dr. Puskas:

...This violates every tenant of due process of law and defiles every American's constitutional right to defend themselves. FAA written appeal procedures state that higher review lies at the circuit court level, but the July decision says simply that there is no legal review process independent of the FAA. No review process. No oversight. Nothing. It's back to the Middle Ages and rule by decree. If that doesn't scare you, it should.

Alfred Adams

12/93 AOPA Pilot

I just cannot believe what I read. Hoover was "tentative" and "imprecise" in his airshow routine. If the FAA finds Hoover's performance sub-par, then where does that leave the rest of us pilots?

I'd like to see the FAA experts do Hoover's routine and then taxi back to the starting point with both engines off.

Hoover, I would fly with you any day, even on one of your bad days.

Joseph J. Glosak

To David Hinson (2/28/94)

Dear Mr. Hinson:

Forgive my bluntness, I mean no disrespect. But, dammit...

You need to withdraw the appeal of the Hoover decision immediately. You need to cut your losses. You need to quickly begin rebuilding the FAA's devastated ethical credibility with those of us, who, for a lot of years, have believed helping the FAA helps aviation.

...You've lost almost all of us with the awful action against Bob Hoover. You'll lose the rest of us if you continue to defend this bureaucratic ugliness. That's what you did by filing an appeal. Now listen.

You need to fly out to Oke City and personally do some soul-searching with that FSDO. Get rid of the remaining co-conspirator who's still drawing taxpayer money; recognize

he professional ethics of the whistle blower. He acted honorably. Then, with, ceremony, apologize to Bob Hoover.

..Why not FIX it? Why start another Balkan War in which the FAA has to be the Serbs? Forget the damn appeal. Ask Bob's forgiveness. Thank him for being an inspiration to you as a pilot as he has been to the rest of us who try to fly with his awesome precision.

Don Riggs

03/20/94
Dear Bob:

..I am writing my Congressmen anyway, but have found them generally scared shitless of the FAA/NTSB! Also, I have noticed, at least in the NW District, an aversion to age: They have not only forced some of their Inspectors into early retirement, but have drummed up charges and disqualified civilian Examiners after the age of 60. I don't know your circumstances, but know that the "Flying Feds" envy the hell out of civilian Airshow rocks!

..just know that I am on your wing, as always!

Jack Hayes

04/09/94
Dear **US Aviator:**

..Words are inadequate to describe the rage I feel toward the FAA, NTSB, and particularly the two "empty suit" FAA Inspectors, Boehler and Kelln, who were pivotal in the removal of Bob Hoover's Medical Certificate...

Name Withheld

04/12/94
Dear **US Aviator:**

have read the articles in support of Bob Hoover... Clearly, the FAA's actions are another example of a "rotten few" individuals' misuse of government bureaucracy. It is truly a said day when the FAA unfairly targets someone like Bob Hoover . Almost anyone who has been to a decent airshow has seen his breathtaking aerobatics routines. Please see that the enclosed check for $10 reaches Bob Hoover. I know it is not much, but perhaps a fund should be set up to pay for his legal defense. Everyone should contribute considering that their tax dollars are being used by the FAA to crucify him.

Kanan Ott

Good Luck!
f I could afford to contribute in proportion to the pleasure of having met the man and watch him fly, this would be the only check you need. Good Luck!

Pete Fearon

04/12/94
Dear **Pacific Flyer**:
...I write you in total indignation and an ultra-high level of (being) pissed off at the Fuzz treatment of Bob Hoover! I could say that the situation is inconceivable, which wouldn't be true after 20+ years of observing the flagrant malpractice of the FAA "Weenies"! After saying that, I must acknowledge the great ones here in the Seattle are with whom I have had the finest relations But they're the minority, the rest "couldn't piss out of a boot with instructions in the heel and a spigot in the toe"!...

Jack Hayes

04/22/94
Dear US Aviator:
...Aviation is suffering, like every other institution, from the complete incompetence of this current administration, and overly excessive government. I doubt if we will see any big advances, since the way it works, is that it looks like things will happen, but political correctness and bureaucrats render it impotent. Bob Hoover is just the beginning of what could happen to us in the future. Common sense and reason have long since departed from our legal system and our government....

Kel DeVries

04/28/94
Dear **US Aviator**:
...There are many out here who are angered by what is happening and realize that it could just as easily be us that some FAA employee decided to axe...

Rich Nadig

05/02/94
Dear FLYING Magazine:
In its mean-spirited, malignant zeal to purge "One of a kind" Bob Hoover from airshows of the United States, the FAA has adopted a technique used by the Soviets before the dissolution of the USSR. Dissidents and other people in disfavor with the apparatchik were routinely rounded up, examined by government-paid psychiatrists who then (Surprise!) always found the "patient" mentally incompetent or "cognitively-impaired"....

Henry Bourne

05/02/94
Dear **US Aviator**:
I wanted to comment on the injustice the FAA is putting to Mr. R.A. Bob Hoover. The FAA kind of reminds me of my very own West Virginia legislature voting themselves an $8500 raise for 60 days work; wish I could do that. We can't go on for much longer supporting a government that is unaccountable and uncontrollable. Who works for whom here? Between the lawyers, politicians, and the FAA, maybe we should start looking for a nice big

boatload of tea to throw overboard.

John "Chris" Toothman

05/13/94
Dear (Sen. Wendell Ford):
...I have been an active general aviation pilot for 23 years, and in so doing, have accumulated about 5000 hours of flying time and hold an Airline Transport Pilot certificate. I am genuinely concerned that if what happened to Bob Hoover happened to me, like most of us in aviation, who are not as famous, I would not have the wherewithal to mount a proper defense against the ever powerful FAA...

Kelly P. Pettit

05/18/94
Dear Senator Phil Graham:
I believe the FAA has made one of the worst mistakes since flying began in this country in the early 1900's. If you are not a pilot, you might not even know his name, but if you are, you will know he is a legend in the flying community...
He did not fail any medical condition listed on the medical certificate (i.e. heart, lungs, along with many other ailments). Hoover was grounded because a couple of FAA Inspectors, attending the Oklahoma City show, filed a report that in their opinion "his flying did not look sharp." In my view, they were probably just jealous that they could not fly as well as Bob Hoover...
The government has no right to take away Bob Hoover's hard earned right to fly with a second class medical. I would trust my family with Bob in any aircraft. If any Senator or congressman or FAA official questions Hoover's ability, I feel sure that Bob would put on a show for you at National airport, and I can assure you that it would be a show you would not want to miss.

Scott Glover

05/18/94
Dear (FLYING magazine):
Bob Hoover is a flying legend and a good friend. As I recall, he has always ruffled the bureaucratic feathers of the FAA. I even presided over a couple of "Hoover incidents" during my tenure. Bob has historically shown an irreverence to "agents with a badge" who know far less about aviation that Hoover and who don't seem to care to learn. However, this latest travesty... is nothing short of revenge by small people who have been given the authority to administer the FAR's as part of a public trust. ..
I don't often take public issue with the FAA, but as my former teammates know, I won't hesitate to counsel the agency if they veer off course. In Hoover's case, the FAA has allowed overzealous bureaucrats with questionable motives to drag it into the mud. And the NTSB didn't have the courage to do what was right. Too bad.

T. Allen McArtor (Former FAA Administrator)

05/19/94

Dear Mr. Vogt (Carl Vogt, NTSB Chairman at the time):

...As a pilot myself, I am quite concerned over the treatment Mr. Hoover is perceived to have undergone. I do not completely understand why he was dropped from flight status. According to the enclosed article, the majority of doctors that have examined him felt that he was indeed fit to fly...

Robert K Dornan, U.S. Congressman, 46th District, CA

To Rep Don Young, AK

...It seems the FAA is far more concerned with preserving their bureaucracy than seeing justice done. If it can happen to one of our finest, it can happen to any of us. We would like to look into the procedure of the FAA and NTSB. We feel they need some congressional oversight.

Donald Kyte, Alaska

06/07/94

Dear (David Hinson):

...A decision to reinstate Bob Hoover to flying status will be very beneficial to your administration's image and reputation for fairness to aviators. The current opinion of most of general aviation (pilots, operators, etc.) is that the FAA actions were not fair. The initial mistake was magnified by subsequent actions within the FAA to back-up its Inspectors.

I strongly believe that your best bet is to "bite the bullet" and reinstate Bob Hoover to flying status.

Robert Schuh

08/03/94

Dear **US Aviator**:

Thanks for organizing the effort on behalf of Bob. His commitment to excellence was a major factor in attracting me to aviation.

The FAA's abuse of power is symptomatic of an excess of power. A response in support of Bob Hoover in some ways is important to our survival as a nation.

James Page

08/05/94

To whom it may concern:

...Many factors were involved in my decision to go into aviation, but certainly one was the inspiration I felt when watching what Bob Hoover could do. I've been following the details of Bob's situation, as best I can, and, in a word, I'm mystified. I can't understand why the FAA would do what it's done. ...Please convey to Bob my heartfelt hope that this matter can be turned around so people can enjoy watching him fly again!

Bill Moe

08/18/94

Dear Bob Hoover:

As an old AME and 22 years-in-a-row Reno fan, I think your flying ability is as good as ever. I'm also a past owner of a Shrike — several times after returning from Reno I've gotten it banked 120 degrees or so, but I've always chickened out and gone the other way back. The Shrike Act is phenomenal!

Keep up the fight — the Feds should be ashamed!

Don Rogers, M.D.

08/24/94

Dear (David Hinson):

It's an outrage that some mindless bureaucrats are allowed to pass on the capability of one of aerobatics' great pilots.

Bob Hoover passed all the physicals. The greatest living pilots vouch for his ability. Perhaps the FAA is what should be graded.

Franklin Reick, President, Flouramics, Inc.

08/26/94

Dear David Hinson:

..It is inconceivable to me that a federal authority chooses to ignore the facts of Mr. Hoover's case, when in reality it is only the one psychiatrists who, typically, sees something unseen by other medical and aviation authorities.

I hope Jack Elliott's article (*in the Newark Star Ledger*) brings sufficient attention to this federal agency fiasco to force your office back into the reality of the situation. If it doesn't, then I hope Mr. Hoover nails you to the wall with an age discrimination and harassment suit to regain his good name and lost income!

Your department should be ashamed of itself!

Eugene Roche, Embarassed Citizen

09/05/94

Dear Friends of Bob Hoover:

Here is a little help. It would be substantially more, but for the fact that I have gone broke in a struggle with the so-called AeroMedical Certification Branch of FAA, over my mere Class III certificate...

The story of their abuses would make a good novel, but I guess that when you turn 70 your case might interfere with their golf appointment or something so you are perceived as fair game too far gone to put up a fight, even if you easily pass tests that 35-year-olds never hear of....

Martin Litton

09/16/94

Dear Friends of Bob Hoover:

...All of us owe a debt to Bob Hoover including those two self-aggrandized FAA lackeys that conspired to remove Bob Hoover from our skies. I wonder if they ever considered the sacrifice that Bob made and the conditions that he encountered while incarcerated in Stalag 1 prison camp, or the knot in the stomach when he took off on each combat mission. Our skies are free, in this country, for all of us to enjoy because of Bob Hoover and his kind.

...I can appreciate what Bob is going through and I hope he realizes that he is the victim of lesser individuals and that the real people are behind him.

Max Kassera

Concerning R.A. Bob Hoover:

Not only every pilot, but every American citizen, should feel a deep and unabiding anxiety about the fascist tactics used by the FAA, NTSB, and their crony doctors and lawyers in stonewalling the evidence in this case. Each of the persons who have contributed to the damaging of Hoover's career and livelihood by the callous and cowardly instigation of the proceedings and subsequently denying, falsifying, and conspiring against the truth should someday suffer the same crushing indignities. Shame on the FAA, the NTSB review board, and shame on the "experts" who feel vindicated by their actions.

Name Withheld

Hope to See You Fly Again at Reno

Dear (Bob Hoover):

I want you to know that you have filled my heart with much joy over many years now. I have some really nice films of you sticking one-wheeled landings in the Shrike with a 45-knot quartering tailwind at Reno. I will fly with you anytime. I can't believe there is anyone who wouldn't.

Hope to see you flying again at Reno.

Bill Garnett

Dear (Bob Hoover):

You're far too great a man and pilot to let the NTSB get away with what I see (and read) as vindictive, petty, narrow-mindedness. You are unappreciated by the narrow provincials of the FAA...

Regards,
"Suitcase"

We the People...

We the people are the government, and we want Bob's medical restored.

Craig Vorwell

(08/22/95)
Don't Let The Bastards Get You Down!
Dear (Bob Hoover):
Our Aero Club this year celebrates its thirtieth year of operation. We are located in the bush and a love flying for the heck of it is common to all of our members. Amongst awards made at our annual celebrations to deserving pilots is our most prestigious award, the Anchor Award. The Anchor is a symbol of the burden bureaucracy places on our flying. It is awarded to the person who, by word or action, contributes the most to the lightening of such burdens... Many of our club members have read of your fantastic exploits with Chuck Yeager. Some of us were delighted to watch your flying demonstrations at the Avalon Airshow. After watching the Shrike Commander being put through its paces and then hearing of your story with the FAA, we knew we had to nominate you for the award.

Forbes Soaring and Aero Club, Australia

08/25/95
Dear Tom Poberezny:
...Hundreds of thousands of people on the continents of North America and Australia have enjoyed and been thrilled by the grace, symmetry, and beauty of Mr. Hoover's aerial performances. They are classic forms of art...

Honorable Mr. Justice A.M. Harradence, Alberta

10/11/95
Dear Sport Aviation:
...Paralleling the views of many American pilots, the FAA has become the laughing stock of the Australian pilot community. It is a very sorry day when an American bureaucracy has become worse than an Australian one. ...I am a Civil Engineer who does not fly for a living, but have a full head of prematurely grey hair in my early 50's. When people make fun of my hair I say, *"Think of me as an airline pilot. Would you rather have someone baby-faced or grey-haired flying the airplane?"* Experience is what counts, and it is sad that with early retirement, airlines literally throw away millions of dollars of hard-won knowledge. ...Hoover's struggles epitomize the narrow-mindedness of the 60-year-old rule.

Robert Hughes, Australia

11/8/95
Dear Bob Hoover:
Congratulations on your victory over the FAA! It was the best news I have heard regarding the aviation world in a long time.
You have never ceased to be an inspiration in and out of the sky; be assured that the importance of this action is not taken lightly by me or by any pilots I know. It was distressing to watch our government unjustly punish you, but it would have been a travesty to let them get away with it!

Albert Morenthaler

11/8/95

Dear Bob Hoover:

I was thrilled to see you at Daytona! And fly you did!

Many of us never doubted and you proved beyond any shadow of doubt that you are the same Bob Hoover of old. You have been a personal hero of mine since the 1950's when I first heard about you flying F-86s. I have really enjoyed the opportunity to know you and I was absolutely beside myself at your recent airshow performance.

When you rolled up to the announcer's stand, all three days, I could just hear everyone in the back of their minds saying, "Take that, FAA!"

J.J. Collmer, President, Collmer Semiconductor, Inc.

Santa Monica Revelations:
An Altogether Different Letter...

In October of 1995, Bob Hoover was scheduled to attend an event in which he, Tony LeVier, John Myers and others were to be honored for their many achievements as test pilots. Hosted at Santa Monica Aviation Museum, the event was to draw a number of dignitaries from around the aviation world... including a somewhat embattled FAA Administrator Hinson, who was also one of the scheduled speakers. Frustrated over being so close to a resolution so many times, Bob decided to write Hinson a letter, include many of the pivotal documents concerning his case, and give it personally to Hinson.

Norb Nester remembers chatting with him about the plan. *"We had been discussing his full surrender of his license (as a way to fly airshows in the USA) and just flying with his Aussie licenses... and hoping the FAA would not step in and do anything about that. But... for historical reasons he did not want to surrender his personal certificate. I understand that.*

But I said if you lose at everything, Bob, and there (are) no more ways for you to go on this thing, those are (some more) options where you might continue to fly. Fortunately, he chose not to... A matter of two weeks before he got his medical back, Bob called me. He said, 'Norb I want to tell you something. I am going to go up here to a little get-together where they are honoring some old has-been like me.' (That was the term he used when he said it) Bob said 'I am going to take a copy of the letter that you wrote. I am going to take a copy of a flight check that I took in Australia, and a copy of the Australian medical examiners report and put them in a folder. I have a mutual friend of Hinson's who has promised me he will get Hinson to read those documents.'"

Long time friend John Myers was the messenger that Bob was talking about. A true aviation pioneer and an amazing man in his own right, Myers had diverted much of a promising legal career by getting involved in the flight operations department at Lockheed and Northrop... eventually becoming one of their pivotal test pilots. He flew such legendary aircraft as the P-38 throughout much of its development program and went on to become the Chief Prototype Test Pilot for the Northrop Company before running a number of aviation test and upgrade programs of his own. Bob, obviously, holds him in very high regard. *"You couldn't ask for a truer friend, Jim... he is a true-blue individual and a very accomplished pilot."* Myers is still flying, by the way, now in his 80s and still owns and pilots his Cessna Citation IISP business jet.

Myers professed to being *"shocked at what had happened to (Bob)... they nearly ruined him, they cost him so much,"* and so when his friend Dave Hinson became available to him, shortly after Bob had told him of receiving some rather pivotal documents from Australia, one thing led to another. Myers remembered that Bob had said *"I sure wish I could get copies of them (the Australian documents) to him..."*

Myers replied, *"Give them to me... I'll make sure he gets them!"* John had known Hinson for a while and maneuvered to get with him privately during the pre-dinner chit-chat. After the usual niceties, he told Hinson that there were some Hoover-related documents that he wanted them to see. Myers asked him to do one thing for him... to look the documents over and give them his full attention long enough to judge the evidence for himself.

Myers remembers Hinson starting to say *"I know all about the Hoover thing...,"* but was interrupted swiftly by the forceful but friendly plea of Myers, *"God damn it, Dave"* he said, *"just promise me that you will read these documents and he consented... and within a few days, that was the end of it."*

Hoover recalled seeing Myers pass him the envelope... *"He took it and put it in his pocket without a word...,"* but learned shortly afterwards that Hinson had promised that he would look everything over personally on the way home and give it his direct attention.... and apparently he did.

Hoover remembered chatting with Hinson a few times during the evening, deliberately avoiding the subject of the documents Myers had given him, *"It didn't seem to be proper to bring it up anymore... I had to trust that he would do what he said and I had great faith in John's effort to get David to look it over. We chatted about a visit I had made to an FBO he once ran (quite a while previously) and such, but we never talked about my medical problems."*

In just a few days, word came down from the FAA that things had suddenly changed... and Dave Hinson apparently started listening to someone beside his "experts."

Chapter 35

Restored: Hoover Flies Again!!

It is not the truth that makes man great, but man who makes the truth great.
Confucius

Not all "Man Fights City Hall" stories have a happy ending. This one does. The FAA "changed" its mind. And when it finally happened, it happened fast.

The pressure mounted, as the evidence was getting too ponderous to refute and a new round of tests basically gave the FAA a reasonable basis to admit that Hoover could fly. All of a sudden, despite the stresses and upsets of a punishing three-year battle against seemingly impossible odds, Bob's condition had *"improved!"* The FAA decided to issue Bob a conditional medical certificate under its "Special Issuance" guidelines.

The FAA backed down and issued Bob a limited medical certificate that basically allowed Bob to fly airshows, do some personal flying, *not* fly passengers for hire, and not a whole lot else.

Bob was issued something of a combination Class 2/Class 3 Certificate in that his privileges were restricted to one year.... with some other restrictions. According to an interview given to *Aviation Consumer* in late October of '95, the FAA's Tony Broderick explained that there was a *"prohibition... against carriage of persons or property for compensation or hire. The technical term means that he can't use that license to fly people for hire or cargo for hire. The reason for that is that we don't look when we are granting a special issuance at what someone says they are going to do with it or what in fact they have done in the past with their license. We look at that license as a document... the medical certificate as a document which permits certain activities in accordance with the Federal Aviation Regulations. If the medical judgement is such that certain activities which would be permitted by an unrestricted certificate should not be because of the medical facts of the case, we restrict the license appropriately. So it isn't really directed at the individual, but it is directed at the potential use of the license and that the restriction is structured or the restrictions are structured such that we are comfortable in defending any permitted use of the license and would not be from a medical viewpoint or some other reason comfortable with the uses that we have restricted. And that's the reason for putting (in) the restriction."*

The FAA's Dr. William Hark explained that Hoover was given *"...a special issuance. The standard is the same for [Class 3 and Class 2 medicals]. We have a long-standing policy in the agency and, to be explicit, in Part 67 of the FARs, that we are willing to consider the right of private pilots to take risks by themselves that might not*

be permitted in the operations by commercial pilots or an airline transport pilot and we have always been willing to permit more for a... I should say be willing for more acceptance for a medical condition or a degree of a medical condition in the case of certifying the private pilot, where if a person was applying for a second class or first class medical certificate. So it is not at all unusual for the agency, were an individual to apply for a first class certificate, to agree only to grant a special issuance for a third or a second, and a person who applies for a second may get only a third. So this again is a very common thing for us and I think we provided for it in the regulations."

Regardless, Bob was going to live to fly again!

The moment that we (at **US Aviator**) found out was a heady one... One October day, as I was packing for a trip, one of my staffers yelled down the hall to me... *"Jim... It's Bob Hoover... He got his medical back!!!"*

I leaped to the phone... no kidding, I must have done Mach Two.

"Jim... I wanted you to be the first to know... Bob Poole (FAA) just called... and he tells me that I'm getting my medical back! Please tell EVERYONE how much their support has meant to me... and that this is the true reason that I'm going to fly again."

Bob was tremendously excited, his voice conveying none of the weary tone that had often accompanied his latest tale of bureaucratic travesty. His mood was elated, upbeat and utterly confident. Bob sounded very much like a little kid on Christmas.

I vaguely remember thanking him for thinking of us in calling to let us know and heading out the door nearly as elated as he, because for once, the good guys had won... but not without one hell of a fight. I was literally heading out the door to the 1995 AOPA Convention, looking forward to an interesting few days in Atlantic City, seeing the latest in Aero-Gadgets and sharing some fun times with our friends.... but now... *Now...* we had something to celebrate!

AOPA 1995 and Our "Lunch" With Bob

Upon arrival at the 1995 AOPA Expo, the word was surprisingly slow in getting around and I have to admit in taking great delight in letting people know all about it. I ran into Phil Boyer and Drew Steketee and shared a few joyous minutes with them recounting our individual conversations with Bob, and I couldn't help noting a real sense of pleasure at the victory.

Sure, such an event was sure to reflect well upon AOPA, who pretty much led the Associations in terms of the fight for Bob's right to fly... but I also saw something more personal... and was pleased to note that this matter was indeed just that. These folks, Phil and Drew, who surely must have had a pretty full plate those days, were pleased as punch over the personal victory. Pretty touching...

On the floor of the AOPA Convention, I was privileged to give hundreds of people first word of this great news. Later, as the FAA Administrator showed up to put as positive a spin on things as he could, though, I started fuming. The FAA said little but was obviously trying to play good guy... after torturing this man for nearly three years, costing him thousands and thousands of dollars, and then making out like they knew he was OK all along. It was almost too much to take... but take it we did, because what they gave back, they could so easily take away again... and raising a ruckus right away didn't seem to be the right thing to do.

But still... they stole three years of his life, and didn't even offer an apology,

instead stating that Bob's "condition" had "stabilized." Yes, Bob's mythical "cognitive defi-cit", a medical condition that has no valid/legal medical definition, and that was based on uncertified tests, and that had been verified by doctors who contradicted themselves... had "stabilized."

AOPA wasted no time in relating this event to its membership. AOPA's Drew Steketee and Warren Morningstar did their best to try to get Bob out to Atlantic City to address the membership but prior commitments prevented that. However, Phil Boyer's long history in the TV business gave him the idea of hiring a satellite truck (the night before, believe it or not) and providing a live (and not inexpensive) direct feed to the assembled AOPA membership gathered together for a luncheon in the Atlantic City Con-vention Center.

Originally, this event was scheduled to be a luncheon with the FAA Administra-tor David Hinson.... but with the excitement of the moment, Hinson was somewhat up-staged. A record number of people attended the luncheon with the Administrator, which opened with a few words from an uncommonly subdued Mr. Hinson. Then, to everyone's delight, Bob Hoover appeared larger than life... on two big display screens, no less.

Bob looked as happy as I can recall. Boyer recalls, *"When you see that face that we all know and love blown up on a twenty-foot screen... with that twinkle in this eye, you know something great has happened... and I was thrilled to have the membership be a part of that. It was just terrific."*

Many have told us that this was one of the best events to ever occur at such an event... one even going so far as to say, *"Man, you don't even see this kind of thing at Oshkosh!"*

One interesting tidbit I gleaned from Boyer was the fact that Hinson was not clued in on this until the last second. *"I wanted to surprise Hinson with Hoover... so he could say 'thank you' in front of the membership."*

Bob spoke directly to Mr. Hinson, offering thanks for Hinson's willingness to reconsider his case in the polite and gracious manner for which he is so well known. Bob then thanked AOPA for its encouragement and assistance. As Bob had said numerous times before, he reiterated that he kept fighting not only for himself, but for all Gen-Av pilots who may find themselves in his shoes one day.

The rest of Hinson's stay was pretty much devoted to a much-anticipated "Meet the FAA" session. In contrast to such previous opportunities, this one included only Ad-ministrator Hinson, instead of a larger cast of characters. Still, it was basically the same old stuff presented on a different day. With the breaking of the Bob Hoover matter, and the majority of people in the room fully aware of the situation, we expected Hinson to try to convince the crowd of the FAA's "good deed" in this matter, but he never uttered a word... a smart move, we thought.

Administrator Hinson began by saying that 1995 had been a great year for gen-eral aviation and that the Clinton Administration had been committed to building a strong and vital Gen-Av sector. He also quoted statistics from the General Aviation Manufactur-ing Association (GAMA) purporting that Gen-Av sales revenue increased 31% over last year. Support for this trend was backed up by Cessna's plans for new aircraft, Piper's emergence out of bankruptcy, Mooney's increased production, etc. Hinson also touted how Gen-Av airports received $314.3 million in block grants in 1994 and $124.2 million in 1995. While receiving such money is important, we were apparently supposed to over-

look the fact that the grant money was down 40% from last year.

Hinson then went on to discuss the General Aviation Coalition and what it had been doing for us, saying the FAA's committed to aiding the industry and the industry's effort to help itself. As examples, Hinson mentioned revised certification and training requirements, a new category for light planes, and a proposed rule that will allow Recreational pilots to self-certify their medical (which ultimately never came about). As a whole, most attendees didn't seem to be buying this, but were instead concerned about the potential for new, less restrictive medical standards. Hinson then moved to aviation safety by saying it was the highest priority, and while the number of accidents for the past 15 years have steadily declined, the rate of accidents has begun to creep upward as a result of fewer people flying.

Hinson also discussed the partnership between the FAA and NASA, which is developing new technologies for Gen-Av, much of the work being conducted at the FAA Technical Center. He stated that the FAA is committed to reducing the number of regulations and briefly mentioned *"the new, less onerous rule on pilot medical standards [that] will be released shortly."* He also mentioned that *"a simpler, less restrictive rule for the certification of pilots and flight instructors is out for comment."*

We heard about FAA budget cuts... again. This was a major topic on the administrator's agenda and while it may have been a fact, most folks in the audience realized this was the beginning of Hinson's so-called support for user fees, and that's exactly what it became by tying it to FAA reform. Hinson said there were changes needed if the FAA was to continue fulfilling its mission as the world's safest and most efficient aviation system. The procurement system makes it very difficult to keep up with new technology and the inflexible personnel system is unable to match resources with personnel needs. His solution: the reform bill introduced by Senators McCain, Ford, and Hollings, which proposed to make the FAA a quasi-independent agency, *paid for by those who use the system*. He admitted that the issue of user fees is a controversial one, but said even "die-hard" opponents should find some aspects appealing.

Four session attendees were then allowed the opportunity to ask the administrator questions, including myself and our friend Glenn McGovern. Kind of elated over the Hoover matter, we were gentler with him than usual, referring to a previous Hinson comment about deregulation as it relates to the (then) proposed rule on training and certification of pilots. I noted that since the FAA spoke of reform and reducing the number of regulations, how could the proposed rule be 132,000 words long? Hinson agreed, but said he expected the final rule to be much shorter... it wasn't.

After the general session, Hinson held a private press conference. We got up close and personal with him... but it seemed like much of the same old thing. He still wouldn't talk *specifically* about what happened to Hoover, even after the matter was resolved... and got on with his stumping for more money for the FAA. Hinson kept banging the drum for more money and laid the groundwork for a move to user fees (ultimately defeated then, but still a black cloud over our collective futures). The FAA's greedy support of user fees to fill its coffers would seem to be capable of decimating our ranks and thus make the FAA's job virtually unnecessary for general aviation, as general aviation simply won't be there... as it would be priced out of the market.

With Hinson's time in the limelight over, the EXPO was all abuzz with the good news and if there was anything that lifted more general aviation spirits than seeing Bob

Hoover show his new medical certificate off on the big screen I can't recall what it was. Everywhere, the buzz was all about Bob, his future and looking forward to seeing him fly again.... something we were surprised to find, even this late in the airshow season, was about to happen in very short order.

Daytona Beach

The somewhat Annual Daytona Beach Airfest was hosted by a friend of Bob's and provided an early chance for him to get back in the saddle. Before we knew it, it was announced that Bob was contracted to fly at the Daytona Beach Airfest, the same show at which the Eagles Aerobatic Team (of which EAA's Tom Poberezny was a member) was making their final farewell... a dramatic ending... and a dramatic beginning.

However, this performance was but three weeks after the FAA had decided to let him fly... and his regular Shrike Commander was down for maintenance, had the smoke system temporarily removed and was not likely to be ready to fly an airshow in time. Hence, F Lee Bailey, to the rescue... again.

Hoover recalls that, *"Lee Bailey had an airplane that he had built up that was just like brand new and he gave it the name of the Hoover Hornet... it was his intent to remanufacture Aero Commanders... to take them, strip them down to the bare metal and put them back together with a full brand new airplane warranty on, not only the airplane, but everything in the airplane! It was a magnificent program.*

So, he said 'my Hoover Hornet is available to you.' It had all my equipment on it or the same type of equipment as I had on my airplane, which was stuck out in Peoria and out of license.

So I planned to use Lee's airplane and told (Daytona) 'YES, yes I can make it'. And then our troubles began. I contacted different people within the FAA, trying to get the airplane on an experimental certificate so that I could use it in the show."

The Aero-Commander Shrike is a certified Standard Category airplane... but not certified for aerobatics... The way that Bob and other performers with similar needs get around that is to "decertify" the airplane and recertify it in the Experimental Category so that aerobatic use does not violate the rules governing that airframe. Normally, decertification is a simple process... and once such a process occurs, a careful inspection by an authorized repairman with Inspection Authorization (an "IA") can get it licensed back in the certificated category it started with (Standard, Utility, etc.). Note that I said that this was "normally" a pretty simple process. But not this time.

Hoover continued his tale of returning to flight status... *"I contacted different people within the FAA, trying to get (Bailey's) airplane on an Experimental Certificate so that I could use it in the show. That particular area of the country (as regards to FAA responsibilities) had never been involved in that particular job and had apparently not done that before.... it's a very simple routine thing that I've done hundreds and hundreds of times over the years.*

Normally, they switched it over in minutes... the paperwork deal. When you go back in the other direction from Experimental to the (Standard) category, there's an inspection required. It's equivalent to a hundred hour inspection.

So it doesn't turn out to be that thorough because there are certain things you

can just look at and you know you don't have to worry about it. The whole profile that I fly is well within the design envelope (so) that there's nothing there to worry about anyhow... a lot of Inspectors never even bother to make me do anything, they just walk around the airplane with me and I show them what to look for and they sign it off. I've done that many dozens and dozens of times over the years. Once, in the past, when my airplane was damaged, we took care of that on a short fuse... we did this overnight (with a borrowed substitute airplane). We went in on Wednesday and the everything was in position on Friday.

Not this time. When I borrowed Lee's airplane these people were not familiar with the ability to go back and forth (between categories) like that. They required us to fly the airplane ten hours after I had done a demonstration which is proof that the airplane wasn't going to fall apart.

And they had me fly it over a restricted area where there were nothing but cotton fields, just boring holes in the sky for 10 solid hours. Luckily, I didn't have to do all of the ten hours. Scott Bailey (who is also a very fine aviator), Lee Bailey's son, did most of that flying.

But the first thing I had to do, of course, was take it out and go through my routine (since I didn't have a low altitude waver yet). So I had to do the routine at a higher altitude and they observed me on the ground (to recertify him personally for his waiver). I stayed up about 1500 feet for the workout. And since I hadn't flown in quite a while, I went through my routine two or three times just to be sure my timing was up to par for them. The first time I flew it off the deck was in the Kissimmee show on Friday for the press!

I felt very, very comfortable that first flight... on Friday. I was even more delighted when I was able to stop right in front of the announcer's stand with both engines still off after completing the energy management maneuver. And the reason I was happy about that is because I had to make a 90-degree turn from the runway to the speaker's platform, so after I made the turn I had to taxi without power and yet I had to have enough speed to come around the 90 degree turn and still stop and make it up to the speakers platform.

It was kind of touch and go; if the wind wasn't just right you couldn't do it. But I was very fortunate to grease it three days in a row right up to the announcer's stand!"

So... come bright and early Saturday November 4th, F. Lee Bailey's beautiful "Hoover Hornet", a lovingly rebuilt Twin Commander that was reconstructed by his Palm Beach Roamer refit group (also headed by Scott), was wheeled out to the airshow display area... and the air of happy anticipation was so thick you could have cut it with a Hartzell prop. The Feds were reportedly pretty cool after the airplane was put through hell quite needlessly (especially since this had to be one of the most exhaustively detailed Commanders in the biz... an incredible piece of work).

Shortly, Bob showed up, bright, cheerful, with no hint of the slightest "Cognitive Deficit" and was kept busy with countless greetings by his many fans. My own moments with him were extraordinary... as we both were obviously pleased to be in a position that we'd nearly given up hope of ever seeing come to pass. And he said the most amazing thing to me.

"Jim", he said, *"I wanted you to know... that it was your efforts that really turned the tide for us"* and I really didn't know what to say to him for that, except for the truth.

"Bob, all we did was work with the truth. We played 'eyeglass' for much of the aviation public... just helping them to see clearer what needed to be seen all along," I said... and I meant it. We'd taken a lot of flak for pushing this matter, and frankly, we still do... but it was *all* worth it right then and there. Bob's thanks said more to me than you could know and the boost we got from that exceeded the negative aspects of all the grief we took... and we'd do it again tomorrow if need be. Really.

Besides that... I got more out of all this then you know. It was a wonderful thing to battle for a just cause, to fight for what you believe in, and champion the honor of a good and talented man. In the course of those three years, American pilots got a wake-up call as they watched Bob struggle to return to flight status. A poorly designed administrative bureaucracy was shown to be corrupt and flawed, and the first truly visible cracks in its armor appeared... and kept growing.

While the whole thing was hell for Bob Hoover, there is no doubt that the unfairness that was thrust upon him will force the FAA to deal with pilots more justly in the years to come... because they simply are sick of the way the FAA can control them... and it seems that they are not willing to put up with this any longer. Yes, we kept the pressure up and covered this issue thoroughly... but we did it for the simple reason that it was the right thing to do... and I have no doubt that while we did play a part in all this, the real impetus behind Bob's medical restoration was the thousands of grass-roots pilots (especially our **US Aviator** readers) who took the time and wrote/called/E-Mailed their elected officials, the FAA, the media and anyone else who might have had an impact on this affair.

If any single group of people can take a large share of credit for this action, it has to rest with people like famed Attorney F. Lee Bailey; Attorney and AOPA General Counsel John Yodice, FAA Inspector Norbert Nester, AOPA's Phil Boyer EAA's, Australia's Dr. Rob Liddell and EAA's Tom Poberezny. These men really put their all into this matter and it is they who should take a bow for such efforts. At a little before high noon on November 4th, 1995, one Robert A. Bob Hoover stepped into the "Hoover Hornet", laid his trademark straw hat carefully to the side, donned a headset and fired up the Twin Commander. He gave me a cheery thumbs up as he prepared to taxi... and then he waited for nearly a minute... seeming to ponder what was ahead for him, his face a mask of total concentration and purpose. Shortly, the power was advanced and he was cleared to taxi... hearing a DAB Ground controller muse to him that it was "just like old times" as he delivered the taxi clearance.

Bob's longtime partner and airshow announcer, Jimmy Driskell, went to work, trumpeting Bob's return as Hoover thundered down the runway just a few feet off the ground, pulled up briskly at airshow center and slow-rolled that beast like he'd been doing it daily for years. It was an immense joy to see... and the crowd loved it... screaming, clapping, hollering and celebrating the return of a genuine American Hero (and right there, I lost it... tears, grins, the works, and I'm not ashamed to say so).

It was twenty minutes of pure magic. Vintage Hoover. Engines stopped and started; the proud Hornet rolled and looped; and Hoover was obviously having a jolly old time of it. Finally, the Hornet roared in at near to 300 mph, both engines were shut down one last time and Bob looped first, then popped right over into a eight-point roll before turning in for home... landing easily and rolling to a graceful and silent stop right smack-dab in front of the announcer's stand.

Absolutely perfect.

Period.

"Cognitive Deficit," my butt! We should all have such so-called deficits....

So... the magic returned, Bob opened the door, put that trademark straw hat back on and stepped humbly from the proud Commander to wave at the crowd and receive thunderous applause from an aviation world that had suddenly gotten one of its most precious treasures returned. Bob waved, smiled, and gave me a wink as hundreds of people made their way out to shake his hand, pat him on the back and borrow a little of his magic... just like old times. One of our best and brightest had returned to the fold... and pilots all over America once again had the right to point skyward at a sleek rolling Commander and say...

"See him? He's one of us."

Chapter 36

Fall-Out: The FAA's Spin Doctors Take Over

"We must remember that a right lost to one is lost to all."
William Reece Smith, Jr.

The FAA could not sit idly by and let Bob simply win. The spin doctors started to work on the matter even as Bob was getting the news of his reinstatement.

FAA Statement on Bob Hoover

(Wednesday, October 18, 1995)

The *Federal Aviation Administration (FAA) today granted noted aviator Robert "Bob" Hoover a restricted second-class medical certificate, allowing the aerobatics pilot to resume performing at air shows in the United States. In addition, Mr. Hoover has been granted full third-class privileges, allowing him to fly as a private pilot.*

Since December 1993, Mr. Hoover has been unable to pilot aircraft under FAA rules because of a medical condition determined by the agency to be disqualifying under the medical standards.

The agency has always been willing to reconsider airmen for medical certification whenever there was a reason to believe that the circumstances that prompted the denial of such certification may have changed. Such is the case with Mr. Hoover. It has been more than two years since the FAA revoked Mr. Hoover's unrestricted medical certificate. The results of new tests conducted this summer and evaluated by outside medical specialists have led the FAA to conclude that Mr. Hoover's condition has stabilized. In light of this, it is appropriate to grant Mr. Hoover a restricted second-class medical certificate that will enable him to resume his air show performances, but under more medical scrutiny than would be required of an airman with an unrestricted second-class medical certificate.

While holders of unrestricted medical certificates are required to take medical tests at least every two years, under his restricted certificate Mr. Hoover will be required to be tested annually and his tests will be more comprehensive.

With appropriate operational restrictions and periodic follow-up evaluations,

the FAA believes that medical certification now can be granted.

The FAA's Federal Air Surgeon apparently was not thrilled at having had to suffer long and hard for the efforts of his staff. Jon Jordan also weighed in on the matter and put his spin on things via an article he did for an FAA publication in the Winter of 1995...

Bob Hoover: The Facts,
by Jon L. Jordan, MD, JD

POSSIBLY IN THE ENTIRE HISTORY of the conduct of the airman medical certification program no one decision has created more controversy than that concerning Mr. Robert A. (Bob) Hoover.

Accusations about the revocation of Mr. Hoover's medical certificate have ranged from allegations of a personal vendetta by agency Flight Standards Inspectors to an agency bias against aging pilots. Many articles in various aviation publications have contained inaccurate and misleading information, designed, I believe, to inflame the reader and to stir controversy. The agency has remained silent on these allegations for two principal reasons: first, to assure non-interference with the legal process as the case wended its way through the judicial system, and second, to preserve, in so far as possible, Mr. Hoover's rights to privacy. A continued "tight lipped" policy no longer appears necessary since the judicial process has ended and many of the medical factors related to the disqualification decision are a matter of public record.

My finding that Mr. Hoover did not meet the medical standards, and the subsequent revocation of his medical certificate, was based on the diagnosis of a significant cognitive deficit and evidence of cerebral pathology. While reports from Flight Standards Inspectors regarding sub-par performance at an airshow led to the special medical evaluation of Mr. Hoover, it was the medical evidence that resulted in his disqualification. The medical determination was made in consultation with nationally recognized experts
in aerospace medicine, neurology, neuropsychology, and psychiatry.

The pressures to find Mr. Hoover qualified were significant, but with the medical evidence available, it was clear that to do so would place the public - and Mr. Hoover - at an unacceptable risk. Following the revocation, the matter of Mr. Hoover's eligibility for certification was pursued through the review process provided by the National Transportation Safety Board and in the Federal courts. The agency's action in revoking the certificate, while reversed by the NTSB's Administrative Law Judge, was affirmed in a clearly written and strongly worded decision by the Full Board. That decision was subsequently affirmed by the United States Court of Appeals for the District of Columbia. The United States Supreme Court refused to hear a further appeal.

Following conclusion of the legal proceedings, Mr. Hoover requested reconsideration. In view of the length of time since his last evaluations, I agreed to consider the special issuance of a medical certificate, to be based on the results of a new assessment. Repeat studies revealed some unexpected normalizing changes in his clinical condition. In view of this new information, I concluded that Mr. Hoover could be issued a second-class medical certificate that, although limited and conditioned on comprehensive follow-up evaluations by a physician of our choosing, would allow him to perform in airshows.

The opportunity for reconsideration that was afforded Mr. Hoover is the oppor-

tunity that is afforded to any airman who seeks medical certification. A decision once made is not considered ever binding if there is a change in circumstances.

While it is regrettable that Mr. Hoover's disqualification created so much controversy, I continue to firmly believe that the original decision was appropriate, given the clinical evidence. In addition, however, I also believe that the final outcome graphically demonstrates the fairness of the certification system and the protection provided airmen by the process we use in applying our certification standards.

But... one of the most intriguing bits of spin control done by the FAA occurred through an interview arranged by Aviation Consumer with FAA heavyweight Tony Broderick, FAA Attorney Susan Caron and FAA AeroMedical Staffer Dr. William Hark. The expertly crafted interview (done by Scott Dyer) revealed a fascinating mind set on the part of the FAA staffers interviewed and did little to convince the aviation world that Bob Hoover hadn't been set up....

The FAA's Anthony J. Broderick Talks About The Hoover Affair

Aviation Consumer: *The first area that I'd like to explore with you is the situation where Bob Hoover has recently been granted a special issuance of his second class medical certificate. Pilots are certainly happy that he has a US medical again that will permit him to fly in air shows. There is certainly the perception that, by granting this special issuance several years after the initial emergency revocation, the FAA has reversed itself under the heat of the criticism and this is an admission that the initial revocation was wrong. Is that accurate?*

Broderick: *No, it's not. That's an unfortunate interpretation of what happened. It's the kind of thing that tends to make some people want to defend their position ad infinitum. We recognized before we took the initial action that it was not going to be popular, and we weren't happy to have to do it, but we have a public responsibility. We recognized when we got new information that indicated that a special issuance was possible that some people would interpret this as FAA just trying to change the tide of public opinion but that really frankly didn't factor into our decision-making at all. What we did is evaluate the information we had in both cases and take the action that we believed was in the best medical judgement of the FAA was the right action to take.*

Aviation Consumer: *What change resulted in Bob Hoover getting a medical now when exams by half a dozen or more doctors on both sides only two years ago resulted in an emergency revocation order?*

Broderick: *Well, one of the difficulties we have in a discussion like this is the fact that we need to protect, by law and for moral reasons, the privacy of individuals. So, we are unable to talk about the detailed medical data that we have recently gotten that is different from the data that is in the public record. But what you can do is look at the data in the public record and recognize that there was a spectrum of both physical measure-*

ments and neuropsychological tests that were taken several years ago. When evaluating data that was recently obtained, the same Federal Air Surgeon and the Deputy Federal Air Surgeon concluded that the condition that they were concerned about several years ago was not present today in the same degree and so they were able to issue a certificate on the basis of that new data. Unfortunately, it's just not possible to go into detailed examination and comparison of before and after records. The only thing we can say is that there is ample medical data to support both decisions.

Aviation Consumer: *Without getting into detailed factual information about the tests and the results of those tests two years ago and most recently, is this a situation where the condition that the Federal Air Surgeon was concerned about several years ago has stabilized, or that it has improved?*

Broderick: *Let me let Dr. Hark answer that question and then I'll make a comment after that.*

Dr. Hark: *Well, "stabilized" was our word. It is a good medical word and we use it. In looking at the situation obviously his overall condition and status has improved or we would not have issued a special issuance. That's as much as I can say about it.*

Broderick: *The only thing that I point out is that there's a long period of time that's expired here and I think it's important to recognize when you talk about the kind of neuropsychological tests that we were looking at and that are in the public record that is a long enough period of time to be able to make judgments about the progression of neuropsychological problems, so clearly we got good data and the decision that the doctors made was that he was in fact qualified for a medical albeit a special issuance medical which has some restrictions.*

Aviation Consumer: *It seems that the granting of the special issuance medical occurred only after the conclusion of the litigation. There has been commentary since then that there was a delay by the FAA until the court action was over. Some interpret this as a punishment for Bob Hoover pursuing his legal rights for review of the agency and the NTSB decision in the courts. Why wasn't this done a year ago?*

Broderick: *The very direct and short answer to that is we had no new data to evaluate a year ago, but let me expand on that. We worked for nearly a year with Mr. Hoover on an informal basis before he and his legal team initiated legal proceedings. When a situation like this arises, we go from a basically cooperative, informal working relationship to an adversarial relationship that is in a different system completely. That's not a decision that we made, but it's a decision that was made by Mr. Hoover and presumably with the advice of counsel. It's not a very appropriate thing in my view to try and pursue or to expect the agency to try and pursue a case like this in two parallel efforts; one in which we have attorneys in an adversarial proceeding that's very formal and the other in which we are trying to work as closely as possible with the applicant and his physician, and that is something that the attorneys clearly understood when they gave him the advice to contest our revocation of his medical. But I also want to point out that at no time did*

ve say, "okay we're not going to consider any more information from you", but the fact
's that none was given to us outside of the courtroom. All of the information there is
public knowledge as to how we evaluated it and what we said about it. So after all of the
different appeals were completed, we began, and I'm actually not sure whether he called
us or we called him.

Caron: His counsel called me after the court decision [by the federal appeals court]. Well,
actually, right before the court decision he agreed to talk to me. We didn't actually start
talking until after the... appellate court decision.

Broderick: So actually, technically we were talking with him before the thing was over,
but at any rate, we then progressed on a reasonably aggressive schedule that involved a
number of evaluations of the new data that the doctors required to provide them the
background that they needed to fairly evaluate the entire case. But quite honestly, I
don't think ten days elapsed between the time that the doctors in our organization reached
their conclusion and discussed it with me and we actually issued the certificate. In fact it
was probably less than that.

Aviation Consumer: During the time following the emergency revocation, Bob Hoover,
of course, got a medical certificate issued in Australia that allows him to perform there.
Did the FAA supply any medical information to the Australian authorities as they considered whether or not to grant him a medical?

Broderick: No, the FAA was not asked for any data about Mr. Hoover, nor did we provide
any to the designee who issued the medical on behalf of Australia, but, as you know, it
was someone in the United States and the situation that the FAA was in was quite widely
known. We're quite confident of that, so apparently they made the decision that they
didn't need the information that we had.

Aviation Consumer: There was a considerable amount of debate in the litigation process
as to whether to compare Hoover's performance on these tests against all adults, or
against all pilots, or to compare his results only with persons of comparable age and
schooling. In evaluating Bob Hoover's condition today, what group was he compared
against? What ultimately was the position of the agency in terms of which norms are the
most appropriate in deciding the neuropsychological condition of a pilot who is applying
for a medical?

Broderick: Again let me let Dr. Hark give you a few words on that.

Dr. Hark: Oh, I think I would have to say that we compared him against all of these. We
considered him against the population, we considered him against pilots and we had a
lot of discussion with our consultants as to what was appropriate. I think ultimately, it
was just basically a subjective assessment of the degree of risk that was present and we
concluded that it was acceptable, in the context of the special issuance with restrictions.
I would hesitate to say that there is one comparison or another comparison that must be
used. You have to look at the whole situation.

Aviation Consumer: *Was a check ride or other practical test of aviation capability part of the process in deciding whether or not to make a special issuance?*

Broderick: *No.*

Dr. Hark: *It was not in the specifics [of what FAA requested of Hoover], however, we have been provided probably recently with a detailed account of a check ride that was done with an Inspector in Australia. We had that and it was acceptable to us.*

Broderick: *But I think it is fair to say that had we not had that we would not have insisted upon a check ride. I mean that's one of the things that we are frustrated about. I mean in a technical sense is that it makes very good common sense to do check rides for situations like this and many other situations that are not easily quantifiable from a medical viewpoint. The difficulty is that we don't have the technology in terms of measuring the performance of the pilot during a check ride and then correlating that performance with future accident-propensity to be able to say that here is the way you ought to do that, and no one has ever proposed for us a protocol that would do that. We do run into that kind of thing, for example, when you debate the Age 60 rule. So if there were such a scheme that was (doctors call it a protocol) that were available, we would eagerly use it, and as a matter of fact, while money isn't all we'd like to have, we do have research that we continue to pursue at the Civil AeroMedical Institute ("CAMI") to explore these kinds of things; and not only that, but to explore the relationship between performance and simulators and other kinds of test batteries, like the CogScreen [a set of neuropsychological tests developed by FAA for pilot evaluation and given to Hoover], for example.*

Aviation Consumer: *There are a number of consent decrees between the Equal Employment Opportunity Commission and some private companies that have significant flight operations under Part 91 such as Boeing, for instance, which require some reporting or simulator performance results as well as neuropsychological and other physical evaluations. Is CAMI pursuing that data to develop protocols that might provide for an integrated analysis of pilot ability between testing and practical skills?*

Broderick: *I honestly don't know. Do you Bill?*

Dr. Hark: *Yes, you mention CAMI specifically and CAMI of course is involved in developing and carrying out some of the research efforts that we have on going. We are aware of the .....I don't want to call it a study, but the interaction between the EEOC and Boeing and some other companies and this began around 1990 with testing with relatively few pilots. At the time EEOC announced that they were collecting this data for use as appropriate in determining the future course of [whether corporate flight departments could retire pilots on reaching a certain age] and they estimated five years. As recently as last week I was attempting to get any such information or reports that have the figures that have been produced or*
collected without success so far, but are still in the process. So we'll have to see. No major announcements have been made as to any salient findings or useful trends.
Aviation Consumer: *Does the Hoover special issuance relate solely to the Class 2 medi-*

cal or is it a special issuance of both his Class 2 and Class 3 medical certificates?

Broderick: *Technically, it's both because the Class 3 is limited in duration for one year, so that's the limit on the Class 3. The Class 2 has a passenger carrying restriction as well.*

Aviation Consumer: *Why is there a prohibition on carrying passengers if it is not an unacceptable safety risk to have Hoover performing at airshows attended by tens of thousands of people?*

Broderick: *There actually isn't a prohibition against carrying passengers. The prohibition is against carriage of persons or property for compensation or hire. The technical term means that he can't use that license to fly people for hire or cargo for hire. The reason for that is that we don't look when we are granting a special issuance at what someone says they are going to do with it or what in fact they have done in the past with their license. We look at that license as a document, the medical certificate as a document which permits certain activities in accordance with the Federal Aviation Regulations. If the medical judgement is such that certain activities which would be permitted by an unrestricted certificate should not be because of the medical facts of the case, we restrict the license appropriately. So it isn't really directed at the individual, but it is directed at the potential use of the license and that the restriction is structured or the restrictions are structured such that we are comfortable in defending any permitted use of the license and would not be from a medical viewpoint or some other reason comfortable with the uses that we have restricted. And that's the reason for putting the restriction.*

Aviation Consumer: *The FARs governing second and third class medical requirements have exactly the same language on mental and psychological standards. Since Hoover has different restrictions on his second class medical than on his third class medical, is there a different standard applied in issuing a second class medical than for the third class, notwithstanding the identity of language in the regulations?*

Dr. Hark: *If he doesn't meet the standard then, by definition, he is given a special issuance. The standard is the same for [Class 3 and Class 2 medicals]. We have a longstanding policy in the agency and, to be explicit, in Part 67 of the FARs, that we are willing to consider the right of private pilots to take risks by themselves that might not be permitted in the operations by commercial pilots or an airline transport pilot and we have always been willing to permit more for a... I should say be willing for more acceptance for a medical condition or a degree of a medical condition in the case of certifying the private pilot, where if a person was applying for a second class or first class medical certificate. So it is not at all unusual for the agency were an individual to apply for a first class certificate to agree only to grant a special issuance for a third or a second, and a person who applies for a second may get only a third. So this again is a very common thing for us and I think we provided for it in the regulations.*

Broderick: *Many people are surprised to read that paragraph of the regulations because it is very explicit about the recognition of the FAA that people, as private individuals,*

may elect to assume a personal risk that isn't appropriate when they are carrying persons or property for compensation or hire.

Aviation Consumer: *In connection with the special issuance, is there a deal where Bob Hoover will retire in a year and surrender his medical?*

Broderick: *No. First I've heard of that, but, no, there isn't.*

Caron: *Maybe we should ask you about this?*

Aviation Consumer: *I've heard rumors that . . . .*

Broderick: *Is that the Australian medical you are talking about?*

Aviation Consumer: *No, we are talking about the U.S. medical.*

Broderick: *No, no.*

Aviation Consumer: *Pilots and commentators have been concerned, very concerned, by the process through which Mr. Hoover's medical certificate was revoked. Much of the trial before NTSB Administrative Law Judge Mullins involved arguments by Hoover's lawyers that the FAA did not call as witnesses the two Inspectors who observed his performance in Oklahoma City in the summer of 1992 and who wrote the reports that started the revocation process. The sense is that the FAA had something to hide by not subjecting these individuals to cross examination to determine what they saw and when they reported it. It also appears that they were, at least initially, listed as potential witnesses at the trial. Why weren't they called as witnesses?*

Caron: *I'd like to preface this by pointing out that Mr. Hoover's counsel subpoenaed them to the hearing. In fact, one of them was present, the other was never actually served with a subpoena. One of them was present [at the trial] and [Hoover's counsel] elected not to call him.*

Broderick: *So they put these people on the list, not us.*

Caron: *Well, we also initially put them on the list, too.*

Aviation Consumer: *Which Inspector was there?*

Caron: *I don't remember their names.*

Aviation Consumer: *There was a Mr. Kelln and a Mr. Boehler.*

Caron: *Mr. Kelln was there. The other thing I'd like to point out is that from the legal standpoint, Mr. Hoover had provided explanations for what happened at that airshow and an explanation for what the Inspectors had seen: He had disclosed that to several of*

the doctors and, in fact, that explanation is contained in the medical records that were put into evidence at the hearing. He also testified to that explanation at the hearing and without exception the doctors heard that explanation, accepted the explanation as being reasonable, so notwithstanding the Inspectors' reports, Mr. Hoover had provided an explanation for what the Inspectors had seen. The doctors said that appears to be a reasonable explanation, so it never was a consideration really once Mr. Hoover had the medical testing.

Broderick: *But even... I mean that's all true... but when you now ask the question again, that you ask, the answer is that the issue of why the Inspectors wrote a report which resulted in getting data which resulted in a certificate being revoked... why the data came in is irrelevant. The whole question in that hearing was not why people provided data to the FAA, but why the FAA decided that the data indicated that the person, Mr. Hoover, was not qualified to hold a medical certificate. So the Inspector testimony and all of this stuff about whether or not they conspired to write a report... all of that kind of stuff is not only untrue, but completely irrelevant to the issues at hand. And it's really unfortunate that people have made comments about this, because, in fact, the fact of the matter is that the Inspectors very promptly reported their concerns to the people at the Civil AeroMedical Institute in Oklahoma City. It happened to be all in the same area, and the only delay that was involved was in their actual documentation of that. I mean that's, in retrospect, unfortunate in large part because it gives rise to all of this unfounded rumor and innuendo, but the fact is that they were very prompt and, as Susan said, there was no question on the part of Mr. Hoover and his team as to whether or not his performance was not quite what you would expect on the day in question. He'd in fact was, as he explained it, due to malfunction of the airplane. So what we have is a situation where the Inspectors saw something which gave them some concerns. Those concerns were, in fact, supported by the testimony of the pilot himself as being legitimate. He gave a different explanation for why it had happened than one might imply or infer from the medical data, but the Inspectors' conduct and the way the process that was followed is one that is widely criticized because it is not fully explained and not understood.*

Caron: *The other thing that really should come out to light is that Mr. Hoover's counsel really had free access to the FAA before the hearing had been initiated. It permitted them to go into the air traffic control tower in Oklahoma City and talk to controllers who may have observed or participated in that airshow. We allowed them free access to these people. Not once did they ever ask to [question before trial] those Inspectors other than taking the step, and that step was not taken until the hearing, to get those subpoenas. They never followed through on it. It really was a red herring that they raised to detract from the medical issue that was being trial at the hearing.*

Aviation Consumer: *Putting aside for a moment the issues of legal relevance to the case that was being tried before Judge Mullins, many pilots are, nonetheless, interested in what the Inspectors saw and heard from the standpoint that they are putting themselves in Bob Hoover's shoes: pilots who deal with FSDO Inspectors are concerned about Inspectors observing things, not writing reports until two months after the fact and then*

not making known what the true bases were in public for their observations. Although there were explanations given by Mr. Hoover for some problems in his routine on the day that he was observed involving oil pump cavitation and a cowl flap problem, there were also some observations by the Inspectors of Mr. Hoover's personal well-being, physical well-being, on the flightline. There is no record that they sought to speak with Mr. Hoover at the airshow. Did they, and if not, why not?

Broderick: I don't know. Susan may know.

Caron: No, as far as I know, they don't. I don't know for sure. Why not, I don't think that something ordinarily that an Inspector asks, who is observing an airshow in an official capacity would do, but Tony can address that.

Broderick: Yeah, I mean, it depends on what the issue is and I don't know what the specific circumstances were. Certainly if an Inspector saw something that looked to them like a performance problem regarding flying capabilities, perhaps violations of the rules, maybe something airworthiness with the airplane, that would be a completely appropriate and expected thing to do. I would only speculate that they were genuinely concerned about what they perceived to be as laymen his basic medical condition and therefore I wouldn't think it necessarily appropriate for them as not being physicians to go and question him and try to understand if he's got a medical problem. They did what they should have done, and that is go to the FAA medical department and asked them to do whatever investigation is appropriate. Indeed, the only thing that I could fault anybody for in this whole thing is the fact that they had a lot of work to do and it took them a number of weeks to get around to completing their documentation on this. Obviously, it would have been better for all concerned had they done that more promptly, but when you have the kind of workload that some FSDO Inspectors do on busy periods, it is understandable why something like this might be put to a lower priority.

Aviation Consumer: I'm not suggesting that an Inspector is competent or required to speak with an individual to determine, medically, his physical condition. However, the reports that were submitted include some statements that Mr. Hoover appeared to be in rather frail physical condition, had difficulty entering and exiting the aircraft and, in another report, a statement that his behavior on the ground seemed tentative and he does not appear physically well. Why wouldn't it have been appropriate for the Inspectors to inquire about how he was feeling, since that certainly might have an effect on the safety of the show that day, if he weren't up to flying?

Broderick: I don't know. I certainly can't speculate as to what the situation was and why they made the judgments that they do. But these folks do this kind of thing for a living. They look at a lot of airshows. They obviously made a judgment that they didn't have the kind of immediate problem that conceivably they could have and I just assume that because of the actions they took. You're right. It might have been appropriate. On the other hand, it might have been a situation where there were a lot of people around and this is not necessarily the best time to ask questions like that and they perhaps didn't want to do that with a large crowd around and circumstances were such that they couldn't

et private time with Mr. Hoover. I don't know. There are all kinds of good reasons why it might have and you have to ask them directly.

Dr. Hark: I did discuss it with one of the Inspectors. You know, people who are laypeople are reluctant to go up to someone of some note and say "you look bad", or "you don't look well", or something of that sort. Out of politeness or whatever the people are reluctant to do this kind of thing. The two Inspectors viewed the show from different vantage points: they weren't together. It was after the show that they were discussing it and realized that they had independently come to the conclusion that the performance just didn't appear to be up to par as expected. This was then discussed with a safety official in the local FSDO, a co-worker there, as well as with their supervisors. In the context of what should we do about this" it was the recommendation of the safety person who said, "Well if you ask me, I'll talk to the medical people" and that was the person who went to the medical certification division and first reported this: it wasn't one of the Inspectors. I'm convinced that this was done out of concern for both Mr. Hoover's well-being as well as the well-being of the people that attend these shows.

Caron: I also spoke to both Inspectors and believe the same thing.

Aviation Consumer: The report written by one Inspector, Mr. Boehler, contains a paragraph which is somewhat intriguing in light of trial testimony by airshow performers on Bob Hoover's behalf that they saw nothing wrong with his performance. It reads: "Comments and remarks from other airshow performers indicated a concern for Mr. Hoover's lack of continuity in performances. Many feel he is not in good physical condition and should not be performing such arduous tasks. Other airshow performers seem to avoid him and he is not included in the group. This is not uncommon when the peers are worried about someone over whom they have no influence." Who talked to Mr. Boehler to tell him that other airshow performers thought that Mr. Hoover was not up to snuff?

Broderick: I don't know.

Caron: I spoke to Mr. Boehler who mentioned that he had spoken to other people. I recall that I called several individuals and inquired whether they had been at the airshow and whether they could give me their impressions of what they had seen.

There were individuals who had reservations about his performance that day and whether or not it was because of the cavitation problem, you know, I really don't know that. But they did corroborate what the Inspector said, as far as the actual performance.

Aviation Consumer: Who were these people?

Caron: I don't remember his name, but one of the people who even testified at the hearing was his announcer who also talked a little bit about it. And that was in the records. As to the other individuals, I don't recall.

Aviation Consumer: Would it be possible for someone to supply me with the names of those other people?

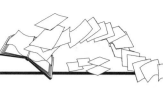

Caron: *To be honest, I don't think I would have the names of them. I can try to contac*
those two people. All I know is I did make several phone calls.
Aviation Consumer: *If some effort could be made, I would appreciate. Do you know i*
they were members of the ACE program?

Caron: *I don't recall.*

Aviation Consumer: *Both you, Tony, and Dr. Hark have made reference to the fact tha*
the Inspectors who observed the airshow made, at least, oral reports to people within th
FSDO and otherwise prior to their writing their formal report about approximately tw
months after the airshow in question. How much time passed between the airshow an
when the first oral reports were made?

Dr. Hark: *Two days.*

Aviation Consumer: *Two days?*

Broderick: *Saturday to Monday?*

Dr. Hark: *Yes. It was the first work day after the show is when they discussed this. I thin*
the following day they went over CAMI.

Aviation Consumer: *Given the seriousness of the concern why then did it take two months*
not just for the written report to the issues, but for the initial letter to Mr. Hoover indicat
ing that his medical status was in need of reevaluation and he would have to submit th
results of additional psychiatric and other tests?

Broderick: *Well, I think the point is that it wasn't viewed as something that was of high*
enough priority to bump the other work that the Inspectors were doing, and that's wha
the initial delay was. I'm not aware of any particular delays from the time that th
[FAA's] medical division got the information that they needed until the time proceeded t
begin discussions with Mr. Hoover and, of course, those discussions went on for a long
time.

Aviation Consumer: *Some critics of the administration's action towards Mr. Hoover have*
complained that the evaluation of whether or not he was fit to hold a second class medi
cal was not made by Dr. Audie Davis at the AeroMedical Branch in Oklahoma City, tha
branch that reviews the lion's share of medical applications in the country, but instead
was made here in headquarters in Washington, DC How did this case get pulled from th
normal channels?

Broderick: *We had an inquiry that came to the Administrator that asked that the Ad*
ministrator review the actions that were in process regarding Mr. Hoover. We frequently
get requests from people to review actions because they are concerned that they may no
be properly taken and it is a common practice with the FAA to ask that the file be sen
from Oklahoma City here to headquarters so that the most senior medical staff gets th

pportunity to review that and get appropriate consultant input if they need it. That's exactly what happened in the case of Mr. Hoover. It wasn't anything that was out of the ordinary given the request that we got. We do that for a lot of people.

Dr. Hark: *Let me note that the FARs specifically provide for review on request by the Federal Air Surgeon if someone is unhappy with a decision and they always have the right to ask for review. And they do this very frequently.*

Aviation Consumer: *This is an in-house appeal, right?*

Dr. Hark: *Yes, yes, but it's explicit in the FARs that anyone denied a medical by someone other than the Federal Air Surgeon can appeal that decision to the Federal Air Surgeon. Many people take advantage of that, to the extent that some of the aviation organizations routinely advise their members to insist on review by the Federal Air Surgeon if they get an adverse decision from [the AeroMedical Division in] Oklahoma City. In this particular case it was brought to the attention of the Administrator, the Administrator expressed specific interest in the case and noted that he wanted to be kept informed of the progress of the case (this was verbally to me directly). It's always the case that once an Administrator has a specific interest in a case, almost routinely, they will bring the case here for final action. The Administrator was assured that the only final action on that case would be taken here and we followed up.*

Broderick: *Which is not unusual.*

Dr. Hark: *No, not at all.*

Aviation Consumer: *My recollection is that Administrator Richards was the FAA's Administrator at that point. Is that right? Was it the letter from T. Allen McArtor [a former FAA Administrator under the Bush Administration] from August of 1992 that caused this to be brought to Washington?*

Dr. Hark: *Yes, that was the whole thing that I was aware of. Whether General Richards had phone calls or any other input I don't know.*

Aviation Consumer: *There was some testimony at the hearing by Bob Hoover that at some point Dr. Davis told one of Hoover's physicians that he should fight the revocation because it was unwarranted. Did Dr. Davis ever express that view internally within the agency?*

Broderick: *Not to me. I don't know of any comment like that.*

Dr. Hark: *Did he express the view that revocation was unwarranted?*

Aviation Consumer: *Yes.*

Dr. Hark: *No.*
Aviation Consumer: *Tony, were you involved in the decision to issue the emergency*

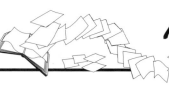

revocation order?

Broderick: *I think I would put the words differently. Obviously, the decision to do that is a medical decision in coordination with legal and the Administrator. In fact, it is important that folks recognize that I don't impose my judgment over the doctors when you are talking about medical issues. But in fact there was quite a group of folks that came down to me to this office to talk about this case and consult on what looked like the course of action before the decision was made. So to that extent I was involved in the decision-making process and the recommendations that were made to the Administrator to do this and certainly was not to say that it was something I didn't know about. I was fully informed about, not only what the course of action was that was recommended to be taken, but the reasons for it.*

Aviation Consumer: *There is a perception that Bob Hoover was the first pilot to be called in for neuropsychological and psychiatric examinations, and reevaluation of his fitness to hold a medical certificate, based upon observations of his day-to-day flying. Is that accurate or have there been others who have been called in for this type of testing?*

Dr. Hark: *He certainly was not the first person to be evaluated for neuropsychological testing. We do have authority for any number of reasons often in sort of the same sequence he was asked to have general internal medical, neurological, and psychiatric examination and it was the finding of some abnormalities by the physician that led on to more extensive psychological evaluations. And again, that is not an unusual sequence of events. We do ask for some evaluations on people and we have on the basis of observed behavior... We have a person who goes into an establishment and starts fighting or does something unusual, something a-social or anti-social or bizarre...*

Caron: *Yet sometimes they are related to flying.*

Dr. Hark: *Yes, sometimes they are related to flying. We have sometimes one crew member sometimes discussing the actions of another crew member saying this wasn't right or will describe it, so that sounds unusual and we say we need to see if something is going on here. I recall we did it with an individual who was an airline captain who had raised a ruckus when asked to go through the security screening back when we first started screening all crew members, then we had one who was very bizarre in his behavior at this particular time. That triggered ..... so as I say there all kinds of reasons. I don't recall .... well when we have a physician or observer of some kind calls or writes the agency with these and describes to us the unusual circumstances or kinds of circumstances which raises the question we do that. In this case we have a couple of agency Inspectors come to us and describe what they think is a change in both actions and appearance which triggered the evaluation. So to say that this is something unusual and never happened before and we singled him out is a mischaracterization.*

Broderick: *Although it is unusual. It is unusual. Another interesting thing is that medical denials are relatively unusual, a very small number. But when you are talking 600/700,000 pilots in the country.*

Dr. Hark: *The denial is considerably less than one percent of the people who apply. We certify many, many people who don't meet the medical standards.*

Broderick: *Well, the interesting number is 99.9% of the people that apply for an FAA medical and provide all the data that we need get a medical. They get either a special issuance or obviously that's a tiny fraction or a regular medical.*

Aviation Consumer: *At some level?*

Broderick: *Right...... but it's one-tenth of one percent of the people that apply and provide us with the data that we need are denied. Now there turns out that there are a number of people each year who when asked for additional data won't give it to us, so we can't ever reach the judgment. The point is that it's quite rare to actually get a denial when you go through the process.*

Caron: *It's even rarer for a case to go to hearing.*

Aviation Consumer: *There are certainly not that many in the reported cases.*

Aviation Consumer: *Two subjects that we touched on briefly in some other questions and answers, Tony, are the Age 60 Rule and CogScreen. Over the last ten years a fair bit of time and probably an equal dose of money has been spent by the FAA in developing the CogScreen battery of neuropsychological tests which have been given to a large number of pilots. My understanding is that there is at least a fair baseline of data that has been developed. What are the FAA's intentions with regard to this test?*

Broderick: *Will it be given to all of us as a routine matter? Not in short term. We hold hope for it, but it's still I will say the developmental kind of stage. We use it.*

Dr. Hark: *Well, it's a little more than developmental. In fact it is published now, is in use by the general medical community, has been released and is marketed and used. I doubt that in the context of simply routine certification that at any time in the immediate future that it or any similar test would be used. Our original reason for beginning to develop it was to find a better tool for the evaluation of people... well for evaluating cognitive function with an eye mainly towards people with a history of head injury or substance abuse or alcoholism, whatever, and that the existing tools are a little too gross and are affected by testing effects and need to be repeated testing. As a rule for something that is easier to administer and would have fewer of those types of problems and we believe that CogScreen has great promise in that respect.*

Broderick: *My use of the word "developmental" – I was thinking more about using it as a surrogate for performance testing which we're still trying to figure out if we can do that for subtle changes in performance which..... we hold hope for that but these things take a long time to develop the huge amount of data that needs to be obtained. It's just a long time.*

Aviation Consumer: *Is there any consideration being given to requiring a battery of tests such CogScreen to go along with a 609 ride in the event of observations of a FAR violation?*

Broderick: *No. Nothing. Nothing that is, again, in the foreseeable future... we don't have any plans to make big changes in medical testing for this kind of thing.*

Aviation Consumer: *I would like to thank you very much for your time, all of your time. It was very nice of you to make yourselves available to bring your expertise into the meeting. Thank you.*

Broderick: *I appreciate your taking the time to read all this stuff that you've read. I mean you are one of the few people.... Well, it's interesting because of the issues that I think someone said and I don't know who... oh, I know who it was, it was O'Leary, the fellow that wrote for* Private Pilot... *said that so many of the aviation community's impressions on this case have been created by stories that they read which had a particular editorial slant rather than from them reading the material that the stories were written about. And in at least one case, in* FLYING *magazine..... clearly that was a story written by an advocate, and that is not necessarily a source of unbiased information, though it is a source of information... and I frankly think that what you have written is one of the few pieces that tries to explain all of the facts and let people judge what they will from that, so we appreciate it.*

It was quite an article... and the conflicts and questions that arise from it are ponderous... especially in terms of the delay between the so-called verbal discussions of Hoover's alleged inadequacies in OKC and the much delayed written reports filed by Boehler and Kelln. For an "Air Safety" matter that was considered important enough to ground Hoover later that year to not be *"viewed as something that was of high enough priority to bump the other work that the Inspectors were doing,"* one certainly wonders what the FAA's priorities were, if indeed, there was any case to support the grounding. The FAA's inability to cite Boehler and Kelln's sources among the other airshow observers was also lamely dealt with (the Dog ate my homework?), and the questions/pseudo-answers about the future of CogScreen were worrisome.

Finally; one of the most frustrating things about this article was the FAA's renewed insistence on quoting the O'Leary article as some kind of vindication... as this had to be the ONLY major aviation article that had supported the FAA's position on Hoover from among the aviation press, at large. It also caused no end of consternation when published (O'Leary indicated that he took a LOT of flak for it) from the aviation world. But... the vast majority of the aviation press did NOT support the FAA grounding of Hoover and even when you discount the letters and articles written by friends and associates of Hoover; there was still an extraordinary amount of data published that not only did not support the FAA position, but debunked it rather thoroughly and convincingly.

Chapter 37

What Happened to Norb?

Revenge... A Dish Best Served up Cold.
Old Klingon Proverb

For those of us who work closely with the Federal Aviation Administration, it is not unusual to hear about the climate of fear that can occasionally exist when FAA employees and associates run afoul of their seniors. The FAA puts a premium, both officially and unofficially, on adhering to the "company line." For those in the FAA who fight City Hall or otherwise do things that the management considers negative, the penalties can become severe.

As a result, there is a significant culture of paranoia on the part of much of the field staff. FAA employees do not feel free to speak out. FAA employees do not feel that they can correct management without risk of damage to their careers. FAA employees will often remain silent about things they consider wrong or even dangerous for fear of repercussions.

There are those, however, that have gone against the grain. There are a few who have, at times, spoken out in order to right wrongs. These people are few and far between, especially those who will speak out "on the record."

We have often received information about the inner workings of the FAA from FAA employees who are scared about what is happening to aviation safety, but the vast majority of those who speak to the media (at least of those who have spoken to us), prefer to do so without getting their names involved.

One of the most infamous examples of how the FAA reacts to those who criticize it from within occurred to FAA Inspector Norbert Nester. Barely three years after the FAA started its campaign to take away Robert A. "Bob" Hoover's medical certificate, Nester got public and vocal about his experiences from inside the very office that generated the initial charges against Hoover. He gave sworn testimony before NTSB Law Judge Mullins that the FAA's initial case against Hoover was the result of two OKC FSDO Inspectors plotting to file false complaints about Hoover as part of some self-aggrandizing ego boost.

Mind you, Nester did not, at first, try to buck the system. He was subpoenaed by Bailey and committed the grievous crime of answering questions honestly... despite a surprising eleventh hour phone call from an FAA Attorney.

What surprised Nester was the fact that FAA Attorney Susan Caron had apparently called to find out what he was going to say and to issue some vague warnings about the repercussions of same... because Nester had not been subpoenaed by the FAA, but by

Hoover's Lead Attorney F. Lee Bailey... and he was unaware of that fact until her call!

So... he didn't play whistle blower, he didn't go off half-cocked... he simply responded to a legal request for testimony and allegedly answered those questions honestly and completely, knowing full well, that *"the FAA was probably going to have me for lunch for saying what I did."*

Remember now, he made his statements under oath, and only *after* being subpoenaed to testify by Hoover's attorneys. As he left, he remembers thinking *"what was going to happen Monday when I showed up for work?"* Nester's moment on the hot seat was fairly brief, but the effects long lasting... as he was soon branded a pariah by his peers and immediate management.

Nester remembers the aftermath well. *"I got a very cold shoulder. Management did not want to have anything to do with me. They were comments pro and con from the Inspector staff. But it was blatantly obvious that I had sinned greatly. No question about it. Comments were made by my operations unit supervisor, by the office manager, by the people that were pro-government, that in essence I had signed my own death warrant.*

It was very cold for a number of days. Then after two weeks of that I was presented with a proposal to suspend me. It was based on the fact that I had supposedly gone AWOL for two hours on a Friday afternoon a couple of weeks before that. And that I had not returned to my office upon the completion of a course at the Aeronautical Center.

They did in fact dock my pay for the time period and they did in fact suspend me. I maintained and filed a grievance with the union. I was not a union member but it was represented. I maintained that it was purely retaliatory because of what I had to say. Everybody else maintained that, too, except the management. In fact, Nancy Adland stood right up and she said, 'Now wait a minute; this is nonsense. Mr. Nester has done exactly the same thing as every other Inspector in this office has previously done on numerous occasions. It is commonly accepted that when you have spent a matter of multiple days or a week at the Aeronautical center, when you are released, you are released like everybody else. The fact that we work in Oklahoma City, a mile and a ½ from the Aeronautical center, is immaterial. We have been a student in a student capacity just like everybody else. Now there is not another Inspector in here that has not done exactly the same thing and not a one of them has ever been reprimanded for that action. This is capricious; it is selective enforcement on your part against him'."

This did no good. Nester reported that, *"From that point on there was everything from micro-management and scrutiny about the work that I did, to actually and openly soliciting complaints from the public against me by Frank Allen. He and Alan King talked to the operators and actively solicited complaints. They were unable to get them from some operators. They got marginal things from others who just didn't like the fact that I was enforcing the regulations and doing my job. To show how contradictory they were, Jim Kelln had previously been the principal operations Inspector for a large flight school at an Oklahoma university. It was a contract operation. They were teaching all the OSU personnel. He had been their principal Inspector for a number of years. It was common knowledge that he had a lot of problems. They had a designated examiner that was also the chief Instructor for the school. He, Bob Robertson, had a number of complaints filed against him or lodged against him through our office by applicants for various certificates. His own employer complained about his lack of performance and*

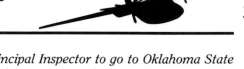
diligence. Frank assigned me as the new principal Inspector to go to Oklahoma State University at Stillwater to this particular facility. 'Do a complete surveillance on it like you would do on any other 141 school,' he said. 'Whatever shakes down, whatever you find we are going to hold them to the letter of the regulations period'.

I said, 'well, that is no different than anybody else'.

Well, I found a lot of paperwork discrepancies, a lot of training records that were not right, and while the man was up for a chief instructor flight check. There were things going on with regards to his pilot examiner's designation also. I rode with a lot of the students. I reviewed a lot of records. I attempted to give him an oral exam as a flight instructor and on two occasions he flunked both of those and I told him he did. The second time I went up it looked like maybe I was going to get the airplane, but that never happened. I never flew with him.

He alleged that I was being a horse's ass, that I was overbearing, that I was everything (negative) that has ever been stated about an operations Inspector. Frank Allen wrote me up in my performance evaluation and I did not get an outstanding or any of that. I got a 'fully successful' but in the PPR, it stated that Mr. Nester surveyed a 141 operator, found numerous discrepancies, diligently adhered to enforcement practices which resulted in, and he listed a number of violation packages... a re-examination of an airman's certificate and a designee. That was the attaboy that I got for doing that. Those came out about April, when they were actually done.

In June, I was put on a performance improvement program because of substandard performance. The very same things that I was applauded for in my PPR in April were the identical items that I was reprimanded for doing and the reason I was being placed on a performance improvement in June. Same operator."

It got worse. *"They were doing everything they could to find fault with me. Frank Allen himself called FAA security and made allegations against me and got them to initiate an investigation into my behavior and performance."*

Nester knew what was happening to him. He had answered questions honestly, under oath and "broken faith" with the implied code of silence that many Inspectors follow when it comes to things that might reflect negatively on the FAA. He grew frustrated and indignant with the system and as he followed the Hoover case, itself, with what he came to strongly believe was nothing less than a bogus vendetta started by others in his office... and the reason that he was not forced to endure harassment... because he had not gone along with the scheme.

There came a point when Nester pretty much had had enough and authored the now famous letter to David Hinson, further exposing the alleged plot by Boehler and Kelln and voluntarily breaking ranks with the conspiracy of silence that surrounded them. Nester admitted that the letter came about as a result of *"pure frustration on my part."*

Norbert related his growing sense of mistrust as he *"sat and listened to all the crap go on in that office. I saw the public harassment and demeaning of individuals. I've watched it all and I saw the infighting and the crap that went on inside the FAA office. The office in Oklahoma City sent out memorandums... where the PR man for the Aeronautical Center sent an interoffice memo that said I am sick and tired of this, I think the old son of a bitch is crazy and they did the world a favor by grounding him. It got hard to take."*

So... the letter went out and was published in a number of publications in short

order, so explosive was the import of what Nester wrote. While he was aware that letter was sure to cause trouble, *"I gave them all the (letter) and said as far as I am concerned it is a public thing and you are free to use it or do whatever you want to do. And they did and I was glad."*

The media response was swift. Nester explained, *"They were pounding the hell out of the government in their publications. I thought that was great at the time. Still do for that matter... but it died down and nothing more came out of it for a while; then one of those publications (that published the content of the letter) appeared in our office. Needless to say things got real icy around my office with regards to me after they saw that letter.*

There was a lot of people saying attaboy and a few people saying 'we are going to hang that SOB.' I got calls from other FSDO offices, from Inspectors. I got calls from just people out of the public, from probably 50 different people around the US who had read that letter or read excerpts from it in different publications. They were just saying we are glad you stood up; we are glad you did.

That is fine, I am glad you did it. Hopefully it steps on them (FAA), that was what it was intended to do. But nothing was coming out of it. Hoover was still getting screwed.

During this time period I developed a bit of rapport with Mr. Hoover. He did not know I had written the letter; he had no clue that I was even thinking about writing a letter. But periodically I've got to admit I just flat felt sorry for the man. Because within a year of being the same age as my dad, they were in the military at the same time, their careers were similar in some respect because of their initial training and different things and some of the equipment that they flew. Obviously my dad was not a test pilot and all that... not in the sense that Hoover was. I guess I felt an incentive for Bob Hoover because of my own father.

So I called him once in a while and talked to him. I asked Bob, 'How are you holding up? How are things going?' He would talk to me. Periodically he would call me just to visit. Not necessarily about his case, just called to visit. At the same time, he would ask, 'How are you holding up? Are they putting the pressure on you?' Things of that nature. He was always a gentleman... always pleasant. Grace under pressure."

Norbert was incensed that despite the negative PR that the FAA was getting, the "Get Hoover" attitude still pervaded his office. *"Jay Nelson never would let up. He was talking to people all over the country, all the time, doing everything he could do to continue to screw Hoover. One event in particular and only one that I can specifically remember that I will tell you about and it is just an example of what happened probably six to eight different times. Jay Nelson came in and said, 'Well I have been talking to my counterpart in Reno, and by god we are going to see to it that Hoover does not get by us here'."*

Norbert remembered thinking, *"Well what business is it of Jay Nelson whether Hoover flies in Reno or not? In the back seat of an airplane or front seat or whatever it is. Yes, he is medically suspended. Everyone knows he can't fly. But if he has a safety pilot with him everyone knows Hoover is flying. The bottom line is, it doesn't mean shit. That is the responsibility of some other FSDO. I got wind of it and so I did some research. I admit I did it. I did it for a period of two years that I was with the government and I don't regret a minutes' worth of it. If I found out that he was going to be someplace, I'd ask him*

what he was going to do exactly. Bob would tell me. So I'd get into the book... and I had a small nucleus of people I could talk to who had access to the inner workings so they could get interpretations on regulations immediately.

I found out through the FAA's computer system that you can go into the archives on previous case histories and learn about a number of different findings. So I would find every conceivable loophole... every way that Hoover could beat the FAA. I ran copies of all those documents and I faxed them to him and would call him and say 'Now Bob...,' the one particular event in Reno is one I remember. I said, 'Now look, when you show up out there they are going to try to stop you from flying. They are going to try to tell you that you can't even ride an airplane. You are not a required crew member'.

Bob told me he was suppose to fly in one of those two-seaters (with another pilot on board), and start the races just like he had before. They were going to try to stop him.

Bob said, 'Well I have an authorization from Jim Bede, and am going to do this. If he is authorizing me to do it, and it is a two-seater airplane, there is no prohibition... I mean they can't refuse to let you into an airplane.'

I said, 'First off, are you going to be in the restricted airspace? Now when I say restricted I am talking about within the box. Are you going to be outside of it?'

He said, 'No, I am going to be above it. I fly up there above it at altitude and observe what goes on. I am not down in the box."

I told him, "'Well then, you are not violating the special provisions because you are not a race participant, and you are outside of the box. You can fly circles around that SOB all day long if you want to.'

I gave him case history and a bunch of stuff and I said 'Bob, let them come out, let them harangue you, let them say and do what they want to do. Let them walk all over their crank and then you pull a piece of paper out and say this is the case history, this is the law, you have no leg to stand on. You'll get to fly and walk off and leave them. I'll be damned if that is not exactly what happened. Had a guy come running up to him that was working the air race... told him 'you are not going to fly today.'

That event took place... It ended up that Hoover calls the office manager. That was the end of it and he went on and did his thing!"

So... Nester suffered... his superiors at the OKC FSDO repeatedly assigned him to tasks for which he was not qualified or trained. And, of course, when he was unable to properly complete the tasks, his personnel ratings were downgraded. It appeared to be a slow and deliberate process.

Nester told other tales of persecution, of invalid personnel actions that were taken against him. And in a Government Agency known for the liberal ways in which they handle personal and sick leave issues; a number of punitive actions, including lost pay and suspensions, were taken against Nester for allegedly being sick more than for which he had credit.

Writing for **US Aviator** in 1995, Aviation Writer and Columnist Bob Cadwalader reported that, "*In the course of our initial investigation, we contacted a number of people familiar with the case. Some were FAA employees sympathetic to Nester and in agreement with his stand against the FAA actions against Bob Hoover. Some were members of the local Oklahoma City aviation community. Virtually all the sources confirmed that the OKC FSDO management was taking various actions against Nester in retaliation for his outspoken opposition to the FAA actions against Hoover.*

The most serious charge made by Nester is that the FSDO manager, Deborah Entricken, made at least one statement to other FSDO employees to the effect that she could do what she wanted to Nester because of whom he was. Due to the nature of the charge, we spent a considerable amount of telephone time trying to confirm this statement. If true, the statement (as well as any actions taken against Nester because of the stated attitude) would be a violation of numerous federal and local laws, not to mention his basic civil rights and his right, as a US citizen, to freedom of speech and expression.

What we learned was not quite the smoking gun we expected to find, but it came close. Two sources within the FSDO informed us that the union to which many Inspectors belong, PASS, had lodged complaints with the FSDO manager regarding unwarranted actions taken against, and the general treatment of, Inspector Nester. Both sources confirmed there have been meetings between the union representative and the FSDO manager to discuss actions taken against Nester. Both sources also expressed familiarity with the alleged statement and, although they recalled it slightly differently, both said the substance of the statement was correct.

These sources also voiced frustration with the FAA's actions against Bob Hoover. Not surprisingly, every source we spoke to, both inside and outside the FSDO, demanded anonymity for fear of retribution.

Shortly before this article was written, Nester told us that a situation very similar to the FAA actions against Bob Hoover appeared to be occurring to him. Nester's supervisor recently informed him that Nester's medical certificate was being revoked by the FAA, and that Nester would soon receive a letter from the regional medical office officially revoking his medical. When Nester asked for the reasons behind the revocation, his supervisor told him it was due to "questions" about medication he had taken during a previous medical leave.

According to Nester, the medications referred to by his supervisor had been prescribed by his physician and had been reported in great detail to the FSDO. He had listed all the medications as well as their side effects, and had specifically informed the FSDO that these medications would affect his ability to fly, as well as prevent him from passing a random drug test. He had further informed the FSDO management that he would stay on medical leave until no trace of the medications were detectable in a drug test. This was to prevent the possibility of affecting the safety and performance of his job as an Inspector on flying status with the FAA.

Shortly after the supervisor told Nester to expect the letter from the medical office, he was told by another FSDO employee that he could no longer take or give flight checks, or be on any flight status with the FAA. When Nester asked this employee why he was taken off flying status, she replied that his supervisor told her that Nester 'had a problem with his medical certificate.' As of this writing, Nester has not received any official communication from any FAA medical office regarding the status of his medical certificate, but he is still not allowed to fly or perform any flight checks. Indications to date are that serious violations of a number of federal rules and regulations have been committed against Norbert Nester. Furthermore, these actions appear to be a direct result of, and in retribution for, his testimony before Judge Mullins and his subsequent statements and letters in support of Bob Hoover. The nature of some of our sources lends great credence to Nester's allegations that his civil rights have been violated, as well as possible criminal violations taking place against him.

We were also able to speak to the FSDO manager, who declined to make any comment whatsoever about Nester's allegations. When asked specifically about her alleged statement to the effect that she could do whatever she wanted to Norbert Nester, she asked if she could call back after speaking to 'someone else about her rights and responsibilities in this matter.' She returned the call within an hour and made only the statement that 'Personnel actions are being taken against Norbert Nester at this time and due to the Privacy Act, I can't make any other comment.'"

Personnel actions *were* taken against Nester... and he eventually wound up without a job... the victim of a suspicious series of coincidences that occurred after his Hoover testimony and associated actions.

From there, Norbert complained that, "*One thing just lead to another; it snowballed; it got out of hand. Every time I turned around I was being suspended, I was reprimanded, I was being called on the carpet for something. It was a continuous process and it began two weeks after I provided testimony.... the end result of why I got fired officially was absenteeism.*"

Norbert, by then, was fully embroiled in a contentious divorce... "*my estranged spouse called FAA security. She alleged I was taking favors from operators, that I was doing all kinds of things. Security investigated me and found, and I happen to know, they found nothing... the operators are very loyal to people they like. They would call me at home and say did you know security is looking at you? They are talking about you and were out here visiting me today. I said, 'well, yeah, I know they are digging around, but you are going to tell them whatever really happened'.*

And they did, and they showed me copies of statements that they wrote. Security ignored all of those. They fabricated their own stories. They created what they want, and they made their recommendations. It ended up that the bottom line was that I ended up in my office with Frank Allen one day... I was on the phone talking to my attorney regarding my domestic problems, late one afternoon. The attorney called me. I did not initiate the call.

Frank came around the corner into my office and said, 'I want to talk to you'. I said, 'Well, Frank give me just a minute and I will get off the phone'.

That was all. And he stood there.

I said, 'Frank would you excuse me, this is a personal thing and I need to finish it and I will be with you in just a couple of minutes'. He just stood there in the doorway, and finally I stepped up from around my desk, I grabbed the door with one hand and slammed it closed. I literally banged it into him.

He opened the damned door and came back in, and I told the attorney I was talking to that 'I have to go, I can not talk to you right now, I will have to get a hold of you later.' I got up and I was livid.

Frank said, 'we are going to talk'.

I said, 'no, we are not going to talk right now'.

I started to step between him and the door frame and he put his arms up and grabbed a hold of me and tried to physically restrain me. I pushed my way on through the door and walked on down the hallway. He was screaming and shouting at the top of this voice, like a mad sixth grade bully who can't get his way with somebody on the playground. I just walked on out and I don't mind telling you, I remembered what I told him. I said 'Oh Frank, that does it, I have to go take a leak'. And I walked out of the

building.

That is one particular event. Another event came up where Frank pointedly told me that he thought I was crazy. He said 'I think you are the one that has a drug and alcohol problem, not your wife'. Yet, I was never subjected to random drug testing. As a supervisor, he never requested that. He never called the guys in white coats and said, 'Hey, come test him, I think he has a problem. But he made this statement to me again.

I talked to Buck Lawson (one of the Supervisors). I said 'Buck, as perverted as it sounds I am afraid this guy going to call CAMI in, and cause me some problems with my medical, which is ultimately going to screw with my job. He said, 'I know Frank is messed up but I don't think that will ever happen.' It ended up that the stress level was so high and I had so many problems with this character that I initially went to the employee assistance program, a counselor approved by the government.

He said, 'Well I can't help you. You need to go see so and so'. He said 'Go see a shrink.' So I did.

I filed a Workers' Compensation claim in October. Now I had been suspended in the first of October for 14 days with no pay. So I am out for 14 days... I come back in, I have a run in with Frank. I am not there but one to two days before this happens, and I said 'piss on the whole bunch of them. I filed a workers' compensation claim for stress, and I left. They never submitted the papers to the Department of Labor for that Workers' Compensation claim. I continued to receive my paycheck, which was electronic deposit, from the latter part of October through... a portion of December. I don't remember exactly. I checked in with them. I advised them that I was not coming back to work, that I was on medication and under doctor's care. In fact, I came to Texas. I spent a couple of weeks trying to wind down, relax and come back to normal and not have a nervous breakdown. I stayed at my parents' house.

I ultimately went back to Oklahoma City, kept the follow-up appointments. The physician released me to go back to work the first few days of January. I called the physician and I said 'wait a minute, I have a question. I have been on these two medications, which will obviously send up all the bells and whistles on any kind of a drug test'.

He said, 'yeah, they will'.

I said, 'What is the time for my body to metabolize these so that I would be able to pass the drug test?'

Well it ended up that he amended his release. I had gone in... I stayed one day and then he amended the release, and it gave me another five or six days, is what it amounted to. So I left. I did not go back for that five or six days. Buck Lawson called me and asked me about it. I said 'Look, here is the amended release and it is because of this, I can't pass the drug screen. I am not fit for duty. I can't perform my job.' And he said 'Well, I don't know what to tell you, the office manager is still on, all I can tell you is it really works a hardship, it makes things difficult...'

So when I go back in, Frank Allen walks in and he throws all the paperwork on my desk for that Workers' Compensation claim. He said 'You filled out the wrong papers. You will have to do it right.' Now we are talking about something that took place over two months before that. It ended up that I checked and I filled out the paperwork that the office had given me... and in fact, (they) gave me the wrong forms.

So I filled out the appropriate forms, I resubmitted the claim and did all that. The next thing out of his mouth is 'Oh, by the way you, are going to have to file for a

request and advancement on your sick leave.' And I said 'why would I request an advance on my sick leave? I have been out on a workman's compensation plan for over 2 months.'

He said, 'Well, there has been a screw up... we made a mistake, we authorized an advance on your sick leave, but we did not have your authority to request that and you have been getting paid and it was our mistake. You shouldn't have been getting paid all that time.' I answered, 'Well, I guess that was your problem, not mine. You authorized it; you get it worked out.'

He said, 'No, that is your problem. You are going to have to fill out a request for advance on sick leave'. I asked why would I want to request an advance on sick leave when I was out on legitimate Workers' Compensation claim and when I had a doctor's statement. It ended up and needless to say I never did get to file for an advance on sick leave.

I was immediately notified that... there was a proposal to terminate my employment at a given date about a week down the road.

I had the opportunity to write the rebuttals and file grievances and reasons why I shouldn't be terminated and all. I did that. I was immediately restricted to the office, and I was not to leave the office under any circumstances during my workday for the next two week period. In other words, I couldn't go see an operator, I could not do an accident investigation, I couldn't do anything. I was committed to the office. They stuck me on freaking counter detail where I was waiting on everybody who walked in, answering all the questions and the telephone, doing menial things and updating computer files, and that type of thing. Unexpectedly, they walked in one afternoon and they handed me paperwork that said effective immediately you are put on administrative leave pending your termination effective the 15th of February. Clean out your desk. No notice, no warning, no nothing. (They) just walked in and laid it on me and that was it. You are done. Needless to say that was the day I left. I walked out with two books that I wanted... that were personal things for me. I left every other government publication, book, and everything else that had been issued to me and walked out.

I never went back. I was fired, technically, for absenteeism, and it was for the three- or four-day time period between then and the original release for return to duty by the psychiatrist. Until the three or four days later when he stated in his amended release for return to duty so that I could actually pass the drug screen. That was the time period... they had called me to say 'Are you coming to work?'.

I said 'No, I am not coming to work. I can't because I would be in violation of DOT orders, FAA policy of everything. I can not come to work until this date. And that was what they needed to fire me.'"

And so Norbert was no longer an FAA employee and his honesty, courage and heroism were rewarded in the way that many government employees who buck the system are rewarded... with unemployment, harassment and the literal destruction of his life. Norbert is not even flying anymore.

"Jim, there is no doubt in my mind, that if I were to start flying again, that I would be grounded again in short order... I guess that part of my life is over. But... you know what? I can't go back on what I did. It was the right thing... it really was."

Chapter 38

The BIG Question... Can It Happen Again?

"You need only reflect that one of the best ways to get yourself a reputation as a dangerous citizen these days is to go about repeating the very phrases which our founding fathers used in the struggle for independence."
Charles Austin Beard

After two years of book research and two decades of concerted pro-aviation activism (four years, alone, since Bob was reinstated), I'd love to tell you that things have changed and the world of aviation is a fairer and more righteous place to work and fly in.... and if I said that, I'd be lying.

Mind you, there have been efforts to make things right... **US Aviator** magazine has been advocating a "Pilot's Bill of Rights" for over a decade... but the best pro-aviation efforts were led by US Senator Jim Inhofe with the introduction of the "Hoover Bill" and the support of a number of aviation associations, such as AOPA, urging their members to let their elected officials know that this is important to them. This effort was designed to carry out reforms in current FAA policies concerning emergency revocation of pilot and operating certificates. The bill was defeated 51-46 in a Senate vote on Thursday, Sept. 24, 1998, though supporters vow it would return in 1999.

Sponsored by Sen. Jim Inhofe (R-Okla.), this measure provided for third-party oversight of emergency revocations by the NTSB where it would review and determine if the FAA had "due cause" to proceed with any such action. This attempt became known as the "Hoover Bill." AOPA, ALPA, the NTSB Bar Association and EAA testified to many other examples in which FAA's revocation powers were abused, leaving their victims only way out being a serious and high-cost legal battle to regain flight status.

AOPA claimed that *"The problem is that FAA now considers almost every certificate action an 'emergency.' FAA's action against world-renowned airshow pilot Bob Hoover is one of the most notorious examples of abuse under the agency's emergency revocation authority."*

AOPA president, Phil Boyer, seemed particularly impressed with the efforts of Oklahoma senator Jim Inhofe, who spearheaded the attempt to make the Hoover Bill into law." Senator *Inhofe made a tremendous effort to get the Hoover Bill passed,"* said Boyer. *"He was able to convince 46 of his colleagues that it is the right thing to do."*

"With this strong base of support now established in the Senate, I believe we will be able to make the Hoover Bill law in the next legislative session."

EAA has noted that, *"Currently, although NTSB rules allow for an expedited appeal of an emergency revocation, the cost burden and time limitations are formidable obstacles to many certificate holders. Additionally, FAA often has months or years to prepare a case while a defendant has a limited opportunity to present a defense or appeal to a federal court. EAA continues to support FAA's ability to use emergency revocation in cases where aviation safety is truly an issue. The use of such power, however, has increased dramatically. Emergency revocation cases brought before the NTSB from FAA has increased from six percent of all enforcement cases in 1989 to 35 percent of all such cases in 1995."*

I have long been impressed with Senator Inhofe, who has spearheaded not only the "Hoover Bill," but a number of other aviation-friendly efforts. The Senator has spoken eloquently and learnedly on the subject and appeared to have the upper hand on this fight, until it came to a Senate vote where it was defeated... then.

Inhofe argued passionately and righteously for passage of the bill and nothing I can say can address it more eloquently than he did on the floor of the senate in late September '98, *"...there is a process that is used by the FAA which is known as the emergency revocation process. This process will allow an Inspector in the event of an alleged violation by a licensed pilot to take away the pilot's certificate. He would take away the certificate under the emergency revocation clause declaring that an emergency exists.*

The problem with this is that many times when you have an Inspector do this, or an examiner take away a certificate, there is not even an emergency nature to the revocation. Consequently, we have many, many cases where the individuals have been abused.

I would like to suggest that Ted Stewart, who is an American Airlines pilot, has been a pilot for over 12 years and presently flying Boeing 767s. In May of 1995, there was an emergency revocation. He was not guilty of anything. There was not an emergency attached to this. There was never any hazard to anyone's health or safety.

However, it was 2 months until he was able to get his certificate back. Then an examiner went back to him in June of 1996 and again revoked his certificate under the emergency revocation. Consequently, for another 2 months he was unable to earn a living. Fortunately, he worked for American Airlines; they were good enough to keep his paychecks coming, but in many cases that is not the case.

I happen to be a very close friend of a man named Bob Hoover. I think most of you can remember who Bob Hoover is. He is considered to be the best performer in the circuit of airshows. In fact, I have flown airshows with him. In 1992—and I was there at the time—an Inspector came in, an examiner for the FAA, and said to him, 'We think you have a problem. We think perhaps there is a mental problem or something'—they didn't really define it—and they revoked his certificate. It wasn't for another 4 years he was able to get his certificate back. In the meantime, he was flying his airshows but outside the United States. Now, very simply, what my amendment does is set up a process whereby if you lose your certificate, you have 48 hours to take it to the NTSB and let the NTSB make a determination as to whether or not there is any kind of an emergency nature to the revocation. After they have looked this over and decided there is no emergency involved to the nature of the revocation, then at the end of 7 days the pilot will get

his certificate back. If there is, then he would not get it back. They can go ahead then and go through the normal adjudication of the violation.

This is something that has been going on for quite some time. We have been concerned about reforming this process. This is a compromise, because this makes it very clear if there is any hazard out there, if there is any risk to anyone's safety, the flying public or the pilot himself, the pilot is not going to be able to fly. It is as simple as that.

A lot of people say that there are only 300 emergency revocations a year. Therefore, it is not really a problem; it doesn't really affect that many people. I suggest to you that if you take 300 people, there might be 20 or 30 of those who make their living flying airplanes for American Airlines or one of the other airlines, in which case that takes them out of their occupation.

The other problem we have is there are 650,000 pilots right now licensed in the United States and they all live in mortal fear that something like this would happen to them."

Senator Inhofe was joined by Senator Frist from Tennessee, who also argued well for the passage of this important bill and said some truly amazing things in the minute or so that he was given to speak his piece on behalf of all the airmen in the USA. ".. I rise in support of the Inhofe amendment. Clearly, the FAA will be against this amendment because they will not voluntarily relinquish anything in terms of regulatory authority. I believe this amendment is reasonable. It provides, in essence, due process for pilots who do have their privileges revoked, with attention given to safety. It really assures accountability within the FAA. As a pilot who has been witness to the potential abuses—and the Senator from Oklahoma has demonstrated several well-documented examples of how the FAA has really unfairly used a necessary power to prematurely revoke certificates—this amendment will address the issue while assuring accountability. I rise in support of the amendment, a more reasonable approach which assures accountability and assures due process."

Unfortunately, there were some credible dissenters, and I found that to be disheartening, both in terms of what they said as well as who they were. Particularly, I believe, in the case of Senator John McCain... a man who has made many sacrifices on behalf of his country... and should know that the cause of freedom and due process are paramount in all things as far as the USA is concerned. McCain addressed the Senate with this statement...

"...I, of course, respect very much the views expressed by Senators Frist and Inhofe, both of whom are pilots. The FAA has objected to this amendment. I believe it goes too far. I understand Senator Inhofe's concerns. They were voiced a couple of years ago on a similar measure when we were doing another bill, the aviation bill. The fact is, we need to address this issue.

I believe this goes too far. I look forward to working with Senator Inhofe and Senator Frist on it, but I am very hesitant to take a measure which could, at the end of the day, possibly endanger safety. That is why I have to oppose this amendment at this time."

Joining the Arizona Senator in his dissent was Senator Ford of Kentucky... "I have to oppose this amendment, also. The FAA must have the ability to act when it believes safety is at risk. The FAA is often criticized for not acting quickly enough on

safety matters. Here they revoke a certificate for safety purposes and we want to make it harder for them to act. Right now the court of appeals has upheld the FAA actions in every case. They do not second guess the agency charged with the regulation of safety, so let's be sure we give the FAA the authority for safety in the air."

Inhofe was not easy to dissuade, however, stepping up to the bat again on the floor of the Senate to further argue for this bill. "...just a few years ago we went through the same thing with the civil penalties of the FAA Act, so there would be someone other than the FAA involved. Prior to that time, the FAA was the judge, the jury, and the appellate court. They made all the decisions and they were protecting their own, because every bureaucracy does this—EPA, IRS, FDA and all the rest of them.

We changed the regulation so the NTSB, then, would be the appellate court for civil penalties, and it has worked very well. The junior Senator from Texas served on the NTSB, and I yield her whatever time she needs."

Senator Hutchinson then affirmed her support of the bill; "I do support the Inhofe amendment. Having served on the National Transportation Safety Board, I can tell you that the NTSB normally does not overturn the FAA revocation of pilots' licenses. But they do, after they go through the process and look at all of the evidence. I think it is quite fair to say if someone is going to be disadvantaged by having a license revoked, that the NTSB could very easily, and quickly, look at the type of evidence that they are going to hear and, without making a final adjudication, determine that this person would or would not be eligible to fly during the pendency of the proceedings.

I think it would introduce a new level in the process. It would be the emergency level. I think the NTSB can handle this. I think they are competent to do it, and I think their record shows that they have done it in the past. I do support the amendment."

Senator Inhofe concluded his remarks by stating, "I will conclude by saying this in no way impairs the flying safety of the flying public or the pilots. The fact that the average time between the alleged violation and the revocation is 132 days pretty much tells you it is not really an emergency problem in most of these cases. I urge you to join the 625,000 pilots and myself in supporting the Inhofe amendment."

Senator McCain got last shot at this bill but did offer something of an olive branch, "...I thank the Senator from Oklahoma. If he does not prevail on this amendment, which I oppose, I want to pledge to him that I will work with him. There have been abuses. He pointed out the case of Mr. Hoover, who was respected and admired by all of us, who was mistreated by the bureaucracy. Unfortunately, there are always cases where these things happen. But I think we have always to keep safety as the paramount concern, and I believe this amendment possibly—I am not saying absolutely—but possibly could endanger the FAA's ability to carry out their primary responsibilities. I thank the Senator from Oklahoma for his deep involvement in this and other aviation issues. I look forward to working with him in addressing what is clearly a problem."

That Was Then, This Is Now...

The Hoover Bill was reborn in early 1999, renamed Senate Bill 722. It provided for a third-party review of emergency revocations by the NTSB. As before, a NTSB review would determine if the FAA had "due cause" to proceed with any emergency revocation. Aviation has actually mobilized itself better than is its custom for this renewed fight.

AOPA alone, sent some 43,000 "Legislative Alert" mail-grams to AOPA members in five key states in February of 1999 where they urged pilots to contact their U.S. Senators right away to vote for legislation that would curb FAA's abuse of its emergency authority to revoke pilot certificates. *"We came within five votes of passing the Hoover Bill in the Senate last year,"* said AOPA's Phil Boyer. *"We think we can change the minds of some of those senators who voted 'no' last time. That's why we've asked AOPA members in Florida, Illinois, Nevada, North Dakota and South Dakota to weigh-in for those key votes."*

The measure was reintroduced by Inhofe on March 25. Sen Inhofe was joined by seven cosponsors on this legislation: Senators Frank Murkowski (R-Alaska), Conrad Burns (R-Mont.), Chuck Grassley (R-Iowa), John Breaux (D-La.), Mike Crapo (R-Idaho), Ted Stevens (R-Alaska) and Bill Frist (R-Tenn.).

At this time, expectations are high that the measure will pass... The legislation was not opposed by the NTSB, either. Changes brought about by the '98 elections seem to promise that this year will find the bill enjoying greater support. In addition, EAA has noted that Senators opposed to the measure last fall *"discovered substantial negative reactions to their votes in their home states."*

Congrats to those who made their feelings so widely and noticeably felt.

That's democracy, folks.

I've oft been ashamed to be part of a generation that has often turned our backs on what is right and wrong... we have walked away from fights because it was politically expedient to do so, we have watched our heroes be killed, we have attacked those who try to stand for something, we have condoned being lied to, we have run away from righteous causes, and we have turned our back on those in need...

Think of it, my generation saw the assassination of John Kennedy, Bobby Kennedy, Martin Luther King, John Lennon... and other amazing thinkers and dreamers who spoke of peace, freedom, and justice.

But... we flyers are a special breed and we do not have to allow such negativity and failure into our own lives. We certainly do not have to allow our joys and freedoms to slip through our fingers. It may sound a mite elitist, but I truly believe that we flyers are better than that... but only if we stand up for ourselves and each other.

The one great and positive result brought about by the Hoover debacle was the fact that the aviation community woke up, albeit temporarily in many cases, and got INVOLVED in what was happening to one of their own, and indirectly, to themselves. Thousands of pilots and aviation devotees all over the world got enraged, involved and actively fought this matter... and made sure the FAA learned that their days of unfairness and illegality were numbered and while we have a long ways to go, as yet, to seeing aviation treated fairly, constitutionally, and respectfully by the FAA, there is no doubt that the straw that broke the camel's back came about due to the immense loyalty pilots felt toward one man who represented what they all wanted to be, themselves... the best flyer in the world.